Research Anthology on Social Media Advertising and Building Consumer Relationships

Information Resources Management Association
USA

Volume I

Published in the United States of America by
    IGI Global
    Business Science Reference (an imprint of IGI Global)
    701 E. Chocolate Avenue
    Hershey PA, USA 17033
    Tel: 717-533-8845
    Fax: 717-533-8661
    E-mail: cust@igi-global.com
    Web site: http://www.igi-global.com

Library of Congress Cataloging-in-Publication Data

Names: Information Resources Management Association, editor.
Title: Research anthology on social media advertising and building consumer
  relationships / Information Resources Management Association, editor.
Description: Hershey, PA : Business Science Reference, [2022] | Includes
  bibliographical references and index. | Summary: "This edited research
  book considers best practices and strategies of utilizing social media
  successfully throughout various business fields to promote products,
  build relationships, and maintain relevancy by discussing common
  pitfalls and challenges companies face as they attempt to create a name
  for themselves in the online world"-- Provided by publisher.
Identifiers: LCCN 2022015784 (print) | LCCN 2022015785 (ebook) | ISBN
  9781668462874 (hardcover) | ISBN 9781668462881 (ebook)
Subjects: LCSH: Internet advertising. | Internet marketing. | Social
  media--Economic aspects. | Customer relations.
Classification: LCC HF6146.I58 .R47 2022 (print) | LCC HF6146.I58 (ebook)
  | DDC 659.14/4--dc23/eng/20220407
LC record available at https://lccn.loc.gov/2022015784
LC ebook record available at https://lccn.loc.gov/2022015785

British Cataloguing in Publication Data
A Cataloguing in Publication record for this book is available from the British Library.

The views expressed in this book are those of the authors, but not necessarily of the publisher.

For electronic access to this publication, please contact: eresources@igi-global.com.

List of Contributors

Table of Contents

Volume I

Section 1
Fundamental Concepts and Theories

Section 2
Development and Design Methodologies

Volume II

Section 4
Utilization and Applications

Section 5
Organizational and Social Implications

Section 7
Critical Issues and Challenges

Preface

Social media has become a key tool that businesses must utilize in all areas of their practices to build relationships with their customer base and promote their products and services. Through social media, businesses have access to a global customer base of which they can reach, interact with, and develop their brand. This technology is no longer optimal as those who do not take advantage of the many benefits it offers continue to struggle with outdated practices. In order for a business to flourish, further study on the advantages social media provides in the areas of marketing and developing consumer relationships is required.

Staying informed of the most up-to-date research trends and findings is of the utmost importance. That is why IGI Global is pleased to offer this four-volume reference collection of reprinted IGI Global book chapters and journal articles that have been handpicked by senior editorial staff. This collection will shed light on critical issues related to the trends, techniques, and uses of various applications by providing both broad and detailed perspectives on cutting-edge theories and developments. This collection is designed to act as a single reference source on conceptual, methodological, technical, and managerial issues, as well as to provide insight into emerging trends and future opportunities within the field.

The *Research Anthology on Social Media Advertising and Building Consumer Relationships* is organized into seven distinct sections that provide comprehensive coverage of important topics. The sections are:

1. Fundamental Concepts and Theories;
2. Development and Design Methodologies;
3. Tools and Technologies;
4. Utilization and Applications;
5. Organizational and Social Implications;
6. Managerial Impact; and
7. Critical Issues and Challenges.

The following paragraphs provide a summary of what to expect from this invaluable reference tool.

Section 1, "Fundamental Concepts and Theories," serves as a foundation for this extensive reference tool by addressing crucial theories essential to understanding the best practice of social media utilization for business processes. The first chapter of this section, "Social Media for Business Purposes: Objectives Pursued and Satisfaction in the Results," by Prof. Aitziber Nunez-Zabaleta of UPV EHU, Leioa, Spain, analyzes the specific work tasks that 302 professional workers from the Basque region in Spain perform on social media (SM) for attaining their objectives, together with the work satisfaction they gain. The final chapter of this section, "How Social Commerce Characteristics Influence Consumers'

Online Impulsive Buying Behavior in Emerging Markets," by Prof. Vu Minh Ngo of Van Lang University, Vietnam and Profs. Nguyen Cao Lien Phuoc and Quyen Phu Thi Phan of University of Economics, The University of Danang, Vietnam, investigates the role of social commerce characteristics in shaping consumers' online impulsive buying behavior. The study's outcomes offer useful insights to both academicians and practitioners.

Section 2, "Development and Design Methodologies," presents in-depth coverage of the design and development of advertising strategies on social media based on consumer buying behavior. The first chapter of this section, "Effects of Social Media Marketing Strategies on Consumers Behavior," by Profs. Shamsher Singh and Deepali Saluja of Banarsidas Chandiwala Institute of Professional Studies, India, investigates how social media affects the decision-making process of consumers and the impacts of various marketing strategies used by firms on social media. The study employs the survey method to collect primary data from 200 customers who have been regularly using social media. Factor analysis and ANOVA has been used to gain insights in the study. The selected respondents are assumed to represent the population in the urban areas of Delhi. The final chapter of this section, "Social Media Advertisements and Buying Behaviour: A Study of Indian Working Women," by Prof. Yuvika Gupta of IMS Unison University, India and Prof. Samik Shome of Institute of Management, Nirma University, India, identifies the factors that are influencing the working women purchase behaviour. It explains that demographic variables such as age and income of working women do play a significant role in online purchases. The key contribution of this paper is to provide the corporate houses an assessment of the extent to which the working women in India are influenced by social media in their online buying behavior.

Section 3, "Tools and Technologies," explores the various tools and technologies used in advertising through social media from implementation to analytics. The first chapter of this section, "Social Media as a Marketing Tool," by Prof. Rajeshwari Krishnamurthy of Great Lakes Institute of Management, India, discusses how social media can be used as a marketing tool. Right from describing the various forms of social media, it touches upon the different methods by which social media are engaged with by a marketer. The tasks of creating awareness, generating interest, encouraging action, resulting in purchase, and doing brand advocacy are all covered. The final chapter of this section, "Paradigms of Public Relations in an Age of Digitalization: Social Media Analytics in the UAE," by Prof. Badreya Al-Jenaibi of The United Arab Emirates University, UAE, explores the uses of social media in public relations (PR) departments in the United Arab Emirates (UAE). It seeks to lay the basis for understanding the place of social media in the UAE and to contribute to the analysis of the issue of social change in the PR offices. The chapter assesses the state of PR in the UAE in relation to global media and highlights needs in this area for both public and private enterprises. Presenting interview data taken from a cross section of 40 organizations throughout the UAE, it addresses perceptions of benefits, challenges, public acceptance, and future strategies of social media in relation to global SM as whole. It finds that barriers to the use and acceptance of SM in PR have mostly been lifted.

Section 4, "Utilization and Applications," describes how advertising and marketing strategies are used and applied in social media. The first chapter of this section, "Maturity Profiles of Organizations for Social Media," by Prof. Edyta Abramek of University of Economics in Katowice, Poland, analyzes case studies of selected organizations in terms of their achievements in the use of social media. The profiling method applied in the study facilitated evaluating the model of the selected organization. The final chapter of this section, "Social Media in Micro-Enterprises: Exploring Adoption in the Indonesian Retail Sector," by Profs. Savanid Vatanasakdakul and Chadi Aoun of Carnegie Mellon University, Doha, Qatar and Prof. Yuniarti Hidayah Suyoso Putra of Macquarie University, North Ryde, Australia, proposes a research model derived from the Unified Theory of Acceptance and the Use of Technology and extended by integrating the task-technology-fit framework, along with price value propositions.

Section 5, "Organizational and Social Implications," includes chapters discussing the impact of social media advertising on both the companies and on the consumers. The first chapter of this section, "Firm's Competitive Growth in the Social Media Age," by Prof. Nermeen Atef Ahmed Hegazy of Cairo University, Egypt, explains social media as a strategic marketing tool which can be used by firms to help gain competitive advantage. It further discusses the techniques applied to social media advertising for firms. The final chapter of this section, "Social Media Marketing and Brand Loyalty Among Online Shoppers in Anambra State, Nigeria: Mediating Effect of Brand Awareness," by Profs. Ebuka Christian Ezenwafor, Adeola A. Ayodele, and Chukwudi Ireneus Nwaizugbo of Nnamdi Azikiwe University, Akwa, Nigeria, examines the mediating effect of brand awareness on social media marketing and brand loyalty among online shoppers in a typical emerging market.

Section 6, "Managerial Impact," covers the internal and external impacts of social media on companies. The first chapter of this section, "Social Media and E-Commerce: A Study on Motivations for Sharing Content From E-Commerce Websites," by Prof. Beatriz Casais of School of Economics and Management, University of Minho, Portugal & IPAM Porto, Portugal and Prof. Tiago Da Costa of Faculty of Economics, University of Porto, Portugal, uncovers which motivations serve as a background for individuals sharing intentions of e-commerce content. The final chapter of this section, "Social Media, Online Brand Communities, and Customer Engagement in the Fashion Industry," by Prof. Guida Helal of American University of Beirut, Lebanon, focuses on theoretical and managerial implications. This chapter considers the influence social media brand communities and social identity may have on a fashion brand.

Section 7, "Critical Issues and Challenges," presents coverage of academic and research perspectives on challenges to using social media as a tool for advertising. The first chapter of this section, "Consumption in the Digital Age: A Research on Social Media Influencers," by Prof. Eda Turanci of Ankara Haci Bayram Veli University, Turkey, examines the relationship between influencers and consumption. The final chapter of this section, "An Empirical Study on Determining the Effectiveness of Social Media Advertising: A Case on Indian Millennials," by Profs. Taanika Arora and Bhawna Agarwal of Amity College of Commerce and Finance, Amity University, India, proposes a conceptual model based on social media advertising, which examines the impact of some identified antecedents such as entertainment, informativeness, credibility, incentives, pre-purchase search motivation, and social escapism motivation on attitude towards social media advertising and further see the impact on purchase intention.

Although the primary organization of the contents in this multi-volume work is based on its seven sections, offering a progression of coverage of the important concepts, methodologies, technologies, applications, social issues, and emerging trends, the reader can also identify specific contents by utilizing the extensive indexing system listed at the end of each volume. As a comprehensive collection of research on the latest findings related to consumer relationships on social media, the *Research Anthology on Social Media Advertising and Building Consumer Relationships* provides managers, business owners, entrepreneurs, researchers, scholars, academicians, practitioners, instructors, and students with a complete understanding of the applications and impacts of social media as a tool for advertising and building brand image. Given the vast number of issues concerning usage, failure, success, strategies, and applications of social media in modern business strategies and processes, the *Research Anthology on Social Media Advertising and Building Consumer Relationships* encompasses the most pertinent research on the applications, impacts, uses, and strategies of social media advertising.

Section 1
Fundamental Concepts and Theories

Chapter 1
Social Media for Business Purposes:
Objectives Pursued and Satisfaction in the Results

Aitziber Nunez-Zabaleta
UPV EHU, Leioa, Spain

ABSTRACT

This article analyses the specific work tasks that 302 professional workers from the Basque region in Spain perform on social media (SM) for attaining their objectives, together with the work satisfaction they gain. The target population consisted of 23,000 professional workers in the Spanish Basque Country region, both employees and self-employed, with a particular interest in the use of new technologies. A sample of 302 professional workers were surveyed. The author found that professional workers are using SM applications to accomplish a wide range of objectives. Employees themselves are using SM for business purposes with their own strategy and on behalf of the company they work for. In addition to the SM strategy of the employees being integrated within the overall business strategy, managers should encourage them to use SM as this all contributes to the better performance of the company.

1. INTRODUCTION

Networking has always played a key role in business success, and the advent first of general social networking sites (SNS) and subsequently of professional ones has constituted a sea change for professional relationships, reinforcing the advantages of having an online network of contacts. This professional or business practice involves an approach that consists in establishing a professional network of contacts for publicising the firm and its business, listening to and learning from others, and locating possible collaborators, partners and investors (NetCity, 2013). This practice is used to expand a business, increase its visibility and improve its network of commercial contacts, and thereby generate business within it (Aral et al., 2013). The activities encompassed by networking pursue different goals depending on the

DOI: 10.4018/978-1-6684-6287-4.ch001

position a person holds within the firm: reinforce the relationship with current customers; have a better understanding of these same customers within a more relaxed atmosphere; elucidate upon the firm or business idea, promote oneself personally for professional development, disclose the firm's new products and services, identify business opportunities, get to know business partners or customers, and re-establish contact with prior acquaintances.

Most of the studies on the use of Social Media (SM) applications and their penetration focus on the strategies of companies themselves, which are used as the unit of analysis. However, there are few studies that deal with employees, even though there are a large number of them using SM on a personal basis, albeit for work purposes and on behalf of the company. Companies pursue strategies on SM that are designed to publicise new products, launch promotions and offers, provide customer services, recruit staff, increase traffic to the corporate website, and improve brand image. There are activities that are normally undertaken by the marketing department, and therefore adopt a communicational approach. Yet what use is made accordingly by the company's employees?

This article seeks to shed light on the specific tasks these employees undertake on SM, and whether or not they are satisfied with the results they are achieving. At the same time, this study aims to find out whether there is a relationship between their satisfaction with these outcomes and six variables (age, gender, type of worker, size of company, type of consumer that the company sells to and the economic sector).

The table below shows some studies focused on workers activity on SM.

2. THEORETICAL REVIEW AND HYPOTHESIS

SM penetration in all areas is now reaching maturity. Almost eight out of every 10 internet users aged between 18 and 55 use SM on a general basis; that is, for as many types of purposes as the options that each network provides (IAB, 2016). On a professional level, SNS in general and professional networks in particular, have meant a new paradigm when establishing and upholding relationships and new ways of doing business.

There are a number of firms that analyze the use of SM for several purposes, sometimes through longitudinal studies, which enable comparisons to be made with prior years and introduce new topics according to trends. One such trend is the use for work purposes, where they are gaining ever-greater importance. Furthermore, there are a series of consultancy firms that conduct studies in the workplace by surveying managers in different areas. According to IAB (2016), 31% of people surveyed say they use them for work purposes (in 2013 just 8% of respondents said they used social tools for work purposes). Another similar study conducted by The Cocktail analysis (2015) found that one out of every five users considers the SNS useful for professional development.

SM activities of the workers may improve business performance, it is an alternative commercial tool, it is used to strengthen the link with customers, fund and recruit staff, identify new business opportunities, monitor the competition, assess a possible internationalization, find information to solve problems and make contacts of professional interest.

Employees can bring many benefits to the companies they work for by using SM on their work tasks. Some of these benefits are shown in Table 2.

Table 1. Research studies focused on the use of SM by employees

Title of the Study	Sample	Aims of the study	Citation
Motivations for Social Networking at Work	285 employees in IBM all over the world	Describes the use of Beehive social network, which has been designed to give support to IBM employees in order to share information, amongst its members	(DiMicco, *et al.*, 2008)
Using Social Media for work: Losing your time or improving your work?	1.799 employees in the insurance sector onto the Greek market	Study of values that make a greater use of SM with work purpuses among employees, making a link between the use and business performance	(Leftheriotis and Giannakos, 2014)
When social networks cross boundaries: a case study of workplace use of Facebook and LinkedIn	450 responses from three groups belonging to Microsoft corporation	Examine attitudes and behaviours in large companies with technological skills through 30 in deepth interviews and observation of different communities belonging to Microsoft company	(Skeels and Grudin, 2009)
Understanding the Influence of Social Media in the Workplace: An Integration of Media Synchronicity and Social Capital Theories.	105 software professionals in China	Analyses the influence of SM on employees work performance, as well as the mechanism through which these employees create value for the work they carry out	(Cao *et al.*, 2012)
Utilization of relationship-oriented Social Media in the selling process: a comparison of consumer (B2C) and industrial (B2B) salespeople	395 sale-people in B2B and B2C markets	Review of SM applications focused on business relationships	(Moore *et al.*, 2013)
Helping workers understand and follow Social Media policies	166 workers currently studying at Middle West universities of United States of America	Discussion about how SM guidelines should be communicated to employees	(O'Connor *et al.*, 2016)

Source: Author's own work

Table 2. Benefits workers can bring to the company associated with the use of SM

Benefits for the company	Studies	Citation
Reduction of transaction costs	Users of the world, united! the challenges and opportunities of Social Media	(Kaplan and Haenlein, 2010)
	Social media's influence on business-to-business sales performance	(Rodríguez *et al.*, 2012)
	How social technologies drive business success	(Millward Brown, 2012)
	Handbook of Social Media management: Value chain and business models in changing media markets	(Friedrichsen, 2013)
Improvement of work performance	Factors of social networking use as a business tool among micro-enterprises	(Alexandra and Kassim, 2013)
	Business performance and Social Media: Love or hate?	(Paniagua and Sapena, 2014)
	The impact of enterprise Social Media on task performance in dispersed teams.	(Suh and Bock, 2015)
Strengthen relationships with employees	Motivations for social networking at work	(DiMicco *et al.*, 2008)
	Adoption of social networking sites: An exploratory adaptive structuration perspective for global organizations	(Sinclaire and Vogus, 2011).
	Understanding the influence of Social Media in the workplace: An integration of media synchronicity and social capital theories	(Cao *et al.*, 2012)
	Exploring factors influencing the use of enterprise social networks in multinational professional service firms	Chin *el al.*, 2015)
Strengthen relationships with Clients and suppliers	Usage, barriers and measurement of Social Media marketing: An exploratory investigation of small and medium B2B brands	(Michaelidou *et al.*, 2011)
	How social technologies drive business success. European survey results.	(MillwardBrown, 2012).
	The role of Social Media in affective trust building in customer–supplier relationships	(Calefato *et al.*, 2015)
Gaining Knowledge of the competitors	Social Media: The new hybrid element of the promotion mix	(Mangol and Faulds, 2009)
	Gaining competitive intelligence from Social Media data: Evidence from two largest retail chains in the world	(He *et al.*, 2015)
	Social Media Monitoring for Companies: A 4W Summarisation Approach	(Rexha *et al.*, 2016)

Source: Author's own work

2.1. Making Professional Contacts and Communicating with Stakeholders

There are many scholars that report the benefits of using SM insofar as they make it easier to contact customers and possible business partners, as well as keep in touch with them (Andzulis et al., 2012; Cruz et al., 2012; Michaelidou et al., 2011; Heinrich et al., 2011). SM may help to generate leads, in other words, to find out who is interested in the firm's products. Firms may gather detailed data on potential customers, whereby they may increase their social capital and reduce the costs of acquiring a new customer (Rodríguez et al., 2012). These detailed data, what's more, enable firms to forge closer ties with their customers, which in turn makes it easier to share information on those products that are best suited to these self-same customers.

Accenture (2011) found that the main objectives that firms pursue through SM are, firstly, to increase their interaction and positive experiences with current and potential customers; secondly, protect, influence and build up brand reputation, and thirdly, create openings for obtaining new income. Companies hence face the challenge of focusing the contacts so that they generate real results such as open innovation, that when powered by SM, they share visions and objectives in order to focus interaction towards useful outcomes (Hitchen et al., 2017). According to a survey conducted by Millward Brown (2012) involving 2,700 professionals from European firms, these individuals are using SM for locating people of professional interest more speedily collaborating and knowledge sharing building up professional relationships and creating communities, as well as reducing the number of emails. As far as interacting and communicating with customers is concerned, this same survey finds that the greatest benefits obtained from the use of SM is perceived to be obtained in the following tasks: greater effectiveness of certain marketing activities, such as reputation, conversion and loyalty; heightened consumer satisfaction; and lower marketing and travel costs, for example. As regards the interaction with suppliers and business partners, the benefits are perceived in quicker access to information, lower communication costs, greater access to experts, as well as a reduction in travel costs.

Leftheriotis and Giannakos (2014) investigated the use of SM for work purposes among 1,799 employees and found that two out of three employees make use of SM in their work irrespectively of their age and more than half of the employees claimed that they use it in order to watch the market/com- petitors. These authors point out that the use of SM is not simply a waste of time for employees, but they also positively impact the employees' performance. He et al. (2014) examined the impact of SM in B2B communication and business performance in small and medium enterprises (SMEs) and report that communication performance can enhance marketing, innovation and collaboration between SMEs.

As regards the sales process Andzulis et al. (2012) state that in the initial approach to potential customers during the first stage of this process, SM applications provide the firm with an opportunity to contact prospective customers, and so start a relationship. In the final stages of the sales process, SM applications may help to clear up doubts and resolve problems with customers, as well as provide testimonials that support the product and generate trust. In sum, SM may shorten the time needed for the sales process thanks to the speedy sharing of information and the proximity acquired with the customer. In the same vain, Itani et al. (2017) report that SM enables two key sales behaviors of competitive intelligence collection and adaptive selling.

2.2. Market Research

The new consumer is defined as someone who is permanently online, has greater power of decision and choice, and above all has the ability to generate and digest information. This means that firms need to listen to the dialogue that arises over their brand, product or service. Hence, the reason they need to monitor these conversations on SM, and thus, besides measuring their reputation online, they can draw conclusions for conducting a specific study. This is another source of information to be considered together with the firm's in-house information, and all the other market research conducted by organizations.

SNS such as Twitter and Facebook are a major source of data on consumer behavior, and they shed light on the strategy competitors use to capture their stakeholders' attention and achieve customer satisfaction (Manthiou et al., 2014). Facebook provides valuable information on market segmentation, which is crucial for sending consumers the right message (Sigue, 2011). As regards the objective of learning more about the market revealed by an analysis of the interviews in that study, for some firms their presence in SM is a way of conducting market research easily and economically: the firm can track the opinions of customers sufficiently interested in the product and, what's more, these social networks can be used to find out about the market performance of other firms in the industry (Banesto, 2013).

Díaz (2015) posits that although there is still a long way to go for fully exploiting SM as a tool for market research, there is no doubt about the role they play in a consumer's life, so they should be included within traditional research in order to obtain more holistic results and a better understanding of the perception of products and services.

2.3. Sharing Information and Knowledge

The recent literature on knowledge management has stressed the importance of those interactive technologies that cater for this process, which largely take the form of virtual communities, which include blogs, wikis and other SM applications (Ardichvili et al., 2003). These new technologies have technical features that give free rein to the desire for involvement in knowledge sharing, and which, furthermore, allow overcoming the traditional barriers that have restricted this activity (McAfee, 2006; Kaiser et al., 2007). The aforementioned survey by Millward Brown (2012) indicates that 80% state that social tools have helped them to improve the way in which teams cooperate and share knowledge with each other. According to this survey, 37% of the professionals polled say they are using social networks for cooperating and sharing knowledge. In turn, McKinsey (Bughin et al., 2009) affirms that when SNS are used efficiently, they drive employees' engagement with projects in which ideas and knowledge are shared. In the same way, knowledge can often be accessed by collaborative means, and identifying the required knowledge and the holders of this knowledge is a step towards knowledge access.

The volume of user-generated content on social media often hinders the internalization of knowledge for open innovation (Wang et al., 2012). According to Lashgari et al. (2018), marketers have begun to realize that becoming involved in communication with end-users will substantially, and perhaps dramatically, improve their business. Therefore, they seek to take advantage of less expensive and more convenient means of communication such as SM. They think that SM bring the possibility of open innovation by involving individuals and experts in various fields in product or service development, an advantage that is often difficult to achieve by traditional media. Hitchen et al. (2017) also say that SM encourages user to interact more frequently than when limited to physical meetings, phone contact, or even e-mail, and makes collaboration on innovative projects easier and more detailed. Mount and Garcia (2014) in turn, suggest that the implementation of SM can create a context for ambidexterity during open innovation in ideation, as users are free to explore and exploit new ideas for improvement. These authors believe that managers need to create an open and inclusive virtual environment in which participants with diverse knowledge can easily contribute, share, and edit content. Managers thus need to become more socialized and engaged with users by communicating and stimulating knowledge generation that is closely aligned with internal processes.

2.4. Staff Recruitment

The use of professional Social networks has been proposed as a tool for finding the right people and profiles for recruitment processes, verify candidates' references, and post job vacancies (Salgado and Ávila, 2014). Digital social networks, especially those with a professional bias, such as LinkedIn, may prove useful for making business contacts and recruiting future employees. According to a report issued by the consultancy Deloitte (Kiron et al., 2013), 23% of firms now use social networks as an aid when selecting candidates and according to workforce management (2011), today's specialists conduct a detailed study of candidate profiles on SM, in what is now referred to as Recruiting 2.0[1], as they seek precise information on what a potential candidate has done, what they can do, and their future aspirations.

Mukiur (2016) points out that specific applications like LinkedIn, Facebook are gaining popularity in business since they are offering opportunities to facilitate the recruitment and attraction of best candidates. One of the results of the survey conducted by this author is that for 40% of human resource managers LinkedIn is the preferred application for the task referred. In the same vein, Robert Half says that HR specialists and hiring managers are increasingly incorporating tools such as Facebook and LinkedIn into their recruiting strategy. Some job candidates invite employers to view their profiles on social networks, hoping the information will help hiring managers see a more complete view of the real person beyond the resume and cover letter.

3. METHODOLOGY

The main aim has been to examine the specific objectives that professionals pursue on the applications making up the Social sphere as the result of the work activities performed.

The target population used here consists of 23,000 professional workers in the Spanish region of the Basque Country, both employees and self-employed, with a particular interest in the use of new technologies and who subscribe to the newsletter that Euskadi+innova[2] delivers each week, reporting on the latest news and events. The questionnaire was administered to the participants via the home page on the Euskadi+innova website, and remained online between 1 February and 15 February 2017, which constituted the data-gathering period. 302 people responded to the survey in an appropriate manner.

As regards the cohort's main characteristics, 51.2% are women, the average age is 40, almost all of them have secondary or higher studies, 70% are in paid employment, and almost all of them work in the third or fourth economic sectors. Almost half work for microenterprises (fewer than 10 employees) and 23.7% for large corporations (more than 250 employees). Finally, only 14% sell to end consumers (B2C)[3], 50.2% solely to other firms (B2B)[4], and 35% operate in both environments (B2B2C)[5].

Contingency tables have been used to conduct independence tests for verifying whether there are significant differences for six of the seven variables studied: three related to the actual worker (gender, age and type of work) and three related to the nature of the firm that employs them (size, economic sector, and type of consumer it sells to).

Statistical verification has involved the Mann-Whitney U-test, the Kruskal-Wallis H test, and the Pearson's Chi square test. The McNemar test has been used to determine the gap between the aims pursued and the positive outcomes obtained (see Appendix 1). This test measures a single characteristic (pursued purpose) on two occasions in order to compare whether the measurements (use and good result) are equal or if, conversely, a significant change occurs. Moreover, the Chi-square of independence has also been used to check whether there are significant differences between those people who consider the results satisfactory and those who do not in relation to six variables: age, gender, type of worker, size of company, type of consumer that the company sells to and the economic sector (see Appendix 2).

The questions used for gathering the information are shown in Table 3.

Table 3. Questions in the questionnaire

Question	Illustration
1. What specific work task do you carry out through SM?	Figure 1
2. Are you getting a satisfactory result?	Figure 1

Source: Author's own work

4. ANALYSIS AND RESULTS

This study hypothesizes that using SM at work help employees to perform their vocational tasks more effectively and innovatively. We postulate that work satisfaction, is positively influenced by using such social streams. To test these hypotheses, online survey has been sent to participants for exploring their opinions.

Figure 1 shows the objectives that the respondents have been asked to choose, with the percentage that say they pursue those objectives on the one hand (light) and on the other those that report satisfactory results or postivie outcome (dark).

As visualized, that the objectives the respondents most commonly meet through SNS are making professional contacts (81.3%); communicating with them (73.5%); announcing events (59%); finding potential customers (53%); participating in groups of discussion in order to share information (50.2%); and, finally, communicating with professional contacts (51.9%). Appendix 1 presents the statistical significance values calculated for each objective and the pertinent work satisfaction. Appendix 2 compares workers who are getting 'work satisfaction' to those who do not.

Figure 1. Percentage of respondents who say they pursue one of the following tasks (dark) and those who report positive outcomes (light). Source: Author's own work based on survey data.

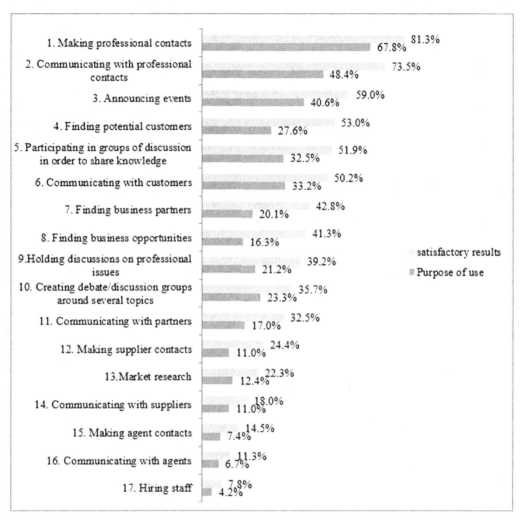

5. DISCUSSION OF RESULTS

The validity of using enterprise SM is questioned for several reasons. These reasons include lacking awareness of the potential validity of using SNS, versatile purposes of using SM applications and reducing time needed for work-based activities. Conversely, business SM encompasses acquiring new contacts, promoting products and interacting with customers. Our findings go hand in hand with the positive influence of using online SNS at work (Leonardi et al., 2013).

We note that finding business contacts and securing a positive outcome are proportional to meeting the vocational objectives. It can be assumed that making contact with other professionals for no specific purpose is easier than working on a contract or implementing agreements. Similarly, keeping in touch with people is easier online either with customers or with business partners and suppliers. Concerning announcing events, the positive outcome is also very close to the purpose. The difference is slightly greater in cases of creating debate or delineating discussions around a given topic. The objectives of making contact with suppliers, potential customers, agents and other business partners, holding discussions on professional matters, and announcing events, were more attainable using online applications than marketing surveys, hiring staff, and finding business opportunities.

Our results show that the main objective is to make professional contacts in general, and to make contact with potential customers in particular. In addition, a high percentage seeks to communicate dynamically with customers. There are several studies that report the generation of leads, or to put it another way, finding potential customers, as the first goal pursued by professionals using SM. According to BtoB Magazine (PuroMarketing, 2013), this is the main challenge for 60% of the professionals in B2B firms. In another study (Accenture, 2011), 65% of the professionals, also working for B2B firms, consider it extremely important to use SM as channels of interaction with customers, potential customers, business partners and other stakeholders

Elsewhere, there is a remarkably low percentage of professionals using these networks for hiring staff. According to the Inesdi Digital Business School (2012), 50% of the companies, although being domestic SMEs, has recruited staff through the Web.

There are significant differences in the reasons people use SM and the ambits in which they say they have recorded a positive outcome. Naturally enough, a SNS used for professional purposes does not always lead to positive outcomes. There are numerous reasons for this. One reason might be a lack of awareness of the potential that each SNS provides; that is, the way of effectively using all its features. This may explain why the best possible performance is not always possible to achieve. Another reason might be that the tool used for each purpose is not always the most suitable one, as each tool has different functions. Another explanation might be that people dedicate less time than needed to activities on SM. The survey does not provide us with conclusive answers on these matters.

Figure 1 shows that those tasks pursued by a high percentage of the professionals polled are also those in which the gap with the positive outcomes obtained is proportionally narrower. This suggests that the professionals are focusing on those tasks that provide them with a satisfactory result, either because they are using the right tool or because they know how to use it properly to achieve their goals.

We have gone deeply into those who say they do not obtain positive outcomes in the tasks they undertake in order to verify whether there are any differences between them and the following characteristics: age, gender, type of worker, size of company and type of consumer that the company sells.

Firstly, regarding potential customers, the self-employed are the ones who in a lower proportion are not satisfied with the result achieved. This is not the same case for contacts with suppliers: employees are generally more satisfied with the outcome. Keeping in touch with professional contacts through SM is proving to be more difficult for workers over the age of 50 than for all the other and interestingly, professionals between the ages of 31 and 40 are the ones least satisfied with the outcome of participating in discussion groups on sundry topics for the purpose of sharing information.

Companies that sell to end consumers are more satisfied than the others with the outcome obtained in terms of keeping in touch with customers. We should not forget that these firms normally have more customers than B2B firms, and it seems more logical that they find it easier to keep in touch via the networks.

There is a remarkably high percentage of professionals in small firms that state they are satisfied with the results obtained in the task "create debate/discussion groups on sundry topics" when we compare them with medium and large companies. Considering that the larger a company is, the more specialized the list of tasks to be performed by each employee, it may be the case that our survey has not reached the people responsible for participating in groups within large companies. In small companies, by contrast, it is more likely that an employee will be called upon to perform a broad range of tasks, including representing the company in fora.

We believe that SM can be utilized to identify new business opportunities and new ideas, or deepen relationship with customers and to enhance collaboration between companies and other parties (Lehtimäki et al., 2009; Gillin and Schwartzman, 2011). Furthermore, SM applications can be a powerful lure for an organization; their interactivity promises to bring more employees into daily contact at lower cost. When used effectively, they also may encourage participation in projects and idea sharing, thus deepening a company's pool of knowledge (Bughin et al., 2009).

Experts from literature, research and practice agree that a strong commitment from an organization's executives and leaders is an essential requirement in handling employees' SM use, as the process of embracing it at the workplace has to start at the core of an organization's culture (Dreher, 2014).

6. CONCLUSION

We found that employees and self-employed are using SM to accomplish a wide range of pursued objectives. Those being the goals pursued in a greater extent are the ones that report a satisfactory outcome. They undertake a number of work tasks, and although in general the percentage of satisfactory outcomes is some way away from the goals, this should not be viewed negatively, quite the opposite, we take it to be a positive result, as it shows that there is a long way to go for developing the use of Sm applications, both separately and in combination with each other. In the case of the main task mentioned (making professional contacts), we found that the results recorded are very close to those expected, we therefore conclude that workers are making good use of SM in this specific task. We may also affirm that those workers who are most active on the social sphere are the ones recording the best results in the tasks they undertake.

This study leads us to believe that the SM applications used by companies and those used by workers do not coincide. Employees themselves are using SM for business purposes with their own strategy in the name and on behalf of the company they work for. We therefore contend that the SM strategies of the companies do not take the activities of the workers online into account. As workers increasingly make greater use of SM applications, it would be of interest for companies to set up behavior guidelines for their employees and include them in the company SM strategy for its better overall management.

We contend that companies should not ignore the opportunity that SM provide: making professional contacts, keeping in touch with stakeholders, announcing events, participating in discussion groups, etc. These opportunities are ways of helping to expand the company at little expense and of accessing new business options. Therefore, in addition to the SM strategy of the employees being integrated within the overall business strategy, managers should encourage them to use SM as this all contributes to the better performance of the company.

7. REFERENCES

Accenture. (2011). Making social media pay: Rethinking social Media's potential to bolster B2B interactions, customer loyalty, revenues and brand reputation. Retrieved from http://www.accenture.com/us-en/Pages/insight-making-social-media-pay.aspx

Alexandra, V., & Kassim, E. S. (2013). Factors of social networking use as a business tool among micro-enterprises. *Paper presented at the International Conference on Research and Innovation in Information Systems (ICRIIS)* (pp. 227-231). IEEE. 10.1109/ICRIIS.2013.6716713

Andzulis, J. M., Panagopoulos, N. G., & Rapp, A. (2012). A review of social media and implications for the sales process. *Journal of Personal Selling & Sales Management, 32*(3), 305–316. doi:10.2753/PSS0885-3134320302

Aral, S., Dellarocas, D., & Godes, D. (2013). Social media and business transformation: A framekork for research. *Information Systems Research, 24*(1), 3–13. doi:10.1287/isre.1120.0470

Ardichvili, A., Page, V., & Wentling, T. (2003). Motivation and barriers to participation in virtual knowledge-sharing communities practice. *Journal of Knowledge Management, 7*(1), 64–77. doi:10.1108/13673270310463626

Banesto, F. (Ed.). (2013). *Observatorio sobre el uso de las redes sociales en las PYMEs españolas.*B. Fundación.

Bughin, J., Chui, M., & Miller, A. (2009). How companies are benefiting from web 2.0: McKinsey global survey results. Retrieved from www.mckinsey.com

Calefato, F., Lanubile, F., & Novielli, N. (2015). The role of social media in affective trust building in customer–supplier relationships. *Electronic Commerce Research, 15*(4), 453–482. doi:10.100710660-015-9194-3

Cao, X., Vogel, D. R., Guo, X., Liu, H., & Gu, J. (2012). Understanding the influence of social media in the workplace: An integration of media synchronicity and social capital theories. *Paper presented at the 2012 45th Hawaii International Conference on System Science (HICSS)* (pp. 3938-3947). Academic Press.

Chin, C. P. Y., Evans, N., & Choo, K. K. R. (2015). Exploring factors influencing the use of enterprise social networks in multinational professional service firms. *Journal of Organizational Computing and Electronic Commerce, 25*(3), 289–315. doi:10.1080/10919392.2015.1058118

Cruz, M., Varajao, J., & Goncalves, P. (2012). The perceived potential of business social networking sites. *International Journal of Web Portals, 4*(1), 1–15. doi:10.4018/jwp.2012010101

Díaz, S. (2015). Las redes sociales y su influencia en la investigación de mercados. Retrieved from http://blog.amai.org/index.php/las-redes-sociales-y-su-influencia-en-la-investigacion-de-mercados/

DiMicco, J., Millen, D. R., Geyer, W., Dugan, C., Brownholtz, B., & Muller, M. (2008). Motivations for social networking at work. *Paper presented at the ACM Conference on Computer Supported Cooperative Work* (pp. 711-720). ACM.

Dreher, S. (2014). Social media and the world of work: A strategic approach to employees' participation in social media. *Corporate Communications, 19*(4), 344–356. doi:10.1108/CCIJ-10-2013-0087

Friedrichsen, M. (2013). *Handbook of social media management: Value chain and business models in changing media markets.* Springer. doi:10.1007/978-3-642-28897-5

Gillin, P., & Schwartzman, E. (2010). *Social marketing to the business customer: Listen to your B2B market, generate major account leads, and build client relationships.* John Wiley & Sons.

Robert Half. (2016). Social media recruiting: 5 mistakes to avoid. Retrieved from https://www.roberthalf.com/blog/evaluating-job-candidates/social-media-recruiting-5-mistakes-to-avoid

He, W., Shen, J., Tian, X., Li, Y., Akula, V., Yan, G., & Tao, R. (2015). Gaining competitive intelligence from social media data: Evidence from two largest retail chains in the world. *Industrial Management & Data Systems, 115*(9), 1622–1636. doi:10.1108/IMDS-03-2015-0098

He, W., Wang, F. K., & Zha, S. (2014). Enhancing social media competitiveness of small businesses: Insights from small pizzerias. *New Review of Hypermedia and Multimedia, 20*(3), 225–250. doi:10.1080/13614568.2014.889225

Heinrich, B., Zellner, G., & Leist, S. (2011). Service integrators in business networks? the importance of relationship value. *Electronic Markets, 21*(4), 215–235. doi:10.100712525-011-0075-x

Hitchen, E. L., Nylund, P. A., Ferràs, X., & Mussons, S. (2017). Social media: Open innovation in SMEs finds new support. *The Journal of Business Strategy, 38*(3), 21–29. doi:10.1108/JBS-02-2016-0015

Hoffman, D. L., & Fodor, M. (2010). Can you measure the ROI of your social media marketing? *MIT Sloan Management Review, 52*(1), 4.

IAB. (2016). Estudio anual de redes sociales. Retrieved from http://www.iabspain.net/wp-content/uploads/downloads/2016/04/IAB_EstudioRedesSociales_2016_VCorta.pdf

Inesdi. (2012). Barómetro sobre las profesiones digitales en la empresa. Retrieved from http://www.infoempleo.com/barometro/default.htm

Kaiser, G. E., Barghouti, N. S., Feiler, P. H., & Schwanke, R. W. (1988). Database support for knowledge-based engineering environments. *IEEE Intelligent Systems, 3*(2), 18–32.

Kaplan, A., & Haenlein, M. (2010). Users of the world, united! the challenges and opportunities of social media. *Business Horizons, 53*(1), 59–68. doi:10.1016/j.bushor.2009.09.003

Kiron, D., Palmer, D., Nguyen, A., & Berkman, R. (2013). Social business study: Shiting out of first gear. *Dupress.* Retrieved from http://dupress.com/articles/social-business-study/

Lashgari, M., Sutton-Brady, C., Solberg Søilen, K., & Ulfvengren, P. (2018). Adoption strategies of social media in B2B firms: A multiple case study approach. *Business & Industrial Marketing, 33*(5), 730–743. doi:10.1108/JBIM-10-2016-0242

Leftheriotis, I., & Giannakos, M. N. (2014). Using social media for work: Losing your time or improving your work? *Computers in Human Behavior, 31*, 134–142. doi:10.1016/j.chb.2013.10.016

Lehtimäki, T., Salo, J., Hiltula, H., & Lankinen, M. (2009). Harnessing web 2.0 for business to business marketing – literature review and an empirical perspective. *Faculty of Economics and Business Administration, 29*, 76.

Leonardi, P. M., Huysman, M., & Steinfield, C. (2013). Enterprise social media: Definition, history, and prospects for the study of social technologies in organizations. *Journal of Computer-Mediated Communication, 19*(1), 1–19. doi:10.1111/jcc4.12029

Mangold, G., & Faulds, D. (2009). Social media: The new hybrid element of the promotion mix. *Business Horizons, 52*(4), 357–365. doi:10.1016/j.bushor.2009.03.002

Manthiou, A., Tang, L. R., & Bosselman, R. (2014). Reason and reaction: The dual route of the decision-making process on facebook fan pages. *Electronic Markets, 24*(4), 297–308. doi:10.100712525-014-0156-8

Sigue, M. (2011). Cómo usar las redes sociales para hacer investigación de mercados. Retrieved from http://www.gestiopolis.com/como-usar-redes-sociales-hacer-investigacion-mercados/

McAfee, A. (2006). Enterprise 2.0: The dawn of emergent collaboration. *MIT Sloan Management Review, 47*(3), 21–28.

Mehrtens, C. (2013). Social media: Their role as support tools in B2B organizations. *Paper presented at the 2Nd IBA Bachelor Thesis Conference,* Enschede, Netherlands. Academic Press.

Michaelidou, N., Siamagka, N. T., & Christodoulides, G. (2011). Usage, barriers and measurement of social media marketing: An exploratory investigation of small and medium B2B brands. *Industrial Marketing Management, 40*(7), 1153–1159. doi:10.1016/j.indmarman.2011.09.009

MillwardBrown. (2012). How social technologies drive business success. european survey results. Retrieved from http://www.millwardbrown.com/docs/default-source/insight-documents/articles-and-reports/Googe_MillwardBrown_How-Social-Technologies-Drive-Business-Success_201205.pdf

Moore, J., Hopkins, C. D., & Raymond, M. A. (2013). Utilization of relationship oriented social media in the selling process: A comparison of consumers (B2C) and industrial (B2B) salespeople. *Journal of Internet Commerce, 12*(1), 48–75. doi:10.1080/15332861.2013.763694

Mount, M., & Martinez, M. G. (2014). Social media: A tool for open innovation. *California Management Review, 56*(4), 124–143. doi:10.1525/cmr.2014.56.4.124

Mukiur, R. M. (2016). Reclutamiento a través de las redes sociales: Reclutamiento 3.0. *Opción, 32*(10).

NetCity. (2013). Proyectos y experiencias de interés. Retrieved from http://asociacionredel.com/wp-content/uploads/2014/06/Netcity.pdf

O'Connor, K. W., Schmidt, G. B., & Drouin, M. (2016). Helping workers understand and follow social media policies. *Business Horizons, 59*(2), 205–211. doi:10.1016/j.bushor.2015.11.005

Paniagua, J., & Sapena, J. (2014). Business performance and social media: Love or hate? *Business Horizons, 57*(6), 719–728. doi:10.1016/j.bushor.2014.07.005

PuroMarketing. (2013). La generación de leads sigue siendo el principal reto para las empresas B2B. Retrieved from http://www.puromarketing.com/53/15905/generacion-leads-sigue-siendo-principal-reto-para-empresas.html

Rexha, A., Kröll, M., & Kern, R. (2016). Social media monitoring for companies: A 4W summarisation approach. *Paper presented at the European Conference on Knowledge Management.* Academic Press.

Rodríguez, M., Peterson, R. M., & Krishnan, V. (2012). Social media's influence on business-to-business sales performance. *Journal of Personal Selling & Sales Management, 32*(3), 365–378. doi:10.2753/PSS0885-3134320306

Salgado, J., & Ávila, R. (2014). Aplicación de las redes sociales en la gestión de los recursos humanos. Retrieved from http://www.udec.cl/exalumnos/node/1727

Senik, Z., Scott-Ladd, B., Entrekin, L., & Adham, K. (2011). Networking and internationalization of SMEs in emerging economies. *Journal of International Entrepreneurship, 9*(4), 259–281. doi:10.100710843-011-0078-x

Sinclaire, J. K., & Vogus, C. E. (2011). Adoption of social networking sites: An exploratory adaptive structuration perspective for global organizations. *Information Technology Management, 12*(4), 293–314. doi:10.100710799-011-0086-5

Skeels, M. M., & Grudin, J. (2009). When social networks cross boundaries: A case study of workplace use of facebook and linkedin. *Paper presented at the ACM 2009 International Conference on Supporting Group Work* (pp. 95-104). ACM. 10.1145/1531674.1531689

Suh, A., & Bock, G. W. (2015). The impact of enterprise social media on task performance in dispersed teams. *Paper presented at the 48th Hawaii International Conference* (pp. 1909-1918). Academic Press. 10.1109/HICSS.2015.229

The cocktail analysis. (2015). *VII obserbatorio redes sociales.*

Urueña, a., Ferrari, A., Blanco, D., & Valdecasa, E. (2011). In ONTSI (Ed.), *Estudio sobre el conocimiento y uso de las redes sociales en España.*

Wang, X., Yu, C., & Wei, Y. (2012). Social media peer communication and impacts on purchase intentions: A consumer socialization framework. *Journal of Interactive Marketing, 26*(4), 198–208. doi:10.1016/j.intmar.2011.11.004

Workforce Management. (2011). Best practices for Recruitment. Retrieved from http://www.workforce.com/

ENDNOTES

[1]   Recruiting 2.0: the process of looking for and selecting employees (staff recruitment) via the internet and social networks

[2]   Euskadi+innova is an agency attached to the Basque Government's Department of Economic and Competitive Development whose remit is to make Basque businesses more competitive.

[3]   B2C: Business to Consumer

[4]   B2B: Business to Business

[5]   B2B2C: Business to Business to Consumer

This research was previously published in the International Journal of E-Business Research (IJEBR), 15(3); pages 35-50, copyright year 2019 by IGI Publishing (an imprint of IGI Global).

APPENDIX 1. STATISTICAL DIFFERENCES FOUND BOTH, FOR OBJECTIVES PURSUED AND SATISFACTORY RESULTS.

Business objectives on the Web 2.0	Pursued objective	Satisfactory results	McNemar test	
			Chi-square	Significance
1. Making new professional contacts	81,3%	67,8%	27,38	0,000
2. Communicating with professional contacts	73,5%	48,4%	28,52	0,000
3. Announcing events	59,0%	40,6%	40,64	0,000
4. Finding potential customers	53,0%	27,6%	60,01	0,000
5. Participating in groups of discussion in order to share information	51,9%	32,5%	38,88	0,000
6. Communicating with customers	50,2%	33,2%	38,08	0,000
7. Finding business partners	42,8%	20,1%	48,4	0,000
8. Finding business opportunities	41,3%	16,3%	59,036	0,000
9. Holding discussions on topics	39,2%	21,2%	39,88	0,000
10. Creating debate/discussion groups	35,7%	23,3%	20,28	0,000
11. Communicating with partners	32,5%	17%	30,81	0,000
12. Making new supplier contacts	24,4%	11%	28,52	0,000
13. Market research	22,3%	12,4%	20,25	0,000
14. Communicating with suppliers	18,0%	11,0%	9,02	0,003
15. Making new agent contacts	14,5%	7,4%	12,03	0,001
16. Communicating with agents	11,3%	6,7%	4,01	0,045
17. Hiring staff	7,8%	4,2%		0,031

APPENDIX 2. DIFFERENCES BETWEEN THOSE WORKERS THAT CONSIDER THEY ARE GETTING SATISFACTORY RESULTS AND THOSE THAT DO NOT.

Work purposes with significative differences for those who said they get satisfactory results	Variable		Percentage of workers who said they get satisfactory results	Prueba Chi Cuadrado		
				Chi-square	Degrees of freedom	Significance
2. Communicating with professional contacts	Age	<30	62,50%	7,643	3	,054
		31-40	6,20%			
		41-50	67,10%			
		>50	36,40%			
4. Finding potential customers	Type of Worker	Employee	40,5%	4,653	1	,031
		Self-employed	57,6%			
5. Participating in groups of discussion in order to share information	Age	<30	78,90 %	9,244	2	,026
		31-40	42,60%			
		41-50	60,70 %			
		>50	63,60%			
6. Communicating with customers	Type of consumer the company sells to	Other companies B2B	54,90%	7,158	2	,028
		End cosumer B2C	88,90%			
		Both other companies and end consumer B2B2C	64,20%			
10. Creating debate/discussion groups	Size of the company	<10	65,20%	9,075	3	,028
		10-49	16,70%			
		50-250	53,80%			
		>250	53,30%			
12 Making new supplier contacts	Type of Worker	Employee		4,330	1	,037

Chapter 2
Social Media Marketing as New Marketing Tool

Sonal Trivedi
Chitkara Business School, Chitkara University, India

Reena Malik
Chitkara Business School, Chitkara University, India

ABSTRACT

Businesses are growing rapidly. They are using different strategies to connect customers. In this process, marketing is the most important thing. Most people use social media, and it has become one of the best platforms for marketing products. On social media, people can share their views and opinions and also get knowledge about the product and its updates. One of the fundamental reasons for utilizing social media in marketing is us a specialized apparatus that makes the organizations open to those interested in their products and makes them visible to the individuals who have no information of their products. These companies utilize social media to make a buzz and learn from and target customers. Therefore, companies need to look at various social media platforms where their customers exist. In this chapter, the concept of social media marketing is discussed with some practical examples of companies applying social media marketing tools.

INTRODUCTION

Economic development is the procedure by which a nation improves the prosperity of its natives through political or financial methods, is impacted by an assortment of components, including Marketing. The term is regularly mistaken for economic growth, which alludes to an expansion in the capacity of an economy to create products or administrations after some time (Sheoran et al. 2018). Truth be told, economic development is just a single critical factor in the financial advancement of a region.

Marketing is viewed as the most critical action in a business enterprise while at the beginning period of advancement it was viewed as the last activity (Mago, 2017). For convenience, the significance of marketing might be clarified as follows:

DOI: 10.4018/978-1-6684-6287-4.ch002

i) Conveyance of Standard of Life to the General Public:

Present day marketing dependably goes for consumer satisfaction (Diaconescu, 2020). Along these lines, the fundamental obligation of marketing is to create goods and services for the society as per their necessities and tastes at a sensible cost.

ii) Reduction in Distribution Cost:

Through effective marketing, the organizations can diminish their distribution expenses to a great extent (Blazheska, Ristovska & Gramatnikovski, 2020). Reduction in the expense of distribution straightforwardly influences the costs of products in light of the fact that the expense of distribution is an important piece of the complete cost of the item.

iii) Enhancing Employment Opportunities:

Marketing contains advertising, sales, distribution, branding and a lot more exercises (Štrach, 2018). So, the advancement of marketing naturally offers to ascend to a requirement for individuals to work in a few zones of marketing. Along these lines, the business openings are conceived.

iv) National Income Growth:

The successful task of marketing activities creates, maintains and builds the demand for products and enterprises in the society (Subhashini & Kowsalya, 2020). To satisfy this expanded need the organizations need to build the dimension of production thus raising their income. This expansion, thusly, builds the national income.

Social Media Marketing can be communicated as the process toward making matter that marketers have customized to the setting of every social media platform so as to initiate client participation and belongingness (Duffett, 2017). But every social media platform is different and hence same content can be shared on all platforms, for few platforms video is apt and for few images can work better (Wang & Kim, 2017). Following graphic shows, the various available social media platforms.

One of the fundamental reasons for using social media in marketing field is that it provides direct information to the company related to customer preferences and awareness regarding their product (Keegan & Rowley, 2017). Additionally, companies use social medial to create buzz for their product in the market (Vinerean, 2017). Social media marketing is applicable at each stage of marketing from customer acquisition to customer retention.

LITERATURE REVIEW

Dwivedi et al. (2020) in their paper explained the opportunities and issues in social media marketing specially related to ethical issues, electronic word of mouth, B2B marketing, mobile marketing, digital content management and artificial intelligence. The findings of the study show that there are ample opportunities of technology like VR and AI in the field of social media marketing.

Jacobson, Gruzd & Hernández-García (2020) studied in their paper the requirement for professional norms in use of consumer data for social media marketing by marketers. The study recommends strategy for marketers to mitigate the concerns of consumers regarding use of their information on social media.

Iankova et al. (2019) explored in their paper the fundamental difference in usage and perceived importance of social media marketing. The study concludes that social media marketing is of less significance as communication channel in B2B.

Chen & Lin (2019) studied the impact of activities of social media marketing on purchase, participation and continuance intention of consumer. The findings of the study show that activities of social media marketing indirectly influence the perceived value and identification of goods.

Tafesse & Wien (2018) studied the impact of social media on company's marketing strategies. The study covers social media analytics, customer engagement initiatives, active presence, and social media strategy.

Bilgin (2018) studied the impact of social media marketing on brand loyalty, brand image and brand awareness. The findings of the study suggest that social media marketing has positive influence on brand image and is most effective in creating brand awareness. It was also found that social media marketing develops brand loyalty also.

Felix, Rauschnabel & Hinsch (2017) in their study explored social media marketing governance, networks and hierarchy, poles of modernism and conservations, social media marketing culture, and generic dimensions. The study also suggests a framework for social media marketing which fulfills the objective and mission of organization.

Alalwan et al. (2017) in their study reviewed and examined 144 articles on social media marketing. The areas which were covered in these articles were impact of social media marketing on firm's performance and brand, customer relationship management, e-WOM and advertisements. After review of these articles, the paper also suggests the scope of future studies in the field of social media marketing.

Godey et al. (2016) focused on the influence of social media marketing activities on creation of brand equity and behaviour of customer. The study was conducted over around 850 luxury brands and measured five parameters of social media marketing i.e. WOM, customization, trendiness, interaction and entertainment. The finding of the study suggested that there is positive influence of social media marketing on brand equity.

Stephen (2016) studied five themes of social media marketing i.e. eWOM, mobile environment, consumer behavior, digital advertising and digital culture. The study throws light on various aspects of consumer experience related to digital environment. The study concludes that majorly social media marketing revolves around eWOM and other aspects are not discovered. Thus, the study suggests that there is requirement of exploring wider scope of social media marketing.

Zhu & Chen (2015) studied the impact of social media advertising on buying decision of consumer of US. The study presents the typology of social media marketing on the basis of following categories – creative outlet, collaboration, self-media and relationship. The finding of the study shows how each element cater to need of consumer.

Dwivedi, Kapoor & Chen (2015) reviewed the literature of 71 articles based on social media marketing to understand SMM as new marketing channel. This study suggests the gap in the field of social media marketing and scope for future research.

Constantinides (2014) studied the present status, effects and nature of social media to understand its role as agent for customer empowerment. The findings of the paper recommend two strategies for social media marketing i.e. passive approach and active approach. Using social media marketing as customer voice is passive approach and using social media marketing as PR channel or direct marketing is active approach. The paper also suggests the future scope of research.

Dahnil et al. (2014) reviewed academic literature related to adoption of social media marketing by SMEs. The finding of the research suggests the level of adoption of social media marketing at global level.

Vinerean et al. (2013) studied the people interacting online and engage in communicating directly about brand. The study was conducted over around 250 social media users and different segments of social media users were identified. The findings of the study are useful for marketers to approach different social media users with different social media marketing strategy.

Paquette (2013) conducted a vast literature review to recognize the concept of social media marketing, virtual brand community, consumer motives, user generated content, and viral advertising. The study also suggests that there is scope of further study on social media marketing opportunities for small retailers.

Saravanakumar & SuganthaLakshmi (2012) explained in their paper the need for companies to realise the significance of social media marketing, use it as promotion mix, use it as communication channel and to build brand equity.

Erdoğmuş & Cicek (2012) focused on the influence of social media marketing on the brand loyalty of consumer. The study was conducted over 338 people who at least follow one brand on social media. The findings of the study suggest that brand loyalty of consumer is positively influenced when consumer directly offers applications on social media, appears on various platforms, offers popular content, offers relevant content and advantageous campaigns.

Neti (2011) explained in his paper the concept of social media marketing, its benefit, growth, strategies, relevance and role in marketing. The findings of the study suggests that social media marketing is gaining popularity day by day and other organizations should also adopt it as marketing strategy.

Akar & Topçu (2011) shows in their study the factors affecting the attitude of consumer towards social media marketing. The study was conducted over undergraduate students to understand their attitude over 32 items. The finding of the study shows that there are six factors which affects the attitudes of consumer.

Hoffman & Fodor (2010) in their study showed paths to effective social media strategy and relevant metrics for social media applications organized by key social media objectives.

Fogel (2010) in his paper studied the current issues in brand and product measurement conversation in social media. The finding of the study shows that companies should include eWOM in their advertising strategy.

Mangold & Faulds (2009) argued in their paper social media as a part of promotion mix. The paper present two views – one traditional and other non-traditional. The traditional view says that social media allows company to talk directly to consumer while non-traditional view says that social media allows consumer to converse with each other which is not control of manager.

Ray (2009) studied the impact of social media marketing investments and explained four perspective for marketers risk management, brand management, digital and financial perspective.

Reuben (2008) in his paper studied 148 universities which are using social media as their marketing mix to reach their target customers. The popular social media platforms identified in this study are Twitter, Flickr, YouTube, MySpace, and Facebook.

The literature review shows that large companies, small businesses, universities and small retailers are using social media marketing in their promotion mix. But social media marketing is still seen as eWOM and its other application are still to be explored. Additionally, it shows that there is no framework for managers to control the WOM on social media. It also shows that there is a gap for research on scope of AI in social media marketing.

RESEARCH METHODOLOGY

Research Aim

The aim of the study is to identify social media marketing as a tool for companies to reach to the end consumer and create brand awareness. The research is done by thorough literature review using journals, book and other data in electronic form. The data from one company using social media in their promotion mix was collected and analyzed.

Research Strategy

The current study is conducted through case study method. Case study method is a method where a situation in analysed in depth (Harrison et al. 2017). Thus, case study method is a descriptive method where a situation is explained and analysed in depth. In the present study, the case of Coco-Cola company is taken to analyse the use of social media marketing by company.

Research Objective

1.   To identify and analyse the way organizations are using social media marketing.
2.   To identify the advantages and disadvantages of social media marketing to businesses.

Research Approach

The research approach used in the current study is deductive as the researcher has first identified the research problem and defined the research questions and then used case study method to identify the impact of social media marketing on businesses. Deductive approach was used in the present study as it helps in establishing relationship between two variables (Woiceshyn & Daellenbach, 2018) i.e. social media marketing in promotion mix of businesses.

Type of Research

The current research is descriptive research as the present study provides answers to research questions of 'how' companies are applying social media marketing and 'what' are its advantages and disadvantages. As descriptive research provides answers to questions like how, what, when and where (Kothari, 2004).

Collection of Data

In the present study, the data is collected from secondary sources such as official statistics, public documents, books, newspaper, magazines, articles, journals, and website of selected company. Secondary data is the data which exists either in published or electronic format (Noor, 2008). The data is collected in a way which ensures integrity (Marczyk and DeMatteo, 2005). Collection of secondary data is more convenient for researcher and further clears the research objective of the researcher.

CASE STUDY

Coca Cola and Facebook

As we all know that coca cola is one the biggest beverage brand in the market selling 3900 beverage choices and in 200 countries with over more than 500 brands. "We communicate exactly the same thing today as we did 125 years ago," M. Berquet (Director of Marketing, Coco-Cola) said, "and that is Coke's unique taste. We try to achieve brand love by communicating that message, and we have always been guided by the same principles: be unique, be simple, be honest and tell brand stories." According to him, brand image can be built through consistency. In one of the tests conducted in 2014, the blindfolded subjects were able to undoubtedly recognize only two shapes i.e. one of egg and another coke bottle. That is definitely an achievement.

One of the contributing factors for this success is the social media marketing on various social media platforms majorly Facebook (Rauschnabel, Praxmarer & Ivens, 2012). Coke uses many Facebook interfaces and products in its use that includes a news feed, posting ads, logout experience, etc. Coke worked with Starcom MediaVest to use the full range of Facebook products and the results that were analyzed with a study conducted by the Kantar Worldpanel study on the same in 2013.

The most noteworthy move of the Facebook marketing took place in 2013 when Coca- Cola launched a multichannel campaign and television and FB focusing a return of the polar bear family made by Ridley Scott (Refer figure 1). The 6-minute promotional video takes their journey across the Arctic and learns about leadership. This Advertisement was broadcast on television into a 30-sec spot in prime time. Over a 3 days period, the company decided to use the FB target block using the logout experience i.e. the ad used to play when the users logged out of their Facebook accounts.

As already mentioned the company is a popular brand in more than 20 countries and hence it has a different strategy of marketing to cover the diverse culture in these countries. Facebook has played a very important role in their social media strategy and we will consider success story for the most profitable cases where Facebook has played a significant role to help coke make huge ROI.

Figure 1. Coco-cola TV commercial used on FB
Source - digitaltveurope.com

European Partners

The European partners of the company coke used the help of a local agency named PauwR Digital marketing to study the local market and audiences and device methods that increase the sale of the product in the local areas (Deighton & Kornfeld, 2011). For this reason, they made advertisements that were both local and personal. They devised the call to an action method, where people were invited to come and try the Fuze Tea which was absolutely free and claimed to return money back if they did not like the product on a refund page available to the customers.

Two types of advertisements were used to link ads and carousel method (Refer figure 2). The former was used if the vendor used to keep only one type of product/flavor and the latter if the vendor has multiple products of flavor.

Facebook contributed very heavily in the entire campaign by helping got make advertisements by using Facebook APIs and the company was able to make over 10,000 + ad creatives as a part of 2,500 ad sets. With the help of this API, the company produced mathematical and statistical adjustments and increase campaign output.

Figure 2. Coke ad on Facebook
Source - www.cocacolaep.com/sustainability/this-is-forward

Coke Brazil

In the autumn of 2017, the coke campaigns with the help of eight Brazilian singers which were Simone and Simaria, Anitta, Luan Santana, Projota, Solange Almeida, PablloVittar, Thiaguinho, Valesca, and Ludmilla (Refer figure 3). The photos of these singers were made available on the coke cans and the final goal was a contract of a musical video by the top 3 singers that were picked by the audience at the end of the promotion (Kačániová & Bačíková, 2016). The winning trio of the promotional campaign was PablloVittar, Simone and Samaria and Luan Santana and hence came the record hit "Hasta la Viste".

Figure 3. Coke Facebook partnership campaign
Source - <u>oglobo.globo.com</u>

Coke's and Facebook's partnership on this campaign involved a number of elements, let it be #Fan-Feat project, live broadcast of the trio' show and messenger live voting of their famous artist, etc. The company not only invested in FB but also much other social media feeds including Vertical Video, Live, Instant Experience ads, ads, Stories, and Insta feed. The result of this strategy was humongous and it was estimated that 3.6 million people were reached in 2 hours and around 600,000 views on Facebook live for a show in Sao Paulo.

Coke Taiwan

Targeting the audience in the age group of 11-20 and 20-30 who were interested in music and drinks, a multilevel campaign as launched consisting of the following objectives:

- To introduce a new bottle design
- The new bottles picturized 3 popular music artists who made promotional videos to make that the point the coke make summer fun and favorable (Refer figure 4).

The company also announced a launch of a new Messenger Bot along with a short video ad. The video was an adaptation of the tv commercial and it was converted in carousel format and uploaded in Instagram stories. It basically advertised the 3 artists featuring new Coca-Cola bottles. When people clicked on the advertisement it takes them to the bot which asked the people questions, increasing interest, and traffic. It encouraged a fun, personal, one-to-one interaction and also created awareness about the promotion in the target audience of young adults. It also created encouraged them to participate in Coca- Cola's lucky draw.

Figure 4. Picture of 3 popular music artists on Coco-Cola bottles
Source – Perez, 2020

Coke and YouTube

Coco-Cola had created its own channel on YouTube with the objective to target young audience which spend their maximum time on iPhones, YouTube and Facebook (Refer figure 5).

Google as of late appealed that YouTube carries a ROI which 78% greater than television advertisements, with the research proposing that companies ought to spend anyplace between five to 25% of their advertisement spending plan on the channel.

The medium "CokeTV'' is a strategy adopted by Coke to catch the attention of social media generation. It is adjoined by Dodie Clark and vloggers Emmanuel "Manny" Brown. This idea was influenced from the success of marketing strategy of Red Bull (Brownbill, Miller & Braunack-Mayer, 2018). The marketing strategy adopted by Red Bull to connect to young generation was to present itself as an energy drink by sponsoring various thrilling sports. It widespread its marketing campaign from all possible digital channels to its own TV channel named RebBull TV.

Coke entered into social media marketing but a bit late from its other competitors. Coke started its own YouTube channel in 2014. But as it is well said its never too late, So Coke at least made its presence on YouTube. It added to Coke's other marketing strategies. It also opted catchy tag lines to attract the attention of consumers. It also added varieties in its product line. It also product line with zero or low sugar content. The marketing Director 'Bobby Britain' says that CokeTV is different from others because it speaks the language of its customers.

"It will be the most engaging platform to reach young adults in GB and Ireland, entertaining them with relevant and authentic content, uniquely served in a way only Coca-Cola can," Britain added.

Figure 5. CokeTV GB and Ireland
Source - Reporter, 2016

CokeTV Great Britain & Ireland

Home   Videos   Playlists   Channels   About

Welcome to CokeTV with Manny and Dodie |
#CokeTVMoment

13K views · 1 month ago

Join Manny and Dodie (doddleoddle) every week,
Thursdays at 4pm for brand new #CokeTVMoments

They'll be going on adventures and doing all sorts of
awesome things with some of their friends from
YouTube including Jake Boys, Caffreezy Helen
Anderson, Jack Howard and loads more!

Subscribe now to never miss a moment!

Read more

Uploads

Manny's PES showdown | Can Dodie and Lucy become pro   Manny gets a Football Freestyle   Can Dodie Master GRAFFITI? |
#CokeTVMoment   footballers? | #CokeTVMoment   lesson from World Champion   #CokeTVMoment
159,206 views · 3 days ago   59,383 views · 1 week ago   231,329 views · 2 weeks ago   182,953 views · 3 weeks ago
CC   CC   CC   CC

Every Dodie #CokeTVMoment

Watch Doddleoddle aka Dodie have fun with her friends and have an amazing #CokeTVMoment in every
episode

Can Dodie and Lucy become pro   Can Dodie Master GRAFFITI? | Dodie and Evan Edinger go   Dodie and Helen Anderson go
footballers? | #CokeTVMoment   #CokeTVMoment   CLIMBING | #CokeTVMoment   STUNT DRIVING !
by CokeTV Great Britain & Ireland   by CokeTV Great Britain & Ireland   by CokeTV Great Britain & Ireland   by CokeTV Great Britain & Ireland
59,383 views · 1 week ago   182,953 views · 3 weeks ago   196,163 views · 1 month ago   110,366 views · 1 month ago
CC   CC   CC

CASE ANALYSIS

Facebook

Case Analysis of the Coke Investment

The entire promotion was largely aimed at creating brand awareness. Using its campaign as a medium Coca-Cola wanted to encourage people to participate in various activities using FB adding as a compliment to the television resulting in a direct impact in sales. Delivering the message to a wider audience this strategy reaped incredible results. According to a study, Facebook leads in incremental sales with an ROI greater than all other media:

- Over 1.4 million unique shoppers reached
- Facebook was able to obtain 27% incremental sales with a mere 2% of gross media budget.
- 18% of the total potential buyers were exposed on the Facebook campaign.
- 3.6 times greater Return of Investment than television ROI.

Case Analysis of the Coke Investment in the European Market

According to Pieter Voogt, Managing Director, PauwR Digital Marketing "This campaign was a win-win-win for Coca-Cola European Partners, the vendors, and customers. For Coca-Cola European Partners Nederland, it provided the ideal solution to supporting thousands of outlets with local relevancy at scale. For vendors, that meant new customers and for the customers themselves, they got to try Fuze Tea for free." During the February–April 2018 campaign, Coca-Cola European Partners saw more than 32,000 people in the Netherlands try Fuze Tea for free.

- Over 1.4 million unique shoppers reached
- 32,170 offers redeemed

Case Analysis of the Coke Investment Brazil

Coca-Cola utilized the music as a base to reach out to the youth on Facebook in a new and way which was notably compelling, giving the target audience a chance to take part in the promotion and campaign. The entire success was only possible because of the combined result of Coca-Cola, FB, JWT, and KOLAB. This promotional method came out to be world's most intelligent way to form a community of fans and approach by giving them a cause and innovative formats like a celebration of the outcome and hand album

- 20-point ad recall in the second phase of the campaign
- 8-point increase in brand favourability
- 8-point increase in top-of-mind for association with music

Case Analysis of the Coke Investment Taiwan

Coca-Cola wanted to engage teens and young adults through its summer 2018 campaign to improve brand favourability as well as brand interest. The results were highly favorable for the company and the major credibility goes to the users of the Bot. The one to one interaction method boosted brand favourability and many customers were engaged with the brand via the bot to the Messenger to show their love for the videos, releasing quality results.

- 65% of the target audience reached
- 22% lift in sales in convenience store channel compared to before the campaign
- 15.6 interactions per person on Messenger

YouTube

In order to handle diminishing popularity of its image among the millennials, Coca-Cola chose to dispatch a channel on Youtube. Youtube is the most-well known video-sharing stage and is extremely mainstream among the youth. Coca-Cola began with youth-driven campaigns like "Share a-Coke" which was an enormous success. For connecting with much more prominent audience Coca-cola began working together with well-known youtubers. Coke has various videos on YouTube which are shot with Athletes, performing artists, and trending youtubers and these videos were trending in top 100.

In Croatia, a Youtube Talent show was launched. The point of the show was to discover new talent from among a huge number of Youtube users..

KPIs

The Key Performance Indicator of Coke marketing strategy is that it keep on submitting new videos on daily basis, kept those videos short and got various followers and likes on YouTube. The cost of this advertisement strategy was low and its reach and impact on people was high. The video of Coke which motivated viewers to share the bottle of coke got millions of likes and share. Thus, this strategy ensures that the video is effective, liked by people and reached to million of viewers. Additionally, it does not cost any additional money to company. It was all possible because of growing popularity of social media and smartphones and availability of internet everywhere.

CONCLUSION

Social media has been a very important source of marketing especially in recent times and many companies rely on the same. Let it be the newer companies who rely majorly on social media for marketing or let it be older companies who are shifting their traditional television advertisement-based approaches to social media marketing ones and earning huge profits. The case study of Coca-Cola confirms the statement as we have seen the shift from their traditional based approaches to social media ones. Facebook, Twitter, and YouTube play a very significant role in the same and location-based strategy is a cherry on a cake to customize the marketing pattern and model as per the geographical and cultural needs to ensure better results. Hence we conclude that social media marketing is a very significant method or part in any marketing strategy.

REFERENCES

Akar, E., & Topçu, B. (2011). An examination of the factors influencing consumers' attitudes toward social media marketing. *Journal of Internet Commerce, 10*(1), 35–67. doi:10.1080/15332861.2011.558456

Alalwan, A. A., Rana, N. P., Dwivedi, Y. K., & Algharabat, R. (2017). Social media in marketing: A review and analysis of the existing literature. *Telematics and Informatics, 34*(7), 1177–1190. doi:10.1016/j.tele.2017.05.008

Bell, E., & Bryman, A. (2007). The ethics of management research: An exploratory content analysis. *British Journal of Management, 18*(1), 63–77. doi:10.1111/j.1467-8551.2006.00487.x

Beverage, F. (2020*). Coca-Cola TV Commercial, 'Snow Polar Bear' Song by Edvard Grieg*. Retrieved 9 November 2020, from https://www.ispot.tv/ad/ZIai/coca-cola-snow-polar-bear-song-by-edvard-grieg

Bilgin, Y. (2018). The effect of social media marketing activities on brand awareness, brand image and brand loyalty. *Business & Management Studies: An International Journal, 6*(1), 128–148. doi:10.15295/bmij.v6i1.229

Blazheska, D., Ristovska, N., & Gramatnikovski, S. (2020). The impact of digital trends on marketing. *UTMS Journal of Economics (Skopje), 11*(1).

Boyatzis, R. E. (1998). *Transforming qualitative information: Thematic analysis and code development.* Sage.

Brownbill, A. L., Miller, C. L., & Braunack-Mayer, A. J. (2018). The marketing of sugar-sweetened beverages to young people on Facebook. *Australian and New Zealand Journal of Public Health, 42*(4), 354–360. doi:10.1111/1753-6405.12801 PMID:29972262

Chen, S. C., & Lin, C. P. (2019). Understanding the effect of social media marketing activities: The mediation of social identification, perceived value, and satisfaction. *Technological Forecasting and Social Change, 140*, 22–32. doi:10.1016/j.techfore.2018.11.025

Clarke, V., & Braun, V. (2013). Teaching thematic analysis: Overcoming challenges and developing strategies for effective learning. *The Psychologist, 26*(2).

Constantinides, E. (2014). Foundations of social media marketing. *Procedia: Social and Behavioral Sciences, 148*, 40–57. doi:10.1016/j.sbspro.2014.07.016

Dahnil, M. I., Marzuki, K. M., Langgat, J., & Fabeil, N. F. (2014). Factors influencing SMEs adoption of social media marketing. *Procedia: Social and Behavioral Sciences, 148*, 119–126. doi:10.1016/j.sbspro.2014.07.025

Dahnil, M. I., Marzuki, K. M., Langgat, J., & Fabeil, N. F. (2014). Factors influencing SMEs adoption of social media marketing. *Procedia: Social and Behavioral Sciences, 148*, 119–126. doi:10.1016/j. sbspro.2014.07.025

Deighton, J., & Kornfeld, L. (2011). *Coca-Cola on Facebook*. Harvard Business School Marketing Unit Case, (511-110).

Diaconescu, M. (2020). Some considerations regarding the new trends in marketing approaches. *Romanian Economic Journal, 23*(77), 2–10.

Duffett, R. G. (2017). Influence of social media marketing communications on young consumers' attitudes. *Young Consumers, 18*(1), 19–39. doi:10.1108/YC-07-2016-00622

Dwivedi, Y. K., Ismagilova, E., Hughes, D. L., Carlson, J., Filieri, R., Jacobson, J., ... Kumar, V. (2020). Setting the future of digital and social media marketing research: Perspectives and research propositions. *International Journal of Information Management*, 102168. doi:10.1016/j.ijinfomgt.2020.102168

Dwivedi, Y. K., Kapoor, K. K., & Chen, H. (2015). Social media marketing and advertising. *The Marketing Review, 15*(3), 289–309. doi:10.1362/146934715X14441363377999

Erdoğmuş, İ. E., & Cicek, M. (2012). The impact of social media marketing on brand loyalty. *Procedia: Social and Behavioral Sciences, 58*, 1353–1360. doi:10.1016/j.sbspro.2012.09.1119

Felix, R., Rauschnabel, P. A., & Hinsch, C. (2017). Elements of strategic social media marketing: A holistic framework. *Journal of Business Research, 70*, 118–126. doi:10.1016/j.jbusres.2016.05.001

Fogel, S. (2010). Issues in measurement of word of mouth in social media marketing. *International Journal of Integrated Marketing Communications, 2*(2).

Godey, B., Manthiou, A., Pederzoli, D., Rokka, J., Aiello, G., Donvito, R., & Singh, R. (2016). Social media marketing efforts of luxury brands: Influence on brand equity and consumer behavior. *Journal of Business Research, 69*(12), 5833–5841. doi:10.1016/j.jbusres.2016.04.181

Harrison, H., Birks, M., Franklin, R., & Mills, J. (2017, January). Case study research: Foundations and methodological orientations. In *Forum Qualitative Sozialforschung/Forum: Qualitative. Social Research, 18*(1).

Hoffman, D. L., & Fodor, M. (2010). Can you measure the ROI of your social media marketing? *MIT Sloan Management Review, 52*(1), 41.

Iankova, S., Davies, I., Archer-Brown, C., Marder, B., & Yau, A. (2019). A comparison of social media marketing between B2B, B2C and mixed business models. *Industrial Marketing Management, 81*, 169–179. doi:10.1016/j.indmarman.2018.01.001

Jacobson, J., Gruzd, A., & Hernández-García, Á. (2020). Social media marketing: Who is watching the watchers? *Journal of Retailing and Consumer Services, 53*, 53. doi:10.1016/j.jretconser.2019.03.001

Kačániová, M., & Bačíková, Z. (2016). Emotional aspects of Facebook textual posts a framework for marketing research. *European Journal of Science and Theology, 12*(6), 187–197.

Keegan, B. J., & Rowley, J. (2017). Evaluation and decision making in social media marketing. *Management Decision, 55*(1), 15–31. doi:10.1108/MD-10-2015-0450

Kothari, C. R. (2004). *Research methodology: Methods and techniques*. New Age International.

Mago, Z. (2017). New trends of marketing communication based on digital games. *European Journal of Science and Theology, 13*(6), 171–182.

Mangold, W. G., & Faulds, D. J. (2009). Social media: The new hybrid element of the promotion mix. *Business Horizons, 52*(4), 357–365. doi:10.1016/j.bushor.2009.03.002

Marczyk, G., DeMatteo, D., & Festinger, D. (2005). *Essentials of research design and methodology*. John wiley & sons, Inc.

Neti, S. (2011). Social media and its role in marketing. *International Journal of Enterprise Computing and Business Systems, 1*(2), 1-15.

Noor, K. B. M. (2008). Case study: A strategic research methodology. *American Journal of Applied Sciences, 5*(11), 1602–1604. doi:10.3844/ajassp.2008.1602.1604

Paquette, H. (2013). *Social media as a marketing tool: A literature review*. Academic Press.

Perez, L. (2020). *Pin on Love Coca Cola*. Retrieved 9 November 2020, from https://www.pinterest.com/pin/597078863078710815/

Rauschnabel, P. A., Praxmarer, S., & Ivens, B. S. (2012). Social media marketing: How design features influence interactions with brand postings on Facebook. In *Advances in Advertising Research* (Vol. 3, pp. 153–161). Gabler Verlag. doi:10.1007/978-3-8349-4291-3_12

Ray, A. (2009). *The ROI Of Social Media Marketing*. Marketing.

Reporter, D. (2016). *Endemol Shine Beyond, Coca Cola Create Coketv*. Digital TV Europe. Available at: https://www.digitaltveurope.com/2016/07/19/endemol-shine-beyond-coca-cola-create-coketv/

Reuben, R. (2008). *The use of social media in higher education for marketing and communications: A guide for professionals in higher education*. Academic Press.

Santana & Juntos. (2020). Retrieved 9 November 2020, from https://oglobo.globo.com/cultura/musica/luan-santana-pabllo-vittar-simone-simaria-lancam-clipe-juntos-22647128

Saravanakumar, M., & SuganthaLakshmi, T. (2012). Social media marketing. *Life Science Journal, 9*(4), 4444–4451.

Sheoran, M., Kumar, D., Kumar, V., & Verma, D. (2018). Understanding the trends of marketing research and its future directions: A citation analysis. *The Bottom Line (New York, N.Y.), 31*(3/4), 191–207. doi:10.1108/BL-04-2018-0022

Singh, Y. K. (2006). *Fundamental of research methodology and statistics*. New Age International.

Stephen, A. T. (2016). The role of digital and social media marketing in consumer behavior. *Current Opinion in Psychology, 10*, 17–21. doi:10.1016/j.copsyc.2015.10.016

Štrach, P. (2018). Emerging Trends in Marketing Communications: Personalization and Eventization. *Marketing Identity, 6*(1/1), 160-167.

Subhashini, M., & Kowsalya, M. (2020). Recent trends in marketing environment. *Studies in Indian Place Names, 40*(40), 439–446.

Tafesse, W., & Wien, A. (2018). Implementing social media marketing strategically: An empirical assessment. *Journal of Marketing Management, 34*(9-10), 732–749. doi:10.1080/0267257X.2018.1482365

This is Forward. (2020). Retrieved 9 November 2020, from https://www.cocacolaep.com/sustainability/this-is-forward/

Triangulation, D. S. (2014, September). The use of triangulation in qualitative research. *Oncology Nursing Forum, 41*(5), 545–547. doi:10.1188/14.ONF.545-547 PMID:25158659

Vartanian, T. P. (2010). *Secondary data analysis*. Oxford University Press. doi:10.1093/acprof:oso/9780195388817.001.0001

Vinerean, S. (2017). Importance of strategic social media marketing. *Expert Journal of Marketing, 5*(1).

Vinerean, S., Cetina, I., Dumitrescu, L., & Tichindelean, M. (2013). The effects of social media marketing on online consumer behavior. *International Journal of Business and Management, 8*(14), 66. doi:10.5539/ijbm.v8n14p66

Wang, Z., & Kim, H. G. (2017). Can social media marketing improve customer relationship capabilities and firm performance? Dynamic capability perspective. *Journal of Interactive Marketing, 39*, 15–26. doi:10.1016/j.intmar.2017.02.004

Weimer, W. B. (1979). *Notes on the methodology of scientific research* (No. 507.2 W45). Academic Press.

Woiceshyn, J., & Daellenbach, U. (2018). Evaluating inductive vs deductive research in management studies. *Qualitative Research in Organizations and Management, 13*(2), 183–195. doi:10.1108/QROM-06-2017-1538

Zhu, Y. Q., & Chen, H. G. (2015). Social media and human need satisfaction: Implications for social media marketing. *Business Horizons, 58*(3), 335–345. doi:10.1016/j.bushor.2015.01.006

Chapter 3
Social Media, Marketing Practices, and Consumer Behavior

Nozha Erragcha
Tunis Business School, University of Tunis, Tunisia

Hanene Babay
University of Monastir, Tunisia

ABSTRACT

This chapter looks at the phenomenon of social media and its consequences on marketing and consumer behavior. To express an opinion, the authors first define the notion of "social media," review their different types as well as the decisive moments that marked their history. Then, they focus on the influence of these media on marketing practices by referring to the changes that have affected the marketing approach from the stage of the market study to the stage of control of marketing actions companies. Finally, they are very interested in the changes that have affected the traditional decision-making process and are announcing useful recommendations to respond to this set of changes.

INTRODUCTION

Since Tim Berners-Lee's shocking invention in 1989, the Web has transfigured the Internet to the point that it has become a synonym for some. Being simple to use, the web has been massively adopted by the general public and its success has generated the need to make it evolve since its first version 1.0 which dates from the 90s. This first version, also called traditional web, is static. It focuses on the distribution of information and does not solicit the intervention of users. Thus, according to this form of the web, the first e-commerce sites were product-oriented sites whose main purpose is to present the products to consumers by offering them online access to information about these products. But the individual consumer of this content could not interact with the website in question. It is compared in its non-interactive design to a television program.

DOI: 10.4018/978-1-6684-6287-4.ch003

Nevertheless, in the early 2000s, new applications appeared on the Web giving users the ability to interact and generate content themselves. As an indication, the YouTube app allows everyone to upload a video for free broadcast worldwide. Other media and applications also appeared as blogs, wikis, podcasts, social networks, social bookmarks, microblogging, etc. Through these applications, the web 2.0 has totally changed perspective and has become a social web that favors the sharing and exchange of information and content (text, video, images or other). Therefore, the intervention of consumers is tolerated or even desired and their opinions are now solicited permanently. They then enrolled in a virtual socialization that offers them a growing pleasure. Little by little, social media has become an integral part of the lives of consumers who now use them to connect with friends and family, keep up to date and even entertain themselves. That's why around 4 billion people around the world today use social media.

The interest and commitment shown by consumers to social media has not been without consequences for marketing. Companies have had to adapt their marketing strategies to exploit the potential offered by these media, particularly to inform, seduce, convince and retain their customers. At the same time, these media have had a very significant impact on consumer behavior, in particular their motivations and brakes with respect to buying online and the way in which their decision-making process works. This process seems to undergo a real metamorphosis that should be considered more closely and draw conclusions and useful recommendations.

More research that delve into aspect of consumer behavior and psychology in the digital economy is deemed necessary (Ling Chang, Ling Tam, & Suki, 2016; Nathan, Fook Chiun, & Suki, 2016; Suki, 2016). Accordingly, this study focus on the rise of social media and the consequences of this boom on marketing and consumer behavior. To do this, they first come back to the definition of social media and their classification in order to clarify the reader about what is called "social media".Then, they will focus on the influence of these media on marketing practices and on the various stages of the decision-making process.

SOCIAL MEDIA - DEFINITION, TYPOLOGY AND HISTORY

What is Social Media?

According to Kaplan and Haenlein (2010), social media is defined as "a group of Internet-based applications that build on the ideological foundations of Web 2.0, and that allow the creation and exchange of user generated content".

In other words, Social media refers to all sites and web platforms that offer so-called "social" features to users. These platforms are based on the collaborative creation of content as well as the exchange of information between individuals (forums, blogs open to comments, etc.). Social media is understood as the different forms of online communication used by people to create networks, communities and collectives to share information, ideas, messages and other content, such as videos.

From this definition, two important characteristics of social media are to highlight:

1. Social media includes online communication, which means that the story of social media can not begin before the invention and the widespread adoption of the Internet.

2. Social media depends on user-generated content. That's why classic websites and blogs are not part of the social media world. Only some people can post on these sites, and there are significant restrictions on the types of content that are downloaded.

These two features make it possible to distinguish social media from other applications on the web and emphasize concepts such as collaboration, interactivity and sharing that particularly characterize this type of media.

Moreover, it is clear that social media contain a wide range of elements. Indeed, social media applications include messaging applications like WhatsApp and Viber, platforms based on profiles like Facebook and LinkedIn, video portals like YouTube, and email clients such as GMail. These elements lend themselves to being categorized according to their own characteristics and the purposes to which they respond. Thus, the authors propose to draw up a typology which highlights the different types of elements constituting the social media in order to better understand this vast notion.

The Different Types of Social Media

Social media apps vary in scope and functionality. Thus, to better understand the potential of social media in the digital strategies of companies, it is essential to understand the specificities of each category or type of social media. Social media can focus on mass targeting or professional networking or sharing photos, videos and knowledge (Kietzmann et al., 2011). The classification depends on the user's use and the need he / she wants to meet and achieve (Kaplan & Haenlein, 2010, Hanna et al., 2011, Kaplan & Haenlein, 2012, Zolkepli and Kamarulzaman, 2011, Kaplan, 2012).

Social Networks

This includes platforms that allow their users to connect to other users with common interests. Usually, they rely on creating a profile to interact with other users. Members are linked bilaterally or through groups. The most popular today are Facebook and LinkedIn.

Platforms Of Social Bookmarking

They record, organize, and manage links to web resources that the user finds useful. Most of them allow to "mark" the links to make easier their reunion and sharing. The most famous are Pinterest and StumbleUpon.

Sharing Services

They allow uploading, sharing photos, videos or audio content on a website to make them accessible anywhere in the world. The majority of these services offer additional social characteristics such as the addition of a user profile or the possibility of commenting on the content. The most popular are YouTube or Flickr.

Micro-Blogging Sites

These are publishing, sharing and discussion services. Each individual member has a public profile where the latest messages are listed. This member can subscribe to other people's profiles and view their publications. These sites focus on short updates that are visible to anyone who has subscribed to receive. The most known sites are Twitter and Instagram.

Forums

This is a public chat room where messages are displayed in chronological order. A message posted by a user could be approved before by a moderator. The content posted by Internet users are categorized by themes, subjects. They are at least temporarily archived.

Blogs

This is a special form of website, with specific features. A blog is characterized by the more or less regular publication of articles, usually classified in reverse chronological order on the main page. Articles are dated and each has a unique URL with a comment box. There are many known and influential blogs. The blog also participates in SEO optimization of a company on a search engine.

Collaborative Media

Social and information sites that tend to relay content in a relatively neutral and factual way. Collaboration, mutual aid and exchange are embodied in this type of social media. These sites are particularly powerful collaborative spaces. The best known are Wikipedia and Commentçamarche.net.

History of Social Media

The history of social media has been marked by decisive moments, relative to the launch of certain sites and platforms whose footprint was particularly salient. These have contributed to the evolution of "social media" as well as the success gained by these media so far. In what follows, the authors will return to the key dates that characterize the history of social media since the advent of web 2.0.

In the year 2000, a site called Hot or Not was launched to invite users to post photos of themselves in order to be rated by other users based on their charm. This site would have fed the lack of confidence of millions of people, which made its success at the time and led to say that it even inspired the creators of Facebook.

In 2002, a dating site called Friendster was launched. This site allows users to meet friends of their friends. This is to create a profile, include "status updates" and indicate mood. The site had a messaging service that also allows sending messages to friends of friends. This site has had incredible success in just one year and has reached a peak of popularity to which the creative company was unprepared. So the servers were and so the users started to connect elsewhere.

In 2003, the "MySpace" site was created as a place for friends. Disappointed users of Friendster service have abandoned it for the benefit of the newborn baby who has become the favorite haunt for millions of trendy teens. This site has made it possible to create public profiles that are customizable and visible to everyone, unlike private Friendster profiles, which are reserved for registered users.

From 2003 to 2005, social media particularly gained ground. Indeed, Mark Zuckerberg has launched Facebook. At the same time, LinkedIn is making an appearance by targeting the business community. Photo sharing sites like Photobucket and Flickr or bookmarks like del.ici.ous or blogging like WordPress are born. YouTube also entered the scene in 2005 with the first video in which a man comments on his visit to the zoo in front of the elephant enclosure. This video has so far made 56 million views. In the same year, the Reddit Community Social News website was also launched.

In 2006, the Facebbok network took off and became a truly global network. Twitter has also taken off.

In 2007, YouTube launched a partnership program with its creators of popular content, which marked a turning point for the site. The microblogging also arrives thanks to Tumblr. This year was also marked by the advent of the hashtag, a symbol that mobilized, promoted and sensitized around critical (and not so critical) social issues.

In 2009, Twitter totally adopted the hashtag after realizing that this symbol is more than just a way to organize content, but a unique language to express ideas and emotions on the Internet. The hashtag energizes the platform and seduces new users.

The year 2009 was also marked by the new family hobby: FarmVille. This addictive social game has even featured in the list of the worst inventions in the world, published by TIME Magazine). Second, users were noticeably attracted by the foursquare geolocation application, which is one of the first applications that allows users to indicate where they are and publish check-ins, recommending certain neighborhoods or cities to their family and to their friends. Since then, this application has been a social phenomenon par excellence.

In 2010, the digital culture was jostled by the adoption of emoji by the Unicode standard. Since this adoption, emojis have become popular at lightning speed and have been legitimized as language. At the same year, Instagram enters the scene by giving birth to the phenomenon of publishing retouched photos with a Polaroid type filter.

In 2011, social networks played a fundamental role in the protest movements against the regime of Zine el-Abidine Ben Ali in Tunisia and later that of Hosni Mubarak in Egypt. The success of these protests sparked similar movements, collectively known as the "Arab Spring," which swept the countries of the Middle East and North Africa in the hope of overthrowing the powers that be and to bring to peoples positive changes. According to several reports, social networks have contributed significantly to the success of these events by allowing organizers to mobilize and shape opinion. The most popular Twitter hashtags (#Egypt, # Jan25, #Libya, #Bahrain and #protest) were tweeted millions of times in the first three months of 2011. Facebook usage has grown throughout the Arab region and doubled in some countries. The government manages to block all access to Facebook and Twitter briefly, but soon activists find other creative ways to organize themselves, inspiring viewers around the world. Since these facts, social networks have acquired an inescapable importance.

Also in 2011, the Snapchat application was launched and was an immediate success because it draws on the ephemeral nature of the moments of life. With this application, users publish content ("snaps") that disappear after 24 hours. This disappearance of snaps seduced teenagers, who were the first to use the application. For teens, Snapchat is the perfect alternative to find their friends - and to flee their family on Facebook.

In 2012, Facebook celebrated a billion users contacted through this network.

2014 was named the Year of the Selfie because of Ellen DeGeneres' selfie at the Oscars, which was retweeted over three million times, setting a new record on Twitter and winning the Twitter award " Golden tweet of the year.

In 2015, the streaming war begins. Meerkat is the first app to create the craze for live video. Shortly after, Twitter launches Periscope and wins the first war of streaming.

In 2016, Facebook launched Facebook LIVE to join the battle of live video. Instagram launched the Stories. With the help of filters, stickers, polls, hashtags and highlights, the Stories manage to make the Instagram application even more addictive, even though it seemed impossible.

The year 2016 was also marked by the crisis of fake news on social media related to the American elections. An information war was cleverly waged using "troll factories" on social media to spread false information (including false statements and conspiracy theories) during US presidential elections. Opinion leaders in mainstream media such as journalists, experts and politicians (up to Hillary Clinton and Donald Trump) are spreading content that is said to have been shared on social networks by bots. Since then, Facebook has revealed that 126 million Americans had been exposed to content published by Russian agents during the elections.

In 2018, representatives of Facebook, Twitter and Google appear before the US Congress to give their testimony in connection with investigations into Russian interference in the US presidential election. At the beginning of 2018, we learn that Facebook has authorized a researcher from Cambridge Analytica, who worked on Donald Trump's presidential campaign, to acquire the data of 50 million users of the social network without their consent. Following this, a campaign named #DeleteFacebook (#DeleteFacebook) spreads on the Internet to protest this scandal by massively suppressing their Facebook profiles. Yet the number of Facebook users seems to continue to climb. BUT, Zuckerberg had to participate in five days of hearings before the US Congress following strong pressure to respond to the problem of protection of personal data. That same year, Instagram launched the IGTV app to allow its users to publish long videos that can last an hour.

All these events, evolutions and revolutions attached to social media seem to have significant consequences for human life on more than one plan. Their fallout seems to be difficult to define definitively. Thus, it is inevitable to be interested in the impact of these social media on marketing and consumer behavior.

INFLUENCE OF SOCIAL MEDIA ON MARKETING

For years, the rate of companies using social media for marketing purposes has visibly increased and the budget allocated by these companies for the implementation of their marketing strategy on these networks continues to grow as well. Companies are increasingly investing in the potential of social media as they offer significant advantages over conventional channels of marketing:

First, social media gives businesses the space they need to reach their target. Indeed, given the surprising increase in the number of connected consumers (no less than 70% of the workforce is well anchored in social media) and the increased time spent by these consumers on these virtual spaces, it is important for any company to be present in order to ensure an omnipresence in the daily lives of its customers.

Secondly, by being present on these media, marketers can easily identify influencer groups that are likely to play the role of promising brand ambassadors and thus contribute to the success of the brand.

And thirdly, all this is done at almost no cost (compared to traditional customer outreach programs) because in most cases, social networking sites are free.

Social media is then associated with a very attractive potential that should never be overlooked. Thus, to ensure a presence that allows them to achieve their profitability, image and sustainability goals, companies are forced to implement a methodical process to properly address the digital space. They must then be aware of the influence of these media on the marketing approach and the opportunities that it is important to grasp to properly carry out each step of this process.

Conduct a Market Research on Social Media

Social media is a unique opportunity for companies that want to do a study of their market. These media provide invaluable information that is relatively inaccessible through conventional data collection methods. In fact, individuals do not behave in the same way when responding to an inquiry as when they are talking with friends or colleagues or when they are under anonymity on a forum. Thus, to access the words of these individuals in these different situations makes it possible to collect information with an essential wealth around the needs and opinions of the consumers. Consumer-to-consumer conversations are particularly relevant because they provide a closer view of reality and help to better understand the public's view.

Nevertheless, the use of social media to carry out a market study does not mean that traditional methods of market research are no longer effective. These media are particularly useful for complementing conventional methods or verifying the results that result from them in order to reach more generalized and realistic conclusions. In addition, thanks to these media, it is possible to carry out several market studies at the same time which would allow the company to improve its performance in several areas including customer service, product development, crisis management, e-reputation, etc. Thus, the use of social media to carry out a market study makes it possible to:

- Access information faster and cheaper

Conducting market research through social media provides very quick access to information that exists on millions of sites, forums, and networks around the world, but also divides, analyzes, and compares data collected as wish the company. On the basis of these data, it is also possible to create different reports, depending on the needs of different teams or departments of the company and as precisely or generally as necessary. This would be significantly more expensive with conventional methods of data collection.

- Validate the results obtained during a classical market study

If the results obtained through traditional methods are reflected on social media, then there is no doubt that these results are accurate.

- Develop a good competitive intelligence

The analysis of the competition is essential to study a market well. Competitive intelligence makes it possible precisely to follow the actions taken by the competitors, to know their marketing strategies, to observe their strengths and weaknesses, to know their products and the services as well as their innovations. As such, social media provide valuable assistance to companies that want to operate a competitive intelligence. Indeed, beyond conversations about the brand itself, the real benefit of conducting a market research with social media is the ability to access discussions about competitors and, above all, from consumer to consumer. This is where the most valuable information is. The collection of such information could inspire the company to react in time. Once the market study is completed, the company could save its requests to continue to observe its audience and access this information at any time.

- Know consumers better

Social media is a huge help in getting to know the intended audience. Indeed, the sample that the company can observe on these media is much larger relative to any panel used. The company could also access the spontaneous personal opinions expressed when consumers discuss with each other. Indeed, there are thousands of conversations on the web just waiting to be analyzed. This concerns both current discussions and those archived on different online discussion platforms. It is then possible to carry out retroactive searches in order to collect the information sought.

- Discover the trends of the sector

Social media monitoring also allows you to discover trends and key topics from conversations around a brand, as well as an entire industry. This allows the company to know and control its environment. In this respect, social media offers an effective tool for quickly accessing important insights for the company. The Brandwatch Signals function does just that by informing the business automatically as soon as a crisis or trend emerges.

Several examples can illustrate the importance of social media in conducting a market study. Two concrete examples are cited in this regard. The first example concerns the banking sector. In fact, one credit card company conducted a classic market survey and another on social media, in order to observe consumers' behavior towards their debts and their financial situation. It turned out that the results obtained were very different. Indeed, while the "physical" group described themselves as responsible with their money, consumers who voted on online discussion forums were much more open about their financial problems. This means that the informality and anonymity provided by these forums can reveal another face of consumers that they dare not show in other situations. It is therefore important to combine the two methods of market research in order to obtain a more realistic view of its market.

The second example is Sony. Indeed, by analyzing the keywords related to its field of activity, the marketing team of Sony realized that the word "mom" returned constantly. For example, Sony was a pioneer in targeting mothers as part of its marketing campaign while its competitors continued to address a young male audience at the time. This example shows how important it is to listen to and analyze discussions on the social web to discover opportunities to exploit. Standby tools enable the company to observe what its customers say beyond its brand or competitors and thereby broaden its knowledge of the market, its players and its audience.

It is also possible, through these media, to analyze the demographic Insights of an audience. Several features make it possible, like Brandwatch Analytics, which offers a very practical feature for market research and sociological studies: Demographics. This feature analyzes, for example, the demographics of twittos that discuss a brand or product in conversations with Brandwatch Analytics and provides access to numerous dashboards and charts to organize this data, as well as to many tools and filters to analyze, understand and derive actuable insights. This feature is not the only one to offer such services. There's also the built-in Snapchat Insights analytics tool that collects multiple types of data including user demographics: age, location, gender, and interests.

Then, in the case where the company wants to launch a given innovation, the social media also offer an essential space to perform product testing on a large sample. Thus, developing a market study seems to be easier but also more exciting and more interesting on these media.

Develop Marketing Strategy on Social MEDIA

Like market research, the development of the marketing strategy has been influenced by the advent of social media. The concepts segmentation, targeting and positioning are now boosted by these media. In fact, beyond the sociodemographic segmentation criteria frequently used in a classic segmentation (age, sex, income, occupation, etc.), segmentation via social media is more and more using psychographic criteria (tastes, hobbies, events, interests, etc.) and behavioral. The likes, comments and shares unveil the expectations and preferences of consumers connected to these media.

Segmentation is a very important step in defining the company's marketing strategy on social media. This segmentation process begins with an analysis of the points of view of the targets as well as their activities: place and condition of life, passions, interests, priorities,... And then the company must think about the way of consumption of its customers: motivations, rhythm, who are their influencers? Who pushes them to consume? ... Then she has to identify on which social networks her audience is most present: Facebook, Twitter, LinkedIn, Quora, Pinterest, Viadeo, Snapchat, Instagram,... Finally she must follow her audience on these social networks through the frequency and type of posts they post, the time they spend on these networks, etc.

The analysis of this information would allow the company to clearly identify the characteristics of its target (persona). It could also easily get in touch with customers interested in its products or services. Through the social media, the company can easily reach a niche clientele, not only locally but also globally thanks to the power of the internet.

Finally, having defined its position relative to the competitors, the company can use social media to communicate this positioning effectively and this, by prioritizing its presence on the social media most consistent with this positioning. In addition, the company is called upon to present content to this audience that attracts it to attract its attention and engage it in a conversation around its offer, thanks to the techniques and tools of content marketing. It can also check via these media if the positioning conveyed is correctly perceived by the target and this, detecting as and when its reactions.

What Influence of Social Media on the Marketing Mix?

Social media has significantly changed the 4P. First, around the product policy, social media have imposed the addition of certain features to the product marketed on these media. Indeed, it is no longer enough to offer consumers features to meet their essential needs. The products offered must be particularly meaningful. They must have additional value that can occur intrinsically and / or through an improved and much richer brand experience. These products are in fact aimed at consumers who use more and more tools such as Facebook, Twitter and comparison sites and reviews, which offer them early knowledge and significantly wider than many companies. They are therefore more demanding and very knowledgeable.

Thus, products must be designed with sophisticated promises to meet the expectations and aspirations of this type of customers.

Regarding pricing policy, companies are more than ever asked to price their products and services in a fair and competitive manner across all distribution channels. Indeed, the extended digital connectivity today imposes price transparency. The most obvious example is travel, especially the sale of airline tickets. In this respect, studies have shown that price is one of the main reasons why consumers go to companies' social media sites. In addition, the Internet and the mobile Web allow customers to check prices. These will publicly claim the company concerned if they detect inconsistencies on it. This can be mobilized in the service of competitors who sell less expensive.

In terms of distribution, apart from retail stores, direct sales, print catalogs and / or the website, the company must be present on social media to ensure a strong presence within a wide range of competing offers. This includes all platforms and applications to reach the target of the company. On these platforms, it is also important to focus on conversations between consumers. Companies need to determine if their prospects, customers and the general public want to socialize around their products and / or brand. This virtual socialization is a real asset for the marketing of the company's products, whether to attract prospects or to retain current customers.

In terms of communication, social media has imposed a revolution in communication practices. In fact, classical marketing relied on its promotional activities to communicate the attributes of the offer to the public in a single direction from business to consumer. Social media, on the other hand, has imposed new rules according to which it is the consumers who make known the performance and the value of the products. Today, communication is not limited to the virtues of the offer but must focus on what makes the special brand, original, different to the point that consumers want to join. Social media marketing is conversation-based rather than product-driven and needs to be integrated at every stage of the buying process, even at the post-purchase stage. This requires constant content and support that helps engage consumers.

Can Social Media Gauge the Effectiveness of the Marketing Strategy?

The commercial strategy undertaken on social media certainly deserves to be evaluated. Indeed, measuring the effectiveness of marketing actions allows the company to adjust its choices and plan future actions. There are several indicators to gauge the effectiveness of these actions. In what follows, the authors will look at the most relevant indicators starting with key indicators, which do not depend on a particular sector of activity, such as community growth and user responses.

The Size Of The Audience

The success of the business strategy is reflected in the correct size of the community on the business page and the fact that the community is active. Nevertheless, checking these indicators on each social network separately is tedious. It also causes a waste of time. Tools such as SEMrush provide all the useful statistics on a single dashboard. These tools can also provide a detailed report on audience engagement for each social network.

Commitment

Companies are certainly interested in detecting customer engagement and seeking to measure that engagement through the reactions and behaviors they display on social media. The signs of commitment are relatively comparable from one social network to another. However, each platform admits its own specificities and the indicators can also have different names and meanings:

Likes

Like is the most standard way people use to respond to content. Being very used and widespread, this modality is present on all social networks. As an indication, Facebook has introduced a number of "reactions" in the form of symbols and emoji to allow users to express their feelings about a post or publication. By a simple click, the consumer individual reveals his attitude towards a given content.

Comments

Comments are the most direct and expressive means of expression of the audience. Through their comments, customers of a particular brand express their appreciations around the offer and express that they wish to interact with the company. In addition, if consumers write positive comments about a brand, it may mean that the brand's efforts are being made in the right direction. On the contrary, the negative comments, if they are numerous, call to diagnose the situation.

Shares

Shares, retweets, and re-releases prove that a particular strategy, offering, or theme has impacted the target audience. Sharing also reflects a level of trust in content and the company that published it. Indeed, when a person shares content, it means that they believe the information is valid and useful.

The Engagement Rate

The size of the community and the number of likes are two important indicators, but they are not representative of each other. One hundred Likes may reflect a high level of success for an account with 1,000 subscribers, but perhaps less for an account that counts 100,000. The Engagement Rate measures the involvement of a hearing, its reactivity to the content published by the company and further its fidelity. It is essential for the company to study this indicator if it wants its subscribers to change from fan to customer. SEMrush's Social Media Tracker tool allows enterprise publications to be ranked by engagement rate to determine the types of content that work best on each social network. This information helps to target audiences' interests in an efficient way.

Other Specific Indicators

Apart from the indicators already mentioned, the company is called upon to collect data related to its own objectives and competitors in order to ensure that it is progressing towards the achievement of these objectives. In this respect, some indicators seem interesting, including:

The Growth Dynamics Of Audiences

It is appropriate for a company to measure the visibility of its products or services to potential customers. Social networks are a good way to do this because they are free and therefore a good option for small businesses with limited budgets. The audience growth indicator is particularly important for young brands who want to see how fast their community is evolving and what type of activity contributes most to growing their audience.

Comparative Indicators

The company must also monitor its competitors especially when it works in a congested business niche. To do this, it is necessary to identify, in particular, the content that best suits them, their strengths and weaknesses, the audiences they neglected to target, the influencers they mention, and so on., to be able to develop a strategy that will allow it to be competitive.

Traffic on Social Networks

Most companies use social networks to generate leads. But, the likes do not make money to the company if they do not lead to a conversion. Thus, it is essential to measure the share of traffic on social networks that directly generates a conversion. Google Analytics is the best tool to see the traffic coming from company accounts on social networks, but SEMrush also allows to compare these results with those of the competitors and to see especially how much of the traffic goes, from the social networks, towards the competitors' websites rather than the company's website.

IMPACT OF SOCIAL MEDIA ON CONSUMER BEHAVIOR

Long before the advent of social media, the buying path was relatively basic. Indeed, consumers went to the store to acquire products that meet their needs, including following the advice of sellers. At that time, media such as television, the press and magazines exerted some influence on the purchasing but the bulk of the consumption was in store when the consumer went there to buy. Today, social media has upset this classic pattern of consumption. Indeed, a study conducted in January 2017 on 3648 women between 18 and 64 years old having bought at least one beauty product during the last three months in the United Kingdom, France, Germany or the United Arab Emirates (survey conducted by GFK for Facebook) showed that 72% of female consumers are influenced by their online experience.

E-commerce accounts for a large share of purchases, but in-store sales remain the most popular channel for consumers (69%). In this respect, it is clear that consumers who appropriate their purchases still in store now go there with a clear idea of what they want. If this is not the case, these consumers use their smartphones in store especially to compare prices directly or to search for information on similar products. These assertions show that the in-store journey and the use of social networks are not contradictory acts. However, the influence of social media on the purchase path is indisputable. This journey has undergone a real revolution, which arouses the interest to study closely the behavior of the connected consumer. The study online consumer behavior goes beyond the traditional field of marketing and in turn becomes a current of research in its own right. Indeed, the advent of web 2.0 has transformed the profile of the consumer and its use of the Internet in the context of buying and consuming.

In this chapter, the authors are particularly interested in the impact of social media on consumer behavior by returning to each step of its decision-making process. They propose to describe the peculiarities of online consumer behavior by going through the main stages of its decision-making process: information retrieval, evaluation of alternatives, purchase and post-purchase evaluation (Engel, Blackwell and Kollat, 1968).

The Online Information Search Phase

During this phase, the consumer will enter a process of research and information processing allowing him to choose the product that best meets his needs (Zaoui et al., 2008). In this respect, social media has upset the situation. Indeed, these media have become the first source of information consulted by consumers, even if these consumers will later choose to make their purchases elsewhere, especially through conventional channels. The primacy granted to these media comes from the fact that they offer an unavoidable convenience in the search for information. The consumer can find on the sites of these media information from several sources at once. They can learn from their knowledge, consult the opinions of other consumer members in interactive groups and visit the pages of companies created on these media. The latest figures and statistics reflecting consumer behavior during this phase are both meaningful and very meaningful. Indeed, according to a study conducted by GlobalWebIndex in 2018, about 54% of social media followers use them to search for products. Consumers are increasingly joining social networks to seek advice and recommendations. In addition, these media are increasingly perceived as sources of credible information and that is why they are relatively privileged compared to official sources such as brand sites. This is because consumers are more likely to trust the opinions of other consumers than the best creative.

Nevertheless, this trend should not deter companies from promoting their products and services via social networks. Indeed, the more the brand selects the content published delicately, the more it manages to capture the attention of its fans and generate interest in the prospects generally.

The Evaluation Phase of Alternatives Online

The search for information on the Internet will allow the consumer to form his evoked set, consisting of alternatives from which he will choose the product or service he will buy on the Internet or in stores (Alba et al., 1997; Howard, 1989; Meyer, 1982; Wu, 2003). The choice of the individual will then be made on the basis of a set of criteria which also served to constitute the evoked ensemble (Andrews and Srinivasan, 1995). The possibilities offered by social media to help the consumer to constitute his evoked whole and to evaluate the various alternatives are immense (Alba et al., 1997) which can cause an information overload and consequently the confusion, the abandonment of research (Biswas, 2004) or the adjournment of the decision (Dhar and Nowlis, 1999). The challenge is to seduce the target with attractive content and a distinctive offer. In addition, we must always seek to identify influencers to help the consumer to focus on the company's offer compared to competing offers. Studies have shown that 49% of consumers rely on influencer recommendations on social networks before making their purchases. (Fourcommunications, 2018). This means that if the consumer has confidence in the influencer, he will tend to buy the product. This statistic shows that brands have every interest in relying on the power of influencers as part of their social media marketing.

Among these influencers, there are consumers who have had a positive experience with the brand. According to a study by GlobalWebIndex (2018), 71% of these consumers tend to recommend the brand to their friends and family. Their testimony is of great credibility. These consumers could greatly influence prospects and guide them towards a definite choice. Thus, the company must make sure to take advantage of the influence that these consumers can have on social networks. In addition, there are opinion leaders who play an important role in these new procurement processes. They can exert a strong influence by distributing, in social networks, articles, photos, video tutorials on certain products, they guide consumers in their choices. Thus, companies could benefit from the influence of these thought leaders to guide the choice of consumers.

The role of influencers is not at all marginalized. Nearly 40% of consumers say they are more likely to buy a brand they see on Facebook or Instagram. This is due in particular to the quality of the visuals posted or the opinions and tests made by the influencers. The brand is then credited by all the voices that boast. Thus, it is no longer just a salesperson who advises the consumer, but it is consumers who redesign the buying process by interacting with each other.

The Phase of Passing the Order Online

In our opinion, the online transaction consists of two phases: the online ordering phase and the online payment phase. The authors chose to separate these two phases because they can be conducted separately on the Internet. Placing an order online is a decision that may depend on several factors that may encourage or slow down consumer behavior in this regard. On the social networks, companies have the opportunity to use purchase incentive techniques to push consumers to place their order. Among these techniques, there is live chat. Customers appreciate this form of interaction with the brand because they benefit from real-time support. The response time is a crucial element of this support by chat, it must be less than 30 seconds, and otherwise the customer could abandon the purchase. Studies have shown that 57% of customers say they will give up their shopping cart if they do not find an answer to their questions quickly. In addition the company must master the organization of these live video to make the customer feel that it is unique and is listening to it despite being solicited by other customers. In addition, this chat support does not automatically lead to boost sales. The customer must be pushed to the purchase of a clever and intelligent way and this, by applying the techniques of sale suitable. These include:

- Make flash sales: The flash sale is a very fashionable concept right now. This is to create a sale with a very limited duration and this, to create a state of emergency, while advancing a very convincing advantage: an interesting discount for example. Combining the limited time and the large reduction will prompt the client to make his decision quickly. In addition, offering gifts or additional benefits would cause the customer to buy from the company that grants him such benefits and not from competitors especially that it is constrained by the limited time of the offer.
- Announce a limited number of products available in stock: when the company displays a limited number of products available, it could prompt the customer to make a quick decision to take advantage of it before the stock runs out. The company can also limit the number of customers who will enjoy its exceptional offer during the live instead of limiting the number of products available.

Online Payment Phase

Buying on the Internet is a remote transaction, with high uncertainty due to the transfer of money and the disclosure of personal information through "open" technology to a virtual vendor "hiding" behind a screen (Hoffman et al., 1999). As such, buying online can be considered risky, and remains one of the most obvious barriers to the development of online shopping (Forsythe and Shi, 2003, Hoffman et al., 1999, Miyazaki and Fernandez 2001, Pavlou 2003, Tan 1999, Tan and Thoen 2001). Looking at the profile of online shoppers and non-shoppers shows that online shoppers are less concerned about the financial risks of buying online, while the majority of non-shoppers are concerned about financial risk and fear for their data financial and personal (Lee and Tan 2003, Swinyard and Smith, 2003). The presence of the consumer on social media means that the consumer already shares personal information with the community. Users of these social media also have the habit of sharing the most personal data in private messages, which reassures these users more. Regarding payment, note that companies and brands that use these media to sell tend to postpone payment upon receipt of the order. This modality is used in particular to provide a remedy for the financial risk perceived by the customers but could be at the origin of certain problems for the companies which send the orders to customers who prove not solvent or who renounce the purchase after have gone through all the previous steps to payment.

Product Delivery Phase

Except for digitized products, whose possession is immediate, there is a gap between the placing of the order and the possession of the product (Zaoui et al., 2008).

The "no immediate possession" of the product is another characteristic of online shopping that hinders some consumers (Zaoui et al., 2008). It has been established that there is a negative relationship between delivery times and the tendency to change from buying an offline circuit to an online circuit (Gupta et al., 2004). Several consumers were also faced with a problem of receiving a product damaged or not meeting the advertised criteria. As such, social networks have been used by companies to reassure customers and prospects in this regard. These companies constantly publish testimonials from their satisfied customers by the company's delivery performance, to provide proof of their professionalism. These testimonials are usually presented in terms of screenshots of private conversations between the company and its customers or in terms of spontaneous thank-you messages sent by customers to the company.

The Online Post-Purchase Phase

Contrary to what one might think, the post-purchase stage is of paramount importance for companies and brands. In fact, it is no longer sufficient to sell one's products and services. The most important thing would be to maintain a privileged and lasting relationship with the customers. That said, studying consumer behavior in the post-purchase phase is essential in order to establish, develop and maintain a lasting customer relationship. The importance of loyalty is well established today and there is a growing need to harness the potential of social media to achieve this goal. Social media can help the company maintain a favorable relationship with its customers through a set of measures such as:

- Create a dialogue with customers: social networks are a particularly interesting communication channel because it allows companies to conduct both a one-to-many communication when the brand speaks to all its subscribers and a one-to-one communication when the brand responds directly to the requests and comments of its consumers. Thanks to these media, the brand and its customers are in constant interaction, which is the basis of maintaining their exchange relationship.

- Generate a base of contacts to promote the brand: social media can bring together diverse and varied profiles of people interested in the brand and who can communicate with each other. For companies, this dynamic is to be maintained to be exploited in order to encourage the most passionate customers to play the role of promising ambassadors of their brands.
- Provide after-sales service: Facebook and Twitter are used by companies to manage after-sales service issues and turn complaints or requests into constructive communication, which could positively impact brand perception.

To do this, it is important to accompany consumers from the curious stage, visitors and try to keep consumers who reach the status of ambassadors. If this happens, dissatisfied customers can hurt the image of the company when they talk about it to others. Thus, the marketing strategy on social media must integrate the 4 steps presented in the visual above. We are talking here about Inbound Marketing. The fourth step of this approach is essential for the company since it allows to optimize the returns on investment and then facilitate the communication strategy on the Internet. Indeed, by increasing customer loyalty, encouraging them to promote it, the company certainly gains in efficiency.

In addition, to better manage consumer behavior in the post-purchase phase, it is important to pay particular attention to virtual communities. Social media has created thousands of virtual communities that have developed spontaneously by fans and continue to be managed by them. In addition, many communities are now managed by the companies themselves. These communities are commercially oriented but manage to create community spirit among members and generate strong brand loyalty (Mathwick, 2002). Virtual communities are generally important because they help businesses better understand the concerns of their consumers, leading to satisfaction and retention (Hagel, 1997). These concerns can be unveiled in many ways including negative comments. In this case, the brand should not see these comments as a danger but rather as an opportunity to propose an individual solution to the dissatisfied consumer. Claims processing is the key to creating a constructive and mutually beneficial relationship with clients.

In the end, it is clear that the process of buying online admits features making it more complex. This offers cyber-consumers more leeway to act and reverse the balance of power with companies. However, it is important for these companies to understand the ways in which they can benefit from them in order to achieve their objectives and to minimize the potential harm affecting their journey.

CONCLUSION

For years, social media has been growing exponentially. Their major asset is simplicity and speed. Indeed, for most users, these media are intuitive, do not require real expertise and have no difficulty in accessing information. It is enough for a user to discover a product, a service or a person that interests him, so that he immediately informs his entire community. The potential of these media is therefore enormous for companies that want to develop their customer base, their brand image and their turnover. Today, the use of these media is inevitable, they acquire a more strategic role.

Social media has also influenced consumer behavior. It is more and more demanding and better informed through the use of the internet and social media. And yet, social media has managed to influence its attitudes, product valuation, purchase intent and loyalty (Safi et al., 2018). The impact of these media is so great that it is illusory to think to have definitively identified.

REFERENCES

Alba, J., Lynch, J., Wietz, B., Janiszewski, C., Lutz, R., & Sawyer, A. (1997). Interactive home shopping: Consumer, retailer, and manufacturer incentives to participate in electronic marketplaces. *Journal of Marketing*, *63*(3), 38–53. doi:10.1177/002224299706100303

Andrews, R. L., & Srinivasan, T. C. (1995). Studying consideration effects in empirical choice models using scanner panel data. *JMR, Journal of Marketing Research*, *32*(1), 30–41. doi:10.1177/002224379503200105

Biswas, D. (2004). Economics of information in he web economy, towards a new theory? *Journal of Business Research*, *57*, 724–733. doi:10.1016/S0148-2963(02)00355-7

Chang, L. D. M., Ling Tam, A. Y., & Suki, N. M. (2016). Moderating effect of races towards consumers' feeling of TCM usage. Handbook of Research on Leveraging Consumer Psychology for Effective Customer Engagement, 306-323.

Dhar, R., & Nowlis, S. M. (1999). Consumer preference for the no-choice option. *The Journal of Consumer Research*, *24*(2), 215–231. doi:10.1086/209506

Engel, J. F., Kollat, D. T., & Blackwell, R. D. (1968). *Consumer Behavior*. New York: Holt, Rinehart &Winston.

Forsythe, S. M., & Shi, B. (2003). Consumer patronage and risk perception in internet shopping. *The Journal of Consumer Research*, *56*, 863–875.

Gupta, A., Su, B., & Walter, Z. (2004). An empirical study of consumer switching from traditional to electronic channels: A purchase-decision process perspective. *International Journal of Electronic Commerce*, *8*(3), 131–161. doi:10.1080/10864415.2004.11044302

Hagel, J. I. (1997). Net gain, expanding markets through virtual communities. *The McKinsey Quarterly*, *1*, 141–153.

Hanna, R., Rohm, A., & Crittenden, V. L. (2011). We're all connected: The power of the social media eco system. *Business Horizons*, *54*(3), 785–807. doi:10.1016/j.bushor.2011.01.007

Hoffman, D. L., Novak, T. P., & Peralta, M. (1999). Building consumer trust online, in (coord.). *Communications of the ACM*, *42*(4), 80–85. doi:10.1145/299157.299175

Howard, J. A. (1989). *Consumer behavior in marketing strategy*. Academic Press.

Kaplan, A. M. (2012). If you love something, let it go mobile: Mobile marketing and mobile social media 4x4. *Business Horizons*, *55*(2), 129–139. doi:10.1016/j.bushor.2011.10.009

Kaplan, A. M., & Haenlein, M. (2010). Users of the world, unite! The challenges and opportunities of Social Media. *Business Horizons*, *53*(1), 59–68. doi:10.1016/j.bushor.2009.09.003

Kaplan, A.M., and Haenlein, M. (2012). Social Media: Back to the Roots and Back to the Future. *Journal of Systems and Information Technology, 14*(2), 101-104.

Kietzmann, J. H., Hermkens, K., McCarthy, I. P., & Silvestre, B. S. (2011). Social media? Get serious! Understanding the functional building blocks of social media. *Business Horizons*, *54*(3), 241–251. doi:10.1016/j.bushor.2011.01.005

Lee, K. S., & Tan, S. J. (2003). E-retailing versus physical retailing, a theoretical model and empirical test of consumer choice. *Journal of Business Research*, *56*(11), 877–885. doi:10.1016/S0148-2963(01)00274-0

Mathwick, C. (2002). Understanding the online consumer: A typology of online relational norms and behavior. *Journal of Interactive Marketing*, *16*(1), 40–55. doi:10.1002/dir.10003

Meyer, R. J. (1982). A descriptive model of consumer information search behavior. *Marketing Science*, *1*, 1.

Miyazaki, A. D., & Fernandez, A. (2001). Consumer perceptions of privacy and security risks for online shopping. *The Journal of Consumer Affairs*, *35*(1), 27–44.

Nathan, R. J., Fook Chiun, D. C., & Suki, N. M. (2016). An online marketing strategies assessment for companies in airlines and entertainment industries in Malaysia. Handbook of Research on Leveraging Consumer Psychology for Effective Customer Engagement, 1-15.

Pavlou, P. A. (2003). Consumer acceptance of electronic commerce: Integrating trust and risk with the technology acceptance model. *International Journal of Electronic Commerce*, *7*(3), 101–134. doi:10.1 080/10864415.2003.11044275

Safi, H., Azouri, M., & Azouri, A. (2018, May). L'influence des réseaux sociaux sur le comportement du consommateur: Le cas de l'industrie des biens luxueux. *La Revue Gestion et Organisation*, *10*(1), 29–35. doi:10.1016/j.rgo.2018.04.001

Suki, N. M. (2016). *Handbook of Research on Leveraging Consumer Psychology for Effective Customer Engagement*. https://www.igi-global.com/book/handbook-research-leveraging-consumer-psychology/149284

Swinyard, W. R., & Smith, S. M. (2003). Why people (dont) shop online: A lifestyle study of the internet consumer. *Psychology and Marketing*, *20*(7), 567–597. doi:10.1002/mar.10087

Tan, S. J. (1999). Strategies for reducing consumers' risk aversion in internet shopping. *Journal of Consumer Marketing, 16*(2), 163.

Tan, Y.-H., & Thoen, W. (2001). Toward a generic model of trust for electronic commerce. *International Journal of Electronic Commerce*, *5*(2), 61–74.

Wu, J., & Rangaswamy, A. (2003). A fuzzy set model of search and consideration with an application to an online market. *Marketing Science, 22*(3), 411–434. doi:10.1287/mksc.22.3.411.17738

Zaoui, I., Ben Ammar Mamlouk, Z., & Trahand, J. (2008). Analyse du processus d'achat sur Internet: nouvelles influences, nouveaux comportements, nouveaux challenges. *Actes du congrès de l'AFM.*

Zolkepli, I. A., & Kamarulzaman, Y. (2011). Understanding social media adoption: The role of perceived media needs and technology characteristics. *World Journal of Social Sciences, 1*(1), 188–199.

This research was previously published in Leveraging Consumer Behavior and Psychology in the Digital Economy; pages 27-45, copyright year 2020 by Business Science Reference (an imprint of IGI Global).

Chapter 4
Social Media, Crowdsourcing, and Marketing

Shivani Inder

https://orcid.org/0000-0002-4805-4118

Chitkara Business School, Chitkara University, India

ABSTRACT

Social media has emerged as a new playing ground for digital marketing. Supporting the resource view of the organization, crowdsourcing is a strong platform for social media marketing. Crowdsourcing on social media for marketing is strengthening companies in terms of saving marketing expenditure; promoting at speed of light; and enhancing the organizational learning, collaboration, and performance. The chapter tries to focus on the relevance of social media, crowdsourcing, and marketing, which help the company to improve, innovate, and cultivate on the crowdsourced wisdom. The future of social media, crowdsourcing, and marketing depends on how companies change the way they perceive stakeholders, business, and processes.

INTRODUCTION

Social media is an expanding and growing platform for communicating expectations among the stakeholders. According to a survey conducted by Misco International Limited, in association with the Ornate Group, it has been found that two out of three business feel that social media is important for sending a message (Times, 2021). According to Kaplan and Haenlein (2010), Social media is "a group of internet based applications that build on the ideological and technological foundations of Web 2.0, and that allow the creation and exchange of user-generated content." Adding to this, Kietzmann, Hermkens, McCarthy and Silverstre (2010) defined social media as media that "employ mobile and web based technologies to create highly interactive platforms via which individuals and communities share, co-create, discuss and modify user-generated content."

Social media made pervasive, substantial alterations in the communications and businesses have been pointed at the centre of a new communication landscape (Kietzmann et al., 2010). Social media is considered as a subset of internet marketing. Businesses mostly prefer to use social media like Facebook

DOI: 10.4018/978-1-6684-6287-4.ch004

(90%), followed by LinkedIn (71%), Instagram (62%) & YouTube (36%) (Times, 2021). 'The honeycomb of social media' offers seven functional blocks like sharing, presence, relationships, identity, conversations, groups and reputation (Kietzmann et al, 2010) at the disposal of companies for the purpose of marketing. For companies to fully leverage social media and reap the benefits of marketing, companies must learn and acquire new skills and strategies (Scott, 2015). Outsourcing the non core activities and diverting such activities to experts helps companies to explore benefits cost effective expert generated solutions. Combining outsourcing with social media, crowdsourcing offers a much desirable strategic way to reach solutions to an array of problems. Businesses can develop capabilities and enhance performance by effectively employing social media resources (Paniagua and Sapena, 2014).

CROWDSOURCING

Management literature has broadly analyzed the outsourcing concept (Parmigiani, 2007). Focusing on the resource based view of the organization, companies attempt to be competitive by channelizing its resources towards the core activities and outsourcing the non-core activities to outside parties and reduce the cost substantially. Therefore, "companies should commit most of their resources to their core competence, while outsourcing the rest of their functions to specialized entities." (Li and Petrick, 2008,p. 237). With internet, technology and globalization on the one edge of organizational environment, information travels at the speed of light. Additionally, companies also try to develop and nurture the mechanisms to attract experts to focus and provide solutions to the problems or work that suits them the most. This brings the attention of the companies to ensure that the experts must come under the ambit or in close proximity of the companies, so that the expertise can be accessed at ease and earliest. In other words, companies are shifting their attention to "folk capital", or "community capital" or "global capital" or "masscapital".

Building on the merge of concepts of 'community' and 'outsourcing', crowdsourcing has emerged as concept of twenty first century. Jeff Howe and Mark Robinson coined the term "crowdsourcing" in 2005. Surwiecki (2005) suggests "many hands make light work" to the concept. Crowdsourcing is "the act of taking a task traditionally performed by a designated agent (such as an employee or a contractor) and outsourcing it by making an open call to an undefined but large group of people" (Howe, 2008). Brabham (2008) defined crowdsourcing as "an online, distributed problem solving and production model." Whitla (2009) elaborated the concept as a process of arranging work for organisations and offering returns to whosoever in the group completes the work. Crowdsourcing is an emerging trend which pools in the wisdom of crowd on internet and helps firms in solving problems or handling tasks that require huge human capital (Li, Hsieh, Lin and Wei, 2020).

SOCIAL MEDIA AND CROWDSOURCING

Crowdsourcing is emerging as a strong platform for social media marketing. Social media contributes in marketing generally by two main forms, i.e. one is to employ crowdsourcers for completing tasks and carrying out marketing of products, and the second is to employ the crowdsourcers as experts for contributing in promoting and advertising campaigns.

Ford et al (2015) point that crowdsourcing offers a unique outsourcing approach as the willing and capable individuals join the task sourced. Saxton et al (2013) points three basic element to crowdsourcing: the crowd, outsourcing and the social network or web. Crowdsourcing is a sort of online movement in which a party i.e. crowdsourcer (may be organization, non profit organization, or individual) makes a call for the achievement of task to a group of people. Individuals participating in the achievement of task get rewards either in the form of monetary rewards, social acknowledgment, skill advancement etc whereas the crowdsourcer achieves the task.

Crowdsourcing plays a crucial role in social media marketing. As whenever the time to make a purchase decision arrives, the probability of trusting a fellow customer is comparatively much higher than a brand. A number of social media platforms have been used crowdsourcing to market brands than just selling products. Social media marketing enables marketers to market a lifestyle, idea or culture rather than just a brand. With crowdsourcing and social media, marketers bring in the brand story to life by embedding audience preferences rather than visual content marketing.

Considering one end of the scale, companies may consider crowdsourcing to carry out activities to spread the word or message regarding the product/service on the network of communities or social circles via social media. For example, a small scale company may crowdsource its promotional material for marketing on social media and distribute it across different communities and locations at a specified period of time. Moreover, social media crowdsourcing enables the companies to modify the message as a response to stakeholder's expectations. Additionally, companies may have crowdsourcers to navigate and analyse the reviews and posts on social media and increase the product visibility.

Over the recent years, marketing practices have started focusing on reading the conversations between different stakeholders and interpreting expectations rather marketing focused on transactions. Considering social network and exchange theories (Morgan & Hunt, 1994) the value of relationships stem out from trust, faith, understanding, commitment, customs etc. Literature has not given the role of social media marketing and crowdsourcing much deserved attention, especially the exploration of ways social media contribute in innovation processes and learning processes of organisations.

Crowdsourcing and online social network complement and contribute in the organizational learning and helps in improving the organization performance (Palacios-Marques, Gallego-Nicholls and Guijarro-Gracia, 2021). Zupic (2013) suggests that social media acts crowdsourcing enabler via two mechanisms i.e. peer-to-peer learning and motivation. Palacios et al (2016) points five emerging trends in relation to crowdsourcing such as problem solving, learning paradigms, open innovation, new product development and collaborative initiative. Pacauskas, Rajala, Westerlund and Mantymaki (2018) investigated user innovation for crowdsourcing based marketing initiatives. They emphasized on the importance of activities and technical features that enable socializing with other participants, support active participation and create a participatory experience. They suggest that crowdsourcing can be leverage for marketing purposes and user innovation as a building block for engagement mechanism in crowdsourcing initiative.

Piller, Vossen and Ihl (2012) highlight the use of crowdsourcing to establish social collaboration between producer and customer for the process of new product development. Businesses generally choose four main channels of social media to increase performance i.e. social capital, customer's revealed preferences, social marketing and social corporate networking (Paniagua and Sapena, 2014).

Alongwith, crowdsourcing equip brands with much user generated content which is much more engaging. Crowdsourcing leads to collective, thoughtful engagement. It offers a multiplayer experience. Marketing on social media via crowdsourcing helps the brands to convert the users into brand advocates and engage users to brands.

Figure 1. Block of social media, medium and business performance
(Source: Adapted from Paniagua and Sapena, 2014)

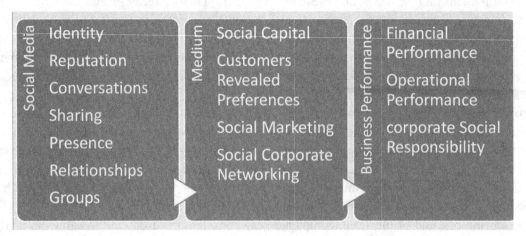

Companies deploy a number of methods to crowdsource social media marketing campaigns like asking for feedback, conducting contests and giveaways, polls, sruveys etc. Nike's Nike idea, Starbuck's MyStarbucks Idea, Threadless.com T-shirt idea project Crowdflower, Lego's Lego factory are the few examples for the companies that have successfully employed the combination of social media and crowdsourcing to promote the business. Toyota crowdsourced its marketing campaign with '#FeelingTheStreet campaign' for a period of six weeks in 2015. Toyota was able to crowdsource best content from social media platforms Instagram and Facebook. The company received more than 1.2 million likes, comments and shares on social media. Additionally, there was a 440% increase year-on-year in ad engagement without any extra expenditure.

Another excellent example for crowdsourcing and social media marketing is of 'Porche' They crowdsourced a campaign on social media with statement "the best expert panel in the world: our fans" to choose an exterior color for the car. This led to huge response of 16,000 likes, 1200 comments for the color Aquablue Metallic to top the list. Considering crowdsourced wisdom, the company released the car on August 2, 2013 and posted its photos on their Facebook page.

Similarly, Mountain Dew and Lays have resorted to crowdsourcing marketing and products on social media.

HOW CROWDSOURCE MARKETING WORKS

Challenges

Though social media provides a platform for crowdsourcing, still crowdsourcing faces a number of challenges like ill-prepared proposals and solutions (Whitla, 2009). Social media, crowdsourcing and marketing has few challenges. The medium offers a lack of credibility as no minimum standard has been established to ensure quality level of local crowdsourcing platforms. As it has been rightly put forward by Jeff Howe "sometimes crowds can be wise, but sometimes they can also be stupid." Establishing the ground for assigning the responsibility and putting procedures to effectively filtering ideas for future consideration is a challenge in case of assigning a marketing campaign through social media crowdsourcing (Hempel, 2006)

Figure 2. Glimpse of Toyota's '#FeelingTheStreet' campaign

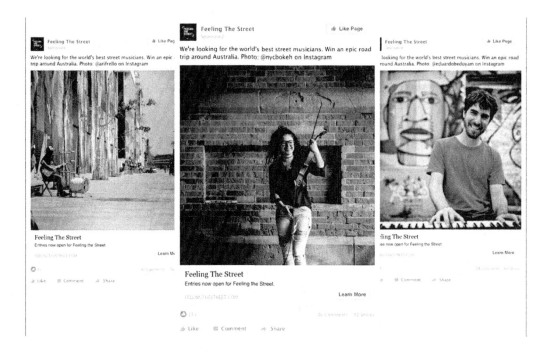

Figure 3. Porsche Facebook post on August 2013

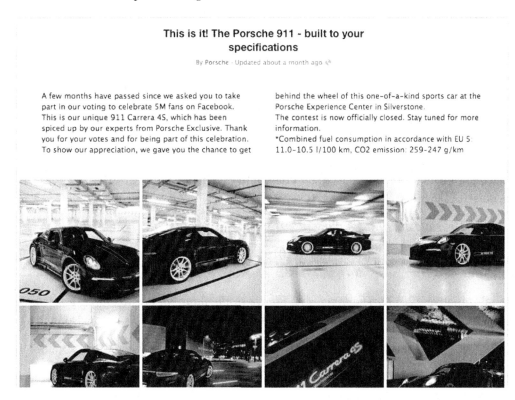

Belsky (2010) points that a large number of participants in the crowd sourced projects are novices that ultimately affect the quality of the work provided. Another challenge is lack of skilled and experienced talents to support growth of local platforms. Out of motivations, Acar (2019) comments that intrinsic and extrinsic motivations have association with quality of solutions, whereas motivations pinned in prosocial and learning have negative relation with solution quality. Ren, Han, Genc, Yeoh & Popovic (2021) find that crowd contributes more creatively in solving generalist tasks than professionals, whereas professionals tend to have more creativity in specialist tasks. Additionally, they also establish understanding on the boundaries on the creativity for crowdsourcing and how to break these boundaries.

Assigning legal ownership of ideas and part work done by an individual need to addressed through formal and legal rules applicable uniformly across countries (Stibbe, 2006). Few other challenges for social media marketing and crowdsourcing are weak payment systems and global levels of competition.

CONCLUSION

In the today's digital and age of social media, the discovery of the capabilities for the firms to stay competitive is not inside the company but stays outside the firm. The chapter tries to postulate the relevance of social media, crowdsourcing and marketing which help the company to improve, innovate and cultivate on the crowdsourced wisdom. The future of social media, crowdsourcing and marketing depends on how companies change the way they perceive about the stakeholders, business and processes.

REFERENCES

Acar, O. A. (2019). Why Crowdsourcing Often Leads to Bad Ideas. *Harvard Business Review*.

Belsky, S. (2010). *Crowdsourcing is broken: How to fix it*. Bloomberg Businessweek.

Brabham, D. C. (2008). Crowdsourcing as a model for problem solving: An introduction and cases. *Convergence*, *14*(1), 75–90. doi:10.1177/1354856507084420

Ebner, W., Leimeister, J. M., & Krcmar, H. (2009). Community engineering for innovations: The ideas competition as a method to nurture a virtual community for innovations. *R & D Management*, *39*(4), 342–356. doi:10.1111/j.1467-9310.2009.00564.x

eYeka. (2015). *The state of crowdsourcing in 2015*. Analyst report #CSReport 2015.

Ford, R. C., Richard, B., & Ciuchta, M. P. (2015). Crowdsourcing: A new way of employing non-employees? *Business Horizons*, *58*(4), 377–388.

HBS Digital Initiative. (2017). *The biggest challenge to the future of crowdsourcing in business*. Retrieved from: https://digital.hbs.edu/platforms-crowds/biggest-challenge-future-crowdsourcing-business/

Hempel, J. (2006). Crowdsourcing: Milk the masses for inspiration. *Business Week*, *25*, 38–39.

Howe, J. (2008). *Crowdsourcing: How the power of the crowd is driving the future of business*. Random House.

Ikediego, H. O., Ilkan, M., Abubakar, A. M., & Victor Bekun, F. (2018). Crowd-sourcing (who, why and what). *International Journal of Crowd Science*, *2*(1), 27–41. doi:10.1108/ijcs-07-2017-0005

Kaplan, A. M., & Haenlein, M. (2010). Users of the world, unite! The challenges and opportunities of Social Media. *Business Horizons*, *53*(1), 59–68.

Kietzmann, J. H., Hermkens, K., McCarthy, I. P., & Silvestre, B. S. (2011). Social media? Get serious! Understanding the functional building blocks of social media. *Business Horizons*, *54*(3), 241–251.

Li, X., & Petrick, J. F. (2008). Examining the antecedents of brand loyalty from an investment model perspective. *Journal of Travel Research*, *47*(1), 25–34.

Li, Y.-M., Hsieh, C.-Y., Lin, L.-F., & Wei, C.-H. (2020). A social mechanism for task-oriented crowd-sourcing recommendations. *Decision Support Systems*, 113449.

Majchrzak, A., & Malhotra, A. (2013). Towards an information systems perspective and research agenda on crowdsourcing for innovation. *The Journal of Strategic Information Systems*, *22*(4), 257–268.

Majchrzak, A., & Malhotra, A. (2013). Towards an information systems perspective and research agenda on crowdsourcing for innovation. *The Journal of Strategic Information Systems*, *22*(4), 257–268.

Miner, T. (2005). The wisdom of crowds: Why the many are smarter than the few, and how collective wisdom shapes business, economies, societies, and nations. *Journal of Experiential Education*, *27*(3), 351.

Morgan, R. M., & Hunt, S. D. (1994). The commitment-trust theory of relationship marketing. *Journal of Marketing*, *58*(3), 20–38.

Pacauskas, D., Rajala, R., Westerlund, M., & Mäntymäki, M. (2018). Harnessing user innovation for social media marketing: Case study of a crowdsourced hamburger. *International Journal of Information Management*, *43*, 319–327.

Palacios, M., Martinez-Corral, A., Nisar, A., & Grijalvo, M. (2016). Crowdsourcing and organizational forms: Emerging trends and research implications. *Journal of Business Research*, *69*(5), 1834–1839.

Palacios-Marqués, D., Gallego-Nicholls, J. F., & Guijarro-García, M. (2021). A recipe for success: Crowdsourcing, online social networks, and their impact on organizational performance. *Technological Forecasting and Social Change*, *165*, 120566.

Paniagua, J., & Sapena, J. (2014). Business performance and social media: Love or hate? *Business Horizons*, *57*(6), 719–728.

Parmigiani, A. (2007). Why do firms both make and buy? An investigation of concurrent sourcing. *Strategic Management Journal*, *28*(3), 285–311.

Paul, W. (2009). Crowdsourcing and its application in marketing activities. *Contemporary Management Research*, *5*(1).

Piller, F., Vossen, A., & Ihl, C. (2012). From social media to social product development: The impact of social media on co-creation of innovation. *Die Unternehmung*, *66*, 7–27.

Ren, J., Han, Y., Genc, Y., Yeoh, W., & Popovič, A. (2021). The boundary of crowdsourcing in the domain of creativity. *Technological Forecasting and Social Change, 165*, 120530.

Saxton, G. D., Oh, O., & Kishore, R. (2013). Rules of crowdsourcing: Models, issues, and systems of control. *Information Systems Management, 30*(1), 2–20.

Scott, D. M. (2015). *The new rules of marketing and PR: how to use social media, blogs, news releases, online video, and viral marketing to reach buyers directly.* John Wiley & Sons.

Stibbe, M. (2006). All contributions welcome. *Director, 60*(4), 76–81.

Surwiecki, J. (2005). *The Wisdom of Crowds: Why the Many Are Smarter than the Few and How Collective Wisdom Shapes Business, Economies, Societies, and Nations.* Doubleday.

Times Malta. (2021). *Two out of the three believe social media 'very important' for their business.* Retrieved from: https://timesofmalta.com/articles/view/two-out-of-three-believe-social-media-very-important.850025

Whitla, P. (2009). Crowdsourcing and its application in marketing activities. *Contemporary Management Research, 5*(1).

Župič, I. (2013). Social media as enabler of crowdsourcing. In *Social Media in Human Resources Management.* Emerald Group Publishing Limited.

This research was previously published in Big Data Analytics for Improved Accuracy, Efficiency, and Decision Making in Digital Marketing; pages 64-73, copyright year 2021 by Business Science Reference (an imprint of IGI Global).

Chapter 5
Finding Your Voice:
Developing a Content Strategy for Social Media That Works!

Karen L. Yacobucci
NYU School of Medicine, USA

Stephen Maher
NYU School of Medicine, USA

ABSTRACT

This chapter aims to provide an indispensable introduction to content marketing based on industry best-practices and help academic libraries navigate this essential but often overlooked marketing practice. The chapter will begin by addressing some of the consistent challenges organizations have starting their social media marketing campaigns and developing a social media strategy. Next, the chapter will focus on defining the tone and voice of their social media messages. Then, it will discuss sustaining the campaign by curating content and avoiding "content fatigue." Finally, the authors share an example of how an academic library but them into practice. They are confident this chapter will give academic librarians the vocabulary and techniques they need to talk and walk their way through meaningful and engaging marketing campaigns for their libraries using social media.

INTRODUCTION

In 1996, Bill Gates wrote and published an essay titled "Content is King" where he declared the Internet was a "marketplace of ideas, experiences, and products-a marketplace of content" (Evans, 2017). Since that time, the predictions Gates made regarding the importance of content on the Internet have largely been accurate. Unlike television or radio, where consumers have advertisements interrupt their entertainment experience, consumers willfully search for content on the Internet. This drive to seek out and consume information by choice has made way for the rise of content marketing.

DOI: 10.4018/978-1-6684-6287-4.ch005

According to the Content Marketing Institute, "Content marketing is the strategic marketing approach of creating and distributing valuable, relevant and consistent content to attract and acquire a clearly defined audience – with the objective of driving profitable customer action" (Content Marketing Institute, 2018).

Simply put, Content Marketing strategically positions content in front of the consumer. But what exactly is content?

Depending upon one's work, content can mean a lot of different things. In the field of marketing and communication, however, content has a very specific meaning and can be described as "the information and experiences that are directed towards an end-user or audience" (Lee, 2013). Other fields see content as an information exchange. It is the tangible information communicated through any point of contact between two or more entities; Business to Consumer (B2C), Business to Business (B2B), and in our case, Library to End-User. Yet it is important to emphasize, the content experience not only comes from the exchange itself, it's also the emotional value that the intended audience derives from that exchange.

With the ever-increasing rise and popularity of various social media platforms, it's no wonder that content marketing and social media seem synonymous. Successful content marketing almost always includes a strong social media component, and for the purpose of this chapter, focus is placed on the creation of a content strategy for social media.

BACKGROUND

One of the challenges in surveying the implementation of content strategy in academic libraries is a matter of terminology. The term "content strategy" has been attributed to web site governance rather than marketing. Rebecca Blakiston has penned a number of articles on web content strategies for academic libraries whereby content is "curated Web content that promotes, explains, and instructs users about various services and resources" (Blakiston, 2013). And Ilka Datig's article envisions "content strategy as a holistic tool that encompasses all library outreach platforms, including websites, social media, and other digital and print materials" (Datig, 2018). Combining web content with marketing is perhaps unavoidable as social media has become more pervasive but, as Darlene Fichter and Jeff Wisniewski assert in their article,

The world of content has changed. Regardless of the specific platforms, tools, or technologies, libraries need to strategically create and deliver content in ways that are efficient, effective, sustainable, and engaging. (Fichter & Wisniewski, 2014)

Although to date literature on academic libraries looking at content strategy strictly in terms of marketing purposes has been scant, librarians have written about marketing and outreach for some time. A recent white paper reported the results from a survey administered by the Association of College and Research Libraries' (ACRL) Marketing and Outreach Information Group. The survey found that many academic libraries do not have dedicated staff for marketing and that when outreach campaigns have launched they have not been analyzed to determine their impact (Park & Dantus, 2018). These results reinforce findings from a study conducted almost 10 years ago wherein although "libraries participate in different types of outreach, they often do so in informal and ad hoc ways without the benefit of systematic and well thought out outreach programs" (Carter & Seaman, 2011). Similar to the term "content strategy", the literature found on the concept of "user persona" is not directly associated with marketing.

The concept is identified in the context of User-centered Design (UCD), a "process focused on optimizing interfaces" typically rather than marketing or outreach (Tempelman-Kluit & Pearce, 2014). Even then it is admitted that the development of user personas based of common needs and patterns among library patrons is rare (Zaugg & Rackham, 2016). These examples support the need to more closely examine the content strategy life cycle in the context of an academic library. The next section will recount a case study where an academic library used the social media platform Twitter to promote scholarly communications among the institution's research faculty.

There are many examples in the literature of academic libraries utilizing Twitter, including the institution in the aforementioned case study (Cuddy, Graham, & Morton-Owens, 2010). Of the web 2.0 social media platforms, Twitter is one of the most widely adopted among academic libraries for marketing purposes (Del Bosque, Leif, & Skarl, 2012; Gunton & Davis, 2012; Milstein, 2009). One of the features of Twitter is the ease in which users can analyze the effectiveness and dissemination of their messages - tweets and retweets. A study of academic libraries at Drexel University examined the account types that retweeted library content - grouping them into categories (e.g. librarians, students, scholars, and university organizations) (Kim, Abels, & Yang, 2012). Another study of Twitter followers from a library at Texas A&M University was found to provide valuable insight into the accounts that receive library information (Sewell, 2013). And libraries have since reported ways to further investigate and understand their Twitter followers and its impact on how it uses its messaging via Twitter (Shulman, Yep, & Tomé, 2015). This would suggest, although not stated in the framework of the content strategy, academic libraries are including Measurement in its use of Twitter.

MAIN FOCUS OF THE CHAPTER

Content Strategy

In order for a Library to successfully translate their message to its intended audience, a comprehensive content strategy will need to be established, specific to the unique, fast paced, and ever-changing needs of social media. There are many different ways to approach content strategy, and this process will undoubtedly go through a series of refinements until an individual library can identify what works best for them. Regardless of whatever strategy is employed, at its core should be four distinct phases which encompass a complete content strategy lifecycle: assessment, creation, promotion, and measurement. Figure 1 illustrates the perpetual flow of a content strategy lifecycle.

Assessment

Before content can be developed for social media channels, completing two initial actions are recommended. The first involves conducting an audit of the current social media landscape and selecting channels that would resonate with the identified target audience. The second action involves evaluating the successes and struggles a library may have already had with social media. Ilka Datig of Nazareth College emphasizes that a library's "first step in applying content strategy is to get the lay of the land by conducting various assessments" which includes a comprehensive content audit (Datig, 2018).

Figure 1. Content strategy lifecycle

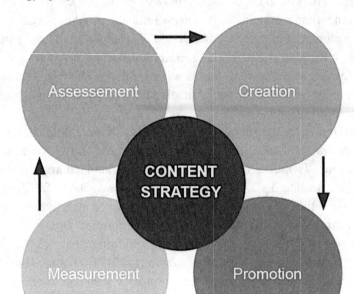

Survey the Landscape

Surveying the current social media landscape can help identify which channels are popular with an intended audience as well as the style of content that they engage with most or has the most use-value for them. Datig writes, "librarians should consider what type of content is most effective at reaching users and creating engagement" (p.66, 2018). For example, if it is determined that users are engaging more with photo or video-sharing platforms, exploring social networks that capitalize on that format, like Instagram or YouTube, could be a better source for sharing as well as a better allocation of a library's time and effort in content creation. In addition, if it is discovered that users seem more interested in sharing music or book recommendations, Spotify and GoodReads would prove to be more meaningful channels for those users.

Libraries that have trouble identifying their audience can learn from organizations similar to theirs. For example, a small academic library looking to jump into social media, but not sure how to begin, can easily start by identifying other academic libraries who already have a strong and successful social media presence and adopt the same platforms and similarly structured content. According to the Pew Research Center, "a majority of Americans use Facebook and YouTube, but young adults are especially heavy users of Snapchat and Instagram" (Pew Research Center, 2018). A survey conducted by the Association of College and Research Libraries (ACRL) discovered similar results. Sabine Dantus and Jennifer Park write, "not surprisingly, this number aligns with the results of this survey, which show Facebook as the most-used social media platform among academic libraries" (Park & Dantus, 2018).

Evaluate Success

The second phase of assessment involves evaluating what a library has already done and identifying the areas with which they have been successful or struggled in regards to social media. Successful social networks are able to consistently engage their users. Although engagement can be a one-off interaction with an audience through social likes and shares it is also the open line of communication developed with an audience over time. In addition to one-off interactions, the way in which an audience engages and communicates through social media should be noted; Are they asking questions? Are they making comments? Which styles of content are receiving more likes and shares? Increased user engagement is a factor which can positively influence a user's perception of brand trust in an online environment (Dessart, Veloutsou, & Morgan-Thomas, 2016).

Fortunately, most social media platforms have some form of performance analytics which makes it easy to identify topic trends, top performing posts, likes, social shares, etcetera. Undoubtedly, content that is consistent, clear, and meaningful will increase the number of followers any network has, as well as increase engagement as is evidenced by performance analytics. When a social network is struggling, performance analytics suffer and less engagement will be seen from users. Social networks that are created and left to languish will fail at drawing the attention of their intended audience.

This two-pronged approach to auditing social media content allows academic libraries to take a closer look and what has and has not worked in their current plan and helps to identify which digital assets or social platforms are best suited for their library's needs.

Creation

After the social media assessment phase, development of content can begin. The creation phase of social media strategy involves identifying the target audience as well as planning and brainstorming content suitable for that audience.

Identify the Target Audience

If a library knows who their target audience is, they can better develop content which is designed to specifically speak to the needs, wants, and desires of that audience. The librarians who manage social media channels successfully have a firm understanding of their audience and are able to craft unique content for them. Their social media strategy has more user engagement, resulting in a a stronger library brand.

One straightforward way to create this level of specified content is to develop a set of user-personas intended to identify the unique drivers of target audiences. User-personas have long been used by web designers and usability experts in order to increase the quality and effectiveness of their work. Now more than ever, social media content managers are using this same practice in order to better identify and communicate with their audience. Essentially, a user-persona is a fictional representation of an ideal user that establishes the who, what, and sometimes the where of any particular group of individuals who make up the target audience or end-user.

For example, a basic user-persona which might be developed for an academic library could be a Research Scientist, who is looking for creative approaches to communicating data. In that simple declaration, the who (the Research Scientist) and the what (looking for creative approaches to communicating data) are established, and specific content which meets that user's needs can be more easily developed.

User-personas can be as basic or as detailed as needed. More detailed user-personas might include a picture, demographic information, level of skill with a variety of technology, reading habits, frustrations, and more. An example of a basic user-persona is illustrated in Figure 2.

For some, creating user-personas may seem like an unneeded extra step, or a distraction that merely detracts from getting the job done, but when carefully created and used to their fullest potential, user-personas can be a powerful tool. Librarian Tara J. Brigham from the Winn-Dixie Foundation Medical Library writes, "personas can assist library staff in gaining insight to what users need and want. This can not only help improve the library's services and access to resources but also might create loyal library users" (Brigham, 2013).

Figure 2. User-persona overview

User-Persona Overview

Persona	Research Scientist	Student	Professor
Goals/Objectives	Looking for creative approaches to communicating data.	Wants to be able to access Library subscribed textbooks from off-campus.	Needs to provide access to relevant coursework in an online environment throughout the semester
Challenges	Has some experience with data visualization tools, but wants to explore using more advanced software for data visualization	Does not know where to find textbooks in the Library catalog.	Looking for a streamlined approach to communicating course material needs with the library.

Content Planning and Brainstorming

As previously mentioned, during the content strategy assessment phase, social media platforms best suited to meet the needs of the library should be identified. Different platforms allow for communication of different types of information and in different ways. Twitter, for example, is a great way to communicate small bursts of information under 280 characters, while Facebook doesn't have limits on the amount of text that can be published. Spotify caters to music lovers, and Instagram primarily delivers information by way of images. Whichever platform is used, content needs to be created which is suitable for that platform.

The following tools and concepts can be used to streamline the content creation process:

Cross-Channel Marketing and Content Development

Simply put, cross-channel marketing, also known as multi-channel marketing, is all about engaging with users across multiple digital channels and on any device, be it a laptop, smartphone, or tablet. At its core, this type of marketing aims to provide an integrated experience for users. When thinking about cross-channel marketing it's important to remember how this effects content development. As previously mentioned, libraries that have more than one social media platform will want to push the same content across all platforms, but content must be designed to fulfill the technical requirements or limitations of each platform. For example, an ideal size for an Instagram square image will be roughly 1080px x 1080px, whereas the ideal size for an image used in a Twitter post would be around 1024px x 512px (Hootsuite, 2018).

When designing content, libraries need to consider the ways in which their audience will engage with those platforms. Ensuring that content can easily be read and understood via mobile devices, desktop computers, or any conceivable device can bring libraries even closer to their users.

Editorial Calendar

Establishing and adhering to an editorial calendar might seem like extra work, but it's a great way to manage the full content lifecycle and maintain quality control. After content has been generated and approved for publication, it should be scheduled in an editorial calendar. Content can be scheduled to coincide with important dates relevant to the library or its parent institution, as well as national observances. Using and adhering to an editorial calendar can also prevent overlapping content from being published, help maintain a consistent editorial tone, and establish a structured workflow.

Furthermore, if balancing multiple social media platforms, an editorial calendar provides the added benefit of tracking which pieces of content have been posted and which have not, all visible in one location. Much like user-personas, editorial calendars can be as basic or complex as you need them to be. Below is an example of a basic editorial calendar created as an Excel spreadsheet.

Figure 3. Editorial calendar example

Author	Description	Content (cut/paste)	Attachments	Platform/Digital Touchpoints	Posting Date	Observances
Karen	Go Red For Womens Heart Health	NYU Health Sciences Library wears red for women's heart health! #GoRed #GoRedForWomen #WearRedDay	<go red image>	Twitter, Facebook	2/2/18	National Wear Red Day, Groundhog Day
					2/3/18	
					2/4/18	
Stephen	#NYUBragMonday	Spotlight on @nyulangone faculty article in @Nature Translational Psychiatry. Chemistry-based molecular signature underlying the atypia of #clozapine http://bit.ly/2m1eYb0 #NYUBragMonday	<image>	Twitter	2/5/18	
Lita		Make an art button that's yours to keep! Join us in the Farkas Breezeway on 2/8. Educators from The Metropolitan Museum of Art will have a table where you can make an art button from your favorite Met image! 2/8/18: 9:00-11:00AM Come and learn about CIAC's Reflecting Art in Nursing Practice spring series!	<image>		2/6/18	
					2/8/18	
Karen	#WeekendReads	"You cannot separate passion from pathology any more than you can separate a person's spirit from his body." [i]Letters to a Young Doctor[/i] by Richard Selzer. Find this book and more at the Sid and Ruth Lapidus Library! #WeekendReads	<image>	Intranet	2/9/18	
Lita		Nurses, want to increase your advanced searching skills? Come to the workshop Tuesday February 13: 9:00AM - Finding the Best Nursing Evidence Every Time. You'll get hands-on practice to bring your searching skills to the next level! Location is Lapidus Library, Consultation Room. Please sign up in FOCUS for 1 hour of CE. (It's a really good class!)	<image>	Intranet, Twitter, Facebook	2/9/18	

Social Media Management Systems

Libraries working with 3 or more platforms may want to invest in a Social Media Management System in order to streamline their workflow. Social Media Management Systems are designed to support social network integrations from a variety of social networking services (i.e., Facebook, Twitter, Instagram, LinkedIn,) which helps to systematize content creation by making modification, scheduling, and publishing easier. Hootsuite, Sprout Social, and Buffer are all examples of social media management systems designed to perform these essential functions all from the convenience of one dashboard.

Promotion

After content has been created and perfected to reach target audiences, developed for one or multiple social media platforms, and built into an editorial calendar, it's ready to be shared with the world.

Here is another area where early stage assessment comes full circle. During that process, libraries may be able to more clearly identify days and times when their audience was more likely to engage with social media. It should be noted that engagement rates do vary between platforms and industry, which means that the best time for a nonprofit organization to post on Instagram will most likely be different for an academic university who posts on Twitter. Experimentation is encouraged when trying to identify best days and times to post. Combinations of different days and times may yield different results and should be noted. In most cases, engagement rates increase when people have down time. That could be at 5am, when they are just waking up and getting ready to start their day, between 12 and 2pm, when they are sitting down to have their lunch, or 5pm when they are getting ready to leave work or commuting home. There are many guides online which can provide input on when to promote content, but ultimately a library's own analytics and measurement will be the best guide. Sharing the right kind of content at the best times ensures that it can be viewed by a larger number of people. Naturally, the more content is viewed, the more chance for engagement it has. Dalal, O'Hanlon, and Yacobucci write, "the more mentions, shares, reposts, retweets, likes, and reviews your content receives, the stronger your brand becomes and the more likely it is your content will continue to be shared and engaged with" (Dalal, O'Hanlon, & Yacobucci, 2017).

Scheduling posts in advance is a great way to automate the publishing process. A social media management system is designed to scheduled content and publish across multiple platforms all at once.

In addition to posting the right content at the right time, many social media platforms provide an option for paid promotion. Paid promotion allows for organizations to pay a platform to advertise specific content as a means to reach a wider audience. Paid promotion is a great way to get content in front of a wider audience, but as the name implies, it does come with a cost.

Measurement

Understanding analytics is essential for auditing, assessing, and improving the performance of social media platforms. Being able to measure the success of these platforms is just as important as the content itself.

Different organizations care about different types of analytics, which is why defining a success matric is recommended. A success matrix combines all the data that is meaningful for communicating and measuring the perceived success or health of an organizations' social media content. This can include the amount of traffic the platform gains in a particular timeframe, the number of social shares, engagement (audience interaction), mentions, influencers, top content, and more.

Different social media platforms report different analytics, and it can be easy to get caught up in a lot of differing data points. Value may not be found in collecting each and every data point, but Libraries should be looking at more than one at any given time, since no single analytic is enough to understand how an audience perceives a library's brand. For example, if a library is interested in knowing if their audience prefers video content over other types of content, they may focus on analytics for most popular posts and social shares, and identify which of those posts included a video and if they outperformed content which did not include a video.

CASE STUDY: CONTENT STRATEGY IN PRACTICE AT THE NYU HEALTH SCIENCES LIBRARY

The following is a real-world example of content strategy in action at an academic library.

Faculty publication metrics had been a growing service among academic libraries (Vieira et al, 2014). Libraries collect data on their institution's faculty publications as a way to demonstrate institutional memory, support promotion, and tenure discussions. Knowledge of this scholarly activity has more than internal value though. By using social media the library can promote these publications not only as a way to market the institution's research productivity but also the library as the means by which people can access and obtain this research.

Several commercial databases offer customizations for users to be alerted when articles on a specific subject area have been published. Databases like Web of Science and Scopus allow authors to set alerts on their own published articles to know when they have been cited in another publication, informing them about the legacy of their research. Government databases like NIH RePORTER allow institutions to track the research productivity associated with grants they have obtained. These customizations can be powerful tools for libraries to develop greater institutional memory on the publications authored by its faculty and students.

As the authors have explained, content marketing is "the information and experiences that are directed towards an end-user or audience". How does information about recent publications authored by individuals affiliated with the academic institution meet this definition and who is the end-user or audience? The following library's approach to content strategy through it's distinctive four phases: assessment, creation, promotion, and measurement attempts to answer these questions.

Assessment

The NYU Health Sciences Library (NYUHSL) is the medical library for the New York University School of Medicine and NYU Langone Health, a network of hospitals and ambulatory care centers across the five boroughs of New York City, Long Island, and beyond. The medical school was ranked third in the nation according to U.S. News and World Report 2018-2019 'Best Graduate Schools' for research, and has won numerous awards over the past several years (U.S. News & World Report, 2018).

In a major metropolitan area like New York where advertising, marketing, and public relations are well-established industries, NYU Langone Health has launched several high profile advertising campaigns to promote its hospital and medical facilities. They have also undergone a major reorganization of its websites to ensure consistency of font, color, and other design elements that define the current NYU Langone Health and NYU School of Medicine brand.

This rebranding process has extended to social media. There is an NYU Langone Health twitter account and many of the research centers and academic departments have accounts as well. Although a comprehensive count has not been taken, several faculty members have twitter accounts that promote their professional and personal research, conference appearances, and article publications.

For almost two decades scholarly research has been published electronically, transitioning away from the print journal or book. The publishers of those print journals, however, have maintained much of the scholarly communications market by successfully transforming its print journals into online or e-journals while keeping the reputation of the journal's name and associations with quality peer-review and editorial practices.

Perhaps one of the most significant changes with this transition from print to electronic publishing is the ability for publishers and large-scale subscribers (i.e. libraries) to track how frequently a journal is read. Internet metrics such as clicks and page-views tell a publisher which articles are garnering the most attention from its audience. These statistics have informed decisions to launch new publications. For libraries, which subscribe to many journals from a single publisher, the usage statistics it receives indicate which journals are more frequently read, informing its decisions on which titles to renew for the following year.

Building upon these Internet 1.0 metrics, social media – and its new platforms for people to discuss, share and create content – introduced ways to deepen the public's engagement with scholarly communications. The most well-known metrics for tabulating how articles are discussed and shared via social media comes from article-level metrics called as altmetrics and are collected by an organization with the same name. The qualitative data Altmetrics (the company) collects can tell authors and publishers how often their content (journal articles, datasets) are being discussed on the Internet. These altmetrics create an impression of the interest surrounding the content. It does not tell the whole story but it can serve as the starting point for understanding an article's impact on scholars in its discipline and broader scholarly community.

Beyond utilizing altmetrics, many publishers have turned to social media as a means to promote its content; new articles, conference proceedings, and newer nontraditional means of scholarly communications such as podcasts. While almost every major academic scholarly publisher has its own Twitter account, many of their individual journal titles also have accounts as well.

For these reasons, NYUHSL chose Twitter as the primary social media platform for this campaign. As a large-scale academic library, NYUHSL subscribes to thousands of journals in the field of health science and STEM related subjects. Promoting faculty publications reinforced one of the central missions of the Library, to provide access to library subscribed content. The next challenge was to identify the best way to share content which reinforces that message to the NYU Langone Health community. Choosing articles authored by researchers at NYU School of Medicine and NYU Langone Health provided a direct approach for this challenge. What made the articles relevant for the NYUHSL Twitter feed was its focus on who authored it, not necessarily what the article was about or its relative meaning to its disciplines. The campaign, therefore, would have two core messages; celebrate the research authored by NYU faculty and emphasize that the library provides access to that research.

Creation

When NYUHSL first launched this Twitter campaign, tweets were limited to 140 characters. Because of this, the Library needed to be economical with what would be said about a particular article. At the same time, the Library also wanted the tweets to denote a human touch rather than an automated copy and paste of an article title and its URL. The Library also wanted tweets to have visual impact, utilizing any images or figures from an article, in order for it to stand out as an end-user scrolled through their Twitter feed. And lastly, the Library wanted to make these tweets engaging by tagging relevant individuals such as the article author(s), using a distinct hashtag, and linking back to our parent institution by always including their Twitter handle.

Before NYUHSL could promote the articles, they first had to find them. For this, the Library utilized bibliographic databases that track publications across multiple publishers and collect extensive metadata about each article. NYUHSL wanted to track articles based on the author's affiliation. If an article was published by an author affiliated with New York University, the bibliographic databases would make that clear. The two databases used for this project were Elsevier's Scopus and Web of Science by Truven Analytics. Although both yielded similar results, in time, it was decided to use only Scopus because of its user interface and ability to easily set email alerts when new articles were added to the database that matched the Library's search criteria.

At least once per week NYUHSL librarians would receive an email with a list of articles co-authored by someone affiliated with NYU. From here the librarians would review the list looking for notable journal titles (e.g. JAMA, The New England Journal of Medicine, Academic Medicine, etc.). Next, the librarians would identify the articles which had significant NYU contribution. This was mainly accomplished by identifying whether or not an NYU author was listed as a first, second, or last author. Finally, catalog holdings were checked to ensure that the Library had subscribed access to the article. If each of these criteria were met, then the content would be written and the Twitter post would be scheduled in the Library's editorial calendar.

Each tweet began with the text, "Spotlight on @nyulangone faculty" (or research), and would go on to briefly describe the article. Occasionally, an article would be authored by someone affiliated with a department or lab with its own Twitter account. In those cases, we would replace the NYU Langone handle with that department or lab's twitter handle.

If an individual author had their own Twitter account, librarians would include that handle as well. In order to identify whether or not an author had a personal Twitter account, librarians would search for their name using Twitter's internal search function. Occasionally adding an "MD" to the search would help narrow the results. Even if a person's name was found on Twitter, account descriptions would be read in order to ensure the account actually belonged to the author. The same process was applied to journals as well. If an article was published in a journal with a Twitter account, then the post would also include the journal's handle.

When describing the article, usually a variation of the title would be enough, but occasionally the abstract would have to be paraphrased. As the article's description was written, possible trending Twitter themes would also be identified and any relevant hashtags would be included. If some were found, a hashtag would be placed in front of the word. The description beginning with "Spotlight on" would then look like something this.

Figure 4. Spotlight Tweet example

NYU HEALTH SCIENCES LIBRARY **NYU HSL** @NYU_HSL   Follow ⌄

Spotlight on @nyulangone research on improving #Senescent Wound Healing in

As previously mentioned, not only was it important to highlight the NYU faculty author, it was equally important to highlight the Library provided access to the article. Including a call-to-action encouraging individuals to read the article provided an opportunity to emphasize the content's connection to the Library. This call-to-action came in the form of a link to the article. Because Library subscribed resources are not available to the public, there was a lot to consider with this inclusion. Each NYU faculty publication tweet had to provide a link to the Library subscribed full-text article, but librarians also had to be cognizant that the general public could also view this content. This could be problematic for the general public attempting to access library subscribed content. Most of the content licensed by NYUHSL has its web proxy protocol embedded into the URL. This protocol prompts individuals to authenticate with institutional login credentials in order to gain access to subscribed content. Although this solved the issue of providing access to authorized individuals, it was a concern that it could have the negative effect of alienating or frustrating the general public. For this reason, it was decided rather than direct users to the article they would be directed to the article's PubMed record.

Maintained by the United States' National Library of Medicine (NLM), PubMed is a search engine for references and abstracts to journal articles and other scholarly publications in the health sciences. Given the size and scale of Pubmed, with nearly 28 million records and the addition of over 500,000 new records every year, the Library was confident that all of the selected articles would be found in PubMed. An additional benefit of directing the Twitter audience to an article's PubMed record was that NLM allows libraries to directly link to subscribed full-text from within the PubMed database by way of OpenURL. OpenURL lets libraries connect users to its subscribed journals through its standardized encoding format and its placement in information platforms (i.e. catalogs and databases) on the Internet (Needleman, 2002). Simply put, although PubMed records can be viewed by anyone, OpenURL lets libraries connect users to its subscribed journals.

Figure 5. PubMed OpenURL example

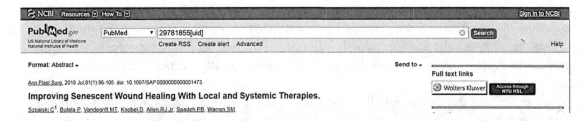

Once it was identified that the Library would point users to the article's PubMed record, the URL itself needed to be considered. URLs vary from publisher to publisher. This variety could impact the character limit of each tweet. Using a URL shortening service like Bit.ly would not only decrease the length of the URL, but also provide another measurable analytic for tracking whether or not the URLs were actually being clicked on.

Figure 6. Full Tweet example

NYU HSL
@NYU_HSL

Spotlight on @nyulangone Dean & CEO Dr. Robert I. Grossman's editorial in @radiology_rsna on #DisasterManagement

Access through NYU HSL

short.med.nyu.edu/29762099

#NYUBragMonday

Disaster Management

Robert I. Grossman, MD

11:32 AM - 27 Aug 2018

Figure 7. Full Tweet example 2

NYU HSL
@NYU_HSL

Spotlight on @nyulangone faculty take on the Technology Crisis in Neuropsychology in @NANneuropsych

short.med.nyu.edu/28541383

#NYUBragMonday

12:44 PM - 30 Oct 2017

Promotion

The library's Twitter account is used to promote a number of library services, such as classes, newly acquired resources, as well as celebrate the work of librarians and staff in supporting the research and education mission of the institution. Based on the Scopus email alerts, the Library had the potential to send tweets about NYU affiliated authored publications multiple times a day, over multiple days. This practice though would risk overwhelming the purpose of the library's Twitter account and, to be quite candid, despite the workflows set in place to create each tweet, would be too time-consuming for librarians to maintain in conjunction with other responsibilities. It was for these reasons that it was decided to schedule these tweets once per week, each Monday.

After refining and scheduling the tweets, the next step was to put internal content management workflows into practice. NYUHSL had already been using the social media dashboard application, TweetDeck, for managing the Library twitter account, but for the purposes of this campaign the Library took advantage of its scheduled tweets feature. With this feature, tweets about articles authored by NYU faculty and researchers could easily be scheduled in advance. This was especially effective when the alert emails contained more than one article that fit the criteria for promotion.

Another benefit of TweetDeck is its ease for adding images to a tweet. Occasionally an article would contain an interesting graphic, like a chart, figure, x-ray, or MRI scan. Images can positively impact user engagement with social media posts. When an image was found in an article, it would be saved, and later included as an attachment to the post via TweetDeck. If the article did not contain a suitable image, often times an image of the Journal's cover would be included.

Over time as theses tweets were perfected, the Library was easily able to coordinate tweets alongside national observances, like Women's History Month. The Library would also plan tweets to coincide with events happening at NYU Langone Health and NYU School of Medicine.

Measurement

One of Twitter's most exciting advantages is how quickly one can witness the impact of their tweets. Whether a tweet is liked or retweeted, it can quickly be identified that what you wrote or shared has been viewed.

Since the campaign began in December 2015, NYUHSL has posted over 140 tweets as part of the faculty publication campaign. Based on Twitter analytics, on average each of these tweets have been liked 1.04 times and retweeted approximately 0.46 times. These may not seem like large numbers, but since incorporating faculty publications into the NYUHSL social media strategy, followers, profile visits, and mentions have all increased dramatically.

Because a link manager was also used for embedding URLs in each post, the Library has been able to track total clicks by date for each URL. The most clicked URL (http://short.med.nyu.edu/28541383) having been clicked on over 130 times. This same tweet was also liked 6 times and retweeted 4 times.

Figure 8. Tweet activity

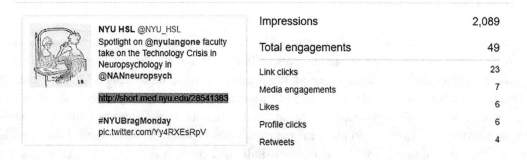

The purpose of the campaign has been twofold, (1) celebrate the research authored by our NYU faculty and (2) emphasize the library provides access to that research. While this campaign has been successful in meeting these goals, there were other benefits in launching this campaign. Tracking an institution's research publications is important for building and maintaining its reputation. It is also important for the authors whose productivity is measured to some degree by their scholarly activity. Although our library was already active in the process of collecting data on the institution's published research and the authors associated with it, the twitter campaign gave its librarians an opportunity to get more familiar with that research and the individual researchers and faculty involved. This gave its librarians a deeper sense of institutional memory seeing more details in the raw numbers such as total publications and citation count.

Another benefit to the campaign has been how it introduced librarians to how Twitter can work as a social marketing tool. Although none of the tweets went viral by industry standards, the Library gained a better understanding of the reach of Twitter and how by promoting the research of its institution's community of scholars. It also strategically positioned the Library as a knowledge-based organization of value. NYU authors with Twitter accounts were able to see that their library recognized their research and valued their contributions to the field of health sciences. For the publishers and journals with Twitter accounts, they saw that NYUHSL recognized their role in the scholarly communication process. This recognition was also seen by other libraries, authors, and scholars from other institutions.

CONCLUSION

Developing a content strategy for social media at any Library can be a rewarding experience. In addition to leveraging its strengths to support an organization's core mission and values, it opens up possibilities for end-users to engage with Libraries in new and innovative ways.

Developing and adhering to a specific content strategy for social media allows libraries to communicate their brand to target audiences. For many academic libraries, Twitter, has been a successful platform to disseminate information about its services and relationships to the scholarly communities it supports. Although marketing and outreach plans have historically been ad hoc endeavors, applying the content strategy framework of Assessment, Creation, Promotion, and Measurement can serve as a model for librarians and staff to carry out and follow-through on their campaigns.

REFERENCES

Blakiston, R. (2013). Developing a Content Strategy for an Academic Library Website. *Journal of Electronic Resources Librarianship*, *25*(3), 175–191. doi:10.1080/1941126X.2013.813295

Brigham, T. J. (2013). Personas: Stepping Into the Shoes of the Library User. *Medical Reference Services Quarterly*, *32*(4), 443–450. doi:10.1080/02763869.2013.837737 PMID:24180652

Carter, T. M., & Seaman, P. (2011). The Management and Support of Outreach in Academic Libraries. *Reference & User Services Quarterly*, *51*(2), 163–171.

Content Marketing Institute. (2018). *Getting Started*. Retrieved August 2, 2018, from https://content-marketinginstitute.com/getting-started/

Cuddy, C., Graham, J., & Morton-Owens, E. G. (2010). Implementing Twitter in a Health Sciences Library. *Medical Reference Services Quarterly*, *29*(4), 320–330. doi:10.1080/02763869.2010.518915 PMID:21058176

Dalal, H. A., O'Hanlon, R., & Yacobucci, K. L. (2017). *Video Marketing for Libraries: A Practical Guide for Librarians*. Rowman & Littlefield. Retrieved from https://books.google.com/books?id=3vK_jwEACAAJ

Datig, I. (2018). Revitalizing library websites and social media with content strategy: Tools and recommendations. *Journal of Electronic Resources Librarianship*, *30*(2), 63–69. doi:10.1080/1941126X.2018.1465511

Del Bosque, D., Leif, S. A., & Skarl, S. (2012). Libraries atwitter: Trends in academic library tweeting. *RSR. Reference Services Review*, *40*(2), 199–213. doi:10.1108/00907321211228246

Dessart, L., Veloutsou, C., & Morgan-Thomas, A. (2016). Capturing consumer engagement: Duality, dimensionality and measurement. *Journal of Marketing Management*, *32*(5–6), 399–426. doi:10.1080 /0267257X.2015.1130738

Evans, H. (2017, January 29). *"Content is King"—Essay by Bill Gates 1996*. Retrieved August 29, 2018, from https://medium.com/@HeathEvans/content-is-king-essay-by-bill-gates-1996-df74552f80d9

Fichter, D., & Wisniewski, J. (2014). Content Marketing and Strategy for Libraries. *Online Searcher*, *38*(6), 74–76.

Gunton, L., & Davis, K. (2012). Beyond broadcasting: Customer service, community and information experience in the Twittersphere. *RSR. Reference Services Review*, *40*(2), 224–227. doi:10.1108/00907321211228282

Hootsuite. (2018, July 18). *Social Media Image Sizes: A Quick Reference Guide for Each Network*. Retrieved November 29, 2018, from https://blog.hootsuite.com/social-media-image-sizes-guide/

Kim, H. M., Abels, E. G., & Yang, C. C. (2012). Who disseminates academic library information on Twitter? *Proceedings of the American Society for Information Science and Technology*, *49*(1), 1–4. doi:10.1002/meet.14504901317

Lee, O. (2013, March). *What is Content? Learn from 40 Definitions*. Retrieved February 20, 2014, from https://www.toprankblog.com/2013/03/what-is-content/

Milstein, S. (2009). Twitter FOR Libraries (and Librarians). *Computers in Libraries, 29*(5), 17–18.

Needleman, M. (2002). The OpenURL: An Emerging Standard for Linking. *Serials Review*, *28*(1), 74–76. doi:10.1080/00987913.2002.10764714

Park, J., & Dantus, S. (2018). *Marketing Academic Library Resources and Services (White Paper)*. ACRL. Retrieved from http:// choice360.org/librarianship/whitepaper

Pew Research Center. (2018). *Social Media Use 2018*. Pew Research Center. Retrieved from http://www.pewinternet.org/2018/03/01/social-media-use-in-2018/

Rouse, M. (2016, June). *What is Content Management System (CMS)*. Retrieved August 2, 2018, from https://searchcontentmanagement.techtarget.com/definition/content-management-system-CMS

Sewell, R. R. (2013). Who is following us? Data mining a library's Twitter followers. *Library Hi Tech*, *31*(1), 160–170. doi:10.1108/07378831311303994

Shulman, J., Yep, J., & Tomé, D. (2015). Leveraging the Power of a Twitter Network for Library Promotion. *Journal of Academic Librarianship*, *41*(2), 178–185. doi:10.1016/j.acalib.2014.12.004

Tempelman-Kluit, N., & Pearce, A. (2014). Invoking the User from Data to Design. *College & Research Libraries*, *75*(5), 616–640. doi:10.5860/crl.75.5.616

U.S. News & World Report L.P. (2018). *New York University (Langone) - Best Medical Schools - US News*. Retrieved August 29, 2018, from https://www.usnews.com/best-graduate-schools/top-medical-schools/new-york-university-04073

Vieira, D., McGowan, R., McCrillis, A., Lamb, I., Larson, C., Bakker, T., & Spore, S. S. (2018). The Faculty Bibliography Project at the NYU School of Medicine. *Journal of Librarianship & Scholarly Communication, 2*(3), 1–15.

Zaugg, H., & Rackham, S. (2016). Identification and development of patron personas for an academic library. *Performance Measurement and Metrics, 17*(2), 124–133. doi:10.1108/PMM-04-2016-0011

ADDITIONAL READING

Anderson, C. L. (2012). LibraryPalooza: A marketing case study. *New Library World, 113*(1/2), 55–64. doi:10.1108/03074801211199040

Colburn, S., & Haines, L. (2012). Measuring Libraries' Use of YouTube as a Promotional Tool: An Exploratory Study and Proposed Best Practices. *Journal of Web Librarianship, 6*(1), 5–31. doi:10.1080/19322909.2012.641789

Deodato, J. (2018). Overhyped Fad or Missed Opportunity? A History of Academic Libraries and the Social Web. *Journal of Web Librarianship, 12*(1), 1–27. doi:10.1080/19322909.2017.1390424

Henner, T. (2014). From the Literature. *Medical Reference Services Quarterly, 33*(2), 227–234. doi:10.1080/02763869.2014.897526 PMID:25023012

Richardson, H. A. H., & Kennedy, M. R. (2014). How to Market Your Library's Electronic Resources. *The Serials Librarian, 67*(1), 42–47. doi:10.1080/0361526X.2014.899289

Rossmann, D., & Young, S. W. H. (2015). Using Social Media to Build Community. *Computers in Libraries, 35*(4), 18–22.

Young, S. W. H., & Rossmann, D. (2015). Building Library Community through Social Media. *Information Technology and Libraries, 34*(1), 20–37. doi:10.6017/ital.v34i1.5625

This research was previously published in Social Media for Communication and Instruction in Academic Libraries; pages 37-54, copyright year 2019 by Information Science Reference (an imprint of IGI Global).

Chapter 6
New Communication Strategies and the Future of Advertising Narration

Murat Koçyiğit

(iD) https://orcid.org/0000-0002-2250-415X

Necmettin Erbakan University, Turkey

ABSTRACT

Nowadays, almost all consumers use social media platforms. Therefore, many consumers share their brand-related experiences on online platforms. Social media platforms have changed the way consumers communicate. It offers consumers the opportunity to contribute to the debate. By means of online media, individuals are no longer just content consumers. Online media users are both content-producing and prosumer. Hence, the prosumer, which produces the content itself and consumes itself, provides the multiple uses in the mass market. It has a comprehensive impact on the purchasing decisions of other consumers. Developing and changing communication technologies are to provide the development of new communication strategies. Moreover, Web 3.0 technology, the third level on the Web, is used by semantic web consumers. Web 3.0 (semantic web) technologies combine information. Semantic Web improves the web experience and makes it more relevant to their search. Web 3.0 stands out with its ability to share meaning and run useful and entertaining web applications.

INTRODUCTION

In the digital world and the age of digital communication, social media is a set of online services that facilitate two-way communication and content sharing. Social media is becoming a productive component of the overall marketing and communication strategies of brands. Brands structure corporate communication, public relations and digital advertising strategies on the basis of social media platforms. Social media platforms increase the online visibility of the brand. These platforms strengthen the brand's relations with the customer. Social media platforms are the best electronic word of mouth channel and have the

DOI: 10.4018/978-1-6684-6287-4.ch006

ability to deliver ad content to more users. The content of digital advertising narrative in social media platforms increases the brand awareness with its interesting and intriguing feature. Given the rapid rise in popularity and the hundreds of millions of worldwide users, social media marketing is quite attractive. Social media platforms with millions of users are an effective digital advertising channel. Digital advertising content reaches millions of users, increasing brand awareness. Social media platforms are becoming the most effective advertising channel that increases brand awareness, brand connotations and brand visibility (Weinberg, 2009; Barefoot & Szabo, 2010). Although many social media messages look like traditional "broadcasts" from one business to many consumers, their interactive component offers an enticing illusion of "one-to-one" communication that invites individual readers to respond (Zimmerman & Sahlin, 2010). The phrase digital advertising narration generally refers to using these online services for relationship selling a subject you already know all about. Social media services or channels make innovative use of new online technologies to accomplish familiar communication, advertising, public relations and marketing goals. Everything already known about marketing and advertising is true. Social media marketing and digital advertising is a new technique, not a new world (Weber, 2007; Dafonte-Gomez, 2014).

Digital advertising has defined a provocative content as a free peer-to-peer communication that results from a defined sponsor using the Internet to convince or influence a viewer to transfer the content to others. In digital advertising campaigns, viral messages about brands spread to potential consumers, and then quickly transferred this information to other potential consumers (Porter & Golan, 2006; Eckler & Bolls, 2011). Digital advertising is to introduce the brand or products or company using social media tools. Digital advertising is a process that allows you to communicate and interact with the masses too good to be able to advance through traditional advertising channels members of online social channels with web sites, products, promote their brands and services, to raise awareness (Koçyiğit, 2017).

SOCIAL MEDIA AND NEW COMMUNICATION STRATEGIES

New communication strategy and tactics are inseparable. Brands can't design a strategy without deep, firsthand knowledge of the tactics brands using, and tactics are aimless without a strategy to guide them. Social media strategy should fit with of brand established identity. One of the worst mistakes a new social media marketer will make is to apply the same strategies from the offline broadcast world to the social web. Before brands launch into a social media conversation, should listen. New communication technologies have introduced new communication strategies. New communication strategies and tactics are as follows (Zarrella, 2010; Zyl, 2009; Musser & O'Reilly, 2006; Hall & Rosenberg, 2009):

- Monitoring: Whether it's a local brand or an international brand, consumers talk about brands on social media. But brands must start listening before participating in conversations. Brands can't respond if they don't know what are being said, where they are being said and who is saying it. Monitoring social media is an ongoing process, and brands should use multiple systems to be sure nothing slips through the cracks the right (or wrong) story can come from anywhere and blow up in brands' face. The first tools brand should be using allow brand to search for brand name and product names; brand should then subscribe to the search results via RSS. Company names, product names, brand names and important employee names should be monitored on social media platforms.

- Responding: After talking about brands on social media, brands should participate in these platforms. Speed is very important, so brands should start planning their responses as soon as possible. A negative interpretation or speech should be directly intervened. Messages that damage the reputation of brands or crisis events must be reacted before spreading in social networks. Brands must show their presence on social media platforms by responding to those who are spoken about themselves.

- Research: When brands begin to monitor what is said about them, they must know who the users on social networks are and how they use those platforms. New communication technologies require new research strategies. Comprehensive research is required for social media platforms. It is necessary to know what social network platforms are used by current and potential customers. Therefore, brands should do a thorough research.

- Integration: One of the central tenets of Web 2.0 is the idea that web applications should be able to share data and play nicely together. Brands social media marketing effort can integrate with at least one other part, and users of one kind of social media are likely to be users of other types; it makes sense to invite those who interact with on Twitter to join page on Facebook.

The importance of social media for Web 2.0 technology and relationship building for brands is increasing day by day. Social media platforms originally developed to facilitate the exchange of personal information (photos, video, messages, audio) to groups of friends and family, these full featured services offer multiple functions. From a brands point of view, many of them support subgroups that offer the potential for more targeted marketing, public relations and advertising. Basic marketing focuses on the need for branding, name recognition, visibility, presence, or top of mind awareness. Social media platforms are an effective channel that allows users to remember the brand name of the product or service. Social media services, of almost every type, are excellent ways to build brand. Social media works for branding as long as brand's name in front of the right people. Brands should plan to segment audiences on social media platforms (Tuten, 2008; Ryan & Jones 2009; Evans, 2008).

With the emergence of social media, digital advertising has gained enormous popularity; online social platforms have significantly changed the way consumers respond to advertising. Social media platforms, such as Twitter, Instagram, LinkedIn, Facebook, enable target consumers to communicate ads to friends, link them to advertisers, or comment on advertising, and post these comments on viral channels and send them as message senders. Accordingly, positive advertising responses indicate the power of using Facebook groups as a platform for digital advertising. When group members redirect digital ads to other friends, they become supportive in the social media ads of this brand, thus increasing the likelihood that your friends will see ads. Advertisers are known to value digital advertising. Participation in social media groups has increased the interest of social network users in digital advertising. Digital advertising narrative is interesting to users. In this context, social network users follow advertising messages with creative content (Chu, 2011; Cooke & Buckley, 2008). Digital advertising is direct and indirect communication, such as sharing all kinds of content with social networking tools. The connotation and awareness of brands is increasing thanks to social media platforms such as blogs, microblogs, social networks, social bookmarking (Koçyiğit, 2017).

Social networks and virtual communities are required to understand the current changes in the business environment. The network potential encouraged by new innovations leads all communities and brands to work faster, create more dependency and manage, and operate in global markets. Obviously, these new trends facilitate the creation of strong social networks and virtual communities, affect the design of websites and, in general, increase the competitiveness of organizations and at the same time turn the business models into all sectors. In particular, the growth of virtual social networks such as LinkedIn, Facebook, Twitter or YouTube, and in general all kinds of virtual communities have been important for the last few years. However, their impact is very broad and is becoming increasingly widespread through various activities ranging from economic and marketing to advertising and politics. In this context, social media platforms, such as corporate networks, professional communities, e-business platforms, research networks, training networks, networks with customers, suppliers and friends' networks, are effective channels for digital advertising narrative (Garrigos-Simon et al., 2012; Constantinides & Fountain, 2008; Garrigos et al., 2011).

In the world of social media, the term engagement refers to the length of time and quality of interaction between brand and followers. Social media is a long-term commitment. In addition to small trials or pilot projects, if brands are not planning to continue, they should not hesitate to begin social media commitment. Any short-term benefits seen aren't worth the effort having to make. Already, many clever brands have found ways to use social media to improve business processes. Although individual applications depend on the nature of the business, brands should consider using social media to immediately identify and fix customer issues or complaints. In this context, new communication strategies on social media platforms are as follows (Zimmerman & Sahlin, 2010; Lincoln, 2009; Grainger, 2010):

- Learn about customer feedback and new product designs or changes.
- Provide tech support to many people at one time; if one person has a question, changes are good that others do, too.
- Find qualified new vendors, service providers and employees using professional networks such as LinkedIn.
- Collect critical market intelligence on your industry and competitors by following content on appropriate social media.
- Use new geolocation services to manage local traffic and acquire new customers at slow times.

Because social media strategies focus on inexpensive ways to reach niche markets with specific messages, they're tailor-made for a guerrilla marketing approach and digital advertising narration. As with all guerrilla marketing activities and digital advertising narration, target one market at a time (Miletsky, 2010; Gunelius, 2011; Safko & Brake, 2009).

SEMANTIC WEB AND ADVERTISING NARRATION

Semantic web (Web 3.0) elements will be included in the future advertising narrative. Web 3.0 is also known as semantic web. Web 3.0 is a term used to describe the evolution of Web use and interaction that involves converting the Web into a database. Web 3.0 attempts to connect, integrate, and analyze data from a variety of data sets to obtain new information flow. Web 3.0 can improve data management, support the accessibility of mobile internet, and simulate creativity and innovation. The semantic web can promote the phenomenon of globalization, increase customer satisfaction, and organize collaboration on the social network. The development of the semantic network is continuing to overcome the problems of the current web. The semantic web can define a data network and work as a global database of many databases. The purpose of the design network of data on the semantic web is the machines first and then the people. Semantic web is a web that can show what the computer can understand. The main purpose of the semantic web is to make the web read by both machines and people. Web 3.0 is a web where the concept of website or webpage disappears, where data isn't owned but instead shared, where services show different views for the same web, the same data. With digital web technology, digital advertising and digital advertising narrative will gain a new dimension. Semantic web technology, creativity and innovation will increase. Furthermore, a fast and collaborative web application will be used. The contents prepared by computers and the contents that the computer can understand will become the basic elements of digital advertising (Aghaei et al., 2012; Hendler, 2009; Naik & Shivalingaiah, 2008). Strategically, the most important change in Web 3.0 is the importance of meaning in the new environment. For this reason, networks are necessary tools to find out what is happening now, what competition is doing, what customers demand, and even discovering technological trends, innovations and expert opinions. They are also vital to creating, influencing and participating in discussions on new innovations and image promotion. The management of social networks for information management is also indispensable because networks can create, share, and learn, and are creativity and innovation resources, as many stakeholders can add value to different products or processes of companies. The customer's transformation from a passive customer to a highly active customer who wants to participate in all production processes and the development of social networks is to change the appearance of the production itself and to ensure that organizations make an interactive connection with the market. Web 3.0 based semantic web are effective in many areas ranging from product promotion, production logistics or distribution to brand positioning, brand communication, brand management or sales service (Garrigos-Simon et al., 2012; Lister et al., 2009). Innovations, combined with the advancement of new information and communication technologies and the development of the Internet, have had a profound impact on the structure of brands and changed the decision-making process. The understanding of developments and transformations from new information and communication technologies through the advancement of social networks and Web 3.0 technology in the new economic and social environment is vital because of the impact of recent innovations in the competitiveness of organizations. In the era of Web 3.0, with new communication technologies, brands change their marketing and digital advertising strategies through data warehousing, data mining, or customer relationship management. With Web 3.0 (semantic web) technology, brands use data from various social networks or other digital channels for digital advertising strategies. The information network makes cross-marketing, digital advertising, public relations and other corporate communication strategies faster and more effective. Web 3.0 technology provides product and service awareness for different users and brands. In addition, Semantic web is the latest technology on the web for personalization, adaptation and creative content creation. Semantic web differentiates digital advertising strategies and social media marketing concept. In addition, the semantic web gives a new dimension to general marketing strategies (Garrigos-Simon et al., 2012; Lassila & Hendler, 2007).

CONCLUSION

The evolution of digital communication technologies, starting with Web 1.0, continues with Web 2.0 and Web 3.0. Web 3.0 technology, expressed as the 3rd generation on the web, has moved the network infrastructure to a very different location. Web technologies that have been developing since the beginning of the 1990s have started to use a wide range of web technologies, including highly intelligent interactions and artificial intelligence techniques (Koçyiğit & Koçyiğit, 2018). The web structure, which makes its transformation more visible with Web 2.0 technology, has evolved from Web-based to human-oriented, machine-oriented intelligent computing techniques. Continuous progress continues in web technologies, where development, transformation and progress continue. These developments and advances also affect digital advertising. Therefore, digital advertising narrator has to keep up with the innovations introduced by Web 3.0 technology.

REFERENCES

Aghaei, S., Nematbakhsh, M. A., & Farsani, H. K. (2012). Evolution of the World Wide Web: From Web 1.0 to Web 4.0 [IJWesT]. *International Journal of Web & Semantic Technology*, *3*(1), 1–10. doi:10.5121/ijwest.2012.3101

Barefoot, D., & Szabo, J. (2010). Friends with Benefits A Social Media Marketing Handbook. San Francisco, CA: No Starch Press.

Chu, S. C. (2011). Viral Advertising in Social Media. *Journal of Interactive Advertising*, *12*(1), 30–43. doi:10.1080/15252019.2011.10722189

Constantinides, E., & Fountain, S. J. (2008). Web 2.0: Conceptual Foundations and Marketing, *Journal of Direct. Data and Digital Marketing Practice*, *9*(3), 231–244. doi:10.1057/palgrave.dddmp.4350098

Cooke, M., & Buckley, N. (2008). Web 2.0, Social Networks and The Future of Market Research. *International Journal of Market Research*, *50*(2), 267–292. doi:10.1177/147078530805000208

Dafonte-Gomez, A. (2014). The Key Elements of Viral Advertising: From Motivation to Emotion in the Most Shared Videos. *Comunicar*, *43*(22), 199–206. doi:10.3916/C43-2014-20

Eckler, P., & Bolls, P. (2011). Spreading the Virus: Emotional Tone of Viral Advertising and Its Effect on Forwarding Intentions and Attitudes. *Journal of Interactive Advertising*, *11*(2), 1–11. doi:10.1080/15252019.2011.10722180

Evans, D. (2008). *Social Media Marketing An Hour A Day*. Indianapolis, IN: Wiley Publishing.

Garrigos, F., Gil, I., & Narangajavana, Y. (2011). The Impact of Social Networks in the Competitiveness of the Firms. A.M. Beckford, & J.P. Larsen (Eds.), Competitiveness: Psychology, Production, Impact and Global Trends. Hauppauge, NY: Nova Science Publishers.

Garrigos-Simon, F. J., Lapiedra Alcami, R., & Barbera Ribera, T. (2012). Social Networks and Web 3.0: Their Impact on the Management and Marketing of Organizations. *Management Decision*, *50*(10), 1880–1890. doi:10.1108/00251741211279657

Grainger, J. (2010). *Social Media And The Fortune 500: How The Fortune 500 Uses, Perceives and Measures Social Media As A Marketing Tool, (Degree of Master of Art*, North Carolina at Chapel Hill).

Gunelius, S. (2011). *30 Minute Social Media Marketing: Step-by-Step Techniques to Spread the Word About Your Business Fast and Free*. New York, NY: McGraw Hill.

Hall, S., & Rosenberg, C. (2009). *Get Connected: The Social Networking Toolkit for Business*. New York, NY: Entrepreneur Press.

Hendler, J. (2009). Web 3.0 Emerging. *Computer, 42*(1), 111–113. doi:10.1109/MC.2009.30

Koçyiğit, M. (2017). A Literature Review on the Viral Advertising Narrative Structure. Yılmaz, R. (Ed.), Narrative Advertising Models and Conceptualization in the Digital Age (pp.167-183). Hershey, PA: IGI Global.

Koçyiğit, M., & Koçyiğit, A. (2018). Değişen ve Gelişen Dijital İletişim: Yazılabilir Web Teknolojisi (Web 2.0), Çakmak, V. ve Çavuş, S. (Eds.), Dijital Kültür ve İletişim (ss.19-48). Konya, Turkey: Literatürk academia.

Lassila, O., & Hendler, J. (2007). Embracing Web 3.0. *IEEE Internet Computing, 11*(3), 90–93. doi:10.1109/MIC.2007.52

Lincoln, S. R. (2009). *Mastering Web 2.0 Transform Your Business Using Key Website and Social Media Tools*. London, UK: Kogan Page.

Lister, M., Dovey, J., Giddings, S., Grant, I., & Kelly, K. (2009). *New Media: A Critical Introduction* (2nd ed.). New York, NY: Routledge.

Miletsky, J. I. (2010). *Principles of Internet Marketing: New Tools and Methods for Web Developers*. Boston, MA: Cengage Learning.

Musser, J., & O'Reilly, T. (2006). *Web 2.0 Principles and Best Practices*. Sebastopol, CA: O'Reilly Media.

Naik, U., & Shivalingaiah, D. (2008). *Comparative Study of Web 1.0, Web 2.0 and Web 3.0* (pp. 499–507). International CALIBER.

Porter, L., & Golan, G. J. (2006). From Subservient Chickens to Brawny Men: A Comparison of Viral Advertising to Television Advertising. *Journal of Interactive Advertising, 6*(2), 30–38.

Ryan, D., & Jones, C. (2009). *Understanding Digital Marketing; Marketing Strategies for Engaging the Digital Generation*. London, UK: Kogan Page.

Safko, L., & Brake, D. K. (2009). *The Social Media Bible: Tactics, Tools, Strategies For Business Success*. New Jersey: John Wiley&Sons Inc.

Tuten, T. L. (2008). *Advertising 2.0 Social Media Marketing in a Web 2.0 World*. Westport, UK: Praeger Publishers.

Weber, L. (2007). *Marketing to The Social Web, How Digital Customer Communities Build Your Business*. Hoboken, NJ: John Wiley & Sons

Weinberg, T. (2009). *The New Community Rules: Marketing On the Social Web* (1st ed.). Sebastopol, CA: O'Reilly Media.

Zarrella, D. (2010). The Social Media Marketing Book. Sebastopol, CA: O'Reilly Media.

Zimmerman, J., & Sahlin, D. (2010). *Social Media Marketing All in One for Dummies*. Indianapolis, IN: Wiley Publisihing. doi:10.1002/9781118257661

Zyl, A. S. (2009). The Impact of Social Networking 2.0 on Organisations. *The Electronic Library, 27*(6), 906–918. doi:10.1108/02640470911004020

KEY TERMS AND DEFINITIONS

Digital Communication Technologies: Starting with Web 1.0, continues with Web 2.0 and Web 3.0. Web 3.0 technology, expressed as the 3rd generation on the web, has moved the network infrastructure to a very different location.

Digital Content: Text, audio, video, games, e-books, e-magazines, e-newspapers, graphics, such as a large medium that includes many different forms.

Semantic Web: Semantic Web (Web 3.0) elements will be included in the future advertising narrative. Web 3.0 is also known as semantic web.

Social Media Platforms: Social media platforms are the best electronic word of mouth channel and have the ability to deliver ad content to more users.

Virtual Communities: The virtual communities are the general name of networks that bring together users on social media and help them to share.

This research was previously published in the Handbook of Research on Narrative Advertising; pages 333-340, copyright year 2019 by Business Science Reference (an imprint of IGI Global).

Chapter 7
Understanding Historical Background of Corporate Social Responsibility (CSR) and Realizing Social Media as a New Horizon in CSR Communication

Melis Kaytaz Yiğit
Yiğit Metal, Turkey

Özge Kirezli
İstanbul Bilgi University, Turkey

ABSTRACT

With globalizing world, formal and the dimensional structure of market competition has been changing dramatically. In such a rapidly changing environment, companies should not just meet unlimited consumer needs, but also adopt a certain social responsibility philiosophy towards the society. In that sense, corporate social responsibility is one of the important concepts that play a role in formation of positive perceptions of the target groups. The purpose of this chapter is to understand the changing nature of corporate social responsibility (CSR) over years, and also find the effect of social media on communicating corporate social responsibility. In that sense, firstly the need for CSR is to be discussed in different perspectives. Alternative definitions are provided over years to sense the evolving nature of the concept. Then in the last part, new media and social media's impact on CSR, as of benefits/challenges provided and alternative social media tools to be used in communication, are discussed.

DOI: 10.4018/978-1-6684-6287-4.ch007

INTRODUCTION

Globalization and technological advancements have dramatically changed the formal and the dimensional structure of market competition. In such a rapidly changing environment, companies should not just meet unlimited consumer needs, but also consider their impact on the society during their operations. As economy' number one rule, resources are scarce, and to ensure the sustainability of the resources companies need to develop a sense of responsibility towards the nature and the society. In that sense, corporate social responsibility (CSR) is one of the important concepts that companies must consider strategically. With corporate social responsibility activities, companies support society's social, economic, environmental and cultural development, and hence, having that responsibility eventually creates positive associations among target markets and contribute their corporate image. In order to create long-term relationships with customers, companies need to start produce products and services according to social and other norms which result in increased profits.

In other words, while corporate social responsibility provides contribution for the society, it can also enhance the business operations. These investments have long term return, but in the end several positive consequences emerge. Having a clear sense of social responsiblity not only affect the image of the institution, but also has a positive effect on company's financial performance. Today's stakeholders and customers, who are non-business stakeholders, are concerned with the social activities of businesses in their buying decisions. For companies, the key point is first of all having a sustainable and strong CSR attitude and then finding effective and efficient ways to communicate with the society.

The purpose of this chapter is to understand the changing nature of Corporate Social Responsibility (CSR) over years, and also quest the effect of social media on communicating Corporate Social Responsibility. In that sense, firstly CSR's evolutionary progress is to be presented. Subsequently communicating CSR philiosophy and actions are detailed. Then in the last part, new media and social media's impact on CSR, as of benefits/challenges provided and alternative social media tools to be used in communication are discussed.

CONTEMPORARY CORPORATE SOCIAL RESPONSIBILITY: HISTORICAL AND DEFINITIONAL EVOLUTION

For several decades, the concept of corporate social responsibility has been deeply discussed by academic and business professionals. However the history of the corporate social responsibility literaly roots back to 1950's, it can be said that the appearance of corporate philanthropy or contributions in the late of Industrial Revolution were the first developments that supported emerge of the concept of corporate social responsibility (Carroll, 2008).

In Murphy's (1978) work, corporate social responsibility was classified in four periods. The first period is up to 1950's and was called "philanthropic" era which companies donation was just delimited to charities. Second period 1953-1967 was termed as "awareness" era, in which companies started to awaken of overall responsibilities of business and community affairs. The period of 1968-1973 was named as "issue" era; in these years companies began to center specific issues rather than general affairs. Finally the period 1974-1980 was named "responsiveness" in which companies started to take CSR issues in their management and organizational actions ((Carroll, 2008). Over the time with the social and technological developments, the definition and the understanding of the corporate social responsibility has changed as well.

In this part of the chapter, by deep literature review, the history and the definitional evolution of the corporate social responsibility is examined as a whole. Starting with the formal birth in 1950's to up to now, all the historical stages and developments of corporate social responsibility are presented in detail.

CSR: The 1950's

Modern literature of the concept of corporate social responsibility was begun in 1953 with Howard R. Bowen's book named Social Responsibilities of the Businessman. In his book Bowen (1953) stated that largest businesses and their actions are at the core of the power and decision making, which substantially affected the lives of citizens (Carroll, 2008). Bowen (1953) was the first author who defines social responsibility; he interpreted social responsibility, as the obligation of businessmen to pursue those, policies, to make those decisions, or to follow those lines of actions which are desirable in terms of the objectives and values of our society" (Carroll, 2008)

Generally decade of 1950 was lack of corporate social responsibility practices between companies; but especially Bowen's proposal was the iniatiative attempt to change the attitudes over corporate social responsibility. After Bowen (1953), a certain number of authors like Selekman (1959), Heald (1957) and Eels (1956) have made a significant contribution to corporate social responsibility literature (Carroll, 2008).

In sum, Frederick (2006) stated that corporate social responsibility in the 1950's has three main ideas. These were identified as; the idea of corporate managers as public trustees, the idea of balancing competing claims to corporate resources, and the acceptance of philanthropy as a manifestation of business support of good causes (Carroll, 2008).

CSR: The 1960's

The meaning of corporate social responsibility was heavily studied in 1960's by the authors. Kaith Davis was the leading author who deeply touched on the corporate social responsibility in his studies. In his 1960s paper he define social responsibility as:

Businessmen's decisions and actions taken for reasons at least partially beyond the first direct economic or technical interest. (Davis, 1960;70).

Davis stated that corporate social responsibility is still indefinite term, but corporations should embrace it in managerial context. With his definition author asserted that corporate social responsibility actions can be long and complicated but in long run, they can provide important economic gains for the firm. Beside these, he remarked the importance businessmen's role on social responsibility in terms of their social power. He believed that, if businessmen want to gain considerable social power, they should act more socially responsible. Davis's social responsibility definition was become commonly accepted viewpoint among authors by the late 1970s and 1980s.

Another important social responsibility definition was come up by William C. Frederick in 1960. For him:

Social responsibility in the final analysis implies a public posture towards society's economic and human resources and a willingness to see that those resources are utilized for broad social ends and simply for the narrowly circumscribes interests of private persons and firms. (Frederick, 1960:60).

From this point of view, he indicated that economic and human resources of the society should not be used for just specific people and firms' interest, moreover it should be used to utilize interest of the whole society. In other words, when trying to gain business goals and objectives, companies should take society's expectations into consideration and should result the business activities in direct proportion to advancing social economic welfare (Carroll, 2008).

When it came up to 1967, with his book named Corporate Social Responsibility, Clarence C. Walton not only revealed many aspects of corporate social responsibility like the role of firms and business person in modern society but also represents different social responsibility models. In his book Walton(1967) stressed the importance of top managers attitudes of corporate social responsibility against society (Carroll, 2008) as:

Social responsibility recognizes the intimacy of the relationships between corporation and society and realize that such relationship must be kept in mind by top managers as the corporation and the related groups pursue their respective goals. (Walton, 1967:18).

Generally in the decade of 1960, corporate social responsibility activities were just newly launched by companies. With the emergence of corporate social responsibility principles like health and safety, corruption, pollution and discrimination, the awareness and implementation of corporate social responsibility by companies and government significantly increased as of 1950's (Heath and Ni, 2008). The basic corporate social responsibility activities of these years were philanthropy, employee improvements, customer relations and stakeholder relations (Heald, 1970).

CSR: The 1970's

1970's first remarkable study produced by Morrell Heald with the named of his book The Social Responsibilities of Business: Company and Community, 1900-1960. Despite not providing specific social responsibility definition, he discussed his book from the perspective of businessmen and indicated that social responsibility is the construct which is closely related to how businessmen define and experience it. From this point of view, he concluded that businessmen in 1970s period were mainly preoccupied with corporate philanthropy and community relations (Carroll, 2008).

Horald Johnson (1971) was another pioneer of this decade with his book named "Business in Contemporary Society. Framework and Issues". In his book, author examined various definitions of corporate social responsibility and analyzed them (Carroll, 2008). The term "Conventional wisdom" was first used by him with the definition of:

A socially responsible firm is one whose managerial staff balances a multiplicity of interests. Instead of striving only for a larger profits for its stockholders, a responsible enterprise also takes into account employees, suppliers, dealers, local communities and the nation. (Johnson, 1971:50).

In his conventional wisdom definition, the term he used "multiplicity of interest" is the first indicator of stakeholder approach. For him, social responsibility is not just about interest of employees and philanthropy-recipients; it includes interest of other specific groups like employees, suppliers, dealers and local communities (Carroll, 2008). Other important points of Johnson view are, profit maximization with implementing social activities and utility maximization that refers businesses' motivation for social responsibility decisions. At the same year, Committee for Economic Development published Social Responsibilities of Business Corporations paper and make major contribution to the topic of corporate social responsibility. The paper defines corporate social responsibility as:

Business functions by public consent and its basic purpose is to serve constructively the needs of society-to the satisfaction of society. (CED, 1971:11).

The committee exhibited interwoven three circles of social responsibility named; inner circle, intermediate circle and outer circle. Inner circle refers to companies' basic responsibilities which provide to exercise economic functions like products, jobs and economic growth. On the other side intermediate circle involves relevant economic functions with consideration of changing social values and priorities. The last circle named outer circle includes emerging business responsibilities which companies deeply involved and act to improve the social environment (Carroll, 2008). Defining these circles, triggered a heightened interest in re-defining relationships between society and businesses.

Along with these outcomes, CED centered new view of corporate social responsibility which consists of business people and educators and their changing social contract with emerging new social responsibilities like environmental conservation, worker safety and expectations of consumers. Improving human rights, became seen as significant responsibility of businesses which at the future induce profit maximization (CED, 1971).

Apart from all these Steiner (1971) emphasized the interpretation and implementation of corporate social responsibility by offering models and criteria. For him, the main goal of businesses is to maintain economic profit but whilst profiting, businesses should also help society to succeed societal goals.

When it came up to 1973, Davis again presented an article and redefine corporate social responsibility in broader sense as:

Corporate social responsibility refers to the firms' consideration of, and response to, issues beyond narrow economic, technical and legal requirements of the firm. (Davis, 1973: 318).

In this decade of 1970s the terms corporate social responsiveness, corporate social performance and corporate social responsibility were mainly used as same manner. In 1975, Sethi separated these terms and revealed "dimensions of corporate social performance" which contains social obligation, social responsibility and social responsiveness. For him social obligation, which is proscriptive in nature, is about economic and legal conditions that refers to corporate behavior against market forces or legal constraints. In other respect, second dimension named social responsibility, which is prescriptive in nature, is about social obligations which promote improving companies corporate behavior level. The third dimension of corporate social performance is social responsiveness. For Sethi social responsiveness refers to company's adaptation of corporate behavior with social needs (Carroll, 2008).

In 1975, the book named Private Management and Public Policy: The Principle of Public Responsibility, Lee Preston and James Post restrained the term of social responsibility and emphasized on the term called public responsibility. The reason why they used term public rather than social is to underline the importance of public policy process. For them, social responsibility is much more about individual opinion and conscience than public responsibility (Carroll, 2008).Then, Eilbert and Parket presented a list of corporate social responsibility activities of the year 1970s and stated the most implemented activities in order of minority hiring, ecology, minority training, contributions of education, and contributions of arts, hard-core hiring, hide core training, urban renewal and civil rights (Carroll, 2008).

Arnold B. Carroll is another significant writer of 1970s with proposing four-part definition of corporate social responsibility which was compounded with corporate social performance (Carroll, 2008). For him the companies which want to implement corporate social performance successfully should consider having three components. First one is, they need to identify basic definition of corporate social responsibility and in second they should discover the social responsibility issues in society an in third they should have know to how to response these issues in other words they need to remark the philosophy (or strategy) to the issues (Carroll, 2008).

Carroll (2008) stressed four components, as economic, legal, ethical discretionary responsibilities, constitutes pyramid of corporate social responsibility corporate social responsibility and defines the concept as:

The social responsibility of business encompasses the economic, legal, ethical and discretionary expectations that society has of organizations at a given point in time. (Carroll, 1979;500).

CSR: The 1980's

In 1980s, there was a few study on defining corporate social responsibility but, much more studies have done to create new themes and alternative concepts like corporate social responsiveness, corporate social performance, public policy, business ethics and stakeholder theory.

In early 1980s, Thomas M. Jones (1980) defined corporate social responsibility from the points of corporate obligations to society which has two features. For him, firstly, obligation should be voluntary adopted and secondly it has to be broad that includes customers, employees, suppliers and neighboring communities (Jones, 1980;59). Beside these in his article Jones addressed the importance of corporate social responsibility process and became the first author who handled corporate social responsibility as a process (Carroll, 1999).

In 1981, Frank Tuzzolino and Barry Armandi proposed corporate social responsibility need-hierarchy framework which based on Maslow's need hierarchy. Concededly Carroll's 1979 corporate social responsibility definition, they executed organizational need hierarchy tool to favor operation of corporate social responsibility. Like Maslow, they indicated that organizations had psychological, safety, afflictive, esteem and self actualization criteria they need to be fulfilled (Carroll, 1999).

When it came up to 1987, Edwin M. Epstein constituted an corporate social responsibility definition on the concepts of social responsibility, responsiveness and business ethics and underlined the beneficial effect of corporate social responsibility on corporate stakeholders.

CSR: The 1990's

In 1990s the there were a few studies that contribute phenomenon of corporate social responsibility. Most of the concepts presented in these years were introduced in 1980s, but it was 1990s that they were used in corporate social responsibility literature. The pioneer themes of this decade were corporate social performance, stakeholder theory, business ethics theory and corporate citizenship (Carroll, 2008).

During 1990s, globalization effected company's structure and most of them become global companies which started to pay significant attention on corporate social responsibility and public affairs. On the other side new themes like global social investment, corporate reputation, community partnership, corporate social policy was also became dominant concepts used. 1990s corporate social responsibility activities included education, culture, arts, health and human services, civic and community, international donees, community partners and Non Governmental Organization partners (Carroll, 2008).

The nonprofit organization named Business for Social Responsibility was created in 1992 which aimed to lead companies to act as socially responsible. According to BSP, with implementing socially responsible business policies and practices the companies not only achieve suitable growth but also they can gain competitive advantage (Carroll, 2008).

Contemporary CSR

In 2000s era, corporate social responsibility literature started to focus on empirical researches rather than theoretical researches. Continuing rapid changes in the world will undoubtedly affect the way in which corporate social responsibility is implemented. According to Steger (2008) there are four powerful drivers that will change corporate social responsibility's scope and implementation process. One of them is stated as the emergence of Asian competition. Countries, especially like China, India and Thailand are developing rapidly and become an important force against Western countries. With having power over the world, these countries will need to gain competitive advantage against Western countries and will give importance on topics like human rights, landscape production or biodiversity which is also improve the scope and the form of application corporate social responsibility activities. On the other side according to Steger (2008) three players, financial institutions, governments and customers will negatively affect corporate social responsibility phenomenon. Financial institutions which has strong power on companies started to ignore any kind of long term activities like "sustainable development". They are just started to focus on merger and acquisition projects and short term financial activities as well. In addition, governments and the customers are in the same position. For author, not only the national governments have seen not to interest in improving their national well-being but also customers are seen as becoming insensitive in environmental issues (Steger, 2008).

Contingency theory of corporate social performance was produced by Byran Husted in 2000 and proved that corporate social performance is the fit between social issue and company strategy developed against this issue. Like Husted there were also various studies (Jones and Mureell, 2001, Smith et al, 2001; Backhaus et al, 2002) that empirically investigated the relationship between corporate social responsibility and corporate social performance and proved corporate social performance as a dimension of corporate social responsibility.

By time, corporate social responsibility was associated with many concepts like stakeholder theory, business ethics, sustainability and corporate citizenship. Lantos's article named as "The Ethically of Altrustic Corporate Social Responsibility" (2002), corporate social responsibility was grounded into three categories named altruistic corporate social responsibility, ethical corporate social responsibility, and strategic corporate social responsibility. When ethical social responsibility refers company's ethic or moral responsibilities to prevent social injuries, altruistic corporate social responsibility defined as company's complimentary helping on societal problems. The third one strategic social responsibility was based on using it as a marketing tool and gain financial obligations legally. This thought was supported by Davis (2005) who argued that corporate social responsibility should be used as business strategy to get competitive advantage.

In 2003 Schwartz and Carroll offered a three-domain approach of corporate social responsibility in a venn diagram. Economic, legal and ethical approaches of corporate social responsibility were presented as a useful implementation of CSR (Carroll, 2008).

In their empirical study on 25 best CSR practices, Philip Kotler and Nancy Lee (2004) categorized six main social initiatives called cause promotion, cause related marketing, corporate social marketing, corporate philanthropy, community volunteering and socially responsible business practices (Kotler and Lee, 2005).

Today's globalizing world expedites communication effectively and enhances responsible behavior of global and local companies (Startk and Kruckeberg, 2005). The expectation of today's society has changing dramatically with the developments of politics, economics and technology. Power and the effect of the civil society groups reshaping conventional stakeholders like consumers, governments and trade unions (Lenssen et al. 2005). In parallel with societal change businesses are also changing in the same manner, to become successful and gain competitive advantage they started to take into account these relevant expectations. Freeman et al. (2006) stated that 21st century is the era of accountability and sustainability, corporate reputation and corporate responsibility at whole. In sum, companies has to engage in social, economic and politic issues to maintain corporate reputation,

Corporate social responsibility has also become global phenomenon, and it penetrated into company's business strategies. Wagner et al. (2009) pointed the positive effect of corporate social responsibility on brand management and purchase intention with consumers. According to Cochran (2007) corporate social responsibility is one of the best way of improving reputation and relationship between stakeholders. In long term it is no doubt that implementing strategic corporate social responsibility creates shareholder value and profit maximization (Falck and Heblich, 2007).

COMMUNICATING CORPORATE SOCIAL RESPONSIBILITY

The development of information age, increasing international competition, interdependence of economic and financial market, diversity, easy accessibility and new channel opportunities have created a new understanding of corporate social responsibility communication. Corporate social responsibility is based upon the communication of inside and outside of the corporation's (Isenmann, 2006).

The need of transparent and proactive communication is one of the key issues of corporate social responsibility (Chaudhri and Wand, 2007). Communication plays a fundamental role in the success of corporate social responsibility activities. In other words, using the right communication strategies both increase success of the works and provide stakeholders exact information about organization and its behavior.

Most commonly, corporate social responsibility communication defined as the communication which designed by corporation itself to spread corporate social responsibility activities (Morsing, 2006). In another definition, corporate social responsibility communication refers to a bridge between social and environmental information and stakeholder interactions. It both executes activities in accordance with the social and environmental statement of stakeholders and also provides the continuity of stakeholder interaction (Podnar, 2008).

Nielsen and Thomsen (2009), in their proposed corporate social responsibility communication model, indicated the significant role of corporate social responsibility communication against corporation's external and internal stakeholders like local communities, employees, Non-governmental organizations (NGOs), traditional and online media, suppliers, customers, investigators and retailers (Coombs and Holladay, 2012).

Generating and raising CSR awareness, can only be achieved through well-prepared communication strategies. In that sense, effective communication of company's social responsibility actions, can help establishing legitimacy (Bebbington et al., 2008), strengthen the company image by communicating the abstract and intangible characteristics of an organization (Schlegelmilch and Pollack, 2005) and nurture a two way communication with stakeholders with web tools (Fieseler et al., 2010). It should also be mentioned that communication in CSR issues, may create negativity in two aspects. Firstly, as Chaudhri and Wang, (2007) stated wrong and mistakable CSR communication can compromise corporate image and brand equity. Both CSR message or action and the channel chosen, might pose a threat for company reputation. Secondly, company may be passive in underlining their responsible attiude to the public. Neglecting usage of various communication channels for disseminating CSR attitude, might be percieved as a careless company image, which might be harmful for public view.

Morising and Schultz (2006) presents three CSR communication strategies based on Grunig and Hunt's (1984) public relation model called stakeholder information strategy, stakeholder response strategy and stakeholder involvement strategy. Stakeholder information strategy is designed by top managements and its communication process build on process of sensegiving which means communication is one-way from organization to stakeholders. In this strategy companies just inform stakeholders about corporate social responsibility decisions and actions. On the other side stakeholders have two options against corporate CSR efforts: support or oppose the company. The other one stakeholder response strategy is based on two way asymmetric communication model which communication flows from public. This communication strategy is also designed by top managers according to considering feedbacks via opinion polls, dialogue, networks and partnerships. At this time the company's communication department started to make market surveys to determine best places that enhance its CSR actions and against, stakeholders respond actions. Unlike stakeholder information strategy, stakeholder response strategy is not limited to just inform stakeholders it also includes demonstrating stakeholders about company's CSR efforts. In the third one stakeholder involvement strategy, CSR communication processes are interactive between stakeholder and company. To determine which CSR effort should company focus is decided by both stakeholder and company's communication department. There is a proactive, frequent and systematic dialogue between them which provides stakeholders to involve corporate CSR efforts (Morising and Shultz, 2006).

Although these three strategies are introduced and explained in depth in the literature with advantages and disadvantages; a few of the today's companies implement stakeholder response strategy and internalize stakeholder's involvement in their CRS communication practices. (Morising and Shultz, 2006). From time to time, companies may act reluctant to communicate CSR activities, not just threat of using CSR for marketing purposes (Van de Ven 2008), but also avoid heightening stakeholders' skepticism towards the company (Schlegelmilch and Pollach, 2005) and losing their trust.

As mentioned earlier, effective CSR communication should evolve plan which not only examines the stakeholders in detail, but also identify the right channel and right message. Before designing CSR communication strategy, managers should search stakeholder's interest and design communication strategy.

The basic model of communication includes six dimensions named source, channel, message, receiver, feedback and noise. To implement effective CSR communication, corporate social responsibility, information should rightly transform to the stakeholders; but at this point, different interests of stakeholders could be problematic as well. Targeted messaging, which effectively meet specific needs of receivers, should be implemented among stakeholders. In addition the factors like target group characteristics, type and the aim of the corporate social responsibility activities determines the channel of corporate social responsibility communication (Coombs and Holladay, 2012). Du et al. (2002) presents a conceptual framework of CSR communication in their study.

Content of the Message

Selecting right CSR message is one of the important things in CSR communication process and also its success. Du et al. (2010) presents a conceptual framework of CSR communication in their study. According to them there are two types of message content: issue and initiative. In other worlds there are two different alternatives of creating CSR messages; one of them is solely address a social issue the other one is constituting CSR message in the direction of social issue that company interested in itself (Du et al.. 2010).

Creating content of the message just about a social issue should be perceived important by society. If not it can cause consumer's doubt on their ulterior motives because of not fitting on their 'schemer schema" (Friestad and Wright, 1994). The issue should be really important to society. To increase credibility of advertising and revive consumer hidden motives, CSR message should focuses on social issue by taking consideration of being logically related to company and its products (Du et al., 2010).

However, nowadays companies mostly use second option in creating CSR message. In this type company selects CSR message according to its initiative and involvement to social issue (Du et al.. 2010). In this case four important factors needed to be considered. One of them is CSR commitment to a social issue. Commitment on social issue can be occur by donating fund, providing other contributions like marketing expertise, human capital or R&D support. Company should select one or several aspects of commitment and intensify all interest over issue. The second one is the strength of CSR impact on social issue. There should provide societal impact or important benefits to supported topic. Beside these factors it should be also focus on CSR motives which means the supported issue should be engage with company itself and adopt consumer motives to not cause stakeholder skepticism. The last important factor is CSR fit which means the perceived fit between social issue and company's business. Using common associations of brand and issue may lead so many advantages like creating or promoting company trust and recognition (Du et al.. 2010).

Selecting the Channel

In addition to, creating right message for stakeholder, selecting proper channel is another crucial factor of CSR communication success. There are various communication channels including press, commercials, magazines, billboards and most importantly internet tools (Du et al.. 2016). While some of the channels can be controlled some of them can not be controlled by company. Controlling mean company has authority on the content of the message and how it used; this can be done by using companies own communication channels like media tools and members of its value chains.

As Coombs and Holladay (2012) mentioned, especially employees should be seen as a CSR communication channel. These internal stakeholders should be well informed about CSR practices in order to better communicate CSR. Their blogs, social media accounts are the most vital tools to can be used as well (Coombs and Holladay, 2012). Their and their family member's word of mouth activity about CSR efforts can be perceived credible by consumers (Du et al.. 2010). Companies should involve their employees and their family member in CSR activities and should see them as valuable communication channel (Coombs and Holladay, 2012).

In addition to employees the other powerful stakeholder group can be seen as consumers in CSR communication channels. Specially, leader consumer or consumer ambassadors who have great viral power can be used as channel via their social media accounts. Companies should act proactive on their social media channels to engage their CSR communication activities with consumers (Du et al.. 2010).

A NEW HORIZON IN CSR COMMUNICATION: STIMULATING STAKEHOLDER ENGAGEMENT THROUGH SOCIAL MEDIA

For years, companies have been benefiting from various channels, to reflect their CSR attitude. In general the channels can be grouped as traditional (newspaper, magazine, CSR reports) and contemporary (social media, internet based applications, mobile applications) methods. As one of contemporaray channel, social media, refer to platforms or internet-based applications that are possible via Web 2.0 (Kaplan and Haenlein, 2010). Kotler et al. (2010) particularly refer to rise of social media as an important enabler of the new wave technology. Definitely, social media is distruptive in terms of changing not just the existing structure but also the future of business. With almost no investment, companies are getting advantage of gaining insights about the market, especially recent trends and changing consumer profile, and design marketing communications, accordingly. Consumers are no longer isolated from each other, now they are active in creating and disseminating any content, providing useful feedbacks to company, which turns them into potential company ambassadors. It is a beneficial and practical way of facilitating relationship between company and its stakeholders. According to recent figures, it seems that companies realized the power of social media. According to Barnes and Lescaut (2014) 80 percent of Fortune 500 companies have one or several Facebook accounts; over 80 percent use Twitter; and over 30 percent of these companies have blogs. With time, these figures are expected to increase due to wide acceptance (Stohl et al, 2017).

In that section, firstly benefits and challenges stemming from using social media for CSR communication are delineated. Then, most popular social media tools are elaborated by indicating their importance and effect in terms of CSR communication.

Benefits and Challenges of Using Social Media for CSR Communication

Rapid growth of digital technology, especially Web 2.0, opened a new dimension in the online channel as two way communication between consumers and companies. Now consumers, not only embrace a wide range of information from various resources, but also share their opinions and experiences to a greater community, freely. Social media is considered as a set of online technology tools that facilitate communication between people by sharing text, video, audio, images and any combination of these (Coombs and Holladay, 2012 ; Safko and Brake,2009). Hence, social media technology opens up a new horizon for information sharing and relationship building practices (Lee et al,2013). In that sense, companies, that are continously seeking alternative ways to reach target audience, preferably at lower cost, are mesmerized with what social media can offer to them. In Kim et al's study (2011) components of interactivity in social media are listed as gathering consumer feedback and opinions, providing live chat platform, engaging in participation via uploading photos, videos etc., and attracting public's attention, celebrating special days/seasons and forming personalized messages about consumers. With accelerating popularity of social media, now consumers are in charge of both messages and media due to convenience in accessing information and media platforms (Kesevan et al,2013). This enhanced two-way communication enabled consumer-to-consumer interaction as in the form of electronic word of mouth (eWOM). According to Hennig-Thureau et al., 2004) consumers are fueled by social interaction, economical incentives, concern for others and potential to improve their social image. By replacing coventional Word of Mouth with Electronic Word of Mouth (eWOM), consumers demonstrate or recommend products, promote specific ethical behaviours or condemn irresponsible acts. In that sense, consumers today continously search for information about corporate philanthropy, to increase their awareness and moreover share this with the community. Hence, this highly effective tool leads companies to revisit their strategies in communicating CSR Programs. Argenti (2009) defends that technology has dramatically changed how corporations engage with stakeholders in two-way conversations about corporate social responsibility. Now it is imperative for companies to integrate social media to their existing communication strategy (Lee et al.,2013).

It is beneficial to mention benefits of social media as a medium for communicating CSR activities. First of all, social media enables companies to listen target audience and trace which specific CSR issues are important for diverse stakeholders. Moreover, company may control the effectiveness of previous CSR initiatives, by assuring if stakeholders are aware and/or knowledgeable of these activites. Secondly, companies can increase the credibility of CSR actions by letting these events to be spread by social media. There is a growing belief about consumer skepticisim about CSR activities announced via company channels (Du et al.,2010). There are specific evidences, showing that consumers react more favorably to CSR activites when they acquire information from a netural source rather than company source (Yoon et al,2006 ; Simmons and Becker-Olsen,2006). Thirdly, stakeholder reactions to specific CSR activities can be measured either by engaging in one to one conversation or following the social media accounts of different parties. In that perspective, social media offers a valuable direct channel for end users, whereby any query or feedback is to be effectively processed. Pressley (2006) summarizes the benefits of CSR communication through social media as inexpensive investment, efficiency, real time communication, public relations and option of online archives

Besides, numerous benefits, social media for CSR communication has some challenges, as well. Unfortunately, such a valuable channel can easily be violated by not following rules of etiquette. As Coombs and Holladay (2012) highlight, social media is a means of allowing people to find out necessary information, not forcing unrequested information onto stakeholders. It is apparent that companies must integrate new social channels in their marketing communication mix to leverage the effect. One other challenge is stated as, companies having little or not control over CSR information disseminated via social media (Schnedier et al,2007). As Friedman (2006) points out, the information flow is multi sourced, interconnected, and nearly impossible to forecast. Especially negative facts can easily be shared for such a convenient channel. Companies need to employ a sustainable and ongoing communication from these social media platforms to measure and detect public opinion which require excessive amount of effort and time to be devoted in that area (Bittner and Leimeister,2011; Etter and Fieseler, 2010). In other words, high reactivity and interconnectivity in social media, necessitate companies to be ready for taking action against any sign of misinformation or manipulation (Lee et al,2013). Also the tone of social media need to be carefully planned, not to be so formal but not reckless as well, to reflect proper corporate image (Etter and Fieseler,2010).

ALTERNATIVE SOCIAL MEDIA TOOLS FOR CSR COMMUNICATION

Traditionally a company used to communicate its CSR efforts through announcement of social reports, advertisements or web sites (Du et al., 2010). Now, thanks to Web 2.0, interactive online conversations are possible via a wide range of alternatives like blogs and microblogs, content communities, social networking sites and social bookmarking or aggregators (Coombs and Holladay, 2012). It is vital to mention each type of these social media tools in the next sections.

Blogs and Microblogs

Blogs and micro blogs are acting as a means of reflecting people's ideas, opinions and experiences which are to be shared with other through links and reposting (Coombs and Holladay,2012). Blogs provide larger area for expression of individuals self interest or favorable/unfavorable experiences, and ofter accompanied with discussion board sor forums. As the name implies micro blogs involve shorter messages like Twitter, whereby message limit is 140 characters (Coombs and Holladay,2012). Launched by 2006, Twitter surely has a unique position within social media platforms where participants write and share up to 140-character messages (Lee et al,2013). In terms of effectiveness, while the impact of traditional media is measured by the number in circulation, the influence of users are usually estimated by the number of followers (Kwak et al. 2010). Also, the number of retweets and mentions represent an enhanced form of indicating actual influence (Cha et al,2010 ; Kwak et al,2010). Namely, as Uzunoglu et al (2017) state, Twitter is extremely influential, facilitating dialogue between stakeholders and organizations in that sense, it is percieved as a valuable platform to communicate CSR-related messages and activities (Uzunoglu et al,2017 ; Colleoni, 2013; Etter, 2013; Lee et al, 2013). Parmelee and Bichard (2012) attribute success of Twitter as its distinct characteristics of being real-time, fast, direct, and concise.

Content Communities

Content communities are born when people come together around some specific issues ar area of interest by providing videos and/or images. Youtube and Flickr can be counted as the most popular content communities. Companies have been devoting considerable amount of budgets to identify and reach "specific target consumers" to convey their CSR perspective and activities. So these platforms are extremely practical in reaching to people under a specific category, such as environmental concern or animal safety, in terms of impact and cost.

Social Networking Sites

Social networking sites are web based services that let people to construct profiles whereby sharing any content (photo, video, news) of your own or viewing others is possible (Coombs and Holladay,2012;

Boyd and Ellison,2007). Most popular social networking sites are Facebook, MySpace and LinkedIn (Coombs and Holladay,2012; Safko and Brake,2009). Surely, Facebook is more widely accepted and used with respect to other social networking sites. According to a Facebook brand community study, it was found that engaging in (writing or reading messages) Facebook page of a company positively influences relationships (Gummerus et al,2012). According to survey by KRC Research (2011), Facebook was named as the most valuable tool for getting in contact with the consumers (%67 of people claimed it), it was followed by blogs (%60), LinkedIn (%58), Twitter (%46) and Foursquare (%44) (Kesevan et al,2013). Brengman and Karimov (2012) claim that companies may show signs of integrity by just offering access to a social media tool through company web site.

Social Bookmarking or Aggregators

Social bookmarking or aggregators are websites whereby, a collection of customer evaluations and feedback. People, place tags or bookmarks on internet content (videos, photos) and all of these tags have certain keywords, and eventually these tags are compiled under these social bookmarking sites. By sharing these same themed tags people gain knowledge about specidic issues. Usually, these sites are used to evoke a sense of awaranesson company's CSR efforts and their reactions to CSR activities (Coombs and Holladay,2012).

HOW TO USE SOCIAL MEDIA WISELY FOR CSR COMMUNICATION?

Recently, it is evident that responsible companies should somehow get in contact with their stakeholders regularly to deliver their CSR attitude or actions (Crane et al, 2016 ; Du et al,2010). In that sense, increased penetration of internet and wide acceptance of social media globally, had given companies an excellent tool to convey their message, withal chance to hear more than what they present from the consumers. According to a research (Imran Ali et al,2015) conducted in Pakistan on employees, customers and investors, majority of the respondents acknowledged that social media is very important to CSR communication. Yet, the same sample believe that social media is a more trustworthy tool, with respect to traditional methods, and positively influence the buying intention of consumers. Also, the individuals are enthusiastic about working for corporations which are successful in communicating their CSR activities through social media.

Companies which use social media as a means of showing how they contribute to a greater community as in the Pepsi Refresh Project, IBM's Smarter Planet, Timberland Earthkeeping, Unilever's Onslaughter (against palm oil deforestation), On the other hand, Non-governmental organizations (NGO) also appreciated the immense effect of social media spread news. Recently, Greenpeace tended to use social media assaults for unethical initiatives of some companies (Nestle, Bp, HSBC, Burger King) especially for palm oil sourcing. Most of the companies immediately changed their ingredients or suppliers to avoid negative public reaction, which is regarded as a success attributed to social media. Nestle changed their ideas on palm oil with respect to 1,5 million views of a Youtube campaign by GreenPeace. Also, BP experiences a crisis about Gulf oil disaster and was subject to many protests from twitter and Facebook, and eventually it is stated that BP lost over 50% of its share price in two months.

In that sense, for transparency and ethics the fundamentals of social media and social responsibility have so much in common. If a business wants to involve in an issue, it sure needs to use social media wisely to leverage the effect. The logic of social media usage in CSR communication is simple and yet effective. First of all, the company needs to have the philiosophy that embrace in reflecting their ethical approach not just boosting sales. So in that sense, it is advised to have clear ojectives and share the news by presenting honesty in their manner. Secondly, it is a must that company must engage in a reciprocal communication with the individuals, since it does not just start a relationship but also establish strong ties with individuals and turn them into company advocates. For long, companies have been using social media for information sharing; however what consumers seek is to engage in a genuine dialogue with the company. There are several stuides confirming companies lack of interest on interactivity (Waters and Willaims, 2011; Etter,2013), but the paradigm is changing to catch the wind to take the advantage of social media. Thirdly, as a crucial part of reciprocity, corporations ahould actively listen public and also ask questions to be a part of the issue that they involve in. Fourthly, negative or unpleasent reactions are unavoidable, but instead of eliminating these reactions, companies should respond to comments and start a persuasion process of turning that negativity to positivity.

CONCLUSION

Since 1980s rapid and radical change in the world had significant effects on business life. Especially increasing globalization and new communication technologies create new business designs within the context of competition. A new global competition brought novel insights; the price focused competition left its place to customer oriented competition that brings customer value to the agenda. These developments lead to emerge of new concepts; new and changing customer expectations make companies to take into consideration of executing social responsibility activities.

On the other side, businesses are involved in an interaction of its environment; this interaction makes necessary of meet some obligations which both benefit society and company. They are the part of an environmental system, and to survive they should accommodate to changing come out. In this adaptation process the best tools that business can benefit is corporate social responsibility.

In recent years corporate social responsibility, dated to 1950's, has become as an important business strategy. In the past, whereas making profit was a sufficient measure of corporate social responsibility; today the responsibilities of companies extend over to benefit of whole society. Corporate social responsibility activities provide coherent stakeholder behavior, deepen their relationship with company and strengthen company's image as well. To achieve all kinds of profitable CSR efforts, companies need to pay attention to corporate social responsibility communication. Effective communication with external and internal stakeholders is the main issue in CSR communication success. Choosing right message content and right communication channel is the most important points to revive stakeholders and consumers extinct motives and also to decrease their skepticism over CSR activity.

Jahdi and Acikdilli (2009) claimed that even the method chosen for CSR communication is important in terms of building company's socially responsible and easily accessible image. In that sense, as new technologies entail companies to involve in continuous learning, CSR modes of communiciation diversified, too. By 2005 only 10 percent of companies are stated as having social media budgets, but by 2010, it reached to almost 30 percent (Kesevan et al,2013). So enlighted by these information, companies need to see social media engagement as a prerequisite for developing and nurturing relationship with stakeholders. Hence, a definite integration with other marketing communication mix is strongly recommended. According to a study, social media users believe that social media is an effective platform to explore companies CSR activities (Cone,2010). However, due to lack of control over messages, negative events can also be easily disseminated. According to same study, fifty-eight percent of people are willing to share their unpleasent experiences through social media (Cone,2010). As Kesevan et al. (2013) indicate, organizations are just on the edge of realizing the tremendous effect and power of social media in terms of earning and ensuring a competitive advantage. So it is not just opening up accounts in Twitter or Facebook, but systematically passing and renewing information to these channels to keep users updated. Hence, companies must definitely be proactive in using social media to reflect their CSR vision and activities.

REFERENCES

Argenti, P. A. (2009). *Digital strategies for powerful corporate communications*. New York: McGraw-Hill.

Backhaous, K. B., Stone, B. A., & Heiner, K. (2002). Exploring the Telationship Between Corporate Social Performance and Employer Attractiveness. *Business & Society*, *41*(3), 292–318. doi:10.1177/0007650302041003003

Barnes, N. G., & Lescaut, A. M. (2014). *The 2014 Fortune 500 and social media: LinkedIn dominates as use of newer tools explodes*. Retrieved from http://www.umassd.edu/cmr/socialmediaresearch/2014 fortune500andsocialmedia/

Bebbington, J., Larrinaga, C., & Moneva, J. M. (2008). 'Corporate social reporting and reputation risk management'. *Accounting. Auditing and Accountability*, *21*(3), 337–361. doi:10.1108/09513570810863932

Bittner, E., & Leimeister, J. M. (2011). Towards CSR 2.0 - potentials and challenges of Web 2.0 for corporate social responsibility communication. *Proceedings of the 11th Academy of Management Annual Meeting*.

Bowen, H. (1953). *Social Responsibilities of the Businessman*. New York: Harper & Row.

Brengman, M., & Karimov, F. (2012). The effect of web communities on consumers' initial trust in B2C ecommerce websites. *Management Research Review*, *35*(9), 791–816. doi:10.1108/01409171211256569

Carrol, A. B. (2008). A History of Corporate Social Responsibility: Concepts and Practices. In The Oxford Handbook of Corporate Social Responsibility (pp. 29-46). Oxford University Press.

Carroll, A. B. (1979). A Three-Dimensional Conceptual Model of Corporate Social Performance. *Academy of Management Review*, *4*(4), 497–505.

Carroll, A. B. (1999). Corporate Social Responsibility: Evolution of a Definitional Construct. *Business & Society*, *38*(3), 268–295. doi:10.1177/000765039903800303

Chaudhri, V., & Wang, J. (2007). Communicating Corporate Social Responsibility on the Internet. *Management Communication Quarterly*, *21*(2), 232–247. doi:10.1177/0893318907308746

Cochran, P. (2007). The Evolution of Corporate Social Responsibility. *Business Horizons*, *50*(2), 449–454. doi:10.1016/j.bushor.2007.06.004

Colleoni, E. (2013). CSR communication strategies for organizational legitimacy in social media? *Corporate Communications*, *18*(2), 228–248. doi:10.1108/13563281311319508

Committee for Economic Development (CED). (1971). *Social Responsibilities of Business Corporations*. New York: CED.

Cone. (2010). *2010 Consumer new media study*. Retrieved October 30, 2011 from http://www.coneinc.com/2010-consumer-new-media-study

Coombs, W. T., & Holladay, S. (2012). Privileging an Activist vs. a Corporate View of Public Relations History in the US. *Public Relations Review*, *38*(3), 347–353. doi:10.1016/j.pubrev.2011.11.010

Davis, I. (2005). What is the Business of Business? *The McKinsey Quarterly*, (3): 104–113.

Davis, K. (1960). Can Business Afford to Ignore Social Responsibilities? *California Management Review*, *2*(3), 70–76. doi:10.2307/41166246

Davis, K. (1973). The Case for and against Business Assumption of Social Responsibilities. *Academy of Management Journal*, *16*(2), 312–322. doi:10.2307/255331

Du, S., Bhattacharya, C. B., & Sen, S. (2010). Maximizing business returns to corporate social responsibility: The role of CSR communication. *International Journal of Management Reviews*, *12*(1), 8–19. doi:10.1111/j.1468-2370.2009.00276.x

Elbert, H. & Parket, I. R. (1973). The Correct Status of Corporate Social Responsibility. *Business Horizons, 16*, 5-14.

Epstein, E. M. (1987). The Corporate Social Policy Process: Beyond Business Ethics, Corporate Social Responsibility, and Corporate Social Responsiveness. *California Management Review*, *29*(3), 99–114. doi:10.2307/41165254

Etter, M. (2013). Reasons for low levels of interactivity. *Public Relations Review*, *39*(5), 606–608. doi:10.1016/j.pubrev.2013.06.003

Etter, M., & Fieseler, C. (2010). On relational capital in social media. *Studies in Communication Sciences*, *10*(2), 167–189.

Falck, O., & Heblich, S. (2007). Corporate Social Responsibility: Doing Well by Doing Good. *Business Horizons*, *50*(3), 247–254. doi:10.1016/j.bushor.2006.12.002

Fieseler, C., Fleck, M., & Meckel, M. (2010). 'Corporate social responsibility in the blogosphere'. *Journal of Business Ethics*, *91*(4), 599–614. doi:10.100710551-009-0135-8

Frederick, W. C. (1960). The Growing Concern over Business Responsibility. *California Management Review*, *2*(4), 54–61. doi:10.2307/41165405

Frederick, W. C. (2006). *Corporation Be Good: The Story of Corporate Social Responsibility*. Indianpolis Dog Ear Publishing.

Freeman, R. E., Velamuri, S. R., & Moriarty, B. (2006). *Company Stakeholder Responsibility: A New Approach to CSR*. Charlottesville, VA: Business Roundtable Institute for Corporate Ethics.

Friedman, T. L. (2006). *The world is flat: A brief history of the twenty-first century*. New York: Farrar, Straus and Giroux.

Friestad, M., & Wright, P. (1994). The Persuasion Knowledge Model: How People Cope with Persuasion Attempts. *The Journal of Consumer Research*, *21*(1), 1031. doi:10.1086/209380

Gummerus, J., Likljander, V., Weman, E., & Pihlstrom, M. (2012). Customer Engagement in a Facebook brand community. *Management Research Review*, *35*(9), 857–877. doi:10.1108/01409171211256578

Heald, M. (1970). *The Social Responsibilities of Business: Company and Community, 1900-1960*. Cleveland, OH: Case Western Reserve University Press.

Heath, R. L., & Ni, L. (2008). *Corporate Social Responsibility*. Institute for Public Relation. Retrieved from http://www.instituteforpr.org/corporate-social-responsibility/

Hennig-Thurau, T., Gwinner, K., Walsh, G., & Gremler, D. (2004). Electronic Word-of-Mouth Via Consumer-Opinion Platforms: What Motivates Consumers to Articulate Themselves on the Internet? *Journal of Interactive Marketing*, *18*(1), 39–52. doi:10.1002/dir.10073

Husted, B. W. (2000). A Contingency Theory of Corporate Social Performance. *Business & Society*, *39*(1), 24–38. doi:10.1177/000765030003900104

Isenmann, R. (2006). CSR Online: Internet Based Communication. In Management Models for Corporate Social Responsibility (pp. 246-253). Springer.

Jahdi, K. S., & Acikdilli, G. (2009). Marketing communications and Corporate Social Responsibility (CSR): Marriage of convenience or short gun wedding? *Journal of Business Ethics*, *88*(1), 103–113. doi:10.100710551-009-0113-1

Johnson, H. L. (1971). *Business in Contemporary Society: Framework and issues*. Belmont, CA: Wadsworth.

Jones, R., & Murrel, A. (2001). Signaling Positive Corporate Social Performance: An Event Study of Family-Friendly Firms. *Business & Society*, *40*(1), 59–78. doi:10.1177/000765030104000105

Jones, T. M. (1980). Corporate Social Responsibility Revisited, Redefined. *California Management Review*, *21*(2), 55–67.

Kaplan, A. M., & Haenlein, M. (2010). Users of the world, unite! The challenges and opportunities of social media. *Business Horizons*, *53*(1), 59–68. doi:10.1016/j.bushor.2009.09.003

Kesavan, R., Bernacchi, M. D., & Mascarenhas, O. A. J. (2013). Word of Mouse. CSR Communication and the Social Media. *International Management Review*, *9*(1), 58–66.

Kotler, P., Kartajaya, H., & Setiawan, I. (2010). *Marketing 3.0: From products to customers to the human spirit*. New York, NY: Wiley. doi:10.1002/9781118257883

Kotler, P. & Nancy, L. (2000). *Corporate Social Responsibility: Doing the Most for Your Company and Your Cause*. Hobeken, NJ: John Wiley & Sons, Inc.

Lenssen, G., Van Den Berghe, L., & Louche, C. (2005). Responding to Societal Expectations. *Corporate Governance*, *5*(3), 4–11.

Morsing, M. (2006). Corporate Social Responsibility as Strategic Auto-Communication: On the Role of External Stakeholders for Member Identification. *Business Ethics (Oxford, England)*, *15*(2), 171–182. doi:10.1111/j.1467-8608.2006.00440.x

Morsing, M., & Schultz, M. (2006). Corporate Social Responsibility Communication: Stakeholder Information, Response and Involvement Strategies. *Business Ethics (Oxford, England)*, *15*(4), 323–338. doi:10.1111/j.1467-8608.2006.00460.x

Murphy, P. E. (1978, November). An Evolution: Corporate Social Responsiveness. *University of Michigan Business Review*.

Nielsen, A. E., & Thomsen, C. (2008). Investigationg CSR Communication in SMEs: A Case Study Among Danish Middle Manager. *Business Ethics (Oxford, England)*, *18*(1), 83–93. doi:10.1111/j.1467-8608.2009.01550.x

Parmelee, J. H., & Bichard, S. L. (2012). Politics and the Twitter revolution. Lanham, MD: Lexington.

Podnar, K. (2008). Communicating Corporate Social Responsibility. *Journal of Marketing Communications*, *14*(2), 75–81. doi:10.1080/13527260701856350

Pressley, L. (2006). *Using social software for business communication*. Unpublished Working Paper LIS 650. Retrieved June 30, 2017 from http://laurenpressley.com/papers/socialsoftware_business.pdf

Preston, L., & Post, J. E. (1975). *Private Management and Public Policy: The Principle of Public Responsibility*. Englewood Cliffs, NJ: Prentice-Hall.

Research, K. R. C. (2011). Civility in America,2011., G. P. (2002). The Ethicality of Altruistic Corporate Social Responsibility. *Journal of Consumer Marketing*, *19*(3), 205–232.

Safko, L., & Brake, D. (2009). *The Social Media Bible*. John wiley &Sons Inc.

Schlegelmilch, B. B., & Pollach, I. (2005). The Perils and Opportunities of Communicating Corporate Ethics. *Journal of Marketing Management*, *21*(3-4), 267–290. doi:10.1362/0267257053779154

Schneider, A. M., Stieglitz, S., & Lattemann, C. (2007). *Social software as an instrument of CSR. Transparency and Social Responsibility Conference*, Lisbon, Portugal.

Schwartz, M. S., & Carroll, A. B. (2003). Corporate Social Responsibility: A Three-Domain Approach. *Business Ethics Quarterly*, *13*(4), 503–530. doi:10.5840/beq200313435

Sethi, S. P. (1975). Dimensions of Corporate Social Performance: An Analytic Framework. *California Management Review*, *17*(3), 58–64. doi:10.2307/41162149

Simmons, C. J., & Becker-Olsen, K. L. (2006). Achieving marketing objectives through social sponsorships. *Journal of Marketing*, *70*(4), 154–169. doi:10.1509/jmkg.70.4.154

Smith, W. J., Wokutch, R. E., Harrington, K. V., & Byran, D. (2001). An Examination of the Influence of Diversity and Stakeholder Role on Vorporate Social Orientation. *Business & Society*, *40*(3), 266–294. doi:10.1177/000765030104000303

Starck, K., & Kruckeberg, D. (2003). Ethical Obligations of Public Relations in an Era of Globalization. *Journal of Communication Management*, *8*(1), 29–40. doi:10.1108/13632540410807529

Steger, U. (2008). Future Perspectives of Corporate Social Responsibility: Where We Are Coming From? Where Are We Heading? In J. Moon & S. Donald (Eds.), *The Oxford Handbook of Corporate Social Responsibility*. OUP.

Steiner, G. A. (1971). *Business and Society*. New York: Random House.

Stohl, C., Etter, C., Banghart, S., & Woo, D. J. (2017). Social Media Policies: Implications for Contemporary Notions of Corporate Social Responsibility. *Journal of Business Ethics*, *142*(3), 413–436. doi:10.100710551-015-2743-9

Tuzzolino, F., & Armandi, B. R. (1981). A Need-Hierarchy Framework for Assessing Corporate Social Responsibility. *Academy of Management Review*, *6*(1), 21–218.

Uzunoglu, E., Turkel, S., & Yaman Akyar, B. (in press). Engaging consumers through corporate social responsibility messages on social media: An experimental study. *Public Relations Review*.

Van de Ven, B. (2008). An Ethical Framework for the Marketing of Corporate Social Responsibility. *Journal of Business Ethics*, *82*(2), 339–352. doi:10.100710551-008-9890-1

Wagner, T., Lutz, R. J., & Weitz, B. A. (2009). Corporate Hypocrisy: Overcoming the Threat of Inconsistent Corporate Social Responsibility Perceptions. *Journal of Marketing*, *73*(6), 77 91. doi:10.1509/jmkg.73.6.77

Walton, C. C. (1967). *Corporate Social Responsibilities*. Belmont, CA: Wadsworth.

Waters, R., & Williams, J. (2011). Squawking, tweeting, cooing, and hooting: Analyzing the communicaiton patterns of government agencies on twitter. *Journal of Public Affairs*, *11*(4), 353–363. doi:10.1002/pa.385

Yoon, Y., Gurhan-Canli, Z., & Schwarz, N. (2006). The effect of corporate social responsibility (CSR) activities on companies with bad reputations. *Journal of Consumer Psychology*, *16*(4), 377–390. doi:10.120715327663jcp1604_9

This research was previously published in Corporate Social Responsibility and Strategic Market Positioning for Organizational Success; pages 59-85, copyright year 2019 by Business Science Reference (an imprint of IGI Global).

Chapter 8
Social Media and Events:
Before, During, and After

Gulser Yavuz
Mersin University, Turkey

Kemal Enes
Mersin University, Turkey

ABSTRACT

Globally, the number of the internet and social media users is increasing day by day. The event industry has been affected by that popularity of social media and so event management and event marketing activities have changed radically. In this research, the importance of the social media in the events, management of the event, and finding how to take advantage of the social media by the marketing of the event are explored. Using of the social media in events was examined in these three parts: before, during, and after the events. Today it is regarded as an important tool used by the event managers of social media platforms and so social media has become an indispensable part of the events.

INTRODUCTION

The habits related to communication are changing. Especially in the last 10 years, the channels used in communication have evolved and new communication channels are becoming more popular. As one of the most striking examples of today, 13 million people followed the marriage of Prince William and Catherine Middleton on the official YouTube channel, rather than the usual communication channel, television. They preferred two-way communication instead of one-way communication of traditional media by making live comments during the entire marriage process.

Social media gained the throne of television, which is the most important communication tool due to the emerging technology and the rapid increase of people's use of internet and mobile technology. TV celebrities are being replaced by influencers and bloggers and people prefer to be in touch around the clock or even 24 hours a day, not just at the beginning, as on TV.

DOI: 10.4018/978-1-6684-6287-4.ch008

This emerging communication technology has a serious impact in many sectors. Especially the event sector is one of the most common areas of this impact. Without social media support, it seems unthinkable for events to take place. Therefore, event management is also evolving with this process and continues to develop in order to benefit from the benefits of social media at a high level.

Communications with participants, stakeholders, and sponsors through social media, especially before, during, and after the event, are supported by social media in some cases carried out only through social media.

BACKGROUND

Key Success Factors of Use of Social Media at Events

Social media is an environment that gives people opportunities at the online social life. Social media is an internet-based group of applications allowing user-centered creation and exchange of content built (Kaplan & Haenlein, 2012, p. 102). Events are a part of real social life. online social life unimaginable without the social media and this indicates social media has a magic role in the events. In order to reach, announce and manage the potential participants social media activities are very important for the success of the events (Grate, 2020). According to the research, although there are existing studies about the social media and events, there has not been enough studies about using social media for the events.

According to investigated the sources during the research process; it is indicated that the using of the social media in activities should be examined in 3 phases such as before the event, during the event and after the event. These phases play a key role in the social media management in the events.

MAIN FOCUS OF THE CHAPTER

Globally the number of the internet and social media users is increasing day by day. Social media is a current and popular topic, especially in recent years. The widespread and increasing popularity of social media has also left its mark on the event industry and social media has become an indispensable part of events. A comprehensive literature review shows that research on the use of social media tools within the scope of event marketing and management processes should be increased. In this context, in order to contribute to the literature, the importance of social media in events and how social media can be used in event management and marketing are tried to be revealed. In this chapter; using of the social media in events was examined in these three parts: before, during and after the events.

Events

Events are an important source of motivation for tourism and play an important role in the development and marketing of many destinations (Getz, 2008). In addition to serving various policy areas such as the recent growth in the number, size, cost, and impact of activities, such as urban and economic development, it also includes various social efforts to promote community integration (Getz, 2012). Activities seen as an integral part of the tourism sector also help to market goods, services, ideas, places or people (Fuchs, 2014, p. 248).

Table 1. Key Success Factors of Use of Social Media at Events.

Scholar(s)	Key Success Factors of Use of Social Media at Events
Atçeken, K., Doğrul, Ü., & Çabuk, S. (2018)	Facebook, Festival, Social Media, Promotion
Aventri. (2019)	Event Marketing, Community Management, Micro-Influencer Marketing, Social Media Management, Social Media ROI, Event Marketing of the Future
Barutçu, S., & Tomaş, M. (2013)	Social Media, Social Media Marketing, Sustainable Social Media Marketing, Efficiency Measurement.
Brooks, R. (2020)	Social Media Marketing, Tweeter marketing, Facebook Marketing, Blog marketing, Using Hashtags, Event Marketing
Bulut, E. (2012).	Social Media, Social Media Tools, Social Media Applications, Political Marketing, Internet
Fuchs, C. (2014)	Social media, Critical theory, Internet, Social media, Web 2.0, social media culture, Social Media and Communication power, Political economy of social media, Google, Facebook, Twitter, Wikileaks, Wikipedia, Social Media and its Alternatives
Getz, D. (2008)	Event tourism; Definitions; Theory; Research
Getz, D. (2012)	Event studies; Discourses; Policy implications; Interdisciplinary theory
Ghazali, A., & Ramli, N. (2014)	Social Media, Event Management, Attendee Satisfaction
Hede, A.-M., & Kellett, P. (2012)	Event marketing, online brand community, social media, Web 2.0
Hoffman, D. L., & Fodor, M. (2010)	Social Media Measurement, Social Media ROI, Social Media Metrics,
Hudson, S., Roth, M., Madden, T., & Hudson, R. (2015)	Music festivals, Marketing, Social media, Brand relationship quality, Emotions
Kaplan, A., & Haenlein, M. (2012).	Social media, Internet, Information exchange, Information, Information management
Lee, S. S., Boshnakova, D., & Goldblatt, J. (2017).	Meeting and Event Technology History, Using the technology, Meeting and Event Search Engine Optimization, Searc technology, Meeting and Event Design Technology, Marketing with wikis websites blogs and podcast, social media technology solutions for event, Mobile applications for event marketing,
Paris, C. M., Lee, W., & Seery, P. (2010)	Social Capital, Web 2.0, Marketing, Consumer Behavior
Potter, B. (2018)	Social media impact on events,
Preston, C. (2012)	Event Promotion, Elektronic event marketins strategies, Merketing events, Social media in events
Van der Wagen, L., & White, L. (2010)	Event Managemt, Marketing, Consept and design, Using social media for sponsorship, financial management for event
We Are social. (2020, 10 07).	Social media statistics,
Yalçın, F. G. (2017, 08 25).	Factors affecting event marketing

The event sector is a large sector affecting many sectors and continues to grow. In the world, many types of events are organized in regional, national, international and global characteristics. For example, in the USA, more than 2,500 music festivals are held annually, while the UK hosts over 70 different beer festivals each year (Preston, 2012, p. 142). Conferences and meetings constitute a large 20% of the direct spending in the UK event sector, and the sector where exhibitions and trade fairs, music and sports events are predominant is worth £ 41.2 million (Luty, 2020).

The business events market, called the Global MICE (Meetings, incentives, conferences and exhibitions) sector, is expected to be worth $ 882.84 Billion in 2018 and $ 1546.69 Billion by 2025. The event sector is attracted by rapid innovations in technology and supported by social media platforms and continues to grow and develop (Heraldkeepers, 2020).

Social Media

Social media is an internet-based group of applications built on the ideological and technological foundations of Web 2.0, allowing user-centered creation and exchange of content (Kaplan & Haenlein, 2012, p. 102). Social media is a new online media group that shares most or all of the features of participation, openness, conversation, community, and connectedness. "Participation" refers to encouraging the contributions and feedback from all interested parties, "openness" means that most social media services are open to feedback and participation, "conversation" refers to two-way communication, the rapid formation of communities that share common interests in "community", "connectedness" refers to developing their connections by making use of connections to other sites, resources, and people (Paris, Lee, & Seery, 2010, p. 533).

There are basically six types of forms of social media. These are social networks (Facebook etc.), blogs, wikis (Wikipedia), podcasts (Apple Itunes), forums, content communities, microblogging (Twitter). Today, the social media term is generally used for all of these platforms (Mayfield, 2020, p. 6).

Studies conducted over the years show that the ranking of the most accessed sites in the world has changes over time. For example, in 2000, the most frequently accessed sites were MSN, Yahoo, Excite, AOL, Microsoft, Daum, sites like eBay and Altavista, while in 2013 Google, Facebook, YouTube, Yahoo, Baidu, Wikipedia, Windows Live, QQ, Amazon, Twitter, Blogspot, LinkedIn, Wordpress websites have been accessed the most. The main reason for this difference is that these platforms now include social networking sites (Facebook, LinkedIn), video sharing sites (YouTube), blogs (Blogspot, Wordpress), wikis (Wikipedia) and micro blogs (Twitter, Weibo). What differentiates these social networking sites and promotes their popularity is that the web pages, web mail, digital image, digital video, discussion group, guestbook, link list or search engine are integrated platforms that combine many media and information and communication technologies (Fuchs, 2014, p. 6).

According to the Global Digital Report, the number of internet users is increasing every day. In 2019, there were 4,388 billion internet users and 5,112 billion unique mobile users worldwide, up 2 percent from the previous year. Although social media use is still not distributed evenly throughout the world, it is seen that the number of active social media users reaches 3.483 billion people. 3,256 of these people use social media through their mobile devices. It is noted that new users have increased dramatically over 10 percent over the previous year. While time spent on social platforms varies between cultures, the average social media user spends 2 hours and 16 minutes on social platforms every day. In terms of active user accounts, social media platforms such as Facebook, YouTube, Instagram and WhatsApp, Facebook Messenger, WBXIN / WeChat messaging applications maintain their top positions (we are social, 2020, p. 8).

It can be said that social media is now a priority for people and institutions from many areas around the world, from politicians to artists, musicians to business people. Traditional media tools, which also played an important role in event management and were the most important communication channel of the era, have changed due to today's technological changes and innovations, and the media tool that is the most effective channel of today has become social media. According to a comprehensive study of event professionals in 2018, 73% of event planners believe that social media is the most effective tool for marketing events (Aventri, 2019, p. 10).

This change is based on changing preferences for many reasons for users. Compared to social media and traditional media, communication in media such as newspapers, radio and magazines, which are traditional media tools, is one-way, while social media can be said to be two-way. For example, at a sporting event, fans share news, information and comments from social media beyond watching. The updating, speed and interaction structure of social media make it more preferable. Unlike traditional media, many journalists, artists, experts, educators, and students can raise themselves heard through blogs or social media networks without any personal or organizational investment (Bulut, 2012, pp. 29-31) .Thanks to social media, people draw their routes, participate in scientific, artistic, recreational, etc. activities, and recommend them. They are able to find knowledge, inspiration, like-minded people, communities and collaborators faster than ever. New ideas, services, business models and technologies are emerging and evolving at a dizzying pace in social media (Mayfield, 2020).

Social media has fundamentally changed the way users share their personal and professional lives and the way they receive, process and act on shared information and ideas, as well as the way events are designed, marketed and sold (Potter, 2018).

If we look at the examples of big events, the Olympic Games, a Special Event, maintains its connection with the Olympic movement and the volunteer community through online social network interfaces. While the Facebook page for the 2012 London Olympics contains around 36 thousand followers (Hede & Kellett, 2012, p. 242) the 2020 Tokyo Olympics Facebook page is followed by 849 thousand people, and the videos posted show thousands of views (Tokyo 2020, 2020). The 2014 FIFA World Cup generated a total of 3 billion Facebook interactions between June 12, 2014, and July 13, 2014. 1.5 billion for the 2016 Rio Olympic Games, 534 million for the Rio Carnival held in Brazil in 2015, and 67 million for the Academy Awards in 2016 interactions were made (Clement, Selected global media and sporting events with the most Facebook interactions as of May 2017, 2020).

Companies that create Facebook pages can promote their products or services through photos and videos, invite their followers to launch or similar large or small events, and carry some services on their corporate websites to Facebook pages with special tools (Bulut, 2012, p. 46). In fact, Facebook has an event application, allowing the event owners to share the event date, time and place, and the remaining time by sending an invitation.

Twitter, one of the most widely used networks and founded in 2006, is an online social networking service that allows users to send text-based status updates and messages up to 280 characters long. These messages are called tweets. As of the fourth quarter of 2019, Twitter has reached 152 million daily active users worldwide. This network, which is also used very actively by famous people, is an important access channel that allows them to communicate with their fans almost instantly, provide news/information and create a public image about themselves. Major sporting events and awards events such as the American Football League Super Bowl, Grammy Awards or Academy Awards bring a lot of raises on Twitter. Online discussions, photos, tweets, or comments allows the users to participate in the success of these events and celebrities (Clement, 2020).

Instagram, another of today's most popular social media platforms, is a photo-sharing social networking service that allows users to take photos and edit them with filters. The platform allows users to share their images online and directly with their friends and followers on the social network. There are more than 1 billion monthly Instagram users worldwide as of June 2018, and about 112 million active Instagram users in the United States, and experts predict that this figure will exceed 120 million users in 2023.

Brands are keen to reach the Instagram audience, as social network users show high engagement rates with the content displayed. Sports content such as the NBA and NFL, as well as sports sites have high-interest audiences on the platform (Clement, 2020) Therefore, it can be said that today's popular social media platforms constitute the most important communication channel that is also referenced for events.

Use of Social Media in Events

From the point of view of events, looking at the management process of social media, it seems that events are evaluated in three stages before, during and after the event.

Before the Event

In order to reach and announce potential participants of the event, social media activities prior to the event are very important and create an important doping for the success of the event. According to brand and content marketing expert Grate (Grate, 2020), bringing an event to the sales stage is no easy task, and half of the struggle to organize it is marketing the event. The inclusion of social media in event strategies and design from the beginning allows this marketing to be effective (Potter, 2018).

In order to effectively and efficiently use social media tools, which are included in the promotional tools in marketing activities, it is necessary to carry out the promotional activities in a planned manner and to take into account the increasing importance of social media in promotion (Atçeken, Doğrul, & Çabuk, 2018, p. 157).

Rozgonyi (2019), an event marketing consultant, states that there are new social media rules for Event Design. According to the author, 4D should be considered when creating an activity design strategy map. These are the concepts of Digital, Direct, Dynamic, Data. Under these topics, event organizers should answer some questions. These are the questions respectively; "How does your event look on social media and where does it live on social media?", "How do you connect with your community through social media?", "How will you tell stories during the event cycle?" and "How will you determine the event's response and return on investment?" (Rozgonyi, 2019).

When used correctly, social media allows the event to reach more people, attract attention and keep interest alive. According to Brooks (2010), social media can be a cost-effective way to recruit participants into a one-time event into a recurring event. The trick is to determine when to use which social media tools. In event management, each social network serves a different purpose and needs to be used correctly. Multiple social media platforms can be used in this process. The first step is to notify people of your activity, make them mark these in their calendars and register them. For this, it is necessary to turn to the place where there are potential participants in the first place. In which of the social networks mentioned above are the contacts included? Various organizations collect and analyze data about social media tools according to the most preferred regions, countries, demographics. These analysis reports will be able to help with which platforms should be weighted in order to promote the event by type (Brooks, 2020).

Events should have a high level of interest, humor or social cause that will allow them to be shared on social media, among friends or communities with similar ideas. If the event does not have a remarkable reason, then the event will have a limited success (Van der Wagen & White, 2010, p. 454). In the planning of the event, that is, before the event takes place and during the event process, it is necessary to make shares that will attract users. By seeing and sharing and interacting with content related to this event, users on social networks can be made more aware of the event.

The best way to get knowledgeable and experienced social media users into a conversation around a topic is to create a hashtag (#). Therefore, it is recommended to create a hashtag first for the event. Although hashtags have been used in Twitter posts, they are now used on all social media platforms. The blowup in the popularity of Instagram is partly due to the use of hashtags to attract people to chat around the images used on this visual platform. Event planners often have some confusion about copyright infringement by using a hashtag, but hashtags are not copyrighted. Since there is no copyright, the biggest problem that can be experienced is the use of duplicate hashtags, so to see if there is a conversation that has started in the process of creating a hashtag, it must be written in the search area and the status of use there should be observed. Related citation address can be examined for examples related to the subject (Hayes-Peirce, 2017).

Yalçın (2020) notes that Twitter also allows you to measure the topics, most influential people, and information density that get the most attention at the event in real time, without the need for an app, thanks to hashtags. Although Facebook is still a little weak in getting a clear result over the hashtag, it emphasizes that the event page feature remains unique, and is very valuable in terms of providing the calendar feature and all the information together. Facebook's Social VR app states that Facebook Spaces enhancements and new features for Facebook Groups will give a magic touch to events (Yalçın, 2017).

Taking advantage of "influencers" in event marketing is a common method. Influencers literally means "the person who affects". Having a large audience of followers on a social media channel, the power to influence their purchasing decisions due to their expertise, knowledge, location or relationship with their audience are called Influencer. Influencers are classified as mega (over 1 million followers), macro (40 thousand-1 million followers) and micro (1,000-40 thousand followers), content style can be described as youtuber, blogger, social media sharers (What is an Influencer?, 2020). It is of great importance to use these influential individuals over the target audience to market events. The story of the event is also enriched when the right influencers are selected and included in the event plans. However, there is a risk that an influencer in the field of activity can positively affect the return on investment, while an improper sharing may have negative consequences (Yalçın, 2017). For this reason, the right influencers should be selected, taking into account the scope, type and size of the event. For example, Mega-Influencers, who are generally movie stars, athletes, musicians, etc., can be used for a large-budget event on a global scale.

To create new eyes on social media posts about the event, PPC (pay per click), an internet advertising model used for direct referral, where advertisers pay advertisers when clicked on online advertisements on social media, can also be used. Publishing PPC ads on social media is not only cost-effective, but also direct guidance to the destination (Social Tables, 2020).

Today, event planners have become event strategists (Solaris, 2020, p. 14). The expectation of planners about the event is actually a great way to share information with potential guests at an early stage of the planned process. If used correctly, social networks can help spread news at a very low cost.

Event planners collect information about the needs and expectations of potential guests and establishes the activity process. Through social media and networks, guests can ask questions, gather ideas, and start a conversation long before the event, which will provide a unique opportunity to create an event that best meets the needs and expectations of their guests.

One of the main reasons people participate in special events is to get in touch with new people, to share ideas with like-minded people that is to be part of a community. If it is possible to create a community on social media platforms, those who intend to participate in the event can establish a good network and communicate with each other before. (Lee, Boshnakova, & Goldblatt, 2017, p. 211). However, as for event trends, networking is the most neglected element, according to a research report prepared by examining more than 2,000 events over two years and interviewing more than 3,000 event professionals. More and more participation in events is achieved because it is desirable to meet the people involved. The chaotic and over-information-laden world of social media offers opportunities to find new peers and partners. In creating networking, planners will need to make effective use of event technologies. In addition, audiovisual effects will continue to be important in providing high-engagement experiences with projection mapping, virtual reality (VR), augmented reality (AR), and mobile event apps, giving planners the chance to incorporate their audience into a story. Because now there are participants who want to be involved in the story. In addition, it is recommended in the report that planners should be more inclusive while networking at events, and they should create a comprehensive network to serve underrepresented audiences such as younger, introverted, disabled, etc. (Solaris, 2020, pp. 10-22).

Atçeken, Doğrul and Çabuk (2018) have followed the 27-day process on their Facebook page in their research on the 5th Mersin Citrus Festival, an international event. For the first time, social media planning was applied to this event and the festivals held in previous years were compared and found that social media had a very important impact on the announcement of the festival, informing visitors about the festival activities, the rate of interaction of visitors and reaching more visitors. As a result of the studies; "total likes" and "engaging users" and "total representation" of the variables identified, which had a very large increase in the proportional change compared to the previous year and moreover, despite the fact that the festival's social media spending was realized with a very low budget and was actively used shortly before the festival, it showed that it is the most known communication tool for visitors. Therefore, it can be said that the advertising and promotion process is more effective when a planned social media supported event is carried out and can be carried out with lower budgets.

During the Event

The sustainability of events increases in direct proportion to the strength of interactions with participants during the event. In order for a good event to be in demand in the future, organizers now encourage participants to use social media. 2 million people follow the Instagram account of the Coachella Music Festival, which is one of the largest music events in the world and lasts for 3 days. During the event, 7 million posts are sent at the end of each concert, and a total of 43 million posts are reached at the end of each day (Baglietto, 2019). In addition, information about new concerts, surprise participants, sponsorship activities that will take place during the festival is shared for 3 days, which allows participants to use the festival more effectively. As in this example, it is possible to increase the number of participants in future events by sharing videos or images of speakers or events to increase the number of potential guests during any event.

As mentioned in the pre-event activities, the purpose of meeting new people, which is one of the main reasons why people participate in events, can be realized more quickly with the use of social media. If this network can be established prior to the event, participants will be able to communicate with each other during the event.

In addition, by increasing interaction with existing participants through social media during the event, participants can be prevented from entering into false expectations, which is a serious mistake for each event planner (Ghazali & Ramli, 2014, p. 8). In this way, it will be possible for participants to leave the event more happily by meeting their expectations. Instant feedback from participants related to the event can also be provided, making small interventions that need to be done during the event, which allows the event to go smoothly (Hudson, Roth, Madden, & Hudson, 2015, p. 70).

By strengthening ties with participants, event social media accounts increase tracking numbers and strengthen the hand of event managers for future sponsorship deals (Lee, Boshnakova, & Goldblatt, 2017, p. 225). Posts made with hashtags, which are available to event participants, especially those starting with Twitter and on many social media accounts such as Instagram and Facebook can reach a very large audience by making them one of the most talked-about topics in a specific region or all over the world. This is a valuable promotion work that cannot be achieved with no advertising budget. All these exchanges increase the awareness of the event and encourage future participants.

The biggest music festivals in the world, Coachella, Tomorrowland, Glastonbury Festival, Sziget Festival, Amsterdam Dance Event, Bestival, manage to be among the trending topics in the world when they take place. Each festival has its own hashtags so that they can reach potential future festival participants (Glastonbury, Tomorrowland, Sziget & More: How Top European Music Festivals Use Social Media, 2020). In addition, Oktoberfest, Cannes Film festival provides information about all programs and instant events with this hashtag and official social media accounts and ensures that the participants have a more effective festival.

Another event-related study examined more than 25 million social media posts sent by the organizers and participants of the 50 most popular events, including everything from music festivals to endurance races, during the calendar year, especially before, during and after the events. As a result, it was found that many people also talked about the event before the event, with the most social media updates being quotes and multimedia shared during the event (36% of all updates). According to the research, one of the most important social media strategies is to create a photo booth (Grate, 2020). Photo booths are booths used in event areas, where participants take photos using various accessories, and these photos can be obtained in special design prints or in the form of social media shares. While these photos can be shared by the participants during or after the event on social media, it is also interesting to share them by the event owners using the event or sponsor hashtags.

Finally, participants ' enthusiasm can be kept alive with small quizzes, reward programs and similar activities that will be held during the event. By obtaining data about the event, strategic decisions can be made more effectively in future events. As an example, in 2019, 67% of social media posts were made by female participants at the Coachella event and the majority of them were between the ages of 25-34, and the invitation of the Blackpink group, which consisted of all women and the majority of the audience was this audience. This group is the first K-pop (Korean pop) supergroup to be invited to Coachella (Baglietto, 2019).

After the Event

The end of the event does not mean the end of social media activities. The most important and beneficial element here is getting feedback. When compared to traditional media and social media, the fact that social media is faster in feedback and measurement is an important factor in its preference. It may take weeks or months to receive or measure the feedback of the message sent in television, newspapers, magazines or open air advertisements, which are the most important tools of traditional media. However, feedback on social media is almost as fast as one-on-one communication (Bulut, 2012, pp. 29-31) This speed can make strategic decisions faster, especially after the event, and better preparation for the next event.

Social media can track how many people reach the desired message on many platforms, such as the number of views of videos on Instagram, the number of tweets posted about the event, or the number of reads of the blog. Observing and analyzing the frequency of use of tweets and hashtags, and the interactions of the tweets (like, commenting, retweeting) even in small events, can guide the organizers by providing a control opportunity.

Event technology allows planners who have now become strategists to save time and focus on creating engaging, interactive event experiences. Event stakeholders use event data and participant feedback from event planners to improve return on investment and achieve event goals. Event technology is used as a useful tool to collect meaningful data and measure participant satisfaction (Aventri, 2019).

When conducting research related to social media, it is necessary to measure the effects of data before and during the event. There are 7 criteria set for this (7-ways-to-measure-social-mediaeffectiveness, 2011): The first is the measurement of brand awareness. Businesses can measure this by the number of followers of their brands, the number of searches, the number of visitors to their websites through links, and the number of keywords searched for related to the brand. The second is the follow-up of honest discussions. Online discussions are honest, explicit discussions between consumers. From these discussions, businesses can receive positive, neutral or negative comments about their brands. Businesses should monitor comments made on their own brands and competing brands through monitoring programs. The third is the measurement of impact area. Businesses can access impact figures by the number of links to their websites. There may be individuals who comment on the brand of the business or like the product on microblogs such as Twitter and social networking sites such as Facebook and LinkedIn. Examining these social media tweets and likes can analyze why individuals like or dislike them. The fourth way of measuring activity is the interaction indicator. It should be aimed to measure the interaction of people between your site and your brand, it is important to see how interested people are in what you say or offer. This means ratings for your brand, the number of good or bad statements, retweets, photos, video views, and new pages of Facebook likes. The fifth way to measure efficiency is popularity. The number of people who subscribe to your email or RSS feeds is the number of followers on Twitter, members of LinkedIn groups, and people who like your Facebook page or other social media sites. Other places to watch include industry gatherings or content communities such as Flickr or YouTube. The sixth is the use of Monitoring Tools. If you don't measure, monitor, and track information you receive from social media sites, it doesn't make much sense to see a lot of activity on Facebook likes or Twitter tweets. Google Analytics and Measure map are two tools that can be used to track and analyze data. In this way, it will be possible to understand how people will react and what needs to be changed by event managers in terms of advertising. The seventh and final criterion is listening and learning. It is necessary to pay attention to any positive, negative or neutral feedback received from social media sites. It is necessary to see what can be learned from these notifications and what needs to be changed. It is necessary to be proactive in monitoring the data and making the necessary adjustments to the advertising and advertising method. It is possible to succeed when you listen carefully to what is being said and make some proposed changes. Event planners must first set criteria to evaluate social media data related to events.

It is seen that Web 2.0 platforms are adopted by event organizations. However, the lack of academic research on this issue cannot fully demonstrate the results of social media contribution in the event sector (Hede & Kellett, 2012, pp. 241-242)Today, many people or organizations agree that social media has somehow come back. However, the uncertainties about how this level of return should be measured will allow organizations to hesitate to actively use social media. (Attraction et al. 2018). The table above is a good guide to the elimination of this hesitation.

Table 2. Relevant Metrics for Social Media Applications

Social Media Application	Brand Awareness	Brand Engagement	Word of Mouth
Blogs	• number of unique visits • number of return visits • number of times bookmarked • search ranking	• number of members • number of rss feed subscribers • number of comments • amount of user-generated content • average length of time on site • number of responses to polls, contests, surveys	• number of references to blog in other media (online/offline) • number of reblogs • number of times badge displayed on other sites • number of "likes"
Microblogging (e.g.,twitter)	• number of tweets about the brand • valence of tweets +/– • number of followers	• number of followers • number of @replies	• number of retweets
Cocreation (e.g., mkcid)	• number of visits	• number of creation attempts	• number of references to project in other media (online/offline)
Social bookmarking (e.g., stumbleupon)	• number of tags	• number of followers	• number of additional taggers
Forums and discussion boards (e.g., google groups)	• number of page views • number of visits • valence of posted content +/–	• number of relevant topics/threads • number of individual replies • number of sign-ups	• incoming links • citations in other sites • tagging in social bookmarking • offline references to the forum or its members • in private communities: number of pieces of content (photos, discus- sions, videos); chatter pointing to the community outside of its gates • number of "likes"
Product reviews (e.g., amazon)	• number of reviews posted • valence of reviews • number and valence of other users' responses to reviews (+/–) • number of wish list adds • number of times product included in users' lists (i.e., listmania! On amazon. com)	• length of reviews • relevance of reviews • valence of other users' ratings of reviews (i.e., how many found particular review helpful) • number of wish list adds • overall number of reviewer rating scores entered • average reviewer rating score	• number of reviews posted • valence of reviews • number and valence of other users' responses to reviews (+/–) • number of references to reviews in other sites • number of visits to review site page • number of times product included in users' lists (i.e., listmania! On amazon.com)
Social networks (e.g., bebo, facebook, linkedin)	• number of members/fans • number of installs of applications • number of impressions • number of bookmarks • number of reviews/ratings and valence +/–	• number of comments • number of active users • number of "likes" on friends' feeds • number of user-generated items (photos, threads, replies) • usage metrics of applications/ widgets • impressions-to-interactions ratio • rate of activity (how often members personalize profiles, bios, links, etc.)	• frequency of appearances in timeline of friends • number of posts on wall • number of reposts/shares • number of responses to friend referral invites
Video and photosharing (e.g., flickr,youtube)	• number of views of video/photo • valence of video/photo ratings +/–	• number of replies • number of page views • number of comments • number of subscribers	• number of embeddings • number of incoming links • number of references in mock-ups or derived work • number of times republished in other social media and offline • number of "likes"

Source: (Hoffman & Fodor, 2010)

In addition to evaluating events, event planners use social media to provide credibility by sharing suggestions and photos of previous events, creating interactive communities between participants before, during and after the event (Roig, Fuentes, & Ramon, 2017, p. 5). This allows your social media-related area to be active and maintain its influence at the end of the event.

Event technology is adopted as a tool used to collect meaningful data about the event and measure participant satisfaction, and it is expected to continue to be used by event organizers in the future (Solaris, 2020, p. 14). Although what needs to be done after the event is generally expressed in this way, advances in technology can open up new and different ways of evaluating it.

SOLUTIONS AND RECOMMENDATIONS

The event sector has many subtitles and is a large and dynamic sector that is in direct and indirect interaction with many sectors. Professionals who organize events that create significant competitive advantages for countries, regions and organizations need to constantly monitor and analyze the everyday life of society, current technology, science and connected sectors.

The source of this information is communication tools. The form of communication is changing in the world and one-way communication is not preferred anymore. It is not a realistic approach to think that activities in which two-way interaction is performed will not use social media, which again has the same feature and allows two-way communication. In this context, event managers should reach out to potential event participants before the event and attract them to their activities, keep the participants' interest alive by establishing uninterrupted two-way communication during the event and increase their level of satisfaction, and use social media to ensure that the effect lasts longer when the event is over, to reach potential participants in the future and to make strategic evaluations about the event. In addition, event organizers have to have a strong social media channel to have a stronger hand in their negotiations with sponsors, so that they can reach out to sponsors with a larger budget.

As of January 2020, today, where it is not possible to ignore an environment where 3.8 billion people in the world are all together, event owners must use social media effectively. Otherwise, event managers will be called dinosaurs by the next generation, like the first generations who refused to use computers, and they will slowly disappear in the future.

As a final word, people in many parts of the world prefer to spend more time in their homes due to the pandemic today. For this reason, internet usage is increasing for news, information, education, sharing and communication purposes. In addition, most of the canceled events have been transferred to virtual environments and as a result of the pandemic, the event sector also changed. This process signals us that the social media tools used as aids in the near future may turn into the main environment and scenes where the events will be held.

FUTURE RESEARCH DIRECTION

The relationship between social media, which has billions of active users and an indispensable part of daily life, and the event sector, which affects many sectors and continues to grow, should be more subject to scientific research. There is limited research in the literature about the effects of social media marketing on events. Especially, researches on ROI for social media activities will contribute to both event literature and event managers in terms of directing their investments correctly and providing time and cost efficiency. Will be able to create a proactive perspective for new events in future researches using social media prediction models regarding events Finally, Factors such as measuring participants' satisfaction during and after the event, how and through what tools they have knowledge of the event and its content, what they expect from the event survey, etc. must be revealed by scientific methods.

Lastly the research focuses on the positive aspects of social media in events. However, in future studies, the negative effects of using social media can be examined.

CONCLUSION

In the globalizing world, using of the social media is increasing rapidly and the period of the people express themselves face to face is getting over. Personal relationships are transferred to social media environments. People meet, have fun and even share their sorrows on these platforms. The YouTube concert of Andrea Bocelli in Italy's famous Duomo Square, where the empty streets of big cities are also reflected, has been watched by 41 million people and liked by 1 million people and became the symbol of the struggle against pandemic. This example shows us, it is not thought that social media should be ignored in the activities that people organize for gathering. Therefore, the importance of social media in activities is discussed in this study and using a social media before, during and after the events are discussed. As a result of the research, it is found that the use of social media in events is very important for the success of the events.

In addition, while the studies in the literature mostly examine the relations between social media and the event, this research makes suggestions on how event professionals will use social media before, during and after the event.

REFERENCES

Atçeken, K., Doğrul, Ü., & Çabuk, S. (2018). Tutundurmada Sosyal Medyanın Önemi: 5. Mersin ULuslararası Narenciye Festivali Örneği. *Akademik Araştırmalar ve Çalışmalar Dergisi, 10*(18), 146–157. doi:10.20990/kilisiibfakademik.428624

Aventri. (2019). *The future of Event Marketing* (2nd ed.). Norwalk: Event.

Baglietto, M. (2019). *What Brands Can Learn From Coachella's Social Media Marketing Mastery*. Retrieved from netbasequid.com web site: https://netbasequid.com/blog/coachellas-social-media-marketing-mastery/

Barutçu, S., & Tomaş, M. (2013). Sürdürülebilir Sosyal Medya Pazarlaması ve Sosyal Medya Pazarlaması Etkinliğinin Ölçümü. *Journal of Internet Applications and Management*, 5-24.

Brooks, R. (2020). *12 Ways to Market Your Event With Social Media*. Retrieved from https://www.socialmediaexaminer.com/12-ways-to-market-your-event-with-social-media/

Bulut, E. (2012). *Pazarlama İletişiminde Yeni Yaklaşımlar Kapsamında Sosyal Medya Uygulamaları ve Etkili Kampanya Örnekleri*. İstanbul: Unpublished masters thesis.

Clement, J. (2020). *Instagram accounts with the most followers worldwide 2020*. Retrieved from Statista web site: https://www.statista.com/statistics/421169/most-followers-instagram/

Clement, J. (2020). *Selected global media and sporting events with the most Facebook interactions as of May 2017*. Retrieved from Statitas: https://www.statista.com/statistics/477371/facebook-sporting-events-interactions/

Clement, J. (2020). *Twitter accounts with the most followers worldwide 2020*. Retrieved from Sttista web site: https://www.statista.com/statistics/273172/twitter-accounts-with-the-most-followers-worldwide/

Fuchs, C. (2014). *Social Media a Critical Introduction*. Sage Publication Inc. doi:10.4135/9781446270066

Getz, D. (2008). Event tourism: Definition, evolution, and research. *Tourism Management, 29*(3), 403–428. doi:10.1016/j.tourman.2007.07.017

Getz, D. (2012). Event Studies: Discourses and Future Directions. *Event Management, 16*(2), 171–187. doi:10.3727/152599512X13343565268456

Ghazali, A., & Ramli, N. (2014). The Relationship Between Social Media Uzage and Event Attendees Satisfaction At Carnival Event. In *Proceedings of the Australian Academy of Business and Social Sciences Conference* (pp. 1-10). Dubai: Australian Academy of Business and Social Sciences.

Glastonbury, Tomorrowland, Sziget & More: How Top European Music Festivals Use Social Media. (2020). Retrieved from Ticketbooth web site: https://www.ticketbooth.com.au/ticketing/blog/glastonbury-tomorrowland-sziget-more-how-top-european-music-festivals-use-social-media/

Grate, R. (2020). *Event Marketing 101: How to Keep Attendees Engaged Before, During and After Your Event*. Retrieved from Buffer Library Web Site: https://buffer.com/library/social-media-event-marketing/

Hayes-Peirce, S. (2017). *Social Media Strategies for Sparking Event Conversations in 2018*. Retrieved from Mpi web site: https://www.mpi.org/chapters/southern-california/chapter-news/single-blog/article/social-media-strategies-for-sparking-event-conversations-in-2018

Hede, A.-M., & Kellett, P. (2012). Building online brand communities: Exploring the benefits, challenges and risks in the Australian event sector. *Journal of Vacation Marketing, 18*(3), 239–250. doi:10.1177/1356766712449370

Heraldkeepers. (2020). *MICE (Meetings, Incentives, Conferencing, Exhibitions) Market Size To Worth USD 1546.69 Billion by 2025 ndustry Analysis, Business Outlook, Current and Future Growth By 2025*. Retrieved from Marketwatch Web Sitesi: https://www.marketwatch.com/press-release/mice-meetings-incentives-conferencing-exhibitions-market-size-to-worth-usd 154669 billion by-2025-industry-analysis-business-outlook-current-and-future-growth-by-2025-2020-08-17

Hoffman, D. L., & Fodor, M. (2010). Can You Measure the ROI of Your Scial Media Marketing. *MIT Sloan Management Review, 52*(1), 41–49.

Hudson, S., Roth, M., Madden, T., & Hudson, R. (2015). The effects of social media on emotions, brand relationship quality, and word of mouth: An empirical study of music festival attendees. *Tourism Management, 47*, 68–76. doi:10.1016/j.tourman.2014.09.001

Kaplan, A., & Haenlein, M. (2012). Social media: Back to the roots and back to the future. *Journal of Systems and Information Technology*, *14*(2), 101–105. doi:10.1108/13287261211232126

Lee, S. S., Boshnakova, D., & Goldblatt, J. (2017). *The 21st Century Meeting and Event Technologies Powerful Tools for Better Planning, Marketing, and Evaluation.* Oakville: Taylor & Francis Group.

Luty, J. (2020). *Direct spending in the events sector in the United Kingdom (UK) as of 2017, by event type.* Retrieved from Statista Web Sitesi: https://www.statista.com/statistics/426464/direct-spending-in-the-events-sector-in-the-united-kingdom/

Mayfield, A. (2020). *What is Social Media.* Retrieved from icrossing Web sitesi: https://www.icrossing.com/uk/sites/default/files_uk/insight_pdf_files/What%20is%20Social%20Media_iCrossing_ebook.pdf

Paris, C. M., Lee, W., & Seery, P. (2010). *The Role of Social Media in Promoting Special Events: Acceptance of Facebook 'Events'. In Information and Communication Technologies in Tourism 2010* (pp. 531-541). Lugano: Springer-Verlag/Wien.

Potter, B. (2018). *The Impact of Social Media on Meetings and Events.* Retrieved from Mpi Web site: https://www.mpi.org/blog/article/the-impact-of-social-media-on-meetings-and-events

Preston, C. (2012). *How to Successfully Promote Events, Festivals, Conventions, and Expositions.* Wiley Press.

Roig, E. M., Fuentes, E. M., & Ramon, N. D. (2017). User-Generated Social Media Events in Tourism. *Sustainability*, 1–23.

Rozgonyi, B. (2019). *New Social Media Rules for Engaging Event Design.* Retrieved from Mpi.org web site: https://www.mpi.org/chapters/chicago-area/chapter-news/single-blog/c-c-articles/2019/08/06/new-social-media-rules-for-engaging-event-design

Social Tables. (2020). *15 Tactics to Sell More Event Tickets Today.* Retrieved from Socialtables web site: https://www.socialtables.com/blog/social-media/drive-event-ticket-sales/

Solaris, J. (2020). *10 events trend for 2020.* Retrieved from eventmanagerblog web site: https://www.eventmanagerblog.com/10-event-trends

Tokyo 2020. (2020). Retrieved from Tokyo 2020 Facebook page: https://www.facebook.com/tokyo2020/about/?ref=page_internal

Van der Wagen, L., & White, L. (2010). *Event management: for tourism, cultural, business and sporting events* (4th ed.). Pearson Pub.

ways-to-measure-social-mediaeffectiveness. (2011). Retrieved from before it's news web site: http://www.sitepronews.com/2011/09/06/7-ways-to-measure-social-mediaeffectiveness-for-your-company-a-spn-exclusive-article/

we are social. (2020). *Digital 2020: Global Digital Yearbook.* Retrieved from Hootsuite Web Site: https://datareportal.com/reports/digital-2020-july-global-statshot

What is an Influencer? (2020). Retrieved from influencermarketinghub.com web site: https://influencer-marketinghub.com/what-is-an-influencer/

Yalçın, F. G. (2017). *Tüm yönleriyle etkinlik pazarlaması ve etkinlik pazarlamasında son trendler.* Retrieved from Digitalage Web site: https://digitalage.com.tr/tum-yonleriyle-etkinlik-pazarlamasi-ve-etkinlik-pazarlamasinda-son-trendler/

ADDITIONAL READING

Abuhashes, M., Al-Khasawneh, M., & Al-Dmour, R. (2019). The Impact of Facebook on Jordanian Consumers' Decision Process in the Hotel Selection, IBIMA. *Business Review*, 1–16.

Alghizzawi, M., Habes, M., & Salloum, S. A. (2018). The role of social media in tourism marketing in Jordan. *International Journal of Information Technology and Language Studies*, 2(3), 59–70.

Chen, S. C., & Lin, C. P. (2019). Understanding the effect of social media marketing activities: The mediation of social identification, perceived value, and satisfaction. *Technological Forecasting and Social Change*, *140*, 22–32. doi:10.1016/j.techfore.2018.11.025

Dedeoğlu, B. B., Niekerk, M., Küçükergin, K. G., Marcello, D. M., & Okumuş, F. (2019). Effect of social media sharing on destination brand awareness and destination quality. *Journal of Vacation Marketing*, *20*(10), 1–24.

Feliciano, J. F. D. G. (2018). Social media networks in the third sector: the road to sustainability. Lisbon: Unpublished masters thesis.

Harb, A. A., Fowler, D., Chang, H. J., Blum, S. C., & Alakaleek, W. (2019). Social media as a marketing tool for events. *Journal of Hospitality and Tourism Technology*, *10*(1), 28–44. doi:10.1108/JHTT-03-2017-0027

Hede, A.-M., & Kellett, P. (2011). Marketing Communications for Special Events: Analysing Managerial Practice, Consumer Perceptions and Preferences. *Journal of Marketing*, *45*(6), 987–1004.

Hills, M. (2015). *Doctor Who: The Unfolding Event.* Palgrave Macmillian. doi:10.1057/9781137463326

Hoyle, L. H. (2020). *Event Marketing.* John Wiley & Sons.

Romero, N. L. (2011). ROI. Measuring the social media return on investment in a library. *Managing Library Finances*, *54*(2), 145–151. doi:10.1108/08880451111169223

Shen, C., Luong, T., Ho, J., & Djailani, I. (2019). Social media marketing of IT service companies: Analysis using a concept-linking mining approach. *Industrial Marketing Management*, *90*, 593 604. doi:10.1016/j.indmarman.2019.11.014

KEY TERMS AND DEFINITIONS

Hashtag: A word or phrase with the symbol "#" in front of it, used on social media websites and apps so that you can search for all messages with the same subject. This function was created on Twitter.

Influencer: Having a large audience of followers on a social media channel, the power to influence their purchasing decisions due to their expertise, knowledge, location or relationship with their audience are called Influencer.

ROI/Return on Investment: Interest or dividends shown as a percentage of the money invested.

Social Media: Forms of media that allows people to communicate and share information in two ways using the internet or mobile phones.

This research was previously published in Impact of ICTs on Event Management and Marketing; pages 139-155, copyright year 2021 by Business Science Reference (an imprint of IGI Global).

Chapter 9
Event Management in Social Media

Murat Seyfi
Gaziosmanpaşa University, Turkey

ABSTRACT

This chapter describes how through globalisation and developments in communication technologies, the lifestyle of people has changed and developed as well. Now, events are re-designed with communication tools and are becoming an important part of social life. This study aims to determine and evaluate the factors affecting perceptions of the audience who take part in events realized via Facebook, or on another online platform. Since this study is implemented through a social media communication device, on an on-line platform, it differs from other studies and gives this area a new perspective. Data acquired from questions were prepared to test the hypothesis of the study were analysed by doing factor analysis and regression tests. The acquired results were discussed.

INTRODUCTION

Event management is an applied science in which inter-disciplinary studies are used. It is a format that is continuously renewing and developing its practices through technology that is constantly changing and developing. In particular, event practices now cease to be ordinary activities and have become a structure that has horizontal and vertical components through recent developments in communication technologies and multi-functional globalization effects. The base for this is that events are creating their own stories with creative, interesting and transmediatic practices. In relation to this, event management and event marketing caused the rise of a new dimension by using technological instruments in all the sub-elements of the process of "strategical communication management".

Events have appeared in different formats and styles throughout the history of humankind. In the ancient era; wars, occupations, religious celebrations and agricultural harvest seasons were bases for events. Today, formats of events have changed through the developments in communication technologies and effects of globalization. Now, events have gained a new memory, place, and space which are

DOI: 10.4018/978-1-6684-6287-4.ch009

different from traditional events. Therefore, factors affecting perceptions of the audience have changed and developed.

Every day, thousands of events are held on social media websites that have billions of users today. Social media and the events held on such websites acquired such a vital place in social life that they have become an important research area. There are almost any research in the literature about the evaluation of the events held on social media. Therefore, focusing on pilot studies rather than studies producing hypothesis will be the right thing to do since various dimensions are in question when the audience is evaluating Facebook events and traditional events. This study conducts a pilot study to determine sub-dimensions of audience perceptions about the event on Facebook. This study analyzes yoga and recovery events held by Seçil Tezgel in Turkey on a Facebook page which is created by herself. The participants of the events are people who want to take online yoga courses and to recover through spiritual methods. This study differs from other studies in that the event was held on a social media website. McLuhan (1964) focuses on the fact that mediums change people's frame of mind rather than the message itself by saying "medium is message". Therefore, people's lifestyle and way of perceiving life are directly influenced by the mediums. In other words, social media devices which came into our lives through communication technologies are not only the inventions people use but also the mediums that re-invent people and their lifestyle. Hence, participant's adaptation process to the digital platform is also analyzed apart from their loyalty and satisfaction.

There are scarcely any studies in the literature about the topic. Therefore, focusing on pilot studies rather than studies producing hypothesis will be the right thing to do since various dimensions are in question when the audience is evaluating Facebook events and traditional events. This study conducts a pilot study to determine sub-dimensions of audience perceptions about the event on Facebook. Within this context, this study differs from other studies and is thought to contribute to the literature.

BACKGROUND

Event is described as a remarkable activity taking place in a specific place and a period of time (Getz, 2007, p.19). Events, from the perspective of the audience, are seen as a medium for recreation and entertainment. Individuals expect to experience happiness and joy-oriented experiences by participating in the events (McLean, 2006, pp.40-41). According to Pira (2004), each event has its own purposes. These purposes might be sustaining social communication or reaching related purposes by creating an environment for the benefit of the institution, affecting the people and carrying the mission and the needs of the event into a general area. However, an event which cannot achieve its aims, even if it is profit-oriented or a charity, becomes insignificant and a loss of resources (Pira, 2004, p.31). Therefore, researching perceptions of the audience in the events is vital in terms of determining sub-factors of participant satisfaction and loyalty.

Event management is the sector that has grown biggest in the leisure industry in the recent years. Therefore, it has been researched exhaustively by both the academicians and experts of the profession (Nicholson & Pearce, 2001). Within this scope, there have been many studies conducted which particularly consider motivation, satisfaction, loyalty, social and cultural effects of participants (Visitors loyalty Gandhi & Shaw 2002; social impacts of event Kim et al., 2010; event motivation Li & Petrick, 2006; building brand image Gwinner et al., 1999; loyalty Gedenk & Neslin, 1999; effects of events Xing & Chalip, 2006). The basis for these studies is to develop communication strategies which will create a behavioral change on event participants, reinforce consumer behaviors, and which are persuasive and encouraging. Potential consumers are motivated to purchase this free-time experience thanks to these communication studies. However, qualified an event product is designed, the event in question will be sealed behind closed doors unless there is a successful advertisement of the event with promotional efforts. The success of the most well-known events (Super Bowl, Olympic Games) depends upon a well-developed strategic communication plan (Goldblatt, 2010). Through globalization and the developments in communication technologies, communication studies have changed and developed. Now, people's participation process to the events begins with their cellphones and on their accounts of social media without leaving their homes thanks to social media devices. Therefore, the relationship between social media and event management deepens each passing day.

DIGITALIZATION OF EVENT MANAGEMENT

Through developments in communication technologies, the lifestyle of people has changed (McLuhan, 1964). The flow of daily life has also undergone a transformation within the post-modern world. Virtual or non-virtual communities which appeared as a result of this transformation developed many opportunities in individual mobility via the internet. Particularly, virtual communities can benefit from high-level education and technology opportunities when compared to conventional communities. Therefore, it is now an obligation to organize events which are unique to individuals' lives. All those free times make free time events acquire a new dimension. This feature formed the basis for large individualization of events, which makes free time experiences a catalyst for individual cultural values and cultural capital. Now, the cultural capital of people and free time events have started to nourish each other. That is to say, events caused societies and individuals to find an important place within their socio-cultural and economic context. For this reason, globalization and technological developments have become driving forces for modern-day events (Argan & Yüncü, 2015, pp. 4-5). In particular, various vital habits of people, the habit of recreation through applications on the internet is in the first place, have entered into an evolution process. In relation to this, social media devices have started to bring people together for different purposes on different platforms (Kaplan & Haenlein, 2010). Developments in communication technologies have particularly brought about practices like integration with social media in terms of event management. Social media has started to be seen as the most critical platform in terms of the function it has; that is, it gives the opportunity to reach the individual directly and enables feedback from the individual. In addition, social webs which have a significant number of followers in the world have acquired the position of webs which are included in plans of event management. Social media integration in events varies each passing day through the developments in communication technologies. The purpose of web-based social media applications that are peculiarly designed for events is including more participants in the application with ease, understandability and quickly, and thus to reach the aimed number of participants. The most frequently used social media based digital platforms are applications like QR code, RFID Radio Frequency Identification, TweetWall, 360 Selfie, Prestagram, SocialBreak, and SocialGoal. In addition, Hashtags, Likes, and Tweets are widely used for events to reach large masses. The more social media develops the more these kinds of applications used in the events will develop, and their numbers will increase (Akay, 2014, pp. 64-68). In the recent years, Facebook, YouTube and especially Twitter have become highly efficient devices to observe event processes. In addition, they have many functions in terms of lead generation. In particular, they make potential customers involve in the process for each stakeholder of the event beyond just simple sales regarding the event. This makes event management acquire a dynamic structure (Rothschild, 2011). Social media has become an important platform as a result of the constant development of the technology and increasing number of the participants. Consequently, each social web appearing on the internet has developed its own format of the event.

There are many studies in the literature about the classification of events. Getz (1997) classified events by considering their contents and extent, Roche (2000) made a classification from the perspective of modernity and mega events, Armstrong (2001) conducted studies to classify events within themselves, Shone and Parry (2004) classified events as free time, cultural, private and personal events, Tassiopoulus (2005) classified them whether they are planned or not, and whether they have a specialty or not. Especially with technological developments in the 2000s, management and practice of events have changed and developed. Therefore, new classification studies and developing new theories within this context have become a necessity. As a result of the literature review, sectoral analyses and in-depth interviews with people who work in this sector by Seyfi (2017), digital events are classified as technology-based events, virtual-on-line events, and transmediatic events. While technology-based events describe people according to their condition of activity or passivity, in virtual on-line events the focus is on on-line or off-line processes of the participants. Within this framework, Facebook events fall into the group of virtual-on-line events.

Facebook and Event Management

Today, Facebook is the most popular social media device having the highest number of users. Facebook was established by Mark Zuckerberg and his friends in 2004 with the purpose of gathering people in the campus together on an on-line platform. Facebook is a profit-oriented, the USA originated institution providing on-line social media and social web service (Carlson, 2010). In 2006, when Facebook was brought into service of everybody, it grew so quickly. Facebook created new applications to develop itself and focused on satisfying the needs of both the business world and the individuals with the increase in the number of its users (Richmond, 2007). By the year 2011, users had the feature of creating their "memorable life events" that bring their characteristics to the forefront. Facebook has become an important event management area with its development each passing day. In particular, Facebook became an important source of information in times of crisis beyond being a communication device (Seyfi & Güven, 2016). Facebook was frequently used when people were gathering together and events were being organized during social events like the Arab Spring (Huang, 2011). As a consequence of the frequent use of Facebook in social, political and cultural events, Facebook event application has started to be often used both in individual and commercial practices. For this reason, Facebook prepared briefing pages for its users on how to organize an event.

According to a 2014 dated report by Pew Research Center, Internet usage rate is 87% in America, and 97% of the users are between the age of 18 and 29. Therefore, re-designing events and in fact, the social life as a whole according to this circumstance have become a necessity. Studies conducted on the topic suggest that participation rate to events has increased more than ever thanks to announcements through social media channels. It is determined that use of Facebook before and about the event is 77%, use of Twitter during the event is 73% and use of Facebook after the event is 55%. Besides, technology orientation directly affects not only the process of the event but also the planning process of the event. Due to all these reasons, the sector is growing each passing day and the evolutionary process continues (Pew Research Center, 2014). Furthermore, the number of the events realized on virtual platforms are also increasing apart from the use of social media. The report of Market Research Media demonstrates that this sector will worth 18 billion dollars by experiencing a 5% growth by the year 2023 (Market Research Media, 2017). Thus, the importance of new communication devices and technological applications in the event management process are increasing day by day.

Through technological developments and social media practices, event management processes have also changed and developed constantly. While conventional events have a specific time and place, events realized on digital platforms have started to create their own memories and places. According to Halbwachs (1992), memory creates the process of an individual's socialization and it is determined by social elements. Since memory cannot stay the same, it has a "reconstruction" function in a community. This explains the organic link between the memory and communities (Huyssen, 2003). Events held on social media platforms also contribute to the memory of the virtual community, which is created by those events. Thus, these kinds of events become a part of social life. On the other hand, constant update of knowledge with events by means of social media puts forward a new concept of place because sharing made on different social media devices adds a new dimension to the events.

Harmonization of Technology and Humans

The event management process has encountered a new function through events organized on digital platforms like Facebook. Different from conventional events, human-technology adaptation seems to be an important function within this new platform. Although the intense use of technology in events supports factors like creativity, speed, and entertainment, participants might feel like bullied unless they can adapt these technological devices. According to a report prepared by AARP Foundation and Microsoft in 2009, participants desire security and accessibility in the environment during the process of technology usage. In addition, participants seek an adaptation process in which they can take responsibilities rather than technology's managing all of the communication process (Rogers, 2009). In the events realized on on-line platforms, it is vital to know from which aspects technological innovations adapt to the society and culture, how the innovations spread in the society, how the individuals perceive and embrace these events and the factors increasing or decreasing the use of technology. Therefore, there have been many studies conducted to explain the relationship between technology and people. Rogers (2003) focuses on the concept of innovation when he develops the Theory of Diffusion of Innovation. According to Rogers, innovation is not only newly discovered technological devices but also a process. For this reason, if individuals come across an object or technology for the first time, which was previously discovered, they perceive it as innovation. Thus, from that moment on, individuals exert effort to embrace and adapt this innovation they come across. When event areas are handled at this point since the event area constantly renews itself, it is a new area for participants, and they must use their communication channels actively in order to embrace and adapt to these innovations.

Fishbein and Azjen (1975) stated that available attitudes in social science studies are prerequisites for determining specific behaviors of individuals. In other words, they drew attention to the relationship between attitude and behavior. Attitude is the tendency to react positively or negatively and is an important element influencing the intention to use or not to use the computer. In addition, attitudes might change on digital platforms and may be re-shaped according to the features of the digital platform (Ma et al., 2005). The basis for this is perceived ease of use and perceived usefulness. Perceived ease of use and perceived usefulness are important elements influencing individuals' intention about using a computer (Davis, 1989). While perceived usefulness was defined by Davis (1989) to point out individuals' tendencies and opinions about increasing their performance in a work that they are doing with the use of technology, perceived ease of use points out easy use of a specific technology and ease of learning how to use this technology. Therefore, perceived ease of use and perceived usefulness of participants in the events realized in digital platforms are vital. It can be anticipated that people may develop many positive attitudes in terms of ease of use against the events to be held on a digital platform, which is widely used by people like Facebook. On the other hand, when the topic is handled from an organizational perspective, a technological change that causes re-shaping of production system will bring about an essential organizational change (Woodward, 1965, p.72). When we consider that events are generally organized by companies, the relationship between organizational change and technological adaptation should be questioned by event managers. Organizations must have the ability to adapt to this change because technology makes the organizational change necessary by changing the structure of organization and management philosophy (Liker et al., 1999, p. 582). This will directly influence event management process.

Hypothesis of the Study

When the evaluation studies about the events are examined, it can be seen that studies are most often conducted to determine people's satisfaction from the event and their loyalty, and events' cultural influences and social benefits (Kim & Petrick, 2005; Parasuraman et al., 1988; Pons, Mourali & Nyeck 2006; Kim et al., 2015; Delamere et al., 2001; Lee & Cho, 2012; Pierce, Stacey & Barkatsas, 2007). Now it is an obligation to conduct different evaluation studies since the technological devices are frequently used in event platforms and the number of the event practices on virtual platforms is increased. The reason behind this is that the events that take place on virtual platforms and conventional events differ greatly from each other in terms of both usage requirements and environmental influences. Therefore, developing hypotheses that analyses the effects of technological devices on both the event and the people' behavior is vital for understanding the topic. Within this framework:

H1: On Facebook events, participant satisfaction influences participant behaviors. Besides, there is a substantial relationship between participant satisfaction and loyalty.

H2: Loyalty is defined as "constant purchasing, frequent purchasing, and word-of-mouth recommendations" (Lee, Kim, and Kim, 2006). Every event organizer wants participants to re-participate in the event. In online events held on Facebook, participant loyalty influences participant's behaviors.

H3: In particular, the place that the event was held directly affected the perception of participants in the event evaluations. Therefore, in events held on Facebook, the behaviors and perception of participants will be directly influenced by Facebook's factors (being online and sharing online etc.).

H4: Individual and social events have always had an important role in the event evaluations. The behaviors and perception of participants on Facebook events are directly influenced by individual and social effects of the event.

Methodology of the Study

The purpose of this study is to conduct a pilot study which aims to determine sub-factors for evaluation of perception of participants in events held on Facebook. As a result of the field research made within this scope, questions developed in studies which aim to evaluate satisfaction and loyalty of participants

(Kim et al., 2015; Yürük et al., 2017; Petrick et al., 2013; Parasuraman et al., 1988) were based in this study. Moreover, questions regarding the adaptation of human to computers (Thüring & Mahlke, 2007; Rosen et al., 2013) and aiming to put forward effects of the Facebook environment were included in the study due to the fact that it was conducted on an online platform. These questions were checked by 5 people who conduct studies in this field, and structural changes were made. As a result of the evaluations, a survey questionnaire is created consisting of 18 questions which are of 5 Likert type. Before factor analysis, whether the data is suitable for factor analysis is examined with KMO (Kaiser-Meyer-Olkin) and Barlett's test. After acquiring meaningful results, it is determined that there are four factors among the 18 questions analyzed whose eigenvalue is higher than 1.

Participants of an event page titled "Şifanın Yolu" which was realized by Seçil Tezgel in Turkey make up the sample of the study. Seçil Tezgel organizes yoga, meditation and recovery events on Facebook being sometimes free of charge and sometimes not. The average number of participants of these events is 150-250. 210 people took part in the event organized in December, before the New Year, and the study was conducted on these people. 106 of the 210 people accepted to take part in the research and answered the questionnaire on Google form. Acquired data were analyzed with the program SPSS. Within the scope of the analyses, factor and regression analyses were conducted

Findings

Descriptive analyses were conducted in order to describe demographical features of the participants. Within this framework, it is determined that 90.6% of the participants are women. Since there is a huge difference between the number of women and men participants there was not an analysis conducted on gender difference. When participation frequency of participants to events on Facebook is observed, it can be seen that 69.8% of the participants said that they participated in more than 7 Facebook events.

Factor Analyses

Factor analysis can be described as a multivariate statistic that aims to find and explore few conceptually meaningful new variables (factors, dimensions) by gathering together various variables that are related to one another (Dunteman, 1989; Renie, 1997; Stevens, 2012). In this study, since the researcher does not have any opinion or prediction about the relationship between the variables regarding the topic that he researches, Exploratory Factor Analysis was conducted in order to reveal the probable relationship between the variables.

In order to test whether the factor analysis was to be made or not, firstly KMO and Barlett tests were made. Since the KMO value was higher than 0.60, that is 0,741, factor analysis could be made. In addition, according to Bartlett test results, $X2=1391,584$, $df=153$ and $p=0.000$ were found significantly at a confidence level. They show that there was a relationship between the variables and so determined that the data have been in conformity with the factor analysis.

After it was seen that the expressions in the research were suitable, factor analysis was made one more time and the dimensions of the factor were determined. As it can be seen from the table, research questions consist of four dimensions.

Through Total Variance Analysis explained, four factors appeared whose eigenvalue was higher than 1. This shows that the scale developed has four dimensions.

Table 1. Demographical features of the participants

	Frequency	Percentage
Where do you live for the most part of your life?		
Big Cities	74	69.8
Small and Medium Scaled Cities	32	31.2
How often do you participate in the events on Facebook?		
I have participated only for 1 time up to now.	6	5.6
1-3 times	18	16.9
4-7 times	8	7.5
More than 7	74	69.8
Your Educational Status		
Primary School	6	5.6
Secondary School	26	24.5
Associate Degree	18	16.9
Bachelor's Degree	40	37.7
Master's Degree	16	15
Your Age?		
21-30	4	3.7
31-40	36	33.9
41-50	44	41.5
51-60	16	15.1
+60	6	5.6

Table 2. KMO and Bartlett's test

Kaiser-Meyer-Olkin Measure of Sampling Adequacy.		,741
Bartlett's Test of Sphericity	Approx. Chi-Square	1391.584
	df	153
	Sig.	,000

Table 3. Total variance explained

Component	Initial Eigenvalues			Extraction Sums of Squared Loadings	
	Total	% of Variance	Cumulative %	Total	% of Variance
1	6,980	38,779	38,779	6,980	38,779
2	2,421	13,447	52,227	2,421	13,447
3	1,712	9,511	61,738	1,712	9,511
4	1,252	6,956	68,694	1,252	6,956

With acquired results through Total Variance Analysis, factor loads were determined in order to determine questions forming four sub-dimensions. From 18 questions that were prepared within the framework of the study, questions whose factor load was lower than 0.5 were considered invalid. Thus, factor loads that make up the sub-dimension of the scale developed were determined in the table.

Since there are not any studies aiming to develop a scale regarding the events held on Facebook, it is not possible to foresee implications. Therefore, Exploratory Factor Analysis was conducted within the context of the study. Four dimensions were determined in the study of determining the dimensions. Since there are not any studies aiming to determine dimensions in the literature, these four dimensions were classified according to questions' conceptuality levels. In addition, the cumulative percentage of these four dimensions is 68,455%, which demonstrates that these dimensions widely involves the research.

Table 4. Dimensions of the questions

	Factor Loading	Cronbach Alfa
Dimension1: Social-Individual Effect		,735
I think I found health, luck, and recovery through participation in this event.	,650	
I can implement the things that I learned from this event.	,653	
My self-confidence increases in Facebook events.	,681	
I really feel good during the event.	,883	
I think this event is beneficial for the society.	,789	
Dimension2: Satisfaction		,702
I am pleased to have participated in recovery events of Seçil Tezgel on Facebook.	,701	
I think this event's being online, on Facebook is economically more suitable for me.	,689	
I think this event's being online, on Facebook saves time for me.	,653	
It is important for me to participate in this event.	,892	
I enjoy Facebook events as much as real-life events.	,782	
Dimension3: Effects of Social Media Environment		,769
I can easily adapt the event on Facebook.	,703	
I like participating in questionnaires and discussions on the event page.	,746	
I like sharing things with other participants. (I like their comments and I answer them)	,701	
It makes me feel happy when I see participants on Facebook.	,708	
It makes me feel confident when I see participants on Facebook.	,682	
Dimension4: Loyalty		,805
I recommend people around me to participate in this kind of events.	,643	
I will participate in this kind of events again.	,830	
I will mention about these events to my friends.	,796	

Linear regression analysis was made in order to determine how sub-dimensions of the event held on Facebook affect the perception of participants. Results of this regression analysis that was conducted to test the hypothesis of the study are as follows:

Table 5. Regression analysis

Independent Variables	Unstandardized Coefficients		Standardized Coefficients	t	Sig.
	B	Std. Error	Beta		
Social and Personal Effect	,278	,000	,316	7.310	,000
Satisfaction	,278	,000	,289	5.595	,000
Effects of Social Media	,278	,000	,363	8.074	,000
Loyalty	,167	,000	,264	9.309	,000

According to the results of multiple regression analyses that were aimed to explain the effects of sub-factors which are social and individual effect, satisfaction, social media effects and loyalty on total satisfaction and loyalty ($p < 0,01$), it is determined that sub-factors are substantially efficient. When Beta values that are standardized according to regression analysis, it is determined that Social and Individual effect ($\beta=0,316; p < 0,01$), Satisfaction ($\beta=0,289; p < 0,01$), Effects of Social Media ($\beta=0,363; p < 0,01$), Loyalty ($\beta=0,264; p < 0,01$) have effects on perception of participants.

CONCLUSION

Events that have been at the center of the social life for centuries is changing and developing each passing day. Especially through the developments in communication technologies, types of events and event management have acquired a new dimension; therefore, studying the dimensions of this new social media-based digital event world has become an obligation. Facebook stands out as a Virtual-On-line Event platform in terms of the abundance of participants and its being prevalent in social media-based digital events. The number of events held on Facebook is increasing each passing day. In relation to this, it is an important field of practice for both individual marketing and entertainment and commercial marketers.

There have been many studies conducted to analyses satisfaction and loyalties of event participants. The main reason underlying these studies' being conducted is to plan event management processes more systematically and to obtain positive outcomes (Cronin et al., 2000). However, both the structure of events and expectations of participants have changed through the development of technology and change of people's lifestyles. In particular, people focused on using their time more efficiently through modernization. Therefore, the number of events taking place on digital platforms is increasing day by day. At first, events organized on Facebook were more of a rendezvous but in time, these events have become the events in which people are active and in which participants invest both their time and money. Correspondingly, many factors affecting satisfaction of participants have appeared. In particular, values like harmonization of technology and humans, time and economy have come to the prominence.

Social media devices like Facebook, YouTube, and Twitter directly affect emotional commitment in the processes of event management and this emotional commitment again directly affects speeches on the event and thus, loyalty between the participant and the event develops organically. Emotional commitment to the event will provide the best opportunity to become different and will support new communication strategies to preserve loyalty between event managers and participants (Hudson et al., 2015). When the contents of "effects of social media" dimension which was determined within the scope of the research are analyzed, especially emotional sharing come to the forefront. Various emotional based factors like participants' sharing with other participants or feeling self-esteem when they see participants on Facebook directly influence the process. According to Lee et al. (2012), emotional sharing via social media influences both potential of participant and satisfaction of participant. Participants keep the interest to the event alive both before the festival and after it through the function of "follow us" on Twitter. Sharings about the event made on various social media devices also create a sustainable story of the event. The concept of multiple intelligence which was put forward by Jenkins (2010) with transmediatic story-telling model appears. Thus, events become platforms which constantly produce information and sharing beyond being a space in which time is spent.

This study aims to gauge and evaluate individual, technological and social effects of digital event world that developed through social media. Within the scope of the aims of this study, factor analyses and regression analyses were made in order to evaluate satisfaction and loyalty of participants in events that were held on social media. As a result of the factor analyses, it is determined that there are four sub-dimensions which are individual-social effect, effects of social media, loyalty, and satisfaction to describe and evaluate social media events. In order to determine the relationship between these four sub-dimensions, regression analyses were made, and it was determined that there are substantial relationships between each of the sub-dimensions. When the contents of these sub-dimensions were analyzed, it was seen that, different from conventional events, factors relating to Facebook and on-line platforms took an important place. This makes re-question of the relationship of events with places from the perspective of digitalization. The dimension of social-individual effects, which was defined within the scope of the study, contains within itself both contents in conventional events and contents relating to Facebook platform. For instance, while the answer to the question "I think this event is beneficial to the society" is sought in conventional events, the event organized on Facebook plays a role in the evaluation of the process. On the other hand, contents like "My self-esteem increases in the environment of the events organized on Facebook" assert a feature of the Facebook platform. Similarly, in addition to the attitudes researched in the studies evaluating conventional events, it was tried to determine attitudes which would reveal effects of social media and on-line platforms in question contents in the other sub-dimension.

Consequently, results of this study suggest that social media-based digital events provide satisfaction to the participants and affect their perceptions in the events. This result supports that this study will be a beneficial source for both sector professionals and individual users.

Further Research and Limitations

Both conventional and virtual events are generally realized by professional companies. However, the events realized on Facebook are at the initial stage in terms of professionalization process since they are quite new. Therefore, there are many difficulties in finding and researching pilot practices. Hence, the study is limited to a single study and the data are only acquired on the online platform.

This study can be a basis for many studies to be conducted. Event management on social webs can be profoundly researched particularly with scale development studies.

Experimental and theoretical studies can be conducted by using new research methods in the studies to be conducted in the future since the topic is quite new and there are not any studies in this area. For instance, events realized on social webs can be profoundly researched by using research methods of netnography and PAR (participatory action research).

REFERENCES

Akay, R. (2014). Etkinlik yönetimi uygulamalarinda yaratici rekabet ve sosyal medyanin entegrasyonu. *The Turkish Online Journal of Design, Art and Communication, 4*(4), 55–70. doi:10.7456/10404100/005

Argan, T. M., & Yüncü, D. (2015). *Etkinlik Pazarlama Yönetimi*. Istanbul: Detay Yayıncılık.

Arsmtrong, J. S. (2001). *Planning Special Events*. Indiana: Indiana University Center on Philanthrophy.

Carlson, N. (2010). At Last—The Full Story of How Facebook Was Founded. Business Insider. Retrieved from http://www.businessinsider.com/how-facebook-was-founded-2010-3

Cronin, J. J. Jr, Brady, M. K., & Hult, G. T. M. (2000). Assessing the effects of quality, value and customer satisfaction on consumer behavioral intentions in service environments. *Journal of Retailing, 76*(2), 193–218. doi:10.1016/S0022-4359(00)00028-2

Davis, F. (1989), *A Technology acceptance model for empirically testing new end user information systems: theory and results* [Doctoral Dissertation]. MIT Sloan School of Management.

Delamere, T. A., Wankel, L. M., & Hinch, T. D. (2001). Development of a scale to measure resident attitudes toward the social impacts of community festivals, Part I: Item generation and purification of the measure. *Event Management, 7*(1), 11–24. doi:10.3727/152599501108751443

Dunteman, G. H. (1989). *Principal component analysis (Quantitative applications in the social sciences)*. Beverly Hills, CA: Sage Publication.

Fishbein, M., & Ajzen, I. (1977). Belief, attitude, intention, and behavior: An introduction to theory and research. *Philosophy & Rhetoric, 10*(2), 130–132.

Gandhi-Arora, R., & Shaw, R. N. (2002). Visitor loyalty in sport tourism: An empirical investigation. *Current Issues in Tourism, 5*(1), 45–53. doi:10.1080/13683500208667907

Gedenk, K., & Neslin, S. A. (1999). The role of retail promotion in determining future brand loyalty: Its effect on purchase event feedback. *Journal of Retailing, 75*(4), 433–459. doi:10.1016/S0022-4359(99)00018-4

Getz, D. (2007). *Event Studies: Theory, Research and Policy for Planned Events*. Oxford: Elseiver Butterworth-Heinemann.

Goldblatt, J. (2010). *Special events: A new generation and the next frontier* (6th ed.). John Wiley & Sons.

Gwinner, K. P., & Eaton, J. (1999). Building brand image through event sponsorship: The role of image transfer. *Journal of Advertising, 28*(4), 47–57. doi:10.1080/00913367.1999.10673595

Halbwachs, M. (1992). *On Collective Memory*. University of Chicago Press.

Huang, C. (2011). Facebook and Twitter key to Arab Spring uprisings: report. *The National* (Vol. 6). Retrieved from http://www.thenational.ae/news/uae-news/facebook-and-twitter-key-to-arab-spring-uprisings-report

Hudson, S., Roth, M. S., Madden, T. J., & Hudson, R. (2015). The effects of social media on emotions, brand relationship quality, and word of mouth: An empirical study of music festival attendees. *Tourism Management*, *47*, 68–76. doi:10.1016/j.tourman.2014.09.001

Huyssen, A. (2003). *Present pasts: Urban palimpsests and the politics of memory*. Stanford University Press.

Jenkins, H. (2010). Transmedia storytelling and entertainment: An annotated syllabus. Continuum. *Journal of Media & Cultural Studies*, *24*(6), 943–958. doi:10.1080/10304312.2010.510599

Kaplan, A. M., & Haenlein, M. (2010). Users of the world, unite! The challenges and opportunities of Social Media. *Business Horizons*, *53*(1), 59–68. doi:10.1016/j.bushor.2009.09.003

Kim, S. S., & Petrick, J. F. (2005). Residents' perceptions on impacts of the FIFA 2002 World Cup: The case of Seoul as a host city. *Tourism Management*, *26*(1), 25–38. doi:10.1016/j.tourman.2003.09.013

Kim, W., Jun, H. M., Walker, M., & Drane, D. (2015). Evaluating the perceived social impacts of hosting large-scale sport tourism events: Scale development and validation. *Tourism Management*, *48*, 21–32. doi:10.1016/j.tourman.2014.10.015

Kim, Y. G., Suh, B. W., & Eves, A. (2010). The relationships between food-related personality traits, satisfaction, and loyalty among visitors attending food events and festivals. *International Journal of Hospitality Management*, *29*(2), 216–226. doi:10.1016/j.ijhm.2009.10.015

Lee, H. S., & Cho, C. H. (2012). Sporting event personality: Scale development and sponsorship implications. *International Journal of Sports Marketing & Sponsorship*, *14*(1), 46–63. doi:10.1108/IJSMS-14-01-2012-B005

Lee, W., Xiong, L., & Hu, C. (2012). The effect of Facebook users' arousal and valence on intention to go to the festival: Applying an extension of the technology acceptance model. *International Journal of Hospitality Management*, *31*(3), 819–827. doi:10.1016/j.ijhm.2011.09.018

Li, X., & Petrick, J. F. (2006). A review of festival and event motivation studies. *Event Management*, *9*(4), 239–245. doi:10.3727/152599506776771526

Liker, J. K., Haddad, G., & Karlin, J. (1999). Perspectives on technology and work organization. *Annual Review of Sociology*, *25*(1), 575–596. doi:10.1146/annurev.soc.25.1.575

Ma, W. W. K., Andersson, R., & Streith, K. O. (2005). Examining user acceptance of computer technology: An empirical study of student teachers. *Journal of Computer Assisted Learning*, *21*(6), 387–395.

Majchrzak, A., Rice, R. E., Malhotra, A., King, N., & Ba, S. (2000). Technology adaptation: The case of a computer-supported inter-organizational virtual team. *Management Information Systems Quarterly*, *24*(4), 569–600. doi:10.2307/3250948

Market Research Media. (n.d.). Retrieved from https://www.marketresearchmedia.com/?p=421

McLean, D. J. (2006). *Philosophy and Leisure. In G. Kassing (Eds.), Introduction to Recreation and Leisure*. United States: Human Kinetics.

Nicholson, R., & Pearce, D. G. (2000). Who goes to events: A comparative analysis of the profile characteristics of visitors to four south island events. *Journal of Vacation Marketing, 6*(3), 236–253. doi:10.1177/135676670000600304

Parasuraman, A., Zeithaml, V. A., & Berry, L. L. (1988). Servqual: A multiple-item scale for measuring consumer perc. *Journal of Retailing, 64*(1), 12.

Pew Research Center. (2015). Social media update 2014. Retrieved from http://www.pewinternet.org/2015/01/09/social-media-update-2014/

Pierce, R., Stacey, K., & Barkatsas, A. (2007). A scale for monitoring students' attitudes to learning mathematics with technology. *Computers & Education, 48*(2), 285–300. doi:10.1016/j.compedu.2005.01.006

Pira, A. (2004). *Etkinlik Yönetimi*. Istanbul: MediaCat Yayınları.

Pons, F., Mourali, M., & Nyeck, S. (2006). Consumer orientation toward sporting events scale development and validation. *Journal of Service Research, 8*(3), 276–287. doi:10.1177/1094670505283931

Rennie, K. M. (1997). Exploratory And Confirmatory Rotation Strategies in Exploratory Factor Analysis. *Paper presented at the Annual Meeting Of The Southwest Educational Research Association*. Academic Press. Retrieved from http://files.eric.ed.gov/fulltext/ED406446.pdf

Roche, M. (1994). Mega-events and urban policy. *Annals of Tourism Research, 21*(1), 1–19. doi:10.1016/0160-7383(94)90002-7

Rogers, M. (1999), *Boomers And Technogy: An Extended Conversation*. AARP. Retrieved from https://assets.aarp.org/www.aarp.org_/articles/computers/2009_boomers_and_technology_final_report.pdf

Rosen, L. D., Whaling, K., Carrier, L. M., Cheever, N. A., & Rokkum, J. (2013). The media and technology usage and attitudes scale: An empirical investigation. *Computers in Human Behavior, 29*(6), 2501–2511. doi:10.1016/j.chb.2013.06.006 PMID:25722534

Rothschild, P. C. (2011). Social media use in sports and entertainment venues. *International Journal of Event and Festival Management, 2*(2), 139–150. doi:10.1108/17582951111136568

Seyfi, M. (2017). *Dijital Etkinlik Yönetimi*. Istanbul: Der Yayınları.

Shone, A., & Parry, B. (2004). *Successful Event Management: A Practical Handbook*. Cengage Learning EMEA.

Stevens, J. P. (2012). *Applied multivariate statistics for the social sciences*. London: Routledge.

Tassiopoulus, D. (2005). *Events-An Introduction. Event Management: A Professional and Developmental Approach* (D. Tassiopoulus, Ed.). Lansdowne: Juta Academic.

Thüring, M., & Mahlke, S. (2007). Usability, aesthetics and emotions in human–technology interaction. *International Journal of Psychology, 42*(4), 253–264. doi:10.1080/00207590701396674

Woodward, J. (1965). *Industrial Organization: Theory And Practice*. London: Oxford University Press.

Xing, X., & Chalip, L. (2006). Effects of hosting a sport event on destination brand: A test of co-branding and match-up models. *Sport Management Review*, *9*(1), 49–78. doi:10.1016/S1441-3523(06)70019-5

Yürük, P., Akyol, A., & Şimşek, G. G. (2017). Analyzing the effects of social impacts of events on satisfaction and loyalty. *Tourism Management*, *60*, 367–378. doi:10.1016/j.tourman.2016.12.016

KEY TERMS AND DEFINITION

Digital Attitude: Attitudes may change according to the digital platform.

Digital Events: Digital events are classified as Technology-based Events, Virtual-On-line Events, and Transmediatic Events.

Diffusion of Innovation: Innovation is a process that continually renews itself.

Dynamic Structure: Versalite communication platforms.

Event Management: Event management is an applied science in which inter-disciplinary studies are used. It is a format that is continuously renewing and developing its practices through technology that is constantly changing and developing.

Modern-Day Events: Using today's technology in event management.

Social Media: Social media is critical platform in terms of the function it has; that is, it gives the opportunity to reach the individual directly and enables feedback from the individual.

This research was previously published in the Handbook of Research on Social Media Applications for the Tourism and Hospitality Sector; pages 149-163, copyright year 2020 by Business Science Reference (an imprint of IGI Global).

Chapter 10
Digital Moms:
Devices, Social Networking Sites, and Perceptions Towards Digital Marketing Strategies

Teresa Treviño
iD https://orcid.org/0000-0003-4993-3701
Universidad de Monterrey, Mexico

ABSTRACT

Given the rise of new technologies and the resultant changes in consumer behavior, marketing practices need to evolve, which requires organizations to rethink their strategies. Having a digital marketing strategy can establish a direct dialog with customers, thereby increasing knowledge about customers, suppliers, and partners, as well as building, consolidating, and maintaining brand awareness. However, little is known about the attitudes and perceptions of consumers toward popular digital marketing tools that can strategically be used in an integrated digital marketing strategy. Therefore, the objective of this research is to understand the perceptions of digital moms toward technology and digital marketing strategies. Following a qualitative and interpretative approach, the results contribute to the literature by (1) addressing the symbolic meanings that technological tools have in the lives of this group of consumers and (2) providing insights on how different digital marketing strategies commonly implemented by brands are perceived by digital moms.

INTRODUCTION

Presently, our social world is going digital. New technologies and tools are changing the way we communicate, interact, and have relationships with others. Consumers around the world are becoming more connected by owning several devices that allow continuous Internet access, enabling them to communicate, find information, make purchases, and interact with brands. This phenomenon, called the "mobile lifestyle," has changed many aspects around companies and brands; therefore, many interesting opportunities arise from these changes.

DOI: 10.4018/978-1-6684-6287-4.ch010

As a first step, managers must understand these changes, and it becomes relevant to analyze the meaning that new technological tools have in consumers' lives. It is well known that people assign meanings to the objects they own; therefore, we can expect something almost similar to occur for digital tools and technology itself. In the past, research has questioned whether new technological tools carry symbolic meanings (Trevino, Lengel, & Daft, 1987). Understanding such meanings and roles in today's context can contribute to a better comprehension of the audiences of brands in the online environment as a prerequisite for successful brand performance (Singh & Sonnenburg, 2012).

From a marketing perspective, it is interesting to understand different online audiences to implement better digital marketing strategies that appeal to a specific target. In Mexico, previous literature has suggested that several groups of Internet users can be classified based on demographics and psychographic characteristics such as teens, executives, silver surfers, and digital moms (IAB México & Millward Brown, 2014). In this chapter, the digital moms' segment will be analyzed, considering that research has recognized this segment to have important implications for online marketing strategies (Treviño, 2017).

Furthermore, with the rise of information and communication technologies (ICTs), marketing practices have also been evolving in response to changes in consumer behavior, and this change requires organizations to rethink their strategies. It is well known that companies are seeking to establish long-term relationships with their customers now require a digital marketing strategy. Previous literature has found that companies report several benefits of having a digital marketing strategy. For example, it helps establish a direct dialog with the customer and increases knowledge about customers, suppliers, and partners. It further assists in building, consolidating, maintaining brand awareness, as well as improving the overall communication process (Tiago & Veríssimo, 2014). Considering the importance of this topic, literature addressing the impact of such marketing efforts is insufficient. Specifically, there is an opportunity to understand how consumers perceive the different digital marketing strategies such as social networking sites, email marketing, search engine optimization (SEO), search engine marketing (SEM), and website design. Research on such topics can help managers develop suitable digital marketing strategies.

Therefore, the objective of this research is to understand the perceptions of digital moms toward technology and digital marketing strategies. Particularly, the results contribute to the literature by (a) addressing the symbolic meanings that technological tools have in the lives of this group of consumers, and (b) providing insights on how digital moms perceive different digital marketing strategies commonly implemented by brands.

The following chapter is structured as follows. First, a description of the digital mom segment as Internet users is provided to understand the context of this study. Next, the literature on the symbolic meanings of technology is addressed. Then, common digital marketing strategies are presented and described as a basis for this research. The methodology employed and results obtained is described. Finally, the chapter concludes with discussing some implications for theory and practice as well as analyzing limitations and possible future research on the topic.

Digital Moms as Internet Users in Mexico

There are 71.5 million Internet users in Mexico, and 44% are between the age group of 12 and 25 years. Research has found several important Internet user groups that are classified regarding their activities and lifestyles, such as the teens, executives, silver surfers, and digital moms (Treviño, 2017; Treviño & Morton, 2016; IAB México & Millward Brown, 2014). The teen segment is interesting as it is comprised young users between 13 and 18 years of age and who use the Internet daily for approximately two to five hours (IAB México & Millward Brown, 2014a). Executive users are employees, staff, and middle managers who surf the Internet on most mobile devices (IAB México & Millward Brown, 2014b).

The silver surfer's segment is Internet users older than 50 years of age, and despite their slow acceptance of new technologies, are progressively active online and enjoy informative websites, travel sites, and other e-commerce sites related to clothes, personal items, and luxury articles (Treviño & Morton, 2016).

Finally, a segment that is increasingly important today is the digital moms' group. This group comprises women who have children younger than 12 years (or older but still living at home), daily spend approximately six hours online, and own several digital devices such as smartphones, tablets, laptops, and desktops (Treviño & Morton, 2016, IAB México, Treviño & Pineda, 2017). Many companies and brands target this group of Internet users because they make frequent online purchases, is very active on social networking sites, search for information, and communicate online. Research has recognized that the digital moms' segment has important implications for online marketing strategies. For example, it is known that digital moms use the Internet to make online recommendations and reviews, as well as to follow brands on social media. This group of online users also enjoys making online purchases and searching for discounts coupons online (Treviño, 2017). Based on the above information, this chapter focuses on understanding the digital moms' segment regarding the symbolic meanings they attach to the technology they own and use. Furthermore, the author intends to shed light on how digital moms perceive the different digital marketing strategies commonly used by brands, in an attempt to obtain knowledge that helps companies implement more engaging strategies.

Technology and Its Symbolic Meaning

Defining technology is important for the understanding of this research. Technology can be defined in a broad sense as the objects, tools, or machines created and used by people to enhance life (Calvert & Terry, 2013). The knowledge behind creating those objects and designing them to perform specific functions can also be considered as technology (Brooks, 1973). However, a more contemporary approach to defining technology is one that considers the relationships between machines, users, and designers. For purposes of this research, technology will be addressed based on Calvert and Terry's (2013) view of considering technology as situated within networked social relations and its use and creative misuse by people. Through this approach, it is assumed that technology has to be understood based on its particular context of design and use.

Today, the rise of different ICTs has provided society with many new communication options. Specifically, the term ICT comprises different communication technologies, such as computer hardware and software, the Internet, wireless networks, cell phones, email, instant messaging, and video-conferencing (TechTerms.com, 2010). ICTs also compose many online tools and word-of-mouth forums such as discussion boards, blogs, consumer product rating websites, and social networking sites such as Facebook and Twitter (Mangold & Faulds, 2009). These ICTs affect the lives of consumers', as through its use they communicate with others, look for information, evaluate, and make various decisions. In general, this phenomenon includes people with the desire to connect, and therefore new interactive technologies and online economies grow and evolve at a fast pace. Considering that technological evolution has brought significant changes in consumers' lives, it becomes interesting to understand what it means to them and how they perceive such tools. By addressing these pointers from a marketing perspective, companies can obtain knowledge as to why people choose one medium over another, as well as why they react differently to digital marketing strategies.

For this purpose, the framework of symbolic interactionism can be relevant as it views society as a dynamic network of communication and understands interactions concerning the meanings people assign to things (Trevino, Lengel, & Daft, 1987). This theoretical approach focuses on understanding the relationship between shared meanings (i.e., symbols) and verbal and non-verbal actions and communications (i.e., interactions) (LaRossa & Reitzes, 1993). More specifically, Blumer (1969) identified three core principles that shed light on this theory: (a) people act toward things and each other based on the meanings they have assigned for them; (b) the meanings come from social interactions with others; and (c) these meanings are managed and transformed by an interpretative process that allows people to make sense of their social worlds. By expanding Blumer's initial principles, it is also relevant to recognize that the symbols and meanings that objects have are embedded in the existing cultural and organizational contexts (Snow, 2001).

When analyzing media choices, the symbolic interactionism approach may be useful in understanding why people use specific technological tools and communication mediums. If every object can be considered a symbol, and therefore, has a meaning, then it is possible to question whether the new technological tools carry symbolic cues (Trevino, Lengel, & Daft, 1987). In sum, it is known that people assign meanings to the objects they own. Therefore, we can expect something almost similar to occur for digital tools and technology itself. Understanding such meanings and roles in today's context can contribute to a better comprehension of the audiences of brands in the online environment as it is a prerequisite for a successful brand performance (Singh & Sonnenburg, 2012).

New Technologies and Digital Marketing Strategies

With the rise of ICTs, marketing practices have also been evolving, causing considerable changes in consumer behavior that require organizations to rethink their strategies. Previous literature has found that companies report several benefits of having digital marketing strategies. For example, it establishes a direct dialog with the customer, increases knowledge about customers, suppliers, and partners, as well as builds, consolidates, maintains brand awareness, and improves the overall communication process (Tiago & Veríssimo, 2014).

However, little is known about the attitudes and perceptions of consumers toward popular digital marketing tools that can be strategically used in an integrated digital marketing strategy. Particularly, it has been found that most investments for the total online marketing budget go into social networking strategies followed by email, paid search, and SEO in that order (Tiago & Veríssimo, 2014). For such reasons, the present chapter will address the following: (a) social networking sites; (b) website design and usability; (c) SEO; (d) SEM; and (e) email marketing. In the next section, these activities will be analyzed as a basis for the present research.

Social Networking Sites

Social networking sites (SNSs) are characterized as interactive media, enabling two-way communication rather than one-directional as in traditional media (Lee & Cho, 2011). These technologies have been designed to be socially oriented to share content, interests, and interact with other members. SNSs are not only used for entertainment; previous research has proven that consumers also take advantage of SNSs to discuss brand experiences and preferences (Araujo & Neijens, 2012).

Through the Internet messages in SNSs can be shared and exchanged at any time, resulting in important implications for marketing and consumer behavior research and practice. For example, people now use this technology to obtain information, evaluate products and services, make purchases, and recommend them to others. A consumer behavior survey on the topic found that 72% of participants had used information on Facebook to make retail and restaurant decisions, and 50% of respondents had tried a new brand because of a recommendation found in SNSs (Empathica, n.d.). It is evident that this online communication between consumers' influences organizations and the overall market. Previous research on this topic has suggested that consumers trust brand pages in SNSs, and more importantly, they consider these pages to influence their purchase decisions (Araujo & Neijens, 2012). As a result, companies are beginning to identify SNSs' tools as an opportunity to conduct several marketing activities. Specifically, this new channel of communication is being used to promote services and/or products. The different abilities of SNSs, such as the creation of groups of people who share the same interests, geolocation technologies, and the integration of applications, make them unique for marketing, advertising, and communication.

Considering the frequent use of SNSs, it becomes interesting to understand this mediums role in consumers' lives as a basis for implementing marketing strategies.

SEO

Search engines, such as Google and Bing, are very important information sources for customers, especially, when they need new products or services. They are useful to search for details, compare prices, analyze customer reviews, and even make purchases. It has been found that many customers use search engines as a starting point for surfing the Internet; therefore, search engines can be considered as a link between users and websites (Baye, De los Santos, & Wildenbeest, 2016).

Concerning marketing, being on top of the organic search engine results is relevant as it has been proven that higher ranking results and more frequent appearance of a website in the search result list can generate more clicks on a company's website (Park, Yu, Yu, & Liao, 2015). Particularly, it is known that users rarely click on links beyond the first search results page; therefore, increasing the search engine ranking is now essential to business success (Sen, 2005; Gudivada, Rao, & Paris, 2015).

The digital marketing technique that works to improve visibility in search engines is SEO. SEO's main objective is to optimize a website in a way that the company receives more organic traffic through searches on search engines as it is based on the premise that more clicks translate into more sales.

Appearing in the organic results in Google depends on several factors and the exact algorithm that Google uses to determine a website's ranking is not known completely; however, the website's relevance to the search query made by a user may be the starting point. In this way, keyword results are crucial for an SEO strategy. In other words, marketers should ensure that the website includes the relevant keywords on all elements of the site, such as the page title, the meta description, head tags, body text, anchor text in links, and alt text in images. Additionally, site quality and brand awareness also impact search engine rankings, since users tend to click on websites that are more trusted, recognized, and have an overall positive reputation (Baye, De los Santos, & Wildenbeest, 2016).

SEM

When a user visits a search engine, he or she enters a specific search query and receives results that are divided into organic and sponsored listings. The organic results are ranked according to relevance and other factors considered by a "secret" algorithm. As previously mentioned, organic rankings can be improved based on several factors and a well-planned SEO strategy. When firms do not have a good organic ranking on search engines, one alternative is to implement an SEM campaign to place ads on the sponsored results. SEM, also known as "paid search" or "pay-per-click" (PPC) advertising, targets customers by placing ads on search engines when users search for specific keywords. A paid search campaign is different from other traditional advertising campaigns because companies are charged only when users click on an ad and not on the number of impressions. Furthermore, when planning a new PPC campaign, companies must select keywords that users might search for when requiring their products or services. Next, advertisers bid on those selected keywords to have them appear alongside the organic search engine results.

SEM is a good option for online companies as it is very easy to set up and can generate important traffic to a company's website (Boughton, 2005). More importantly, this traffic is generally interested in a company's offering because SEM delivers ads to users who are already searching for the product or service (Boughton, 2005). Ad placement depends on several factors. First, search engines consider the bid for each keyword. In other words, the more a company is willing to pay per click, the higher the ad placement on the sponsored results. Just as in organic results, generally, higher rankings translate into greater traffic. Furthermore, Google also considers keyword relevance with the ad and ad relevance with the landing page to assign a quality score that will also determine ad placement. Therefore, Google provides an incentive for companies to bid only on relevant keywords, to write targeted ads, and to direct users to relevant landing pages (Boughton, 2005).

SEM is one of the fastest growing digital marketing tools in the industry as more companies are investing in this strategy to reach potential customers, as online search volume grows rapidly (Sen, 2005; Dou, Lim, Su, Zhou, & Cui, 2010).

Email Marketing

Email marketing can be defined as a form of direct marketing that uses electronic mail to communicate commercial messages to an audience (Fariborzi & Zahedifard, 2012). This digital marketing tool is one of the oldest, and it has proven to be beneficial for companies despite the high number of junk or spam emails, as it provides a direct communication channel with customers (Ryan, 2016). Email marketing has been considered the most cost-effective digital marketing tool for acquisition and retention due to the low cost of sending large numbers of emails and the high response rates obtained. In other words, email marketing has the highest return on investment among other marketing tools (Jenkins, 2008; Fariborzi & Zahedifard, 2012).

Among the benefits that email marketing affords to companies, the possibility of building a direct interaction with customers that work to establish a long-term relationship with them is one. Additionally, with email marketing, companies can easily measure the success of their marketing efforts by tracking information about the number of emails sent, open rates, click rates, best days, and times to send campaigns, among others (Fariborzi & Zahedifard, 2012).

Some of the disadvantages of email marketing relate to the volume of emails received by people each day; thus, there is the risk that a company's email could become lost in a full inbox or even get classified as spam. For these reasons, research has focused on determining the factors that can increase the open rate of emails. First, customers will welcome regular emails regarding of brands they recognize and from which they are expecting to receive communication. Second, if customers identify that a certain company will always provide valuable content, then there is more probability of having higher open rates (Ryan, 2016). Additionally, research has suggested the importance of personalization of emails, for example, adding consumer-specific information such as the recipient's name. It has been found that by personalizing emails, the probability of the recipient opening it increases by 20%, sales increase by 31%, and the number of users unsubscribing from the email newsletter reduces by 17% (Sahni, Wheeler, & Chintagunta, 2018).

In sum, email marketing has been regarded as a valuable marketing tool that delivers short messages with a clear value proposition and a call to action for users. Popular email marketing campaign objectives include attracting potential customers, persuading them to repurchase, building loyalty and preference, and announcing or reminding about special events or news (Carmen & Nicolae, 2010).

Website Design

Despite the increasing use of other online tools by companies—especially SNSs—having a well-planned website is still crucial for most organizations. In fact, all the digital marketing techniques we reviewed previously in this chapter are basically designed to drive traffic to the website. It is important to understand that the purpose of the website is to convert received traffic into leads or customers that will ultimately result in actual profits. These conversions will only be possible if the website serves the customer by enhancing the consumer's experience with the brand and does not only provide information about the company.

Website design is a digital marketing technique that should not be discounted, that is, when planning the content, structure, and "look and feel" of their website, companies should always bear in mind the conversion goals being pursued. For example, a conversion objective can be an actual transaction when the customer makes an online purchase or a subscription to the email newsletter, submits a question, or the download of a whitepaper from the website (Ryan, 2016).

Overall, the user experience that a company provides through their website is one of the main determinants to drive conversion. It is also crucial to design the company's website with the target market in mind to achieve a successful user experience. Identifying what customers will want while surfing the website can be the first step when starting the design or redesign process (Ryan, 2016). Furthermore, web usability also impacts user experience as it focuses on delivering a simple and easy-to-use design. The theory of web usability suggests that websites should be designed in a way that users can find the information they are looking for and accomplish their goals effortlessly.

Research on website design has suggested several factors that determine a successful website. Particularly, meta-analyses of papers related to website design have found that information quality/business content, ease-of-use /navigation efficiency, page loading speed/responsiveness, visual appearance, security, personalization, and marketing/customer focus are the major categories that make a website successful (Gehrke & Turban, 1999; Park & Gretzel, 2007). Furthermore, studies have also suggested that the design of a website can be divided into visual, navigational, and informational dimensions. If this is not planned sufficiently, it could lead to consumer irritation and feelings of discomfort (Hasan,

2016). Other research on this topic identified that the general content and appearance of the website are two factors that ranked as most important for users and significantly impact behavior. Interestingly, the overall evaluation of the website is influenced by the perceptions of web design quality. These results imply that the appearance of a website is highly important for users as it will determine their overall evaluations and lead to higher usage intentions (Al-Qeisi, Dennis, Alamanos, & Jayawardhena, 2014).

Taking this into consideration, website design can be regarded as an important technique for a successful digital marketing strategy. Considering that companies are investing in digital marketing strategies by implementing a mix of the different tools described above, it is important to understand how customers perceive such strategies and the attitudes they have toward them.

Methodology

The choice of method is a crucial step in any research project. Choosing a method depends on the goal of the investigation, the nature of the phenomenon, and the level of theoretical maturity (Smith, 1983; Bryman, 1984; Edmonson & McManus, 2007). Given that the phenomenon of interest requires a deep understanding of the meanings and perceptions that consumers give to digital marketing strategies, a qualitative methodology was used as it seemed appropriate. Furthermore, the digital marketing literature is scant and can be classified as "nascent-phase," particularly from the customer's perspective, for exploring perceptions and attitudes toward companies' online marketing strategies. Therefore, through qualitative methods researchers can discover the meanings of consumers' actions (Hudson & Ozzane, 1988; Healy et al., 2007).

Data Collection

The data collection process was divided into two phases (Figure 1). Phase one included four focus groups and five in-depth interviews conducted by the author in late 2014 and early 2015. Furthermore, Phase 2 included twenty in-depth interviews and two focus groups conducted by a group of four marketing students supervised by the author (Tables 1 and 2). The data of the second phase were collected in early 2018. The analysis of data collected at different periods allows the researcher to understand the phenomenon more deeply since the author contains five years' worth of data on the digital moms' segment and their online behavior. Furthermore, the triangulation of data derived using several methods is useful to ensure the validity and credibility of the research (Miles & Huberman, 1994).

Sample

Considering that research on digital marketing mainly focuses on teens and millennials as their subjects, this research intends to shed light on another relevant consumer group for the marketing literature: the digital moms. As previously discussed, these online users show notable implications for branding, consumer behavior, and marketing strategy. Therefore, to be included in this study, women must meet the following criteria: (a) have children who live at home; (b) use the Internet daily; (c) own at least one device with Internet access; and (d) maintain at least one active account on a social networking site, chat forum, blog, or any other communication forum on the web. Participants were chosen through convenience and snowball sampling (Miles & Huberman, 1994; Flick, 2009).

Figure 1. Research phases

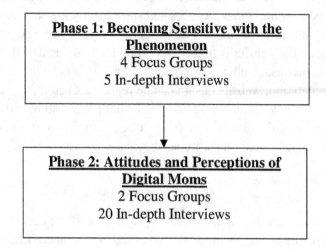

RESULTS

As women become mothers, they experience life differently. Being responsible for another individual who requires constant attention demands a considerable amount of time and effort. Participants of the present research take their "mom" role very seriously; therefore, they perform their activities and interests in their free time. Findings suggest that the Internet and the different tools used for accessing it represent an important part of their daily activities. It is known that consumers choose to use and buy products not only for the functional attributes but also for the meanings they convey (Belk, 1988). By considering these factors, several symbolic meanings of the digital technological tools were derived from the narratives of participants. This facilitated the researcher to understand the context of each mother (Table 3).

Symbolic Meanings of the Internet and Devices

Security: Being Available

One of the most recurrent themes that participants refer to when talking about technological tools and devices they use is security. Mothers reflected on the fact that possessing a smartphone helps them feel more secure when leaving home, as well as at other times because it allows them to be in touch with their family and friends. Older mothers find this issue paradoxical as the lack of such technology during their adolescence did not prevent them from feeling secure. However, nowadays, they find it difficult to leave the house without their smartphones. For example, two participants comment on how the smartphone helps them feel more secure in critical times and how they still believe they are safer if they can be reached:

Look, in 2009, when the city began to be unsafe, it is amazing how the cellphone helped you feel a little safer, then, it is something that remained. (It helped me) by being communicated... (Maricela, 40)

When I forget my cellphone... oh my God, what if something happens? So, I go back for it (the cell phone)... really, I see the telephone as a means for security... (Carolina, 30)

Table 1. Demographics of focus group participants

Name	Age	Occupation	Kids
Phase I			
Group 1			
Alejandra	46	Sales agent	3
Rosario	44	Sales agent	3
Sandra	47	Own business	3
Josefa	48	Insurance agent	3
Yolanda	33	Entrepreneur	2
Group 2			
Ana	41	Home keeper	3
Irene	42	Home keeper	3
Maruca	48	Student	2
Juliana	40	Home keeper	2
María	52	Home keeper	2
Group 3			
Carolina	30	Employee	2
Elisa	33	Home keeper	1
Mirna	29	Graphic designer	1
María del Rosario	26	Home keeper	1
Group 4			
Teresa	30	Home keeper	2
Karla	32	Teacher	2
Paula	33	Employee	1
Isabel	32	Home keeper	3
Gaby	29	Teacher	2
Phase II			
Group 1			
Susana	35	Home keeper	2
Saralicia	31	Home keeper	1
Ailin	31	Home keeper	2
Fernanda	34	Own business	5
CatalinaD	27	Own business	1
Group 2			
AnaGeorgina	32	Home keeper	2
Mislene	35	Home keeper	1
Michelle	35	Own business	4
Georgina	31	Artist	3
Lynette	42	Real estate	2
Lyu	38	Own business	2

Table 2. Demographics of in-depth interview participants

Name	Age	Occupation	Kids
Phase I			
Claudia	40	Home keeper	2
NancyM	36	Employee	2
Maricela	40	Teacher	3
Gina	32	Home keeper	3
NancyS	41	Home keeper	3
Phase II			
MarianaV	29	Own business	1
MarianaG	32	Own business	1
Catalina	33	Own business	3
RosaMaría	46	Architect	2
Liliana	45	Home keeper	3
Cynthia	44	Home keeper	2
DanielaD	30	Own business	1
Gabriela	35	Own business	2
Maridy	33	Lawyer	1
Myriam	32	Employee	1
Tatiana	32	Own business	1
AnaSofia	31	Home keeper	2
Ana	37	Own business	2
Alma	28	Home keeper	1
Verónica	46	Own business	2
MarianaM	37	Own business	4
DanielaF	40	Own business	2
Teresa	28	Employee	1
Mayerling	31	Employee	1
AnaSylvia	30	Own business	2

Maricela's and Carolina's narratives are examples of how the cellphone has become a security medium in their daily routine. Being available for others and knowing that they can communicate with their family at any given moment translates into a calming sense of security given the unsafe environment in which they feel they live.

Control: Parental Tool

Another implication of possessing devices with Internet access is family control. This is, in fact, related to the security feeling previously described, but is further directed toward other family members, especially the children. Mothers refer to IT devices, such as smartphones and tablets, as tools that help them with some childcare tasks. IT allows parents to monitor their children in different ways, which mothers translate into a control feeling that they like and need. This symbolic meaning was present for both mothers with young and older children. Younger mothers benefit from video calls to monitor their children when they are alone with the nanny. It serves as a good way to observe what the child is doing and how he or she is being treated:

When we have to go out (of the house), we leave them with our domestic employee, but we call them on FaceTime... 'how are you, are you going to bed now'? [...] So, everything is via FaceTime, 'let me see what you are doing, turn around the camera to see who is with you.' (Juliana, 40)

For older mothers, smartphones offer other ways to help them monitor their teenagers or young adults. For example, María reflects on how she sometimes needs to look for her son when he does not answer at night:

I have an application called Friends because I have a 23-year-old boy that likes to go out at night, so... most of the time he forgets to tell me where is he going, so I see the Friends app, and the GPS tells me where he is... 'oh, ok, he is at his friend's house.'(María, 52)

The sense of control that smartphones provide to mothers can be suggested by the previous examples provided by Juliana and María. It is interesting how IT devices have also translated into a parental tool that they find useful to keep track of their children, despite their age.

Dependence: Connected 24/7

A third meaning found within the participants' narratives was the need to be connected at all times and the dependence they have developed for these devices. Digital moms find it difficult to leave their devices and daily Internet access, even when on vacation. Additionally, this dependence is likened to specific behaviors, such as expecting them and other people to answer their messages and calls immediately and to assume that what is shared on SNSs is known by everyone. Even though they admit that this dependence on Internet access may sometimes stress them, it is something that they cannot live without.

It creates me a conflict, and I realize it now that I just went on vacation... It is sad...you are at the beach, which such a divine view, and you can see everyone sitting, with their iPhones... but, we are at the beach! [...] we went on vacations, and we were all with our iPhones, at morning, at evening, and night. In the past, when you went on vacations, you did not need it (the iPhone) that was the last thing you thought about... (Juliana, 40)

Juliana's example indicates how even on vacations she experiences dependence on her smartphones; however, a desperation feeling is also present when lacking an Internet connection:

It happens to me that when I go to the United States, they tell me at home, you have to turn off your Data Roaming, because it is very expensive, and so and so... When I am at McAllen or any other part of the USA, I am desperate looking for a place with Wi-Fi so I can communicate. (María, 52)

Mothers who participated in this study reflected on how they were aware that this dependence is sometimes not justified, particularly when they feel desperation and anxiety to find Internet access even if they are not expecting an important call. However, they accepted this form of communication as inevitable as it is now part of their daily lives.

Adaptation/Change: The Challenge to Keep Up With IT

The use of digital technology also symbolizes adaptation and change for digital moms. In their narratives, it is evident how, despite being active users of technology and devices with Internet access, they still struggle to keep up each new generation of IT and do not consider themselves to be tech-savvy. Hence, participants reflected on how they have to try to understand new technologies and how to use them to not become obsolete in this rapidly changing world.

For example, one participant reflects the struggle in adopting new technology:

We need to change with the technological advance, and that change is difficult to me... because I didn´t live it, I am not used to this change...and my kids are all the time with that (technology) [...] they were born that way, in this new era... and I have a hard time accepting this, so this is a conflict between my kids and me. (Irene, 42)

Additionally, participants commented that this change has also influenced the tools they use in their homes. As technology becomes increasingly mobile, many devices in the home become obsolete. For example, traditional landline telephones are becoming less common as more people own personal mobile phone and can be reached in this manner. In the same manner, the home computer, or desktop, is also becoming obsolete as household members have access to a laptop, tablet, or smartphone.

In fact, I have nine months without a telephone in my home because it is no longer needed... everything is by cell phone. You do not use the cellphone that much actually to make calls. Everything is now via WhatsApp. (Sandra, 47)

The computer in my house is now obsolete because everything we do is in the iPad or iPhone. (Juliana, 40)

These examples suggest that mothers are also coping with technological advance. The home telephone, where all members of the family received phone calls to the same number, is practically obsolete as personal mobile devices allow direct contact at any time. Additionally, a similar phenomenon is occurring with the desktop computer, which was used as a family computer, and is now being replaced by laptops or tablets owned by individual members in the family. The symbolic meanings that these cultural and technological changes bring to mothers include the struggle to adapt and keep up with the latest generation of technology, even though they use and enjoy their current IT.

Perception of Digital Marketing Tools

This research also attempts to understand how digital moms perceive companies' different online marketing efforts by analyzing the most common digital marketing tools: (a) advertising on SNSs; (b) SEO;

(c) SEM; (d) email marketing; and (e) website design. In the next section, results about digital moms' perceptions are presented.

Table 3. Symbolic Meanings of Technological Tools

Meaning	Description
Technological Tools	
Security	Feeling secure by the possession of the device
Control	Family control by monitoring children's activities
Dependence	The necessity of being connected at all times
Adaptation/Change	Keeping pace with the new generation IT

Source: Author

Advertising on SNSs

Digital moms reported as being active on Facebook, Instagram, Twitter, Pinterest, and YouTube. Particularly, Facebook is the platform where they search for information on new products, services, and brands in general. Furthermore, they trust Facebook's company pages because they can contact brands directly, look for reviews, and form communities with other customers. As some participants commented:

Nowadays, I believe it is an advertising medium [Facebook], I do not know if it is the strongest medium, but I believe so... I get to learn about things, like concerts and all that stuff, by social networks... or promotions, for example, HEB sometimes advertises in their social networks about the Halloween promotion...2X1...well, you take advantage of this, right? (Claudia, 40)

Some [Facebook brand pages] have helped me as a mother...For example, when I was breastfeeding [...] I did not understand how (to breastfeed). So, I went to the Facebook page of the brand "Liga de la Leche." each time I had questions, I consulted this page. It was great. (Paula, 33)

Furthermore, Instagram is used by moms to be informed about news, products, and services. Participants reported following international accounts. Instagram was also reported as being useful in learning about small and local business, as many new companies use advertising on Instagram in the form of paid ads, as well as through local influencers.

[I use Instagram to learn about] more local things. I have learned about places (restaurants and stores), and I have tried them because of their advertising on Instagram.(Teresa, 28)

Digital moms have mixed attitudes toward social network advertising. For example, it was found that Facebook's right column advertising is perceived negatively and that participants rarely click or respond to such ads. On the contrary, Facebook's newsfeed ads and Instagram's paid ads and influencer marketing were found to have a positive overall perception among participants. As two moms commented:

The worst thing that they can do to me is that they show me the ads on the right [of the screen, in Face-book], I cannot stand it! (Maricela, 40)

I feel that sometimes [the advertising] gives me the opportunity to get to know new things that are related to my interests. I would say that what I see in the ads are things that I like.(Alma, 28)

SEO

True to expectations, organic results that appear in the top positions are given higher credibility by participants. Digital moms in this study reported that they preferred clicking on the first results on the organic section once they make a search query. As one participant mentioned:

I feel that the first result [on the search results page] is the only one correct.(Rosa María, 46)

Furthermore, results suggest that besides the position of the website on the results page, the content is also important for clicking a link. Participants reported that they first read the title of the link and then read the description about the website they intend to visit. With this information, they form a perception about the results and finally decide which website to visit. This highlights the importance of a good SEO strategy that includes using keywords with a relevant header, meta-descriptions, and a display URL. One participant reflected on the process through which she selects a link on the search results page:

I read the title first; then I read a little bit about what is under the title [the meta description]. (Mayerling, 31)

SEM

Interestingly, participants in this study recognized that the search results page is divided into two sections: the organic results and the sponsored results. They can identify whether a result link is an advertising link or not and, in general, they reported a negative attitude toward sponsored results. Digital moms are good users of technology and are frequent users of the Internet. For these reasons, even though they do not understand exactly how SEM works—as in who pays whom and when—they recognize that companies are paying to appear on the sponsored section of the results page of a search engine. As one participant mentioned:

I do not like to click on the sponsored results because those are the ones [companies] are paying for, so they are not necessarily the most popular results, so I do not trust them. (Myriam, 32)

Website Design

Digital moms use SNSs, such as Facebook and Instagram, almost as search engines to look for new products and services. However, they reported that when they find a company they are interested in through these SNSs, they sometimes visit their official website to look for further information. A company's website is rated by digital moms based on the design and overall look and feel. Consistent with previous research on the topic, a poor design can lead participants to abandon the website.

Furthermore, the usability is also important: digital moms reported that in general, they look for simple and easy-to-use sites. Additionally, if the website is an e-commerce site, meaning that users can purchase products, then digital moms look for good-quality images regarding size and zoom options to analyze the product, detailed descriptions, and reviews by other customers. As one participant mentioned:

When I visit a website, if I do not like what I see and inspire me, I close it and look for another one. (Teresa, 28)

Email Marketing

Finally, email marketing was also analyzed to understand participants' perceptions toward this digital media strategy. In general, it was found that digital moms believe that receiving too many emails from a company is annoying. If they receive many emails with advertising by brands every day in their inbox, they have mixed feelings toward this kind of digital marketing strategy. Participants reported to rarely open emails from companies and that this was only when they intended to make a purchase and they recall receiving an email from such brand.

When I have a specific need, when I am going to buy, let say kid's clothes, I open [the emails] from kids' brands. (Mariana M, 37)

You know, I do like it (to receive emails from brands) because, you can say, I received today something but I do not need it today, so I delete it (it does not matter)... but sometimes, there are things that I am looking for, and I go and check (the inbox)... Groupon, Kidzania, or others, I say, let me check what I have. (Then I decide.)(Irene, 42)

This finding suggests that email marketing can be good for brand awareness even though this cus-tomer segment does not open the received email regularly, they are aware of the brands in their inbox and return to them when needed (Table 4).

Table 4. Attitudes toward digital marketing tools

Digital Marketing Tool	Digital Moms' Attitude
Social networking site advertising	Participants generally have positive attitudes toward ads on social media except for Facebook right column ads.
Search engine optimization	Participants value and have positive attitudes toward the first organic results on search engines.
Search engine marketing	Participants show a negative attitude toward paid ads on the results page of search engines.
Website design and usability	Participants value and have positive attitudes toward a well-designed website that is easy to navigate.
Email marketing	Participants have a generally positive attitude toward emails received by brands, but only open them when they have a specific need for a product or brand.

Source: Author

DISCUSSION AND CONCLUSION

There is evidence to suggest that consumers attach meanings to different IT tools and devices. On the one hand, devices have several attached meanings such as security, family control, dependence, and adaptation. Digital moms feel a sense of security by having a smartphone as it enables them to contact or be contacted by family and friends. The security feeling is also related to dependence on IT devices and technology itself. Results indicate that there is an urge to be connected at all times and people also expect to obtain an immediate response from others. This can lead to a vicious circle, starting with the fear of feeling insecure, which in turn increases the use of mobile devices to feel safe. Regular usage of these devices increases our abilities as well, and we get used to this easy and rapid form of communication. This phenomenon is common in today's society as the fear of not having access to our smartphone and devices can be found in other segments of the population as well.

Additionally, there is now a term that addresses this situation: "nomophobia." Nomophobia refers to "no-mobile-phone phobia" and describes extreme dependence on one's smartphone. For this research particularly, the dependence expressed by participants stems from the desire to achieve excellence in all mom-related activities throughout the day as well as being reachable and reaching others at any given moment. It is interesting to question whether women are more prone to developing dependence or addiction to mobile phones than men, as women have a greater propensity to communicate with others and to develop affective relationships.

New forms of communication are drastically different from the traditional ones. Consumers have now replaced telephone calls with instant messages. Therefore, some protocols, such as invitations, announcements, and notifications that once were sent via physical letters, have been replaced by WhatsApp messages and social networking messages and alerts. Additionally, IT devices also represent a means of family control by digital moms as they take advantage of the available technologies to monitor their children. Tools such as video calls and GPS (Global Positioning System) monitoring allow them to keep track of their children's activities throughout the day. Finally, despite digital moms being active users of technology, they still struggle to keep up with newer-generation IT. The use of IT devices represents a constant challenge to become knowledgeable and not be left behind. For older digital moms, the use of such technologies is not considered natural, as they grew up without digital technologies, and, for this reason, they feel a certain lag compared with younger mothers.

On the other hand, SNSs, especially Facebook, showed interesting meanings associated by consumers. One meaning commonly found on Facebook is a nostalgic feeling derived from the reconnection with old friends and family who are not physically close. Consumers find this SNS to be a tool that allows them to reunite with people they care about but have been distanced with for some or the other reason. Additionally, there is a strong sense of community attached to SNSs such as Facebook and WhatsApp. In fact, there are some characteristics consistent with Muñiz and O'Guinn (2001), such as shared consciousness, rituals and traditions, and a sense of moral responsibility.

Furthermore, as consumers display such symbolic meanings toward IT devices and SNSs, companies are now using digital marketing strategies to reach consumers online. This research particularly explored the generalized attitudes toward five of the most common digital marketing strategies used by organizations. It noteworthy that four out of the five strategies explored were positively perceived: SNSs advertising, SEO, website design and usability, and email marketing. However, ads on social media need to deliver a clear, unique value proposition to digital moms and, more importantly, should be placed in a natural, non-invasive manner. Participants reflected on how advertising that flows naturally with their consumption of social media content is useful and even enjoyable, such as ads on Facebook's newsfeed (as it appears along the content of their Facebook friends), as well as ads on their Instagram stories. However, ads on Facebook that are located on the right of the screen were clearly perceived as a desperate attempt to target customers and participants rejected them.

Furthermore, these negative attitudes for those particular ads on Facebook also stem from the fact that the ads are normally related to past searches and participants commented that they did not like to be exposed in that manner. Finally, an interesting finding of this research is related to SEM, considering the recent increase of the total digital marketing budget dedicated to this strategy by organizations. We can be certain on the fact that ads on search engines' results pages are: (a) identified by participants so they can clearly understand and locate results that are sponsored by a company; (b) not valued and often ignored; and (c) are not trusted by participants. These results demand further research to identify if other types of online users respond better to this specific digital marketing strategy.

Overall, these results shed light on the perceptions of digital moms toward technological tools and digital marketing strategies. Particularly, results contribute to the literature by (a) addressing the symbolic meanings that technological tools have in their lives and (b) providing insights of how digital moms perceive different digital marketing strategies commonly implemented by brands. In sum, managerial implications derived from these results as brands targeting this group of Internet users can use both symbolic meanings and perceptions to inspire a creative and holistic digital marketing strategy.

LIMITATIONS AND FUTURE RESEARCH

No research is without limitations. Particularly, this study focused on one segment of Internet users in Mexico and used a qualitative method to collect information; therefore, these results cannot be generalized to all consumers. Digital moms are characterized as frequent users of online technologies, and it can be assumed that they are more educated on digital marketing techniques that are applied by companies. As mentioned earlier, it becomes interesting to understand how different segments of online users react toward the same digital marketing strategies proposed in this study. This can have important managerial implications as companies seek knowledge regarding which digital marketing strategy to implement based on the target consumer group.

Furthermore, future research can also consider the timeline or sequence of the purchase decision process, which involves different digital marketing strategies or whether usage frequency makes any difference in the attitudes toward them. For example, considering that SEM is generally received negatively by participants in this study, it would be interesting to shed light on when online users' value and use paid results over organic one on the search engine results page. Hopefully, this research can serve as a basis and inspiration for further research on the topic.

REFERENCES

Al-Qeisi, K., Dennis, C., Alamanos, E., & Jayawardhena, C. (2014). Website design quality and usage behavior: Unified Theory of Acceptance and Use of Technology. *Journal of Business Research*, *67*(11), 2282–2290. doi:10.1016/j.jbusres.2014.06.016

Araujo, T., & Neijens, P. (2012). Friend me: Which factors influence top global brands participation in social network sites. *Internet Research, 22*(5), 626–640. doi:10.1108/10662241211271581

Baye, M. R., De los Santos, B., & Wildenbeest, M. R. (2016). Search engine optimization: What drives organic traffic to retail sites? *Journal of Economics & Management Strategy, 25*(1), 6–31. doi:10.1111/jems.12141

Belk, R. W. (1988). Possessions and the extended self. *The Journal of Consumer Research, 15*(2), 139–168. doi:10.1086/209154

Blumler, J. G. (1979). The role of theory in uses and gratifications studies. *Communication Research, 6*(1), 9–36. doi:10.1177/009365027900600102

Boughton, S.B. (2005). Search engine marketing. *Perspectives in Business, 2*(1), 29-33.

Brooks, H. (1973). The technology of zero growth. *Daedalus, 102*(4), 139–152.

Bryman, A. (1984). The Debate about Quantitative and Qualitative Research: A Question of Method or Epistemology? *The British Journal of Sociology, 35*(1), 75–92. doi:10.2307/590553

Calvert, M., & Terry, J. (Eds.). (2013). *Processed lives: gender and technology in everyday life.* Routledge.

Carmen, P., & Nicolae, P. A. (2010). Email marketing campaigns: The easiest path from organizations to consumers–an exploratory assessment. *Annals of Faculty of Economics, 1*(1), 737–742.

Dou, W., Lim, K. H., Su, C., Zhou, N., & Cui, N. (2010). Brand positioning strategy using search engine marketing. *Management Information Systems Quarterly, 34*(2), 261–279. doi:10.2307/20721427

Edmonson, A., & McManus, S. (2007). Methodological Fit in Management Field Research. *Academy of Management Review, 32*(4), 1155–1179.

Empathica. (n.d.). *White paper: What is the Opportunity for "SoLoMo" (Social.Local.Mobile.) to Improve the Customer Experience?* Author.

Fariborzi, E., & Zahedifard, M. (2012). E-mail Marketing: Advantages, Disadvantages and Improving Techniques. *International Journal of e-Education, e-Business, e-. Management Learning, 2*(3), 232.

Flick, U. (2002). An introduction to qualitative research. *Sage (Atlanta, Ga.).*

Gehrke, D., & Turban, E. (1999, January). Determinants of successful website design: relative importance and recommendations for effectiveness. In HICSS (p. 5042). IEEE. doi:10.1109/HICSS.1999.772943

Gudivada, V. N., Rao, D., & Paris, J. (2015). Understanding search-engine optimization. *Computer, 48*(10), 43–52. doi:10.1109/MC.2015.297

Hasan, B. (2016). Perceived irritation in online shopping: The impact of website design characteristics. *Computers in Human Behavior, 54*, 224–230. doi:10.1016/j.chb.2015.07.056

Healy, M. J., Beverland, M. B., Oppewal, H., & Sands, S. (2007). Understanding retail experiences-the case for ethnography. *International Journal of Market Research, 49*(6), 751–778. doi:10.1177/147078530704900608

Hudson, L. A., & Ozanne, J. L. (1988). Alternative ways of seeking knowledge in consumer research. *The Journal of Consumer Research, 14*(4), 508–521. doi:10.1086/209132

Jenkins, S. (2008). *The truth about email marketing.* FT Press.

LaRossa, R., & Reitzes, D. C. (1993). Symbolic interactionism and family studies. In Sourcebook of family theories and methods (pp. 135-166). Springer US. doi:10.1007/978-0-387-85764-0_6

Lee, S., & Cho, M. (2011). Social media use in a mobile broadband environment: Examination of determinants of Twitter and Facebook use. *International Journal of Mobile Marketing, 6*(2), 71–87.

Mangold, W. G., & Faulds, D. J. (2009). Social media: The new hybrid element of the promotion mix. *Business Horizons, 52*(4), 357–365. doi:10.1016/j.bushor.2009.03.002

IAB Mexico & Millward Brown. (2014). *Estudio de consumo de medios entre internautas mexicanos.* Author.

IAB Mexico & Millward Brown. (2014a). *Estudio de consumo de medios entre internautas mexicanos. Segmento Teens.* Author.

IAB Mexico & Millward Brown. (2014b). *Estudio de consumo de medios entre internautas mexicanos. Segmento Ejecutivos.* Author.

IAB Mexico & Millward Brown. (2014c). *Estudio de consumo de medios entre internautas mexicanos. Segmento Digital Moms.* Author.

Miles, M., & Huberman, M. (1994). *Qualitative Data Analysis: An Expanded Sourcebook* (2nd ed.). Thousand Oaks, CA: SAGE Publications, Inc.

Muniz, A. M. Jr, & O'Guinn, T. C. (2001). Brand community. *The Journal of Consumer Research, 27*(4), 412–432. doi:10.1086/319618

Park, L. S., Yu, J., Yu, S., & Liao, L. (2015). *Search engine optimization for category specific search results.* U.S. Patent 9,116,994.

Park, Y. A., & Gretzel, U. (2007). Success factors for destination marketing websites: A qualitative meta-analysis. *Journal of Travel Research, 46*(1), 46–63. doi:10.1177/0047287507302381

Ryan, D. (2016). *Understanding digital marketing: marketing strategies for engaging the digital generation.* Kogan Page Publishers.

Sahni, N. S., Wheeler, S. C., & Chintagunta, P. (2018). Personalization in Email Marketing: The Role of Non-informative Advertising Content. *Marketing Science, 37*(2), 236–258. doi:10.1287/mksc.2017.1066

Sen, R. (2005). Optimal search engine marketing strategy. *International Journal of Electronic Commerce, 10*(1), 9–25. doi:10.1080/10864415.2005.11043964

Singh, S., & Sonnenburg, S. (2012). Brand performances in social media. *Journal of Interactive Marketing, 26*(4), 189–197. doi:10.1016/j.intmar.2012.04.001

Smith, J. K. (1983). Quantitative versus Qualitative Research: An Attempt to Clarify the Issue. *Educational Researcher, 12*(3), 6–13. doi:10.3102/0013189X012003006

Snow, D. A. (2001). Extending and broadening Blumer's conceptualization of symbolic interactionism. *Symbolic Interaction*, *24*(3), 367–377. doi:10.1525i.2001.24.3.367

TechTerms.com. (2010, January 4). *ICT*. Retrieved Dec 11, 2018, from http://www.techterms.com/definition/ict

Tiago, M. T. P. M. B., & Veríssimo, J. M. C. (2014). Digital marketing and social media: Why bother? *Business Horizons*, *57*(6), 703–708. doi:10.1016/j.bushor.2014.07.002

Trevino, L. K., Lengel, R. H., & Daft, R. L. (1987). Media symbolism, media richness, and media choice in organizations a symbolic interactionism perspective. *Communication Research*, *14*(5), 553–574. doi:10.1177/009365087014005006

Treviño, T. (2017). Madres digitales en Monterrey, México: Estudio de hábitos, comportamientos y actitudes en Internet. *Revista Argentina de Investigación en Negocios*, *3*(2), 71–79.

Treviño, T., & Morton, F. (2016). Online Shopping in Mexico: Exploring the Promising and Challenging Panorama. In Mexican Business Culture: Essays on Tradition, Ethics, Entrepreneurship and Commerce and the State (pp. 166-182). McFarland & Company.

Treviño, T., & Pineda, J. L. (2017). *Mamás Digitales en México: ¿Por qué se conectan con las marcas en Internet?* El Financiero.

KEY TERMS AND DEFINITIONS

Bing: Originated from MSN Search, it is a search engine developed by Microsoft to provide standard web search, as well as specialized searches for news, shopping, images, videos, maps, and other categories.

Email Marketing: A valuable and digital marketing tool that delivers short messages with a clear value proposition and a call to action for users.

Global Positioning System (GPS): It is a satellite-based navigation system composed of 24 satellites put into orbit by the US Department of Defense.

Pay-per-Click (PPC): It is a digital advertising model where the advertiser pays an amount (fixed or determined by auction) when a user clicks on one ad.

Protocol: Formal description of message formats and rules that guide the exchange of messages between computers.

Silver Surfer: Internet user older than 50 years of age.

Social Networking Sites (SNSs): It is an interactive media enabling two-way communication rather than one-directional as in traditional media.

Usability: The extent to which a product can be used by specified users to achieve goals with efficiency and satisfaction.

This research was previously published in the Handbook of Research on Digital Marketing Innovations in Social Entrepreneurship and Solidarity Economics; pages 260-280, copyright year 2019 by Business Science Reference (an imprint of IGI Global).

Chapter 11
Background of "Pinned" Images:
Lifestyle Advertising in Social Media

Aslı Sezgin

https://orcid.org/0000-0002-4557-7351

Osmaniye Korkut Ata University, Turkey

Zaliha İnci Karabacak

https://orcid.org/0000-0002-4931-556X

TOBB University of Economics and Technology, Turkey

ABSTRACT

The presence of a hidden enforcement is a matter in social media networks, whose contents are made attractive by rich images illustrating the rearrangement of the living spaces belonging to the followers of these networks. Every detail of private life including personal appearance, spaces where time is spent with friends, food is consumed, coffee is drunk, and houses are decorated, is presented through charming images. Inspired by these images, people have started to make their preferences regarding what mobile phone to use, what sports to practice, or what films to watch. The content of social media has begun to draw attention to "lifestyle advertising" and has provided a convenient ground for the advertising industry. Pinterest is a network where images reflecting modern people's daily habits, including consumption, are pinned in order to serve as sources of inspiration. In this study, the perfect living spaces which have been fictionalised as models in the images shared on Pinterest will be investigated in terms of "lifestyle advertising" and in comparison to real life.

INTRODUCTION

The impact of social media on various areas of daily life is now considered an undiscussable reality. Today, as a result of research on social media and its effects, it can be stated that these networks and the sharings made on them have a manipulative influence on every aspect of life.

DOI: 10.4018/978-1-6684-6287-4.ch011

The use of social media, mainly as part of the routine activities of the young generation, which is also called the digital generation, offers the opportunity to realize social interaction in a digital environment. Gaming websites, video websites and blogs offer a medium for entertainment and communication for today's people, who have evolved in a technological sense over the years and have managed to remove the time-space barrier. In this environment, communication opportunities increase, social connections are easily established and even technical skills can be developed (O'Keeffe & Clarke-Pearson, 2011). People with common ground can communicate with each other in this environment whenever and wherever they wish.

In recent years, with the help of multimedia, a new daily living space that we can design and share at will and which has entertaining as well as communicative content, has been created in the new digital environment. This also entails, among other things, the evolution of daily lifestyles. The developments in consumer electronics and interaction methods, and the facilities provided to access the Internet allow the creation of this new life. Easily accessible multimedia content, communication and information infrastructure supporting user access and smart devices offering user-friendly digital content are also important opportunities for the creation of a new digital lifestyle (Hofmann, & Thomas, 2008).

People's ability to access information and entertainment must play an important role in the content provided by Web 2.0 technology. Media content is created, shared and consumed by users. Those that meet the expectations and requirements can gain access easily through the customized content (Hofmann, & Thomas, 2008).

One of the most important issues that draw attention to the new lifestyles, which have become fictionalised in the digital environment, is the presentation of the content according to the expectations and requirements mentioned above. In social media, content with a high degree of attractiveness encourages consumption.. Social media networks, which millions of people can access free of charge (Zarella, 2010), offer a customized advertising content that can reach more users with less cost than the traditional media environment.Lifestyle advertising draws people's attention under the heading of social media advertisement.

These advertisements make customers purchase a product by creating changes in attitude and behavior through persuasion and enable them to have the lifestyle they imagine. Advertisements have an important role in expanding and adopting new lifestyles which emerge with social mobility, through the values and symbolic meanings imposed on products (Erdoğan, 2014).

The increase in the production of similar products has caused the advertising texts to become more and more similar. This inadequacy of traditional advertising texts has led to the emergence of lifestyle facts in advertisements texts (Karaçor as cited in Şimşek, 2002). Flueckiger (2009) emphasizes that lifestyle advertisements tend to have intense nostalgia which is ahistorical, offering merely the most delightful view of an imaginary experience.

In this study, Pinterest has been selected to be analysed as a social media network where different lifestyles with different attractive contents are submitted. Pinterest, which has increased its number of users and market value since 2010, is defined as a visual-based online network. Some general evaluations of this social media were determined in a study conducted in order to describe Pinterest in terms of its content and users (Mittal, Gupta, Dewan, & Kumaraguru, 2013). According to the subject, content and scope of this study, these evaluations can be summarized as follows:

- The most common issues among users are design, fashion, photography and food.
- 95% of the shared content consists of pre-published web content.

- Pinterest users do not conceal their personal information, and trademark sharings draw attention (Mittal, Gupta, Dewan, & Kumaraguru, 2013).

Based on this study, which aims to study the content of users' lifestyles shared on Pinterest and the consumption preferences presented in these lifestyles, the assumption regarding lifestyle advertising has been carried out through images in social media networks. With this purpose, an evaluation of the consumption-based new digital lifestyles, which are fictionalized through Pinterest images, will be carried out via the method of interpretation of these images with a critical point of view.

BACKGROUND

Virtual Lives Fictionalized in the World of Images

The digital revolution that began in the 1990s has brought along different problems for producers and consumers alike, due to the use of media technologies in the industrial environment. While consumers are in a dilemma on how to make a selection from a large number of products with different appeals (Rickard, 2006), producers intend to seek different ways to widely benefit from the new media technologies in a competitive environment. In this context, social media networks represent the easiest and most accessible sharing environment for both users and consumers.

Web 2.0 technologies offer different approaches to everyday life practices. Perhaps the most striking of these are cameras that are featured in every mobile phone, offering the opportunity to capture even the most ordinary moment of day. Because computers now incorporate high technology and are endowed with increasing digital storage capabilities, they offer new opportunities, enabling people to take and send photos instantly. Taking photos has begun to turn into a social activity, as a result of these sharings. The number of digital images are rapidly increasing in online media as they are transmitted through these nets. As a consequence, a large number of practices emerge for coding and editing of these images (Rubinstein & Sluis, 2008). This has brought along new perspectives in the cultural sense, as well as a change in the consumption habits as mentioned above.

In the present day, when computers and internet technology have completely altered the sense of entertainment, the internet and, consequently, the new media applications, have replaced television and domestic family entertainments. With the help of technology, social media networks use images extensively as part of the digital lifestyle and add new features to this environment day by day. Photos are edited through filters within a few seconds, without the need for any further processing, and it has now become possible to store a large number of photographs. Any user who does not have information of how to take a professional photography, in the digital environment, he can take photographs with remarkable features in a short time, with the help of design applications (Rubinstein & Sluis, 2008).

Social media has substantially changed and expanded the means of communication among people, communities and organizations, by giving a different point of view to the traditional communication approach (Kietzmann, Hermkens, McCarthy & Silvestre, 2011). Now, organizations establish a two-way communication, accessing their target groups through social media, not only through face-to-face communication. As a consequence, a more professional approach has been adopted regarding the subject of social media, and the institutionalized organizations are preparing strategies and receiving expert support in this regard.

The habitants of the virtual social world live more freely than they actually do, in an environment which most would like to have in their real life. This free virtual environment is furnished with rich visual content, creating a new way of fictionalized lives.

Up-to-dateness is also very important in this environment where activities are fast and intense. Likes, wishes can change rapidly according to the social media content. Companies have become aware of the need to hold on to the social media environment so as to commercially increase the demand for their products and services.

Social media enables companies to reach their consumers on a timely and direct basis at much lower costs and higher efficiency than conventional communication tools do (Kaplan & Haenlein, 2010).

The different features of the virtual life that are established by the social media are also remarkable. For example, in the virtual social life, users can simultaneously interact with other users. Besides, the users in this environment can also submit their own completely customized content (Kaplan & Haenlein, 2009).

Social media, with its high visual character, visuality has come into prominence, can effectively make sense of our perceptions, beliefs, environment, the world, because of this visual feature. When compared to traditional media, intensive use of visuality also provides technological and financial facilities (Heverly, 2008). Personal space has been redefined, and its boundaries have been redrawn in this new world where human life is redefined as well. Social media is regarded as an important communication channel that also changes the social relations and habits by opening private life to sharing and to the sense of wonder (Houghton & Joinson, 2010). Pinterest social media network, which constitutes the research aim of this study, should be considered as an important social media environment, where visuality comes into prominence, where users make sharings with the main idea of inspiration, which can be influential in the formation of a new lifestyle through pinned ideas in the digital world of the 21st century.

Pinned Images: Pinterest

Pinterest, which met with its users for the first time in March 2010, is a social media network that has been rapidly appropriated and popularized by the private and public sectors. Pinterest, where users share their favorite contents according to their interests, and where collections created by users are also included, comes with the slogan *World's idea catalog* in many countries, especially in America and Japan.

Pinterest, which functions as a digital pinboard, allows users to pin the images they displayed on the Internet onto their own pinboard. Users who pin any image or video on the internet, record these images on the pinboards they organize. Being able to add up to 500 characters to the images they record, users can also follow other pinboards and comment on them. Pinterest is a social media application with a constantly increasing popularity, especially in terms of sharing ideas as well as inspiration topics. The personal use of Pinterest has more than just institutional usage. Pinterest, where inspiring images are collected from different sources, has recently begun to be used for promotional purposes in the fields such as the world of business and the education sector (Hansen, Nowlan, & Winter, 2012).

Among the notable features of Pinterest, the creation of image collections is preferred by users for having a feature other than sharing. Pinterest, which differs from other popular social media networks precisely due to this feature, also offers important data to researchers in analyzing user behaviors (Feng, Cong, Chen, & Yu, 2013). In a study aimed at analyzing user behavior on Pinterest, Feng et al. (2013) investigated the topological features of this social network, images commonly used, sources of images, and popular Pinterest users. As a result of the research, it was emphasized that Pinterest users mainly focus on daily life practices, that they prefer to pin the images in decoration, gastronomy, fashion categories, and that this should be regarded as an ideal advertising and marketing platform, especially for retail companies.

When the sharings on Pinterest are examined in detail, it can be observed that the areas of delight, pleasure, power, entertainment and optimism are mosly included in the images that users have added to their pinboards. The users acting as content curators are redesigning their lifestyles at their own will. In this social media network, it is possible to observe the sources of happiness of others through images (Lewallen & Behm-Morawitz, 2016). Female users in particular take inspiration from many issues related to living spaces, such as refreshments culture, fashion, and home decoration.

Lifestyle Advertising

Peoplpe'sifestyles have always attracted the attention of the marketing staff. Behaviors, emotions, attitudes, thoughts have been investigated to find out what people need and want. People are evaluated under different categories according to their individual desires, spare time activities, and income status, through lifestyle marketing perspective. Lifestyle ensures a better division of consumers according to more detailed and specific evaluations, instead of grouping them based on general demographic characteristics. Many researches focus on lifestyle in the process of obtaining more comprehensive and diverse information about individuals (Krishnan, 2011).

Economic developments, demographic trends and new technologies also affect the extent and scale of consumption culture considerably. Consumption culture indicates the culture in which identities, perceptions, values, desires shape mass production and consumption (Singh, 2011). Lifestyle advertising is also a reflection of this 'consumer culture.'

'Lifestyle', the name given to the forms of behavior that represent individuality and elitism, briefly represents a life model. Lifestyle is the way of using form, attitude, goods, places and time, depending on the cultural structures. Accordingly, lifestyle is also related to the concept of consumption. Consumer habits, shaped within hedonist, financial, and aesthetic dimensions come into existence in the modern lifestyle. The concept of lifestyle has begun to develop with the adoption of consumption culture (Alyakut, 2017).

Lifestyle maintains a variety of important factors according to Joseph Plummer's study as it seen in Table1.

Lifestyle advertising presents itself as natural, ordinary and routine while affectting consumer behaviour (Moon, 1990).

Minimizing the loss of meaning in the advertisement translation in the international advertising context, and using as few words as possible for this purpose is one of the important factors in lifestyle advertising (Şimşek, 2002). Moon (1990) points out that the majority of advertising depends on visual imagery, whilelittle or no information at all affects consumers in a non-rational way.

In addition to their interest in the lifestyle marketing sector, consumers have begun to need a media environment with a customized, rich content that will enhance the living standards in their daily lives with limited leisure time. This environment has two basic components. The first is that it provides for the content to be controlled by consumers, while the second is that consumers can have access to measurable data about what they watch, follow, or the content they produce (Coopers, 2006).

Table 1. Key lifestyle factors

Activities	Interests	Opinions
Work	Family	Themselves
Hobbies	Home	Social issues
Social events	Job	Politics
Vacation	Community	Business
Entertainment	Recreation	Economics
Club Membership	Fashion	Education
Community	Mood	Products
Shopping	Media	Future
Sports	Achievements	Culture

Source: Plummer as cited in Padhy, 2011

Social Media Marketing

Social media networks are powerful tools for sharing information, shaping ideas, connecting domains and cultures, ensuring participation and realizing communication intensely. It has become possible to develop personal and social aspects through these networks, and lifestyles have begun to reshape depending on these networks. In this sense, brands want to take advantage of the influential position of social media networks to reach consumers (Kulandairaj, 2014). New and effective channels have begun to be used as methods of interpersonal communication. Although social media networks that inform producers and consumers under different headings are used mostly by young people, they also offer a communication environment in which consumers of almost every age group can receive information. Messages reach to many people in a digital environment through social media networks. Companies have started to allocate more budget for social media marketing, which is increasingly becoming important among interactive marketing methods (Sago, 2010).

Packer (2011), in the strategic approach that he developed for the marketing topic in social media, briefly summarizes the steps that must be followed to achieve success with this new marketing method:

- **Discovery Phase:** It is the stage that will provide the development of the brand, in which the marketing objectives are identified, and, accordingly, the purpose of the social media networks is set forth. At this stage, it is especially necessary to collect the data regarding the habits of social media use of the target group.
- **Pilot Project Implementation:** It is the phase in which preliminary information about the brand is transferred on the social media networks and implemented based especially on observations; no sale has been made at this point and the pilot scheme is tested.
- **Design and Application Phase:** The messages are designed in accordance with the data obtained at this stage. The messages that followers look for are shared, and marketing-intended communication content is designed.
- **Assessment Phase:** It is the phase in which social media sharing is carried out, and the communication that is established with the target group in this environment is evaluated.

Social media marketing makes the exchanges between consumers and organizations easier. Additionally, it offers the marketers many advantages such as providing inexpensive access to consumers and various ways to interact and engage with consumers positioned at different points in the purchase cycle (Tuten & Solomon, 2014).

Facebook, Twitter, LinkedIn, YouTube, Google+, Instagram and Pinterest are the platforms used most by marketers. Among the major social networks, Pinterest dropped sharply from %45 to %40 (Stelzner, 2016). Besides, blogs, which can be integrated with almost every other tool and platform, create very important central points for social media marketing actions (Zarrella, 2009).

The anagement of social media marketing is performed in two ways by organizations. One way is to create internal positions to manage, and the other one is to hire agencies, consultants and service providers (Tuten & Solomon, 2014).

Millward Brown Digital, the leading digital research specialist in the world, offers digital solutions that will provide brand growth, increase marketing efficiency, while helping customers improve their brands. Millward Brown, which works for the marketing staff to recognize consumers, also provides guidance on media planning. In the researches made by Millward Brown on Pinterest, the studies conducted on the brand measurement of this social media network are remarkable (Millward Brown Digital, 2015).

Methodology and Findings

Within the context of the industrial lifestyle, advertisements are instructive on how products will be consumed. Yet now, since goods are consumed more than needed, ads have become a catalyst for consumption culture by being associated with concepts, such as prestige, identity, difference, and status that manipulate consumption (Yavuz, 2013). It is observed in today's market conditions, in which new communication technologies dominate that lifestyle, ads are frequently featured in social media in order to increase consumption within the context of social media marketing.

For this study, the sharings which emphasize personally distinctness and those presenting lifestyles through visual appeal were selected from all Pinterest sharings..The selected images were analyzed and interpreted through a descriptive analysis with a critical point of view. The aim was to determine the content of advertisements included in the presentations of these lifestyles and, thus, to get an idea about the new lifestyles in social media networks.

A descriptive analysis is a type of qualitative data analysis which involves the summarization and interpretation of data obtained by various data collection techniques according to predefined themes. In descriptive analyses, the researcher can use citations directly in the interpretation of data. The aim here is to present the acquired facts to the reader in a summarized and interpreted way. The theme and categories that will define the frame of data analysis are created in the first step of descriptive analysis. After defining the data in these categories, the findings should be explained and associated (Özdemir as cited in Yıldırım & Şimşek, 2010).

In this study, the randomly selected images for descriptive analysis, and the categories included in pinboards, which are used extensively on Pinterest, are given in Table 2.

While determining these categories, the most common sharing categories among the users on the Pinterest social media network were taken into account. Pinterest's use of high quality photos in particular, which transfers information about product categories and styles instead of bringing the brand to the forefront, and the creation of boards according to people's interests, were highlighted in the research on e-commerce, and in the discussions where the marketing of social media come into prominence (Eticaretmag, 2012). The categories selected in this study were chosen by taking into consideration interests such as technology, food and beverage, fashion, sports, decoration and cosmetics.

Table 2. Descriptive analysis categories

1	Technology
2	Eating-Drinking
3	Fashion
4	Sport
5	Decoration
6	Cosmetics

In lifestyle advertising, the display of products, without using any introductory word to present them, draws people's attention to visuals of all categories. On Pinterest image, the category of technology in Figure 1 represented by the Apple brand, was showcased through laptop computers and mobile phones, connecting them with the modern person who uses technology in daily life.

The effect of placing 'pleasure-focused life' in the center of consumption has had influences on the adoption of consumption as a culture in the capitalist sense. Consumption has become a behavior carried out with symbolic purposes rather than being requirement-driven. Instead of the functionality of products, their indication of values created in society life are more significant. These values make people consume as they desire to be part of the selected group. While daily life is aestheticized in advertisements, qualities such as high status are also promised (Güneş & Aydın, 2016).

Companies take advantage of advertising messages that focus on emotions, because they can make the difference when it comes to products with similar features. While Apple puts forward the concept of a consistent brand in the marketing environment where all its competitors are also involved, it also intends to achieve an important position in the minds of the consumers. In doing so, it uses the Apple logos in different colors and appeals. Apple prefers to use a strategy that aims to seduce consumers (Pinson & Brosdahl, 2014). The products that promise consumers a different social status is remarkable in Apple's marketing strategy. The user profile exhibiting his distinctiveness in every environment in modern living spaces is remarkable in the Apple images in Pinterest sharing.

When we evaluate today's modern people in the practices of everyday life, we can state that they represent themselves through socio-psychological consumption behavior. Consumption habits should be evaluated in the context of urban spaces. These spaces make sense of life again through new dominations. Objects, symbols and values are evaluated within the assumptions of the capitalist social system in modern daily life (Tellan, 2008).

As the preferences in the consumption process satisfy the needs directly, we can state that they are identified based on the cultural characteristics, habits, behavioral patterns supporting lifestyle (Riley, 1994). These preferences also determine needs over time, and consumption is driven by lifestyle habits. When Starbucks's images on Pinterest are reviewed, they are a reflection of a lifestyle.

When Starbucks Corporation's marketing strategy is analysed, it is observed that there is a strong relationship between coffee and self-esteem. However, it is clear that coffee production, consumption and advertising strategy are influenced by capitalism rather than by this love. Coffee, which is among the most valuable commodities after petroleum, has become a lifestyle symbol along with Starbucks, which uses together different aromas, music, colors and decorations (Ruzich, 2008).

Figure 1. Technology: Apple Macbook
Source: https://tr.pinterest.com/pin/173247916893367754/

Starbucks reflects the physical environment of its stores in this virtual environment using the virtual world of social media effectively and enabling its customers to follow innovations (Chua & Banerjee, 2013).

Symbols that represent Paris and make people recall spring season, along with pink-coloured maca-rons and Starbuck mugs produced in almost every colour, were used in images of Starbucks posted on Pinterest. One can see a particular arrangement in this picture, where pink color is predominantly used, while Paris, one of the fashion capitals, is centered especially on female consumers who make references to the lifestyle offered by Starbucks.

Consumption in modern life, with emotional benefits including images and symbolic elements com-ing into prominence, is characterised by the evaluation and purchase of symbols. As the true self of the individuals (who am I?), and their ideal self (who do I want to be?) develop, the importance of images, behaviors, feelings, goals, roles and values emerge. Ultimatelly, we are what we decide to consume. The products that, thus, become the symbol of status are important in shaping our social life. The brand and the symbolic meaning attached to it have an effective role in the determination of this status (Azizağaoğlu & Altunışık, 2012). For example, the modern and free woman has been associated with wearing a Guess bag. As Figure 3 shows it, the image of a woman wearing a Guess bag is considered to be iconic of the modern woman and has been shared on Pinterest in the category of fashion. One of the fashion products that have become a symbol of high status is now part of lifestyle. The image of the woman whose face we cannot see gives information about her social status through the bag brand she wears.

Figure 2. Eating-drinking: Starbucks
Source: https://tr.pinterest.com/pin/460915343094869225/

Figure 3. Fashion: Guess
Source: https://tr.pinterest.com/pin/142004194480903656/

Consumption in modern times is no longer connected to necessity, but should be carried out based on pleasure. This idea is also obvious in what has become known as "healthy life". The concept of health is discussed not only as a physiological event, but also as a socio-cultural event. The framework of being healthy has also begun to be determined by the culture of consumption. Purposes such as hedonism, vanity, belonging to a group or a culture are now realized by means of aestheticized products. The concept of healthy life and the multitude of products that give the promise of providing such as a lifestyle have created a new market. Media and social media in particular have been used as an important tool for this market through visual language (Atilla & İşler, 2012). Adidas brand products, which are associated with the image of a free and modern female with a fit body, as shown in Figure 4, are similar to the relationship between brand and social status, indicated in Figure 3. Adidas brand is considered representative of a lifestyle identified with a healthy life, as emphasized in Figure 4.

Figure 4. Sport: Adidas
Source: https://tr.pinterest.com/pin/368802656974511874/

The characteristics of consumption culture are conveyed by media products, and the new marketing concept positions people according to their lifestyles, thus underlying their social status. Metropolises are of utmost importance for these lifestyles. Consumption is different in metropolitan life, in which pleasures has come to replace necessity. The clues about how to manage to live well are conveyed to the people who desire a good life (Ülken, 2015). Figure 5 illustrates the way Ikea brand products have successfully tried to turn Scandinavian style decoration into a consumption behaviour, especially in recent years, and have redefined the concept of a regular home bath through a minimalist approach to home decoration.

Figure 5. Decoration: Ikea
Source: https://fr.pinterest.com/pin/369224869427619324/

As envisaged by Ikea, the decoration products fit into place through their geometric forms and pastel colors and are objects of the brand's "less is more" philosophy (Döl & Avşar, 2013). The vision and mission of Ikea in what concerns space design, home accessories and furniture sectors, is to create a better daily life for the majority of people, regardless of their social status (Batı, 2009). From this point of view, the image selected as an example in the decoration category in Figure 5 is different from the previous examples. The social status Ikea intends to create expresses plainer lifestyle that is accessible to the majority.

The transformation of the woman into a visual object, especially because of the messages conveyed by the media, has obliged the female to follow beauty standards. The concept of beauty presented by the media is particularly obvious in advertisements. It goes without saying that for females, beauty has always been an important matter and concern. However, a female, influenced by the images presented by the media, attributes her happiness particularly to the products that will "beautify" her. These marketed products have now become the source of happiness. The ideal woman, as depicted by the media, is a female who takes care of her physical appearance (Oğuz, 2010). A set of the same brand products of make-up brushes and cosmetics which illustrate females' passion for beauty were given as an example for the cosmetics category in Figure 6.

In modern lifestyle, women desire to make a difference in their image by resorting to all kind of beauty products. In this context, face in particular plays an important role in what female beauty means. Female consumers have become conscious of their physical appearance, sometimes adhering to visuals that support unreal beauty. The images related to cosmetics on Pinterest show how beauty products have sometimes become an obsession (note the multitude of brushes a woman has to possess in order to be just like the rest), conducting to impulsive buying behavior (Villi & Kayabasi, 2013).

Figure 6. Cosmetics: Nars
Source: https://tr.pinterest.com/pin/547257792200101639/

FUTURE RESEARCH DIRECTIONS

The emphasis laid by the present book on symbols and on language in marketing strategies was exemplified in this chapter by Pinterest social media network, in which symbols are intensively used, while words remain in the background. Although the current chapter is just a small reference research for future studies, it dwells on the idea that social media networks, as new application areas for advertising and marketing strategies, will gradually become more important.

If one takes into account the fact that social media affect the purchasing behavior of individuals in their capacity of "consumers" more and more, the importance of the virtual lifestyles offered through these networks should be understood in terms of advertising and marketing platforms. More detailed quantitative and qualitative analyses should be performed from different perspectives, to the advantage of marketers and advertisers. Not only will its visual richness attract the attention of the consumers, but its data collecting power will also allow for consumers' behaviors to be analysed, and this is an important aspect that needs to be further investigated by the studies pertaining to this field.

The effect provided by the strategy of limited amount of text and bigger number of visuals in the performance of the so-called "lifestyles" of various users can be the subject of different researches, especially when sociocultural and demographic variables are taken into consideration.

CONCLUSION

In the introductory section of the present chapter, the topic of marketing strategies was investigated within the scope of current trends. The structure of the new media and social media networks, which are increasingly gaining importance within the more general mass media landscape, directly reaches and allows the interaction with consumers. In this context, Pinterest was selected as an examplary social media network, illustrative of the new trends. The "inspirational" nature of Pinterest as a idea catalog, one of the social media networks that brings the power of visuality to the forefront, makes it a very strong channel in the field of marketing as well.

Since the new media has come to replace the role and position in daily life once occupied by the conventional media, avoiding the influence of the world of images presented by lifestyles is impossible as it has become part of our modern life. These images, which are now at the tip of our fingers through mobile phone applications, offer us a new way of life, whose boundaries have been drawn by certain consumption habits.

Pinterest should nowadays be considered an important social media network that promises new lives, with its high-resolution photographs, with its slogan "inspire", in which the consumption behavior lurks in the background. In the present study, the lifestyles of individuals living in modern, luxurious, attractive, healthy environments decorated with minimalist lines, enjoying a certain social status are transferred through Pinterest in six different categories that have been analysed by means of the descriptive analysis method. Although these lifestyle features do not appear at first glance, certain brands are coming into prominence, which necessitates that the issue should be viewed in the context of the lifestyle advertising. All messages are transmitted through images in this customized advertising content. Thus, access to the consumer and memorability are provided and performed at a high rate, in today's world where the visual culture dominates.

Advertisers who are aware of the social media's capacity to reach a large number of users within a short period can transmit to the users the messages intended to market their products even through personal sharings. Pinterest also presents the aesthetized products as a source of delight and pleasure through pinned images on pinboards, and encourages their consumption due to their symbolic meanings thus promising to achieve the desired lifestyle.

REFERENCES

Alyakut, Ö. (2017). The Changing Homes in Postmodern Society: Semiological Examination of House Advertising that Promise New Life Style. *Journal of Communication Theory and Research, 44*, 243–262.

Atilla, G., & Didar, B. İ. (2012). A Qualitative Pre-Study On Healthism as a Consumer Object. *Dumlupınar University Journal of Social Science, 34*, 221–230.

Azizağaoğlu, A., & Altunışık, R. (2012). Postmodernism, Symbolic Consumption and Brand. *Journal of Consumer and Consumption Research, 4*(2), 33–50.

Chua, A. Y. K., & Banerjee, S. (2013). Customer Knowledge Management Via Social Media: The Case of Starbucks. *Journal of Knowledge Management, 17*(2), 237–249. doi:10.1108/13673271311315196

Döl, A., & Avşar, P. (2013). Re-evaluating the Conception of Object within the Context of Minimalism. *İdil, 2*(10), 1-11.

Eticaretmag. (2012). Pinterest Using Guide for E-Commerce Companies. Retrieved from http://eticaret-mag.com/e-ticaret-sirketleri-icin-pinterest-kullanim-rehberi/

Feng, Z., Cong, F., Chen, K., & Yu, Y. (2013). An Empirical Study of User Behaviors on Pinterest Social Network. *2013 IEEE/WIC/ACM International Joint Conferences on Web Intelligence (WI) and Intelligent Agent Technologies (IAT)* (Vol. 1, pp. 402-409).

Flueckiger, B. (2009). Lifestyle, Aesthetics and Narrative in Luxury Domain Advertising. *Popular Narrative Media*, 2(2), 195–212. doi:10.3828/pnm.2009.6

Gençyürek Erdoğan, M. (2014). *The Construction of Lifestyles in Tourism Advertisements: Semiological Analysis*. Unpublished Masters Thesis, Başkent University Institute of Social Sciences, Turkey.

Güneş, S., Selda, K., & Aydın, Ö. (2016). The Presentation of Luxury Lifestyles on Decoration Magazine Advertisements within the Frame of Consumption Culture: Example of Home Art Decoration Magazine. *Journal of Yaşar University*, *11*(43), 220–239.

Hansen, K., Nowlan, G., & Winter, C. (2012). Pinterest as a Tool: Applications in Academic Libraries and Higher Education. *The Canadian Journal of Library and Information Practice and Research*, 7(2). doi:10.21083/partnership.v7i2.2011

Heverly, R. A. (2008). Growing Up Digital: Control and the Pieces of a Digital Life. In T. McPherson (Ed.), *Digital Youth, Innovation, and the Unexpected* (pp. 199–218). Cambridge, MA: The MIT Press.

Hofmann, G., & Thomas, G. (2008). Digital Lifestyle 2020. *IEEE MultiMedia*, *15*(2), 4–7. doi:10.1109/MMUL.2008.24

Houghton, D. J., & Joinson, A. N. (2010). Privacy, Social Network Sites and Social Relations. *Journal of Technology in Human Services*, *28*(1-2), 74–94. doi:10.1080/15228831003770775

Kaplan, A. M., & Haenlein, M. (2009). The Fairyland of Second Life: Virtual Social Worlds and How to Use Them. *Business Horizons*, *52*(6), 563–572. doi:10.1016/j.bushor.2009.07.002

Kaplan, A. M., & Haenlein, M. (2010). Users of The World, Unite! The Challenges and Opportunities of Social Media. *Business Horizons*, *53*(1), 59–68. doi:10.1016/j.bushor.2009.09.003

Kietzmann, J., Hermkens, K., McCarthy, I. P., & Silvestre, B. (2011). Social Media? Get Serious! Understanding the Functional Building Blocks of Social Media. *Business Horizons*, *54*(3), 241–251. doi:10.1016/j.bushor.2011.01.005

Krishnan, J. (2011). Lifestyle – A Tool for Understanding Buyer Behavior. *Journal of Economics and Management*, *5*(1), 283–298.

Kulandairaj, A. J. (2014). Impact Of Social Media On The Lifestyle of Youth. *International Journal of Technical Research and Applications*, *2*(8), 22–28.

Lewallen, J., & Behm-Morawitz, E. (2016). Pinterest or Thinterest? Social Comparison and Body Image on Social Media. *Social Media+ Society, 2*(1), 1-9.

Millward Brown Digital. (2015). Millward Brown Digital and Pinterest Partner to Provide Platform Measurement. Retrieved June, 23, 2017 from https://www.millwardbrowndigital.com/press/millward-brown-digital-and-pinterest-partner-to-provide-platform-measurement/

Mittal, S., Gupta, N., Dewan, P., & Kumaraguru, P. (2013). The Pin-Bang Theory: Discovering the Pinterest World. Retrieved from https://arxiv.org/abs/1307.4952

Moon, R. (1990). Lifestyle Advertising and Classical Freedom of Expression Doctrine. *McGill Law Journal. Revue de Droit de McGill, 36,* 76.

O'Keeffe, G. S., & Clarke-Pearson, K. (2011). The Impact of Social Media on Children, Adolescents, and Families. *Pediatrics, 127*(4), 800–804. doi:10.1542/peds.2011-0054 PMID:21444588

Oğuz, G. Y. (2010). How Beauty Turns into a Promise for Women: An Analysis on Cosmetic Advertisements in Women's Magazines. *Journal of Selçuk Communication, 6*(3), 184–195.

Özdemir, M. (2010). Qualitative Data Analysis: A Study on Methodology Problem in Social Sciences. *Journal of Eskişehir Osmangazi University Social Sciences, 11*(1), 323–343.

Packer, R. (2011). Social Media Marketing: The Art of Conversational Sales. Retrieved from http://wsiinstitute.com/media/ec/SocialMedia MarketingWhitepaper. pdf

Pinson, C., & Brosdahl, D. (2014). The Church of Mac: Exploratory examination on the loyalty of Apple customers. *Journal of Management and Marketing Research, 14,* 1.

Pricewaterhouse Coopers. (2006). *The Rise of Lifestyle Media: Achieving Success in the Digital Convergence Era. A Report by Technology Centre, Pricewaterhouse Coopers.* New York: Pricewaterhouse Coopers International Limited.

Rickard, S. (2006). Colour My World. The Consumption Junction Meets Digital Lifestyle. *Paper presented at the conference of the Australian and New Zealand Communication Association,* Adelaide, Australia.

Riley, M. (1994). Marketing eating out: The influence of social culture and innovation. *British Food Journal, 96*(10), 15–18. doi:10.1108/00070709410072463

Rubinstein, D., & Sluis, K. (2008). A life more photographic. *Photographies, 1*(1), 9–28. doi:10.1080/17540760701785842

Ruzich, C. M. (2008). For the love of Joe: The language of Starbucks. *Journal of Popular Culture, 41*(3), 423–442. doi:10.1111/j.1540-5931.2008.00529.x

Sago, B. (2010). The influence of social media message sources on millennial generation consumers. *International Journal of Integrated Marketing Communications, 2*(2), 7–18.

Şimşek, G. (2002). Transformability of Advertising Campaigns and Lifestyle Advertising in Europe; Same Advertisement, Different Geography, Different Culture and Meanings. Istanbul University Faculty of Communication Journal, 14.

Singh, P. R. (2011). Consumer Culture and Postmodernism. *Consumer Culture and Postmodernism in Postmodern Openings, 5*(5), 55–88.

Stelzner, M. A. (2016). *2016 Social Media Marketing Industry Report.* Social Media Examiner.

Tellan, D. (2008). Production of Daily Life and Advertisements. *Journal of Communication Theory and Research,* 27-53.

Tuten, T. L., & Solomon, M. R. (2014). *Social Media Marketing.* London: SAGE Publications.

Ülken, F. B. (2015). Life Style Representation in Istanbul Life Magazine. *Karadeniz Technical University Communication Research Journal, 1*(9), 39–57.

Villi, B., & Kayabaşı, A. (2013). Analysis of the Factors Affecting Impulsive Buying Behaviours of Women in Cosmetics. *The International Journal of Economic and Social Research, 9*(1), 143–165.

Yavuz, Ş. (2013). The Role of Adversing in Turkish Society's Transformation into a Consumer Society. *Journal of Communication Theory and Research, 36,* 219–240.

Zarrella, D. (2009). *The Social Media Marketing Book.* Canada: O'Reilly Media.

ADDITIONAL READING

Cario, J. E. (2012). *Pinterest Marketing: An Hour A Day.* John Wiley & Sons.

De Mooij, M. (2010). *Consumer Behavior and Culture: Consequences for Global Marketing and Advertising.* Atlanta, GA: Sage.

Jing, Y., Liu, D., Kislyuk, D., Zhai, A., & Xu, J., Donahue, & Tavel, S. (2015). Visual Search at Pinterest. In *Proceedings of the 21th ACM SIGKDD International Conference on Knowledge Discovery and Data Mining* (pp. 1889-1898). 10.1145/2783258.2788621

Mangold, W. G., & Faulds, D. J. (2009). Social Media: The New Hybrid Element of the Promotion Mix. *Business Horizons, 52*(4), 357–365. doi:10.1016/j.bushor.2009.03.002

Miles, J., & Lacey, K. (2013). *Pinterest Power: Market Your Business, Sell Your Product, and Build Your Brand on the World's Hottest Social Network.* McGraw-Hill.

Mittal, S., Gupta, N., Dewan, P., & Kumaraguru, P. (2014). Pinned it! A Large Scale Study of the Pinterest Network. In *Proceedings of the 1st IKDD Conference on Data Sciences* (pp. 1-10). 10.1145/2567688.2567692

Saravanakumar, M., & Sugantha Lakshmi, T. (2012). Social Media Marketing. *Life Science Journal, 9*(4), 4444–4451.

Van Dijck, J. (2013). *The Culture of Connectivity: A Critical History of Social Media.* Oxford: Oxford University Press. doi:10.1093/acprof:oso/9780199970773.001.0001

KEY TERMS AND DEFINITIONS

Image: A visual representation of a thing, person, animal by photography, painting, digital technologies.

Lifestyle Advertising: To market a a certain type of lifestyle by associating it with a promoted brand, product, or service.

Modern Life: Life based on consumption.

New Media: Different forms of electronic and interactive communication like the internet, web sites, computer games, e-mail, social networks, blogs, wikis.

Pinterest: A type of social bookmarking site where people pin images.

Social Media Marketing: A way of internet marketing based on social networks and applications.

Social Media Networks: Social media sites, such as Facebook, Twitter, Pinterest, YouTube, and so on, which enable people to share photos, videos, music.

This research was previously published in The Role of Language and Symbols in Promotional Strategies and Marketing Schemes; pages 267-284, copyright year 2019 by Business Science Reference (an imprint of IGI Global).

Chapter 12
How Social Commerce Characteristics Influence Consumers' Online Impulsive Buying Behavior in Emerging Markets

Quyen Phu Thi Phan
University of Economics, The University of Danang, Vietnam

Vu Minh Ngo
https://orcid.org/0000-0002-0997-4720
Van Lang University, Vietnam

Nguyen Cao Lien Phuoc
School of Economics, The University of Danang, Vietnam

ABSTRACT

With the rapid development of social commerce, consumers may easily purchase products they did not plan to purchase or do not really need when they surf social networking websites and browse posts. However, the literature on social commerce pays little attention to the extant knowledge of online impulse buying behavior (OIBB), especially in emerging markets. This study investigates the role of social commerce characteristics in shaping consumers' online impulsive buying behavior. Data was collected from 240 Vietnamese consumers with experience in online shopping. Using a Partial Least Square 3.0 analysis, the results indicated that socialization and availability of information significantly influence the urge to buy impulsively, but do not influence impulsive behavior. In contrast, personalization and product selection influence both the urge to buy impulsively and impulsive behavior. The findings also indicated that gender and age do not impact online impulsive buying behavior. Study outcomes offer useful insights to both academicians and practitioners.

DOI: 10.4018/978-1-6684-6287-4.ch012

INTRODUCTION

Consumers often act impulsively when making online decisions. Online shoppers have easy access to products, ease of purchasing, a lack of social pressures, and an absence of delivery efforts. Therefore, about 40% of all online expenditures occur as a result of impulsive buying (Verhagen & Van Dolen, 2011a). With the rapid development of social commerce, consumers, when surfing social networking websites and browsing posts, such as Facebook, Twitter, and Pinterest, may easily purchase products they had not planned on purchasing or that they do not really need. Consumers can find interesting links to shopping websites on these platforms. Under these circumstances, impulsive buying is unavoidable, especially with regard to social commerce (Huang, 2016). Surprisingly, the literature on social commerce pays little attention to the extant knowledge of online impulse buying behavior (OIBB), especially in emerging markets.

Social commerce (s-commerce) has changed the role of the customer as well. Consumers become the central focus for companies when they can interact, get trustworthy advice, search and purchase goods and services, and hence become the uniqueness of s-commerce (Kim & Park, 2013). However, many questions on how customers behave in social commerce environments remain practically unanswered (Hajli, Sims, Zadeh, & Richard, 2017; Li, 2017). To the authors' knowledge, there are several studies about online impulsive buying behavior in social commerce. For instance, Leong et al. (2018) investigated the effects of utilitarian-, hedonic-, and trust-motivations on participation that influences the urge to purchase and, ultimately, impulsive purchasing in social commerce environments. Chung et al. (2017) examined the impact of shopping value on the urge to buy restaurant products and services. However, this present study differs from the extent literature in a significant way: it is focused on how social commerce characteristics shape online impulsive buying behavior.

Additionally, considering the effect of other factors on consumer behavior, one should pay attention to the conditions of local market and diversity cultural forces, which could influence the way consumers behave when impulse buying (Yu & Bastin, 2010). However, impulsive buying has been much studied in the context of Western countries, while the Asian context has largely remained oblivious (Badgaiyan & Verma, 2015). Impulsive buying behavior is of specific interest in emerging economies, such as like India (Mittal, Sondhi, & Chawla, 2015). Several researchers have indicated that Asian consumers may engage in less impulsive purchasing than do consumers in Western countries (Hoyer et al., 2012). Yu and Bastin (2010) indicated that impulse buying in emerging markets would contribute to the literature because Southeast Asian countries are regions that have the most active social media users in the world. Vietnam represents an emerging country and is ranked seventh among the countries with the largest number of Facebook users and the highest e-commerce adoption rate in Southeast Asia (Tung, 2017). However, the behavior of Vietnam consumers is rarely understood. Therefore, another emerging research gap is to empirically investigate the influence of predictor variables on impulse buying within the Vietnam context, which can significantly contribute to the existing literature of social commerce.

The originality of the current study rests on answering the limitations by: (1) investigating the influences of unique characteristics on OIBB and, (2) analyzing the relationship between the urge to buy impulsively and impulsive buying behavior within emerging markets. Consequently, this study seeks answers to the research gaps.

Accordingly, this study is posed to examine the following research question: "How do social commerce characteristics influence consumers' online impulsive buying behavior in emerging markets?" To this end, the primary goal of this study is to provide a better understanding of factors of the social commerce environment, which determine online impulsive buying behavior (OIBB). Based on the Stimulus–Response (S-R) theory (Mehrabian & Russell, 1974), the authors' identified a set of characteristics of social commerce platforms (socialization, personalization, product selection, and information availability) and hypotheses on how they may shape OIBB. Additionally, this study attempts to empirically investigate the OIBB of Vietnamese consumers and to extend the existing research on online impulse buying, especially in the Vietnamese context.

The study's theoretical contributions are twofold. First, it confirms the role of social commerce characteristics for testing online impulsive buying behavior. This answers the call of Li (2017) for publications aimed at studying the process and uniqueness of how consumers behave impulsively in social commerce environments. Despite this call, there has not yet been a similar study published. Therefore, this research study explores how social commerce environments influence OIBB. Second, this study provides guidelines for marketing managers who use social media platforms as strategy tools when entering developing countries.

LITERATURE REVIEW

Definition of Constructs

In the S-R theory, the stimuli are the features of the online environment that customers interact with. Stimuli (S) are social commerce characteristics that affect consumers' response in this study. Previous studies identified various characteristics of social commerce environments based on the motivation theory and the unified gratification theory (UGT) (Mikalef et al., 2013; Lin & Lu, 2011). Similarly, consistent with the typology of Mikalef et al. (2017) and Zhang et al. (2014), the authors considered four social commerce characteristics, namely, information availability, personalization, product selection (utilitarian motivations), and socialization (hedonic motivation). These characteristics capture various aspects of social commerce platforms that facilitate user gratification (Mikalef et al., 2017).

Firstly, socialization is described as the ability to participate in interactions among consumers during the browsing of products on social commerce platforms. Consumers are enabled to replicate the experience of socializing in a synchronous manner (Mikalef et al., 2017). The activities of socializing on social commerce websites has been made much more comfortable and more user-friendly, so that users can communicate with friends and share experiences relating to pages/products, or message threads in products or on brand communities (Hajli, 2015; Osorio & Papagiannidis, 2019).

Another interesting characteristic of social commerce platforms is personalization. The authors defined personalization as the ability to provide consumers with customized advertisement based on their preferences. Online retailers present advertisements of new products or update the latest trends that are in line with the recommended content and user interests (Zhang et al., 2014).

Additionally, information availability is one of the key characteristics in online shopping. It is defined as the amount products and/or service information available on the social commerce platforms (Mikalef et al., 2013). Wang and Doong (2010) stated that the accuracy and amount of information available about products or services influences consumers' purchasing decisions. Information content is an important resource for online consumers because they recognize their need for particular goods or services based on need-related information provided on social commerce platforms, which influences their purchasing decision (Hajli, 2015; Aydin, 2019).

Last but not least, the wealth of information about a variety of products or services is a highlighted feature of online retailing environments. In this study, product selection is the degree to which users believe that there is a range of available products on social commerce platforms (Mikalet et al., 2017). With a wealth of information provided, consumers will spend considerable time looking at various products, which leads to positive feelings, and they tend to review the page content more intensively (Hsu & Tsou, 2011; Huang, 2016).

Online impulsive buying behavior, as an unplanned purchasing decision, consists of two dimensions, namely, the urge to buy impulsively and the actual impulsive buying behavior (Chan, Cheung, & Lee, 2017). The urge to buy impulsively is a state of desire that is experienced upon encountering an object in the shopping environment (Badgaiyan & Verma, 2015). Additionally, impulse buying is defined as "a sudden and immediate purchase with no pre-shopping intentions either to buy the specific category or to fulfill a specific buying task" (Beatty & Ferrell, 1998, p. 170). The relationship between the urge to buy impulsively and the actual impulsive buying behavior has been debated. Previous scholars indicated that impulsive buying behavior happens after experiencing an urge to buy (Rook, 1987; Beatty & Ferrell, 1998), whereas more recent scholars argued that the urge to buy did not always result in actual impulsive buying (Badgaiyan & Verma, 2015; Shen & Khalifa, 2012).

Consequences, the important question remains as to how various social commerce characteristics influence the constructs "urge to buy impulsively" and "impulsive buying behavior." Therefore, this study refers to the urge to buy impulsively, and actual impulsive buying behavior refers as response variables.

HYPOTHESIS DEVELOPMENT

Impulsive Buying Behavior and Urge to Buy Impulsively

Researchers Beatty and Ferrell (1998) explored an important distinction needs to be made relating to the construct of the "urge to buy impulsively" (desire) and "impulsive buying behavior" (behavior). They stated that the spontaneous urge to buy impulsively is a state of desire that is experienced before actually performing an impulse buying behavior. The more consumers experience the urge, the more they are more likely to make an impulse purchase. The relationship between the urge to buy impulsively and impulsive buying has been described as a chain effect at the response stage in studies done of both offline and online. Badgaiyan and Verma (2015) provided evidence regarding the relationship of the urge to buy impulsively and impulsive buying behavior. When consumers browse longer, they experience more and more urges and, in turn, increase their likelihood of engaging in an impulse purchase. Therefore, the following hypothesis is introduced:

Hypothesis One: Urge to buy impulsively positively affects impulsive buying behavior.

Effects of Social Commerce Characteristics (S) on Urge to Buy Impulsively and Impulsive Buying Behavior

Social commerce environments provide platforms on which consumers can socialize with peers. The foremost motives for people to go shopping are social interaction and enjoyment (Kim & Eastin, 2011). In a social commerce context, consumers are able to share information and the shopping experience with those who have the same interests (Wolfinbarger & Gilly, 2001). During socialization, consumers build their network to receive benefits from social activities while shopping (Zhang et al., 2014). They are more likely to interact with others who have in depth knowledge about brands and products. When the frequency of interaction increases, they may find social commerce to be more enjoyable and involving (Pagani et al., 2011). This will lead consumers to search for more information about a product they are interested in purchasing or to imitate other consumers' styles, and then may ultimately impulsively buy (Mikalef et al., 2017; Xiang et al., 2016). Previous studies suggested that impulsive buying behavior is influenced by a consumer's positive emotions (Weinberg & Gottwald, 1982). Therefore, consumers who prefer online shopping as a mean of social interaction and a way to relax, have a higher tendency to make an impulse purchase from the Internet (Ozen & Engizek, 2014). Thus, the following hypothesis is proposed:

Hypothesis Two: Socialization positively affects (a) urge to buy impulsively, and (b) impulsive buying behavior.

Personalization is a unique medium for offering advertisements that fit consumers' interests (Park, Shin, & Ju, 2014). Based on consumers' personal information when they join social media websites or consumers' navigation history exchanged between sites, online retailers can directly advertise to target customers on a one-to-one basis. Consumers can easily find out about products and services based on their location or their historical information (e.g. profiles, prior interaction), which is suggested by social media platforms.

Saad and Metawie (2015) indicated that impulsive buying is associated with feelings and psychological motivations instead of thinking and functional benefits. Consumers with positive moods have reduced decision complexity and shorter decisions times, which lead to facilitating a greater desire to reward themselves and, thus, stimulates impulse buying. According to the literature on impulsive behavior, one of the main reasons that consumers tend to buy impulsively and impulse buy is the retailers' up and cross-selling strategies (Chang et al., 2011). In a social commerce context, online vendors apply this strategy through product recommendations, suggested coordinated items, sale items, and new products based on consumers' preferences. Product recommendations impact consumers' sense of vision and if they are easily stimulated by product attributes, they will buy products impulsively (Xiang et al., 2016). The following hypothesis is developed based on the literature:

Hypothesis Three: Personalization positively affects (a) the urge to buy impulsively, and (b) impulsive buying behavior.

Consumers are not able to touch products on the Internet; consumers often want to acquire full information (e.g. size, color, design, and fabric) before purchasing specific products to substitute for a more sensory experience, which can lead to consumer impulse purchases (Park et al., 2012). In order to collect information, consumers may actively web browse to determine a product's desirability. If social commerce platforms do not provide enough information about a consumer's needs, it can break the consumer's mood, and then the consumer will tend to find an alternative way. In contrast, the availability of information that meets a consumer's needs makes the consumer more likely to enjoy the shopping experience. Thus, the consumer will actively engage in more exploratory browsing on the web, which results in more unplanned purchases (Xiang et al., 2016). If the information provided is more detailed and specific, then consumers tend to focus their attention. Thus, the following hypothesis is proposed:

Hypothesis Four: Information availability positively affects (a) the urge to buy impulsively, and (b) impulsive buying behavior.

Consumers tend to shop online when their product expectations are met or exceeded (Fram & Grady, 1995). Social commerce sites allow marketers to display their full range of products without having to stock them in their inventory (Mikalef et al., 2017). With a wealth of information, consumers will spend considerable time looking at products, which leads to positive feelings involving an urge to buy (Huang, 2016). Additionally, a wide range of product categories enhances shopping efficiency because of the increased access to comparable items and it enables better product choices. Park et al. (2014) indicated that variety of selection in shopping malls encourages consumers to browse. When consumers spend more time browsing for products or service, it leads to encountering more stimuli, which increases the likelihood of impulsive buying (Verhagen & Van Dolen, 2011b). The hypothesis follows:

Hypothesis Five: Product selection positively affects (a) the urge to buy impulsively, and (b) impulsive buying behavior.

The Control Variables: Age, Gender and Income

Age, gender, and income have been considered as control variables regarding to both the "urge to buy impulsively" and "impulsive buying behavior." First of all, studies have revealed that consumers' impulsive behaviors are related to gender. Male and female consumers have different social roles and personality factors that affect the act of consuming. Studies indicated that women are more emotionally and psychologically rooted than men, suggesting that they are more susceptible to impulse buying (Coley & Burgess, 2003). In this regard, Ghani et al. (2011) found that there was no significant difference between males and females when it came to impulse buying, and that men and women had the same level of susceptibility to impulse purchases. In contrast, Mai et al. (2003) stated that men were more impulsive in purchasing as compared to women. Thus, it can be safely hypothesized that:

Hypothesis Six: Gender is moderated significantly related to (a) the urge to buy impulsively, and (b) impulsive buying behavior.

Interestingly, the factors that have been linked to impulse buying are also likely to be influenced by age. Santini et al., (2017) believed that young consumers look for products that satisfy their needs, increasing their desire to purchase. In addition, young consumers can be affected by their peers much of time, which leads them to increase their impulse buying. Badgaiyan and Verma (2015) explained that young consumers have less control over their emotions; therefore, they have higher impulsive buying tendencies than older consumers. It is thus, hypothesized that:

Hypothesis Seven: Age is significantly related to (a) the urge to buy impulsively, and (b) impulsive buying behavior.

RESEARCH METHOD

Data Collection

This study employed an online survey questionnaire for data collection. The target social networking website was Facebook. Furthermore, the online survey excluded respondents who did not have previous experience with Facebook commerce. The previous studies identified Generations Y as the target users of social media (Nadeem, Juntunen, & Juntunen, 2017). Therefore, the ages of the target respondents were 18 to 35. The link to the questionnaire was posted on Facebook. Initially, a pretest was conducted for the scale. Two academic experts carefully examined the translation, wording, structure, and content. Their useful feedback was used to improve the scale to ensure that initial reliability and validity were at acceptable levels.

After the questionnaire was finalized, a pilot test was conducted with 80 respondents. The final questionnaire was distributed in 2019 over a period of one month. A total of 268 respondents answered the questionnaire. There were 28 responses discarded because they had no experience purchasing on Facebook or they failed to answer a question, resulting in a final sample consisting of 240 valid responses. Most respondents were female (70.4%). In total, 30.4% of the respondents were between 18 and 24 years old. A second group included respondents between 25 and 29 years of age (45%), followed by a group of respondents between 30 and 35 years of age (24.6%) (see Table 1).

Measures

The measurement for the construct was adapted from the extant literature and revised to suit the context of social commerce. Four constructs of social commerce characteristics (e.g. socialization, personalization, information availability, product selection) were adapted from To et al. (2007) and Mikalef et al. (2013, 2017). The scale for "urge to buy impulsively" was adapted from Verhagen and Van Dolen (2011). The last scale, which is "impulsive buying behavior," was adapted by Badgaiyan and Verma (2015). All items were measured using a seven-point Likert scale ranging from (1) "strongly disagree" to (7) "strongly agree."

Common Bias Method

To determine the presence of a common method variance bias among the proposed variables, the authors tested for common-method variance, employing Harman's single factor test. By loading all items onto one factor, the exploratory factor analysis indicated that items do not belong to one single factor, excluding the possibility of common-method bias.

DATA ANALYSIS AND RESULTS

In order to test the hypothesis, Smart PLS 3.0 M3 software was used. There were two main steps: the evaluation of measurement, and the evaluation of the structural model.

Table 1. Sample characteristics

	Characteristics	Frequency (n=240)	Percent (%)
Gender	Male	71	29.6
	Female	169	70.4
Age	18-24	73	30.4
	25-29	108	45
	30-35	59	24.6
Education level	High school and lower	3	1.3
	College	19	7.9
	Bachelor	146	60.8
	Graduate	72	30
Occupation	Worker	83	34.6
	Business	25	10.4
	Household	4	1.7
	Employee	52	21.7
	Student	66	27.5
	Others	10	4.2
Frequency purchasing on Facebook	<= 1 time a week	18	7.5
	Several times a week	22	9.2
	<= 1 time a month	87	36.3
	Several times a month	113	47.1
Facebook usage frequency	<=1 time a day	14	5.8
	Many times a day	218	90.8
	<= 1 time a week	7	2.9
	Several times a week	1	0.4
Which products you often purchase on Facebook	Fashion	209	87.08
	Cosmetic	144	60
	Electronic	76	31.67
	Travel	32	13.33
	Food	140	33.6
	Others	16	6.67

Measurement Model

To test the reliability and validity of the latent variables, a two-step approach was employed. In the first step, an exploratory factor analysis (EFA) was conducted for initial evaluation of the following measurement scales: socialization, personalization, product selection, and information availability. A principal component analysis and VARIMMAX rotation were employed for factor structure identification because the authors assumed some correlation between the factors in the model. The Kaiser-Meyer-Olkin (KMO) statistics were 0.881, indicating that the data was satisfied for factor analysis. As shown in Appendices 1, all indicator loaded on the intended factors and were higher than 0.6.

In the second step, the authors examined the reliability and validity of the instrument. Table 2 lists the Cronbach's alpha values, the average variance extracted (AVE), composite reliability (CR), and factor loading. As shown in the table, all the constructs have composite reliability and Cronbach's alpha is higher than 0.7, suggesting the constructs' reliability (Hair et al., 2013). For construct validity, both convergent validity and discriminant validity were examined. Convergent validity was evaluated by testing both the average variance extracted (AVE) and indicator loadings. All AVE values were higher than the recommended level of 0.5. The standard loadings of all items were above the desired of threshold of 0.7 (Fornell & Larcker, 1981), as seen in Table 2.

Table 2. Items and scales sources

Items	Factors Loading	Cronbach Alpha	Composite Reliability	AVE
Socialization				
SC1	0.885			
SC2	0.925	0.836	0.902	0.755
SC3	0.792			
Personalization				
PER1	0.866			
PER2	0.893	0.831	0.899	0.748
PER3	0.834			
Product Selection				
PS1	0.863			
PS2	0.873	0.849	0.909	0.768
PS3	0.893			
Information Availability				
INF1	0.895			
INF2	0.907	0.821	0.893	0.736
INF3	0.765			
Urge to buy impulsive				
UPL1	0.853			
UPL2	0.865	0.772	0.87	0.785
UPL3	0.923			
UPL4	0.901			
Impulsive buying behavior				
IPL1	0.901			
IPL2	0.932	0.908	0.936	0.697
IPL3	0.639			

Discriminant validity was assessed using (1) Fornell-Larcker and (2) cross-loading criteria. Table 3 presents the square root of the AVE in bold along the diagonal, verifying the condition of being higher than the correlation between constructs (Fornell & Larcker, 1981). The heterotrait–monotrait ratio (HTMT) was evaluated to determine the discriminant validity. The critical threshold for the HTMT was 0.85. The HTMT should be less than 0.85 in order to establish discriminant validity (Henseler et al., 2015).

Table 3. Assessment of discriminant validity

Constructs	INF	PER	PL	PS	SC	UPL
Information Availability (INF)	*0.859*	0.683	0.578	0.636	0.624	0.578
Personalization (PER)	0.534	*0.865*	0.679	0.616	0.661	0.619
Impulsive Behavior (PL)	0.467	0.539	*0.840*	*0.676*	0.621	0.800
Product Selection (PS)	0.536	0.518	0.555	*0.876*	0.641	0.591
Socialization (SC)	0.526	0.552	0.510	0.544	*0.869*	0.579
Urge to buy impulsive (UPL)	0.504	0.539	0.699	0.521	0.506	*0.891*

HYPOTHESIS TESTING: STRUCTURAL EQUATION MODELING

After testing the measurement validity and reliability, the authors tested the proposed hypotheses using a bootstrap resampling method with 5000 sub-samples (Hair et al., 2014). The findings are show in Table 4. The model explains a 45.8% of variation in the "urge to buy impulsively" and 57.3% in "impulsive buying behavior." First, "urge to buy impulsively" was found to be statistically significant in explaining impulsive buying behavior, with $p > 0.001$, thus supporting hypothesis H1.

Second, the effect of socialization and information availability on urge to buy impulsively were found to be statistically significant, supporting hypotheses H2a and H5a; however, both effects of socialization and information availability on impulsive buying behavior were found to be not statistically significant, and did not support hypotheses H2b and H5b.

Thirdly, personalization and product selection were found to influence both the "urge to buy impulsively" and "impulsive buying behavior," supporting hypotheses H3a, H3b, H4a and H4b. (See Table 4).

Additionally, with regard to the control variables, the results indicated that the construct "urge to buy impulsively" and "impulsive buying behavior" were found insignificantly related to both age and gender; therefore, hypotheses H6ab and H7ab were not supported.

Discussion of Findings

The positive relationship between the urge to buy impulsively and actual impulsive buying behavior was demonstrated in prior studies (Beatty & Ferrell, 1998; Badgaiyan & Verma, 2015). This present study shows a consistent result confirming this positive relationship. That is to say, the former is a desire for impulse buying and the latter fulfills this desire. More interestingly, it must be noted that even if the felt urge to buy impulsively turns out to be necessarily preceding the stage of impulsive buying, the actual impulsive buying behavior may not happen. The urge to buy impulsively is an emotional state for having impulsive buying behavior (Verhagen & Van Dolen, 2011).

Table 4. Summary of results related to hypotheses testing

	Hypothesis	t-Value	β-Value	Decision
H1	Urge to buy impulsive→ Impulsive behavior	7.516	0.000***	Supported
H2a	Socialization → Urge to buy impulsively	2.242	0.025**	Supported
H2b	Socialization → Impulsive behavior	1.512	0.131	Not supported
H3a	Personalization → Urge to buy impulsively	3.520	0.000***	Supported
H3b	Personalization → Impulsive behavior	2.357	0.018**	Supported
H4a	Product Selection → Urge to buy impulsively	3.114	0.002**	Supported
H4b	Product Selection → Impulsive behavior	3.237	0.001***	Supported
H5a	Information availability → Urge to buy impulsively	2.516	0.012**	Supported
H5b	Information availability → Impulsive behavior	0.139	0.889	Not supported
H6a	Gender → Urge to buy impulsively	0.680	0.05	Not supported
H6b	Gender → Impulsive behavior	0.167	0.013	Not supported
H7a	Age → Urge to buy impulsively	1.071	0.076	Not supported
H7b	Age → Impulsive behavior	0.781	0.059	Not supported

Socialization was found to impact the urge to buy impulsively. Socialization reflects interactions among consumers using technology. In the social commerce setting, consumers are able to replicate the experience of socializing in a synchronous manner (Mikalef et al., 2017). The activities of socializing over social commerce websites has been made much easier and more user-friendly because users can communicate with friends, share experiences relating to pages and products, or message threads in products or on brand communities (Hajli, 2014). This finding is consistent with Huang's (2016) study that stated that friends' comments have a considerable influence on consumers' desires to buy something. In contrast, socialization was found to be an insignificant influence on consumers' impulsive buying behavior. This result is consistent with the study of Wang and Xiao (2009, p. 4), which stated that impulse purchasing is "an immediate experience, often concurrent with a feeling of excitement and urgency."

Similarly, information availability has a significant effect on the urge to buy impulsively, but has an insignificant effect on impulsive buying behavior. The results of this present study revealed that consumers who had more product-related information available to them were more likely to have the desire purchase. This is consistent with Chen et al.'s (2016) study, which indicated that textual information quality influences the "urge to purchase impulsively." Information availability reflects service quality and time savings, which have a positive influence on the urge to purchase (Leong et al., 2018). However, this characteristic of social commerce environments does not affect impulse purchasing. Thus, overwhelming users with unnecessary information will not influence their impulsive buying behavior. Mikalef et al. (2017) confirmed that the amount of available information did not affect consumer purchase intentions or electronic word of mouth (eWOM) intention.

Secondly, personalization and product selection positively and significantly influences both the urge to buy impulsively and impulsive buying behavior. The essence of personalization is confirmed in social commerce environments because the environment provides only and exactly what each customer wants at the right time. In social commerce environments, this function becomes more efficient when e-retailers have the very best understanding of the consumers' needs based on those consumers' historical searching, or the information consumers have provided on a specific platform. Consumers not only feel the urge to purchase impulsively, but also to engage in impulsively behavior.

Meanwhile, product selection would influence consumers' desires because e-retailers have enhanced shopping efficiency, which has provided changes and variety, resulting and in a relief from boredom. Offering a variety of products has a direct and positive effect on impulsive buying behavior. A similar idea was suggested by Park et al.'s (2011) study wherein results revealed a direct and negative effect of product selection on impulsive buying behavior. While consumers were less likely to purchase on impulsive according to the study by Park et al. (2011), this present study suggests that product selection encourages consumers' impulse purchases. Also, a previous study by Mikalef et al. (2017) showed that product selection did not impact behavioral intention. This result may be due to the differences in context of the study when compared to the present study's context, wherein product selection has been validated to have a direct and positive effect on impulsive buying behavior. It is an interesting and, perhaps, distinctive finding in emerging markets.

Vietnamese consumers appear most interested in a greater variety of products. They tend to shop online when their product expectations are met or exceeded. This is especially true when social commerce platforms promote a wide variety of products that align with the consumers' needs enabling consumers to make the best possible selection.

CONCLUSION

Theoretical Implications

This study contributed new insights to understanding the determinants of online impulse purchasing both Information System (IS) and marketing perspectives. First, this study applied the S-R model to investigate the characteristics of the social commerce environments that influence consumers' urge to buy impulsively and impulsive buying behavior. The authors expanded on Mikalef et al.'s (2017) study by showing that social commerce constructs influence not only planned behavior, but also unplanned behavior. Therefore, the findings of this study can enrich the understanding of academics and researchers regarding the impact of social commerce environments.

Second, this study confirms the appropriateness of using the S-R theory for testing online impulsive-buying behavior and the urge to buy impulsively and, thus, offers a valid theoretical perspective for the facet of online consumer behavior. By introducing social commerce constructs as stimulus, this study provides a deeper understanding of what takes place in consumers' minds unconsciously before an impulse purchase is made.

Third, several new relationships have also been empirically validated in the emergency market. The findings have stressed that the impact of socialization and information availability on impulsive buying behavior appeared to be different when compared to the impacts of these factors on the urge to buy impulsively. While all of the characteristics of social commerce environments were found to be supported for the urge to buy impulsively, only personalization and product selection were found to significantly influence actual impulsive buying behavior. The results show that that "urge to buy impulsively" is a prior stage of impulsive buying behavior (Beatty & Ferrell, 1998; Badgaiyan & Verma, 2015). Socialization and information availability were found to be unrelated to "actual impulsive buying behavior" while still being found to significantly affect the "urge to buy impulsively." This implies that the impact of socialization and information availability has not lead to actual impulsive buying behavior, thus, consumers may feel temporarily out of control, but then, they pay more attention to behavioral consequences.

Fourth, the mediating role of the "urge to buy impulsively" reveals that consumers have to process stimuli and have a desire before engaging in impulsive buying behavior. Additionally, the internal process can lead to consumers' impulsive purchasing behavior or may only stop their desire. Finally, the theoretical model was validated in the newly emerged F-commerce context of developing countries.

Practical Implications

Besides the theoretical implications, this study also contributed significant practical implications. First, consumers with high socializing are the desire to buy a product at sudden. Facebook retailers may create a fan club where consumers can interact with one another and share information. In addition, personalization is crucial to the urge to buy impulsively and impulsive buying behavior. So, to stimulate impulsive buying behavior, online retailers should create personalized content that is meaningful and targeted to a specific kind of consumer. More specifically, online retailers can communicate with consumers in a human way and create meaningful conversations that are based on the core interests of their target consumers. This allows them to build engagement and consumers' trust. Moreover, personal recommendation agents will increase a good shopping experience by reducing the overlap, or redundancy of information, which creates an encouraging environment for customers.

Furthermore, offering a variety of product selections to specific consumers allows them to easily find items that match their needs and interests. Although previous studies found that a range of products may distract consumers from making the best selection (Mikalef et al., 2017). However, this study showed that a variety of products stimulate consumers' desires as well as their decisions to purchase impulsively. In order to direct sell products via Facebook to the right consumers with the right offer, online retailers should build carousels featuring a range of products in one post to avoid too much information. In addition, consumers are likely to visit a store if the retailers provide product availability information online. Online retailers need to provide accurate information and show consumers the benefits of products and services, which will create the feelings that consumers will get when they own the products, which will then increase the consumer's desire to buy.

LIMITATIONS AND FUTURE RESEARCH

The present study exhibited some important insights. Still, it is not without limitations, which need to be considered for future research. First, the data were collected for the study from various types of products (e.g. clothing, cosmetics, food, etc.) and is limited geographically to Vietnam consumers who shop online. Future studies should attempt to define the extent to which impulsive behaviors are triggered by different products and services, which will help researchers and managers to develop strategy for different products and services. Additional research should test the moderating effect on the relationship between social commerce features and impulse buying behavior, such as demographic variables or situational factors, which would help deepen an understanding about consumers' impulsive buying behavior. In addition, it would be interesting to compare two models, such as the differences between developing and developed countries.

ACKNOWLEDGMENT

This research was supported by the Internal Grant Agency of the Faculty of Management and Economics, Tomas Bata University in Zlin, grant No. IGA/FaME/2018/015.

REFERENCES

Aydin, G. (2019). Examining Social Commerce Intentions Through the Uses and Gratifications Theory. *International Journal of E-Business Research*, *15*(2), 44–70. doi:10.4018/IJEBR.2019040103

Badgaiyan, A. J., & Verma, A. (2015). Does urge to buy impulsively differ from impulsive buying behaviour? Assessing the impact of situational factors. *Journal of Retailing and Consumer Services*, *22*, 145–157. doi:10.1016/j.jretconser.2014.10.002

Beatty, S. E., & Ferrell, M. E. (1998). Impulse buying: Modeling its precursors. *Journal of Retailing*, *74*(2), 169–191. doi:10.1016/S0022-4359(99)80092-X

Chan, T. K. H., Cheung, C. M. K., & Lee, Z. W. Y. (2017). The state of online impulse-buying research: A literature analysis. *Information & Management*, *54*(2), 204–217. doi:10.1016/j.im.2016.06.001

Chang, H. J., Eckmanb, M., & Yanb, R. N. (2011). Application of the stimulus-organism-response model to the retail environment: The role of hedonic motivation in impulse buying behavior. *International Review of Retail, Distribution and Consumer Research*, *21*(3), 233–249. doi:10.1080/09593969.2011.578798

Chen, J. V., Su, B. C., & Widjaja, A. E. (2016). Facebook C2C social commerce: A study of online impulse buying. *Decision Support Systems*, *83*, 57–69. doi:10.1016/j.dss.2015.12.008

Chung, N., Song, H. G., & Lee, H. (2017). Consumers' impulsive buying behavior of restaurant products in social commerce. *International Journal of Contemporary Hospitality Management*, *29*(2), 709–731. doi:10.1108/IJCHM-10-2015-0608

Coley, A., & Burgess, B. (2003). Gender differences in cognitive and affective impulse buying. *Journal of Fashion Marketing and Management*, *7*(3), 282–295. doi:10.1108/13612020310484834

Fornell, C., & Larcker, D. F. (1981). Structural equation models with unobservable variables and measurement error: Algebra and statistics.

Fram, E. H., & Grady, D. B. (1995). Internet buyers. Will the surfers become buyers? *Direct Marketing*, *58*(6), 63–65.

Ghani, U., Imran, M., & Ali Jan, F. (2011). The impact of demographic characteristics on impulse buying behaviour of urban consumers in peshawar. *International Journal of Academic Research*, *3*(5).

Hair, J. Jr, Sarstedt, M., Hopkins, L., & Kuppelwieser, G., V. (2014). Partial least squares structural equation modeling (PLS-SEM) An emerging tool in business research. *European Business Review*, *26*(2), 106–121. doi:10.1108/EBR-10-2013-0128

Hajli, N. (2015). Social commerce constructs and consumer's intention to buy. *International Journal of Information Management, 35*(2), 183–191. doi:10.1016/j.ijinfomgt.2014.12.005

Hajli, N., Sims, J., Zadeh, A. H., & Richard, M. O. (2017). A social commerce investigation of the role of trust in a social networking site on purchase intentions. *Journal of Business Research, 71*, 133–141. doi:10.1016/j.jbusres.2016.10.004

Henseler, J., Ringle, C. M., & Sarstedt, M. (2015). A new criterion for assessing discriminant validity in variance-based structural equation modeling. *Journal of the Academy of Marketing Science, 43*(1), 115–135. doi:10.100711747-014-0403-8

Hoyer, W. D., MacInnis, D. J., Pieters, R., Chan, E., & Northey, G. (2018). *Consumer Behavior. Asia – Pacific Edition, State.* South Melbourne, Victoria: Australia Cengage Learning Australia.

Hsu, H. Y., & Tsou, H.-T. (2011). Understanding customer experiences in online blog environments. *International Journal of Information Management, 31*(6), 510–523. doi:10.1016/j.ijinfomgt.2011.05.003

Huang, L.-T. (2016). Flow and social capital theory in online impulse buying. *Journal of Business Research Flow, 69.*

Kim, S., & Eastin, M. S. (2011). Hedonic tendencies and the online consumer: An investigation of the online shopping process. *Journal of Internet Commerce, 10*(1), 68–90. doi:10.1080/15332861.2011.558458

Kim, S., & Park, H. (2013). Effects of various characteristics of social commerce (s commerce) on consumers' trust and trust performance. *International Journal of Information Management, 33*(2), 318–332. doi:10.1016/j.ijinfomgt.2012.11.006

Leong, L. Y., Jaafar, N. I., & Ainin, S. (2018). Understanding Facebook Commerce (F-Commerce) Actual Purchase from an Artificial Neural Network Perspective. *Journal of Electronic Commerce Research, 19*(1).

Li, C. Y. (2017). How social commerce constructs influence customers' social shopping intention? An empirical study of a social commerce website. *Technological Forecasting and Social Change, 0–1*(129).

Lin, K. Y., & Lu, H. P. (2011). Why people use social networking sites: An empirical study integrating network externalities and motivation theory. *Computers in Human Behavior, 27*(3), 1152–1161. doi:10.1016/j.chb.2010.12.009

Mai, N. T. T., Jung, K., Lantz, G., & Loeb, S. G. (2003). An exploratory investigation into impulse behavior in a transitional economy: A study of urban consumers in Vietnam. *Journal of International Marketing, 11*(2), 13–35. doi:10.1509/jimk.11.2.13.20162

Mehrabian, A., & Russell, J. A. (1974). *An approach to environmental psychology.* MIT Press.

Mikalef, P., Giannakos, M., & Pateli, A. (2013). Shopping and word-of-mouth intentions on social media. *Journal of Theoretical and Applied Electronic Commerce Research, 8*(1), 17–34. doi:10.4067/S0718-18762013000100003

Mikalef, P., Giannakos, M. N., & Pappas, I. O. (2017). Designing social commerce platforms based on consumers' intentions. *Behaviour & Information Technology, 36*(12), 1308–1327. doi:10.1080/01449 29X.2017.1386713

Mittal, S., Sondhi, N., & Chawla, D. (2015). Impulse buying behaviour: An emerging market perspective. *International Journal of Indian Culture and Business Management*, *11*(1), 1–22. doi:10.1504/IJICBM.2015.070246

Nadeem, W., Juntunen, M., & Juntunen, J. (2017). Consumer segments in social commerce: A latent class approach. *Journal of Consumer Behaviour*, *16*(3), 279–292. doi:10.1002/cb.1632

Osorio, C. A., & Papagiannidis, S. (2019). A study of networking and information exchange factors influencing user participation in niche social networking sites. *International Journal of E-Business Research*, *15*(2), 1–21. doi:10.4018/IJEBR.2019040101

Ozen, H., & Engizek, N. (2014). Shopping online without thinking: Being emotional or rational? *Asia Pacific Journal of Marketing and Logistics*, *26*(1), 78–93. doi:10.1108/APJML-06-2013-0066

Pagani, M., & Mirabello, A. (2011). The influence of personal and social-interactive engagement in social TV web sites. *International Journal of Electronic Commerce*, *16*(2), 41–68. doi:10.2753/JEC1086-4415160203

Park, E. J., Kim, E. Y., Funches, V. M., & Foxx, W. (2011). Apparel Product Attributes, Web Browsing, and E-Impulse Buying on Shopping Web-Sites. *Journal of Business Research*, *65*(11), 1583–1589. doi:10.1016/j.jbusres.2011.02.043

Park, E. J., Kim, E. Y., Funches, V. M., & Foxx, W. (2012). Apparel product attributes, web browsing, and e-impulse buying on shopping websites ☆. *Journal of Business Research*, *65*(11), 1583–1589. doi:10.1016/j.jbusres.2011.02.043

Park, M.-S., Shin, J.-K., & Ju, Y. (2014). Social networking atmosphere and online retailing. *Journal of Global Scholars of Marketing Science*, *24*(1), 89–107. doi:10.1080/21639159.2013.867681

Rook, D. W. (1987). The buying impulse. *The Journal of Consumer Research*, *14*(2), 189–199. doi:10.1086/209105

Saad, M., & Metawie, M. (2015). Store Environment, Personality Factors and Impulse Buying Behavior in Egypt: The Mediating roles of Shop Enjoyment and Impulse Buying Tendencies. *Journal of Business and Management Sciences, 3*(2), 69-77.

Santini, F. D. O., Ladeira, W. J., Vieira, V. A., Araujo, C. F., & Sampaio, C. H. (2017). Antecedents and consequences of impulse buying: a meta-analytic study. *RAUSP Management Journal*, (September).

Shen, K. N., & Khalifa, M. (2012). System design effects on online impulse buying. *Internet Research*, *22*(4), 396–425. doi:10.1108/10662241211250962

Thurstone, L. L. (1923). The Stimulus-Response Fallacy in Psychology. *Psychological Review*, *30*(5), 354–369. doi:10.1037/h0074251

To, P. L., Liao, C., & Lin, T. H. (2007). Shopping motivations on Internet: A study based on utilitarian and hedonic value. *Technovation*, *27*(12), 774–787. doi:10.1016/j.technovation.2007.01.001

Tung. (2017). *Vietnam has the highest e-commerce adoption rate in Southeast Asia: EIU Report*. Retrieved from https://e27.co/vietnam-most-online-shoppers-southeast-asia-report-20181105/

Verhagen, T., & Van Dolen, W. (2011). The influence of online store beliefs on consumer online impulse buying: A model and empirical application. *Information & Management*, *48*(8), 320–327. doi:10.1016/j. im.2011.08.001

Wang, H. C., & Doong, H. S. (2010). Argument Form and Spokesperson Type: The Recommendation Strategy of Virtual Salespersons. *International Journal of Information Management*, *30*(6), 493–501. doi:10.1016/j.ijinfomgt.2010.03.006

Wang, J., & Xiao, J. J. (2009). Buying behavior, social support and credit card indebtedness of college students. *International Journal of Consumer Studies*, *33*(1), 2–10. doi:10.1111/j.1470-6431.2008.00719.x

Weinberg, P., & Gottwald, W. (1982). Impulsive consumer buying as a result of emotions. *Journal of Business Research*, *10*(1), 43–57. doi:10.1016/0148-2963(82)90016-9

Wolfinbarger, M., & Gilly, M. C. (2001). Shopping online for freedom, control, and fun. *California Management Review*, *43*(2), 34–55. doi:10.2307/41166074

Xiang, L., Zheng, X., Lee, M. K. O., & Zhao, D. (2016). Exploring consumers' impulse buying behavior on social commerce platform: The role of parasocial interaction. *International Journal of Information Management*, *36*(3), 333–347. doi:10.1016/j.ijinfomgt.2015.11.002

Yu, C., & Bastin, M. (2010). Hedonic shopping value and impulse buying behavior in transitional economies: A symbiosis in the Mainland China marketplace. *Brand Management*, *18*(2), 105–114. doi:10.1057/bm.2010.32

Zhang, H., Lu, Y., Gupta, S., & Zhao, L. (2014). What motivates customers to participate in social commerce? the impact of technological environments and virtual customer experiences. *Information & Management*, *51*(8), 1017–1030. doi:10.1016/j.im.2014.07.005

This research was previously published in the International Journal of E-Business Research (IJEBR), 16(3); pages 74-88, copyright year 2020 by IGI Publishing (an imprint of IGI Global).

Section 2
Development and Design Methodologies

Chapter 13
Effects of Social Media Marketing Strategies on Consumers Behavior

Shamsher Singh
Banarsidas Chandiwala Institute of Professional Studies, India

Deepali Saluja
Banarsidas Chandiwala Institute of Professional Studies, India

ABSTRACT

In the information age, social media is growing rapidly and at a faster pace. Social media is playing an important role in the day-to-day life of individuals. Using social media has become the everyday routine. Many social media sites display different types of advertisements by which the decision-making process is generally getting affected. Social media is much more than just a medium of sharing information. The present study is an attempt to understand how social media affects the decision-making process of consumers and the impacts of various marketing strategies used by firms on social media. The study employs the survey method to collect primary data from 200 customers who have been regularly using social media. Factor analysis and ANOVA has been used to gain insights in the study. The selected respondents are assumed to represent the population in the urban areas of Delhi.

INTRODUCTION

What is the similarity between Ex US President Barack Obama, Indian super star Amitabh Bachchan, Indian Minister Narender Modi, present US President Donald Trump and Chinese seasoning and processed food maker Chings Secret? All these celebrity are using social networking for their brand promotion. Narender Modi has 40 million follower on face book followed by Donald Trump with 20 million, (Quartz India, 2017) Obama has a fan following of over a million, Bachchan of over three lakhs, Chings Secret has built over one lakh followers through social media. Today everyone is using some social networking site or the other. If they are a professional they use LinkedIn. If they have a flair for

DOI: 10.4018/978-1-6684-6287-4.ch013

writing, they are either a regular blogger or use micro blogging sites like Twitter. If they are interested in connecting with their old friends or finding new ones they are likely to use Facebook, Orkut and many others. And there are several other social networking sites which cater to varied tastes, like Flickr for photography and YouTube for videos, music and movies. Invariably, more often than not, users on these sites are discussing a brand / product / service. These individuals are using social media to share views, and news about brands. Consequently, from the point of a brand promotion and management, social media becomes a significant tool.

Social media are media for social interaction, using highly accessible and scalable publishing techniques. Social media uses web-based technologies to turn communication into interactive dialogues. Kaplan and Heinlein (2010) define social media as "a group of Internet-based applications that build on the ideological and technological foundations of Web 2.0, which allows the creation and exchange of user-generated content". Social media is the medium to socialize. They use web-based technology to quickly disseminate knowledge and information to a huge number of users. They allow creation and exchange of user-generated content. Facebook, Twitter, Hi5, Orkut and other social networking sites are collectively referred to as social media. Social media represents low-cost tools that are used to combine technology and social interaction with the use of words. These tools are typically internet or mobile based like Twitter, Facebook, MySpace and YouTube.

Social Media, today, is among the 'best opportunities available' to a brand for connecting with prospective consumers. Social Media Marketing is the new mantra for several brands since early last year. Significantly different from conventional marketing strategies, Social Media Marketing (SMM) offers three distinct advantages.

- It provides a window to marketers to not only present products / services to customers but also to listen to customers' grievances and suggestions.
- It makes it easy for marketers to identify various peer groups or influencers among various groups, who in turn can become brand evangelist and help in organic growth of a brand.
- All this is done at nearly zero cost (as compared to conventional customer outreach programmes) as most of the social networking sites are free.

Social media marketing helps in generating exposure to businesses, increasing traffic /subscribers, building new business partnerships, rise in search engine rankings, generating qualified leads due to better lead generation efforts, selling more products and services and reduction in overall marketing expenses. The use of social media sites as part of a company's marketing strategy has increased significantly in the past couple years. As Swedowsky (2009) stated, businesses can not afford to ignore the benefits of using social media. In the past, consumers often just had the opinions of a few friends before making a significant purchase. The use of social media can increase number of opinions from just a few to hundreds or even thousands. Swedowsky reiterated that social media continues to abound for both businesses and the consumer.

Online access is no longer a luxury, it is a necessity. Businesses have also realized that consumers use social media because it is fun. They can easily share their ideas, photos, videos, likes and dislikes with each other. Businesses realize that importance of having increased interaction with consumers and retailers, and the use of social media gives them the opportunity to more efficiently meet the demand of their customers.

Many firms now use social media to enhance their marketing scheme. Firms also use social media for promotions and to survey groups for past purchases and interests. One has to be careful, however, when reading the reviews of any firm on a social media outlet. It is obvious that the use of social media to enhance marketing, is here to stay, so one must consider all possible avenues to positively use it to increase advertising and improve marketing. It is also obvious that there are benefits, drawbacks, and challenges associated with any social media strategy, and these must be addressed before a specific social media strategy is implemented. The purpose of social media should be to enhance a business branding and permit their biggest fans (i.e., super fans) to just talk about them. Businesses need to assist in facilitating the social media inputs and discussions.

The present article has made an attempt to find how the social media influences the consumer behaviour in general and in the urban area like Delhi in particular. The present study has used the survey method to collect the primary data from 200 respondents in Delhi who has been using the social media at least for last 6 months and are well versed with the uses of social media by the different organisations.

LITERATURE REVIEW

Social media includes online networks (e.g., Facebook, MySpace, and LinkedIn), wikis (e.g., Wikipedia), multimedia sharing sites (e.g., YouTube and Flickr), bookmarking sites (e.g., Del.icio.us and Digg), virtual worlds (e.g., Second Life), and rating sites (e.g. Yelp) (Edwards, 2011). The distinctive characteristic of social media is that it is a personalized user generated media. Users exercise greater control over its use and content generation (Dickey and Lewis, 2011).

Consumers are no more willing to listen what business organizations want them to listen rather they want business organizations to listen what they say. This attitudinal and behavioral transition in consumers is the impact of social media emergence and it is a big challenge for business firms to deal with it (Kietzmann et al., 2011). This situation signals that business firms should identify those factors of social media that affect the consumer attitude towards the product related information embedded in social media content. This may enable businesses to develop the affective social media promotional strategies. Social media has become the core of the marketing communication as some business gurus say that if business firms do not participate in social media they are not part of cyberspace anymore. Social media enables businesses to contact the end users directly and timely relatively at lower cost than traditional media (Kaplan and Haenlein, 2010).

With the rise in social networks, a new era of content creation has emerged, where individuals can easily share experiences and information with other users (Chen. 2011a) Social media provide opportunities for businesses to become more attractive universally (Chen 2011b). Today a large number of social media platforms have been developed that smooth the progress of sharing information and generation of content in an online context (Chen et al. 2011a). There are a number of social media that facilitate these activities, such as Wikipedia, Facebook, YouTube and Twitter. Individuals apply different social media tools, such as online forums and communities, recommendations, ratings and reviews, to interact with other users online. In fact, individuals are attracted online to exchange information and receive social support (Ridings & Gefen 2004).

Since the inception of social media, various studies have been conducted to examine its different aspects particularly those that drive the individuals to participate in social media. For instance, Daugherty et al. (2008) attempted to explore the factors motivating consumers to create social media content. Cheong and Morrison (2008) examined the consumers opinions about the recommendations and information implanted in user-generated content and producer generated content. Sun et al. (2009) studied the factors that support or inhibit users' knowledge sharing intentions in virtual. Imran and Zaheer (2012) in their study of social media theories argues that if more users of the social media produce the same views in the form of blogs, posts, scraps, reviews, comments etc., about a product it makes product related information credible. This postulation is in line with the assumption of social impact theory (Latane, 1981) which proposes as the number of people increases in a social group influence on target individual's attitude and behavior increases.

Social media users (e.g. members of Facebook) often share their product or brand related experiences and information in the form of posts, comments, and ratings. Individuals are influenced by the actions of others, entertained by their performance and sometimes persuaded by their arguments (Latane, 1981). Consumers rely on multiple sources to determine the credibility of information produced by online communities and bloggers. (Flanagin et al., 2011). (Cheung, Lee, and Rabjohn, 2008; Metzger, et al 2010).In addition, they also rely on the ratings of others, the number of posts, and the usefulness of the information presented (O'Reilly and Marx, 2011). User-generated information in the form of ratings and recommendations from others helps a consumer to assess the credibility of user generated contents (UGC). People join online social networks to search for technical specification of their desired products and brands, check out the new collections in different product categories, people read product related reviews or threads on social media to make the well-considered buying decisions (Muntinga, et al., 2011).

Social media explosion has changed the communication landscape around the globe (Edwards, 2011). It had affected the marketer and consumer relationship. Consumers are no more willing to listen what business organizations want them to listen rather they want business organizations to listen what they say (Kietzmann et al., 2011). Today young consumers believe more in the product related content or information created which other consumers generate on social networking sites, multi media sites, blogs, and so on than producer or company produced product related content, despite being personally unknown or unrelated to the user (Jonas, 2010). Nowak, et al (1990) suggested that a simple model of individual influence, operating in accordance with some general principles of social impact, if extended to reflect how individuals influence and are influenced by each other over time, can lead to plausible predictions of public opinion. Williams and Williams (1989) postulated that social impact varies depending on the underlying purpose of compliance.

Previous research has demonstrated that traditional media publicity can affect marketing outcomes (Agrawal and Kamakura 1995; Elberse 2007; Trusov et al., 2009), similarly online consumer-generated content such as online reviews can also affect sales (e.g.. Chevalier and Mayzlin 2006), and sometimes even negative publicity can have a positive marketing effect (Ahluwalia et al 2000; Berger, et al., 2010). Users perceive advertising differently depending on the social network, which suggests user motivations for online social networking may play a vital role in defining consumer's responses to social media marketing According to Chi (2011) social media is not only for advertising, but it can also be a tool for brands or services to connect with their consumers. Social media allows consumers and prospective consumers to communicate directly to a brand representative. Since most consumers are using the social media as tool to search and purchase items, brands or services use this advantage to advertise their products. The analysis of consumer behavior is central for marketing success, especially since most potential consumers are using the internet and different online socializing tools. The online audience is a booming market worldwide, however giving its globalized nature a level of segmentation is needed cross-culturally (Vinerean, et,.al, 2013)

Social media can build brand attitudes that affect buying behavior. The good image of brand or product can lead the consumer to make decision on their purchases. When consumer's friend on social media shares or recommends services or products on their social media, it affects brand attitude and influences their decision-making. Yet, advertising on social media, which is provided by commercial sources affect both consumer brand attitudes and purchasing intention (Yang, 2012). From that information, it helps marketers plan their marketing strategies. Many marketers use social media for marketing campaigns. It is the easy way to communicate with consumers; also it is inexpensive to advertise their brands or services.

In the marketing literature, scholars have specifically emphasized the effects of online word of mouth through social media activities (Kimmel and Kitchen 2014). Organizations have realized social media to be a new set of business processes and operations that may help firms increase sales (Dewan and Ramaprasad 2014). The study of Abdul Razak,and Latip.(2016) revealed that there are a few factors that influences the usage of social media marketing by SMEs. These factors were identified as usefulness, ease of use and enjoyment.

Areeba, et,.al, (2017) found that marketers need to consider the strategic role of consumer engagement in arousing purchase intention. They also need to strategically enhance their social media marketing communication so that the maximum benefits of engaging customers can be reaped. Marketers should consider offering some additional support to consumers through their social media page design, for example, allow space for consumers to share their related experiences and opinions of using certain products or services with other consumers. This kind of information can help other consumers to decide on what they want to purchase.

Jack Ma, the founder of Chinese e-commerce firm, Alibaba, said that failure to utilise the social network platform as a media to interact with consumers and other business associates or prospects and potentials may lead them to be excluded from the industry, thereby, losing their position in the market (Barhemmati & Ahmad, 2015). Consumer engagement on social networking sites is largely supported by an emotional attachment which is directed to enhance their purchase behavior. Such an engagement would lead to increased consumer loyalty who can then promote the brand and its products to other consumers in the virtual world (Asperen, Rooij, & Dijkmans, 2017)

Dehghani and Tumer (2015) find that Facebook advertising can significantly affect the brand image and brand equity by offering greater interactivity, personalisation and feedback. This process can in turn, affect consumer purchase intentions. Pjero and Kercini (2015) in their study focusing on social media and its influence on consumer behaviour observe that information about products and services offered in the virtual world can positively impact the purchase intentions of consumers. A consumer may be influenced by eWOM (electronic word-of-mouth) by other users.

In today's borderless world, people throughout the globe are using social media in real time for various purposes of communication, with majority spending almost a quarter of their daily time, surfing social networks Companies offering services and products are determined to get the attention of social network consumers thus, these companies are redesigning their marketing strategies and policies. Among these is the strategy of integrating social media into their marketing scheme, one aspect of change that is hoped to project their products, services and brands to the outside world(Forbes, 2017).

The advertising quality on the social networking website is an important factor from user point of view. Social media has strong influence and impact on decision making of customers, however many a time the information available on social media website does not make user comfortable while making decision and they have to search for other sources of information before making buying decision. The organisation likely to use social media as part of their marketing strategies must ensure that sufficient information is provided to the uses so that they are comfortable in making purchase decision (Singh,2016)

There has been little research to explore the implications for the sales force on social media and the communication technology usage patterns associated with it. It would seem that this is a vital gap for sales force research and practice. In particular, social media, such as Facebook, LinkedIn, and now Google+, and communication technology, such as mobile Internet and the smart phone, appear to be more than simple extensions of traditional technology such as static phones, desktops, and even laptops. Today, salespeople often do not have a choice as to whether or not they are contactable. The rise of global business exacerbates such a situation, meaning salespeople might feel that they are on call 24 hours a day and are expected to respond to communications immediately whatever time they come through from anywhere in the world. (Marshall,et al., 2012).

Customer engagement has become a "strategic imperative" for businesses since "engaged customers play a key role in viral marketing activity by providing referrals and/or recommendations for specific products, services, and/or brands to others" (Brodie et al. 2011). Customer-oriented salespeople have often sought new ways to interact and engage with customers to co-create value (Jones, et al., 2003). Bowden (2009) suggests that customer engagement involves a calculative commitment, which forms the basis for consequent buying behavior; leads to an emotional commitment, which forms the basis for buyer loyalty and increases buyers' involvement and trust.

Customer engagement is often considered to be highly correlated with trust and commitment in buyer–seller relationships. Push strategies that utilize large professional networks to disseminate referrals are likely to be more effective when customers are highly engaged. Customer engagement can be increased by providing opportunities to seek, give, and pass opinions (Chu and Kim 2011) about products and services in online communities, wikis, and creative works–sharing sites (e.g., YouTube, Flickr). Such co-created value represents a dynamic and swelling fountain of knowledge for existing and future customers, which can be used to increase buyer involvement and trust.

OBJECTIVES AND HYPOTHESES

This study seeks to find out the impact of social media marketing strategies on consumer behaviour . In pursuance of the above objectives, the following hypotheses were formulated for testing:

$H_{01:}$ There are no significant variations in the customer response for social media marketing strategies based on respondents' gender.

H_{02}: There are no significant variations in the customer response for social media marketing strategies based on respondents' age group.

H_{03}: There are no significant variations in the customer response for social media marketing strategies based on respondents' education level.

H_{04}: There are no significant variations in the customer response for social media marketing strategies based on respondents' occupation.

H_{05}: There are no significant variations in the customer response for social media marketing strategies based on respondents' income.

H_{06}: The advertising quality on the social networking website in not an important factor for decision making by consumers.

H_{07}: Social Media does not have any impact on professional or personal life of users.

H_{08}: The content of social media does not have any impact on decision making by consumers.

H_{09}: Social media does not have any influence on decision making process of consumers related to any field.

H_{010}: The information on social media website does not make user comfortable while making decision.

H_{011}: Brand/ Organisation present on social media website does not have any influences on decision making process by consumers.

METHODOLOGY

The study has employed both primary and secondary data. The secondary data has been used to gain in the in depth knowledge of social media networking sites, where as primary data has been collected from the social media user to find their responses on the various aspects of social media marketing.

Based on the literature review on different aspects of social media a well structured questionnaire was developed. Prior to the final survey, the questionnaire was pre tested using a sample of respondents similar in nature to the final sample. The goal of pilot survey was to ensure readability and logical arrangements of questions. The final questionnaire was administered to 200 customers who were using the one or other social media sites by means of face-to-face interviews.

Limitations of the Study

The study has been carried out in the National Capital Region, which is metropolitan city area where the education level and income level of population is very high as compare to rest of India. Also there is high penetration of internet user especially in the young generation which uses the social media networking site for their personal as well professional uses. The finding of the study cannot be generalised for the whole country, hence the finding of the research can be generalised only for urban areas only.

Research and Statistical Tools Employed

The research and statistical tools employed in this study are, ANOVA, T test and Factor Analysis . SPSS 16 was used to perform statistical analysis. The reliability of the data was carried out by using Cronbach's Alpha Value. T Test and ANOVA was employed to find the significant factor which will determine the overall customer satisfaction. The third major analysis carried out was a factor analysis to examine the underlying or latent dimensions within variables of overall satisfaction (Hair, Anderson, Tatham and Black, 1998). Both Bartlett's test of spherecity and measure of sampling adequacy (MSA) were also carried out to ensure that the requirements of factor analysis were met.

DATA ANALYSIS AND INTERPRETATION

The analysis of this data was divided into following sections:

1. **Demographic profile of Respondents:** Table 1.
2. **Reliability and Validity:** Table 2.
3. **Factor Analysis:** Table 3,4&5.
4. **ANOVA:** Table 6 to 10.
5. **T- Test Computation:** Table 11.

Table 1 indicates the respondent's profile. There are 57% Male and 43% female. Students are largest respondents (4%) followed by Govt. Service (27%) and private service (24%) . Most of the respondents are either graduate (36%) or post graduate (40.%). There are 48% respondents in the 15-25 years age category, 30% in the 25-40 years category and only 22% respondents are in above 40 years. The profile of respondents indicates they are young, educated and decently employed. They belong to the new generation who are using the social networking sites for different purposes such as to connect with their friends, relatives & peers, for networking to make a opinion or to express their view point .

Table 1. Demographic profile of Respondents

Variable	Characteristics	Frequency	Percentage
Gender	Male	114	57
	Female	86	43
Occupation	Government service	54	27
	Private service	48	24
	Student	98	49
Education	Post Graduation	80	40
	Graduation	72	36
	10+2	40	20
	Others	8	4.0
Age group	15-25 yrs	96	48
	25-40 yrs	60	30
	40 yrs & above	44	22
Annual Income	"Less than Rs 100000"	58	29
	Rs.1000001to 300000	62	31
	Rs 300001to 500000	50	25
	Rs 500001and above	30	15
	Total	**200**	**100**

RELIABILITY AND VALIDITY

Table 2 shows the result of reliability analysis- Cronbach's Alpha Value. This test measured the consistency between the survey scales. The Cronbach's Alpha score of 1.0 indicate 100 percent reliability. Cronbach's Alpha scores were all greater than the Nunnaly's (1978) generally accepted score of 0.7. In this case, the score was 0.775 for the service quality provided by the banks.

Table 2. Reliability Statistics

Cronbach's Alpha	Cronbach's Alpha Based on Standardized Items	N of Items
.775	.723	19

Factor Analysis

Overall, the set of data meets the fundamental requirements of factor analysis satisfactorily (Hair et al, 1998). The Kaiser-Meyer-Olkin Measure of sampling adequacy is 0.522 which is above the acceptable level of 0.5 In analyzing the data given, the 14 response items were subjected to a factor analysis using the principal component method. Using the criteria of an Eigen value greater than one, six clear factors emerged accounting for 60.20% of the total variance. As in common practice, a Varimax rotation with Kaiser Normalization was performed to achieve a simpler and theoretically more meaningful factor solution. The Cronbach alphas score for all the factors was 0.775 (Table 2). There are six clear factor emerges from factor loadings as highlighted in Table 10. These six factors represent different elements of social networking site that form the underlying factors from the original 14 scale response items given.

Table 3. KMO and Bartlett's Test

Kaiser-Meyer-Olkin Measure of Sampling Adequacy.		.522
Bartlett's Test of Sphericity	Approx. Chi-Square	102.762
	df	91
	Sig.	.188

Referring to the Table 10, first factor represents elements of social networking sites directly related to availability of informations, therefore it is labeled as "Information factor". These elements are "social media website as source of informations, quality of advertisement on websites and field of decision making". Second factor is directly related to specific reason for using social media website; it is therefore labeled as "User factor". Third factor is directly related to favourite social media site and therefore named as "Preference factor". Fourth factor represent the impact of social media website therefore it is labeled as "Impact factor" These elements are "impact on the professional life, impact on decision making, influence of social media website on decision making and field of decision making". Fifth factor is related to time spent on website and, comfort of making purchasing decision therefore it is named as "Decision factor". Sixth factor is related to type of social media website and type of advertisement viewed on these website and therefore it is labeled as "Advertisement factor".

Table 4. Total variance explained

Component	Initial Eigenvalues			Extraction Sums of Squared Loadings			Rotation Sums of Squared Loadings		
	Total	% of Variance	Cumulative %	Total	% of Variance	Cumulative %	Total	% of Variance	Cumulative %
1	1.783	12.733	12.733	1.783	12.733	12.733	1.559	11.139	11.139
2	1.591	11.364	24.097	1.591	11.364	24.097	1.424	10.168	21.307
3	1.406	10.043	34.140	1.406	10.043	34.140	1.373	9.806	31.113
4	1.337	9.550	43.691	1.337	9.550	43.691	1.362	9.730	40.843
5	1.183	8.448	52.139	1.183	8.448	52.139	1.357	9.695	50.538
6	1.129	8.067	60.206	1.129	8.067	60.206	1.354	9.669	60.206
7	.930	6.642	66.849						
8	.804	5.741	72.590						
9	.780	5.570	78.160						
10	.728	5.201	83.361						
11	.696	4.971	88.331						
12	.619	4.423	92.755						
13	.545	3.893	96.648						
14	.469	3.352	100.000						
Extraction Method: Principal Component Analysis.									

RESULTS AND IMPLICATIONS

ANOVA has been employed to find the significant factor of social media website based on the demographic factor and to test the first five hypotheses. The significance level of 0.05 has been used as cut off for either acceptance or rejection the hypothesis. The analysis of variance based on gender indicates that the significance level is higher than 0.05 hence we accept the H_{01} and conclude that there is no significant variation in the customer response for social media marketing strategies based on respondents' gender.

The analysis of variance based on respondents' age group indicate that significance level is either less or equal to 0.05 in the attribute such as "time spent on site, type of advertisement viewed and impact on the professional life, hence we reject H_{02} and conclude that there are significant difference in the customer response for social media marketing strategies based on respondents' age group. The marketing managers may consider this important aspects while designing their marketing strategies for social media website.

The analysis of variance based on respondents' education level shows that the significance level is equal to 0.05 in the attribute s "specific reason for using social media website", hence we reject H_{03} and conclude that there are significant difference in the customer response for social media marketing strategies based on respondents' education level. Respondents uses the social media website for different purposes such as making purchase decision, friendship, professional purposes etc.

The analysis of variance based on respondents' occupation shows that the significance level is more than 0.05 level for all attributes hence we accept the H_{04} and conclude that there are no significant difference in the customer response for social media marketing strategies site based on respondents' occupation . The analysis of variance based on respondents' income shows that the significance level is more than 0.05 level for all attributes hence we accept the H_{05} and conclude that are no significant variations in the customer response for social media marketing strategies based on respondents' income. This further strengthens the arguments that the marketer can have similar Marketing strategies for all income groups.

Table 5. Rotated Component Matrix[a]

Characteristics	Component					
	1	2	3	4	5	6
Social Media Website	-.026	-.107	.196	-.026	.287	**.690**
Favourite Social Media Site	.114	.165	**.604**	-.381	.135	.043
Time Spent on site	.277	.292	-.047	.015	**.671**	.131
Preferred Time Slot of using social media website	.048	-.773	.196	-.023	.001	.139
Specific Reason for using social media website	-.089	**.744**	.325	.054	.052	.017
Social media website as Source of Informations	**.495**	-.253	-.014	-.140	.239	-.339
Type of Advertisement viewed	-.043	-.045	-.152	.032	-.067	**.610**
Quality of Advertisement on websites	**.634**	-.150	-.170	.297	-.041	.152
Impact on the Professional Life	.408	-.061	.320	**.609**	-.095	.202
Impact on Decision Making	.102	.087	-.028	**.633**	-.341	.354
Influence of Social media website on Decision Making	.263	.059	-.612	**.364**	.091	.169
Field of Decision Making	**.712**	.058	.153	-.035	-.054	-.091
Comfort of making Purchasing Decision	-.187	-.117	.022	.105	**.777**	.008
Impact of Brand or Organisation	.147	.166	.029	**.733**	.006	.146
Extraction Method: Principal Component Analysis. Rotation Method: Varimax with Kaiser Normalization. [a] Rotation converged in 17 iterations						

In order to test the remaining hypothesis the one sample T- test was carried out. This "significance value" is the P-value. It is the probability of a test score indicating the higher value or more [in the direction of the alternative hypothesis] if the null hypothesis is true. The smaller the number, the rarer our test score is under H_0 and the more likely that the null hypothesis isn't true. Using the .05 significance level as our cutoff, we find the P-value of .000 to be in our rejection region. Based on the significance value (.000) we reject null hypothesis H06 and conclude that the advertising quality on the social networking website is an important factor from user point of view. Similarly based on the significance value (.000) we reject null hypothesis H07 and conclude that Social Media does have impact on professional or personal life of users. Similarly based on the significance value (.000) we reject the entire remaining null hypothesis. This indicate that he content of social media does have impact on decision making by consumers and influences their decision making. It seems that many a time, information available on social media website is not sufficient enough to make user comfortable while making decision but it does have influence in their decision making also the Brand/ Organisation present on social media website does influences their decision making .

Table 6. Computation of ANOVA on the basis of gender

		Sum of Squares	df	Mean Square	F	Sig.
Social Media Website	Between Groups	8.876	1	8.876	2.901	.092
	Within Groups	299.874	98	3.060		
	Total	308.750	99			
Favourite Social Media Site	Between Groups	.160	1	.160	.044	.835
	Within Groups	357.880	98	3.652		
	Total	358.040	99			
Time Spent on site	Between Groups	.253	1	.253	.411	.523
	Within Groups	60.257	98	.615		
	Total	60.510	99			
Preferred Time Slot of using social media website	Between Groups	3.682	1	3.682	2.518	.116
	Within Groups	143.318	98	1.462		
	Total	147.000	99			
Specific Reason for using social media website	Between Groups	3.815	1	3.815	.652	.421
	Within Groups	573.575	98	5.853		
	Total	577.390	99			
Social media website as Source of Informations	Between Groups	.913	1	.913	.405	.526
	Within Groups	220.877	98	2.254		
	Total	221.790	99			
Type of Advertisement viewed	Between Groups	1.948	1	1.948	.895	.347
	Within Groups	213.362	98	2.177		
	Total	215.310	99			
Quality of Advertisement on websites	Between Groups	2.406	1	2.406	1.146	.287
	Within Groups	205.834	98	2.100		
	Total	208.240	99			
Impact on the Professional Life	Between Groups	.235	1	.235	.112	.739
	Within Groups	205.765	98	2.100		
	Total	206.000	99			
Impact on Decision Making	Between Groups	.940	1	.940	.526	.470
	Within Groups	175.060	98	1.786		
	Total	176.000	99			
Influence of Social media website Decision Making	Between Groups	1.810	1	1.810	.897	.346
	Within Groups	197.750	98	2.018		
	Total	199.560	99			

continues on following page

Table 6. Continued

		Sum of Squares	df	Mean Square	F	Sig.
Field of Decision Making	Between Groups	.001	1	.001	.000	.983
	Within Groups	320.109	98	3.266		
	Total	320.110	99			
Comfort of making Purchasing Decision	Between Groups	.901	1	.901	.513	.475
	Within Groups	172.099	98	1.756		
	Total	173.000	99			
Impact of Brand or Organisation	Between Groups	2.150	1	2.150	1.094	.298
	Within Groups	192.610	98	1.965		
	Total	194.760	99			

Table 7. Computation of ANOVA on the basis of age group

		Sum of Squares	df	Mean Square	F	Sig.
Social Media Website	Between Groups	17.257	5	3.451	1.113	.359
	Within Groups	291.493	94	3.101		
	Total	308.750	99			
Favourite Social Media Site	Between Groups	23.313	5	4.663	1.309	.267
	Within Groups	334.727	94	3.561		
	Total	358.040	99			
Time Spent on site	Between Groups	6.459	5	1.292	2.247	.056
	Within Groups	54.051	94	.575		
	Total	60.510	99			
Preferred Time Slot of using social media website	Between Groups	3.214	5	.643	.420	.834
	Within Groups	143.786	94	1.530		
	Total	147.000	99			
Specific Reason for using social media website	Between Groups	30.635	5	6.127	1.053	.391
	Within Groups	546.755	94	5.817		
	Total	577.390	99			
Social media website as Source of Informations	Between Groups	12.025	5	2.405	1.078	.378
	Within Groups	209.765	94	2.232		
	Total	221.790	99			
Type of Advertisement viewed	Between Groups	22.736	5	4.547	2.220	.059
	Within Groups	192.574	94	2.049		
	Total	215.310	99			
Quality of Advertisement on websites	Between Groups	5.556	5	1.111	.515	.764
	Within Groups	202.684	94	2.156		
	Total	208.240	99			

continues on following page

Table 7. Continued

		Sum of Squares	df	Mean Square	F	Sig.
Impact on the Professional Life	Between Groups	21.238	5	4.248	2.161	.065
	Within Groups	184.762	94	1.966		
	Total	206.000	99			
Impact on Decision Making	Between Groups	6.917	5	1.383	.769	.574
	Within Groups	169.083	94	1.799		
	Total	176.000	99			
Influence of Social media website Decision Making	Between Groups	10.552	5	2.110	1.050	.393
	Within Groups	189.008	94	2.011		
	Total	199.560	99			
Field of Decision Making	Between Groups	6.436	5	1.287	.386	.857
	Within Groups	313.674	94	3.337		
	Total	320.110	99			
Comfort of making Purchasing Decision	Between Groups	5.568	5	1.114	.625	.681
	Within Groups	167.432	94	1.781		
	Total	173.000	99			
Impact of Brand or Organisation	Between Groups	12.209	5	2.442	1.257	.289
	Within Groups	182.551	94	1.942		
	Total	194.760	99			

Table 8. Computation of ANOVA on the basis of education

		Sum of Squares	df	Mean Square	F	Sig.
Social Media Website	Between Groups	15.994	3	5.331	1.748	.162
	Within Groups	292.756	96	3.050		
	Total	308.750	99			
Favourite Social Media Site	Between Groups	5.276	3	1.759	.479	.698
	Within Groups	352.764	96	3.675		
	Total	358.040	99			
Time Spent on site	Between Groups	2.030	3	.677	1.111	.349
	Within Groups	58.480	96	.609		
	Total	60.510	99			
Preferred Time Slot of using social media website	Between Groups	5.460	3	1.820	1.234	.302
	Within Groups	141.540	96	1.474		
	Total	147.000	99			
Specific Reason for using social media website	Between Groups	44.914	3	14.971	2.699	.050
	Within Groups	532.476	96	5.547		
	Total	577.390	99			

continues on following page

Table 8. Continued

		Sum of Squares	df	Mean Square	F	Sig.
Social media website as Source of Informations	Between Groups	4.167	3	1.389	.613	.608
	Within Groups	217.623	96	2.267		
	Total	221.790	99			
Type of Advertisement viewed	Between Groups	3.686	3	1.229	.557	.644
	Within Groups	211.624	96	2.204		
	Total	215.310	99			
Quality of Advertisement on websites	Between Groups	3.272	3	1.091	.511	.676
	Within Groups	204.968	96	2.135		
	Total	208.240	99			
Impact on the Professional Life	Between Groups	4.598	3	1.533	.731	.536
	Within Groups	201.402	96	2.098		
	Total	206.000	99			
Impact on Decision Making	Between Groups	4.068	3	1.356	.757	.521
	Within Groups	171.932	96	1.791		
	Total	176.000	99			
Influence of Social media website Decision Making	Between Groups	5.167	3	1.722	.851	.470
	Within Groups	194.393	96	2.025		
	Total	199.560	99			
Field of Decision Making	Between Groups	7.839	3	2.613	.803	.495
	Within Groups	312.271	96	3.253		
	Total	320.110	99			
Comfort of making Purchasing Decision	Between Groups	2.214	3	.738	.415	.743
	Within Groups	170.786	96	1.779		
	Total	173.000	99			
Impact of Brand or Organisation	Between Groups	5.560	3	1.853	.940	.424
	Within Groups	189.200	96	1.971		
	Total	194.760	99			

Table 9. Computation of ANOVA on the basis of occupation

		Sum of Squares	df	Mean Square	F	Sig.
Social Media Website	Between Groups	5.336	2	2.668	.853	.429
	Within Groups	303.414	97	3.128		
	Total	308.750	99			
Favourite Social Media Site	Between Groups	.969	2	.485	.132	.877
	Within Groups	357.071	97	3.681		
	Total	358.040	99			

continues on following page

Table 9. Continued

		Sum of Squares	df	Mean Square	F	Sig.
Time Spent on site	Between Groups	1.429	2	.715	1.173	.314
	Within Groups	59.081	97	.609		
	Total	60.510	99			
Preferred Time Slot of using social media website	Between Groups	8.073	2	4.037	2.818	.065
	Within Groups	138.927	97	1.432		
	Total	147.000	99			
Specific Reason for using social media website	Between Groups	19.615	2	9.808	1.706	.187
	Within Groups	557.775	97	5.750		
	Total	577.390	99			
Social media website as Source of Informations	Between Groups	8.528	2	4.264	1.939	.149
	Within Groups	213.262	97	2.199		
	Total	221.790	99			
Type of Advertisement viewed	Between Groups	2.504	2	1.252	.571	.567
	Within Groups	212.806	97	2.194		
	Total	215.310	99			
Quality of Advertisement on websites	Between Groups	7.713	2	3.856	1.865	.160
	Within Groups	200.527	97	2.067		
	Total	208.240	99			
Impact on the Professional Life	Between Groups	3.088	2	1.544	.738	.481
	Within Groups	202.912	97	2.092		
	Total	206.000	99			
Impact on Decision Making	Between Groups	4.006	2	2.003	1.130	.327
	Within Groups	171.994	97	1.773		
	Total	176.000	99			
Influence of Social media website Decision Making	Between Groups	1.800	2	.900	.441	.644
	Within Groups	197.760	97	2.039		
	Total	199.560	99			
Field of Decision Making	Between Groups	4.726	2	2.363	.727	.486
	Within Groups	315.384	97	3.251		
	Total	320.110	99			
Comfort of making Purchasing Decision	Between Groups	4.306	2	2.153	1.238	.294
	Within Groups	168.694	97	1.739		
	Total	173.000	99			
Impact of Brand or Organisation	Between Groups	1.788	2	.894	.449	.639
	Within Groups	192.972	97	1.989		
	Total	194.760	99			

Table 10. Computation of ANOVA on the basis of annual income

		Sum of Squares	df	Mean Square	F	Sig.
Social Media Website	Between Groups	3.749	3	1.250	.393	.758
	Within Groups	305.001	96	3.177		
	Total	308.750	99			
Favourite Social Media Site	Between Groups	12.340	3	4.113	1.142	.336
	Within Groups	345.700	96	3.601		
	Total	358.040	99			
Time Spent on site	Between Groups	3.713	3	1.238	2.092	.106
	Within Groups	56.797	96	.592		
	Total	60.510	99			
Preferred Time Slot of using social media website	Between Groups	4.853	3	1.618	1.093	.356
	Within Groups	142.147	96	1.481		
	Total	147.000	99			
Specific Reason for using social media website	Between Groups	14.850	3	4.950	.845	.473
	Within Groups	562.540	96	5.860		
	Total	577.390	99			
Social media website as Source of Informations	Between Groups	13.615	3	4.538	2.093	.106
	Within Groups	208.175	96	2.168		
	Total	221.790	99			
Type of Advertisement viewed	Between Groups	2.109	3	.703	.316	.813
	Within Groups	213.201	96	2.221		
	Total	215.310	99			
Quality of Advertisement on websites	Between Groups	4.058	3	1.353	.636	.594
	Within Groups	204.182	96	2.127		
	Total	208.240	99			
Impact on the Professional Life	Between Groups	6.970	3	2.323	1.121	.345
	Within Groups	199.030	96	2.073		
	Total	206.000	99			
Impact on Decision Making	Between Groups	4.257	3	1.419	.793	.501
	Within Groups	171.743	96	1.789		
	Total	176.000	99			
Influence of Social media website Decision Making	Between Groups	3.933	3	1.311	.643	.589
	Within Groups	195.627	96	2.038		
	Total	199.560	99			
Field of Decision Making	Between Groups	1.564	3	.521	.157	.925
	Within Groups	318.546	96	3.318		
	Total	320.110	99			

continues on following page

Table 10. Continued

		Sum of Squares	df	Mean Square	F	Sig.
Comfort of making Purchasing Decision	Between Groups	10.579	3	3.526	2.084	.107
	Within Groups	162.421	96	1.692		
	Total	173.000	99			
Impact of Brand or Organisation	Between Groups	5.443	3	1.814	.920	.434
	Within Groups	189.317	96	1.972		
	Total	194.760	99			

Table 11. T- Test Computation

Statement	Test Value = 0					
	t	df	Sig. Value (2-tailed)	Mean Difference	95% Confidence Interval of the Difference	
					Lower	Upper
Interesting Advertisement Quality	15.445	99	.000	2.24000	1.9522	2.5278
Impact on Professional / Personal Life	15.251	99	.000	2.20000	1.9138	2.4862
Influence on Decision Making	16.763	99	.000	2.38000	2.0983	2.6617
Impact on Decision Making	21.938	99	.000	2.90000	2.6377	3.1623
Comfort in Purchasing Decision	19.500	99	.000	2.60000	2.3354	2.8646
Brand/ Organisation Influences on Decision making	18.519	99	.000	3.33000	2.9732	3.6868

FUTURE DIRECTION AND MANAGERIAL IMPLICATIONS

The study is descriptive in nature and provides the useful information regarding customer perspective of social media sites and how it is influencing their decision making. This study has brought an important finding that irrespective of gender, occupation and income of the customer, the marketing professional may design their marketing strategies which should have focus on broader segmentation or mass segmentation . The organisation must have their presence on the social networking sites in order to optimize their marketing promotion. The marketing only on the social media is not an ideal strategy; however it can be complementary to the traditional promotional media. Managers while deciding the promotional mix, they should include the promotion on social media websites as well. Future research can be carried out based on the findings of this study to establish its effect on customer decision making and how it affects the satisfaction. This research did not study the association between customer satisfaction and retention of customers. Additional research may well explore the relationship between these two constructs.

CONCLUSION

The empirical evidence based on ANOVA indicates that there are not significant variance in customer responses based on the gender, occupation and income. This indicate that the customer irrespective of their gender, occupation and income view the social media networking site in similar way. However there are significant variance on the bases of age and education of the respondents. This study bring out the significant characteristic of social media " such as time spent on site, type of advertisement viewed, specific reason for using social media website and impact on the professional life". The organisation should take in to account while designing their marketing strategies. The result of T- test indicate that advertising quality on the social networking website is an important factor from user point of view. Social media has strong influence and impact on decision making. The organisation likely to use social media as part of their marketing strategies may ensure that sufficient information is provided to the uses so that they are comfortable in making purchase decision. It was found that brand/ organisation which are present on social media website does influences purchase decision making of customers, which suggest that organisation should carefully choose the contents of the advertisement on social media. Factor analysis have brought six factor representing different elements of social networking sites These factors are "information factor, user factor, preference factor, impact factor, decision factor and advertisement factor". This brings out the important factor regarding how the manager should plan their marketing strategy depending upon the focus of the strategy.

REFERENCES

Abdul Razak, S.B., & Latip, N.A.B. (2016)."Factors That Influence The Usage of Social Media In Marketing. *Journal of Research in Business and Management, 4*(2), 1-7.

Agrawal, J., & Kamakura, W. A. (1995). The Electronic Worth of Celebrity Endorsers: An Event Study Analysis. *Journal of Marketing, 59*(July), 56–62. doi:10.2307/1252119

Ahluwalia, R., Robert, B., & Unnava, H. (2000). Consumer Response to Negative Publicity: The Moderating Role of Commitment. *JMR, Journal of Marketing Research, 37*(2), 203–214. doi:10.1509/jmkr.37.2.203.18734

Asperen, M., Rooij, P., & Dijkmans, C. (2017). Engagement-based loyalty: The effects of social media engagement on customer loyalty in the travel industry. *International Journal of Hospitality & Tourism Administration, 17*(4), 1–17.

Barhemmati, N., & Ahmad, A. (2015). Effects of social network marketing (SNM) on consumer purchase behavior through customer engagement. *Journal of Advanced Management Science, 3*(4), 307–311. doi:10.12720/joams.3.4.307-311

Berger, J., Sorensen, A. T., & Rasmussen, S. J. (2010). Positive Effects of Negative Publicity: When Negative Reviews Increase Sales. *Marketing Science, 29*(5), 815–827. doi:10.1287/mksc.1090.0557

Bowden, J. L.-H. (2009). The Process of Customer Engagement: A Conceptual Framework. *Journal of Marketing Theory and Practice, 17*(1), 63–74. doi:10.2753/MTP1069-6679170105

Brodie, R. J., Hollebeek, L. D., Jurić, B., & Ilić, A. (2011). Customer Engagement: Conceptual domain, fundamental preposition and implication of research. *Journal of Service Research*, *14*(3), 252–271. doi:10.1177/1094670511411703

Chen, J., Xu, H., & Whinston, A. B. (2011a). Moderated online communities and quality of user-generated content. *Journal of Management Information Systems*, *28*(2), 237–268. doi:10.2753/MIS0742-1222280209

Chen, Y., Fay, S., & Wang, Q. (2011b). The role of marketing in social media: How online consumer reviews evolve. *Journal of Interactive Marketing*, *25*(2), 85–94. doi:10.1016/j.intmar.2011.01.003

Cheong, H. J., & Morrison, M. A. (2008). Consumers' reliance on product information and recommendations found in UGC". *Journal of Interactive Advertising*, *8*(2), 38–49. doi:10.1080/15252019.2008.10722141

Cheung, C. M. K., Lee, M. K. O., & Rabjohn, N. (2008). The impact of electronic word of-mouth: The adoption of online opinions in online customer communities. *Internet Research*, *18*(3), 229–247. doi:10.1108/10662240810883290

Chevalier, J. A., & Mayzlin, D. (2006). The Effect of Word of Mouth on Sales: Online Book Reviews. *JMR, Journal of Marketing Research*, *43*(August), 345–354. doi:10.1509/jmkr.43.3.345

Chi, H.-H. (2011). Interactive Digital Advertising VS. Virtual Brand Community: Exploratory Study of User Motivation and Social Media Marketing Responses in Taiwan. *Journal of Interactive Advertising*, *12*(1), 44–61. doi:10.1080/15252019.2011.10722190

Chu, S. C., & Kim, Y. (2011). Determinants of Consumer engagement in electronic word of mouth (eWOM) in social networking sites". *International Journal of Advertising*, *30*(1), 47–75. doi:10.2501/IJA-30-1-047-075

Daugherty, T., Eastin, M. S., & Bright, L. (2008). Exploring consumer motivations for creating user-generated content. *Journal of Interactive Advertising*, *8*(2), 16–25. doi:10.1080/15252019.2008.10722139

Dehghani, M., & Tumer, M. (2015). A research on effectiveness of Facebook advertising on enhancing purchase intention of consumers. *Computers in Human Behavior*, *49*(1), 597–600. doi:10.1016/j.chb.2015.03.051

Dewan, S., & Ramaprasad, J. (2014). Social Media, Traditional Media, and Music Sales. *Management Information Systems Quarterly*, *38*(1), 101–121. doi:10.25300/MISQ/2014/38.1.05

Dickey, I. J., & Lewis, W. F. (2011). *An Overview of Digital Media and Advertising*. Information Science Reference.

Edwards, S. M. (2011). A social media mindset. *Journal of Interactive Advertising*, *12*(1), 1–3. doi:10.1080/15252019.2011.10722186

Elberse, A. (2007). The Power of Stars: Do Star Actors Drive the Success of Movies? *Journal of Marketing*, *71*(October), 102–120. doi:10.1509/jmkg.71.4.102

Flanagin, A. J., Metzger, M. J., Pure, R., & Markov, A. (2011). User-generated ratings and the evaluation of credibility and product quality in ecommerce transactions. In *Proceedings of the 44th Hawaii International Conference of System Sciences*. ACM Digital Library. 10.1109/HICSS.2011.474

Forbes. (2017). *4Tips To Help Your Business Flourish On Social Media*. Retrieved from https://www.forbes.com/sites/jpmorganchase/ 2017/03/20/4-tips-to-help-your-business-flourish-on-socialmedia/#605da1987dd2

Hair, J., Anderson, R., Tatham, & Black, W. (1998). Multivariate Data Analysis (5th ed.). PHI.

India, Q. (2017). *It's official, Narendra Modi is the most followed world leader on Facebook*. Accessed on 22 -10- 2017, retrieved from https://qz.com/917170/its-official-narendra-modi-is-the-most-followed-world-leader-on-facebook/

Jonas, J. R. O. (2010). Source credibility of company-produced and user generated content on the internet: An exploratory study on the Filipino youth. *Philippine Management Review*, *17*, 121–132.

Jones, E., Busch, P., & Dacin, P. (2003). Firm Market Orientation and Salesperson Customer Orientation: Interpersonal and Intrapersonal Influences on Customer Service and Retention in Business-to-Business Buyer-Seller Relationships. *Journal of Business Research*, *56*(4), 323–340. doi:10.1016/S0148-2963(02)00444-7

Kaplan, A. M., & Michael, H. (2010). Users of the world, unite! The challenges and opportunities of social media. *Business Horizons*, *53*(1), 59–68. doi:10.1016/j.bushor.2009.09.003

Kietzmann, J. H., Hermkens, K., McCarthy, I. P., & Silvestre, B. S. (2011). Social media? Get serious! Understanding the functional building blocks of social media. *Business Horizons*, *54*(3), 241–251. doi:10.1016/j.bushor.2011.01.005

Kimmel, A. J., & Kitchen, P. J. (2014). Word of mouth and social media. *Journal of Marketing Communications*, *20*(1-2), 2–4. doi:10.1080/13527266.2013.865868

Latane, B. (1981). The Psychology of Social Impact. *The American Psychologist*, *36*(4), 343–356. doi:10.1037/0003-066X.36.4.343

Marshall, G. W., Moncrieff, W. C., & John, M. (2012). Revolution in Sales: The impact of Social media and Related technology on the Selling environment. *Journal of Personal Selling & Sales Management*, *32*(3), 349–363. doi:10.2753/PSS0885-3134320305

Metzger, M. J., Flanagin, A. J., & Medders, R. B. (2010). Social and heuristic approaches to credibility evaluation online. *Journal of Communication*, *60*(3), 413–439. doi:10.1111/j 1460-2466.2010.01488.x

Mir, I., & Zaheer, A. (2012). Verification of social impact theory claims in social media context. *Journal of Internet Banking and Commerce*, *17*(1), 1–15.

Muntinga, D. G., Moorman, M., & Smit, E. G. (2011). Introducing COBRAs: Exploring motivations for brand-related social media use. *International Journal of Advertising*, *30*(1), 13–46. doi:10.2501/IJA-30-1-013-046

Nowak, A., Szamrejand, J., & Latane, B. (1990). From Private Attitude to Public Opinion: A Dynamic Theory of Social Impact. *Psychological Review*, *97*(3), 362–376. doi:10.1037/0033-295X.97.3.362

Nunnaly, J. (1978). *Psychometric theory*. New York: McGraw-Hill.

O'Reilly, K., & Marx, S. (2011). How young, technical consumers assess online WOM credibility. *Qualitative Market Research*, *14*(4), 330–359. doi:10.1108/13522751111163191

Pjero, E., & Kercini, D. (2015). Social media and consumer behavior – How does it works in albania reality? *Academic Journal of Interdisciplinary Studies*, *4*(3), 141–146.

Ridings, C.M. & Gefen, D. (2004). Virtual community attraction: why people hang out online. *Journal of Computer-Mediated Communication, 10*(1), 1-10.

Singh, S. (2016). Role of Social Media Marketing Strategies on Customer Perception. *Anveshak-International Journal Of Management*, *5*(2), 27–41. doi:10.15410/aijm/2016/v5i2/100695

Sun, S.-Y., Ju, T. L., Chumg, H.-F., Wu, C.-Y., & Chao, P.-J. (2009). Influence on Willingness of Virtual Community's Knowledge Sharing: Based on Social Capital Theory and Habitual Domain. *World Academy of Science, Engineering and Technology*, *53*, 142–149.

Swedowsky, M. (2009). *Improving Customer Experience by Listening and Responding to Social Media.* Retrieved September 8, 2013, from http://blog.nielsen.com/ nielsenwire/consumer/improving-customer-experienceby-listening- and-responding-to-social-media/

Toor, A., Husnain, M., & Hussain, T. (2017). The Impact of Social Network Marketing on Consumer Purchase Intention in Pakistan: Consumer Engagement as a Mediator. *Asian Journal of Business and Accounting*, *10*(1), 167–199.

Trusov, M., Bucklin, R., & Pauwels, K. (2009). Effects of Word-of-Mouth Versus Traditional Marketing: Findings from an Internet Social Networking Site. *Journal of Marketing*, *73*(September), 90–102. doi:10.1509/jmkg.73.5.90

Vinerean, S., Cetina, I., & Tichindelean, M. (2013). The effects of social media marketing on online consumer behavior. *International Journal of Business and Management*, *8*(14), 66–69. doi:10.5539/ijbm.v8n14p66

Williams, K. D., & Williams, K. B. (1989). Impact of source strength on two compliance techniques. *Basic and Applied Social Psychology*, *10*(2), 149–159. doi:10.120715324834basp1002_5

Yang, T. (2012). The decision behaviour of Facebook users. *Journal of Computer Information Systems*, *52*(3), 50–59.

This research was previously published in Modern Perspectives on Virtual Communications and Social Networking; pages 146-173, copyright year 2019 by Information Science Reference (an imprint of IGI Global).

Chapter 14
The Dynamics of Social Media Marketing Content and Customer Retention

Michelle Willis
University of Hertfordshire, UK

ABSTRACT

Social media platforms are the key tools to facilitate online engagement; however, to stimulate a discussion, the content published on the platforms is significant as it must appeal to different consumers. The quality of the content and platform type is key to successful engagement. Maintaining positive relationships with consumers is a vital activity for many brands in social media. Trust, satisfaction, fairness, and mutual dependency are key factors to retaining customers. Moreover, positive brand attitudes and higher purchase intentions were found to be linked to positive evaluations of companies' social media postings. To maintain value, firms use social media platforms that facilitate consumer-to-consumer as well as consumer-to-business engagement. Drawing from social influence theory, this chapter explores how social media marketing content (SMMC) impacts customer retention.

INTRODUCTION AND RATIONALE

Maintaining positive relationships with consumers is a vital activity for many brands in social media. Trust, satisfaction, fairness and mutual dependency are key factors to retaining customers (Nguyen & Mutum, 2012; Koufaris & Hampton-Sosa, 2004; Martínez & del Bosque, 2013). Moreover, positive brand attitudes and higher purchase intentions were found to be linked to positive evaluations of companies' social media postings (Beukeboom, Kerkhof, & de Vries, 2015). To maintain value, firms use social media platforms that facilitate consumer-to-consumer as well as consumer-to-business engagement. However, there is no general classification of what counts as engagement (Vivek, Beatty, & Morgan, 2010) due to the many types of social media platforms and usage purposes.

DOI: 10.4018/978-1-6684-6287-4.ch014

Online engagement does not solely depend on the medium of technology; Shin's (2018) study on virtual reality environments, described as a type of social media platform (Ngai, Moon, Lam, Chin, & Tao, 2015), concluded that technical quality does not directly impact value or experience. For VR, content that encourages active conversation or community gaming is what motivates human-media interaction and facilitates users' online experience. Harrigan, Soutar, Choudhury & Lowe (2015) agree, stating that customer relationship orientation is needed to drive social media technology. Additionally, the interpersonal communication among users, including communication with the brand, can impact how content is perceived by the majority of observers. Lu, Fan, & Zhou (2016) propose that the presence of social media increases the consumers' trust. This means that exposure to socially shared posts by active sharers can increase the likelihood of purchase intentions, because trust can be established if material content is shared by a mass network or by central social networks.

Various scholars have developed taxonomies of social media in specific areas of study (Kaplan & Haenlein, 2010; Kietzmann, Hermkens, McCarthy, & Silvestre, 2011; Tafesse & Wien, 2017; Vilnai-Yavetz & Levina, 2018). Kietzmann *et al.* (2011) developed the Honeycomb social media model, which focuses on addressing seven functional building blocks: identity, conversation, sharing, presence, relationships, reputation and groups. The model provides guidance on how companies can respond to various audience needs with the social media platforms they use. Kietzmann *et al.* (2011) affirm that their framework is useful for analysis of the increasing number of social media platforms and their various capabilities towards specific user communities. However, the model views the various social media platforms subjectively and focuses on the technology value. The model does not consider the possible social influence that induces online users to engage. Therefore it is important to understand social media content from the perspective of consumers and the social influence behind the content that observers acknowledge to impact their decision-making.

Tafesse & Wien (2017) developed a framework that categorises different social media posts for different online activities from the perspective of customer management and message strategy. The model details various categories of post content and their purpose, providing guidance on maintaining online customer interactions. However, the types of post content categorised in the study were based on a single-message strategy. Customers have multiple interests and reasons for using social media, therefore marketers would likely be expected to generate post content with more than one message strategy. An issue in generating content for brands is posting content that encourages consumers to share or interact based on the content that also benefits the firm.

Akpinar & Berger's (2017) study addresses what type of content is effective and valuable. Their study's findings implied that content that evokes emotion impacts consumers' decision to share or interact. However, Akpinar & Berger (2017) implied that whether the content is emotionally or informatively appealing will depend on the purpose of attracting the consumer. This is supported by Pressgrove, McKeever & Jang (2018) who investigated the likelihood of content being shared on Twitter. Pressgrove *et al.* (2018) concluded that while positive emotions can evoke content sharing, if it does not have a practical significance to the observer, the likelihood of content sharing reduces. Yet unlike Akpinar & Berger's (2017) study, Pressgrove *et al.* (2018) do not specify what content is categorised as informative information or an emotional content, or consider the various engagement purposes. Individuals are likely to use social media platforms for various reasons, so responses will vary.

The studies of Vilnai-Yavetz & Levina (2018) and Fu, Wu & Cho (2017) were undertaken from the perspective of the non-financial motives for sharing e-business content. Both found that self-expression, community connection and belonging were key motivations. It is important for firms to understand how they can develop their social media strategies, by understanding how online consumers access content and what influences them to become interactive based on firm-generated content. However, the study does not consider the non-active social media users who form the majority of the online population. Although that population may be irrelevant to viral sharing activity, it can be argued that their decision to remain with an airline can still be majorly influenced by the type of content posted and shared by the company and its followers.

With the majority of online users being observers rather than content contributors, it is important to understand the extent to which they are socially influenced by followers or company-generated content to remain with airline brands. This can be developed from Dholakia, Bagozzi, & Pearo's (2004) decision-making and participation variable on online communities' frameworks. Two of the main variables include an individual's desire and intention to act and commit with others within an online community. If individuals have a strong social influence over other online consumers, the likelihood of brands being positively perceived by a mass number of social networks would be greater than directly posting content to them. This can be the case even if grouped consumers share similar motivations and values or if the content is directed to a particular audience.

Muller & Peres (2018) analysed the key components of social media networks, such as the quality of networks and their key characteristics that define social influence status. The two key messenger groups identified are market mavens and social hubs; these have access to large volumes of marketplace information or online networks and engage in online activities. These two groups impact consumers' perception of marketing messages and encourage them to share the content. This indicates that the type of information these two main groups deliver and their position in the social media community can impact consumers' brand perception. However, it is important to understand whether the observing social media users perceive these two groups significant to influencing their purchasing intentions and decision to remain with brands.

THEORETICAL CONTEXT

Some scholars define social media as an Internet-based application that builds on technological foundations, consisting of a series of words, images and audio hosted by well-known sites such as Facebook, YouTube, Instagram and blogs (Yates & Paquette, 2011; Bertot, Jaeger, & Hansen, D., 2012; Berthon, Pitt, Plangger, & Shapiro, 2012). In contrast, other scholars define social media as platforms of interaction through user-generated content, promoting the encouragement of individuals or communities to socialise, learn, play, engage and exchange information at their convenience (Kietzmann *et al.*, 2011; Bonsón, Torres, Royo, & Flores, 2010; Fischer & Reuber, 2011; Ozuem, 2016). Although there is no single definition of what social media is, it is clear that social media can be used as a method of online communication to redefine how services are delivered to retain customers (Ayertey, Ozuem, & Appiah, 2018). In general, social media has been defined as a technology and community engagement platform. In addition, there have been various studies of social media that have primarily focused on researching the effects of its activity and connection to online behavioural patterns (Kuksov, Shachar, & Wang, 2013; Blazevic, Wiertz, Cotte, de Ruyter, & Keeling, 2014; Bertot, Jaeger, & Grimes, 2010; Stokinger & Ozuem, 2018).

Kuksov *et al.*'s (2013) study focused on the impact online participants have on companies' management of their brands. Kuksov *et al.* state that brand managers are no longer the key stakeholders for presenting a brand, as social media has more effectively enabled consumers to contribute content. Bertot *et al.* (2010) highlight the notion that social media facilitates collaboration, participation and empowerment to enable online users to interact. This, according to Hennig-Thurau, Malthouse, Friege, Gensler, Lobschat, Rangaswamy, & Skiera (2010) is more effective because consumer-generated content spreads more quickly and is more readily available. In addition, Gensler, Völckner, Liu-Thompkins, & Wiertz (2013) argue that consumer-generated brand stories add to a brand's identity. Consequently, when consumers volunteer content or their own networks, they impact not only the image of the brand but also the authenticity of the brand's social identity. However, the availability of technology that enables interaction does not mean that users will respond in the same way even when provided with equal access to do so. Gensler *et al.* (2013) and Bertot *et al.* (2010) do not specifically mention the various motivations online users have to participate in social media or how firms can use social media to encourage online observers to take part in online discussions.

Every online user will deliver different volumes and types of engagement, resulting in brands receiving different response outcomes for their online content. Blazevic *et al.* (2014) studied the extent to which an individual will probably participate in online interaction in contrast to another who will not, even when equal access and motivational settings are available. The study aimed to examine the difference between online and offline interaction behaviours. Blazevic *et al.*'s study (2014) recorded three themes that characterise general online social interaction behavioural patterns:

1. **The Level of Interaction:** The amount of interactive behaviour from different participants, from lurking to contributing content
2. **Social Preferences:** The level of wanting to be a part or a creator of online community interaction or a discussion
3. **Enjoyment in Interaction:** The extent to which an individual enjoys the online interactive exchange with others

These themes suggest that interactivity is a feature not only linked to technology but also to the consumer focused in the online discussion. Wiertz & de Ruyter (2007) support this argument that online interaction does not solely depend on the medium of technology, but on the individuals who make the decision to use those facilities. Blazevic *et al.* (2014) found that there is a clear distinction between online and offline communication, which they determined from the groups involved in online communication. When communicating online, individuals are more likely to interact with strangers, rather than people they are familiar with. Consequently, the participation or disclosure of information online may be different, or limited, in contrast to the disclosure of information in conversations in an offline environment. This means that there is a difference in types of online consumers, the lurkers or observers, and the contributors that post or participate in online activities (Schlosser, 2005).

Various researchers have found that active contributors constitute a small population in contrast with the number of lurkers, who mainly observe content posted by others (Cothrel & Williams, 1999; Kozinets, 1999; Preece, Nonnecke, & Andrews, 2004). Therefore, technology platforms do not guarantee consumer engagement, and each user, even with common interests and goals, will respond differently to content posted online. Yet it is important to note that individuals who are active posters may be more willing to communicate in online situations rather than offline. Consequently, mass online content is still likely to be generated by the small population of contributors, but it will depend on the nature of the interaction in which they are participating.

Brands that publish SMMC on their fan pages are one method of producing popularity among other brands and encouraging online interaction. De Vries, Gensler, & Leeflang (2012) argued that a range of characteristics of brand posts can impact the brand's popularity. The first characteristic discussed is the vividness of the post, emphasising that the features of the content generate a variety of attitudes towards the brand. Various researchers have found that stimulating the vividness of the post can be achieved through different forms of online features, such as pictures and animations (Fortin & Dholakia, 2005; Goldfarb & Tucker, 2011; Goodrich, 2011). Such elements that augment the richness of a post's features can generate different perspectives of the brand from various observers (Coyle & Thorson, 2001). Consequently, the response will vary amongst individuals who develop their own attitudes towards such richness that is published. Therefore interactivity will be different across different post and communication channels, which is another key feature examined in the study. Liu & Shrum (2002) explain that the form of the medium of communication that enables groups to interact with each other is vital when communicating online. In contrast, Blazevic *et al.* (2014) disagree that the technology platform is the most important characteristic of online interaction. Nevertheless, it is the platform that impacts the effectiveness of, and access to, online interaction, therefore there is a connection between online interaction levels and the technology platform that enables such interaction.

Additionally, de Vries *et al.*'s (2012) study of brand-related content specifically focuses on the characteristics of information and entertainment. Muntinga, Moorman, & Smit (2011) point out that individuals consume brand-related content to obtain information concerning the brand and its products or services. This implies that brand posts that contain informative content about the brand are more likely to retain a certain volume of popularity. However, another essential point de Vries *et al.* mention is the content that retains consumers' psychological attachment to the brand. According to Taylor, Lewin & Strutton (2011) advertisements with entertaining characteristics can impact the perception of the brand through the advertisement, which can potentially increase the consumers' psychological connection with the brand (Raney, Arpan, Pashupati, & Brill, 2003). While this is the case, it is important for firms to consider the objectives of enhancing the online interaction or the response they aim to attain in relation to the content they publish.

For example, de Vries *et al.* found that entertainment brand posts can contain unrelated content which thus negatively impacts the brands' objective as to how they are perceived. However, in contrast, Berger & Milkman's (2012) work on what makes online content viral found that content will most likely be shared if it evokes high emotions. The study suggested that consumers share content for the purposes of self-presentation, as positive content may reflect a positive image of the sender. Considering the findings in the studies referred to on the relationship between content and online consumers, it can be argued that the online engagement objectives must match the purpose of the content posted. Although online participants have different levels of need regarding what experience they want from the content and the social media tools, brands using social media must incorporate customisation into their posting activity.

Similarly, Kim & Ko (2012) concluded that the entertainment, interaction and trendiness characteristics are important for application to marketing social media activities for luxury fashion brands. By way of contrast, their study deemed the element of customisation and word-of-mouth (WOM) to be equally important. Moon (2002) proposed that consumers perceive personalisation as having a practical and symbolic value. Bernritter, Verlegh, & Smit (2016) confirmed that brand symbolism is a great benefit for for-profit firms due to the emotional attachment it generates from customers, therefore increasing their likelihood to endorse brands through social media. In this way, personalisation can impact consumers' perspectives of the brand's symbol and values, encouraging the practice of individualism amongst online users (Dunne, Lawlor, & Rowley, 2010). When examining customisation of international marketing, Markus & Kitayama (1991) assert that understanding cross-cultural differences is vital, as a significant example of customisation in online international marketing (Lim, Leung, Sia, & Lee, 2014; Roth, 1995).

Likewise Hudson, Huang, Roth, & Madden's (2016) research in marketing focused primarily on the cultural dimensions of individualism and collectivism, which can be linked to Hofstede's (1984) cultural dimension study. However, establishing the extent to which a country's culture impacts social media activity is difficult, as individual countries also have sub-groups that can be categorised under different social media activities. These individual studies similarly imply that incorporating customisation into social media posts is significant to retaining online engagement. If firms aim to maintain a continuation of online WOM, it is vital to publish content that matches consumers' interests and connects them with other networks with similar interests. This also contributes to maintaining online consumers' interaction, and it is essential to consider the various activities and reasons that motivate individuals to be active on social media platforms that support brands' social media activity.

TECHNOLOGY PLATFORMS AND TAXOMOMIES

Focusing on the subject of social media, the key significant factor is the technology platforms, including Facebook, Twitter, YouTube and Wikipedia. While these platforms are some of the most globally used, the definition of social media is not limited to the platforms mentioned above (Aichner & Jacob, 2015). As there are various types and formats of social media, there is no methodical way in which social media can be categorised. Thus, it is important to distinguish the different types of social media by the definitions of their intended use. Ngai *et al.* (2015) define six categories of different social media platforms as:

- Media sharing sites
  - Platforms such as YouTube and Instagram that enable users to upload and share audio or visual material online with other people or communities.
- Blogs/microblogs
  - These sites are where individuals can post their own written material online for people to read and comment upon the material or subject. Microblogs are mostly for short and high-frequency posting, whereas blogs are similar to a personal online journal. (e.g. Twitter, Tumblr and Blog sites).
- Social bookmarking sites
  - This is the activity of saving and organising specific web contents through the use of tags in order to share with other online users.
- Virtual/online communities
  - These enable the sharing of specific information and interests through interactive tools.
- Social networking sites
  - These are platforms such as Facebook and LinkedIn that facilitate connecting individuals who may share common interests, or building friendships or promoting acquaintance among individuals. These sites allow individuals to post profiles of themselves and upload pictures and videos.

- Virtual worlds
  - Users can create their own personal identity in computer-generated environments to explore communicating with others and joining in activities.

The definitions of these types of social media indicate that the perceived advantages of social media platforms affect the consumers' motivation to use them. Therefore it is clear that the type and purpose of SMMC will be implemented using the method that best suits the aims and objectives of the material posted in regard to generating consumer interaction and engagement.

Over time the various motivations of consumers using social media have increased from 'lurking' to being active participants. As the motivations of use have increased so have studies to understand the usage behaviour of consumers. So with results not drawing the same conclusions or definitions of social media, there is no generally accepted taxonomy to classify social media as a whole. Yet while there is no generally accepted taxonomy, various researchers have found taxonomies for specific studies of social media, especially in the types of users and their motivations for social media usage. For instance, Kaplan & Haenlein (2010) proposed a taxonomy of social media based on media theories, social presence and media richness, and social processes theories, self-presentation and self-disclosure. Taking into account the type of media and its degree of richness, the study focuses on measuring the media richness of six types of social media and the levels of interaction they enable. To illustrate this, Kaplan & Haenlein (2010) found that blogs score the lowest for media richness due to their basic text-based activity, whereas content communities like YouTube and social networking sites like Facebook scored higher for media richness and social presence due to their combination of text-based communication and sharing of other media content such as pictures and videos. This study helps identify the effectiveness of different social media platforms, but it does not consider the various activities that users can undertake using the social media platforms.

Tafesse & Wien (2017) developed a framework that categorises different social media posts for different online activities and communities. These are:

- **Emotional Brand Posts:** Posts consisting of emotion-laden language, inspiring stories or humour to arouse affective responses
- **Functional Brand Posts:** Posts highlighting the qualities of products or services, or benefits of companies and their performance criteria
- **Educational Brand Posts:** help consumers acquire new knowledge or skills
- **Brand Resonance:** Posts highlighting the main characteristics of a brand's identity and image, including logos, slogans and celebrity associations
- **Experiential Brand Posts:** Highlight the personified qualities of the brand, which can come in the form of visualised product launches, sponsored events or festivals
- **Current Event:** Posts commenting on current themes such as cultural holidays or events to initiate conversations
- **Personal Brand Posts:** Posts tailored around consumer relationships, preferences and experiences
- **Employee Brand Posts:** Posts about a company's employees and their roles within the company and even their personal interests
- **Brand Community:** Posts used to promote or reinforce a brand's online community. This involves tagging and user-generated content to encourage users' participation

- **Customer Relationship:** Customer feedback reviews and testimonies to improve the impact of customer relationship in social media channels and encourage others to submit feedback
- **Cause-Related Brand Posts:** These are created by companies to promote social causes they are supporting and aim to inspire customers to support them
- **Sales Promotion Posts:** The purpose of these posts is to attract consumers toward a buying decision; these include price discounts, coupons and product competitions

The social media post categorisation provides a framework that can be used to inspire new brand post ideas and encourage daily customer interaction on social media, and to improve content strategies. The framework supports determining which category of posts should be published frequently and which ones are more likely to generate consumer engagement. However, the limitation to Tafesse & Wien's (2017) framework is that it does not consider brand posts that incorporate multiple messages into a single post. Therefore measuring the effectiveness of a post category becomes complicated if the post's message cannot be linked to a specified category. Furthermore, the model does not provide an in-depth understanding of how online users are influenced by social factors or networks to engage or share content.

Although it is important to know the various online activities, it is important to understand the various characteristics linked to consumers' psychological or social reasons for interacting through social media or sharing particular content. Vilnai-Yavetz & Levina's (2018) study focuses on addressing four non-financial motives for sharing e-business content: self-enhancement; hedonism; community and belonging; and society and business community. Similarly, Fu *et al.* (2017) examined the social and psychological motivations of content sharing on Facebook. The two broad categories they developed were self-interest (achievement, self-expression, loneliness) and communal incentives (connection, altruism, and group joy). This supports that though consumers may share interest in types of content, there are various consumer behavioural characteristics that social media posts must consider to generate the customers' response to act within the social media community.

In comparison, Kietzmann *et al.* (2011) developed the Honeycomb social media model, which focuses on addressing seven functional building blocks: identity, conversation, sharing, presence, relationships, reputation, and groups. Their study addresses these features of social media and how companies respond to them, providing an understanding of the audience for each social media platform and what their engagement needs are. The Honeycomb framework primarily focuses on the ways in which social media activities vary and impact consumers' online activity. While the framework does not provide specific examples of external social influences that motivate consumers to comply with brands' SMMC or activities, it is a useful framework relating to the strategic development of SMMC.

SOCIAL MEDIA MARKETING AND VIRAL MARKETING

Social media platforms have a high volume of online users encountering many brands and their fan pages. A key marketing method suitable for social media applications is viral marketing, as the community element of social media enables brands to take advantage of the large group of people available to transfer marketing messages to their online networks. Some researchers have therefore combined viral marketing and social media marketing into their study (Kozinets, de Valck, Wojnicki, & Wilner, 2010). Viral marketing is a method that uses consumer-to-consumer communication to spread information about a company's product or service. Viral marketing provides the advantage of rapidly transmitting marketing messages to a mass audience (Kaplan & Haenlein, 2011) without the high investment costs of other traditional advertising (Liu-Thompkins, 2012). Viral marketing has been studied in literature under a variety of subject areas including word-of-mouse and word-of-mouth marketing (Kozinets *et al.*, 2010). Previous research on the determinants of viral marketing success has primarily focused on the features of the content (Shehu, Bijmolt, & Clement, 2016; Pressgrove *et al.*, 2018; Peng, Agarwal, Hosanagar, & Iyengar, 2018) and seeding strategies (Hu, Lin, Qian, & Sun, 2018; Muller & Peres, 2018; Hinz, Schulze, & Takac, 2014).

Features of content often primarily focus on creating effective viral messages that encourage consumers to pass the message to others. Kaplan & Haenlein (2011) developed the Viral Marketing Process Model which identifies three main elements in creating viral marketing, one of which includes the content of the marketing message. Akpinar & Berger's (2017) study investigated the likelihood of content becoming viral based on the viewers' emotional response. Their results from the study indicated that content with more emotional appeal was more likely to be shared than informatively appealed content. Additionally, the study concluded that submitting content that has emotional appeal contributes to boosting brand evaluation and purchase intent. In comparison, Pressgrove *et al.* (2018) found that content evoking positive emotions is more likely to go viral than content evoking negative emotions. However, in contrast their study found that only content with practical value was shared on the basis that it was viewed as having practical value or information relevant enough to share with others. Although Pressgrove *et al.* (2018) was based on a study of the platform Twitter, other sites like Facebook and Instagram that have frequent sharing and posting may have different conclusions as to why content goes viral.

As mentioned earlier, social media users range from being simple observers to active sharers of content. Viral marketing can only occur if consumers are willing to share and promote a brand (de Bruyn & Lilien, 2008). It can be argued that the impact of viral marketing campaigns reaching mass audiences is strongly influenced by key consumer seeds that have a strong social influence in online communities. Samadi, Nagi, Semenov, & Nikolaev (2018) developed the two-level network model which separates the potential seeds or influencers from the regular 'influencees'. The first level contains the influencers that can support a campaign through sharing content consentingly, resulting in the content reaching the 'influencees' who are part of the second stage of the model. However, this study is based on the process of 'paid bloggers' being employed or sponsored to generate or share content, and does not provide assumptions for voluntary activation of potential seeds.

Muller & Peres (2018) analysed components such as the quality of networks and identified key messengers and their characteristics to support the viral message process, as follows:

- **Market Mavens:** As the group who are typically the first to receive the message, these individuals have access to large volumes of marketplace information and engage in online discussions with other consumers to spread information.
- **Social Hubs:** These are individuals with large numbers of online connections who pass marketing messages to a large population of consumers.

Kaplan & Haenlein's (2011) model has limitations to providing an understanding of the 'seeds' impacting the successful spread of viral messages. While the model provides general groups that could impact the process of viral marketing, the model does not specify the social position of seeds that have particular influence over other online consumers. A consumer's social network position within an online community can be defined by his/her relationship with other networks (Kiss & Bichler, 2008; Susarla, Oh,

& Tan, 2012). If the individual is central to the online network it is he/she who impacts other consumers' perception of the marketing messages or encourages other networks to share the content the main seed has shared with them (Muller & Peres, 2018). The development of online communities through social media has extended consumer influence beyond immediate close friends to acquaintances and strangers (Duan, Gu, & Whinston, 2008). Therefore mass networks involved in viral marketing may be a significant factor in influencing individuals to join viral marketing campaigns with heavily populated networks. However, this may be more relevant once a viral campaign has established viral attention, hence the small numbers of fundamental consumers at the start of the process are significant in contrast to targeting a large population at the beginning. Overall, despite research into content and senders and receivers, there is limited understanding on what the main drivers are for successful viral marketing efforts (Ferguson, 2008; Kalyanam, McIntyre, & Masonis, 2007). Yet it can be argued that message content and the influence of key individuals that share it are essential fundamentals to viral marketing.

Social Influence Theory

Social influence is considered essential when studying human behaviour; with regard to social media, it is possible that individuals' online behaviour is impacted by the volume of individuals active online. Social influence occurs when an individual adapts his/her behaviour or beliefs to the behaviour of others in the social system (Leenders, 2002). Scholarly research regarding social and communication networks, opinion leadership, source credibility and uses and consumer indulgence can provide insights into the marketing process and motivations of participants (Phelps, Lewis, Mobilio, Perry, & Raman, 2004). Face-to-face interactions are not essential for social influence, as influence is based on the information about other individuals (Robins, Pattison, & Elliott, 2001). With technology in social media advancing further, the role of social influence may be vital to influencing the usage of the various types of technology platforms (Tsai & Bagozzi, 2014).

Trusov, Bodapati & Bucklin (2010) studied the types of social network users that influence others. They believed that aspects of online social networks like MySpace and Facebook are similar to types of interactions found on consumer product review sites. However, they found that differences in different social network sites were too numerous for them to be treated in the same way. These differences included the volume of people involved and the motives and nature of interactions in online communities. Previous studies had focused more on aggregated group influence than individual influence within groups (Dholakia, Bagozzi, & Pearo, 2004; Godes & Mayzlin, 2004). Trusov *et al.* (2010) found that having a long list of networks does not have a significant influence. Hence it is likely that online users will rely on a small percentage of individuals they are connected to online, supporting the concept that the information or nature of the influencer is key.

Bagozzi & Dholakia's (2002) study adopted a marketing lens to identify two key social influence variables: group norms and social identity. By incorporating the social psychological model of goal-directed behaviour and social identity theory, Bagozzi & Dholakia modelled group participation as a function of individual and social determinants. However, their model has limitations. First, they consider social influence variables to be caused by external forces, and do not consider the background or experience of group norms or social identity. Furthermore the study is limited to virtual communities and does not consider the distinctions among different virtual communities. Dholakia *et al.*'s (2004) study is built on Bagozzi & Dholakia's (2002) framework, but includes the background experience of social influences in the model. Dholakia *et al.*'s model comprises three factors: value perception, social influence variables and decision making, and participation. The value perception consists of five individual value groups:

- **Purposive Value:** Value derived from accomplishment of a pre-determined instrumental purpose (including giving and receiving information).
- **Self-Discovery:** Understanding the notable, unique aspects of one's self through social interactions, supporting individuals to determine their preferences and values.
- **Maintaining Interpersonal Interconnectivity:** The social benefits resulting from online social networks.
- **Social Enhancement:** Value obtained from gaining acceptance and approval from other members, and the image they develop from being a contributor.
- **Entertainment Value:** A result from having fun interacting with others.

Finally there are three main decision-making and participation variables, namely:

- **Desire:** An individual's motivation to favour acting as part of an online community
- **We-Intentions:** An individual's commitment to co-operate actively in agreement with others
- **Participation Behaviour:** Frequency of online behaviour

Dholakia *et al.* (2004) hypothesised that strong group norms indirectly generate consent among members regarding when and how they engage in online interactions. In other words, group norms encourage mutual agreements among members regarding participation details. Research on group negotiation shows that group norms enable co-operative motivation among group members (Weingart, Bennett, & Brett, 1993). Therefore the stronger the group norms, the greater the likelihood of individuals' choice to jointly accommodate their preferences and commitments with others.

Cheung & Lee (2009) investigated important aspects of the social influence processes and their roles in influencing online behaviour. Their model illustrates that intentions to continue using a virtual community are determined by satisfaction, commitment and group norms. These are then affected by online users' needs for purposive value, self-discovery, entertainment value, social enhancement, and maintaining interpersonal inter-connectivity. The model focuses on two behavioural intentions of online members: the intention to continue use and the intention to recommend. Cheung & Lee concluded that satisfaction has the strongest impact on the intention to recommend, as satisfied consumers will engage favourably with firms (Yang & Peterson, 2004). This aspect of satisfaction can be applied to the context of a virtual community. If members are satisfied with their experience, they are more likely to share their positive experiences.

However, Cheung & Lee did not find a connection between satisfaction and commitment. It can be argued that the sense of belonging impacts commitment, which can link with group norms that individuals share with others (Helal & Ozuem, 2018). In this way they generate satisfaction due to the virtual community facilitating individuals' social position in the community. However, this study was only applied to understanding virtual communities. With more social media platforms allowing social interaction it is important to apply an understanding of users' engagement on different platforms. Cheung, Chiu, & Lee's (2011) study hypothesised that individuals with strong social identity generate strong intentions to interact online. Yet it is important to note that individuals' perspectives of online interaction will affect the social influence they accept. So the behavioural outcome of individuals generated will be different even when they are provided with equal access to online platforms. Moreover, it is important to understand the social factors rather than the intended social action (Cheung & Lee, 2009; Dholakia *et al.,* 2004).

According to Prentice-Dunn & Rogers (1985) social influence is strong when individuals belong to groups. Hence it can be argued that when individuals have limited knowledge, the social influence is likely to be high. For example, Cohen & Golden (1972) and Venkatesan (1966) found that social influence is high if product quality detail is unclear. This perspective can be applied to users on social media who may place value on brands based on the volume of online WOM which may reduce individuals' uncertainty. An understanding of human behaviour can be drawn from Kelman's (1958) social influence theory. Kelman states that an individual's attitudes, beliefs and behavioural outcomes are influenced by others through three processes, which are:

- **Compliance**: is assumed to occur when individuals accept influence and adopt the encouraged behaviour to gain rewards or avoid punishment
- **Identification:** Occurs when individuals adopt a behaviour to create or maintain a connection with other individuals or groups
- **Internalisation:** is the adoption of decisions based on finding similarity of one's value systems with other group members

According to Cheung & Lee (2010) earlier models of human behaviour have primarily centred on subjective norms of social influence, which can be linked to the compliance process of Kelman's theory. The limitation of Kelman's model however is that it does not measure the growth of relationships between variables, such as social factors and social identity, or apply them to measuring social interaction. Kelman's research was primarily focused on attitude change, tested scientifically, in contrast to investigating a social community, which limits the understanding of variables influencing social interaction in social media. However, Kelman's theory can contribute to extended studies of different users on social network sites, as many social media may well move through the three different processes. This is supported by Karahanna, Straub, & Chervany (1999) and Taylor & Todd (1995) who compared experienced and inexperienced Internet users, finding that subjective norms are less influential in decisions for usage among experienced users.

CONCLUSION AND MANAGERIAL IMPLICATIONS

Social media has the potential to increase firms' value as a result of maintaining an online interaction with their customers. As well as using social media to connect with peers, many individuals require organisations to adopt a similar level of interaction with their consumers (Hanna, Rohm, & Crittenden, 2011; Ansarin & Ozuem, 2015). Therefore many firms are expected to increase their use of social media as a medium to maintain personal communication with their customers and monitor their online interaction behaviour. According to Trainor (2012), CRM is defined as a customer-facing activities and technology activity combined to create online conversations and develop customer relationships. Wang & Kim (2017) further point out that CRM involves firms managing knowledge about the customers' buying habits in order to personalise product and service offers for individual customers. Research by Xiang, Du, Ma & Fan (2017) has identified social media as significant in motivating users to engage in knowledge-sharing and has recognised that social media incorporates a 'human side' in customer knowledge management (Carlson *et al.*, 2018).

A good relationship between firms and customers is vital for CRM. However, what makes a good relationship in CRM is not always clear. A study by Hajli, Shanmugam, Papagiannidis, Zahay, & Richard (2017) implied that customers' social participation with preferred brands in online communities impacts the relationship quality regarding trust, loyalty and enhancing customer-brand relationships. Kamboj, Sarmah, Gupta, & Dwivedi's (2018) study tested Hajli *et al.*'s (2017) study by assessing the effects of social media participation motivations, including building interpersonal relations, entertainment, brand likeability, information seeking and incentives, and the consequent effect of customer participation on brand trust and brand loyalty. According to Kamboj *et al.* (2018) the findings of the study supported that customer participation in online brand communities leads to brand trust and loyalty and to co-creation of SMMC. The study therefore establishes a link between brand trust and brand loyalty through brands' social media communities.

Kamboj *et al.*'s (2018) findings can be confirmed by Sashi's (2012) model of the process of customer engagement, which confirms that customer engagement focuses on satisfying customers by providing superior value to build trust and commitment in long-term relationships in order to compete with other suppliers. Social media interaction facilitates the process of forming permanent relationships between sellers and buyers. The process of creating a customer engagement cycle has been used in reference to the purchase cycle process which represents customers' stages of purchase decision-making. Sashi (2012) has highlighted the notion that social media enables frequent, faster and richer interactions among groups of people. However, his study does not take different social media platforms into account or examine the advantages and disadvantages of each stage of the engagement cycle regarding social media use. Understanding how social media platforms like Facebook or YouTube combine with CRM to produce affective and calculative commitment is vital. This can be studied with the research into social influence.

According to Üstüner & Godes (2006) social media technology has the potential to support firms in obtaining effective sales through CRM, by enabling them to understand their customers' perspective of the brand. The application of social media to CRM can also support firms in developing strategies for customer solutions and improving the effectiveness of online operations to manage the high demand from customers. Yet while social media is viewed as significant in customer knowledge management, particularly for the personalisation of service and product offers and encouraging consumers' motivation to share knowledge (Moe & Schweidel, 2017; Ozuem and Tan, 2014), it is important to point out that social media alone will not have a direct impact on maintaining online customer relationships. Consequently, the firms' capabilities in facilitating and managing social media platforms and the discussions taking place on them will generate the effectiveness of social media in CRM. Trainor, Andzulis, Rapp, & Agnihotri's (2013) study concluded that social media technology should be used to develop capabilities in online consumer relationships. Therefore social media is vitally significant in maintaining online communication and customer knowledge management, but firms have to organise effective social media activities to generate customer interaction in order to obtain the required information and sustain customers' satisfaction with the brand.

REFERENCES

Aichner, T., & Jacob, F. (2015). Measuring the degree of corporate social media use. *International Journal of Market Research*, *57*(2), 257–276. doi:10.2501/IJMR-2015-018

Akpinar, E., & Berger, J. (2017). Valuable Virality. *JMR, Journal of Marketing Research*, *54*(2), 318–330. doi:10.1509/jmr.13.0350

Ansarin, M., & Ozuem, W. (2015). Social media and online brand communities. In Computer-Mediated Marketing Strategies: Social Media and Online Brand Communities (pp. 1-27). IGI Global.

Ayertey, S., Ozuem, W., & Appiah, D. (2018). Service Failure and Recovery Strategy in Computer-Mediated Marketing Environments. *Global Business and Technology Association Conference*.

Bagozzi, R. P., & Dholakia, U. M. (2002). Intentional social action in virtual communities. *Journal of Interactive Marketing*, *16*(2), 2–21. doi:10.1002/dir.10006

Berger, J., & Milkman, K. L. (2012). What makes online content viral? *JMR, Journal of Marketing Research*, *49*(2), 192–205. doi:10.1509/jmr.10.0353

Bernritter, S. F., Verlegh, P. W., & Smit, E. G. (2016). Why nonprofits are easier to endorse on social media: The roles of warmth and brand symbolism. *Journal of Interactive Marketing*, *33*, 27–42. doi:10.1016/j.intmar.2015.10.002

Berthon, P. R., Pitt, L. F., Plangger, K., & Shapiro, D. (2012). Marketing meets web 2.0, social media, and creative consumers: Implications for international marketing strategy. *Business Horizons*, *55*(3), 261–271. doi:10.1016/j.bushor.2012.01.007

Bertot, J. C., Jaeger, P. T., & Grimes, J. M. (2010). Using ICTs to create a culture of transparency: E-government and social media as openness and anti-corruption tools for societies. *Government Information Quarterly*, *27*(3), 264–271. doi:10.1016/j.giq.2010.03.001

Bertot, J. C., Jaeger, P. T., & Hansen, D. (2012). The impact of polices on government social media usage: Issues, challenges, and recommendations. *Government Information Quarterly*, *29*(1), 30–40. doi:10.1016/j.giq.2011.04.004

Beukeboom, C. J., Kerkhof, P., & de Vries, M. (2015). Does a virtual like cause actual liking? How following a brand's Facebook updates enhances brand evaluations and purchase intention. *Journal of Interactive Marketing*, *32*, 26–36. doi:10.1016/j.intmar.2015.09.003

Blazevic, V., Wiertz, C., Cotte, J., de Ruyter, K., & Keeling, D. I. (2014). GOSIP in cyberspace: Conceptualization and scale development for general online social interaction propensity. *Journal of Interactive Marketing*, *28*(2), 87–100. doi:10.1016/j.intmar.2013.09.003

Bonsón, E., Torres, L., Royo, S., & Flores, F. (2012). Local e-government 2.0: Social media and corporate transparency in municipalities. *Government Information Quarterly*, *29*(2), 123–132. doi:10.1016/j.giq.2011.10.001

Carlson, J., Rahman, M., Voola, R., & De Vries, N. (2018). Customer engagement behaviours in social media: Capturing innovation opportunities. *Journal of Services Marketing*, *32*(1), 83–94. doi:10.1108/JSM-02-2017-0059

Cheung, C. M., Chiu, P. Y., & Lee, M. K. (2011). Online social networks: Why do students use facebook? *Computers in Human Behavior*, *27*(4), 1337–1343. doi:10.1016/j.chb.2010.07.028

Cheung, C. M., & Lee, M. K. (2009). Understanding the sustainability of a virtual community: Model development and empirical test. *Journal of Information Science*, *35*(3), 279–298. doi:10.1177/0165551508099088

Cheung, C. M., & Lee, M. K. (2010). A theoretical model of intentional social action in online social networks. *Decision Support Systems*, *49*(1), 24–30. doi:10.1016/j.dss.2009.12.006

Cohen, J. B., & Golden, E. (1972). Informational Social Influence and Product Evaluation. *The Journal of Applied Psychology*, *56*(1), 54–59. doi:10.1037/h0032139

Cothrel, J. P., & Williams, R. L. (1999). On-Line Communities: Helping Them Form and Grow. *Journal of Knowledge Management*, *3*(1), 54–60. doi:10.1108/13673279910259394

Coyle, J. R., & Thorson, E. (2001). The effects of progressive levels of interactivity and vividness in web marketing sites. *Journal of Advertising*, *30*(3), 65–77. doi:10.1080/00913367.2001.10673646

De Bruyn, A., & Lilien, G. L. (2008). A multi-stage model of word-of-mouth influence through viral marketing. *International Journal of Research in Marketing*, *25*(3), 151–163. doi:10.1016/j.ijresmar.2008.03.004

De Vries, L., Gensler, S., & Leeflang, P. S. (2012). Popularity of brand posts on brand fan pages: An investigation of the effects of social media marketing. *Journal of Interactive Marketing*, *26*(2), 83–91. doi:10.1016/j.intmar.2012.01.003

Dholakia, U. M., Bagozzi, R. P., & Pearo, L. K. (2004). A social influence model of consumer participation in network-and small-group-based virtual communities. *International Journal of Research in Marketing*, *21*(3), 241–263. doi:10.1016/j.ijresmar.2003.12.004

Duan, W., Gu, B., & Whinston, A. B. (2008). The dynamics of online word-of-mouth and product sales—An empirical investigation of the movie industry. *Journal of Retailing*, *84*(2), 233–242. doi:10.1016/j.jretai.2008.04.005

Dunne, Á., Lawlor, M. A., & Rowley, J. (2010). Young people's use of online social networking sites–a uses and gratifications perspective. *Journal of Research in Interactive Marketing*, *4*(1), 46–58. doi:10.1108/17505931011033551

Ferguson, R. (2008). Word of mouth and viral marketing: Taking the temperature of the hottest trends in marketing. *Journal of Consumer Marketing*, *25*(3), 179–182. doi:10.1108/07363760810870671

Fischer, E., & Reuber, A. R. (2011). Social interaction via new social media: (How) can interactions on Twitter affect effectual thinking and behavior? *Journal of Business Venturing*, *26*(1), 1–18. doi:10.1016/j.jbusvent.2010.09.002

Fortin, D. R., & Dholakia, R. R. (2005). Interactivity and vividness effects on social presence and involvement with a web-based advertisement. *Journal of Business Research, 58*(3), 387–396. doi:10.1016/S0148-2963(03)00106-1

Fu, P. W., Wu, C. C., & Cho, Y. J. (2017). What makes users share content on Facebook? Compatibility among psychological incentive, social capital focus, and content type. *Computers in Human Behavior, 67*, 23–32. doi:10.1016/j.chb.2016.10.010

Gensler, S., Völckner, F., Liu-Thompkins, Y., & Wiertz, C. (2013). Managing brands in the social media environment. *Journal of Interactive Marketing, 27*(4), 242–256. doi:10.1016/j.intmar.2013.09.004

Godes, D., & Mayzlin, D. (2004). Using Online Conversations to Study Word-of-Mouth Communication. *Marketing Science, 23*(4), 545–560. doi:10.1287/mksc.1040.0071

Goldfarb, A., & Tucker, C. (2011). Online display advertising: Targeting and obtrusiveness. *Marketing Science, 30*(3), 389–404. doi:10.1287/mksc.1100.0583

Goodrich, K. (2011). Anarchy of effects? Exploring attention to online advertising and multiple outcomes. *Psychology and Marketing, 28*(4), 417–440. doi:10.1002/mar.20371

Hajli, N., Shanmugam, M., Papagiannidis, S., Zahay, D., & Richard, M. O. (2017). Branding co-creation with members of online brand communities. *Journal of Business Research, 70*, 136–144. doi:10.1016/j.jbusres.2016.08.026

Hanna, R., Rohm, A., & Crittenden, V. L. (2011). We're all connected: The power of the social media ecosystem. *Business Horizons, 54*(3), 265–273. doi:10.1016/j.bushor.2011.01.007

Harrigan, P., Soutar, G., Choudhury, M. M., & Lowe, M. (2015). Modelling CRM in a Social Media Age. *Australasian Marketing Journal, 23*(1), 27–37. doi:10.1016/j.ausmj.2014.11.001

Helal, G., & Ozuem, W. (2018). Social Identity Matters: Social Media and Brand Perceptions in the Fashion Apparel and Accessories Industries. In Digital Marketing Strategies for Fashion and Luxury Brands (pp. 326-361). IGI Global.

Hennig-Thurau, T., Malthouse, E. C., Friege, C., Gensler, S., Lobschat, L., Rangaswamy, A., & Skiera, B. (2010). The Impact of New Media on Customer Relationships. *Journal of Service Research, 13*(3), 311–330. doi:10.1177/1094670510375460

Hinz, O., Schulze, C., & Takac, C. (2014). New product adoption in social networks: Why direction matters. *Journal of Business Research, 67*(1), 2836–2844. doi:10.1016/j.jbusres.2012.07.005

Hu, H. H., Lin, J., Qian, Y., & Sun, J. (2018). Strategies for new product diffusion: Whom and how to target? *Journal of Business Research, 83*, 111–119. doi:10.1016/j.jbusres.2017.10.010

Hudson, S., Huang, L., Roth, M. S., & Madden, T. J. (2016). The influence of social media interactions on consumer–brand relationships: A three-country study of brand perceptions and marketing behaviors. *International Journal of Research in Marketing, 33*(1), 27–41. doi:10.1016/j.ijresmar.2015.06.004

Kalyanam, K., McIntyre, S., & Masonis, J. T. (2007). Adaptive experimentation in interactive marketing: The case of viral marketing at Plaxo. *Journal of Interactive Marketing*, *21*(3), 72–85. doi:10.1002/dir.20086

Kamboj, S., Sarmah, B., Gupta, S., & Dwivedi, Y. (2018). Examining branding co-creation in brand communities on social media: Applying the paradigm of Stimulus-Organism-Response. *International Journal of Information Management*, *39*, 169–185. doi:10.1016/j.ijinfomgt.2017.12.001

Kaplan, A. M., & Haenlein, M. (2010). Users of the world, unite! The challenges and opportunities of Social Media. *Business Horizons*, *53*(1), 59–68. doi:10.1016/j.bushor.2009.09.003

Kaplan, A. M., & Haenlein, M. (2011). Two hearts in three-quarter time: How to waltz the social media/viral marketing dance. *Business Horizons*, *54*(3), 253–263. doi:10.1016/j.bushor.2011.01.006

Karahanna, E., Straub, D. W., & Chervany, N. L. (1999). Information technology adoption across time: A cross-sectional comparison of pre-adoption and post-adoption beliefs. *Management Information Systems Quarterly*, *23*(2), 183–213. doi:10.2307/249751

Kelman, H. C. (1958). Compliance, Identification, and Internalization: Three Processes of Attitude Change. *The Journal of Conflict Resolution*, *2*(1), 51–60. doi:10.1177/002200275800200106

Kietzmann, J. H., Hermkens, K., McCarthy, I. P., & Silvestre, B. S. (2011). Social media? Get serious! Understanding the functional building blocks of social media. *Business Horizons*, *54*(3), 241–251. doi:10.1016/j.bushor.2011.01.005

Kim, A. J., & Ko, E. (2012). Do social media marketing activities enhance customer equity? An empirical study of luxury fashion brand. *Journal of Business Research*, *65*(10), 1480–1486. doi:10.1016/j.jbusres.2011.10.014

Kiss, C., & Bichler, M. (2008). Identification of influencers—measuring influence in customer networks. *Decision Support Systems*, *46*(1), 233–253. doi:10.1016/j.dss.2008.06.007

Koufaris, M., & Hampton-Sosa, W. (2004). The development of initial trust in an online company by new customers. *Information & Management*, *41*(3), 377–397. doi:10.1016/j.im.2003.08.004

Kozinets, R. V. (1999). E-Tribalized Marketing? The Strategic Implications of Virtual Communities of Consumption. *European Management Journal*, *17*(3), 252–264. doi:10.1016/S0263-2373(99)00004-3

Kozinets, R. V., De Valck, K., Wojnicki, A. C., & Wilner, S. J. (2010). Networked narratives: Understanding word-of-mouth marketing in online communities. *Journal of Marketing*, *74*(2), 71–89. doi:10.1509/jmkg.74.2.71

Kuksov, D., Shachar, R., & Wang, K. (2013). Advertising and Consumers' Communications. *Marketing Science*, *32*(2), 294–309. doi:10.1287/mksc.1120.0753

Leenders, R. A. J. (2002). Modeling Social Influence Through Network Autocorrelation: Constructing the Weight Matrix. *Social Networks*, *24*(1), 21–48. doi:10.1016/S0378-8733(01)00049-1

Lim, K. H., Leung, K., Sia, C. L., & Lee, M. K. (2004). Is eCommerce boundary-less? Effects of individualism–collectivism and uncertainty avoidance on Internet shopping. *Journal of International Business Studies*, *35*(6), 545–559. doi:10.1057/palgrave.jibs.8400104

Liu, Y., & Shrum, L. J. (2002). What is interactivity and is it always such a good thing? Implications of definition, person, and situation for the influence of interactivity on advertising effectiveness. *Journal of Advertising*, *31*(4), 53–64. doi:10.1080/00913367.2002.10673685

Liu-Thompkins, Y. (2012). Seeding viral content: The role of message and network factors. *Journal of Advertising Research*, *52*(4), 465–478. doi:10.2501/JAR-52-4-465-478

Lu, B., Fan, W., & Zhou, M. (2016). Social presence, trust, and social commerce purchase intention: An empirical research. *Computers in Human Behavior*, *56*, 225–237. doi:10.1016/j.chb.2015.11.057

Markus, H. R., & Kitayama, S. (1991). Culture and the self: Implications for cognition, emotion, and motivation. *Psychological Review*, *98*(2), 224–253. doi:10.1037/0033-295X.98.2.224

Martínez, P., & del Bosque, I. R. (2013). CSR and customer loyalty: The roles of trust, customer identification with the company and satisfaction. *International Journal of Hospitality Management*, *35*, 89–99. doi:10.1016/j.ijhm.2013.05.009

Moe, W., & Schweidel, D. (2017). Opportunities for innovation in social media analytics. *Journal of Product Innovation Management*, *34*(5), 697–702. doi:10.1111/jpim.12405

Moon, Y. (2002). Personalization and personality: Some effects of customizing message style based on customer personalities. *Journal of Consumer Psychology*, *12*(4), 313–326. doi:10.1207/15327660260382351

Muller, E., & Peres, R. (2018). The effect of social networks structure on innovation performance: A review and directions for research. *International Journal of Research in Marketing*. doi:10.1016/j.ijresmar.2018.05.003

Muntinga, D. G., Moorman, M., & Smit, E. G. (2011). Introducing COBRAs: Exploring motivations for brand-related social media use. *International Journal of Advertising*, *30*(1), 13–46. doi:10.2501/IJA-30-1-013-046

Ngai, E. W., Moon, K. L. K., Lam, S. S., Chin, E. S., & Tao, S. S. (2015). Social media models, technologies, and applications: An academic review and case study. *Industrial Management & Data Systems*, *115*(5), 769–802. doi:10.1108/IMDS-03-2015-0075

Nguyen, B., & Mutum, D. S. (2012). A review of customer relationship management: Successes, advances, pitfalls and futures. *Business Process Management Journal*, *18*(3), 400–419. doi:10.1108/14637151211232614

Ozuem, W. (2016). User-generated content and perceived customer value. In *Competitive Social Media Marketing Strategies* (pp. 50–63). IGI Global. doi:10.4018/978-1-4666-9776-8.ch003

Ozuem, W., & Tan, K. (2014). Reconciling Social Media with Luxury Fashion Brands: An Exploratory Study. In Digital Arts and Entertainment: Concepts, Methodologies, Tools, and Applications (pp. 1546-1574). IGI Global.

Peng, J., Agarwal, A., Hosanagar, K., & Iyengar, R. (2018). Network Overlap and Content Sharing on Social Media Platforms. *JMR, Journal of Marketing Research*, *55*(4), 571–585. doi:10.1509/jmr.14.0643

Phelps, J. E., Lewis, R., Mobilio, L., Perry, D., & Raman, N. (2004). Viral Marketing or Electronic Word of-Mouth Advertising: Examining Consumer Responses to Pass Along Email. *Journal of Advertising Research*, *44*(4), 333–348. doi:10.1017/S0021849904040371

Preece, J., Nonnecke, B., & Andrews, D. (2004). The Top 5 Reasons for Lurking: Improving Community Experiences for Everyone. *Computers in Human Behavior*, *20*(2), 201–223. doi:10.1016/j.chb.2003.10.015

Prentice-Dunn, & Rogers, R.W. (1985). Effects of Public and Private Self Awareness on Deindividuation and Aggression. *Journal of Personality and Social Psychology*, *43*, 503–513.

Pressgrove, G., McKeever, B. W., & Jang, S. M. (2018). What is Contagious? Exploring why content goes viral on Twitter: A case study of the ALS Ice Bucket Challenge. *International Journal of Nonprofit and Voluntary Sector Marketing*, *23*(1), e1586. doi:10.1002/nvsm.1586

Raney, A. A., Arpan, L. M., Pashupati, K., & Brill, D. A. (2003). At the movies, on the web: An investigation of the effects of entertaining and interactive web content on site and brand evaluations. *Journal of Interactive Marketing*, *17*(4), 38–53. doi:10.1002/dir.10064

Robins, G., Pattison, P., & Elliott, P. (2001). Network Models for Social Influence Processes. *Psychometrika*, *66*(2), 161–190. doi:10.1007/BF02294834

Roth, M. S. (1995). The effects of culture and socioeconomics on the performance of global brand image strategies. *JMR, Journal of Marketing Research*, *32*(2), 163–175. doi:10.2307/3152045

Samadi, M., Nagi, R., Semenov, A., & Nikolaev, A. (2018). Seed activation scheduling for influence maximization in social networks. *Omega: The International Journal of Management Science*, *77*, 96–114. doi:10.1016/j.omega.2017.06.002

Sashi, C. M. (2012). Customer engagement, buyer-seller relationships, and social media. *Management Decision*, *50*(2), 253–272. doi:10.1108/00251741211203551

Schlosser, A. E. (2005). Posting Vs. Lurking: Communicating in a Multiple Audience Context. *The Journal of Consumer Research*, *32*(2), 260–265. doi:10.1086/432235

Shehu, E., Bijmolt, T. H. A., & Clement, M. (2016). Effects of Likeability Dynamics on Consumers' Intention to Share Online Video Advertisements. *Journal of Interactive Marketing*, *35*, 27–43. doi:10.1016/j.intmar.2016.01.001

Shin, D. (2018). Empathy and embodied experience in virtual environment: To what extent can virtual reality stimulate empathy and embodied experience? *Computers in Human Behavior*, *78*, 64–73. doi:10.1016/j.chb.2017.09.012

Stokinger, E., & Ozuem, W. (2018). The intersection of social media and customer retention in the luxury beauty industry. In Digital Marketing and Consumer Engagement: Concepts, Methodologies, Tools, and Applications (pp. 1305-1328). IGI Global.

Susarla, A., Oh, J. H., & Tan, Y. (2012). Social networks and the diffusion of user-generated content: Evidence from YouTube. *Information Systems Research*, *23*(1), 23–41. doi:10.1287/isre.1100.0339

Tafesse, W., & Wien, A. (2017). A framework for categorizing social media posts. *Cogent Business and Management*, *4*(1), 1284390. doi:10.1080/23311975.2017.1284390

Taylor, D. G., Lewin, J. E., & Strutton, D. (2011). Friends, fans, and followers: do ads work on social networks?: how gender and age shape receptivity. *Journal of Advertising Research*, *51*(1), 258–275. doi:10.2501/JAR-51-1-258-275

Taylor, S., & Todd, P. (1995). Assessing IT usage: The role of prior experience. *Management Information Systems Quarterly*, *19*(4), 561–570. doi:10.2307/249633

Trainor, K. J. (2012). Relating social media technologies to performance: A capabilities-based perspective. *Journal of Personal Selling & Sales Management*, *32*(3), 317–331. doi:10.2753/PSS0885-3134320303

Trainor, K. J., Andzulis, J. M., Rapp, A., & Agnihotri, R. (2013). Social media technology usage and customer relationship performance: A capabilities-based examination of social CRM. *Journal of Business Research*, *67*(6), 1201–1208. doi:10.1016/j.jbusres.2013.05.002

Trusov, M., Bodapati, A. V., & Bucklin, R. E. (2010). Determining influential users in internet social networks. *JMR, Journal of Marketing Research*, *47*(4), 643–658. doi:10.1509/jmkr.47.4.643

Tsai, H-T., & Bagozzi, R.P. (2014). Contribution behavior in virtual communities: cognitive, emotional, and social Influences. *MIS Quarterly*, *38*(1), 143–163.

Üstüner, T., & Godes, D. (2006). Better sales networks. *Harvard Business Review*, *84*(8), 102–112. PMID:16846193

Venkatesan, M. (1966). Experimental Study of Consumer Behavior, Conformity and Independence. *JMR, Journal of Marketing Research*, *3*(4), 384–387. doi:10.2307/3149855

Vilnai-Yavetz, I., & Levina, O. (2018). Motivating social sharing of e-business content: Intrinsic motivation, extrinsic motivation, or crowding-out effect? *Computers in Human Behavior*, *79*, 181–191. doi:10.1016/j.chb.2017.10.034

Vivek, S. D., Beatty, S. E., & Morgan, R. M. (2012). Customer engagement: Exploring customer relationships beyond purchase. *Journal of Marketing Theory and Practice*, *20*(2), 127–145. doi:10.2753/MTP1069-6679200201

Wang, Z., & Kim, H. G. (2017). Can Social Media Marketing Improve Customer Relationship Capabilities and Firm Performance? Dynamic Capability Perspective. *Journal of Interactive Marketing*, *39*, 15–26. doi:10.1016/j.intmar.2017.02.004

Weingart, L. R., Bennett, R. J., & Brett, J. M. (1993). The impact of consideration of issues and motivational orientation on group negotiation process and outcome. *The Journal of Applied Psychology*, *78*(3), 504–517. doi:10.1037/0021-9010.78.3.504

Wiertz, C., & de Ruyter, K. (2007). Beyond the Call of Duty: Why Customers Contribute to Firm-hosted Commercial Online Communities. *Organization Studies*, *28*(3), 347–376. doi:10.1177/0170840607076003

Xiang, Z., Du, Q., Ma, Y., & Fan, W. (2017). A comparative analysis of major online review platforms: Implications for social media analytics in hospitality and tourism. *Tourism Management*, *58*, 51–65. doi:10.1016/j.tourman.2016.10.001

Yang, Z., & Peterson, R. T. (2004). Customer perceived value, satisfaction, and loyalty: The role of switching costs. *Psychology and Marketing*, *21*(10), 799–822. doi:10.1002/mar.20030

Yates, D., & Paquette, S. (2011). Emergency knowledge management and social media technologies: A case study of the 2010 Haitian earthquake. *International Journal of Information Management*, *31*(1), 6–13. doi:10.1016/j.ijinfomgt.2010.10.001

KEY TERMS AND DEFINITIONS

Consumer Engagement: A communication connection between an organisation and consumers through different channels of communication. This can be linked to the customers experience in communicating with organizations regarding its products and services and how effective it is in retaining customer satisfaction.

Influencer Seeding: Influential individuals within a large network that promote brands and their messages on various social media channels to attract the larger target audience to brands. These individuals are highly significant to starting viral marketing campaigns.

Message Strategy: A plan on how to attract target markets to a brand, its services and products and equity through creative and persuasive marketing messages.

Social Influence: The change in behavior, opinions, and emotions of an individual caused as a result of their perception of themselves in relation to the influence, group, or society. Social influence can be seen in socialization, conformity, obedience, compliance, and sales and marketing.

Social Media: Communication channels facilitated through websites and applications linked to social networking, forums, wikis, and microblogging dedicated to community interaction, collaboration, and content sharing.

User-Generated Content: Content such as images, videos, text, and audio that have been created and posted on social media platforms by unpaid contributors or fans of a brand.

Viral Marketing: A marketing technique that encourages online users to share marketing messages to other users or sites, potentially increasing the message's visibility and effect to a larger audience.

This research was previously published in Leveraging Computer-Mediated Marketing Environments; pages 1-21, copyright year 2019 by Business Science Reference (an imprint of IGI Global).

Chapter 15

Examination of Empirical Studies on Customer Engagement, Online Engagement, and Social Media Engagement

Pınar Yürük-Kayapınar
 https://orcid.org/0000-0002-7460-6465
Trakya University, Turkey

ABSTRACT

Customer engagement is more than a purchase between a customer and a business. Activities such as active participation of the customer in the business, loyalty to the brand, continuous exchange of information are a few of the customer engagement activities. Today, with the developing and changing internet technologies, the concept of customer engagement is also handled from a different angle. Because both businesses and customers have started to use internet technologies in all their activities. This situation led to the emergence of the concepts of online engagement and social media engagement. Thus, customers are now making all their interactions with the business online or through social media accounts. The aim of this chapter is to discuss the process from customer engagement to online and social media engagement and to present empirical studies on these topics.

INTRODUCTION

The change in information and communication technologies, the intensification of competition, the rapid spread of the internet, and the new order that emerged with these changes and developments, led to the emergence of great differences especially in the marketing practices and strategies of businesses. The fact that technology is the focus of all activities has triggered the rapid transformation of the marketing sector, entering a new period and the emergence of new approaches in marketing. In addition to

DOI: 10.4018/978-1-6684-6287-4.ch015

this change in marketing, there have been differences in the behavior and habits of consumers, and new preferences and expectations have emerged. Changing consumer and customer behaviors and marketing approaches have led to the emergence of new concepts in marketing, and some concepts to be handled differently with developing technology. One of these concepts is customer or consumer engagement. Because all activities of consumers such as purchasing a product, participating in an activity, collecting information, comparing products, commenting on products, repurchasing, sharing their experiences with others have changed. The main reason for this is the rapid development of technology and the world's effort to keep up with technology. As the technology changes consumer behavior, new factors related to customer engagement have begun to be taken into consideration.

When the literature is examined, it is seen that the concepts of customer engagement, consumer engagement, brand engagement, media engagement, advertising engagement are discussed, and the concept of customer and consumer engagement is used the most. Today, online consumers and social media engagement have been added to the engagement literature, with consumers beginning to use the internet for shopping. Along with these concepts, the traditional concept of engagement has been differentiated, businesses have had the opportunity to get closer to a much wider audience, and concepts have emerged that can instantly measure the behavior and responses of consumers, based on the establishment of a reciprocal, interactive connection and communication with consumers.

Customer engagement behaviors go beyond transactions, and may be specifically defined as a customer's behavioral manifestations that have a brand or firm focus, beyond purchase, resulting from motivational drivers (Van Doorn, et al. 2010). Customer engagement is a component of relationship marketing, which is applicable to both offensive and defensive marketing strategies, aimed at attracting, building, maintaining, and enhancing relationships with potential and existing customers (Vivek, Beatty & Morgan, 2012). In the same study, in which customer engagement is theoretically examined, it is determined that the basic components of customer engagement are participation and involvement for both current and potential customers, as well as value, trust, affective commitment, word of mouth, loyalty and brand community involvement are potential results of customer engagement. Van Doorn et al. (2010), in his study that theoretically examines customer engagement, it was examined between the businesses antecedents (customer-based, firm-based and context-based) and consequences. However, it was emphasized that word-of-mouth (WOM) activity, recommendations, helping other customers, blogging, writing reviews, and even engaging in legal actions are the basic behaviors of customer engagement.

The rapid change of the internet and changes in the consumer caused the concept of customer engagement to change. As a result of using the concept of engagement with the internet, it has revealed the concept of online engagement. On online platforms, this form of engagement is commonly referred to as online engagement and is addressed from the perspective of measuring undertaken actions, such as the click-through rates (CTR), page views, etc., with different measures being applied depending on the possibilities offered by the platform (Cvijikj & Michahelles, 2013). Online engagement can be regarded as a psychological state of users characterized by interactive, cocreative user experiences with a focal agent and object. Calder, Malthouse & Schaedel (2009), who examined customer engagement for a website, developed 2 types of online engagement according to the results of this study. The first is personal engagement, and the second is social-interactive engagement. It was determined that social interactive engagement controls personal engagement and later affects advertisements.

Another concept used with online engagement is social media engagement. But measurement factors are different from each other. Social media is one of the more prevalent channels through which customers engage with a brand or firm, and businesses are recognising the need to engage where current and potential customers are paying most attention (Baird & Parasnis, 2011).

According to the short literature study located above, the following aims are planned to be made in this chapter. Firstly, the concept of customer engagement will be discussed. After these concepts are explained theoretically, empirical studies in the literature on these concepts will be examined. In these studies, other variables that are considered and associated with the concept of engagement will be discussed and the results of these studies will be examined. Secondly, the concepts of online engagement and social media engagement will be mentioned. After explaining these concepts that are generally used together, empirical studies in the literature on these concepts will be examined. In these studies, other variables that are dealt with and associated with the concept of online engagement and social media engagement will be investigated and the results of these studies will be discussed.

BACKROUND

Customer Engagement

The concept of customer management has changed over time. Until the 1990s, customer transactions were often focused on monetary value. The factors used to measure the profitability of the business were recency, frequency, monetary and value. The goals of businesses have changed over time. With the change in the goals of the businesses and the emergence of marketing periods, the main goal was to establish good relations with customers. During this period, researches were conducted on how long a customer will stay in the business by understanding the customer lifetime value. As a result of the researches, it has been revealed that customer satisfaction is not sufficient in order to create customer loyalty and gain profit. The important thing is to keep customers busy. With this goal, the engagement period, in which satisfaction and emotions take place in the process of managing customers, has entered (Pansari & Kumar, 2017).

Customer engagement is defined as (Bowden, 2009): "*a psychological process that models the basic mechanisms by which a service brand creates customer loyalty for its new customers and the mechanisms by which loyalty can be maintained for its customers who purchase again.*" Therefore, engagement includes feelings of trust, honesty, pride and passion for a brand (McEwen, 2004). And another definition of customer engagement is (Pansari & Kumar, 2017): "*as the mechanics of a customer's value addition to the firm, either through direct or/and indirect contribution.*" According to this concept, direct contributions constitute of customer purchases, while indirect contributions constitute of customer referrals, customer influence, customer knowledge, social media messages from consumers about the brand and customer feedback to the brand (Kumar et al. 2010). These direct and indirect contributions provide tangible and intangible benefits to the business or brand. Tangible benefits result in market share, high profits and high incomes, while intangible benefits result in contributions such as permission marketing, privacy sharing, increased engaged customers, increased trust in customers (Pansari & Kumar, 2017). Therefore, the goal of businesses is to create long term customer engagement. To do this, businesses have to consider two key factors. The first is to strengthen psychological connections and create experiences. The second is to transform psychological and experiential commitment into a sense of self towards the business. Thus, the customer will feel the long term engagement and will not easily give up the business (Harmeling et al. 2017). Also, when customers use businesses' websites, many businesses ask them to evaluate their websites. So they do this to get customers involved in the process. For example, in a contest, Lays asked its customers to develop a new chip and stated that the winner of this contest will own 1% of the turnover of the new product. This situation enabled customers to participate more actively (Verhoef, Reinartz & Krafft, 2010).

It is assumed that the customer engagement manages the emotion and satisfaction of customers. Also, different customers will have very different emotional intensity and satisfaction levels. Therefore, Pansari & Kumar (2017) created a matrix consisting of four basic strategies to manage emotion and satisfaction.

- If a consumer feels high emotion and high satisfaction with the brand, this is called *'True Love'*.
- If a consumer feels low emotion but high satisfaction with the brand, this situation is called *'Attraction'*.
- If a consumer feels high emotion but low satisfaction with the brand, this situation is called *'Passion'*.
- If a consumer feels low emotion but low satisfaction with the brand, this situation is called *'Indifference'*.

Online Engagement and Social Media Engagement

With the introduction of Web 2.0, the internet has become more efficient for both customers and businesses that create content. With Web 2.0, platforms such as YouTube, Facebook, Twitter where users can contribute their content and create personal content such as Blogger or Wikipedia have also emerged. With the power of this internet environment, businesses and customers have begun to change direction (Ulker-Demirel, 2019). Consumers become more active and more effective on businesses when they use the ever-evolving communication platform. They carry out all their activities online. Considering this change, businesses act together with consumers in order to attract customers and increase their profits (Rasool, Shah & Islam, 2020). Changing direction has also changed the way customers engage businesses. Customers began to express or share what they wanted to say, their appreciation for the brand, or their contribution to businesses in the online environment. This situation led to the emergence of the concept of online engagement. Online engagement refers to the customer's involvement in the brand or business, either directly or indirectly, using internet technologies in an online environment. Therefore, online engagement is the realization of traditional customer engagement using internet technologies.

Another concept included in online engagement and used with it is engagement through social media. Social media accounts are very important in the concept of online engagement. Customer engagement in online social platforms Cheung, Lee & Jin (2011, p. 3) as follows: "the level of a customer's physical, cognitive, and emotional presence in connections with a particular online social platform". This behavior is an active digital behavior that is created for the brand or business or provides high personal engagement to the consumer in an online environment. This active behavior defined in the digital environment occurs at 3 levels (Valentini et al., 2018):

- *Consuming:* It is a type of behavior that is limited to only seeing the images and videos of the brand or its products. In this type of behavior, you only have to like posts and follow topics.
- *Contributing:* This type of behavior involves active participation. The individual actively participates in conversations involving the brand or product. Like commenting on social media posts.

- *Creating:* It is the type of behavior that requires the highest level of activity. There is a high level of interaction. It includes actions such as creating, uploading, publishing content related to the product and the product. It is the behavior that is constantly followed by other users.

Social media engagement is based on interaction, and usually certain posts are responded immediately, regardless of who posted the message. Social media is an important concept in engagement because it enables both the business, the brand and the customers to establish a two-way connection in a real-time dialogue, create value together and provide an improved customer experience (Riley, 2020). For example, on the pages of brands on Facebook, there are 3 basic variables for measuring online engagement. liking, commenting and sharing. A post with many likes and shares may indicate that its content is of interest, increasing its probability of being liked by someone, and thereby leading to a dissemination of the brand message to additional potential customers through the Facebook algorithm (Luarn, Lin & Chiu, 2015). Another example is YouTube. YouTube engagement is based on both participation and consumption. Participation is measured by like, dislike, comment, share and upload, while consumption is measured by view and read comments (Khan, 2017). In addition a high number of comments on a post represents the degree of success or impact, because it suggests that users invested their time to share their opinions (Sabate, Berbegal-Mirabent, Cañabate & Lebherz, 2014). In the study of Gummerus, Liljander, Weman & Pihlström (2012) investigated the effects of customer engagement behaviors on perceived relationship benefits and relationship outcomes in a Facebook brand communities, the following results were obtained: the influence of customer engagement behavior on satisfaction is partially mediated by social benefits and entertainment benefits, while the effect of transactional engagement behavour on satisfaction is fully mediated through the same benefits. The effect of customer engagement behavior on loyalty is mediated through entertainment benefits. Another study examining the relationships between content type, media type and posting time, and social media engagement revealed that entertaining and informative content significantly increased the level of engagement. Also, posts created on workdays increase the level of comments, while posting in peak activity hours will reduce the level of engagement (Cvijikj & Michahelles, 2013). In another study with the same results as this study, it was emphasized that media and content type of posts exert a significant effect on user online engagement (Luarn, Lin & Chiu, 2015).

EMPIRICAL STUDIES ON CUSTOMER ENGAGEMENT, ONLINE ENGAGEMENT And SOCIAL MEDIA ENGAGEMENT

In the short literature study above, the literature on customer engagement, online engagement and social media engagement has been theoretically discussed and analyzed. In this section, some of the empirical studies conducted in the 2020 on these concepts will be examined. The studies examined were explained in detail what the purpose of the study was, which analysis method was used, how much the sample was and what the results were obtained from the analyzes. In addition to all these, the table shows in which journal the studies were published and which variables were used in the study.

Wang (2020) examined the relationship between branded mobile application adoption and customer engagement. This study, which uses a data set of more than 15,000 customers, analyzes digital interactions between applications, spending and e-mail blocking of customers. According to the results, it has been revealed that customers increase their interaction on branded websites, especially after adopting and using a branded mobile application. Also, low-tier customers show a more significant increase in cross-platform interaction than customers who are already loyal. High-spending customers show a higher increase in spending and promotion responses than low-tier customers.

Rietveld et al. (2020) analyzed Instagram posts using machine learning models. 46.9 K Instagram posts from 59 brands were used as the sample, and the Negative Binomial model was used to explain the customer engagement. According to the results obtained, it shows that visual emotional and informative objections encoded to the content produced by the brand affect customer engagement in terms of likes and comments. It has also been revealed that positive high and negative low arousal images increase customer loyalty. It is that emotional appeal affects the customer relationship more than informative appeals for both visual and textual modalities. Except for informative branding objections, it has been found that informative objections have a negative impact on customer engagement.

Ho & Chung (2020) investigates how customer engagement through various social media communities of mobile apps affects brand value and relationship equity and repurchase intention. In this study, 485 customers of Gogoro, Taiwan's largest electric scooter company, were used as a sample and tested by structural equation modeling. According to the results obtained, customer equity is positively affected by the mobile apps' customer engagement. This result shows that existing customers increase their repeat purchasing intention. Also, the repurchase intention is positively affected by the customer equity across value, relationship and brand developments.

The main purpose of the Molinillo, Anaya-Sánchez & Liebana-Cabanillas (2020)'s study is to examine the impact of social support and community factors (community driven, community identification and community trust) on customer engagement and customer loyalty towards social commerce websites. For this purpose, surveys were collected from 437 Facebook users. According to the findings, customer engagement is a key factor of four dimensions of customer loyalty (one transactional: repurchase intention and three non-transactional: willingness to co-create, stickiness intention and positive eWOM intention) towards social commerce websites. Also, customer engagement is significantly affected by social support and two community factors (community identification and community trust).

Another study was conducted in the tourism sector. In this study by Fang, Zhang & Li (2020), they aim to analyze the relationship between physical attractiveness of service employees, service expertise, desire for social interaction and customer engagement in the tourism sector. For this purpose, they use the experimental method based on interviews and scenarios. As a result of the analysis, the following results were found: Customer engagement is affected by physical attractiveness of service employees. In addition, desire for social interaction mediates this effect. And finally, the relationship between physical attractiveness of service employees and desire for social interaction is moderated by service expertise.

Parihar and Dawra (2020), aimed at the role of customer engagement in turning the committed customer into a loyal customer in the context of online service. For this purpose, it investigates the effects of commitment dimensions on customer engagement dimensions and their effects on loyalty. In this study conducted with the survey method, structural equation modeling was used to test the relationships. As a result of the analysis, the following results were found: Commitment, customer engagement and loyalty are related to each other. Affective and continuance commitment, two of the commitment dimensions, has been revealed to have significant and positive relationship with customer engagement. In addition, two of the 3 dimensions of the customer engagement (Customer influence behavior, Customer knowledge behavior) were found to be in an significant and positive relationship with loyalty.

Another study is related to artificial intelligence. Artificial intelligence is at the focal point of technology development and information technology disciplines. Therefore, in the near future, many studies on artificial intelligence will be conducted and it will settle in the very center of human life. Prentice,

Weaven & Wong (2020) aims to test the relationship between artificial intelligence service quaility, artificial intelligence customer satisfaction and customer engagement. Data has been collected from hotel customers in Australia who have used artificial intelligence tools before. According to the results, it was analyzed that there is a significant relationship between artificial intelligence service indicators, service quality perceptions, artificial intelligence satisfaction and customer engagement. It considerably moderation the impact of artificial intelligence preference between in the relationship of information quality and satisfaction.

Ou et al. (2020) continued his research based on both individual and corporate characteristics of customer engagement. At the individual level, it establishes a relationship chain that extends from customer engagement to attitudinal and behavioral loyalties through impulsive behavior. At the corporate level, it examines a cross-level impact from brand equity in this relationship chain from the service environment. Two different surveys were conducted. According to the results, the service environment has a direct and moderating effect on customer engagement. It has been revealed that brand equity has only moderating effects on certain loyalty characteristics.

Kosiba et al. (2020) examines the impact of consumer banking customers' sense of trust in the bank on customer engagement in Ghana. In this study, an intercept approach was used to select the participants and a questionnaire was applied to the participants. Structural equation modeling was made on the collected data. The results obtained show that trust in service has a positive relationship with emotional engagement cognitive engagement and behavior engagement. In addition, economy based trust has a positive relationship with emotional engagement cognitive engagement and behavior engagement. Trust factors have a positive relationship with both customer engagement, cognitive engagement, and behavior engagement. However, no significant relationship has been determined between the years of being a bank customer and customer engagement.

Touni et al. (2020) conducted his study on Facebook brand communities. The aim of the study is to examine the customer-brand experience and customer engagement as two of the key drivers of customer engagement, as well as to explore the quality of a hotel's brand relationship with the Facebook brand community. In this study, in which 347 Facebook users were selected as a sample, structural equation modeling was applied to the collected data. According to the results, it is confirmed that customer and brand relationships are the driving force for customer engagement. With hotel brand communities built on Facebook, CE has an mediating effect on the way from customer-brand experience to brand relationship quality.

Another study is about social media engagement. Lee et al. (2020) explores how social media posts and comments by destination marketing organizations improve customer engagement. For this purpose, Facebook event pages of 72 destination marketing organizations were used and panel data analysis was applied as the analysis method. Research results show that a destination marketing organizations' social media efforts are positively correlated with customer engagement. And destination marketing organizations with a high level of information in their messages have more customer engagement on their Facebook event pages.

Another study was conducted in the banking sector. Islam et al. (2020) is about how bank websites can make customer engagement more effective in order to increase customer trust and customer loyalty. For this purpose, an online survey was conducted and data were collected from 598 public and private bank customers in India. Structural equation modeling was made on the collected data. As a result of the analysis, the following conclusions have been reached: It has been revealed that website features consisting of website interactivity, website aesthetics, customization, ease of use and telepresence have a positive effect on customer engagement. In addition, positive relationships between customer engagement, customer trust and customer retention have also been identified.

Garg et al. (2020) examines the relationship between social media analytic practices and business performance and the mediating role of customer engagement in this relationship. Therefore, a sample group of senior and mid-level managers was formed in India, as well as retail and information technology consultants. A total of 281 data were obtained from individuals with titles such as Digital Marketing Executive / Digital Marketing Specialist, Management Consultant, Analytics Manager, Customer Relationship Manager, Marketing Director, Engagement Manager. And structural equation modeling has been done. According to the results, it has been analyzed that there is an important and positive relationship between social media analytic practices and business performance. In addition, customer engagement has an intermediary role in this relationship.

Vo, Chovancová & Tri (2020) aimed to increase the number of online bookings by increasing customer satisfaction and customer engagement behavior in e-service of up-scale hotel websites in Vietnam. In addition to this purpose, they wanted to test the mediation relationship between customer satisfaction, website quality and customer engagement behavior. 332 people who made online reservations were courtesy online and face to face, and these data were analyzed with Partial Least Structural Equation Modelling. The findings obtained are as follows: It has been revealed that the website service quality increases customer satisfaction and affects customer engagement behaviors and brand loyalty. In addition, it provides a partial mediating effect on the relationship between customer satisfaction, website service quality and customer engagement behaviors.

Acharya (2020) aimed to examine the effects of brand familiarity, customer brand engagement and self-identification on word-of-mouth communication. Questionnaires were conducted with 458 people and the data were tested by structural equation modeling. According to the results obtained, brand familiarity has a positive effect on customer brand engagment. Self-identification also positively affects word-of-mouth communication. Two dimensions of customer brand engagement (cognitive processing and affection) have a positive effect on self-identification. However, no significant impact was found between the activation dimension of customer brand engagement and self-identification.

The study of Kim, Yoo & Yang (2020) is about online engagement. This study on the online engagement of social media media users focuses on flow theory, which is important to understand customer engagement in the online environment. The aim of the study is to examine flow factors and investigate the influence of social media users on positive attitudes and continuance intention. For this purpose, 516 questionnaires were collected online from South Korea and structural equation modeling was performed on the collected data. According to the results, challenge, information quality and system quality are important variables in the flow. Flow affects positive attitudes and continuance intention. Also, an important relationship was found between skill and flow. Positive attitude is a very important determinant for continuance intention.

Another study related to online engagement is to analyze the posts about products or brands published by digital influencers on Instagram. A qualitative analysis was performed by applying the semiotic image analysis and the critical incidents technique. The results obtained by examining the posts of digital influencers on Instagram are as follows: It has been determined that digital platforms reveal and strengthen different forms of interaction for consumers. Especially in Instagram, engagement extends the value creation process as it attributes social roles to the person (Silva et al., 2020).

Antoniadis et al. (2020) 's study also examines the factors that increase engagement levels in social networking sites. The study was conducted on 12 brand pages promoting food products, 501 posts were included in the study, and the features of the posts that attracted the attention of consumers were examined in these posts. The results obtained are as follows: it turns out that visuality, posting on workdays, and responsiveness increase post levels and popularity. Posting durations, on the other hand, were examined to have no effect on participation levels.

Herrera et al. (2020) examined the effect of experiential marketing on online consumer engagement in the fashion industry in Aguascalientes. A questionnaire was applied to young people between the ages of 20 and 34, and structural equation modeling was made on the data obtained. According to the results, a direct and positive relationship has emerged between online engagement and experiential marketing. But this relationship is not substantial.

Levy & Gvili (2020) examine the impact of shoppers' culture and product involvement on engagement in price negotiations on online shopping sites. For this purpose, consumer culture theory and the elaboration likelihood model has been used to examine the effects of culture and involvement on engagement in price negotiation. And 2 separate studies were designed to test this purpose. The first is the study done with eBay transaction data, the second is the study done in a controlled laboratory environment. The first study revealed positive effects of collectivism and shoppers' engagement in price negotiations. In the second study, the moderator effect of eWOM on the relationship in the first study was determined. Moreover, when buyers shared information on price negotiation, it was observed that the positive effect of collectivism on the negotiation was diminished and the effect of engagement strengthened.

Sadek & El Mehelmi (2020) aimed to measure the impact of customer brand engagement on brand satisfaction, loyalty and trust through the online brand experience. 392 people were reached with the online questionnaire, the study was conducted in the Egyptian banking sector and tested with structural equation modeling. The results show that customer brand engagement has a significant positive impact on brand satisfaction, trust and loyalty through online brand experience.

In their studies, Rachman & Mayangsari (2020) aims to determine the communication styles that Instagram consumers interact with local fashion brands and examine the relationship between Instagram content of fashion brands and consumer engagement. The results obtained from the online survey are as follows: The type of content of the features of Instagram posts (entertainment, informative, and remuneration posts) increases customer engagement. It turned out that entertainment in particular has a very significant impact on customer engagement.

In the study of Chen (2020) investigates to what extent news content affects news engagement on Facebook and how social networks have a mediating effect on this effect. There are 3 basic news consumption factors to determine how much perceived news engagement on Facebook explains: news content attributes, social networks, and news engagement. It shows that social networks have a smaller impact on online news distribution than is believed, while also mediating the influence of news content on social media news engagement. As a result, it was determined that the production of news content is not the only factor that concerns readers while users interact with news on social media. The variety of social networks that spread content is also important.

Yasin et al. (2020) aimed to examine the relationships between five personality dimensions (Neuroticism, Extraversion, Openness, Agreeableness, Conscientiousness), online-brand community engagement, intention to forward online company generated contents and intention to forward user generated content. Customers of banks operating in Palestine were selected as a sample and a total of 685 data were analyzed using structural equation modeling. According to the results, personality traits of extraversion, conscientiousness and openness have a positive effect on online brand community engagement. In addition, online brand community engagement plays an important role in terms of intention to forward online company generated contents and intention to forward user generated contents.

Lee, In & Lee (2020) is to examine the relationship between customer engagement and customers' experiential quality through social media. This study of hospitals also explores the role of service characteristics in a hospital that can shape the interactions between patients and the hospital. 669 data were collected from the hospital (The rankings of social media friendly hospitals, the Hospital Compare database, the Center for Medicare and Medicaid (CMS) cost report, the CMS impact file, the Healthcare Information and Management Systems Society Analytics database and the Dartmouth Atlas of Health Care). According to the results, there is a positive and important relationship between hospital's social media engagement and experiential quality. In addition this, offline engagement is an important determinant of experiential quality.

Dabbous & Barakat (2020) aims to examine the impact of content quality and brand interactivity in social media on consumers' brand awareness and purchase intentions. In addition, it is investigated whether hedonic motivation, consumer engagement and brand awareness mediate the relationship between social media stimuli and offline purchase intention. For this purpose, structural equation modeling was applied to test the relationships. According to the results: 1.Content quality and brand interactivity have a positive significant impact on brand awareness. 2. Content quality and brand interactivity have a positive significant impact on both the hedonic and utilitarian motives to engage in social media. 3. Hedonic motive has a significant positive impact on consumer engagement in social media. 4. Brand awareness and consumer engagement have a positive significant impact on offline purchase intention. 5. Brand awareness mediates the positive relation between content quality, brand interactivity and offline purchase intention. 6. Hedonic motive mediates the positive relation between content quality, brand interactivity and consumer engagement. 7. Consumer engagement acts a mediator in the relation between hedonic motive and offline purchase intention.

The aim of the Kumar & Kumar (2020) studies is to develop a model expressing the role of online brand community based benefits (experience based and self esteem based) and community engagement investment in predicting brand community engagement levels. For this reason, data were collected from 925 members of the firm that creates online branding communities. Structural equation modeling was used to test the model. The results show that the experience and self-esteem benefits of customers increase brand community engagement. Perceived community engagement investment positively drives brand community engagement. In addition, brand community engagement positively affects brand community commitment and brand loyalty.

Li & Xie (2020) aimed to examine the impact of image content on social media engagement in their study. For this purpose, they have two basic questions: Are picture social media posts more popular than those without pictures? Why are pictures with certain attributes more interesting than some other pictures? They used data sets from Twitter and Instagram on major airlines and sports vehicle brands to find answers to these two basic questions. According to the results, image content in both product categories on Twitter has a significant and strong positive impact on user engagement. It turns out that high-quality and professionally shot images lead to consistently higher engagement across both platforms for both product categories. Another result is that the effect of the colourfulness varies according to the product category. While the presence of a human face in the picture and the harmony of the text ensure higher user engagement on Twitter, the same engagement cannot be achieved on Instagram.

Nguyen et al. (2020) examined how social media engagement and electronic word of mouth activities changed the perceived brand image and students' enrolment intentions. The results obtained from a sample of 445 students in Vietnam are as follows: eWOM seeking activities and perceived brand image have a mediating effect on the effect of social media participation on enrolment intention. Compared to their postgraduate colleagues, potential undergraduate students' perceptions of an institution's brand image are more strongly influenced by eWOM seeking activity on social media.

The purpose of the study of Oliveira & Fernandes (2020) is to validate and adapt the model proposed by Linda Hollebeek and colleagues in 2014, to examine its driving forces and consequences. For this purpose, data has been collected from 243 luxury brand followers on Instagram. According to the results of the research, the brand's self expression feature, as well as consumer involvement, significantly affects social media engagement for luxury brands.

In the studies of Cheung, Pires & Rosenberger (2020), it was aimed to examine the effects of social media marketing elements (entertainment, customization, interaction, electronic word of mouth-eWOM and trendiness) on consumer brand engagement and brand knowledge. Data were collected from 214 experienced social media users in Hong Kong through the online survey. Structural equation modeling was made on the collected data. Interaction, word of mouth and trendiness directly affect the consumer's brand loyalty. In addition, interaction, electronic word of mouth-EWOM and trendiness has emerged as the main factors that strengthen brand awareness and brand knowledge.

Nguyen, Hunsaker & Hargittai (2020) aimed to investigate the relationship between online social participation of adults and social capital in their study. Data were collected from adults aged 60 and over. According to the results, internet skills have a moderation role in the relationship between online social engagement and social capital. Older adults with more Internet skills are more often involved in certain online social events related to online bridging.

FUTURE RESEARCH DIRECTIONS

This study theoretically examines the concepts of customer engagement, online engagement and social media engagement. The subjects included in the study provide a guide on which points related to these concepts should be focused more. This study also examines what empirical studies are about customer engagement, online engagement and social media engagement. But only 2020 was taken. Studies to be examined in a longer period will be more guiding. In addition to the literature review in the first part of the study, an empirical study on these issues will provide a better understanding of the subject. It is hoped that the study will serve as a resource for future studies and contribute to the literature in addition to the previous ones.

CONSLUSION

Rapidly changing and developing information and communication technologies, the rapid spread of the internet have caused changes in the behavior of both businesses and customers, and has led to different approaches to marketing. One of the concepts that has changed in marketing is the customer engagement. Today, with these changes, the concepts of online engagement or social media engagement have started to be used more. Because customers now make their communications with the business or the brand, and their purchases online.

Table 1. Journals' name and variables of the studies in 2020

References	Journals	Variables
Wang (2020)	Computers in Human Behavior	PC Web Interactions, Mobile Web Interactions, App Interactions, Spending, After App Release, App Adopter, Email Response
Rietveld et al. (2020)	Journal of Interactive Marketing	Likes, Comments, Positive high arousal, Negative high arousal, Positive low arousal, Negative low arousal, Visual brand centrality, Visual product centrality, Textual brand mention, Textual product mention, Textual deal mention, Textual price mention, Textual product location mention, Textual target audience mention, Control differentiation, control esteem, control knowledge, Control relevance, Control followers, Control count.
Ho & Chung (2020)	Journal of Business Research	Perceived mobile apps' customer engagement, value equity, Brand equity, Relationship equity, Repurchase intention, Perceived brand equity.
Molinillo, Anaya-Sánchez & Liebana-Cabanillas (2020)	Computers in Human Behavior	Social support, Community drivenness, Community Identification, Community trust, Willingness to Co-create, Stickness Intention, Positive eWom Intention, Repurchase Intention.
Fang, Zhang & Li (2020)	Annals of Tourism Research	Physical attractiveness of service employees, Service expertise, Desire for interaction, Tourists' customer engagement.
Parihar & Dawra (2020)	Journal of Product & Brand Management	Affective commitment, Customer referral behavior, Customer influence behavior, Continuance commitment, Customer knowledge behavior, Loyalty, Customer Engagement.
Prentice, Weaven &Wong (2020)	International Journal of Hospitality Management	Artificial Service Performance, Artificial Information Quality, Artificial System Quality, Artificial Preference, Artificial Information Satisfaction, Artificial System Satisfaction, Customer Engagement.
Ou et al. (2020)	Journal of Hospitality & Tourism Research	Service environment, brand equity, customer engagement, Impulsive Behavior, Attitudinal Loyalty (Revisit Intention, WOM, Willingness to Pay More), Behavioral Loyalty (Length of Stay, Budgeted Spending, Actual Spending, Frequency of Visit)
Kosiba et al. (2020)	The Service Industries Journal	Trust in service provider, Emotional Engagement, Cognitive Engagement, Behavioral Engagement, Economy based trust.
Touni (2020)	Journal of Hospitality& Tourism Research	Customer Involvement in Facebook, Customer Brand Experience, Customer Engagement, Brand Reputation, Brand Relationship Quality.
Lee et al. (2020)	Journal of Travel Research	Customer engagement, Visitors destination marketing organization efforts, Information richness, fan size, Post length, Comment length, event category, event scope, event size.
Islam et al. (2020)	International Journal of Bank Marketing	Website interactivity, Website aesthetics, Customization, Ease of use, Telepresence, Customer Engagement, Customer trust, Customer retention.
Garg et al. (2020)	International Journal of Information Management	Social media analytics practices, Business performance, Customer Engagement.
Vo, Chovancová & Tri (2020)	Journal of Quality Assurance In Hospitality & Tourism	Website service quality (Customer cognition of website, information and interface and trust), customer satisfaction, customer engagement behavior, brand loyalty.
Acharya (2020)	South Asian Journal of Business Studies	Brand familiarity, Customer brand engagement (cognitive, affective and activation), self-identification, word of mouth.
Kim, Yoo & Yang (2020)	Journal of Hospitality & Tourism Research	Challenge, Skill, Interactivity, Information quality, System Quality, Concentration, Enjoyment, Time Distortion, Flow, Positive Attitude, Continuance Intention.
Herrera et al. (2020)	Advances in Management & Applied Economics	Experiential marketing (Sensorial, Cognitive, Affective, Behavior, Social), Online Engagement (Stimulation and inspiration, social facilitation, Temporal, Self-Esteem and citizenship, Instrinsic Enjoyment, Utilitarian, Participation and socialization, Community).

continues on following page

Table 1. Continued

References	Journals	Variables
Levy & Gvili (2020)	International Journal of Advertising	Constant, Transaction Involvement, Shopper's activity, Experience, price, country, Collectivistic Culture, Individualistic cultures, Engagement in price negotiation.
Sadek & El Mehelmi (2020)	Journal of Business and Retail Management Research	Customer brand engagement, Online brand experience, brand satisfaction, brand loyalty, brand trust.
Rachmah & Mayangsari (2020)	KnE Social Science	Customer engagement, post characteristics (entertainment, informative, and remuneration posts).
Chen (2020)	Mass Communication and Society	Perceived relevance of news, news engagement, Emotionality, Homophily, social media engagement, tie strength.
Yasin et al. (2020)	Economic Research-Ekonomska Istraživanja	Personality dimensions (Neuroticism, Extraversion, Openness, Agreeableness, Conscientiousness), Online-brand community engagement, Intention to forward online company generated contents and Intention to forward user generated content.
Lee, In & Lee (2020)	Journal of Services Marketing	Social media engagement (Online engagement, offline engagement) Service Complexity, Experiential Quality.
Dabbous & Barakat (2020)	Journal of Retailing and Consumer Services	Content quality, Brand Interactivity, Utilitarian Motive, Hedonic Motive, Brand Awareness, Customer Engagement, Purchase Intention.
Kumar & Kumar (2020)	Journal of Retailing and Consumer Services	Perceived community benefits (experiences and self esteem), Community relationship investment, Brand ownership, Brand community engagement, Brand community commitment, brand loyalty.
Li & Xie (2020)	Journal of Marketing Research	Image Content (Mere presence, Image characteristics), Text Content, Attention, engagement.
Nguyen et al. (2020)	Higher Education Research & Developmentt	Social media engagement, eWOM seeking activities, Student type, perceived brand image, enrolment intention.
Oliveira & Fernandes (2020)	Journal of Strategic Marketing	Consumer involvement, brand expressiveness, components of consumer brand engagement, brand image, brand loyalty.
Cheung, Pires & Rosenberger (2020)	Asia Pacific Journal of Marketing and Logistics	Entertainmet, Interaction, Trendiness, Customisation, eWOM, Consumer Brand engagement, Brand awareness, brand image.
Nguyen, Hunsaker & Hargittai (2020)	Information, Communication & Society	Online Social Engagement, social capital internet skills.

When the literature is reviewed, it is seen that there are a lot of studies, both theoretical and empirical, especially on customer engagement. There are studies that have been applied in many sectors such as finance, health and tourism and have been handled with different factors. In this study, since there are a lot of studies on these issues, only the studies published in 2020 until today have been considered and analyzed. When we look at the studies in general, it is seen that different studies using internet technologies instead of traditional engagement concept started to be carried out, especially in 2020. There is a lot of work done especially with social media networks, interactions, likes, comments, followers, eWOM, artificial intelligence, website interactivity, social media analytics are commonly used variables.

REFERENCES

Acharya, A. (2020). The impact of brand familiarity, customer brand engagement and self-identification on word-of-mouth. *South Asian Journal of Business Studies.*

Antoniadis, I., Paltsoglou, S., Vasios, G., & Kyratsis, P. (2020). Online engagement factors on posts in food Facebook brand pages in Greece. In *Strategic Innovative Marketing and Tourism* (pp. 365–373). Springer. doi:10.1007/978-3-030-36126-6_40

Baird, C. H., & Parasnis, G. (2011). From social media to social customer relationship management. *Strategy and Leadership*, *39*(5), 30–37. doi:10.1108/10878571111161507

Bowden, J. L. H. (2009). The Process of Customer Engagement: A Conceptual Framework. *Journal of Marketing Theory and Practice*, *17*(1), 63–74. doi:10.2753/MTP1069-6679170105

Calder, B. J., Malthouse, E. C., & Schaedel, U. (2009). An experimental study of the relationship between online engagement and advertising effectiveness. *Journal of Interactive Marketing*, *23*(4), 321–331. doi:10.1016/j.intmar.2009.07.002

Chen, V. Y. (2020). Examining news engagement on Facebook: Effects of news content and social networks on news engagement. *Mass Communication & Society*, *23*(6), 1–25. doi:10.1080/15205436.2020.1798462

Cheung, C. M. K., Lee, M. K. O., & Jin, X.-L. (2011). Customer Engagement in an Online Social Platform: A Conceptual Model and Scale Development. *Thirty Second International Conference on Information Systems*, 1–8.

Cheung, M. L., Pires, G., & Rosenberger, P. J. (2020). The influence of perceived social media marketing elements on consumer–brand engagement and brand knowledge. *Asia Pacific Journal of Marketing and Logistics*, *32*(3), 695–720. doi:10.1108/APJML-04-2019-0262

Cvijikj, I. P., & Michahelles, F. (2013). Online engagement factors on Facebook brand pages. *Social Network Analysis and Mining*, *3*(4), 843–861. doi:10.100713278-013-0098-8

Dabbous, A., & Barakat, K. A. (2020). Bridging the online offline gap: Assessing the impact of brands' social network content quality on brand awareness and purchase intention. *Journal of Retailing and Consumer Services*, *53*, 101966. doi:10.1016/j.jretconser.2019.101966

Fang, S., Zhang, C., & Li, Y. (2020). Physical attractiveness of service employees and customer engagement in tourism industry. *Annals of Tourism Research*, *80*, 102756. doi:10.1016/j.annals.2019.102756

Garg, P., Gupta, B., Dzever, S., Sivarajah, U., & Kumar, V. (2020). Examining the relationship between social media analytics practices and business performance in the Indian retail and IT industries: The mediation role of customer engagement. *International Journal of Information Management*, *52*, 102069. doi:10.1016/j.ijinfomgt.2020.102069

Gummerus, J., Liljander, V., Weman, E., & Pihlström, M. (2012). Customer engagement in a Facebook brand community. *Management Research Review*, *35*(9), 857–877. doi:10.1108/01409171211256578

Harmeling, C. M., Moffett, J. W., Arnold, M. J., & Carlson, B. D. (2017). Toward a theory of customer engagement marketing. *Journal of the Academy of Marketing Science, 45*(3), 312–335. doi:10.100711747-016-0509-2

Herrera, V. J. R., Carrillo, E. P. M., Herrera, S. E. V., & Villar, F. R. C. (2020). Influence of Experiential Marketing on Online Engagement of the Consumer in the Fashion Industry in the City of Aguascalientes. *Advances in Management and Applied Economics, 10*(4), 1–8.

Ho, M. H. W., & Chung, H. F. (2020). Customer engagement, customer equity and repurchase intention in mobile apps. *Journal of Business Research, 121*, 13–21. doi:10.1016/j.jbusres.2020.07.046

Islam, J. U., Shahid, S., Rasool, A., Rahman, Z., Khan, I., & Rather, R. A. (2020). Impact of website attributes on customer engagement in banking: A solicitation of stimulus-organism-response theory. *International Journal of Bank Marketing, 38*(6), 1279–1303. doi:10.1108/IJBM-12-2019-0460

Khan, M. L. (2017). Social media engagement: What motivates user participation and consumption on YouTube? *Computers in Human Behavior, 66*, 236–247. doi:10.1016/j.chb.2016.09.024

Kim, B., Yoo, M., & Yang, W. (2020). Online engagement among restaurant customers: The importance of enhancing flow for social media users. *Journal of Hospitality & Tourism Research (Washington, D.C.), 44*(2), 252–277. doi:10.1177/1096348019887202

Kosiba, J. P., Boateng, H., Okoe, A. F., & Hinson, R. (2020). Trust and customer engagement in the banking sector in Ghana. *Service Industries Journal, 40*(13-14), 960–973. doi:10.1080/02642069.2018.1520219

Kumar, J., & Kumar, V. (2020). Drivers of brand community engagement. *Journal of Retailing and Consumer Services, 54*, 101949. doi:10.1016/j.jretconser.2019.101949

Kumar, V., Aksoy, L., Donkers, B., Venkatesan, R., Wiesel, T., & Tillmanns, S. (2010). Undervalued or overvalued customers: Capturing total customer engagement value. *Journal of Service Research, 13*(3), 297–310. doi:10.1177/1094670510375602

Lee, M., Hong, J. H., Chung, S., & Back, K. J. (2020). Exploring the Roles of DMO's Social Media Efforts and Information Richness on Customer Engagement: Empirical Analysis on Facebook Event Pages. *Journal of Travel Research*, 1–17.

Lee, Y., In, J., & Lee, S. J. (2020). Social media engagement, service complexity, and experiential quality in US hospitals. *Journal of Services Marketing, 34*(6), 833–845. doi:10.1108/JSM-09-2019-0359

Levy, S., & Gvili, Y. (2020). Online shopper engagement in price negotiation: The roles of culture, involvement and eWOM. *International Journal of Advertising, 39*(2), 232–257. doi:10.1080/02650487.2019.1612621

Li, Y., & Xie, Y. (2020). Is a picture worth a thousand words? An empirical study of image content and social media engagement. *JMR, Journal of Marketing Research, 57*(1), 1–19. doi:10.1177/0022243719881113

Luarn, P., Lin, Y. F., & Chiu, Y. P. (2015). Influence of Facebook brand-page posts on online engagement. *Online Information Review, 39*(4), 505–519. doi:10.1108/OIR-01-2015-0029

McEwen, W. (2004). Why satisfaction isn't satisfying. *Gallup Management Journal Online,* 11. https://news.gallup.com/businessjournal/14023/why-satisfaction-isnt-satisfying.aspx

Molinillo, S., Anaya-Sánchez, R., & Liebana-Cabanillas, F. (2020). Analyzing the effect of social support and community factors on customer engagement and its impact on loyalty behaviors toward social commerce websites. *Computers in Human Behavior, 108,* 105980. doi:10.1016/j.chb.2019.04.004

Nguyen, L., Lu, V. N., Conduit, J., Tran, T. T. N., & Scholz, B. (2020). Driving enrolment intention through social media engagement: A study of Vietnamese prospective students. *Higher Education Research & Development,* 1–16. doi:10.1080/07294360.2020.1798886

Nguyen, M. H., Hunsaker, A., & Hargittai, E. (2020). Older adults' online social engagement and social capital: The moderating role of Internet skills. *Information Communication and Society,* 1–17. doi:10.1080/1369118X.2020.1804980

Oliveira, M., & Fernandes, T. (2020). Luxury brands and social media: Drivers and outcomes of consumer engagement on Instagram. *Journal of Strategic Marketing,* 1–19. doi:10.1080/0965254X.2020.1777459

Ou, J., Wong, I. A., Prentice, C., & Liu, M. T. (2020). Customer Engagement and its Outcomes: The Cross-Level Effect of Service Environment and Brand Equity. *Journal of Hospitality & Tourism Research (Washington, D.C.), 44*(2), 377–402. doi:10.1177/1096348019897360

Pansari, A., & Kumar, V. (2017). Customer engagement: The construct, antecedents, and consequences. *Journal of the Academy of Marketing Science, 45*(3), 294–311. doi:10.100711747-016-0485-6

Parihar, P., & Dawra, J. (2020). The role of customer engagement in travel services. *Journal of Product and Brand Management, 29*(7), 899–911. Advance online publication. doi:10.1108/JPBM-11-2018-2097

Prentice, C., Weaven, S., & Wong, I. A. (2020). Linking AI quality performance and customer engagement: The moderating effect of AI preference. *International Journal of Hospitality Management, 90,* 102629. doi:10.1016/j.ijhm.2020.102629

Rachmah, R. R., & Mayangsari, L. (2020). Online Engagement Factors on Instagram Local Fashion Brand Accounts. *KnE Social Sciences,* 446-458.

Rasool, A., Shah, F. A., & Islam, J. U. (2020). Customer engagement in the digital age: A review and research agenda. *Current Opinion in Psychology, 36,* 1–5. doi:10.1016/j.copsyc.2020.05.003 PMID:32599394

Rietveld, R., van Dolen, W., Mazloom, M., & Worring, M. (2020). What you feel, is what you like influence of message appeals on customer engagement on Instagram. *Journal of Interactive Marketing, 49,* 20–53. doi:10.1016/j.intmar.2019.06.003

Riley, J. (2020). Sustaining customer engagement through social media brand communities. *Journal of Global Scholars of Marketing Science, 30*(4), 344–357. doi:10.1080/21639159.2020.1766990

Sabate, F., Berbegal-Mirabent, J., Cañabate, A., & Lebherz, P. R. (2014). Factors influencing popularity of branded content in Facebook fan pages. *European Management Journal, 32*(6), 1001–1011. doi:10.1016/j.emj.2014.05.001

Sadek, H., & El Mehelmi, H. (2020). Customer brand engagement impact on brand satisfaction, loyalty, and trust in the online context. Egyptian Banking Sector. *The Journal of Business and Retail Management Research*, *14*(3), 22–33. doi:10.24052/JBRMR/V14IS03/ART-03

Silva, M. J. D. B., Farias, S. A. D., Grigg, M. K., & Barbosa, M. D. L. D. A. (2020). Online engagement and the role of digital influencers in product endorsement on Instagram. *Journal of Relationship Marketing*, *19*(2), 133–163. doi:10.1080/15332667.2019.1664872

Touni, R., Kim, W. G., Choi, H. M., & Ali, M. A. (2020). Antecedents and an outcome of customer engagement with hotel brand community on Facebook. *Journal of Hospitality & Tourism Research (Washington, D.C.)*, *44*(2), 278–299. doi:10.1177/1096348019895555

Ulker-Demirel, E. (2019). Development of Digital Communication Technologies and the New Media. In *Handbook of Research on Narrative Advertising* (pp. 164–175). IGI Global. doi:10.4018/978-1-5225-9790-2.ch015

Valentini, C., Romenti, S., Murtarelli, G., & Pizzetti, M. (2018). Digital visual engagement: Influencing purchase intentions on Instagram. *Journal of Communication Management (London)*, *22*(4), 362–381. doi:10.1108/JCOM-01-2018-0005

Van Doorn, J., Lemon, K. N., Mittal, V., Nass, S., Pick, D., Pirner, P., & Verhoef, P. C. (2010). Customer engagement behavior: Theoretical foundations and research directions. *Journal of Service Research*, *13*(3), 253–266. doi:10.1177/1094670510375599

Verhoef, P. C., Reinartz, W. J., & Krafft, M. (2010). Customer engagement as a new perspective in customer management. *Journal of Service Research*, *13*(3), 247–252. doi:10.1177/1094670510375461

Vivek, S. D., Beatty, S. E., & Morgan, R. M. (2012). Customer engagement: Exploring customer relationships beyond purchase. *Journal of Marketing Theory and Practice*, *20*(2), 122–146. doi:10.2753/MTP1069-6679200201

Vo, N. T., Chovancová, M., & Tri, H. T.VO. (2020). The impact of E-service quality on the customer satisfaction and consumer engagement behaviors toward luxury hotels. *Journal of Quality Assurance in Hospitality & Tourism*, *21*(5), 499–523. doi:10.1080/1528008X.2019.1695701

Wang, R. J. H. (2020). Branded mobile application adoption and customer engagement behavior. *Computers in Human Behavior*, *106*, 106245. doi:10.1016/j.chb.2020.106245

Yasin, M., Porcu, L., Abusharbeh, M. T., & Liébana-Cabanillas, F. (2020). The impact of customer personality and online brand community engagement on intention to forward company and users generated content: Palestinian banking industry a case. *Economic Research-Ekonomska Istraživanja*, *33*(1), 1985–2006. doi:10.1080/1331677X.2020.1752277

ADDITIONAL READING

Aksoy, L., van Riel, A., Kandampully, J., Wirtz, J., den Ambtman, A., Bloemer, J., ... Canli, Z. G. (2013). Managing brands and customer engagement in online brand communities. *Journal of Service Management, 24*(3), 223–244. doi:10.1108/09564231311326978

Brodie, R. J., Hollebeek, L. D., Jurić, B., & Ilić, A. (2011). Customer engagement: Conceptual domain, fundamental propositions, and implications for research. *Journal of Service Research, 14*(3), 252–271. doi:10.1177/1094670511411703

Cabiddu, F., De Carlo, M., & Piccoli, G. (2014). Social media affordances: Enabling customer engagement. *Annals of Tourism Research, 48*, 175–192. doi:10.1016/j.annals.2014.06.003

Coulter, K. S., Gummerus, J., Liljander, V., Weman, E., & Pihlström, M. (2012). Customer engagement in a Facebook brand community. *Management Research Review, 35*(9), 857–877. doi:10.1108/01409171211256578

Davis Mersey, R., Malthouse, E. C., & Calder, B. J. (2010). Engagement with online media. *Journal of Media Business Studies, 7*(2), 39–56. doi:10.1080/16522354.2010.11073506

Dessart, L. (2017). Social media engagement: A model of antecedents and relational outcomes. *Journal of Marketing Management, 33*(5-6), 375–399. doi:10.1080/0267257X.2017.1302975

Dessart, L., Veloutsou, C., & Morgan-Thomas, A. (2015). Consumer engagement in online brand communities: A social media perspective. *Journal of Product and Brand Management, 24*(1), 28–42. doi:10.1108/JPBM-06-2014-0635

Jaakkola, E., & Alexander, M. (2014). The role of customer engagement behavior in value co-creation: A service system perspective. *Journal of Service Research, 17*(3), 247–261. doi:10.1177/1094670514529187

Kumar, V., Rajan, B., Gupta, S., & Dalla Pozza, I. (2019). Customer engagement in service. *Journal of the Academy of Marketing Science, 47*(1), 138–160. doi:10.100711747-017-0565-2

Vicente, M. R., & Novo, A. (2014). An empirical analysis of e-participation. The role of social networks and e-government over citizens' online engagement. *Government Information Quarterly, 31*(3), 379–387. doi:10.1016/j.giq.2013.12.006

KEY TERMS AND DEFINITION

Customer Engagement: It refers to the individual consumer participation or involvement in the activities of businesses. Like buying a product, commenting on the product, being loyal to the brand.

Engagement: To be attached to anything, to participate, initiative.

Online Engagement: It is the realization of customer engagement using internet technologies. The customer does all activities online.

Online Interaction: Online interaction is that in marketing, consumers communicate or interact with each other, with the business or with the brand, and this is done in an online environment.

Social Media Engagement: It stands for customer engagement done through social media networks. The customer buys products from their social media accounts, communicates with the brand, shares their thoughts about the brand or product on their social media account.

Social Networking Sites: It refers to the social media networks people use such as Facebook, Twitter, Instagram, YouTube.

Web 2.0: It is a network where internet technologies are changing and developing rapidly and consumers adapt to these developments and changes.

This research was previously published in Insights, Innovation, and Analytics for Optimal Customer Engagement; pages 25-48, copyright year 2021 by Business Science Reference (an imprint of IGI Global).

Chapter 16
Digital Demands Convergence of Strategies, Media, and Messages:
Firms Mix Content, Social, and Native Marketing

Kenneth E. Harvey
Xiamen University Malaysia, Malaysia

Luis Manuel Pazos Sanchez
Xiamen University Malaysia, Malaysia

ABSTRACT

Even before the world wide web, integrated marketing communications (IMC) was gaining acceptance across all fields of business and industry. However, the explosion of online and mobile marketing has caused a convergence of marketing strategies at the same time that all forms of media are converging onto digital platforms. This has become more than just a "Digital Age." For marketers it is the age of multimedia, the age of coordinated omnichannel communications with an increasing emphasis on mobile, the age of personalization, and an age that blends free and friendly inbound marketing with paid advertising that looks more and more like the organic content that surrounds it. This chapter explores the ongoing impact of the convergence of media, strategies and technologies on the 4 P's of the traditional marketing mix.

INTRODUCTION

Professionals understand that advertising is only one part of marketing. They understand the important role of public relations and branding. They understand that the marketing mix even includes important elements of the products, their pricing and the place where they are sold. Nonetheless, advertising seemed

DOI: 10.4018/978-1-6684-6287-4.ch016

to be the driving force behind marketing as long as traditional media were the dominant channels for promotional messages. All that has changed in the Digital Age.

One of the biggest sources of sales leads now is so-called content marketing or inbound marketing (not exactly synonymous but largely overlapping). Because this marketing is free (not counting labor and other in-house expenses), this would have certainly been part of many PR Department's responsibilities 10 years ago. But those working on content marketing must also be involved, almost by definition, with native advertising. Native advertising is created to look like organic content around it but requires payment to achieve greater reach. Indeed, on Facebook if you have a business site and begin making regular posts, you will be asked if you want to promote your free post. That means you will pay to have it placed on people's timelines who are not among your organization's friends and followers. That immediately makes it native advertising. A BI Intelligence report estimates that native ads will make up 74% of all U.S. digital display ad revenue by 2021 – bringing in, as illustrated in Figure 1, an estimated $36.3 billion, compared with $12.6 billion for non-native advertising (Boland, 2016), and the trend is growing almost as fast internationally. With these major opportunities taking place largely on social media, many organizations have a separate team to oversee theses promotional activities under the Integrated Marketing Communications (IMC) umbrella.

Figure 1. Native display advertising (advertising created to look like the organic content that surrounds it) is growing rapidly while non-native advertising has gone stagnant
Source: Boland, BI Intelligence (2016)

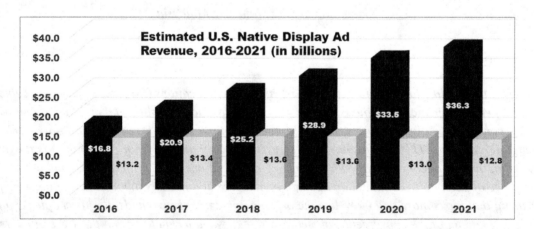

The IMC concept of placing marketing, advertising, branding, public relations, direct sales, and other promotional messaging all under one marketing executive in order to coordinate these activities began before the World Wide Web. But even though digital marketing almost demands an integrated approach, adapting IMC to the digital world still requires some effort. The *Journal of Research in Interactive Marketing* asked Payne, Peltier, and Barger (2017) to provide some insights, suggestions and research topics required to help make this transition. They felt that digital communications enhance organizations' ability to engage consumers with a unified message across channels. The intersection of IMC strategies and tactics with effective omnichannel marketing could allow for a more profitable relationship, they said. The authors noted that this is a new area of academic research and proposed an omnichannel version of the IMC framework to help guide academic inquiries. In reviewing academic literature linking personal and electronic communication in the current omnichannel environment, they recommended five major areas where research is needed:

- Research that better links omni-channel and IMC theory and practice.
- Conceptual and empirical research that helps operationalize the consumer-brand engagement construct, including its antecedents and consequences.
- Build understanding of off- and on-line consumer-brand touchpoints and how they may enhance engagement and profitability.
- How omnichannel IMC best monetizes buyer-seller relationships.
- Omnichannel IMC in other consumer decision contexts.

Melero, Sese and Verhoef (2016) expressed similar feelings that IMC integration into the digital world was in its infancy. While in theory omnichannel marketing coincides with IMC in creating "synergistic management of the available channels and customer touchpoints to enhance the customer experience and to improve performance," accomplishing that in the real world is one of the biggest challenges facing executives. They noted several key issues, including "adopting a customer centric approach, unifying all touchpoints across all channels, delivering personalized customer experiences, integrating the available channels, delight customers across channels, redefining the role of the physical store and embracing mobile marketing."

Batra and Keller (2016) also noted the difficulties encountered in this transition because "consumers, brands, and the media are fundamentally changing in profound ways. With the explosion of new media, consumers are dramatically shifting both their media usage patterns and how they utilize different media sources to get the information they seek, which thus influences when, where, and how they choose brands. Perhaps more than ever, their attention is divided, often due to multitasking, and they are seemingly in a perpetual state of partial attention." Because of the nature of new media, there are "increased social influences on purchase." The power of "word of mouth" communications and advocacy "have become especially important" and "brand messaging is even less under the marketer's control" (p. 122). Batra and Keller offered their own illustrations of the new "dynamic, expanded consumer decision journey," "factors that affect consumer communication processing," and a new "IMC conceptual framework" as it now exists. They challenged readers to consider their proposed paradigm with which to envision the new ecosystem, along with their other illustrations as new ways to model the changing effects of marketing communication. They also recommended some research priorities, noting "a paucity of scholarly research on the changing nature of how consumers seek, acquire, and integrate brand-relevant information in today's dramatically new media environment" (pp. 137-139). One of their specific research priorities was the "tremendous importance" of mobile marketing, noting that "there will undoubtedly be a number of uniquely original considerations that firms will have to factor in."

Nonetheless, coordinating the efforts of separate teams has not always proven easy. Recent studies suggest that despite the wide acceptance of this IMC philosophy, many campaigns still happen in a fragmented, isolated manner.

"It's surprising," says Rebecca Honeyman, Hotwire VP and GM of the firm's New York office. "After years and years of preaching about having one campaign and telling a coherent story, no one is practicing what they preach." Part of the problem, according to Honeyman, is that marketers tend to have one team in charge of direct marketing, another in charge of brand marketing, another in charge of communication, etc., as well as working with a handful of different agencies, each with their own individual teams (Britt, 2015).

The rise of new communication technologies has led modern marketing departments now to include marketing technologists and data scientists responsible for handling new marketing communication tech and Big Data, respectively. A 2017 study by Chief Marketing Technologist found that 27% of marketing executives had restructured their departments to leverage the use of these technologies. The study also indicated that 53% of respondents were moving towards creating a new role to have someone specifically in charge of new marketing technology (Brinker, 2017). Those organizations not making these changes are probably continuing to experience the frustrations expressed in previous studies.

A global survey of B2B marketing executives in 2013 (Ramos, 2013, p. 2-4) found that 97% of the executives felt as if they were "navigating chaos," with more than one-third feeling "overwhelmed" by the new marketing challenges, frequently related to technology. About 60% of the executives had looked for more tech-savvy marketing professionals to help, but 47% had failed to fill the need. It appears that today's marketing graduates do not possess the necessary technical skills, either, which led to the current trend to add technical specialists to the team and teach them what they need to know about marketing. Such technical skills are needed to gather consumer data and then apply it to achieve the growing demand for personalization. Personalization comes from the automated gathering and use of data and is now among the highest priorities for marketing executives (Researchscape International, 2015; Neustar, 2015; Adobe, 2015).

Still in 2017 marketing executives are expressing frustration that their team is unable to perform their most technical advertising efforts. Programmatic advertising uses computer programming to find, negotiate, contract and sometimes fulfill the advertising with as little human involvement as possible. It is expected to facilitate 84% of all U.S. digital display ad spending in 2019 (eMarketer, 2017a) in spite of that fact that most marketing executives are unhappy about having to use specialists from outside agencies to do so. Some 87% of marketing executives say they want to bring at least part of the programmatic advertising function in-house. But after several years of failure in this effort, 96% admit that the outside agencies will still have to play a major role going forward (Johnson, 2017). With technologists on the marketing team, however, the executives will undoubtedly continue their efforts to take over more programmatic functions.

Thus, we see that the need for an integrated marketing department is much greater now than when the concept first became popular before the creation of the Web. For savvy marketers being able to speak with a single voice across communication platforms as the ideal standard.

A NEW LOOK AT OLD CONCEPTS

This chapter will focus on how modern marketing is integrating new tools and tactics with old concepts. Advertising is still a very important part of marketing, of course, and we will cover additional revolutionary changes in advertising in a separate chapter. In this chapter we will review changes in the traditional 4 P's of marketing:

1. **The Products:** The goods and services to be offered.
2. **The Promotions:** The marketing communication to attract prospective customers.
3. **The Place:** Where the product is made available for purchase.

4.   **The Price:** At which the products are offered within the competitive marketplace.

Indeed, Web and mobile technologies have revolutionized all 4 P's of marketing.

Products

Product strategies remain as varied as there are industries. One strategy that continues to stand out is the "long tail" product strategy (Anderson, 2006). Digital products can be "inventoried" now profitably even with relatively few sales per item. A traditional music store might carry 1,000 of the most popular recordings, but an online music store can carry more than 100,000 digital music products and make much greater profit even if the extra 90,000 products only sell a few copies per year. Online digital product sales on a chart begin with a few hundred items with a lot of sales, followed by a long, long tail of items with only a few sales.

Of course "products" in the 4 P's also include services, and the mega-success of Uber (Suslo, 2016; Tobias, 2016) in pairing consumers wanting to save money on taxi services with Uber drivers trying to make some extra money in their free time, is such an example. Launched in 2009, Uber is valued at $63 billion – more than such traditional businesses as Ford and General Motors. A similar example is AirBnB, which after just 10 years of offering international "couch surfing" has far more capacity than the Marriott Hotel chain, with 3 million listings, and is valued at $30 billion. In the process, it raised $3 billion from investors, of which it has only spent $300 million. Company officials believe they will be earning $3.5 billion a year by 2020 before taxes, making it among the top 15% of the Fortune 500 companies (Murray, 2017; Roberts, 2017).

Promotion

Most companies have now integrated digital marketing tools into their overall marketing strategies, and expectations are that mobile will eventually dominate the digital world – with paid online advertising surpassing all other forms of advertising in expenditures by 2021 (eMarketer, 2017b). But some of the most effective marketing available is free.

Inbound/Content Marketing

"Inbound marketing" and "content marketing" are free marketing strategies that have become some of the most important of the Digital Age, and, as suggested earlier, they don't fall exactly into any of the other promotional categories. Lieb (2011) asserted that content marketing is a "pull strategy" rather than an instrument for "push marketing" like traditional advertising. It emphasizes information and dialogic communication rather than selling. When consumers want it, they are provided "with relevant, educational, helpful, compelling, engaging, and sometime entertaining information" (p. 1). Holliman and Rowley (2014) said digital content marketing relates to "creating, communicating, distributing, and exchanging digital content that has value for customers, clients, partners, and the firm and its brands" (p. 287). Feng and Ots (2015) noted that "Instead of advertising, the shift is towards publishing. Companies of all types and sizes flood the market with articles, white papers, videos, podcasts, Facebook posts, and tweets. Reshaped to look like digital newsrooms, corporate communications teams begin to prioritize and produce high-quality brand content." They also concluded that "as a rising phenomenon, content marketing is a relatively unexplored area of academic research" (p. 1).

"Inbound marketing" was a related term coined by one of the top online marketing consulting agencies, HubSpot, in 2006 (Chernov, 2014, p. 12). Most professional marketers are familiar with both terms, but there is disagreement on whether they are the same or how they are related. HubSpot surveyed over 6,000 marketing professionals in June 2014 to see how they considered the terms to relate. The majority (59%) considered "content marketing" to be a subset of "inbound marketing." Of the remaining respondents 33% were divided fairly equally between the other three options, that they were synonymous terms, that they were totally distinct concepts, or that inbound marketing was a subset of content marketing (Chernov, p. 13). So, for our purposes we will proceed as the majority of marketers believe the terms do relate and suggest that they are correct in that "content marketing" suggests strategies that provide content (usually free educational content) that attracts people toward the company and its paid products and services. "Inbound marketing," as the superset of content marketing, would include additional strategies that provide the same effect. For example, "fremiums" (free trial offers) could be considered part of inbound marketing but not content marketing. In reality the vast majority of inbound marketing efforts also fall into the subset category of content marketing.

The most popular forms of inbound marketing, according to the HubSpot survey, are, in order (Chernov, p. 11):

1. Blogging.
2. Organically growing SEO (influenced strongly by all inbound marketing techniques).
3. Content distribution, in general.
4. Webinars.
5. Visual content.
6. Interactive content (games, etc.).
7. How-to videos.
8. Online tools.
9. Fremium trials.

Other key takeaways from HubSpots survey include (Chernov, p. 6-10):

- Inbound marketers who routinely track ROI in their inbound marketing efforts are 1,200% more likely to report a year-to-year increase in ROI. Chernov says a major reason for this is that tracking ROI results in an organization increasing inbound budget and utilization since, if done well, is much more cost-effective than outbound marketing (traditional advertising, phone solicitations, trade shows, etc.).
- Inbound marketing helps a company to be found on the Internet. Marketers who blog are 1,300% more likely to drive positive ROI than those who don't.
- Organization leaders and communication practitioners prioritized the purposes of inbound marketing exactly the same and with almost identical scores. These are, in ranked order:
  ○ Increasing the number of contacts/leads.
  ○ Converting contacts/leads to customers.
  ○ Reaching the relevant audience.
  ○ Increasing revenue derived from existing customers.

- ◦ Proving the ROI of our marketing activities.
- ◦ Reducing the cost of contacts/leads/customer acquisition.
- Inbound marketing is becoming more important to vendors and marketing agencies. "More companies are running inbound than ever before," writes Chernov (p. 9), but marketing agencies are more committed to inbound than vendors. About 47% of the agency respondents reported that inbound marketing was their primary lead generator, as opposed to about 27% of the vendors. In both cases, about 40% of their leads were attributed to neither inbound nor outbound marketing and probably included such sources as referrals.
- Inbound is becoming a vital part of sales. More than 25% of HubSpot's respondents reported that their sales teams are themselves employing inbound tactics. But more important was the response by sales staff themselves in answering the question, "Which lead sources have become more important over the last 6 months?" The top four in order were email marketing, social media, SEO and blogs. Ranked last was traditional advertising, followed by direct mail, pay per click (PPC), trade shows and telemarketing.
- While organization staff members provide content for most inbound marketing worldwide, guests and freelancers show the greatest ROI.
- For North American B2B companies with 1-200 employees, the average cost per lead is about 66% less for inbound marketing than outbound marketing. For larger companies inbound marketing leads are about 40% less expensive.
- Respondents were from around the world, and the results showed that these are global trends, with little variance between locations.

In authoring an earlier 2014 survey study involving 1,099 e-commerce marketing and business professionals from 45 countries in six continents, Mallikarjunan (pp. 10-19) concluded that of those organizations that reported a positive ROI from inbound marketing, 72% were blogging at least once a week. Those that blog were 155% more likely to report a positive ROI. Blogging also helps generate more indexable pages that lead to more and higher listings in organic searches. Of companies that reported that most of their customers come from organic or direct traffic, 69% blog at least weekly. Other findings from the study included:

- Once inbound marketing attracts a visitor to an organization's website, 25% of the marketers follow up primarily with email and 24% primarily via social media (p. 29).
- Businesses that emphasize educational content in their inbound marketing are 527% more likely to report a positive ROI than those that emphasize coupons (p. 33).
- Organic searches are credited with driving the most traffic to a website (22%), although such inbound techniques as blogging, videos, podcasts, webinars and e-books all help achieve higher SEO. Social media, at 17.4%, are credited with providing the second-most impact on traffic, followed by PPC and email.

Social Media

Social media are a primary platform for free inbound or content marketing, as already discussed. But they are also a primary platform for paid native advertising – advertising prepared to blend in with the organic content around it. In social media, it would appear in users' timeline or news feed as a "sponsored" post. And frequently native advertising is the very same content that an organization placed on its own social media site free, but which they then pay to "promote" on other people's sites who are not among their own site's friends, fans or followers. Just like social media organic postings, native advertising can take many forms: a video, a photograph, story text, a multimedia story, an infographic, etc. The main difference is that it's paid. And native advertising does not solely appear in social media, although that is a favored venue. It could also be a paid story in a printed newspaper, for example. It's simply ad content that mirrors its surrounding content. Native advertising has become so popular that it is expected to make up 74% of all U.S. digital display ad revenue by 2021 (Politt, 2017). This social media discussion relates to both free social media postings and to paid advertising, now typically of the native advertising type.

In the 2017 Social Media Marketing Industry Report, 92% of the 5,700 respondents said the social media are important to their business marketing efforts (Stelzner, 2017, p. 7,9), although only 38% said they could measure the ROI of their social media activities. While some of their promotional activities are free, the efforts still represent costs to the organization. Forty-one percent of respondents indicated that they spend more than 11 hours a week on social media, and 64% spend at least six hours (p. 12). While Facebook is the most-used social medium by marketers (commonly used by 94%, compared with second-place Twitter, by only 68%), 53% of the respondents said they had seen a decline in exposure of their free postings on Facebook, blaming it on the company's new algorithm, and another 43% were not sure (p. 11, 19). Other social media commonly used by marketers are LinkedIn (56%), Instagram (54%), YouTube (45%), Pinterest (30%), and Snapchat (7%). Despite their doubts about Facebook, 39% said they posted more on the medium in the current year than previously, and only 15% posted less. More importantly, 68% said they planned to post more in the future, and only 3% said they would post less. Similarly positive plans were stated for the other social media, however (p. 27-32).

Few among social media researchers has gained more notoriety and acclaim nor addressed online PR and marketing from a more scientific perspective than Dan Zarrella. Widely recognized as a "social media scientist," Zarrella began is research with the online marketing company HubSpot. The use of inbound strategies, especially free ebooks and webinars, helped HubSpot soar to the top of the online marketing consulting industry, and Zarrella became their superstar. He spoke at Harvard and has now published four books on the subject, including, *The Science of Marketing: When to Tweet, What to Post, How to Blog, and Other Proven Strategies*, *The Facebook Marketing Book*, *Zarrella's Heirarchy of Contagiousness: The Science, Design and Engineering of Contagious Ideas*, and *The Social Media Marketing Book*. Zarrella calls much of the consulting conducted by other organizations "superstition based." Even when it comes from surveys of executives, those reflect popular trends – not necessarily scientifically founded principles. Besides working with databases with thousands or even millions of files, he has analyzed content of successful inbound marketers and conducts experiments to test resulting hypotheses. Here are several of his findings among many that should be given more attention in future research (Zarrella, 2013).

- **"Conversation" Does NOT Build Reach:** He could find no good examples of organizations that have built large followings with social media "conversation." In analyzing millions of tweets, those with a higher number of followers are those NOT conversing but rather those that are essentially broadcasting interesting content.
- **Best Message Timing has Many Variables:** While there are clearly peaks of traffic for emailing, Tweeting or Facebooking, getting an organization's own message out effectively may be by

messaging during non-peak times to avoid the clutter. The timing of messages should be a matter of experimentation for individual marketing organizations, depending on purpose, content, etc.

- **Social Calls to Action Work:** Social marketers have been hesitant to ask their audience to retweet or to "like" their messages, but social calls to action do work. To ask followers to "please retweet" leads to more than four times as many retweets than making no such request.
- **Social Media Should be Part of an SEO Strategy:** There is a strong correlation between the number of tweets, Facebook shares and LinkedIn shares with the number of inbound links an organization's website has from other websites. In other words, the more exposure a site has on social media, the more frequently those who control other websites create links to the target site.
- **PPC and Emailing Programs also Build SEO:** Analyzing organic search traffic to the HubSpot website, Zarrella found a positive correlation of higher organic search rates with paid search tactics, such as pay-per-click ads, and also with higher emailing rates, such as times when they are sending out information about new ebooks or webinars to people in their database.
- **Be Interesting, not Self-Promoting:** In analyzing the content of tweets, Zarrella found that the more an organization refers to itself, the fewer followers it has. In other words, talk about interesting things, but don't talk about yourself too much.

Programmatic Advertising

Programmatic advertising is not limited to any specific channel, Internet device, target audience or message content. Programmatic ads can be display, video or native ads. They can also be aimed at desktop computers, mobile devices or even include traditional, non-digital media. It is the method, not the substance that counts. The key to programmatic is to make as many of the decisions as possible by computer in order to deal with the fragmented online media market and massive consumer data. Much of the growth is being driven by mobile, where respondents saw the greatest opportunity for programmatic advertising in 2015 – 33%, compared to 20% for the next highest, video advertising. In 2014 mobile was the second most purchased type of programmatic advertising at 69%, only behind display (86%) and ahead of video (67%) (eMarketer, 2015a). The growth of programmatic quickly went global. Even in 2014 Asian advertisers increased programmatic by 329% -- significantly more than North American advertisers (PulsePoint, 2015).

The top advantages to programmatic, a WBR Digital survey found (2015, p. 9), were, (1) improved media buying efficiency and targeting, according to 91% of the respondents; (2) improved customer experience through relevant messaging, according to 90% of respondents; and (3) improved media ROI or conversions, according to 87% of the respondents.

Programmatic advertising is new enough that many advertising professionals still don't know what it is, and if they know what it is, they don't know if and how they can implement it. Indeed, hiring trained professionals to bring it in-house is almost impossible. In late 2012 it was estimated that 90% of all brand marketers had never even heard of programmatic advertising (Gutman, 2012), but by 2014 it became the fastest-growing trend, with mobile programmatic spending increasing 291% and desktop spending increasing 245% during the year (Pulsepoint, 2015). The growth rate slowed in 2015 to 51%, in 2016 to 46%, an estimated 28% in 2017, and an expected 20% in 2018 (eMarketer, 2017c). If those estimates are correct, programmatic advertising will be used in nearly 82% of all digital display ad spending in America in 2018 and 84% in 2019. That will approach $33 billion in U.S. digital ad spending in 2017, an estimated $39 billion in 2018, and $46 billion in 2019.

While programmatic tools made it cost-effective to locate, contract and interact with far more of the advertising sellers who were previously ignored by most advertisers, there was also the problem of individualizing advertising messages appropriate for the difference audiences. As an eMarketer report (2015b), "Creating ads on the fly: Fostering creativity in the programmatic era," explained, to do this effectively requires a change in infrastructure and mindset. Companies active in social media may find this easier to respond to different situations and create new messages on the fly, but others still seeing this from the customer service or direct mail perspective have difficulty adapting. So, programmatic advertisers and agencies are trying to make this also part of the programmatic system. In 2015 63% of the programmatic marketers were already using data signals to help personalize messages. Matt Cohen, the founder and president of the agency OneSpot, explained their process to eMarketer:

For each piece of content we'll create several different sizes of display ads, mobile ads, social ads and soon, native ads. We have a crawler that automatically looks at the client's content, pulls out the headlines, the video, thumbnail, the full video, the photo. It also does an analysis of the content to figure out what it's about, what are the keywords in it and so forth. Then it goes into an ad studio where the client can review it, and alternate variations can be created. … [T]he chance that you're going to have something for anybody in your target audience is extremely high, and you're likely to have something that's actually really good for that specific person.

While these efforts sound exciting, what we have seen in reality is that not all of the corporate clients are satisfied with the agencies' efforts. Developing and tracking programmatic advertising has been very challenging from the start. Because of the technical complexity of programmatic advertising, most advertisers had to contract outside agencies to do the work. In the WBR Digital study (2015), retailers reported good return on investment (ROI), but multichannel analytics were considered lacking. About 36% said analytics were spread across multiple platforms – inefficient but with solid visibility, but another 36% reported that analytics capabilities were still under development, and 20% said analytics provided only fractured visibility across several platforms. Respondents to the Advertiser Perceptions study (2015) indicated that they would spend more money on programmatic if such problems were fixed. Some 40% wanted clear evidence of ROI, and 30% wanted greater transparency in ad placement, including assurance that their ads were being placed in an environment compatible with the brand. Bringing programmatic functions in-house would give advertisers more control, which 59% of the advertisers said was their intention in 2015, but 61% of the agencies surveyed were skeptical that even large companies could accomplish that because of the lack of expertise available in the labor market.

That was in 2015, and a 2017 study by Adweek and Accenture Interactive found that the frustration had not diminished but rather increased (Johnson, 2017). Instead of 59% wanting to bring at least part of programmatic in-house, in 2017 that desire had spread to 87% of the advertisers for much the same reasons – lack of agency transparency, according to 74% of the respondents, lack of measurement tools according to 73%, lack of targeting control according to 66%, and loss of trust according to 53% of the advertisers. Of the largest advertisers, 71% believe they now have the in-house expertise to do some of their own programmatic work, but 96% admit that the agencies will still have to play a major role going forward because of the technical complexities.

Some ad publishers would also like to cut out the agencies in the middle, blaming them for buying cheap, low-quality ad inventory and selling it to advertisers for a higher profit (Chen, 2017). "There are brand safety issues. Even when brands think they know where they're running ads, they don't totally ever know," Paul Josephsen, CMO of Adslot, told eMarketer (2017d).

Transparency is another big issue. Publisher revenue from media has gone down, but technology providers are still taking a massive cut of what's supposed to be working media dollars. And finally, there's fraud. It's not just fake news that brands have to fight against -- it's clickbait as well.

In response to such problems, some advertisers are moving their ad purchases from open exchanges to private marketplaces (PMPs). More than 25% of North American programmatic advertisers planned to make this move "to ensure their ads appear across higher-quality publishers' sites" (Guaglione, 2017). Others are participating in header bidding to ensure higher-quality publications. Header bidding is still done in automated fashion, but it allows advertisers to pay more in order to make specific advertising choices among the publisher's inventory of sites. While a PubMatic analysis of header bidding in the third quarter of 2017 showed an increase of 220% from a year earlier, an eMarketer study revealed that it is so new that only 25% of programmatic advertisers had a good understanding of what it is, and relatively few have implemented the strategy (eMarketer, 2017e). Advertisers are particularly concerned with the lack of visibility and analytics for mobile, which makes up the bulk of programmatic advertising. Thus, the growth of mobile PMP channels was 153% in Q3 of 2017, year-over-year, and it was also the driver for header bidding (Guaglione, 2017). "Mobile, once regarded as the third screen, is quickly becoming the first screen for many consumers globally, which has accelerated header bidding on mobile," said PubMatic CEO Rajeev Goel.

Some of the trust and satisfaction issues have arisen because of the rapid growth of new agencies to address the growing demand of advertisers. To help address these trust issues, organization have been developed to rank agencies and advise advertisers which are most likely to provide satisfactory service. Pixalate, one of the leading global intelligence platforms and real-time fraud protection services, provides three separate trust indexes to help advertisers. The Pixalate Seller Trust Indexes rank the relative quality of programmatic advertising sellers based on Pixalate's proprietary technology that analyzes more than 100 billion monthly impressions. These ratings, revised monthly, can be downloaded at http://www.pixalate. com/sellertrustindex/global/?utm_campaign=Emarketer%20Ad%2011.16.17&utm_source=ppc#!global.

Advertisers, agencies, buyers/sellers and publishers make for a sometimes complicated relationship, even when the buying and selling of programmatic advertising is automated. "What makes a good programmatic publisher for us is someone who is transparent, and is open to having conversations about their tech offerings and what's on their road map in terms of products of data. That helps us think about synergies that they might not have thought of," said Melissa Bonnick, VP of programmatic strategy at Havas' trading desk, Affiperf, in an interview with AdExchanger (Sluis, Liyakasa and Weissbrot, *2017)*. Top programmatic advertising publishers make things simple and transparent to make it easy to buy with a single conversation. They don't require direct negotiating or charge extra for programmatic advertising. They offer unique audience data of value to certain advertisers. And they keep buyers informed of any changes. According to AdExchanger, some of the most aggressive programmatic advertising publishers, not including Facebook and Google, include NBC Universal, The Weather Co. (subsidiary of IBM), The Washington Post, AOL (now Oath), Hulu and Turner/CNN. These large companies see programmatic as a way to become increasingly competitive with Google and Facebook.

Place

The place to explore products and to make purchases in the digital world is typically a company website. … but more and more is apps in your mobile phone. The website influences and is influenced by the other three P's. Web pages to display and demonstrate products and services must be created, and because of the long-tail aspect, there may be many product pages. Then how do you get people to come to the virtual store? As noted previously, inbound marketing tools provide more searchable content for an organization's website. A HubSpot study of its own 7,000+ customers revealed that those with 51-100 web pages of content on their site achieve 48% more traffic than those with fewer than 50 pages of content. But those with over 1,000 pages of content average 3,500% more traffic. Inbound marketing techniques, such as blogging and free ebooks, provide those 1,000 pages of searchable content (HubSpot, 2014). Other inbound marketing requires customized landing pages to become part of the website. A business might place a video on YouTube promoting a new product or buy PPC advertising on Facebook to promote a free webinar, but the website landing page provides the details, requests the visitors' contact information, etc.

The greater power of video also impacts the design and content of a website. Almost 95% of online marketers believe video is the most powerful tool for digital marketing, and website video can increase conversion rates by 60% (Aberdeen, 2014). The 2017 Video in Business Benchmark Report prepared by Vidyard (2016, p. 18) details how customers who use their video platform are enhancing visitors' website experience with video. What are they creating?

- 59% "explainer videos"
- 51% product feature videos
- 45% how to or educational videos
- 44% customer testimonials
- 37% thought leader interviews
- 32% talking head style videos
- 29% live action videos
- 28% pre-recorded demos
- 23% live streaming
- 20% cultural content

Many organizations have failed to fully prepare their websites for easy mobile access. This is important since there are now 4.5 times as many mobile broadband subscriptions in the world than fixed-wire broadband subscriptions, according to the International Telecommunications Union (2017). In a live webcast eMarketer CEO Geoff Ramsey (2015) noted that 86% of so-called Millennials complain that most commercial websites are still not mobile-friendly, and 71% of them find that most online businesses fail to offer a mobile app as an alternative. Ramsey noted that of the billions of dollars in purchases made on mobile devices, 72% are via mobile apps and 28% on websites. Mobile customers who arrive to a website that does not accommodate mobile almost always go a competitor's website thereafter. Mobile users don't mind scrolling up and down on a web page, but they hate scrolling left and right.

According to Adobe, of 2,146 executives who responded to the question, "Over the next five years, what is the primary way your organization will seek to differentiate itself from competitors?" the No. 1 priority for 44% of the respondents was "Customer service/customer experience – making it easy, fun, valuable and/or pleasurable to shop from us" (Adobe, 2015, p. 15). The design and functionality of an online organization's "place" has a powerful effect on prospective customers.

Figure 2. More than 2,000 marketing executives respond to this question: Where does your organization place the highest emphasis in terms of improving the customer experience on your organization's website? Source: Adobe (2015)

Catering to the Omnichannel Customer

The number of m-commerce buyers in the U.S. increased from 57 million to 136 million between 2012 and 2016 and is predicted to double again between 2017 and 2020 in the U.S. (eMarketer, 2017f, p. 2-8). Despite whatever inconveniences may still exist in making mobile purchases, 136 million Americans (64% of all U.S. adult Internet users) had purchased products via mobile devices by 2016. By 2017 mobile represented 35% of all e-commerce sales and is predicted to reach 54% by 2021. Thus, the stakes are high for businesses to adapt to the needs of the mobile consumers. In 2017 only 22% of retail executives reported having mobile websites implemented and working well, 38% had sites set up but needing improvements, and 22% were still making plans for the future. At the same time, only 14% had a mobile app established and working well, 39% had one that needed improvements, 31% were making plans for the future. Their adaption to mobile went down from there. About 9% were effectively making mobile offers within their store, 14% were trying, and 43% were making plans, and only 8% were effectively helping consumers locate products in-store with a mobile app or website, 14% were making an effort, and 44% were making plans. The top priority of North American retailers overall was to increase their digital business by adapting to the needs of mobile (54%), followed by enhancing their marketing (46%). The potential for rapid increase may be seen in two statistics, that while a quarter of all online revenue comes from mobile, more than half of the mobile shopping carts are abandoned before the sale takes place. While the order size of purchases made by desktop may be substantially larger, during the first three quarters of 2017 the number of mobile retail orders was nearly equal to desktop – 48% to 52% (eMarketer, 2017g, p. 1-3).

In part because of the rapid growth of mobile commerce and e-commerce overall, advertisers are putting more and more of their advertising dollars into digital advertising (eMarketer, 2017b). In 2016 digital advertising surpassed TV ad sales in America, and by 2021 it is expected to surpass all other advertising sales combined. As already discussed, that may be a low estimate since digital advertising was expected to approach 41% in 2017, and the dwindling TV audience could cause even more advertising to move from traditional to digital media. Mobile, meanwhile, is the medium of choice now for search advertising. Consumers are using their mobile search capabilities while they are on the go. So mobile search and mobile display advertising together accounted for 70% of all digital advertising in 2017, even though mobile still only accounted for 35% of all e-commerce in 2017 in the value of purchases.

It has taken several years for advertisers to recognize the value of mobile advertising beyond actual sales. Search advertising, of course, is major part of that, but there is much more. The sales funnel, especially in retail sales, is becoming increasingly omnichannel in nature (eMarketer, 2017h). Omnichannel retailing is defined by eMarketer as "the practice of using all available shopping channels to buy or sell goods and services," including "in-store, internet, mobile and catalog sales" (p. 3). Many of the omnichannel strategies revolve around mobile. Digital overall is considered to influence 56% of all in-store sales, as of 2016 (p. 4). Conducting digital research before purchasing is one way that consumers are influenced prepurchase, but they also spend 13% more in-store than do other consumers, and 59% of retailers felt omnichannel customers were more profitable than others (p. 7, 9). The two top omnichannel strategies implemented by retailers include buying online but picking up in-store, which more than doubled from 21% to 44% of retailers in 2016, and in-store return or exchange of online purchases, which soared from 18% to 61% of retailers during that time (p. 13).

Other digital influences on shoppers include visiting a retailer's website or app (58%), using a search engine (54%), visiting other sites or apps (37%), using a digital map (31%), looking at digital images/photos (24%), and calling or emailing the retailer prior to shopping in-store (p. 19). Other options supported by consumers include being able to instantly order out-of-stock items by phone for home delivery (23%), to select items digitally and then be directed to them in-store (22%), and being informed by smartphone about special offers linked to the store (13%). Consumer who engage with a retailer with more channels (including ads, social media and email newsletters) are more likely to purchase from that retailer on a weekly basis. Those who engage in 10 or more channels are about 50% more likely to purchase in-store and 100% more likely to purchase digitally on a weekly basis than those who engage less (p. 21). In the U.S. 67% of smartphone users do mobile research along with in-store visits. That is a growing trend globally, as well, including 59% in China, 52% in Germany, 47% in the UK, and 45% in Japan (p. 22). In-store, the most common mobile activities include comparing prices (77%), checking email for offers and coupons (58%), checking a retail app for special deals (50%), looking for product information and reviews (47%), using a mobile wallet (33%), and ordering items from a different retailer (17%) (p. 23). Young adults 18-26 especially use omnichanneling opportunities, such as shopping digitally and purchasing in-store (46%) or shopping in-store and purchasing digitally (32%) (p. 24). Allowing customers to buy online and then pick up in-store is by far the most-used strategy by retailers, now being offered by 53% of respondents and planned for implementation within one year by 42% more (p. 31). A poll by the e-tailing group found that 64% of consumers picked up mobile purchases in-store at least monthly (p. 33). A different survey by RIS News seemed to suggest fewer per month, but questions were not exactly the same. It concluded that 19% of U.S. internet users buy online and pick up in-store at least twice a month and 60% a few times a year. The survey did not offer an option of once a month (p. 34). Again younger internet users are more likely to use this service – 87% of millennials and 79% of Gen X consumers (p. 37), but those Boomers who do this are more likely to make other purchases when they go to pick up their digital purchase, compared with 75% of millennials and 63% of Gen X buyers (p.38).

Price

Pricing is certainly affected by online promotional efforts, virtual storefronts and the digitization of products. Generally, the digital economy is pushing prices lower. Technology is providing opportunities to use innovative strategies that can disrupt any industry still trying to do traditional business as usual, as the hospitality and transportation industries are experiencing because of AirBnB and Uber. But even the pricing of products that are essentially free to produce is a science. The lowest price does not always achieve the most unit sales, much less the greatest profits. A friend laughs about how she tried futilely to give away a litter of new puppies on Craigs List until she decided instead to charge $50 apiece. Apparently a free puppy is not perceived to be a quality puppy. The same has been found to be true for digital books. A $1 book does not necessarily sell more copies than the same book priced at $3 or $5 or $10. Pricing research must frequently be done on specific product lines to be most effective, but other pricing research can give organizations some idea of the most likely considerations. However, according to executives who responded to Adobe's question about their organization's "primary way … to differentiate itself from competitors" over the next five years, only 5% made price the top priority. (Adobe, 2015, p. 15)

RESEARCH DIRECTIONS AND CHALLENGES

Let's review some of the mind-bending changes in marketing over the past few years and consider academia's role in related research. In 2012 when mobile advertising represented only 2.6% of all ad spending, Shintaro Okazaki foresaw that mobile marketing was about to erupt, but noted that already there was a lack of academic research to parallel industry practice (Okazaki, 2012). Lamberton and Stephens (2016) looked at marketing research from 2000 to 2015 related to digital, social media, and mobile channels and found that researchers from academia and industry have frequently not been aligned, presenting many opportunities for collaboration, growth, and knowledge. In their report they called for academic and industry researchers to work together to address the critical issues in the rapidly evolving marketing ecosystem.

We are at a point in practice where digital marketing is just marketing, simply because almost all marketing activities a firm might consider now can have some kind of digital aspect. [It is] crucial that digital/ social media/mobile marketing researchers work to close the academic-practitioner gap. (Lamberton & Stephens, 2016, p. 168)

By 2017, Americans spent almost as much of their media time each day on digital media as traditional media (5 hours, 53 minutes for digital to 6 hours, 8 minutes for traditional), and people spent most of that digital time on mobile – 3 hours, 17 minutes on average (eMarketer, 2017c). Digital media time will soon exceed traditional, and advertising follows the audience. By 2021, eMarketer projects that digital advertising will surpass all traditional advertising combined and collect over 51% of advertising revenues in America (eMarketer, 2017b). While mobile display advertising is growing rapidly, mobile search dominates. Together mobile search and mobile display accounted for 70% of all digital advertising in 2017, and such trends are now global in nature.

The frenzied pace at which digital marketing is growing and transforming has top marketing executives frustrated and grasping for any research, training and assistance they can get (Ramos, 2013). The growing intertwining of marketing and technology has caused a large proportion of corporate marketing teams to begin hiring IT and database graduates instead of market graduates to provide the breadth of skills they require (Brinker, 2017). One of the most challenging of technologies for marketers is programmatic advertising, which is projected to be used in locating, contracting and fulfilling 84% of all digital display advertising by 2019 (eMarketer, 2017a). And not even the in-house technology experts that the corporations are hiring can figure out this technology. In 2017 85% of the marketing executives wanted to take programmatic responsibilities away from outside consultants and bring it in-house (Johnson, 2017), but 96% admitted that their teams were not yet capable of taking over more than a small part of those functions. These challenging issues in the marketing industry raise questions about university marketing programs being able to keep pace with common industry practices, let alone scholars' ability to achieve industry-relevant research that full-time industry researchers are not already producing.

While conducting research for this chapter, a key-word search for articles about IMC, content marketing, onmichannel, conversation marketing, experience marketing, digital marketing, mobile marketing, social media marketing, messaging marketing, and programmatic advertising in the websites of the Journal of Marketing Research, Journal of Marketing Science, Journal of Consumer Research, The Journal of the Academy of Marketing Science and others for the years 2016 and 2017 yielded marginal results, suggesting many possible areas of collaboration between industry and academia.

Promotion is not the only one of the 4 P's facing such dramatic changes. E-commerce and m-commerce are still far behind brick-and-mortar operations, but the question of when digital commerce exceeds traditional commerce also seems to be more when than if. E-commerce in America has a long way to go, but it has climbed from 4.2% of all retail commerce in the first quarter of 2010 to 9.1% in the third quarter of 2017 and is picking up steam, rising about one percentage point per year (Statista, 2017). Indications are that a few innovations could lead to massive disruption in the marketplace. For example, while the value of m-purchases is still low, the number of m-commerce buyers in the U.S. (people who have made purchases via their mobile device) increased from 57 million to 136 million between 2012 and 2016 and is predicted to double again between 2017 and 2020 in the U.S. (eMarketer, 2017f, p. 2-8). Another facet to this new reality is the acknowledgment that nearly 45% of all marketing emails today are opened on a mobile device. Yet many marketers fail to optimize landing pages and websites in general to accommodate the platform. This is despite Google estimates that 61% of users are unlikely to return to a mobile site they had trouble accessing. And, even worse, 40 percent of those users will visit a competitor's site instead (Aufreiter, Boudet & Weng, 2014). If 136 million Americans (64% of all U.S. adult Internet users) have purchased products via mobile devices in spite of numerous inconveniences, what will happen when organizations make their websites more mobile-friendly and simplify the purchasing process? As consumers become accustomed to the new retail ecosystem and businesses finally adapt their websites to mobile, consumers' actions can change very rapidly, as suggested by tipping point theory, and innovation and investment tend to be drawn to the vacuum created by such an opportunity within a free marketplace, as suggested by push-pull theory.

Email itself is still a vital topic of research for academics and industry researchers. Lost in all the hype about social media, according to Aufreiter et al. (2014), is the fact that email remains a significantly more effective way to acquire customers than social media — nearly 40 times that of Facebook and Twitter combined. That's because 91% of all U.S. consumers still use email daily – about half of those accessing via mobile, and the rate at which emails prompt purchases is not only estimated to be at least three times that of social media, but the average order value is also 17% higher. More precisely, email is part of the omnichannel approach that uses social media and inbound marketing strategies to get consumers to visit a special landing page on advertisers' website where they voluntarily share their email address and other personal information. They are typically asked during that process if it would be OK for the company to send them related information. Once they say yes, email marketing begins, and a click from that email will send them back to the website (or mobile app) for more information and/or to make the purchase. Email specifically and this entire omnichannel process deserves more attention from researchers.

And research issues related to the 4 P's *Place* are also confusing and challenging because of increasing interaction between digital and traditional commerce. The sales funnel is increasingly omnichannel (eMarketer, 2017h), and digital overall is considered to influence 56% of all in-store sales, as of 2016 (p. 4). The fact that the vast majority of search advertising is mobile suggests that the consumers access it especially when they are on the move and ready to make a purchase. Retailers are now rapidly adjusting to this new omnichannel ecosystem, with about half of all retailers in America now allowing consumers to buy online but pick up in-store, and over 60% allowing in-store return or exchange of online purchases (p. 13). These practices that were rare in 2015 will be the norm in 2018. And many of the mobile shopping activities are increasingly being conducted even while the consumers are inside a brick-and-mortar store making their purchase decision, including (p. 23) comparing prices by 77% of the mobile consumers, checking email for offers and coupons (58%), checking a retail app for special deals (50%), looking for product information and reviews (47%), using a mobile wallet (33%), and ordering items from a different retailer (17%).

I don't think we need to analyze all 4 P's to see that the marketing environment is dramatically changing faster than it takes most academics to conduct their research part-time and then achieve publication. Almost by definition industry-relevant research will be out of date before it is published.

Access to 'Big Data'

At the same time it seems clear that without access to Big Data, academics and small industry researchers will simply not have the tools to compete with researchers at the major corporations who have access to both massive amounts of historic data and real-time data. Ethical questions and issues of access to data are already being raised. Knowledge is power, and data is knowledge. It should be evident why Facebook paid $19 billion dollars to buy Whatsapp, even though the messaging application generates no revenue through advertising or through any other means. Why was it so valuable? The answer, at least in part, is data. Without access to such data, academic researchers can become second-class, at best, or not even in the competition. To access such data, researchers may have to pursue partnering opportunities with industry research teams. What do academic researchers offer industry? Research expertise. A large portion of industry research is based on surveys, and as one of the top industry researchers, Dan Zarrella (2013), has noted, is frequently "superstition based" and reflects popular trends rather than reality. The surveys show correlations that do not reveal causation. Industry researchers do some content analysis but seldom venture into any kind of experimentation in their research.

Industry Frustrations as Academic Opportunities

In a half-full perspective, the frustrations of marketing executives do not only indicate big challenges to academic researchers but also big opportunities. If the executives admit the challenge is essentially too big for them to handle, then at least for some academic researchers that is an opportunity to shine. But it means they have to be or become the smartest person in the room, so to speak. While the marketing executive is frustrated by too many changes occurring in too many fronts, an academic researcher might focus on a single issue to achieve expertise recognized not only by his peers but by industry. That, again, suggests some partnering and consulting opportunities that could separate them even further from other researchers. Perhaps a tech-savvy marketing academic could partner with a cutting-edge technology guru to achieve the cross-disciplinary expertise required to master programmatic advertising and begin addressing the many issues for which executives want answers. With the right credentials and commitment, the executives would invite such a research team into their facilities to help them figure out how to bring programmatic advertising in-house, as the vast majority of executives say they want to do but cannot.

While not as big a technical challenge as programmatic, executives are also frustrated that they cannot keep up with all the changes in social media and the potential impact on marketing. Despite most modern executives already using social media marketing tactics, about 90% of them have serious questions about how to use it most effectively, and 80% say they need more expert training (Stelzner, 2017). This is another area were academics should take notice. One study that may be indicative of potential academic contributions to the industry is the social media research by Ashley and Tuten (2015). Their study found that different levels of consumer engagement in social media channels and messages depend on consumer needs, motives, goals, and consumer interpersonal relationships with brands. Their study underlines the importance of frequent updates and incentives for participation. In their research several creative strategies were associated with customer engagement, specifically experiential, image, and exclusivity messages. They found that despite the value of these creative approaches, most branded social content can be categorized as functional. If nothing else, their study points to the many opportunities for future research inherent in the context of social media.

Ascarza, Ebbes, Netzer and Danielson (2017) were able to cooperate with a mobile telecommunication provider to conduct field experimentation involving about 6,000 customers. The study demonstrated how a social media campaign could be used to increase consumption and reduce churn among targeted customers, but it also found a spin-off benefit. Without any targeted communication nor offering any direct incentives, they achieved 28% of the same positive results with customers who had first-degree connections with the targeted customers.

While it may still be challenging for an academic to make himself into the solution to executives' needs, it is easier than programmatic advertising and achievable by many academics willing to focus studies and research on social media. Running social media experiments with commissionable products available at Clickbank.com, one non-academic developed his own social media formula and made about $800,000 in three years while doing it (Penberthy, 2015). He has now become a much-sought-after trainer within the marketing industry. Penberthy used the omnichannel approach mentioned previously, but enhanced his success specifically by focusing on production of short, free marketing videos on YouTube linked to strong website landing pages. His videos were so focused that over 50% of his visitors provided their contact information for follow-up emailed information and, in many cases, sales conversion. Another narrow field within social media is the fastest-growing paid advertising tactic – native advertising, which also ties into viral marketing concepts. The "superstition research" suggests that the key is achieving the "wow" or shock factor, but little research has turned that artistic approach into any kind of science.

Another narrower and less-competitive area of expertise possible for a focused academic researcher could include how to use mobile as more than a "scaled-down version of the Web" (Ask, 2014). Suggested areas of research and application include how to:

- Drive spontaneous purchases with flash sales directed at people based on their location. Geo-targeted marketing is enabled by mobile and can be sent, for example, just to those within one mile of a store. There has been some experimentation with messaging just as a customer approaches the counter to buy. These marketing messages could help upsell or cross-sell a customer. There has been some research in this field, but many opportunities still abound.

- Offer new or greatly personalized services available for digital delivery or digital scheduling, such as monitoring, coaching, just-in-time training, Uber-like services, etc., or cheaper pay-as-you-go services. In Africa this can even include utilities like electricity. They can't afford 24/7 service but can order it as needed. Perhaps trained on-demand child care or elderly care.

- Counter targeting offers. Amazon has experimented with counter-geo-targeting. When it could detect that a consumer was shopping in a store, it sent special offers to steal those purchases. And, in another of the few examples of academic-industry cooperative research studies, Andrews, Luo, Fang and Ghose (2016) took this idea a step further to compare the profitability of geo-targeted offers to retailers' own customers versus making those offers to competitors' customers through GPS-activated mobile messaging technology. They concluded that retailers making special offers to customers already in their own store actually lose profit they otherwise could have retained, while making those offers to competitors' customers successfully allows retailers to profit from sales they would not have made otherwise and possibly retain the buyers as new long-term customers.

A large portion of websites are not yet "mobile-friendly." As noted in this chapter, only 22% of retail executives report having mobile sites that are working well, and only 14% have a mobile app (eMarketer, 2017h). This can be devastating since not only are customers not able to make online purchases in reasonable fashion, but search engines such as Google have revamped their search algorithms to penalize non-mobile websites since most searches are now done with mobile devices. This represents another area in which an academic could achieve expertise and, at the same time, more opportunities to partner with companies in conducting research. The most common skills to build mobile-friendly websites is HTML5, the coding achieved with the newest versions of web-building software sold by Adobe and other vendors. Becoming expert at app development might start by working with a company like Build-Fire, a no-coding-required app builder that is a leader in the SaaS (software as a service) industry. The company business model is based on the premise that they can help content marketers build apps from scratch to enable them to bring their stories right into the Web and mobile preferences of their target audiences. Ian Blair, the CEO and founder of BuildFire.com, swears by his company's mission statement, "Build your app for free and pay only when you publish" (Growth Everywhere, 2017). In only four years BuildFire has become one of the most promising SaaS companies, developing along the way over 3,000 apps across various industries. To be "expert enough" to partner with many companies might just require introducing them to this service and showing them how it works.

To be useful to industry, achieving expertise in one such area may be the key. And once the industry values an academic's professional expertise, research opportunities could abound.

Bigger Picture Research

There are bigger-picture issues to be researched. Tipping point, multi-step (viralization), and push-pull theories can be illustrated and supported with numerous case studies, and in the process perhaps refined as Clayton Christensen (2014) has done with his disruptive innovation theories over the past decade. Christensen points out that to be of real value, a theory should be predictive. With the rapid changes occurring in the marketing industry, there are more opportunities to test theories in a predictive manner than ever before.

Sociological and psychological issues are certainly not dead. As noted earlier, Americans are now spending 12 hours of every day tuned in to some kind of media (eMarketer, 2017c), evenly split between digital and traditional media (6:08 hours traditional vs. 5:53 digital, and digital is expected to surpass traditional media within the next two years). A Gallup poll found that Americans are becoming more and more dependent on their smartphones, to the degree of being addicts (eMarketer, 2015c). A growing portion of users feel compelled to check their mobile phone for messages every few minutes. More than half of all women under 49 said they would be very or somewhat anxious if they misplaced their smartphone for one day. For males of that same age group, the percentage of anxious respondents was about 40%. But this may be more than just a sign of addiction but rather fulfillment of predictions that humans and technology are evolving together. That is what Kevin Kelly (2007), the founding executive editor of Wired magazine, suggested in his famous talk 10 years ago. He said that, in essence, the internet was one giant machine with billions of parts, including all the computers, the servers, the mobile devices, the car sensors, etc., connected to it. Together they included 55 trillion links that function very similar to and in about the same number as the synapses in the human brain, along with 1 quintillion transistors that number and work about the same as neurons in a brain. Thus, the internet in 2007 was similar in size and function to one human brain ... but doubling in its power and capacity every two years. With such exponential growth, he predicted that by 2040 it will have the power of 6 billion human brains and exceed the processing capacity of all humanity. With the internet of things, he said, we would see an "embodiment" of the internet – a blending of the atomic and digital realities. With XML and other programming changes, the internet would then go beyond its page-to-page connections to data-to-data or idea-to-idea connections. The page-to-page connections of the Web required humanity to give up some privacy, but idea-to-idea connections even more so. No more secrets. Nearly total transparency. But then he concluded: "We will become completely co-dependent on it. ... It will lead to total personalization, which means total transparency. ... Marshall McLuhan said that 'Machines are the extension of the human senses.' I am saying that humans will be the senses of the Machine. ... We are the web. We are going to be the Machine. ... We could call it 'the One' ... and the ONE is us." Ten years later, we are seeing much of what Kelly predicted now coming to pass, with even more of it clearly approaching on the horizon. Just a few years ago we expressed fear about the Big Data controlled by corporations, but today consumers expect the personalization that can only come from such data. Today we are spending most of our waking hours connected to media, and we feel compelled to carry with us everywhere our mobile portal into that great, all-knowing Machine. And now there is talk about putting chips into our bodies, first to keep us safe and then perhaps to enhance our mental capabilities – perhaps linking our brains directly to the "ONE." Ideas that have scared us are gradually becoming part of our reality. That should provide some research topics for academia to consider.

CONCLUSION

The IMC philosophy of embracing an integrated approach to marketing communications continues to be at the forefront of marketing theory. In practice, however, there is evidence that not all marketers are implementing it effectively. The 4 P's of the traditional marketing mix remain a necessary point of reference in today's light-speed digital media environment. Innovative product strategies such as long-tailing are not only having a positive impact on ROI but are extending the availability of low-demand products, generating greater costumer satisfaction. Promotion is progressively being dominated by mobile. Inbound or content marketing is now one of the most important marketing tools of the Digital Age, along with its paid counterpart, native advertising. Most marketing professionals are now aware of these powerful tools, and their growing implementation is transforming the world of marketing. The use of social media, content marketing and video all enhance search engine optimization (SEO). Web pages with video are 53 times more likely to get on the front page of a Google search. Video also greatly enhances conversion rates on website landing pages, has greater reach as social media content, and achieves greater click-through rates within marketing emails. Despite marketing executives expressing that video is the most powerful advertising content, and despite most of them saying they want to increase their video content, the percentage of marketers actually doing so has remained stagnant over recent years. It is another area in which about 75% of them say they need more training, and it may suggest that effective IMC teams also need to expand to include a video expert.

Websites and mobile devices are now the new place to shop and make purchases. If a company's website is not mobile friendly it is sure to lose customers in as short as 7.6 seconds. Digital customers are increasingly less tolerant to navigational inconveniences and want to be able to shop and purchase at their own convenience using whatever platform they prefer. Virtual store fronts and the digitization of products is impacting pricing and promotions like never before. Lowest prices no longer guarantee higher sales. Personalization is an inbound marketing tactic that although more technically difficult to deploy is ranked as having progressively greater importance. However, personalization is still limited by access to real-time data and by the boundaries of contextual communication. Omnichannel marketing uses customer data to make personal connections and to achieve campaign integration. This means omnichannel marketing is about reaching consumers through all available traditional and digital channels in a personalized, just-in-time fashion.

Programmatic advertising is a form of intelligent automated media buying that is taking paid advertising into a new paradigm. Programmatic advertising expands the opportunities of billions of companies to find space, negotiate rates and place advertisements through a cost-saving automated system. However, marketing executives are frustrated with its lack of transparency, their lack of ability to control targeting, and the lack of measurement tools.

All of these changes in the marketing ecosystem present challenges to professional marketers and to academic researchers. An era of cooperative research might produce win-win results.

REFERENCES

Aberdeen Group. (2014). *Analyzing the ROI of video advertising*. Retrieved from http://go.brightcove.com/bc-aberdeen-analyzing-roi-b

Accenture. (2015). *Seamless retail research report 2015: Maximizing mobile to increase revenue*. Retrieved from https://www.accenture.com/_acnmedia/Accenture/Conversion-Assets/Microsites/Documents15/Accenture-Seamless-Retail-Research-2015-Maximizing-Mobile.pdf

Adobe. (2015). *Quarterly digital intelligence briefing: Digital trends 2015*. Retrieved from http://offers.adobe.com/content/dam/offer-manager/en/na/marketing/Target/Adobe%20Digital%20Trends%20Report%202015.pdf

Anderson, C. (2006). *The long tail: Why the future of business is selling less of more*. New York, NY: Hyperion Books.

Andrews, M., Luo, X., Fang, F., & Ghose, A. (2016). Mobile ad effectiveness: Hyper-contextual targeting with crowdedness. *Marketing Science*, *35*(2), 218–233. doi:10.1287/mksc.2015.0905

Ascarza, E., Ebbes, P., Netzer, O., & Danielson, M. (2017). Beyond the target customer: Social effects of customer relationship management campaigns. *JMR, Journal of Marketing Research*, *54*(3), 347–363. doi:10.1509/jmr.15.0442

Ashley, C., & Tuten, T. (2015). Creative strategies in social media marketing: An exploratory study of branded social content and consumer engagement. *Psychology and Marketing*, *32*(1), 15–27. doi:10.1002/mar.20761

Ask, J. A. (2014). *Mobile is not a channel*. Retrieved from http://urbanairship.com/lp/forrester-report-mobile-is-not-a-channel?ls=EmailMedia&ccn=150730eMarketerForrChannel&mkt_tok=3RkMMJWWfF9wsRohvK3IZKXonjHpfsXw6egoUa%2BxlMI%2F0ER3fOvrPUfGjI4JRcRlI%2BSLDwEYGJlv6SgFQrbCMbNs3bgEWxA%3D

Aufreiter, N., Boudet, J., & Weng, V. (2014). Why marketers should keep sending you e-mails. *McKinsey Quarterly*. Retrieved from https://www.mckinsey.com/business-functions/marketing-and-sales/our-insights/why-marketers-should-keep-sending-you-emails

Batra, R., & Keller, K. L. (2016). Integrating Marketing Communications: New findings, new lessons, and new ideas. *Journal of Marketing*, *80*(6), 122–145. doi:10.1509/jm.15.0419

Boland, M. (2016). *Native ads will drive 74% of all ad revenue by 2021*. Retrieved from http://www.businessinsider.com/the-native-ad-report-forecasts-2016-5?r=US&IR=T&IR=T

Brinker, S. (2017). *Martech and the modern marketing org*. Retrieved from http://chiefmartec.com/2017/10/martech-modern-marketing-organizational-structures/

Britt, P. (2015, August 5). Marketing campaigns still aren't integrated [Web log post]. Retrieved from http://www.dmnews.com/multichannel-marketing/marketing-campaigns-still-arent-integrated/article/430940/

BuildFire. (2017). *About us*. Retrieved from https://buildfire.com/about-us/

Chen, Y. (2017). *Publishers' programmatic woes: 'We get punished by being premium.'* Retrieved from https://digiday.com/media/publishers-programmatic-woes-get-punished-premium/

Chernov, J. (2014). *State of Inbound 2014*. Cambridge, MA: Hubspot.

Christensen, C. M. (2014). Disruptive innovation. In *The encyclopedia of human-computer interaction* (2nd ed.). Retrieved from https://www.interaction-design.org/encyclopedia/disruptive_innovation.html

eMarketer. (2015a). *Expect more programmatic ads to pop up on mobile*. Retrieved from http://www.emarketer.com/Article/Expect-More-Programmatic-Ads-Pop-Up-on-Mobile/1012291/1

eMarketer. (2015b). *Programmatic creative: Look to existing processes for guidance*. Retrieved from http://www.emarketer.com/Article/Programmatic-Creative-Look-Existing-Processes-Guidance/1012434

eMarketer. (2015c). *How many smartphone users are officially addicted?* Retrieved from http://www.emarketer.com/Article/How-Many-Smartphone-Users-Officially-Addicted/1012800?ecid=NL1001]

eMarketer. (2017a). *eMarketer releases new us programmatic ad spending figures*. Retrieved from https://www.emarketer.com/Article/eMarketer-Releases-New-US-Programmatic-Ad-Spending-Figures/1016698

eMarketer. (2017b). *US ad spending: eMarketer's updated estimates and forecast for 2017*. Retrieved from https://www.emarketer.com/Report/US-Ad-Spending-eMarketers-Updated-Estimates-Forecast-2017/2002134

eMarketer. (2017c). *eMarketer updates us time spent with media figures*. Retrieved from https://www.emarketer.com/Article/eMarketer-Updates-US-Time-Spent-with-Media-Figures/1016587

eMarketer. (2017d). *What's plaguing programmatic advertising?* Retrieved from https://www.emarketer.com/Article/Whats-Plaguing-Programmatic-Advertising/1016600

eMarketer. (2017e). *Understanding header bidding*. Retrieved from https://www.emarketer.com/Article/Understanding-Header-Bidding/1016582?ecid=NL1001

eMarketer. (2017f). *Mobile commerce roundup 2017*. Retrieved from https://on.emarketer.com/Roundup-20171019-Mobile-Commerce-Download-ThankYou.html?aliId=833594723

eMarketer. (2017g). *Mobile purchasing reaches tipping point*. Retrieved from https://on.emarketer.com/Roundup-20171019-Mobile-Commerce-Download-ThankYou.html?aliId=833594723

eMarketer. (2017h). *StatPack: US omnichannel retail*. Retrieved from https://www.emarketer.com/public_media/docs/eMarketer_US_Omnichannel_Retail_StatPack_2017_1.pdf

Feng, S., & Ots, M. (2015, May). *Content marketing: A review of academic literature and future research directions*. Paper presented at Emma Conference at the Business School of the University of Hamburg, Hamburg, Germany.

Growth Everywhere. (2017). *How content marketing as a growth channel propelled BuildFire into a 7-figure ARR SaaS company* [Video file]. Retrieved from https://www.youtube.com/watch?v=pO_1Pd6KKfM&feature=youtu.be

Guaglione, S. (2017). *Report: Header bidding is thriving*. Retrieved from https://www.mediapost.com/publications/article/310271/report-header-bidding-is-thriving.html

Gutman, B. (2012). Kellogg proves ROI of digital programmatic buying. *Forbes*. Retrieved from http://www.forbes.com/sites/marketshare/2012/11/09/kellogg-proves-roi-of-digital-programmatic-buying/

Holliman, G., & Rowley, J. (2014). Business to business digital content marketing: Marketers' perceptions of best practice. *Journal of Research in Interactive Marketing, 8*(4), 269–293. doi:10.1108/JRIM-02-2014-0013

Johnson, L. (2017). *Why 86% of brands plan to take part of their programmatic spend in-house*. Retrieved from http://www.adweek.com/digital/why-86-of-brands-plan-to-take-part-of-their-programmatic-spend-in-house/

Kelly, K. (2017). *The next 5,000 days of the Web*. Retrieved from https://www.ted.com/talks/kevin_kelly_on_the_next_5_000_days_of_the_web?utm_campaign=tedspread--a&utm_medium=referral&utm_source=tedcomshare

Lamberton, C., & Stephens, A.T. (2016). A Thematic Exploration of Digital, Social Media, and Mobile Marketing: Research Evolution from 2000 to 2015 and an Agenda for Future Inquiry. *Journal of Marketing, 80*, 146–172.

Lieb, R. (2011). *Content marketing: Think like a publisher – how to use content to market online and in social media*. Indianapolis, IN: Que Publishing.

Mallikarjunan, S. (2014). *The state of ecommerce marketing*. Cambridge, MA: Hubspot. Retrieved from http://offers.hubspot.com/state-of-ecommerce-marketing-2014

Melero, I., Sese, J. F., & Verhoef, P. C. (2016). Recasting the customer experience in today's omni-channel environment. *Universia Business Review, 50*, 20–37. Retrieved from https://ubr.universia.net/article/view/1739/redefiniendo-experiencia-cliente-el-entorno-omnicanal

Murray, A. (2017). The rise and rise of Airbnb. *Fortune*. Retrieved from http://fortune.com/2017/02/15/airbnb-gallagher-book-inequality-jobs/

Neustar. (2015). *5 ways to engage those slippery omni-channel shoppers*. Retrieved from https://hello.neustar.biz/omnichannel_wp_retail_mktg_lp.html?utm_medium=Advertising-Online&utm_source=Shop.org&utm_campaign=2015-eBook-Shop.org

Payne, E. M., Peltier, J. W., & Barger, V. A. (2017). Omni-channel marketing, integrated marketing communications and consumer engagement: A research agenda. *Journal of Research in Interactive Marketing, 11*(2), 185–197. doi:10.1108/JRIM-08-2016-0091

Penberthy, J. (2015). *Weird YouTube method pulls in $816,481.53*. Live webinar presented 30 July 2015.

Politt, C. (2017). *2016 native advertising trends for publishers*. Retrieved from https://www.huffingtonpost.com/chad-pollitt/2016-native-advertising-t_1_b_10570340.html

PulsePoint. (2015). *Programmatic intelligence report 2014*. Retrieved from http://www.pulsepoint.com/resources/whitepapers/pulsepoint_intelligence_report.pdf

Ramos, L. (2013). *The B2B CMO role is expanding: Evolve of move on.* Retrieved from http://solutions.forrester.com/Global/FileLib/Reports/B2B_CMOs_Must_Evolve_Or_Move_On.pdf

Ramsey, G. (2015). *The State of Mobile 2015.* eMarketer live webcast 25 March 2015.

Researchscape International. (2015). *Trends and priorities in real-time personalization.* Retrieved from http://www.evergage.com/blog/survey-findings-trends-priorities-in-real-time-personalization/

Roberts, D. (2017). Why Airbnb's success is so surprising. *Yahoo! Finance.* Retrieved from https://finance.yahoo.com/news/why-airbnbs-success-is-so-surprising-151121189.html

Sluis, S., Liyakasa, K., & Weissbrot, A. (2017). *The top 10 programmatic publishers.* Retrieved from https://adexchanger.com/publishers/top-10-programmatic-publishers/

Statista. (2017). *Quarterly share of e-commerce sales of total U.S. retail sales from 1st quarter 2010 to 3rd quarter 2017.* Retrieved from https://www.statista.com/statistics/187439/share-of-e-commerce-sales-in-total-us-retail-sales-in-2010/

Stelzner, M. (2015). *2015 Social Media Marketing Industry Report.* Retrieved from https://www.socialmediaexaminer.com/social-media-marketing-industry-report-2015/

Stelzner, M. (2017). *2017 social media marketing industry report.* Retrieved from https://www.socialmediaexaminer.com/report/

Suslo, E. (2016). *6 key success factors behind Uber growth.* Retrieved from https://taxistartup.com/blog/6-key-success-factors-behind-uber-growth/

Tobias, J. (2016). *Uber: The driving force behind its success.* Retrieved from https://www.thestrategy-group.com.au/uber-the-driving-force-behind-its-success/

WBR Digital. (2015) *Creating optimal customer journeys with programmatic marketing.* Retrieved from http://info.mediamath.com/rs/824-LSO-662/images/MediaMath_Creating_Optimal_Customer_Journeys_Programmatic_Marketing_FINAL.pdf?mkt_tok=eyJpIjoiWW1Wak4yVXhZV0ppWldaaCI-sInQiOiJcL0dWMVd5YmVwZEdpV09kUzJLaFZrSkpuWjJZZU9qSmMwTG5yc2pcL2kxTDdlTnlscF-wvMW5scUR4cHRkR2hUR0tOQTU1RUhKa2IyIyODNXRlwvS1wvZ3ZPKzdVTUFSeGGduWkN0RG-dubVBPdnJ6K0dEOFBjZTNtUEt4bFVwQUpxXC9FUEdaZiJ9

Zarrella, D. (2013). *The science of marketing: when to tweet, what to post, how to blog, and other proven strategies.* Hoboken, NJ: John Wiley & Sons.

KEY TERMS AND DEFINITIONS

Big Data: Refers to increasingly large volumes of structured and unstructured data made available with the rise of the internet and artificial intelligence to process these data volumes. Main characteristics of big data include high volume, high velocity (growth rate), and high variety.

Inbound Marketing: Typically, free marketing, overlapping with social media marketing and content marketing. Social media postings, blogs, white papers, ebooks, webinars, videos, and freemiums all attract prospective customers to the brand willingly. In contrast, outbound marketing includes cold calling, trade shows, traditional advertising, and direct mail or email, which is often considered intrusive. Content marketing is sometimes seen as synonymous with inbound marketing, but by most marketers seen as a subset, excluding freemiums and other free offers not valued strictly for their content.

Integrated Marketing Communications (IMC): An approach to achieve marketing campaign objectives through coordinated use of different promotional methods, including advertising, public relations, direct marketing, sales, point-of-purchase materials, and social media, that reinforce each other.

Internet of Things: When physical objects with unique identifiers are interconnected on a network and create wholly integrated self-functioning systems by seamlessly sharing data on the network without any human intervention.

Native Advertising: Any advertising—online or offline—designed to blend in with the non-advertising content around it. Online, it relates particularly to social media, but is paid advertising that mimics organic postings but are indicated as "sponsored." As such, advertisers can have them placed in the news feed of potential customers meeting their criteria.

Omnichannel or Cross-Channel Marketing: Relates closely to personalized marketing because marketing messages are not fully personalized until they can follow the customer or prospective customer across different social, programming, advertising or technical channels. To do so, this also requires the use of a system to gather and organize data and provide real-time access.

Personalization: As related to marketing it is the increased use of big data to personalize marketing messages to prospective customers. It may be in the form of personalized email, videos, shopping basket recommendations, customer service, etc.

SaaS: Stands for software as a service. It is an emerging new industry lead by companies like BuildFire who offer affordable and easy to develop application platforms, sometimes on the basis of build first pay when you publish.

This research was previously published in Diverse Methods in Customer Relationship Marketing and Management; pages 137-162, copyright year 2018 by Business Science Reference (an imprint of IGI Global).

Chapter 17
The Role of Motivational Factors for Determining Attitude Towards eWOM in Social Media Context

Muhammad Bilal

School of Economics and Management, Beijing University of Posts and Telecommunications, China

Zeng Jianqiu

School of Economics and Management, Beijing University of Posts and Telecommunications, China

Umair Akram

 https://orcid.org/0000-0002-9980-6164

Guanghua School of Management, Peking University, China

Yasir Tanveer

Lyallpur Business School, Government College University, Faisalabad, Pakistan

Muhammad Sohaib

School of Public Administration, Xian Jiaotong University, China

Muhammad Ahsan Ali Raza

School of Economics and Management, Beijing University of Posts and Telecommunications, China

ABSTRACT

Social media channels provide a critical opportunity for sharing electronic word-of-mouth (eWOM) communication. eWOM has been considered a prominent factor in shaping consumer behavior. The purpose of this is to examine the effect of website quality, social support, emotional experience, and subjective norms on the attitude of eWOM. Furthermore, the personal interactivity role as moderator is examined. An online survey was conducted from 756 consumers in China. Structure equation modeling (SEM) was employed for data analysis by using AMOS 23. The results indicate that above-mentioned determinants positively influence on attitude and eWOM. Personal interactivity significantly moderates the relationship between attitude toward eWOM and eWOM. Perceived behavioral control (PBC) has a positive direct effect on eWOM. This study provides useful and valuable insights regarding potential determinants of eWOM in Chinese perspective. Theoretical and managerial implications are discussed.

DOI: 10.4018/978-1-6684-6287-4.ch017

1. INTRODUCTION

In recent years, social media has been emerging as the most influential media to a piece of exchange information between consumers and marketers around the globe (Chu and Kim 2018). It enables users to provide their opinions, evaluations, and consumption experiences without time-based limitations (Tien, 2018). The social media has provided an opportunity wherein consumers can share their reviews related to products and services, namely known as electronic word-of-mouth (eWOM) (Hayes, Shan, and King 2018).

eWOM can be defined as "any positive or negative statement made by potential, actual, or former customers about a product or company, which is made available to a multitude of people and institutions via the internet" (Hennig-Thurau et al., 2004). Social media have become the most usual channels of eWOM communication because of their interactivity, ubiquity, and mobility. Nowadays, communication is witnessed on different social media channels like social networking sites (SNSs), online review sites, online discussion forums, and blogs (Sohaib et al., 2019). Consumers and merchants could initiate eWOM communication. The interactive communication among them in social media usually revolves around products and services. The benefits of social media usage have been significantly improving the eWOM motivations, but the interpersonal connection remains unclear.

Related studies have explored key drivers of eWOM and their effects on decision making, and attitude toward website and brand (Wang et al., 2016; Hu and Kim, 2018). However, numerous studies have been conducted related to the primary motivation elements that drive attitude toward eWOM in social media (Sohaib et al., 2018). The current study closes the research gap by using the theory of planned behavior (TPB) and to investigate the potential effects of social media characteristics on eWOM. TPB signifies three motivational factors of a behavior: behavioral beliefs are the prospective outcomes of a behavior, normative beliefs are expected actions of important referents, and control beliefs are likely consequences that may facilitate the performance of a behavior. Therefor TPB provides the reason to measure the association of social support, emotional experience, and website quality with the attitude towards eWOM.

Last but not least, personal characteristics and individual cultural values have been understudied. However, few studies have examined the moderating role of personal interactivity (Lee and An, 2018). Interactivity can develop an interactive relationship and persuade communication among consumers. Thus, personal interactivity moderates the association among attitude toward eWOM and intentions toward eWOM.

According to the above research situations, this study postulates the following research questions:

RQ1: What significant factors are associated with the attitude towards eWOM?
RQ2: Does personal interactivity play a moderating role in this research?

The rest of the study is organized as follows: the second section provides the literature review related to relevant constructs, propose hypotheses, and empirical model. After that, we describe the research methodology, analysis, and outcomes. Finally, this study key finding discussed in detail and provides an outlook on future research.

2. LITERATURE REVIEW AND DISCUSSION

2.1. Theory of Planned Behavior

TPB explained that intentions represent the motivations of behavior. The rational effort of an individual indicates eager to invest in behavior (Cho, 2017) TPB refers to the motivational part of behavior.in addition it shows the effort that a person is ready to trust in a behavior. Human action is consisting on different kinds of beliefs: Behavioral beliefs produce the outcomes of the behavior, in Normative beliefs people are think they should perform or not in a particular behavior and Control beliefs are related to the presence of the factor that may performance or non-performance of the behavior (Jen-Ruei Fu et al., 2015) in their overall respective aggregates, behavioral belief is direct influence on an individual attitude toward behavior is favorable or unfavorable behavior, normative belief involve to rise social action or subjective norms, in control beliefs outcome of perceived behavior control.

In prior literature result identified that attitude toward eWOM, subjective norms, and PBC significantly influence on eWOM in social media (Cheah et al., 2015). Attitude toward the customer target behavior, subjective norms are social factor that influence the customer behavior. these norms depend on opinion which can seek from close friends circle and family member what they individual do or perform the behavior, perceived behavior control play essential role to predict the person perception of the difficulty or easier to perform the specific behavior of interest (Harb et al., 2019).

2.2. Electronic Word-of-Mouth

eWOM is an expended form of word-of-mouth (WOM), which mention information to consumer require from original sources such as friends and family (Engel, Blackwell, and Kegerreis 1969). eWOM is the assessment of features regarding service or product by sharing information among users around the world (Barretto, 2014). Hennig-Thurau et al. (2004) who defined eWOM refers to "any positive or negative statement made by potential, actual, or former customers about a product or company, which is made available to a multitude of people and institutions via the Internet." Shin et al. (2014) regarded eWOM as "the spreading of online reviews, arguments, and recommendations that pertain to personal experiences with specific products or service providers intending to generate persuasive effects on the targeted consumers." Whereas in the context of WOM, people share information with friends and family, they also share eWOM on social media. It provides an opportunity for consumers with passive and active behavior. Passive user prefers to read and search other user's online opinions and recommendations. On the other side, the active user shares their experiences and post online reviews (Khammash and Griffiths, 2011).

The rapidly growing social media provides information sharing channels. These can be useful to share experiences with others (Ma et al., 2015). According to Kozinets et al. (2010), the internet shapes the channels such as discussion forums, review sites that helpful for consumers in the form of eWOM. The past studies have found that eWOM has significant importance about consumer buying decision making, for instance, a tendency to preferred (Liu, 2006), product adoption (Algesheimer and Wangenheim, 2006) experience about products and services (Hennig-Thurau, 2004), and involvement (Muniz and O'Guinn, 2001).

Social media has become one of the best platform channels for eWOM exchange information daily between consumers, through this platform makes opinion leader share profile relating to the product and service of brands. The users can share their opinion via pictures, texts were written, application, even videos. eWOM becomes more reliable, enjoyable, and authentic by this useful content (Erkan and Evans, 2014). In addition, the social media platform facilitates the dissemination of eWOM information among a large number of people (Sohn, 2014); people can share their opinion through the post which they agree with (Chu & Kim, 2011) due to this reason, consumer becoming addicted to social media to gain knowledge about products and company, (Naylor et al., 2012).

2.3. Attitude Toward eWOM

According to Fu et al. (2015), attitude is explained as the far-reaching influence of "goodness" or "badness" of eWOM communication. In this article, we choose the definition given by Fu et al. (2015). Attitude toward information is considered as an influential factor that influences on eWOM intention. Furthermore, it observes how consumer impact on several idea and object. Before information sharing through opinion and feedback on the internet, peoples are likely to know about whether or not such behavior is an appropriate channel. The consumer may think that they should share their comments and opinion online because sharing one content with goods and service is the moral liability to benefit the peoples. According to Phau and Sari (2004) commonly, people are likely to express views on online media if they think it is useful. Therefore, consumers with a favorable attitude towards eWOM communication are eagerly express their online feedback. In prior studies, consumer attitude in relation has been discussed (Fu et al., 2015). Two dimensions of attitude identify which are the effective and cognitive attitude. Effective attitude is the size to which a person likes an object; in cognitive attitude is a single belief about it. (Yang and Yoo, 2004). In the online era, the attitude seems to have a strong influence on consumer behavior intention. (Bruner and Kumar, 2000). It is considering the biggest determinants of a single behavior (Ajzen and Fishbein, 1975).

3. HYPOTHESES DEVELOPMENT AND RESEARCH MODEL

3.1. Website Quality

According to Yusuf et al. (2018), website quality is the perception of customer information seeking and giving. Defined by Yusuf et al. (2018), website quality is measured with two crucial dimensions, which are system and service quality. The better quality of social networking sites attracts its users, where they continue to exchange information on it (Ahn et al., 2007). Consumer perception affects by store environment in online (Ha and Lennon, 2010). Consumer view can be changed about the website by a smooth transaction. (Ahn et al., 2007). The modern website features like an image, feature, font color, animated, background color, interactivity, and sound positively affect the moods and attitude think by online trader (Fiore et al., 2005).

Moreover, prior scholars found precise website quality dimensions which are response time, emotional appeal, ease of understanding, visual appeal, tailored communications, consistent image, intuitive operations, relative advantage, trust, innovativeness, online completeness and fit-to-task, all of with the potential to satisfy the website users' demands. Consumer response on the web is an essential antecedent in consumer attitude towards eWOM. Thus, we will measure the association of website quality and attitude toward e-WOM.

H1: Website quality is positively related to attitude towards eWOM.

3.2. Emotional Experience

Prior research found the probable association between negative emotion and no willingness to recommended (Jang and Namkung, 2009; Lee et al., 2008), and WOM (Ladhari, 2007) in positive emotion online buying that make customer experience happier, memorable and unique (Walls et al., 2011). Moreover, previous studies have evaluated that emotion plays a vital role in consumer online buying behavior and decision-making process (Ladhari et al., 2008). In the context of attitude towards eWOM, emotion level derived from unique, through positive suggestion, the unforgettable and well-cut experience could make customer loyalty and brand ambassador. Based on this, an emotional experience to a consumer may establish a substantial review-generating element in online buying services.

H2: Emotional experience is positively related to attitude towards eWOM.

3.3. Social Support

In social media, group member shares opinions and experiences with others that use to make to a better decision. They are also forwarding message about emotional bonding, for example, affection and sympathy (Molinillo et al., 2019). In the context of online society, social media is providing the best platform for users to receive information from strangers and friends, because of social interaction among them. Which can give the output in positive response (Bai et al., 2015; Lee et al., 2003).

Social support can be defined as "information leading the subject to believe that he is cared for and loved, esteemed, and a member of a network of mutual obligations" (Cobb, 1976). As indicated by Schaefer et al. (1981), "social support can have a number of independent components serving a variety of supportive functions." Importantly in the online channel, it has several-dimensions fabrication, which adds up emotional support and informational support. (Schaefer et al., 1981). In an online setting, emotional support is the evaluated perceive by he/she, frequently which refers to the provision of caring, concern, love empathy, encouragement, and understanding (Ommen et al., 2008) while informational support consists on guidance and advice or valuable information which can reduce the consumer threats. (Liang et al., 2011). The discussions provide solid theoretical reasoning for the interaction between social support and attitude towards eWOM.

H3: Social support is positively related to attitude towards eWOM.

3.4. Subjective Norm

Subjective norm is explained as "the perceived social pressure to perform or not to perform the behavior" (Charu Sijoria et al., 2018). In prior researcher has identified two types of behavior that may influence an individual behavior like a descriptive norm and the injunctive norm. (Park and Smith, 2007). The descriptive norms would be like to rewarded individual behavior when other group member satisfied or admire the same, whereas injunctive norms influenced individual through a specific behavior like sharing or reading online information (Park and Smith, 2007). According to Lim and Dubinsky (2005) gives the best explanation of the association between attitude and subjective norms. Because of an associated individual with others, the theory of cognitive dissonance explained that an individual attitude towards eWOM behavior might change. The suggestion from others and advice become the reason to rise attitude towards eWOM. With the evidence of prior research indicate that the subjective norm influences the attitude towards eWOM.

Subjective norm is a peer, friends, and social pressure which represent the individual opinion whether this behavior should adopt or not (Chu and Kim 2011) identified normative interpersonal plays a crucial part in eWOM behavior. According to Kelman (1958), subjective norms directly affect eWOM by compliance, internalization, and identification. Compliance explains the strength of consumer's conformance to their group norms. Interaction is the social process that affects the person by other group people through belief, attitude, and form of their self-belief. Identification helps to keep relationship with others and suggest to be like and care others community members feeling (Liang et al., 2013). Khalil and Michael (2008) identified that family, friends, neighbor, and peer as subjective norms have a positive relation to individual online purchase. According to Jen-Ruei Fu et al., (2015), some of the online consumers feel they do not like to see themselves as opinion leader or nuisances. It enables them to share their information or suggestion about a positive or negative experience.

H4: Subjective norms are positively associated with the attitude towards eWOM.
H5: Subjective norms are associated with eWOM.

3.5. Perceived Behavioral Control

PBC is the degree of personal perception, whether the performance specific behavioral control is easy or difficult. The essential and beneficial resources (e.g., knowledge, information technology, ability). Furthermore, consumer confidently thinks they have better PBC than eWOM communication. Prior studies suggest that behavioral intention can improve individual perception about behavioral intention. (Ajzen, 1991). This line provides that PBC and eWOM are positively associated.

H6: PBC is positively associated with eWOM.

3.6. Attitude and eWOM

The relationship between attitude towards eWOM and eWOM has been discussed in several studies, based on this study its identified that attitude is an influential factor on eWOM (Kudeshia and Kumar, 2017). On the other hand, it shows that attitude may influence on eWOM, either positively or negatively. Yang and Yoo (2004) explain the process of attitude in two different dimensions, which are cognitive attitude and affective attitude. The effective attitude significantly determines eWOM rather than cognitive attitude. According to Zhao et al. (2016) attitude of user indirectly influence on eWOM through online user engagement. In previous studies found that attitude towards eWOM significantly shapes the consumer behavior and eWOM (Cheung et al., 2008; Jalilvand and Samiei, 2012).

H7: Attitude towards eWOM positively effects on eWOM.

3.7. Moderating Effect of Personal Interactivity

Tarhini et al., (2017) has found the moderating effects of personal cultural values, perceived flexibility advantages, and experience in the context of online services, but studies on personal interactivity are critical to determining the moderating role of it. Personal interactivity considers information sharing and receiving related to the product via online, such as suggestion, opinion, and feedback (Shipps and Phillips, 2013). Social media and online buying plays a significant part in developing affiliations and provide an opportunity to interact with others through information sharing. Jo and Kim (2009) suggest that in the context of eWOM, personal interactivity plays a vital role in consumer selection of the best product, and consumer satisfaction with their online experience.

Interactivity is critical in online buying communication because it is measured as one of the advantages of online media (Hoffman and Novak, 1996; Li et al., 2014a). The interactivity provides a two-way communication channel between the site visitors and users. Harris and Goode (2010) explain that interactivity is an essential part of the service firm and has a significant favorable influence on the consumer's online experience. Absence of face to face interaction with each other, social media channel provides a brick and mortar wholesale and retail stores. Indeed, new communication channel interactivity user may maintain a relationship or sharing information with others in a fast and better way than non-interactive users. Furthermore, in the light of past studies interactivity show the effectiveness in extending user attention spans improving their better achievement and enhancing the value of their user (Cherrett et al., 2009; Dror et al., 2011). Thus, this study evaluates that online user interactivity positively moderates between attitude towards eWOM and eWOM. Figure 1 shows the conceptual framework.

H8: Personal interactivity positively moderates between attitude towards e-WOM and e-WOM.

Figure 1. Conceptual framework

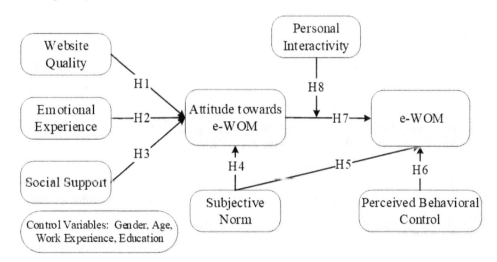

5. METHODOLOGY

5.1. Sampling

This research study was conducted to comprehend the concept of eWOM based consumer attitudes towards eWOM through the associated influence of online buying environment; emotional and social factors, particularly social norms. An online questionnaire was used to collect responses of Chinese citizens using social media platform (Wechat application). Data were collected on this specific application, which means that all respondents were using this application to communicate in their social circles. Location of respondent rests irrelevant due to its virtual nature. The survey, initially written in English, was translated into Chinese since the respondents were Chinese. For utmost consideration, proficient translators were hired to translate survey items from English to Chinese and back to English to eliminate any misconception. The questionnaire was pilot tested by 45 graduate students who were experienced in online shopping to ensure clarity of instructions and scale items. Instructions were revised to increase clarity, and it has been revealed that all items were well communed and understood.

In total, 756 responses were collected in three months from March-May 2019. Eighty-three responses were eliminated from data set based on partial and void replies. Hence, 673 final responses were considered for further analysis to validate the latent constructs of this study. Respondents were 18 years of age or older; the majority was between 26 and 35 years (59.0%), followed by 36–40 years, and above 40 years and 18-25 years (15.6% and 13.7%, 12.6% respectively). Most respondents were students (40.8%); the next most significant number in occupation was business (31.6%). The sample size is well educated as most of the respondents were masters qualified (44.1%) followed by graduate students (27.5%). The largest group of participants (93.7.6%) was shopping online for over four years. Most were using social media for over three hours a day (87.5%).

5.2. Instrument

All measurement scales were derived from reliable (Cronbach's alpha $\geq$ .70) instruments found in previous studies. For website quality, three measurement items each for information design, navigation design, and information design were adapted from Cyr (2008), Egger (2001) and Cheskin (1999, 2000). Five items scale of eWOM was adopted from Ha (2004). Stewart and Segars (2002) and Wang and Hajli's (2015) scale was adopted to measure social support. Emotional experience was measured on the six-item scale rationalized by Serra-Cantallops et al., (2018). Attitude towards eWOM was measured on the five-items scale established by Zainal et al. (2017). Subjective norm (three items) and PBC (three items) were measured on a scale adapted from Liao et al. (2007). Personal interactivity was measured on the three-item scale developed by Lee and An (2018). All items were measured using a five-point Likert scale ranging from 1 (strongly disagree) to 5 (strongly agree). Table 1 shows the descriptive statistics of the sample.

5.3. Reliability and Validity

Based on possible interactions between different variables and their influences on customer's eWOM in WeChat background, validation of measures were confirmed by using SEM that is used in two steps: confirmatory factor analysis (CFA) and hypotheses testing. First, AMOS 22.0 was employed to run CFA to estimate the factor structure and the model fit of the latent variables. Next, the structural model was examined to test the hypothesized relationships between exogenous and endogenous variables.

In the CFA, items were retained if they loaded above 0.50 on one factor (Arnold and Reynolds, 2003) and below 0.30 on other factors (Klein, 1998). The measurement model exhibited good model fit (chi-square = 339.51, df = 2.32, CFI =0.91, RMSEA =0.05, RMR =0.05, GFI= 0.91, AGFI= 0.89, NFI=0.97). The constructs exhibited reliability with (a) coefficient alpha estimates ranging from 0.78 to 0.91, well above the 0.70 thresholds (Hair, Black, Babin, Anderson, and Tatham, 1998), (b) composite reliability (CR) estimates exceeding the recommended 0.70 threshold for all constructs, and (c) average variance extracted (AVE) exceeding the recommended 0.50 threshold (Fornell and Lacker, 1981; Hair et al., 1998; Nunnally, 1978). The results are presented in Table 2.

Table 1. Descriptive statistics of sample

No.	Characteristics	Category	Frequency	%
1	Gender	Male	235	34.918
		Female	438	65.082
2	AGE	18-25	85	12.630
		26-30	188	27.935
		31-35	203	30.163
		36-40	105	15.602
		Above 40	92	13.670
3	Education Level	Intermediate/High School	61	9.064
		Bachelors	185	27.489
		Masters	297	44.131
		Doctoral/PhD	37	5.498
		Others Diplomas	93	13.819
4	Occupation	Student	275	40.862
		Employee	179	26.597
		House Wife	6	0.892
		Business	213	31.649
5	Online Shopping Experience	>1 Years	0	0.000
		1 – 2 Years	25	3.715
		3 – 4 Years	17	2.526
		< 4 Years	631	93.759
6	Social Media Usage	≤1 hour	27	4.012
		2 hours	57	8.470
		3 hours	341	50.669
		4 hours	171	25.409
		≥ 5 hours	77	11.441

Table 2. Reliability and convergent validity

Constructs	Items	Means	SD	Item Loading	CR	AVE	Cronbach's	KMO
Information Design	3	3.131	0.714	0.78-0.91	0.813	0.571	0.892	0.71
Navigation Design	3	3.245	0.521	0.88-0.95	0.902	0.691	0.987	0.78
Visual Design	2	4.24	0.831	0.79-0.92	0.783	0.603	0.788	0.64
Emotional Experience	6	3.113	0.642	0.78-0.88	0.912	0.662	0.915	0.77
Social Support	3	3.311	0.446	0.81-0.89	0.943	0.645	0.879	0.79
Attitude toward e-WOM	5	3.021	0.932	0.79-0.94	0.851	0.671	0.912	0.61
Subjective Norm	3	4.142	0.454	0.88-0.93	0.815	0.702	0.889	0.83
Perceived Behavioral Control	3	3.212	0.231	0.76-0.89	0.737	0.736	0.834	0.73
Personal Interactivity	3	4.013	0.743	0.76-0.87	0.891	0.689	0.862	0.67
Electronic Word-Of-Mouth	5	3.589	0.332	0.87-0.91	0.913	0.751	0.781	0.74

Maximum likelihood factor loadings indicated convergent validity for the underlying constructs, which were high and significant (Wixom and Watson, 2001). That is, all factor loadings exceeded 0.5 and were highly significant ($p < .001$). Discriminant validity indicates that each of the latent variables represents a distinct construct (Scott and Robert, 1998). This was determined by comparing the item loadings associated with a factor to its cross-loading on other factors. Each loading on the factor was higher than their cross-loadings on unintended factors (Henseler and Chin, 2010). Discriminant validity was also confirmed because the correlations between the factors were smaller than the respective square root of the AVEs as noted on the bolded values on the diagonal in Table 3 (Fornell and Larcker, 1981). Sampling adequacy was measured through the Kaiser–Meyer–Olkin (KMO) test, and all values were found to be higher than 0.50.

SEM was applied as a quantitative method to measure the proposed hypotheses and empirical model. Table 4 results explained the indices of structural model, which shows a good fit of model, chi-square = 351.23, df = 2.11, CFI =0.94, RMSEA =0.04, RMR =0.04, GFI= 0.90, AGFI= 0.92, NFI=0.97.

For H1-4, website quality, emotional experience, social support, and subjective norm were found to have a significant effect on attitude towards eWOM; the coefficient values were 0.62, 0.32, 0.34 and 0.87 respectively with significant p-value which indicates that high-quality websites, emotional experience of online consumer with social support and subjective norms rouse attitudes towards eWOM>. Hence, H1-4 were supported. For H5-7, subjective norms perceived behavioral control, personal interactivity, and attitude towards eWOM were found to have a significant impact on eWOM. These hypotheses (H5-7) were supported according to their significant p-value and coefficient values 0.67, 0.32, and 0.73, respectively.

For H8, SEM was applied to test the moderating effects of personal interactivity on eWOM. The results indicate that personal interactivity is a significant moderator, with a coefficient of 1.29 with the significant p-value. Hence, H8 is supported (Table 4).

Table 3. Discriminant validity and common methods bias

Constructs	ID	ND	VD	EE	SS	ATeWOM	SN	PBC	PIN	eWOM	Eigen Values	% of Variance	Cumulative %
ID	*0.755*										2.43	27.61	27.61
ND	0.313**	*0.831*									2.19	19.39	47
VD	0.242*	0.431***	*0.776*								2.67	13.21	60.21
EE	0.351**	0.503**	0.316	*0.831*							1.42	12.37	72.58
SS	0.322***	0.513**	0.430*	0.540**	*0.803*						2.31	10.28	82.86
ATeWOM	0.279**	0.493***	0.271**	0.342**	0.101*	*0.819*					1.76	5.31	88.17
SN	0.521**	0.445***	0.331**	0.444***	0.294***	0.191**	*0.837*				1.23	4.32	92.49
PBC	0.391**	0.439**	0.432**	0.350***	0.341***	0.497***	0.318**	*0.857*			1.19	2.91	95.4
PIN	0.254***	0.459**	0.481***	0.395*	0.310**	0.312**	0.321***	0.127***	*0.83*		1.13	3.31	98.71
eWOM	0.210**	0.329***	0.420***	0.432**	0.233*	0.402***	0.412***	0.279***	0.219***	*0.866*	1.3	1.29	100

NOTE: ID = Information Design, ND = Navigation Design, VD = Visual Design, EX = Emotional Experience, SS = Social Support, ATe WOM = Attitude toward e-WOM, SN = Subjective Norm, PBC = Perceived Behavioral Control, PI = Personal Interactivity, e-WOM = Electronic Word-Of-Mouth, Notes: Italic diagonal values are the square root of average variance extracted (AVE) which should be higher than diagonal values of the correlation coefficient to satisfy discriminant validity, * $p < 0.05$; ** $p < 0.01$; *** $p < 0.001$.

Table 4. Results of model fit

Fit	CMIN/df	P-Value	RMSEA	CFI	GFI	AGFI	NFI	RMR
Recommend value	< 3	*p*< 0.05	<0.08	> 0.90	> 0.90	> 0.80	> 0.90	<0.08
Measurement Model	2.32	0.005	0.05	0.91	0.91	0.89	0.97	0.05
Structure Model	2.11	0.001	0.04	0.94	0.90	0.92	0.97	0.04

6. DISCUSSION

In the context of social media, the main objective of this paper to predict the factor and determinant of online user review in eWOM Platforms. This paper contributes the factor influencing information sharing and intention to adopt eWOM communication channel ineffective social media platforms. Fang (2014) found that social media may encourage the eWOM user to share information in the scenario of images, notes, video, status update, or suggestion that can be shared on the sender personal web page. This part of the paper discusses the one by one every hypothesis followed by the theoretical and practical implication. Furthermore, limitations and future directions are discussed.

H1: In our study, we found that website quality has a direct effect on attitude toward eWOM in a social media environment. An excellent response to the consumer from website change the attitude of other online users to review the product information and service. This study confirms that if website quality is higher than consumer shows a positive attitude towards eWOM, as well as a willingness to participating in online media. This present paper suggested that site-level variables (i.e., website quality attribute, and features interactivity) would affect attitude towards eWOM through the e-Satisfaction. Moreover, our result found that website quality has the most substantial positive impact on attitude towards eWOM.

H2: As mentioned in the literature, social support has a significant impact on attitude towards eWOM in the Chinese social media environment. In prior research identified that the influence of their friends, family, society, and other community member play a vital role in consumer during opinion giving and acceptance. Individuals who have more considerable interpersonal influence and susceptibility are tending to seek information from others (Hsu and Tran, 2013). For instance, consumers usually rely on the information shared by others in social media groups.

H3: In the light of present paper result reveal that emotional experience has a positive influence on the product reputation, eWOM communication, and ultimately on customer attitude.

Moreover, emotional experience has a significant impact on consumer behavioral intention, company reputation, and consumer satisfaction in an eWOM generation. In the past studied Yong-Ki Lee et al. (2008) suggested that positive emotional experience change the feeling dimension (attractive, proud, excited, pleased, contented). In this study, we suggest that the emotional experience plays an active role in consumer attitude towards eWOM.

H4, H5: In prior research indicates that subjective norms have positively associated with the attitude towards eWOM and eWOM. Sohaib et al. (2018) identified that the theory of planned behavior subjective norms significantly influences on behavior intention. The current study shows the same finding that subjective norms play a significant role in personal attitude towards eWOM and behavior intention. We also highlight the influence of subjective norms on the components of TPB in the context of eWOM communication. This study result is similar to past studies.

H6: This study found that PBC significantly influences on e-WOM communication.TPB identified that PBC has influenced on both behavioral and behavior intention (Han, Kim, & Lee, 2018). PBC has a direct impact because it is considered as an actual ability to perform a particular behavior. Previous studies results described that attitude toward e-WOM, subjective norms, and PBC effects on e-WOM in social media (Cheah et al., 2015).

H7: Our result shows that Positive attitude towards e-WOM has enhanced positive influence on consumer intention and motivate to spread e-WOM on the social media platform. In the light of past studies identified that attitude effectively and actively influence consumer attitude to share positive reviews (Cheah et al., 2015). In this study, we provide the TPB as evidence to understand e-WOM. Besides, consumers with positive online consumption experiences tend to have a more favorable attitude, and share more positive e-WOM, through the social media platform.

H8: We found that personal interactivity positively moderates the relationship between the attitude towards e-WOM and e-WOM. Marija Nakevska et al. (2017) suggest that interactivity and interaction elements may influence consumer behavior and personal experience. According to Shapiro et al. (2017), interactivity is a two-way communication channel that motivates and interacts with other active participants. The recent and rapid development of the internet has enhanced interactivity provided by social media (online forums, instant posting, social media service), as compared to offline marketing. Our result shows that a high level of personal interactivity changes the user attitude and like to spread e-WOM. Table 5 shows model structural SEM direct and indirect moderation.

Table 5. Model structural SEM direct and indirect (moderation)

H	Relationship	Estimates	SE	CR
H1	Website quality → Attitude towards eWOM	0.62	0.183	2.141***
H2	Emotional Experience→ Attitude towards eWOM	0.32	0.157	2.349***
H3	Social Support → Attitude towards eWOM	0.34	0.231	2.132**
H4	Subjective Norm → Attitude towards eWOM	0.87	0.198	1.999***
H5	Subjective Norm → eWOM	0.67	0.176	2.465**
H6	PBC → eWOM	0.32	0.211	2.891**
H7	Attitude towards eWOM → eWOM	0.73	0.243	2.761***
Moderating Effect				
H8	Attitude toward eWOM * Personal Interactivity → eWOM	1.29	0.341	3.274***

Notes: SE = Standard Error; CR = Critical Ratio. ***p-value < 0.001

6.1. Theoretical and Practical Implications

This empirical study results contribute theoretically and practically. In past research shows the motives for, opinion giving, opinion receiving, antecedents, and their impact on e-WOM communication. It also highlights the significance of e-WOM in the social media context. The product-related information via social media considers the best credibility platform to encourage the other users for sharing related information. This primary study objective is to deeply research about online user perception and their e-WOM behavior, to examine and to empirically measure the moderating role of personal interactivity.

This study result is mainly contributing to the literature of website quality, social support, emotional experience, attitude towards eWOM, subjective norms, PBC, and eWOM, in the context of Chinese social media. For instance, web quality, emotional experience, and social support dimension have played a vital and most influential role in online user attitude towards e-WOM. Moreover, TPB association with subjective norms PBC and attitude towards e-WOM. The attitude towards e-WOM identified as a critical factor that shapes predictor of behavioral intention (Al-Debei et al., 2013). Prior studies in the context of online shopping and social media have also considered that attitude is a primary element of e-WOM (Hsu et al., 2014). The empirical result shows that the well-established website can play a vital role in generating e-WOM. It suggests that online social media groups should focus on above discussions to motivate consumer's attitude towards e-WOM.

This research paper provides significant practical implications. It is identified that social media channels such as WeChat, QQ have become essential platforms to share personal information and experiences, among others. We observed that social media users' share information about relating concern with others. It is the best platform for users to obtain information. It is also vital for companies or service providers to understand how to engage these social media groups.

Furthermore, marketing practitioners engage their consumers base directly via social media group. It involves online users to engage in e-WOM communication. Specifically, Chinese social media users share their product experiences with others using the social media platform. This study suggests that online marketing managers should pay attention to encourage consumers to sharing positive e-WOM related to brand or service. In such a scenario, the manufacturer and service provider firms can get quick feedback about their product to improve the quality and service. For instance, a good storytelling approach can become more reliable to encourage Chinese consumers to spread e-WOM via social media interaction.

6.2. Limitations and Future Direction

These study results are not without limitations. First, this empirical study asked respondents to recall recent online shopping and service experience before responding to the survey. In future studies, an experimental approach can be used. This approach will provide a deeper understanding and better results. Second, this study has only studied the motivations to share eWOM in the social media context. In future studies, eWOM motivations towards different online platforms such as review sites, shopping sites can be examined. It can highlight the different motivations to share the information on unlike online media.

ACKNOWLEDGMENT

This paper is supported by the research on big data in application for education of BUPT(2018Y0403), and the research project of cyberspace school at BUPT

REFERENCES

Ahn, T., Ryu, S., & Han, I. (2007). The impact of Web quality and playfulness on user acceptance of online retailing. *Information & Management, 44*(3), 263–275. doi:10.1016/j.im.2006.12.008

Ajzen, I. (1991). The theory of planned behavior. *Organizational Behavior and Human Decision Processes, 50*(2), 179–211. doi:10.1016/0749-5978(91)90020-T

Al-Debei, M. M., Al-Lozi, E., & Papazafeiropoulou, A. (2013). Why people keep coming back to Facebook: Explaining and predicting continuance participation from an extended theory of planned behaviour perspective. *Decision Support Systems, 55*(1), 43–54. doi:10.1016/j.dss.2012.12.032

Algesheimer, R., & Wangenheim, F. V. (2006). A network based approach to customer equity management. *Journal of Relationship Marketing, 5*(1), 39–57. doi:10.1300/J366v05n01_04

Arnold, M. J., & Reynolds, K. E. (2003). Hedonic shopping motivations. *Journal of Retailing, 79*(2), 77–95. doi:10.1016/S0022-4359(03)00007-1

Bai, Y., Yao, Z., & Dou, Y. F. (2015). Effect of social commerce factors on user purchase behavior: An empirical investigation from renren. com. *International Journal of Information Management, 35*(5), 538–550. doi:10.1016/j.ijinfomgt.2015.04.011

Barreto, A. M. (2014). The word-of-mouth phenomenon in the social media era. *International Journal of Market Research, 56*(5), 631-654.

Bruner, G. C. II, & Kumar, A. (2000). Web commercials and advertising hierarchy-of-effects. *Journal of Advertising Research, 40*(1-2), 35–42. doi:10.2501/JAR-40-1-2-35-42

Cheah, I., Phau, I., & Liang, J. (2015). Factors influencing consumers' attitudes and purchase intentions of e-deals. *Marketing Intelligence & Planning, 33*(5), 763–783. doi:10.1108/MIP-05-2014-0081

Cherrett, T., Wills, G., Price, J., Maynard, S., & Dror, I. E. (2009). Making training more cognitively effective: Making videos interactive. *British Journal of Educational Technology, 40*(6), 1124–1134. doi:10.1111/j.1467-8535.2009.00985.x

Cheung, C. M., Lee, M. K., & Rabjohn, N. (2008). The impact of electronic word-of-mouth: The adoption of online opinions in online customer communities. *Internet Research, 18*(3), 229–247. doi:10.1108/10662240810883290

Cho, Y. (2017). A consumer satisfaction model based on the integration of EDT and TAM: Comparative study of Korean and US consumers. *Asia Pacific Journal of Marketing and Logistics, 29*(5), 978–993. doi:10.1108/APJML-07-2016-0127

Chu, S. C., & Kim, J. (2018). The current state of knowledge on electronic word-of-mouth in advertising research. *International Journal of Advertising, 37*(1), 1–13. doi:10.1080/02650487.2017.1407061

Chu, S. C., & Kim, Y. (2011). Determinants of consumer engagement in electronic word-of-mouth (eWOM) in social networking sites. *International Journal of Advertising, 30*(1), 47–75. doi:10.2501/IJA-30-1-047-075

Cobb, S. (1976). Social support as a moderator of life stress. *Psychosomatic Medicine, 38*(5), 300–314. doi:10.1097/00006842-197609000-00003 PMID:981490

Cyr, D., Kindra, G. S., & Dash, S. (2008). Web site design, trust, satisfaction and e-loyalty: The Indian experience. *Online Information Review, 32*(6), 773–790. doi:10.1108/14684520810923935

Dror, I., Schmidt, P., & O'connor, L. (2011). A cognitive perspective on technology enhanced learning in medical training: Great opportunities, pitfalls and challenges. *Medical Teacher, 33*(4), 291–296. doi:10.3109/0142159X.2011.550970 PMID:21456986

Egger, F. N. (2001, June). Affective design of e-commerce user interfaces: How to maximise perceived trustworthiness. In *Proc. Intl. Conf. Affective Human Factors Design* (pp. 317-324). Academic Press.

Engel, J. F., Kegerreis, R. J., & Blackwell, R. D. (1969). Word-of-mouth communication by the innovator. *Journal of Marketing, 33*(3), 15–19. doi:10.1177/002224296903300303

Erkan, I., & Evans, C. (2014). The impacts of electronic word of mouth in social media on consumers' purchase intentions. In *Proceedings of the International conference on digital marketing (ICODM2014)* (pp. 9-14). Academic Press.

Fang, L., Mishna, F., Zhang, V. F., Van Wert, M., & Bogo, M. (2014). Social media and social work education: Understanding and dealing with the new digital world. *Social Work in Health Care, 53*(9), 800–814. doi:10.1080/00981389.2014.943455 PMID:25321930

Fiore, A. M., Jin, H. J., & Kim, J. (2005). For fun and profit: Hedonic value from image interactivity and responses toward an online store. *Psychology and Marketing, 22*(8), 669–694. doi:10.1002/mar.20079

Fishbein, M., & Ajzen, I. (1975). *Belief, attitude, intention and behaviour: An introduction to theory and research.* Reading, MA: Addison-Wesley. Retrieved from http://people.umass.edu/aizen/f&a1975.html

Fornell, C., & Larcker, D. F. (1981). Evaluating structural equation models with unobservable variables and measurement error. *JMR, Journal of Marketing Research, 18*(1), 39–50. doi:10.1177/002224378101800104

Fu, J. R., Ju, P. H., & Hsu, C. W. (2015). Understanding why consumers engage in electronic word-of-mouth communication: Perspectives from theory of planned behavior and justice theory. *Electronic Commerce Research and Applications, 14*(6), 616–630. doi:10.1016/j.elerap.2015.09.003

Ha, H. Y. (2004). Factors influencing consumer perceptions of brand trust online. *Journal of Product and Brand Management, 13*(5), 329–342. doi:10.1108/10610420410554412

Ha, Y., & Lennon, S. J. (2010). Online visual merchandising (VMD) cues and consumer pleasure and arousal: Purchasing versus browsing situation. *Psychology and Marketing, 27*(2), 141–165. doi:10.1002/mar.20324

\Hair, J. F., Black, W. C., Babin, B. J., Anderson, R. E., & Tatham, R. L. (1998). Multivariate data analysis.

Han, B., Kim, M., & Lee, J. (2018). Exploring consumer attitudes and purchasing intentions of cross-border online shopping in Korea. *Journal of Korea Trade, 22*(2), 86–104. doi:10.1108/JKT-10-2017-0093

Harb, A. A., Fowler, D., Chang, H. J., Blum, S. C., & Alakaleek, W. (2019). Social media as a marketing tool for events. *Journal of Hospitality and Tourism Technology*, *10*(1), 28–44. doi:10.1108/JHTT-03-2017-0027

Harris, L. C., & Goode, M. M. (2010). Online servicescapes, trust, and purchase intentions. *Journal of Services Marketing*, *24*(3), 230–243. doi:10.1108/08876041011040631

Hayes, J. L., Shan, Y., & King, K. W. (2018). The interconnected role of strength of brand and interpersonal relationships and user comment valence on brand video sharing behavior. *International Journal of Advertising*, *37*(1), 142–164. doi:10.1080/02650487.2017.1360576

Hennig-Thurau, T., Gwinner, K. P., Walsh, G., & Gremler, D. D. (2004). Electronic word-of-mouth via consumer-opinion platforms: What motivates consumers to articulate themselves on the internet? *Journal of Interactive Marketing*, *18*(1), 38–52. doi:10.1002/dir.10073

Henseler, J., & Chin, W. W. (2010). A comparison of approaches for the analysis of interaction effects between latent variables using partial least squares path modeling. *Structural Equation Modeling*, *17*(1), 82–109. doi:10.1080/10705510903439003

Hsu, M. H., Chuang, L. W., & Hsu, C. S. (2014). Understanding online shopping intention: The roles of four types of trust and their antecedents. *Internet Research*, *24*(3), 332–352. doi:10.1108/IntR-01-2013-0007

Hsu, Y., & Tran, T. H. C. (2013). Social relationship factors influence on EWOM behaviors in social networking sites: empirical study: Taiwan and Vietnam. International Journal of Business. *Human Technology*, *3*(3), 22–31.

Hu, Y., & Kim, H. J. (2018). Positive and negative eWOM motivations and hotel customers' eWOM behavior: Does personality matter? *International Journal of Hospitality Management*, *75*, 27–37. doi:10.1016/j.ijhm.2018.03.004

Jang, S. S., & Namkung, Y. (2009). Perceived quality, emotions, and behavioral intentions: Application of an extended Mehrabian–Russell model to restaurants. *Journal of Business Research*, *62*(4), 451–460. doi:10.1016/j.jbusres.2008.01.038

Jo, S., & Kim, Y. (2003). The effect of web characteristics on relationship building. *Journal of Public Relations Research*, *15*(3), 99–223. doi:10.1207/S1532754XJPRR1503_1

Kelman, H. C. (1958). Compliance, identification, and internalization three processes of attitude change. *The Journal of Conflict Resolution*, *2*(1), 51–60. doi:10.1177/002200275800200106

Khammash, M., & Griffiths, G. H. (2011). 'Arrivederci CIAO.com, Buongiorno Bing.com'—Electronic word-of-mouth (eWOM), antecedences and consequences. *International Journal of Information Management*, *31*(1), 82–87. doi:10.1016/j.ijinfomgt.2010.10.005

Klein, A. (1998). Firm performance and board committee structure. *The Journal of Law & Economics*, *41*(1), 275–304. doi:10.1086/467391

Kozinets, R. V., De Valck, K., Wojnicki, A. C., & Wilner, S. J. (2010). Networked narratives: Understanding word-of-mouth marketing in online communities. *Journal of Marketing*, *74*(2), 71–89. doi:10.1509/jm.74.2.71

Kudeshia, C., & Kumar, A. (2017). Social eWOM: Does it affect the brand attitude and purchase intention of brands? *Management Research Review*, *40*(3), 310–330. doi:10.1108/MRR-07-2015-0161

Ladhari, R. (2007). The effect of consumption emotions on satisfaction and word-of-mouth communications. *Psychology and Marketing*, *24*(12), 1085–1108. doi:10.1002/mar.20195

Ladhari, R., Brun, I., & Morales, M. (2008). Determinants of dining satisfaction and post-dining behavioral intentions. *International Journal of Hospitality Management*, *27*(4), 563–573. doi:10.1016/j.ijhm.2007.07.025

Lee, M. S., & An, H. (2018). A study of antecedents influencing eWOM for online lecture website: Personal interactivity as moderator. *Online Information Review*, *42*(7), 1048–1064. doi:10.1108/OIR-10-2017-0275

Lee, Y. K., Lee, C. K., Lee, S. K., & Babin, B. J. (2008). Festivalscapes and patrons' emotions, satisfaction, and loyalty. *Journal of Business Research*, *61*(1), 56–64. doi:10.1016/j.jbusres.2006.05.009

Li, L., Zhang, L., & Willamowska-Korsak, M. (2014). The effects of collaboration on build-to-order supply chains: With a comparison of BTO, MTO, and MTS. *Information Technology Management*, *15*(2), 69–79.

Liang, S. W. J., Ekinci, Y., Occhiocupo, N., & Whyatt, G. (2013). Antecedents of travellers' electronic word-of-mouth communication. *Journal of Marketing Management*, *29*(5-6), 584–606. doi:10.1080/0267257X.2013.771204

Liang, T. P., Ho, Y. T., Li, Y. W., & Turban, E. (2011). What drives social commerce: The role of social support and relationship quality. *International Journal of Electronic Commerce*, *16*(2), 69–90. doi:10.2753/JEC1086-4415160204

Liang, T. P., Ho, Y. T., Li, Y. W., & Turban, E. (2011). What drives social commerce: The role of social support and relationship quality. *International Journal of Electronic Commerce*, *16*(2), 69–90. doi:10.2753/JEC1086-4415160204

Liao, C., Chen, J. L., & Yen, D. C. (2007). Theory of planning behavior (TPB) and customer satisfaction in the continued use of e-service: An integrated model. *Computers in Human Behavior*, *23*(6), 2804–2822. doi:10.1016/j.chb.2006.05.006

Lim, H., & Dubinsky, A. J. (2005). The theory of planned behavior in e-commerce: Making a case for interdependencies between salient beliefs. *Psychology and Marketing*, *22*(10), 833–855. doi:10.1002/mar.20086

Liu, Y. (2006). Word of mouth for movies: Its dynamics and impact on box office revenue. *Journal of Marketing*, *70*(3), 74–89. doi:10.1509/jmkg.70.3.074

Molinillo, S., Anaya-Sánchez, R., & Liébana-Cabanillas, F. (2019). Analyzing the effect of social support and community factors on customer engagement and its impact on loyalty behaviors toward social commerce websites. *Computers in Human Behavior*, 105980. doi:10.1016/j.chb.2019.04.004

Muniz, A. M. Jr, & O'guinn, T. C. (2001). Brand community. *The Journal of Consumer Research*, *27*(4), 412–432. doi:10.1086/319618

Nakevska, M., van der Sanden, A., Funk, M., Hu, J., & Rauterberg, M. (2017). Interactive storytelling in a mixed reality environment: The effects of interactivity on user experiences. *Entertainment Computing*, *21*, 97–104. doi:10.1016/j.entcom.2017.01.001

Naylor, R. W., Lamberton, C. P., & West, P. M. (2012). Beyond the "like" button: The impact of mere virtual presence on brand evaluations and purchase intentions in social media settings. *Journal of Marketing*, *76*(6), 105–120. doi:10.1509/jm.11.0105

O'Leary-Kelly, S. W., & Vokurka, J., R. (1998). The empirical assessment of construct validity. *Journal of Operations Management*, *16*(4), 387–405. doi:10.1016/S0272-6963(98)00020-5

Ommen, O., Janssen, C., Neugebauer, E., Bouillon, B., Rehm, K., Rangger, C., ... Pfaff, H. (2008). Trust, social support and patient type—Associations between patients perceived trust, supportive communication and patients preferences in regard to paternalism, clarification and participation of severely injured patients. *Patient Education and Counseling*, *73*(2), 196–204. doi:10.1016/j.pec.2008.03.016 PMID:18450408

Park, H. S., & Smith, S. W. (2007). Distinctiveness and influence of subjective norms, personal descriptive and injunctive norms, and societal descriptive and injunctive norms on behavioral intent: A case of two behaviors critical to organ donation. *Human Communication Research*, *33*(2), 194–218.

Pfeil, U., & Zaphiris, P. (2009). Investigating social network patterns within an empathic online community for older people. *Computers in Human Behavior*, *25*(5), 1139–1155. doi:10.1016/j.chb.2009.05.001

Phau, I., & Puspita Sari, R. (2004). Engaging in complaint behaviour: An Indonesian perspective. *Marketing Intelligence & Planning*, *22*(4), 407–426. doi:10.1108/02634500410542770

Reza Jalilvand, M., & Samiei, N. (2012). The effect of electronic word of mouth on brand image and purchase intention: An empirical study in the automobile industry in Iran. *Marketing Intelligence & Planning*, *30*(4), 460–476. doi:10.1108/02634501211231946

Schaefer, C., Coyne, J. C., & Lazarus, R. S. (1981). The health-related functions of social support. *Journal of Behavioral Medicine*, *4*(4), 381–406. doi:10.1007/BF00846149 PMID:7338894

Serra-Cantallops, A., Ramon-Cardona, J., & Salvi, F. (2018). The impact of positive emotional experiences on eWOM generation and loyalty. *Spanish Journal of Marketing-ESIC*, *22*(2), 142–162. doi:10.1108/SJME-03-2018-0009

Shapiro, A. M., Sims-Knight, J., O'Rielly, G. V., Capaldo, P., Pedlow, T., Gordon, L., & Monteiro, K. (2017). Clickers can promote fact retention but impede conceptual understanding: The effect of the interaction between clicker use and pedagogy on learning. *Computers & Education*, *111*, 44–59. doi:10.1016/j.compedu.2017.03.017

Shin, D., Song, J. H., & Biswas, A. (2014). Electronic word-of-mouth (eWOM) generation in new media platforms: The role of regulatory focus and collective dissonance. *Marketing Letters*, *25*(2), 153–165. doi:10.100711002-013-9248-z

Shipps, B., & Phillips, B. (2013). Social networks, interactivity and satisfaction: Assessing socio-technical behavioral factors as an extension to technology acceptance. *Journal of Theoretical and Applied Electronic Commerce Research*, *8*(1), 35–52. doi:10.4067/S0718-18762013000100004

Sijoria, C., Mukherjee, S., & Datta, B. (2018). Impact of the antecedents of eWOM on CBBE. *Marketing Intelligence & Planning*, *36*(5), 528–542. doi:10.1108/MIP-10-2017-0221

Singh, J., & Wilkes, R. E. (1996). When consumers complain: A path analysis of the key antecedents of consumer complaint response estimates. *Journal of the Academy of Marketing Science*, *24*.

Sohaib, M., Hui, P., Akram, U., Akram, Z., & Bilal, M. (2018). How non-economic motivations affect electronic word-of-mouth: Evidence from Chinese social media. *International Journal of Information Systems and Change Management*, *10*(4), 311–332. doi:10.1504/IJISCM.2018.098392

Sohaib, M., Hui, P., Akram, U., Majeed, A., Akram, Z., & Bilal, M. (2019). Understanding the justice fairness effects on eWOM communication in social media environment. *International Journal of Enterprise Information Systems*, *15*(1), 69–84. doi:10.4018/IJEIS.2019010104

Sohn, D. (2014). Coping with information in social media: The effects of network structure and knowledge on perception of information value. *Computers in Human Behavior*, *32*, 145–151. doi:10.1016/j.chb.2013.12.006

Stewart, K. A., & Segars, A. H. (2002). An empirical examination of the concern for information privacy instrument. *Information Systems Research*, *13*(1), 36–49. doi:10.1287/isre.13.1.36.97

Tarhini, A., Hone, K., Liu, X., & Tarhini, T. (2017). Examining the moderating effect of individual-level cultural values on users' acceptance of E-learning in developing countries: A structural equation modeling of an extended technology acceptance model. *Interactive Learning Environments*, *25*(3), 306–328. doi:10.1080/10494820.2015.1122635

Tien, D. H., Rivas, A. A. A., & Liao, Y. K. (2018). Examining the influence of customer-to-customer electronic word-of-mouth on purchase intention in social networking sites. Asia Pacific Management Review.

Walls, A. R., Okumus, F., Wang, Y. R., & Kwun, D. J. W. (2011). An epistemological view of consumer experiences. *International Journal of Hospitality Management*, *30*(1), 10–21. doi:10.1016/j.ijhm.2010.03.008

Wang, T., Yeh, R. K. J., Chen, C., & Tsydypov, Z. (2016). What drives electronic word-of-mouth on social networking sites? Perspectives of social capital and self-determination. *Telematics and Informatics*, *33*(4), 1034–1047. doi:10.1016/j.tele.2016.03.005

Wang, Y., & Hajli, N. (2015). Co-creating brand value through social commerce. In Handbook of Research on Integrating Social Media into Strategic Marketing (pp. 17-34). Hershey, PA: IGI Global. doi:10.4018/978-1-4666-8353-2.ch002

Wixom, B. H., & Watson, H. J. (2001). An empirical investigation of the factors affecting data warehousing success. *Management Information Systems Quarterly*, *25*(1), 17–41. doi:10.2307/3250957

Yang, H. D., & Yoo, Y. (2004). It's all about attitude: Revisiting the technology acceptance model. *Decision Support Systems*, *38*(1), 19–31. doi:10.1016/S0167-9236(03)00062-9

Yusuf, A. S., Che Hussin, A. R., & Busalim, A. H. (2018). Influence of e-WOM engagement on consumer purchase intention in social commerce. *Journal of Services Marketing*, *32*(4), 493–504. doi:10.1108/JSM-01-2017-0031

Zainal, N. T. A., Harun, A., & Lily, J. (2017). Examining the mediating effect of attitude towards electronic words-of mouth (eWOM) on the relation between the trust in eWOM source and intention to follow eWOM among Malaysian travellers. *Asia Pacific Management Review*, *22*(1), 35–44. doi:10.1016/j.apmrv.2016.10.004

Zhao, Y., Liu, Y., Lai, I., Zhang, H., & Zhang, Y. (2016). The impacts of attitudes and engagement on Electronic Word of Mouth (eWOM) of mobile sensor computing applications. *Sensors (Basel)*, *16*(3), 391. doi:10.339016030391 PMID:26999155

This research was previously published in the International Journal of Enterprise Information Systems (IJEIS), 16(2); pages 73-91, copyright year 2020 by IGI Publishing (an imprint of IGI Global).

Chapter 18
User-Generated Content and Consumer Brand Engagement

Muhammad Naem
University of Worcester, UK

Sebastian Okafor
University of Cumbria, UK

ABSTRACT

Debates on the importance of user-generated content (UGC) and consumer brand engagement have increasingly gained attention amongst researchers, practitioners, marketing managers, and business leaders. UGC is a concept popularized in the 21st century with the advent and rise of Web 2.0 technology. Web 2.0 has gained recognition due to its novel features that include openness, participation, and the facilitation of the creation and sharing of content. It revolutionized interactions amongst people, and users are now able to share and create personalized content on the internet instead of merely using the content available. The primary objective of this chapter is to evaluate the influence of UGC on consumer brand engagement and discuss its impact on customers and organizational marketing practices.

INTRODUCTION

User Generated Content (henceforth UGC) which is alternatively known as 'user created content' is content published by users on various online platforms (Shneiderman, Preece & Pirolli, 2011). UGC has been described as content created by a consortium or an individual and published through diverse online platforms (McNally et al., 2012). Leung (2009) notes that UGC is any form of content that is developed by users of a service or system and published openly on an associated online platform or system. Most traditional UGC definitions describe the importance of online platforms and technologies that support the generation of such content. These online platforms and technologies are forms of social media, social computing, Web 2.0, collective action tools, social Web, read/write Web, consumer-generated media, virtual communities, computer-mediated communication, online communities, and socio-technical systems (Shneiderman, Preece & Pirolli, 2011). However, prior research presents a clear restriction

DOI: 10.4018/978-1-6684-6287-4.ch018

upon the definition of UGC: when any user copies any content and uploads or posts it on a social media application then he/she is not creating new content or fulfilling the criteria for UGC. UGC is something which generates the content with transformativity or originality or a combination of both (Kaplan and Haenlein 2010). Other researchers have highlighted the fact that UGC became popular in 2005. UGC comprises various forms of media content that should meet three conditions. The content must be published on any social networking sites or website; it must be created outside professional practices and routines and it needs to highlight some unique or creative effort (Kumar et al., 2016). However, most social media applications are used with the purpose of forwarding the copied content of others. All types of social media have their own culture, norms, architectures and unique features. Users visit social media sites with different intentions and interact in diverse ways. McNally et al. (2012) describe the various forms of UGC such as audio, multimedia productions, individual texts, images, and videos. These are distributed through Flickr, Facebook, YouTube, and personal blogs. They are also distributed across software applications or modifications that are generated to operate within hardware platforms or in existing databases (e.g. game or virtual world modifications, iPhone apps, and utilities that influence publicly available databases); and informal or formal groups that generate and disseminate UGC (such as Linex or Apache, open source software, and Wikipedia).

It has become necessary for nations to make a policy framework in order to create and distribute UGC because these contents can bring creative expressions, innovation, and economic growth (Tang, Fang & Wang, 2014). In certain situations, UGC can bring revenue for its creators though voluntary donations, direct payments, content licensed to third parties and advertising revenues. About 80.7 percent of US internet users are seriously consider product reviews before making a purchase decision (eMarketer, 2016). Marketing communication using social media tools such as Facebook, YouTube, Twitter, and Flicker has increasingly gained the attention of many fashion brands, service providers and consumers.

The recent past has witnessed the advent of a new capability acquired by humans. The internet has become omnipresent, enabling users to share newly generated content with other users by delineating their buying intentions, product, and transaction-based experiences (Chaffey & Ellis Chadwick, 2016; Ozuem, 2016). Content generated by users can be accessed via applications ('apps') or websites viewed by visitors with an internet connection. Such content can include textual comments, video, images, profiles, votes, usernames, 'hearts' and likes and other media (Ryan & Jones, 2012). Adverts however are not considered to be examples of the type of User Generated Content (UGC) seen on social media platforms (Ryan, 2014). Voluntary contributors contribute UGC to increase numbers and support each other, generating new content that involves a wide range of creative media. Other users co-create such content beyond the prevailing professional traditional environments. UGC as a concept was popularised in the early 21st century with the advent of "Web 2.0" (Charlesworth, 2014).

Web 2.0 has brought about dramatic changes, often characterised by participation, openness, and sharing. This has revolutionised interactions amongst people and users are now able to share and create personalised content on the internet instead of simply using content already available (Weiger et al., 2011). UGC has rapidly evolved as a result of Web 2.0 and has also increased the participation of users in creating such content (Wan & Ren, 2017; Ozuem et al., 2016). Its popularity is increasing because users can create audio, video, text, and other files on the internet and share content with each other on platforms like YouTube, Blogs, Twitter and Facebook, amongst others (Goh et al., 2013). Due to the growth in popularity of sophisticated mobile phone cameras, the creation of video content on the internet has increased exponentially (Kim et al. 2010; Ozuem & Mulloo, 2016).

UGC in the context of social media can be defined as the sum of all ways of supporting the sharing of unique content by using social media applications (Kumar et al., 2016; Kim & Johnson, 2016). Kaplan and Haenlein (2010) have highlighted the importance of social media for UGC, noting that ten hours of content is uploaded on YouTube every minute. Social media and UGC are closely related and complement each other. Various types of UGC exist on online platforms such as on Twitter, YouTube, Flicker, Wikipedia, Facebook, Tumblr, Pinterest, google+, LinkedIn, Reddit, and Instagram. UGC is generated by many online communities on platforms such as google business TripAdvisor and Zagat, Yelp, and OpenTable, and is also generated by corporate websites such as eBay, and Amazon (Kaplan and Haenlein 2010; Shneiderman, Preece & Pirolli, 2011), according to whom the nature of UGC can vary based on the diverse online applications. UGC can also appeal to corporations who integrate it into their websites and third party selling websites. Less attractive to the commercial world are cross-platform applications such as Viber, WhatsApp, WeChat, Imo, and Tango.

THEORETICAL CONTEXT

UGC is content published on social media or is publicly accessible via networking websites and is created exclusively through amateur practices and routines. It therefore depends on creative effort to some extent (Evans, 2012). UGC in marketing refers to brand-related content created by anyone who does not officially represent the business at issue. UGC can take many forms including podcasts, videos, reviews or social networking updates (Thomsett-Scott, 2014; Ozuem et al., 2016). Barefoot & Szabo, (2010) identify UGC across different media formats including digital video, question-answer debates, wikis, blogging, forums, podcasting social networking, review sites, mobile-phone photography and social media. Content-based sharing sites like Buzzfeed are popular UGC formats.

Any kind of content can be regarded as UGC provided three criteria are met. First, content must have been published, otherwise it cannot be regarded as UGC. (Willis & Wang, 2016) Secondly, the content created must be original; i.e. it must be the work of the content creator (Jiao et al., 2018). Thirdly, content must be created without reward, i.e. it must not be paid content. It must be created by the user voluntarily (Chari et al., 2016). Moreover, Smith & Chaffey (2012), indicate that online communities provide a platform of communication to internet users to enable people to interact with friends and family and discuss a wide array of topics. They exchange pictures, videos, texts, and other materials which are called UGC, which also includes content generated by consumers with respect to their shopping experiences, and is therefore content which consumers share with each other online (Kumar et al., 2016; Jin & Phua, 2016).

UGC can be produced and then shared by an end user of any website or online service (Sterne, 2010). It includes content produced or shared by users who are subscribers or members of an online service rather than produced and shared by the online service or website itself (Herrero et al., 2015; Ozuem & Lancaster, 2014). Other common alternative terms used in place of UGC are conversational media or Consumer Generated Media (CGM) (Stareva, 2014; Ryan & Jones, 2014; Ozuem & Lancaster, 2015). Typically, UGC is created online as it can be easily uploaded and shared with family and friends through social media websites (Brown, 2012). In other words, content that is produced and shared by fans or unpaid contributors qualifies as UGC. Many of these posts, videos and photos are part of what can be termed UGC (Odden, 2012). UGC is a source of that content created by consumers, influencers, social media followers or fans that follow and support various brands (Carvão, 2010; Akehurst, 2009; Tirunillai & Tellis, 2012). Such content, whether in the form of a blog, Wiki, podcast, social image, video or social media post created by a third-party user is then used by businesses on their social media networking or websites for the promotion of their brand(s) (Powell et al., 2011). Such content typically acts as a free source of advertising because it comes at no, or little cost (Cha et al., 2009). Simply put, UGC is content that is not produced by the company itself but by consumers or users (Scott, 2015). Although there exists no single universally accepted definition of UGC, the OECD (2006) defines UGC as having three distinct characteristics: "*i) content made publicly available over the Internet, ii) which reflects a certain amount of creative effort., and iii) which is created outside of professional routines and practices*" (OECD, 2007, p. 4). If these characteristics are present, the content qualifies as UGC. First, the content must be published online. If it is not published online, then it does not qualify as UGC. Secondly, the content must be innovative in nature. Lastly, it must be a personal creation rather than a professional creation.

UGC came into being as a result of content contributed by consumers in the form of audio, video, digital images, blogs, and arguments extracted from posts and other media contributions across the spectrum of social media. Content that is contributed by voluntary donators posted in the form of posts, podcasts, wikis, tweets, pics, videos or audio files or images, blog posts and testimonials is created with the aim of promoting brands that consumers follow on social media (Rodgers & Thorson, 2017). In other words, third party users create the content. UGC offers the option to share content with other networks posted by users in relation to a brand (Dodson, 2016).

At present, the most popular UGC content is available in the form of videos and photos, to the extent that some 44% of adult internet users generate such content (Ryan, 2014). According to Statista, (2017) millennials quite commonly create photos as a form of UGC. Product reviews are also popular, constituting some 29% of UGC content on the web. The new options generated in relation to media drive, more through consumer-created content in the online world, and less through publishers, are called 'user-generated content (UGC)' (Dodson, 2016). UGC is defined as media that is produced as a result of a contribution made through Web 2.0 online technologies. The content is created by the user instead of by professionals receiving regular funding (Smith & Chaffey, 2012). From this definition, it is evident that it is the general public that creates UGC. However, there has been some debate about the uses of UGC in business. In the field of marketing for example, UGC is taken to be content that has an 'unofficial' capacity (Mathieson, 2010) and is created in relation to a brand. This content may take the form of reviews, social media posts, podcasts and videos amongst others. A brand is considered to be based on content generated by a user if followers, associates or colleagues have not had a hand in creating it. UGC refers to media contributed and shared by people online. The Interactive Advertising Bureau (IAB) suggests UGC must have the capacity to engage people and to cultivate conversation. Since marketing now implicates people as users, UGC has given rise to terms like "peer-created content" and "Consumer-Generated Content" (CGC) quite outside of traditional industrial classifications (Schaffer et al., 2013).

Any matter that is selected, prepared and distributed in written and graphical form constitutes publishing activity. Matter is available in the form of magazines, books and newspapers, although UGC content does not come under this purview (Martínez-Navarro & Bigné, 2017). Research has identified that UGC is bound within groups as well as in media, whereas published books are not. (Sheldrake et al., 2011). Traditionally, publishing is intended for published material. However, books available electronically and newspapers available online are considered as examples of publishing, therefore printing does not necessarily require publishing (Evans, 2012). Roberts et al., (2016) following a history of two published editions in about two hundred and forty years is now solely available online. However digital publishing has made its way into the sphere of printed publishing and so the definition of publishing has increasingly blurred boundaries. Technological innovations, in particular, have altered ideas about publishing.

There is now a need to review the concept of publishing in the context of new conditions that have emerged with the dawn of social media. In this context, publishing refers to the dissemination of information to the public (Mahoney & Tang, 2016). However, the public exists at a number of different levels, and in order to understand this, the concept above needs to be examined in closer detail. "General public" indicates that a contributing user does not specify any particular receiver (Agresta et al., 2011). Online content is accessible by a vast and unlimited audience. Limited public access indicates that the contributing user does not specify explicitly a particular receiver but addresses a limited audience. Platforms establish limitations that need e-registration before accessing the reading (Brake, 2014). For instance, if the content is offered to registered users only but registration is open for everyone, the audience will remain confined to users who are already registered. This limited public is bifurcated into "known limited public" and "unknown limited public" (Thomsett-Scott, 2014). The "known limited public" has no particular specified receiver despite the fact the audience is limited to known people. One example of this is the sharing of content between friends as a group on social networks. This is evidence of similarity of 'known-limited public' with private platforms (Barefoot & Szabo, 2010).

The "unknown limited" public denotes an audience that is not limited to known people. The sharing of content within a close community of friends in social networks is a pertinent example of this. If specified receivers are taken to be a limited audience, this is referred to as **private**. In the light of the above, private communication does not fall within the purview of UGC that encompasses the transmission of messages on an individual or group basis on platforms like WhatsApp, email, Viber, WeChat and Imo. This suggests that messages transmitted through email and SMS as well as instantaneous messages, faxes, written letters and telephone calls fall beyond the jurisdiction of UGC (Barefoot & Szabo, 2010). However, communication that takes place at a private level is considered an element akin to activity on social media platforms. For example, social networks enable the general public to create and publish content. They allow private messages to be shared between a limited public. One thing peculiar to social media is that users who develop and contribute content are not bound to delineate their audience except by limiting it (Smith & Zook, 2011).

Reach indicates the tally of individuals that receive a message. When a contributor limits the audience to a lesser extent, the message will likely gain the maximum potential to reach the audience. With lemmatising the audience, the extent of increased intimacy is expected to grow (Evan, 2012). Features are highlighted with reference to the varying degrees of intimacy and reach. This phenomenon of content generated by the general public can be adapted to replace the age-old conception of sender-receiver at contributor and audience levels. Based on such a connection, a user that publishes a message is regarded as a contributor. It is not imperative that contributors are involved in the creation of content. Whether a contributor is involved in content creation or not, in social media, a contributor is seen in the capacity of author and is denoted as such (Evan, 2012).

UGC refers to content that users publish online using an online platform such as social media that contains content generated by users who are not required to possess any specialised programming skills. A company contributes content on a platform like social media encompassing the category of user. Generally, a 'user' refers to a social media user (Brown, 2012). When companies contribute content to a platform like social media this is called UGC (Odden, 2012). A user may be an individual, either skilled or unskilled and is not necessarily acting in a professional or corporate capacity. In this context, a company that contributes content to social media is not considered to be developing UGC. This suggests that an individual who utilises a social media platform is called a user (Powell et al., 2011).

A URL is used as an identifier on search engines to conduct a search of web pages rather than specific content. This does not resonate with the concept of UGC. A single web page carries a single URL but also carries a number of entries from social media contributed by diverse authors (Scott, 2015). In terms of social media, UGC is the smallest unit of contribution made by a single author at a specific time. Content created on the basis of collaboration is generally contributed by many authors (Brown, 2012).

Volunteers regularly contribute content in the form of information, data or media on the web in a presentable, meaningful form. Examples are wikis, restaurant ratings and videos (Kim & Lee, 2017). Moreover, Simon, (2016) noted that when it comes to finding a product rating or a service, customer views make voluntary entries difficult. Recent research found that business-generated content is brand-related quite contrary to user-generated (Schulz et al., 2013). Furthermore, Smith et al., (2012) added that UGC is the outcome of professional work carried out behind the scenes. Such content is inexpensive and has generally undergone development, and users provide it without any charge. The phenomenon of supplying content proves rewarding when it is recognised (Marine-Roig & Anton Clavé, 2016). Content that has the capacity to entertain or inform, gives the impression of real data contributed by others without influence from other media channels (Susarla et al., 2012).

A content unit generated by a user comprises staple data along with metadata. Core data provides staple data information as the content. Metadata is based on information in relation to a core area (Chung, Han & Koo, 2015). Metadata involves the publication date, author ranking in society and expert opinions while still constituting UGC. This work includes expressions obtained through one click as UGC. Examples include 'likes' recorded on Facebook, thumbs up comments on YouTube and 'plus one' ratings on Google. Other users' score ratings based on content units generated by users are called peer ratings (Lu & Stepchenkova, 2015). Social media as well as UGC features represent "Web 2.0" which is also called the "participative web". Web 2.0 is not a new web era. Rather, it is viewed as a leaning propensity trend (Wilson et al., 2012).

The influx of blogs in the contemporary online world as well as videos from YouTube, podcasts and comments on blogs or news articles highlights this dimension (Zhan et al., 2017). Anyone can create content on the internet provided s/he is computer-literate and has access to the internet. Many years ago, corporations and individuals with technical know-how tended to create web content in subjective areas online (Flanagin et al., 2014). Different web forums, chat rooms (Internet Relay Chat), online games and multi-user domains were developed as examples (Fox et al., 2012). Many users have subsequently come to realise that participatory facets pertain to the web. Users are free to make and rate comments while viewing the news, although most encounter an overlap of comments from communities watching on- and offline on social digital networks such as Facebook (Kim, 2012).

UGC is any type of media crafted by consumers or end users that is made publicly available to other users via industry databases and websites or via social media (Roberts et al., 2016). It can include written materials such as forum posts, blog entries and reviews or audio-visual or image-based files (photographs, video clips, audio recordings or GIFs). UGC is essentially any material created outside professional marketing practices and publicised online (Adler & Sillars, 2011). It takes various forms but most relevant and common are consumer-produced recommendations and reviews (Sheldrake & Sheldrake, 2011). Webster et al. (2014), make a comparison between UGC and marketer-generated content. Consumers have become pivotal authors of brand stories since content is easily shared on the social media network and is dynamic (Seadle & Greifender, 2014). Every type of UGC has a different impact on the minds of consumers, so gaining a better understanding of the taxonomy of UGC is essential (Pan & Zhang, 2011). UGC may also be regarded as User Created Content (UCC). However, there does not exist any universal definition of UGC. Research into UGC is ongoing and is considered a growth area in marketing academia (Davis, 2015).

Three characteristics are the subject of debate amongst various scholars. Li et al. (2016), observed that UGC represents the experience and comments of consumers in relation to the products and services delivered to them by brands or companies. Moreover, Granitz, N. & Forman, (2015) observed that UGC represents any content which the public creates online. It is a personal form of content and not a professional one. Heba et al., (2018) indicates that the main feature of UGC is that it is generated voluntarily and by amateurs who are not generating content professionally online. Moreover, Chow & Shi, (2015) observed that self-creation is the most central feature of UGC. It is created without any external or professional help. Xie & Lee, (2015) observed that due to sophisticated online platforms, it is now increasingly difficult to distinguish between UGC and professional content. Bao (2017) argued that many professionals have taken to the internet to generate content which looks like UGC. Such content is used for product reviews and personal experiences about products, but there is a recognised need to develop a classification of UGC that might make it easier for marketers to use it in their marketing activities (Chaffey et al., 2016; Ryan & Jones, 2012; Charlesworth, 2014). Therefore, the ensuing discussion will review the overall taxonomy of UGC and how it relates to marketing objectives.

Switching Focus: Traditional Media to Online Social Media

Nowadays, businesses are switching their focus from traditional media to online social media and they are using sources such as blogs, social networking websites, viral marketing and wikis (Ozuem & Azemi, 2017; Hutton and Fosdick, 2011). Due to this advancement in technology many opportunities have been created for businesses (Ozuem & Lancaster, 2012; Ozuem et al., 2018). For instance, customer communication can be achieved through these media and relationships between businesses and consumers have been strengthened (Abed et al., 2015a, b; Ozuem, 2004). Social media is essentially an internet-enabled platform facilitating a flow of information in the form of decentralised user content through public memberships (Abrahams et al., 2012). In other words, social media can be defined as a group of applications that are based on internet, building on foundations such as the ideology and technology of Web 2.0. This allows the creation and exchange of content that is generated by users (Kaplan and Haenlein, 2010, p. 60). Social media is also referred to as a content-generating network. This involves reviewing content online, obtaining real-time feedback, building customer relationships and facilitating discussions (Rodriguez et al., 2012). In addition, user networks and communities can also increase their presence on social media networking sites (Curran and Lennon, 2011). Abrahams et al. (2012), explain that through social media networking sites, propagating information is easier and has led to decentralised levels of content amongst users. However, there are many other networks that provide the opportunity for users to share their views on products. There is therefore a need to discuss the similarities and differences between social media and other UGC networks.

UGC and social media share the same strong relationship (Rodgers & Thorson, 2017). When they are combined, something magical is created based on the individual strength of each element. Marketers can build strong customer relationships and can strengthen their brands by executing UGC campaigns on social media. The concept of UGC is not new; it was introduced several years ago. However, this phenomenon has recently gained momentum because of the rapid growth of the internet and the easy accessibility this provides, based on instant connectivity and intelligent software (Clark et al., 2017; Hansen & Lee, 2013). Since the internet and technology are at everyone's fingertips, consumers have been granted new powers to make themselves heard and to influence ideas such as sales and marketing (Hansen & Lee, 2013; Ozuem & Azemi, 2018). Three types of UGC exist in the online environment. First, social media UGC can be found on social media websites such as Facebook, Wikipedia, Twitter, YouTube, Tumblr, Pinterest, Instagram, Reddit, google+ and LinkedIn. Secondly, UGC is created by online communities that rate and review products. Such online communities include Yelp, OpenTable, google business, Zagat and Trip Advisor. Thirdly UGC can be created on corporate websites and third-party sales websites such as Amazon and eBay. Online review websites like Zagat, Trip Advisor, OpenTable and Yelp are common platforms for consumers to express opinions and share experiences about purchasing products and services (Leibtag, 2014).

Users consider UGC information to be more trustworthy and relatable compared to information generated by marketers (Seadle & Greifender, 2014). However, it is necessary to understand the difference between the nature UGC among different networks because the nature of UGC is quite different on company own website, third party selling websites (eBay, Amazon) and on instant messages networks (WhatsApp, Viber, WeChat, Imo etc). To address this issue, a definition of social media should be considered. Charlesworth, (2015;1) stated that *"what is understood by social media is still open to some debate"*, furthermore defining (2015;1) social media as a *"collective term for the various social network and community sites including such online application as blogs, podcasts, reviews and wikis"*. According to this definition, both online communities and social media websites are examples of social media networks. Regarding the use of both kinds of online network, it is obvious that social media networking is not only used for rating and reviewing products (Rossmann et al., 2018) but also to socialise with friends and family. However, online communities such as Zagat, Trip Advisor, OpenTable and Yelp are used particularly to review and rate products. Based on this observation, community websites and social media sites are quite different.

Brands' own websites and third party selling websites such as Amazon and eBay are other sources that amass UGC (Chen & Lurie, 2013). Once again, the question arises as to whether or not to consider UGC created by brands and third-party websites as examples of UGC and social media. Any website where users can add content but cannot control the site is defined as a social media site (Han, 2018). Based on this definition of social media, community websites, third-party selling websites and social media sites are very similar, and differences are difficult to highlight. However, it can be argued that all media can be considered as qualifying as social media, so there is need to more strictly define social media and UGC for the purposes of this research.

From the above definitions of social media, it can be concluded that it existed long before the digital revolution (Chaffey & Ellis-Chadwick, 2016). In the early days, social media was used as source of connection among communities of like-minded people who used to share views on all issues from politics and the latest trends to the best way to cultivate tomatoes (Charlesworth, 2015). However, these connections were strongly limited by location and by the available communications technology of the past (Ryan, 2017; Ozuem et al., 2008). If users at that time wanted to discuss a brand, organisation or product they could do so only with close associates, family or friends (Ryan, 2017; Estrella-Ramón & Ellis-Chadwick, 2017). The digital generation has removed these restrictions (Charlesworth, 2014). In the digital world people can spread UGC across the globe instantly via hand-held devices, tablets, watches, wearables, PCs and laptops (Dodson, 2016; Zhang et al., 2016; Davis, 2015). The above definition of a social circle suggests that UGC created in the form of product ratings on review websites (community websites) and on corporate websites cannot be considered examples of social media enabled UGC. According to Tirunillai & Tellis, (2012), a discussion about conventional social circles is not restricted to any specific topic. However, people cannot communicate easily on Amazon, eBay, Yelp, Zagat, and Trip Advisor because community websites and third party selling websites like eBay or Amazon only allow product ratings to be generated. Community websites, selling websites and corporate websites cannot therefore be considered as examples of social media for the purposes of this research. Estrella-Ramón & Ellis-Chadwick, (2017) indicate that people can freely communicate and share their views about anything on social media networks such as Twitter, YouTube and Facebook. This research therefore only looks at UGC created on social media sites such as Twitter and Facebook, but it will nonetheless take a detailed look at the nature of UGC on social media sites.

Definitions of social media offer mixed perceptions regarding the difference between UGC on social media and UGC on corporate and community websites. Kaplan and Haenlein (2010) associate social media sites with digital technology by describing social media as a group of internet-based applications that build on the technological and ideological foundation of Web 2.0. These applications facilitate the exchange and creation of UGC. Furthermore, social media is defined by Gensler et al., (2013) as Web 2.0 which is the sum of open-sourced user-controlled, and interactive online applications used to expand the knowledge, market power and experience of users as participants in social and business processes. These Web 2.0 applications support the creation of networked informal users and they facilitate a flow of knowledge and ideas by allowing the efficient generation, sharing, editing, refining and dissemination of informational content (Evans, 2012; Zhang et al., 2016; Schaffer et al., 2014; Agresta et al., 2011). Based on this definition it is clear that corporate websites, social media sites and third-party selling websites all are considered as examples of UGC. The argument here is that company websites, third-party selling websites (eBay, Amazon) and community website cannot be considered examples of UGC. Therefore, community websites such as Zagat, TripAdvisor, OpenTable, Yelp and third party selling websites such as Amazon and eBay are not considered to be examples of social media sites. Moreover, Statista statistics (2018) suggest the penetration of social media in the UK has taken place on social websites only (see Chart 2.1 below). Therefore, due to the restrictions placed on discussion types on third party websites (e.g. eBay, Amazon), corporate websites and community networks (e.g. Trip Advisor, Yelp) these can be rejected as examples of social media UGC (see Figure 2-2 of the Pyramid of UGC Sources). This study specifically considers social media networks as examples of UGC. Pinterest, Twitter and Facebook are amongst the most high-profile examples of social media, and they operate, and work entirely or mostly based on UGC. Moreover, online forums, product reviews and rating websites as well as classified websites also depend on UGC, but these should not be considered as forms of social media UGC. UGC includes blog posts, tweets, testimonials, videos, pictures and everything in between. Peer-reviewed endorsements of brands rather than brand-endorsed messages count as UGC.

Brand-Related User-Generated Content (UGC)

Brand-oriented UGC represents content which is created with reference to a brand and is intended to be brought to the notice of other users as well (Tang et al. 2014). It provides useful information to consumers who are in the process of arriving at a decision about buying products or services (Yadav et al., 2016). eMarketer (2016) report highlighted that 80.7% of internet users in the US regard product reviews by other consumers as influential factors for arriving at a purchasing decision. The importance, relevance and influence of UGC related to brands is increasingly enabling potential customers to make decisions about brands (Munar & Jacobsen, 2013)

Positive responses from consumers can be generated by brand-oriented UGC which includes favourable attitudes with respect to a brand if the brand-oriented UGC is in favour of the brand (Ryan, 2014). It is also important to note that the influence of UGC also depends on the person who generates it. Social media has enabled users to generate and share content with each other. Among those who are in the social circle of consumers it is easier to get within the reach of UGC (Ransbotham et al., 2012). This is also referred to as creating eWOM and brings people together who share the interests of those within their personal network (Yadav et al., 2016). Consumers are also increasingly being exposed to UGC shared by celebrities on their social media pages. Twitter is increasingly becoming a source for politicians and celebrities to share information about what they like or dislike (Ransbotham et al., 2012; Munar, A.M. & Jacobsen, 2013). Existing research has shown that posts by celebrities can influence followers, even if the content is brand-related (Schultz, 2017). However, the extent to which such posts influence consumers who are making a buying decision and the extent to which brand perceptions are affected are not clear. In this, study the relative effectiveness of celebrities and friend posts on social media in relation to brands is examined (Ransbotham et al., 2012). Furthermore, with regard to the fact that brand-related UGC influences other consumers (such as observed by Lu et al. 2014), it is worth noting the nature of responses from recipients of UGC towards these two constructs (Ryan & Jones, 2012).

Sources of Brand-Oriented UGC

Information is an important feature of social media, as everyone is informed about others due to social media (Shao, 2009). The UGC which users usually encounter is the one shared by their friends. Friends represent the major social circle of a person present on social media. People have brought real-life friendships and relationships online (Liu et al., 2011).

Existing research shows that the buying decisions of people are influenced by views shared by their friends. This is called referent power and describes a situation in which people like to identify with popular views held by their friends (Williams et al., 2010). It is supplemented by reward power whereby people believe that by sharing popular views they are rewarding each other. Further, coercive power also underpins this idea in the sense that people believe they are rendered socially isolated if they go against the popular view (Barreda & Bilgihan, 2013). Apart from the venues of traditional marketing, the factor which most influences people is that of friendship affecting the decisions of people through the power of social media (Zeng et al., 2016). Nearly 60% of consumers note their buying decisions were influenced by friends' posts on social media (Diffley et al., 2018).

However, it is important to distinguish between casual friends and close friends. Close friends enjoy influential power with respect to each other. They also interact with each other more frequently than with casual friends and have reciprocal relationships with each other (Malthouse et al., 2016). They are likely to share their feelings and experiences more closely, and more openly and frequently with each other (Merrilees, 2016). Close friends are also likely to share promotional messages with each other. The intensity of relationships is higher and better in close friendships, which is why people attach importance to information passed on by close friends (Kamboj & Sarmah, 2018).

The variations in UGC types are endless. Some major examples include Podcasts, Forums, user-created blog posts, user-created videos, reviews, Facebook posts or comments and blog comments (Dempster & Lee, 2015; Weber & Henderson, 2014; Statista, 2018). Customer feedback is an open-ended type of feedback that comes in the form of FAQs, Q&As or any other direct feedback that directs a brand social media team (Armstrong et al., 2017). Certain platforms that not only allow customers to ask questions, but also to answer them, providing additional integrity to responses because they are produced by the end users of products. Reviews and ratings are comparatively straightforward and include the number of 'likes' on a product Facebook page (Brake, 2014). This is a clear example of UGC as it allows consumers to create direct feedback about products depending on the system being used. Nielsen (2017), showed that peer reviews are long-lasting and durable. The sites on which they appear are highly credible and feature reviews from other customers. The filter options that are a feature of some systems ensure that only verified customers can review, while others are open-ended platforms (Chaffey, 2006; Schultz, 2016). Marketers can enhance current levels of transparency and trust in brands by allowing user-generated images. Beyond fashion, it is exciting for customers to receive mail about a new product and to see others unboxing products (Zahay, 2015). However, the authenticity of UGC does not rely only on the fact that it is user-generated. More crucial is that UGC is unpaid and also serves the purposes of marketing brands (King et al., 2014; Weber & Henderson, 2014). This renders UGC a version of online WOM marketing, although the content is not necessarily generated with the intention of promotion, particularly because modern users are cautious about marketing messages (Armstrong & Kotler, 2014). For example, a satisfied consumer at a restaurant or Samsung/Apple service centre can generate voluntary posts about their experience, on, for example, Instagram – which of course counts as UGC. However, the brand can take advantage of this activity, but it remains necessary for the brand to be aware of response strategies to address both positive and negative customer feedback. Thus, the next section explores how UGC stimulates customer behaviour in diverse ways.

UGC and Consumer Behaviour

The nature of interactions between people is increasingly changing due to the enhanced democratisation of content available online (Scott, 2015). The focus of companies is shifting from influencing the consumers to playing the role of mediator between consumers for the content they are generating (Wen, 2009). Nevertheless, UGC is a legitimate source of feedback from consumers. Consumers provide opinions and feedback as a result of UGC that can help business in terms of customer relationship management and product development (Gu, Tang & Whinston, 2013). This can occur in both a structured and an unstructured manner. This has resulted in the expansion of consumer-oriented intelligence online. The advent of the internet enabled people to discuss their experiences with industry or companies (Stoel & Muhanna, 2016). They became able to interact with countless numbers of other consumers and able to highlight their personal experiences with the brand, bringing into the limelight their experience before other consumers (Chern et al., 2015). UGC is also becoming an addiction that gives users a sense of recognition and status. When they are appreciated, or their views are welcomed on the basis of their experience they feel a sense of recognition within their circle. That is why UGC is increasingly becoming a source of eWOM (Estrella-Ramón et al., 2017) and positive eWOM has a direct positive influence on customer relationships and buying behaviour (Luo et al., 2016; Zhang et al., 2013; Chern et al., 2015; Gu, Tang & Whinston, 2013)

Nevertheless, consumers are increasingly empowered by the internet, particularly in light of Web 2.0 and they can create content and influence brands and other consumer opinions with the content they are creating. Consumers are not passive anymore; they are becoming increasingly active. The internet has also facilitated two-way communication between consumers and brands. Therefore, UGC has the effect of influencing brand loyalty (Kizgin et al., 2018; Ozuem & Thomas, 2015). Previously, business marketers were able to influence the opinions of consumers (Viswanathan et al., 2018). Today, this is achieved by consumers as they can interact without the constraints of geographical boundaries, and they can influence opinion, which is considered a form of UGC. They can opine freely about the products and services they consume from various brands (Kao et al., 2016; Roberts & Kraynak, 2008). With the help of social media, consumers are able to generate, create, exchange, and edit information online and they can support or critique a particular brand overtly via UGC on social media (Du Plessis, 2017). Peer review feedback is regarded as a more reliable source of marketing as compared to online marketing campaigns (Kao et al., 2016; Hautz et al., 2014). This has the effect of driving brand loyalty amongst customers (Ozuem et al., 2016). The profitability of business is also notably influenced by UGC (Akar & Topcu, 2011; Hautz et al., 2014).

Customer satisfaction increases in line with the quality of customer online reviews and this ultimately leads to higher customer purchasing intentions since positive discussion about brands improves customer confidence because they feel they are dealing with a reliable brand (Yadav et al., 2016). As online reviews are easily understandable and objective in nature, they strongly influence the intentions of customers based on reviews that are subjective and emotive (Leibtag, 2014). Detailed videos and written content provide information to people on various products and in imaginative ways (Goodman et al., 2013). The impact of online reviews on consumer behaviour has become an interesting topic for both practitioners and researchers (Ozuem & O'Keeffe, 2015; Seadle & Greifender, 2014). Online stores and brands publish rich information (Yeh, 2015; Prendergast et al., 2010) that has made it easy for customers to access multiple sources of information about brands and products. This is particularly the case in terms of customer reviews about online shopping on social media (Chakravarty et al., 2010). Although positive reviews are generally appreciated, negative reviews cannot be ignored (Feng & Liu, 2018). Regardless of whether the product or brand is of a supreme quality, an unsatisfied customer will post negative reviews that might have a negative impact on the brand and might influence new customers. These negative reviews can influence other consumers to perceive that the product is of lower quality, thus damaging buying intentions and brand trust (Lee & Choeh, 2018). All types of UGC on social media sites impact on customer trust, which will be discussed in the next section.

Customer Trust

Online reviews of consumers on social media in relation to products or services can be highly influential. A number of studies suggest that online reviews strongly influence product choices and risk perception (Sparks et al., 2016: Palmer, 2009; Matzat & Snijders, 2012). Although all consumer reviews are not equally valued, reviews by family members and close friends on social media are highly influential in terms of driving purchase decisions (Wen, 2009; Hsu et al., 2013; Lee, 2017). The value of UGC as feedback can be measured on the basis of the extent to which it is influential and useful. In terms of the usefulness of UGC, negative feedback has a great impact on brand trust amongst new customers and existing customers (Yan & Du, 2016) since it damages perceptions of trustworthiness (Kandampully et al., 2015). For sellers it is very important to understand how to react to negative reviews. The next section will discuss this aspect in detail. However, it should be acknowledged that if a business attracts only positive reviews this attracts suspicion. Brands, however, cannot satisfy everyone (Liang & Corkindale, 2016; Lee & Wu, 2015; Zhou & Duan, 2015). Negative reviews suggest that brands hide nothing, and positive reviews create high trust relationships with customers (Zhang et al., 2015). Online feedback can benefit brands as they add elements of transparency and truth to the brand image that eventually lead to customer trust (Sun, 2013; Wang & Li, 2016; Munar & Jacobsen, 2013).

Moreover, online reviews on social media are considered new forms of recommendations similar to traditional communications by means of word of mouth (Zheng et al., 2015). Customers who contribute content to social media reviews tend to be previous customers who intend to remain anonymous, whereas sources of traditional WOM are generally known and therefore not anonymous (Ryan & Jones, 2012). The number of customer reviews is another concern in terms of online customer reviews as it is useful for identifying reputation. It also holds clues as to the market performance of specific products or services (Mayzlin and Chevalier, 2006; Ozuem et al., 2017). Moreover, Charlesworth, (2014) suggests that the quantity of online reviews also acts as a reference point in winning the confidence of online customers. These ideas will be discussed in future sections of this chapter.

Customers form expectations about a specific product or service on the basis of multiple sources of information such as the brand name and the price of products or services (Mathieson, 2010). Previous experiences of products also have a bearing (Mayzlin et al., 2016). Moreover, Kaur et al., (2018) focused on determining how consumer social media reviews post-purchase can determine levels of both expectations and uncertainty. Customers form pre-purchase expectations about products partly based on online reviews which influence their later buying decisions. Online consumer reviews are generally characterised by volume, variance and valence (Homburg et al., 2015; Richard & Habibi, 2016). Numerous studies have explored how social media consumer reviews influence customer buying decisions. According to recent meta-analysis, the volume and valence of reviews positively influences customer trust and this in turn impacts on buying decisions (Saboo et al., 2016; Floyd et al., 2014). Following a purchase, expectation-confirmation leads to high levels of the post-purchase satisfaction and reduces return probabilities. Similarly, review volumes mitigate return probabilities ((Seadle & Greifender, 2014). This suggests that positive social media reviews also impact on customer buying return decisions.

MANAGERIAL IMPLICATIONS AND CONCLUSION

It is evident from previous studies that UGC is dynamic and complex, as is the impact of UGC on other consumers (Nielsen Company, 2014; Ayeh et al. 2013). Moreover, Tafesse, (2016) observed that consumer choice is influenced by UGC that consumers encounter on social media because people are more influenced by their friends and family. Furthermore, he observed that UGC is more effective in terms of influencing consumer decision making as compared to media campaigns and advertisements, because customers place more trust in their friends than in marketers. Furthermore, Herrero et al., (2015) observed that the product ratings provided on social media are regarded as more reliable by other consumers; certainly, more so than the ratings provided by industry experts. Moreover, Kamboj et al., (2018) observed that negative UGC is more influential than positive UGC because it consists of in-depth information about products. As such, negative comments are the principal reason why customers switch brands in certain circumstances. However, UGC is keenly followed in some industries such as in the travel industry which is heavily influenced by customer reviews and ratings (Ayeh et al. 2013). Moreover, Ye et al., (2010), observed that where UGC acts in support of a particular travel company and increases by 10%, subsequent bookings increased by 5%. Moreover, Yang et al., (2017) observed that UGC provides weak brands with a stronger position in the market. UGC is also regarded by various researchers as a source of eWOM. However, eWOM might be positive or negative (Renton & Simmonds, 2017; Sabate et al., 2014; Pfeffer et al., 2014). These ideas will be discussed in detail further on in this chapter.

There are two-fold repercussions of the new environments that have supported the growth in social media (Hu et al. 2014). Consumer behaviour is highly influenced by UGC as it amounts to eWOM for other consumers (Ring et al. 2016). This has the effect of influencing buying decisions. Hong et al. (2017), observed that social media UGC is increasingly becoming a prominent source of influencing the decisions of consumers to transact with a particular brand. Gao (et al. 2015) observed that UGC might take the form of a negative or positive comment about a product or service. These comments are made through social media channels. There are different manners and forms of UGC such as those generated in discussion forums online. Examples include blogs, Tweets and Facebook pages. This content has the effect of influencing buying decisions online and offline (Hong et al. 2017). UGC can also amount to a boycott of a brand or company whereby other consumers realise that their fellow consumers were severely affected by the brand's policies or products and services (Fay & Larkin, 2017). UGC can also take the form of mailbags, personal emails, electronic mailings, blog posts, comments on social media, instant messaging, and social media reviews (Gao et al., 2015). However, this research considers social media UGC only. An important feature of UGC is that it is generated by consumers and is not therefore created professionally. Further, UGC on social media is often regarded as more trustworthy by consumers compared with the narratives they find on other media platforms. This is perhaps because people trust their friends and families over marketers (Fay & Larkin, 2017). Sandars and Walsh (2009) observed that since UGC is generated by consumers it is considered reliable and trustworthy by other consumers. Smith (et al. 2012) observed that UGC is equivalent to eWOM and is thus considered reliable by both brands and consumers. Floyd et al. (2014), observed that social influence is a crucial factor behind purchasing decisions and that is why UGC is influential in purchases made by other consumers. The results of research conducted by Geissinger & Laurell, (2016) showed that 70% of consumers looked for consumer reviews before making a buying decision. They typically carried out a search on social media beforehand. Besides, Labrecque, (2014) observed that 78% of consumers believe in the content that is shared by other consumers and value this over industry data. Moreover, Breitsohl et al., (2015) observed that 60% of consumers trust posts by other consumers when it comes to products or services. Some 49% of consumers shape their buying behaviour in the light of such content. Additionally, Breitsohl et al., (2015) observed that those consumers who employed social media platforms arrived at better decisions in terms of product purchases compared with those who did not rely on such a platform. This suggests that UGC on social media impacts customer behaviour in many ways.

REFERENCES

Abed, S., Dwivedi, Y. K., & Williams, M. D. (2015a). Social media as a bridge to e-commerce adoption in SMEs: A systematic literature review. *The Marketing Review*, *15*(1), 39–57. doi:10.1362/14693471 5X14267608178686

Abrahams, A. S., Jiao, J., Wang, G. A., & Fan, W. (2012). Vehicle defect discovery from social media. *Decision Support Systems*, *54*(1), 87–97. doi:10.1016/j.dss.2012.04.005

Adler, L., & Sillars, R. (2011). *2010; The Linked Photographers' Guide to Online Marketing and Social Media*. Cengage Learning.

Agresta, S., Bough, B. B., & Miletsky, J. I. (2011). *Perspectives™ on Social Media Marketing*. Boston: Cengage Learning.

Akehurst, G. (2009). User generated content: The use of blogs for tourism organisations and tourism consumers. *Service Business*, *3*(1), 51–61. doi:10.100711628-008-0054-2

Armstrong, G., & Kotler, P. (2014). *Marketing: an introduction (12ᵗʰ ed.)*. Harlow: Pearson Education Limited.

Armstrong, G., Kotler, P., & Opresnik, M. O. (2017). *Marketing: an introduction (13ᵗʰ ed.)*. Harlow: Pearson Education Limited.

Ayeh, J. K., Au, N., & Law, R. (2013). "Do we believe in TripAdvisor?" Examining credibility perceptions and online travelers' attitude toward using user-generated content. *Journal of Travel Research*, *52*(4), 437–452. doi:10.1177/0047287512475217

Bao, T. T., & Chang, T. S. (2016). The product and timing effects of eWOM in viral marketing. *International Journal of Business*, *21*(2), 99.

Barefoot, D., & Szabo, J. (2009). *Friends with Benefits: A Social Media Marketing Handbook, 1;1st; edn*. San Francisco, CA: No Starch Press.

Barreda, A., & Bilgihan, A. (2013). An analysis of user-generated content for hotel experiences. *Journal of Hospitality and Tourism Technology*, *4*(3), 263–280. doi:10.1108/JHTT-01-2013-0001

Brake, D. (2014). *Sharing our lives online: risks and exposure in social media*. Basingstoke, UK: Palgrave Macmillan. doi:10.1057/9781137312716

Breitsohl, J., Kunz, W. H., & Dowell, D. (2015). Does the host match the content? A taxonomical update on online consumption communities. *Journal of Marketing Management*, *31*(9-10), 1040–1064. doi:10.1080/0267257X.2015.1036102

Brown, E. (2012). *Working the Crowd - Social media marketing for business* (2nd ed.). Swindon, UK: British Informatics Society Ltd.

Brown, J., Broderick, A. J., & Lee, N. (2007). Word of mouth communication within online communities: Conceptualizing the online social network. *Journal of Interactive Marketing*, *21*(3), 2–20. doi:10.1002/dir.20082

Carvão, S. (2010). Embracing user generated content within destination management organisations to gain a competitive insight into visitors' profiles. *Worldwide Hospitality and Tourism Themes*, *2*(4), 376–382. doi:10.1108/17554211011074038

Cha, M., Kwak, H., Rodriguez, P., Ahn, Y. & Moon, S. (2009). Analyzing the video popularity characteristics of large-scale user generated content systems. *IEEE/ACM Transactions on Networking*, *17*(5), 1357-1370.

Chaffey, D. (2006). *Internet marketing: strategy, implementation and practice* (3ʳᵈ ed.). Prentice Hall/Financial Times.

Chaffey, D., & Ellis-Chadwick, F. (2016). *Digital marketing* (6th ed.). Harlow: Pearson Education.

Chakravarty, A., Liu, Y., & Mazumdar, T. (2010). The Differential Effects of Online Word-of-Mouth and Critics' Reviews on Pre-release Movie Evaluation. *Journal of Interactive Marketing*, *24*(3), 185–197. doi:10.1016/j.intmar.2010.04.001

Chan-Olmsted, S. M., Cho, M., & Lee, S. (2013). User perceptions of social media: A comparative study of perceived characteristics and user profiles by social media. *Online Journal of Communication and Media Technologies*, *3*(4), 149–178.

Chari, S., Christodoulides, G., Presi, C., Wenhold, J., & Casaletto, J. P. (2016). Consumer Trust in User-Generated Brand Recommendations on Facebook. *Psychology and Marketing*, *33*(12), 1071–1081. doi:10.1002/mar.20941

Charlesworth, A. (2014). *Digital marketing: a practical approach* (2nd ed.). London: Routledge. doi:10.4324/9780203493717

Chen, H., & Huang, C. (2013). An Investigation into Online Reviewers' Behaviour. *European Journal of Marketing*, *47*(10), 1758–1773. doi:10.1108/EJM-11-2011-0625

Chen, Z., & Lurie, N. H. (2013). Temporal contiguity and negativity bias in the impact of online word of mouth. *JMR, Journal of Marketing Research*, *50*(4), 463–476. doi:10.1509/jmr.12.0063

Chern, C., Wei, C., Shen, F., & Fan, Y. (2015). A sales forecasting model for consumer products based on the influence of online word-of-mouth. *Information Systems and e-Business Management*, *13*(3), 445–473. doi:10.1007/10257-014-0265-0

Chow, W. S., & Shi, S. (2015). Investigating Customers' Satisfaction With Brand Pages In Social Networking Sites. *Journal of Computer Information Systems*, *55*(2), 48–58. doi:10.1080/08874417.2015.11645756

Chu, S. C., & Kim, Y. (2011). Determinants of consumer engagement in electronic word-of-mouth (eWOM) in social networking sites. *International Journal of Advertising*, *30*(1), 47–75. doi:10.2501/IJA-30-1-047-075

Chung, N., Han, H., & Koo, C. (2015). Adoption of travel information in user-generated content on social media: The moderating effect of social presence. *Behaviour & Information Technology*, *34*(9), 902–919. doi:10.1080/0144929X.2015.1039060

Clark, M., Black, H. G., & Judson, K. (2017). Brand community integration and satisfaction with social media sites: A comparative study. *Journal of Research in Interactive Marketing*, *11*(1), 39–55. doi:10.1108/JRIM-07-2015-0047

Curran, J., & Lennon, R. (2011). Participating in the conversation: Exploring adoption of online social media. *Academy of Marketing Studies Journal*, *15*(1), 21–38.

Davis, K. (2015). *Offerpop sifts gold from user-generated content: platform aggregates rich social data with an emphasis on visuals for the entire customer journey*. Haymarket Media, Inc.

Dempster, C., & Lee, J. (2015). *The Rise of the Platform Marketer: Performance Marketing with Google, Facebook, and Twitter, Plus the Latest High-Growth Digital Advertising Platforms*. John Wiley & Sons Inc. doi:10.1002/9781119153863

Diffley, S., McCole, P., & Carvajal-Trujillo, E. (2018). Examining social customer relationship management among Irish hotels. *International Journal of Contemporary Hospitality Management, 30*(2), 1072–1091. doi:10.1108/IJCHM-08-2016-0415

Dodson, I. (2016). *The Art of Digital Marketing: The Definitive Guide to Creating Strategic, Targeted, and Measurable Online Campaigns* (1st ed.). Hoboken, NJ: John Wiley & Sons Inc.

Dodson, I. (2016). *The digital marketing playbook.* Wiley-Blackwell.

Du Plessis, C. (2017). The role of content marketing in social media content communities. *South African Journal of Information Management, 19*(1), e1–e7. doi:10.4102ajim.v19i1.866

Duan, W., Gu, B., & Whinston, A. B. (2008). The dynamics of online word-of-mouth and product sales—An empirical investigation of the movie industry. *Journal of Retailing, 84*(2), 233–242. doi:10.1016/j.jretai.2008.04.005

Dutot, V., & Bergeron, F. (2016). From strategic orientation to social media orientation: Improving SMEs' performance on social media. *Journal of Small Business and Enterprise Development, 23*(4), 1165–1190. doi:10.1108/JSBED-11-2015-0160

Dwivedi, Y. K., Kapoor, K. K., & Chen, H. (2015). Social media marketing and advertising. *The Marketing Review, 15*(3), 289–309. doi:10.1362/146934715X14441363377999

eMarketer. (2016). *Internet users rely on reviews when deciding which products to purchase.* Available at: www.emarketer.com/Article/Internet-Users-Rely-on-Reviews-Deciding-Which-Products-Purchase/1014465

Estrella-Ramón, A., & Ellis-Chadwick, F. (2017). Do different kinds of user-generated content in online brand communities really work? *Online Information Review, 41*(7), 954–968. doi:10.1108/OIR-08-2016-0229

Evans, D. (2008). *Social Media Marketing.* Sybex.

Evans, D. (2012). *Social Media Marketing: An Hour a Day* (2nd ed.). Sybex.

Feng, J., & Liu, B. (2018). Dynamic Impact of Online Word-of-Mouth and Advertising on Supply Chain Performance. *International Journal of Environmental Research and Public Health, 15*(1), 69. doi:10.3390/ijerph15010069 PMID:29300361

Feng, J., & Papatla, P. (2012). Is Online Word of Mouth Higher for New Models or Redesigns? An Investigation of the Automobile Industry. *Journal of Interactive Marketing, 26*(2), 92–101. doi:10.1016/j.intmar.2012.01.001

Flanagin, A. J., Hocevar, K. P., & Samahito, S. N. (2014). Connecting with the user-generated Web: How group identification impacts online information sharing and evaluation. *Information Communication and Society, 17*(6), 683–694. doi:10.1080/1369118X.2013.808361

Floyd, K., Freling, R., Alhoqail, S., Cho, H. Y., & Freling, T. (2014). How Online Product Reviews Affect Retail Sales: A Meta-analysis. *Journal of Retailing, 90*(2), 217–232. doi:10.1016/j.jretai.2014.04.004

Fox, A. K., Bacile, T. J., Nakhata, C., & Weible, A. (2018). Selfie-marketing: Exploring narcissism and self-concept in visual user-generated content on social media. *Journal of Consumer Marketing*, *35*(1), 11–21. doi:10.1108/JCM-03-2016-1752

Gao, G., Greenwood, B. N., Agarwal, R., & McCulllough, J. (2015). Vocal Minority and Silent Majority: How Do Online Ratings Reflect Population Perceptions of Quality? *Management Information Systems Quarterly*, *39*(3), 565–589. doi:10.25300/MISQ/2015/39.3.03

Geissinger, A., & Laurell, C. (2016). User engagement in social media – an explorative study of Swedish fashion brands. *Journal of Fashion Marketing and Management*, *20*(2), 177–190. doi:10.1108/JFMM-02-2015-0010

Gensler, S., Völckner, F., Liu-Thompkins, Y., & Wiertz, C. (2013). Managing Brands in the Social Media Environment. *Journal of Interactive Marketing*, *27*(4), 242–256. doi:10.1016/j.intmar.2013.09.004

Ghose, A., Ipeirotis, P. G., & Li, B. (2012). Designing Ranking Systems for Hotels on Travel Search Engines by Mining User-Generated and Crowdsourced Content. *Marketing Science*, *31*(3), 493–520. doi:10.1287/mksc.1110.0700

Goh, K., Heng, C., & Lin, Z. (2013). Social Media Brand Community and Consumer Behavior: Quantifying the Relative Impact of User- and Marketer-Generated Content. *Information Systems Research*, *24*(1), 88–107. doi:10.1287/isre.1120.0469

Goodman, G. F., Schaffer, N., Korhan, J., & Safko, L. (2013). *2014; Social Marketing Digital Book Set*. John Wiley & Sons Inc.

Granitz, N., & Forman, H. (2015). Building self-brand connections: Exploring brand stories through a transmedia perspective. *Journal of Brand Management*, *22*(1), 38–59. doi:10.1057/bm.2015.1

Gu, B., Tang, Q., & Whinston, A. B. (2013). The influence of online word-of-mouth on long tail formation. *Decision Support Systems*, *56*, 474–481. doi:10.1016/j.dss.2012.11.004

Hansen, S. S., & Lee, J. K. (2013). What Drives Consumers to Pass Along Marketer-Generated eWOM in Social Network Games? Social and Game Factors in Play. *Journal of Theoretical and Applied Electronic Commerce Research*, *8*(1), 53–10.

Hautz, J., Füller, J., Hutter, K., & Thürridl, C. (2014). Let Users Generate Your Video Ads? The Impact of Video Source and Quality on Consumers' Perceptions and Intended Behaviors. *Journal of Interactive Marketing*, *28*(1), 1–15. doi:10.1016/j.intmar.2013.06.003

He, S., & Wen, N. (2015). A Cautious Pursuit of Risk in Online Word-Of-Mouth: The Effect of Truncated Distribution on Consumer Decisions. *Advances in Consumer Research. Association for Consumer Research (U. S.)*, *43*, 736.

Herrero, Á., Martín, H. S., & Hernández, J. M. (2015). How online search behavior is influenced by user-generated content on review websites and hotel interactive websites: 1. *International Journal of Contemporary Hospitality Management*, *27*(7), 1573–1597. doi:10.1108/IJCHM-05-2014-0255

Homburg, C., Ehm, L., & Artz, M. (2015). Measuring and managing consumer sentiment in an online community environment. *JMR, Journal of Marketing Research*, *52*(5), 629–641. doi:10.1509/jmr.11.0448

Hong, H., Xu, D., Xu, D., Wang, G. A., & Fan, W. (2017). An empirical study on the impact of online word-of-mouth sources on retail sales. *Information Discovery and Delivery*, *45*(1), 30–35. doi:10.1108/IDD-11-2016-0039

Hsu, C., Chuan-Chuan Lin, J., & Chiang, H. (2013). The effects of blogger recommendations on customers' online shopping intentions. *Internet Research*, *23*(1), 69–88. doi:10.1108/10662241311295782

Huang, Y., Chen, C. H., & Khoo, L. P. (2012). Products classification in emotional design using a basic-emotion based semantic differential method. *International Journal of Industrial Ergonomics*, *42*(6), 569–580. doi:10.1016/j.ergon.2012.09.002

Hutton, G., & Fosdick, M. (2011). The globalisation of SM, consumer relationships with brand evolve in the digital age. *Journal of Advertising Research*, *51*(4), 564–570. doi:10.2501/JAR-51-4-564-570

Jiao, Y., Ertz, M., Jo, M., & Sarigollu, E. (2018). Social value, content value, and brand equity in social media brand communities: A comparison of Chinese and US consumers. *International Marketing Review*, *35*(1), 18–41. doi:10.1108/IMR-07-2016-0132

Jiao, Y., Gao, J., & Yang, J. (2014). Social value and content value in social media: Two ways to flow. *Journal of Advanced Management Science*, *3*(4), 299–306.

Jin, S. V., & Phua, J. (2016). Making Reservations Online: The Impact of Consumer-Written and System-Aggregated User-Generated Content (UGC) in Travel Booking Websites on Consumers' Behavioral Intentions. *Journal of Travel & Tourism Marketing*, *33*(1), 101–117. doi:10.1080/10548408.2015.1038419

Kamboj, S., & Sarmah, B. (2018). Construction and validation of the customer social participation in brand communities scale. *Internet Research*, *28*(1), 46–73. doi:10.1108/IntR-01-2017-0011

Kamboj, S., Sarmah, B., Gupta, S., & Dwivedi, Y. (2018). Examining branding co-creation in brand communities on social media: Applying the paradigm of Stimulus-Organism-Response. *International Journal of Information Management*, *39*, 169–185. doi:10.1016/j.ijinfomgt.2017.12.001

Kandampully, J., Zhang, T., & Bilgihan, A. (2015). Customer loyalty: A review and future directions with a special focus on the hospitality industry. *International Journal of Contemporary Hospitality Management*, *27*(3), 379–414. doi:10.1108/IJCHM-03-2014-0151

Kao, T., Yang, M., Wu, J. B., & Cheng, Y. (2016). Co-creating value with consumers through social media. *Journal of Services Marketing*, *30*(2), 141–151. doi:10.1108/JSM-03-2014-0112

Kaplan, A. M., & Haenlein, M. (2010). Users of the world, unite! The challenges and opportunities of Social Media. *Business Horizons*, *53*(1), 59–68. doi:10.1016/j.bushor.2009.09.003

Kaur, P., Dhir, A., Rajala, R., & Dwivedi, Y. (2018). Why people use online social media brand communities: A consumption value theory perspective. *Online Information Review*, *42*(2), 205–221. doi:10.1108/OIR-12-2015-0383

Kim, A. J., & Johnson, K. K. (2016). Power of consumers using social media: Examining the influences of brand-related user-generated content on Facebook. *Computers in Human Behavior*, *58*, 98–108. doi:10.1016/j.chb.2015.12.047

Kim, J. (2012). The institutionalisation of YouTube: From user-generated content to professionally generated content. *Media Culture & Society*, *34*(1), 53–67. doi:10.1177/0163443711427199

Kim, M., & Lee, M. (2017). Brand-related user-generated content on social media: The roles of source and sponsorship. *Internet Research*, *27*(5), 1085–1103. doi:10.1108/IntR-07-2016-0206

Kim, S. H., Park, N., & Park, S. H. (2013). Exploring the Effects of Online Word of Mouth and Expert Reviews on Theatrical Movies' Box Office Success. *Journal of Media Economics*, *26*(2), 98–114. doi:10.1080/08997764.2013.785551

King, C., So, K. K. F., & Sparks, B. (2014). Customer Engagement with Tourism Brands: Scale Development and Validation. *Journal of Hospitality & Tourism Research (Washington, D.C.)*, *38*(3), 304–332. doi:10.1177/1096348012451456

King, C., So, K. K. F., Sparks, B. A., & Wang, Y. (2016). The Role of Customer Engagement in Building Consumer Loyalty to Tourism Brands. *Journal of Travel Research*, *55*(1), 64–78. doi:10.1177/0047287514541008

King, R.A., Racherla, P. & Bush, V.D. (2014). What We Know and Don't Know About Online Word-of-Mouth: A Review and Synthesis of the Literature. *Journal of Interactive Marketing, 28*(3), 167-183.

Kizgin, H., Jamal, A., Dey, B. L., & Rana, N. P. (2018). The Impact of Social Media on Consumers' Acculturation and Purchase Intentions. *Information Systems Frontiers*, *20*(3), 503–514. doi:10.100710796-017-9817-4

Kumar, A., Bezawada, R., Rishika, R., Janakiraman, R., & Kannan, P. K. (2015). From Social to Sale: The Effects of Firm Generated Content in Social Media on Customer Behavior. *Journal of Marketing*, *80*(1), 7–25. doi:10.1509/jm.14.0249

Kuo, Y., & Hou, J. (2017). Oppositional Brand Loyalty in Online Brand Communities: Perspectives on Social Identity Theory and Consumer-Brand. *Journal of Electronic Commerce Research*, *18*(3), 254.

Labrecque, L. I. (2014). Fostering Consumer–Brand Relationships in Social Media Environments: The Role of Parasocial Interaction. *Journal of Interactive Marketing*, *28*(2), 134–148. doi:10.1016/j.intmar.2013.12.003

Le, T. D. (2018). Influence of WOM and content type on online engagement in consumption communities: The information flow from discussion forums to Facebook. *Online Information Review*, *42*(2), 161–175. doi:10.1108/OIR-09-2016-0246

Lee, I. (2017). A study of the effect of social shopping deals on online reviews. *Industrial Management & Data Systems*, *117*(10), 2227–2240. doi:10.1108/IMDS-09-2016-0378

Lee, K., & Carter, S. (2011). Global marketing management. *Strategic Direction*, *27*(1). doi:10.1108d.2011.05627aae.001

Lee, S., & Choeh, J. Y. (2018). The interactive impact of online word-of-mouth and review helpfulness on box office revenue. *Management Decision*, *56*(4), 849–866. doi:10.1108/MD-06-2017-0561

Lee, T. Y., & Bradlow, E. T. (2011). Automatic marketing research using online customer reviews. *JMR, Journal of Marketing Research*, *48*(October), 881–894. doi:10.1509/jmkr.48.5.881

Lee, Y., & Wu, W. (2015). Effects of Medical Disputes on Internet Communications of Negative Emotions and Negative Online Word-of-Mouth. *Psychological Reports*, *117*(1), 251–270. doi:10.2466/21. PR0.117c13z1 PMID:26226491

Leibtag, A. (2014). *2013; The Digital Crown: Winning at Content on the Web*. Morgan Kaufmann Publishers Inc.

Leung, L. (2009). User-generated content on the internet: An examination of gratifications, civic engagement and psychological empowerment. *New Media & Society*, *11*(8), 1327–1347. doi:10.1177/1461444809341264

Li, Y. M., Chen, H. M., Liou, J. H., & Lin, L. F. (2014). Creating social intelligence for product portfolio design. *Decision Support Systems*, *66*, 123–134. doi:10.1016/j.dss.2014.06.013

Li, Y. M., & Shiu, Y. (2012). A diffusion mechanism for social advertising over microblogs. *Decision Support Systems*, *54*(1), 9–22. doi:10.1016/j.dss.2012.02.012

Liang, W. K., & Corkindale, D. (2016). The Effect of Online Word-of-Mouth on Risk Assessment for an Experience Service as Price Acceptability Changes. *Services Marketing Quarterly*, *37*(3), 156–170. doi:10.1080/15332969.2016.1184540

Liu, Q., Karahanna, E., & Watson, R.T. (2011). Unveiling user-generated content: Designing websites to best present customer reviews. Elsevier Inc.

Liu, X., Burns, A. C., & Hou, Y. (2017). An Investigation of Brand-Related User-Generated Content on Twitter. *Journal of Advertising*, *46*(2), 236–247. doi:10.1080/00913367.2017.1297273

Lu, Q., Ye, Q., & Law, R. (2014). Moderating Effects of Product Heterogeneity Between Online Word-Of-Mouth and Hotel Sales. *Journal of Electronic Commerce Research*, *15*(1), 1.

Lu, W., & Stepchenkova, S. (2015). User-Generated Content as a Research Mode in Tourism and Hospitality Applications: Topics, Methods, and Software. *Journal of Hospitality Marketing & Management*, *24*(2), 119–154. doi:10.1080/19368623.2014.907758

Luo, B., Zhang, Z., Liu, Y., & Gao, W. (2016). What does it say and who said it? The contingent effects of online word of mouth in China. *Nankai Business Review International*, *7*(4), 474–490. doi:10.1108/NBRI-12-2015-0035

Mahoney, L. M., & Tang, T. (2016). *Strategic Social Media: From Marketing to Social Change* (1st ed.). Hoboken, NJ: Wiley-Blackwell. doi:10.1002/9781119370680

Malthouse, E. C., Calder, B. J., Kim, S. J., & Vandenbosch, M. (2016). Evidence that user-generated content that produces engagement increases purchase behaviours. *Journal of Marketing Management*, *32*(5-6), 427–444. doi:10.1080/0267257X.2016.1148066

Marine-Roig, E., & Anton Clavé, S. (2016). A detailed method for destination image analysis using user-generated content. *Information Technology & Tourism*, *15*(4), 341–364. doi:10.100740558-015-0040-1

Martínez-Navarro, J., & Bigné, E. (2017). The Value Of Marketer-generated Content On Social Network Sites: Media Antecedents and Behavioral Responses. *Journal of Electronic Commerce Research*, *18*(1), 52.

Mathieson, R. (2010). *The On-Demand Brand: 10 Rules for Digital Marketing Success in an Anytime, Everywhere World* (1st ed.). Amacom, Saranac Lake.

Matzat, U. U., & Snijders, C. C. (2012). Rebuilding trust in online shops on consumer review sites: Sellers' responses to user-generated complaints. *Journal of Computer-Mediated Communication, 18*(1), 62–79. doi:10.1111/j.1083-6101.2012.01594.x

McNally, M. B., Trosow, S. E., Wong, L., Whippey, C., Burkell, J., & McKenzie, P. J. (2012). User-generated online content 2: Policy implications. *First Monday, 17*(6). doi:10.5210/fm.v17i6.3913

Merrilees, B. (2016). Interactive brand experience pathways to customer-brand engagement and value co-creation. *Journal of Product and Brand Management, 25*(5), 402–408. doi:10.1108/JPBM-04-2016-1151

Moon, S., Park, Y., & Seog Kim, Y. (2014). The impact of text product reviews on sales. *European Journal of Marketing, 48*(11/12), 2176–2197. doi:10.1108/EJM-06-2013-0291

Munar, A. M., & Jacobsen, J. K. S. (2013). Trust and Involvement in Tourism Social Media and Web-Based Travel Information Sources. *Scandinavian Journal of Hospitality and Tourism, 13*(1), 1–19. doi:10.1080/15022250.2013.764511

Odden, L. (2012). *Optimise: How to Attract and Engage More Customers by Integrating SEO, Social Media, and Content Marketing.* Somerset: Wiley.

OECD. (2006). *OECD Information Technology Outlook, 2006.* OECD. Available at www.oecd.org/sti/ito

OECD. (2007). *Communication Outlook, 2007.* Paris: OECD.

Ozuem, W. (Ed.). (2016). *Competitive social media marketing strategies.* IGI Global. doi:10.4018/978-1-4666-9776-8

Ozuem, W., & Azemi, Y (Eds.). (2017). *Digital Marketing Strategies for Fashion and Luxury Brands.* IGI Global.

Ozuem, W., & Azemi, Y. (2018). Online Service Failure and Recovery Strategies in Luxury Brands: A View from Justice Theory. In Digital Marketing Strategies for Fashion and Luxury Brands (pp. 108-125). IGI Global. doi:10.4018/978-1-5225-2697-1.ch005

Ozuem, W., Howell, K. E., & Lancaster, G. (2008). Communicating in the new interactive marketspace. *European Journal of Marketing, 42*(9/10), 1059–1083. doi:10.1108/03090560810891145

Ozuem, W., & Lancaster, G. (2012). Technology-induced customer services in the developing countries. In *Service science research, strategy and innovation: Dynamic knowledge management methods* (pp. 185–201). IGI Global. doi:10.4018/978-1-4666-0077-5.ch012

Ozuem, W., & Lancaster, G. (2014). Recovery strategies in on-line service failure. In A. Ghorbani (Ed.), *Marketing in the cyber era: Strategies and emerging trends* (pp. 143–159). Hershey, PA: IGI Global. doi:10.4018/978-1-4666-4864-7.ch010

Ozuem, W., & Lancaster, G. (2015). Examining the Dynamics of Value Propositions in Digital Books: A Social Constructivist Perspective. In Handbook of Research on Scholarly Publishing and Research Methods (pp. 295-311). IGI Global. doi:10.4018/978-1-4666-7409-7.ch015

Ozuem, W., & Mulloo, B. N. (2016). Basics of mobile marketing strategy. In *Competitive Social Media Marketing Strategies* (pp. 155–172). IGI Global. doi:10.4018/978-1-4666-9776-8.ch008

Ozuem, W., & O'Keeffe, A. (2015). Towards Leadership Marketing: An Exploratory and Empirical Study. In Marketing and Consumer Behavior: Concepts, Methodologies, Tools, and Applications (pp. 1570-1590). IGI Global.

Ozuem, W., Patel, A., Howell, K. E., & Lancaster, G. (2017). An exploration of consumers' response to online service recovery initiatives. *International Journal of Market Research*, *59*(1), 97–115.

Ozuem, W., Pinho, C. A., & Azemi, Y. (2016). User-generated content and perceived customer value. In *Competitive Social Media Marketing Strategies* (pp. 50–63). IGI Global. doi:10.4018/978-1-4666-9776-8.ch003

Ozuem, W., Prasad, J., & Lancaster, G. (2018). Exploiting online social gambling for marketing communications. *Journal of Strategic Marketing*, *26*(3), 258–282. doi:10.1080/0965254X.2016.1211728

Ozuem, W., & Thomas, T. (2015). Inside the Small Island Economies: Loyalty Strategies in the Telecommunications Sector. In Handbook of Research on Global Business Opportunities (pp. 316-349). IGI Global.

Ozuem, W., Thomas, T., & Lancaster, G. (2016). The influence of customer loyalty on small island economies: An empirical and exploratory study. *Journal of Strategic Marketing*, *24*(6), 37–41. doi:10.1080/0965254X.2015.1011205

Ozuem, W. F. (2004). *Conceptualising marketing communication in the new marketing paradigm: A postmodern perspective*. Universal-Publishers.

Palmer, A. (2009). *Study: Online Shoppers Trust Customer Reviews More than Friends.* Progressive Grocer.

Palmer, R., Cockton, J., Cooper, G., & Sc, M. (2007). *Managing marketing*. London: Butterworth-Heinemann.

Pan, Y., & Zhang, J. Q. (2011). Born Unequal: A Study of the Helpfulness of User-Generated Product Reviews. *Journal of Retailing*, *87*(4), 598–612. doi:10.1016/j.jretai.2011.05.002

Papthanassis Rodgers, S. L., & Thorson, E. (2017). *Digital advertising: theory and research* (3rd ed.). Abingdon, UK: Routledge. doi:10.4324/9781315623252

Pfeffer, J., Zorbach, T., & Carley, K. M. (2014). Understanding online firestorms: Negative word-of-mouth dynamics in social media networks. *Journal of Marketing Communications*, *20*(1-2), 117–128. doi:10.1080/13527266.2013.797778

Powell, G., Groves, S., & Dimos, J. (2011). *ROI of Social Media: How to Improve the Return on Your Social Marketing Investment, 1* (1st ed.). Hoboken, NJ: Wiley.

Prendergast, G., Ko, D., & Siu Yin, V. Y. (2010). Online word of mouth and consumer purchase intentions. *International Journal of Advertising*, *29*(5), 687–708. doi:10.2501/S0265048710201427

Ransbotham, S., Kane, G. C., & Lurie, N. H. (2012). Network Characteristics and the Value of Collaborative User-Generated Content. *Marketing Science*, *31*(3), 387–405. doi:10.1287/mksc.1110.0684

Rathore, A. K., Ilavarasan, P. V., & Dwivedi, Y. K. (2016). Social media content and product co-creation: An emerging paradigm. *Journal of Enterprise Information Management, 29*(1), 7–18. doi:10.1108/JEIM-06-2015-0047

Renton, M., & Simmonds, H. (2017). Like is a verb: Exploring tie strength and casual brand use effects on brand attitudes and consumer online goal achievement. *Journal of Product and Brand Management, 26*(4), 365–374. doi:10.1108/JPBM-03-2016-1125

Richard, M., & Habibi, M. R. (2016). Advanced modeling of online consumer behavior: The moderating roles of hedonism and culture. *Journal of Business Research, 69*(3), 1103–1119. doi:10.1016/j.jbusres.2015.08.026

Ring, A., Tkaczynski, A., & Dolnicar, S. (2016). 2014; "Word-of-Mouth Segments: Online, Offline, Visual or Verbal? *Journal of Travel Research, 55*(4), 481–492. doi:10.1177/0047287514563165

Roberts, M. L., Barker, M. S., Zahay, D. L., Bormann, N. F., & Barker, D. (2016). *Social media marketing: a strategic approach* (2nd ed South-Western.

Rodgers, S. L. & Thorson, E. (2017). Digital advertising: theory and research (3rd ed.). Routledge.

Rossmann, A., Ranjan, K. R., & Sugathan, P. (2016). Drivers of user engagement in eWoM communication. *Journal of Services Marketing, 30*(5), 541–553. doi:10.1108/JSM-01-2015-0013

Ryan, D. (2014). *Understanding digital marketing: marketing strategies for engaging the digital generation* (3rd ed.). London: KoganPage.

Ryan, D. (2017). *Understanding digital marketing: marketing strategies for engaging the digital generation* (4th ed.). London: KoganPage.

Ryan, D., & Jones, C. (2012). *Understanding digital marketing: marketing strategies for engaging the digital generation* (2nd ed.). London: Kogan Page.

Ryan, D., & Jones, C. (2014). *The Best Digital Marketing Campaigns in the World II, Second* (1st ed.). London: Kogan Page Ltd.

Sabate, F., Berbegal-Mirabent, J., Cañabate, A., & Lebherz, P. R. (2014). Factors influencing popularity of branded content in Facebook fan pages. *European Management Journal, 32*(6), 1001–1011. doi:10.1016/j.emj.2014.05.001

Saboo, A. R., Kumar, V., & Ramani, G. (2016). Evaluating the impact of social media activities on human brand sales. *International Journal of Research in Marketing, 33*(3), 524–541. doi:10.1016/j.ijresmar.2015.02.007

Sadek, Elwy, & Eldallal. (2018). The impact of social media brand communication on consumer-based brand equity dimensions through Facebook in fast moving consumer goods: The case of Egypt. *Journal of Business and Retail Management Research, 12*(2).

Sandars, J., & Walsh, K. (2009). 2008; "The use of online word of mouth opinion in online learning: A questionnaire survey. *Medical Teacher, 31*(4), 325–327. doi:10.1080/01421590802204403 PMID:18937096

Schaffer, N., Safko, L., Korhan, J., Goodman, G. F., Stratten, S., & Zarrella, D. (2013). *Social Marketing Digital Book Set* (1st ed.). Hoboken, NJ: John Wiley & Sons Inc.

Schultz, C. D. (2016). Insights from consumer interactions on a social networking site: Findings from six apparel retail brands. *Electronic Markets, 26*(3), 203–217. doi:10.100712525-015-0209-7

Schultz, C. D. (2017). Proposing to your fans: Which brand post characteristics drive consumer engagement activities on social media brand pages? *Electronic Commerce Research and Applications, 26*, 23–34. doi:10.1016/j.elerap.2017.09.005

Schulz, S., Pauw, G., Clercq, O., Desmet, B., Hoste, V., Daelemans, W., & Macken, L. (2016). Multimodular Text Normalisation of Dutch User-Generated Content. *ACM Transactions on Intelligent Systems and Technology, 7*(4), 1–22. doi:10.1145/2850422

Scott, D. M. (2015). *The New Rules of Marketing and PR: How to Use Social Media, Online Video, Mobile Applications, Blogs, News Releases, and Viral Marketing to Reach Buyers Directly* (5th ed.). New York: John Wiley & Sons Inc. doi:10.1002/9781119172499.ch02

Seadle, M. & Greifender, E. (2014). *Structuring the digital domain*. Emerald Group Publishing Ltd.

Shao, G. (2009). Understanding the appeal of user-generated media: A uses and gratification perspective. *Internet Research, 19*(1), 7–25. doi:10.1108/10662240910927795

Sheldrake, P., & Sheldrake, P. P. I. (2011). *The Business of Influence: Reframing Marketing and PR for the Digital Age, 1* (1st ed.). New York: Wiley.

Shneiderman, B., Preece, J., & Pirolli, P. (2011). Realizing the value of social media requires innovative computing research. *Communications of the ACM, 54*(9), 34–37. doi:10.1145/1995376.1995389

Simon, J.P. (2016). User generated content – users, community of users and firms: toward new sources of co-innovation? *Info, 18*(6), 4-25.

Smith, A. N., Fischer, E., & Yongjian, C. (2012). How Does Brand-related User-generated Content Differ across YouTube, Facebook, and Twitter? *Journal of Interactive Marketing, 26*(2), 102–113. doi:10.1016/j.intmar.2012.01.002

Smith, P., & Chaffey, D. (2012). *Emarketing excellence*. St. Louis, MO: Taylor and Francis. doi:10.4324/9780080504896

Smith, P. R., & Zook, Z. (2011). *Marketing communications: integrating offline and online with social media* (5th ed.). London: Kogan Page.

Sparks, B. A., So, K. K. F., & Bradley, G. L. (2016). Responding to negative online reviews: The effects of hotel responses on customer inferences of trust and concern. *Tourism Management, 53*, 74–85. doi:10.1016/j.tourman.2015.09.011

Stareva, I. (2014). *Social Media and the Rebirth of PR: The Emergence of Social Media as a Change Driver for PR* (1st ed.). Hamburg: Anchor Academic Publishing.

Statista. (2018). *How do online customer reviews affect your opinion of a local business?* Available at https://www.statista.com/statistics/315751/online-review-customer-opinion/

Sterne, J. (2010). *Social media metrics: how to measure and optimise your marketing investment.* Hoboken, NJ: John Wiley & Sons.

Stoel, M. D., & Muhanna, W. A. (2016). Online word of mouth: Implications for the name-your-own-price channel. *Decision Support Systems, 91,* 37–47. doi:10.1016/j.dss.2016.07.006

Sun, H. (2013). Moderating Role of Online Word of Mouth on Website Attributes and Consumer Trust in E-commerce Environment. *Journal of Applied Sciences (Faisalabad), 13*(12), 2316–2320. doi:10.3923/jas.2013.2316.2320

Susarla, A., Oh, J., & Tan, Y. (2012). Social Networks and the Diffusion of User-Generated Content: Evidence from YouTube. *Information Systems Research, 23*(1), 23–41. doi:10.1287/isre.1100.0339

Tafesse, W. (2016). An experiential model of consumer engagement in social media. *Journal of Product and Brand Management, 25*(5), 424–434. doi:10.1108/JPBM-05-2015-0879

Tang, C., Mehl, M. R., Eastlick, M. A., He, W., & Card, N. A. (2016). A longitudinal exploration of the relations between electronic word-of-mouth indicators and firms' profitability: Findings from the banking industry. *International Journal of Information Management, 36*(6), 1124–1132. doi:10.1016/j.ijinfomgt.2016.03.015

Tang, L. (2017). Mine Your Customers or Mine Your Business: The Moderating Role of Culture in Online Word-of-Mouth Reviews. *Journal of International Marketing, 25*(2), 88–110. doi:10.1509/jim.16.0030

Tang, T., Fang, E., & Wang, F. (2014). Is neutral really neutral? The effects of neutral user-generated content on product sales. *Journal of Marketing, 78*(4), 41–58. doi:10.1509/jm.13.0301

Thomsett-Scott, B. C. (2014). *Marketing with Social Media: A LITA Guide.* Chicago: ALA TechSource.

Tirunillai, S., & Tellis, G. J. (2012). Does Chatter Really Matter? Dynamics of User-Generated Content and Stock Performance. *Marketing Science, 31*(2), 198–215. doi:10.1287/mksc.1110.0682

Viswanathan, V., Malthouse, E. C., Maslowska, E., Hoornaert, S., & Van den Poel, D. (2018). Dynamics between social media engagement, firm-generated content, and live and time-shifted TV viewing. *Journal of Service Management, 29*(3), 378–398. doi:10.1108/JOSM-09-2016-0241

Wan, F., & Ren, F. (2017). The Effect Of Firm Marketing Content On Product Sales: Evidence From a Mobile Social Media Platform. *Journal of Electronic Commerce Research, 18*(4), 288–302.

Wang, P., Sun, L., & Peng, L. (2013). Modeling product attitude formation process in online word-of-mouth. *Nankai Business Review International, 4*(3), 212–229. doi:10.1108/NBRI-07-2013-0025

Wang, X., & Li, Y. (2016). How Trust and Need Satisfaction Motivate Producing User-Generated Content. *Journal of Computer Information Systems, 57*(1), 49–57. doi:10.1080/08874417.2016.1181493

Weber, L., & Henderson, L. L. (2014). *The Digital Marketer: Ten New Skills You Must Learn to Stay Relevant and Customer-Centric.* John Wiley & Sons Inc.

Webster, J. G. (2014). *Marketplace of Attention: How Audiences Take Shape in a Digital Age.* MIT Press.

Weiger, W. H., Wetzel, H. A., & Hammerschmidt, M. (2017). Leveraging marketer-generated appeals in online brand communities: An individual user-level analysis. *Journal of Service Management*, *28*(1), 133–156. doi:10.1108/JOSM-11-2015-0378

Wen, I. (2009). Factors affecting the online travel buying decision: A review. *International Journal of Contemporary Hospitality Management*, *21*(6), 752–765. doi:10.1108/09596110910975990

Williams, R., van der Wiele, T., van Iwaarden, J., & Eldridge, S. (2010). The importance of user-generated content: The case of hotels. *The TQM Journal*, *22*(2), 117–128. doi:10.1108/17542731011024246

Willis, E., & Wang, Y. (2016). Blogging the brand: Meaning transfer and the case of Weight Watchers' online community. *Journal of Brand Management*, *23*(4), 457–471. doi:10.1057/bm.2016.16

Wood, N. T., & Burkhalter, J. N. (2014). Tweet this, not that: A comparison between brand promotions in microblogging environments using celebrity and company-generated tweets. *Journal of Marketing Communications*, *20*(1-2), 129–146. doi:10.1080/13527266.2013.797784

Xie, K., & Lee, Y. (2015). Social Media and Brand Purchase: Quantifying the Effects of Exposures to Earned and Owned Social Media Activities in a Two-Stage Decision Making Model. *Journal of Management Information Systems*, *32*(2), 204–238. doi:10.1080/07421222.2015.1063297

Xie, K. L., Zhang, Z., Zhang, Z., Singh, A., & Lee, S. K. (2016). Effects of managerial response on consumer eWOM and hotel performance: Evidence from TripAdvisor. *International Journal of Contemporary Hospitality Management*, *28*(9), 2013–2034. doi:10.1108/IJCHM-06-2015-0290

Xue, F., & Zhou, P. (2010). 2011; "The Effects of Product Involvement and Prior Experience on Chinese Consumers' Responses to Online Word of Mouth. *Journal of International Consumer Marketing*, *23*(1), 45–58. doi:10.1080/08961530.2011.524576

Yadav, M., Kamboj, S., & Rahman, Z. (2016). Customer co-creation through social media: The case of 'Crash the Pepsi IPL 2015'. *Journal of Direct, Data and Digital Marketing Practice*, *17*(4), 259–271. doi:10.1057/dddmp.2016.4

Yan, Y. & Du, S. (2016). Empirical Study for the Influence Factors of Customer Satisfaction Based on B2C Online Shopping. *Revista Ibérica de Sistemas e Tecnologias de Informação, E14*, 300.

Yang, J., Zheng, R., Zhao, L., & Gupta, S. (2017). Enhancing customer brand experience and loyalty through enterprise microblogs: Empirical evidence from a communication framework perspective. *Information Technology & People*, *30*(3), 580–601. doi:10.1108/ITP-09-2015-0219

Yeh, C. (2015). Online word-of-mouth as a predictor of television rating. *Online Information Review*, *39*(6), 831–847. doi:10.1108/OIR-01-2015-0033

Yoo, B., Donthu, N., & Lee, S. (2000). An examination of selected marketing mix elements and brand equity. *Journal of the Academy of Marketing Science*, *28*(2), 195–211. doi:10.1177/0092070300282002

Yoon, S., & Han, H. (2012). Experiential approach to the determinants of online word-of-mouth behavior. *Journal of Global Scholars of Marketing Science*, *22*(3), 218–234. doi:10.1080/21639159.2012.699219

Zahay, D. (2015). *The impact of digital shopping channels on multi-channel marketing and attribution in the changing retail landscape*. Emerald Group Publishing Ltd.

Zhan, Y., Liu, R., Li, Q., Leischow, S. J., & Zeng, D. D. (2017). Identifying Topics for E-Cigarette User-Generated Contents: A Case Study From Multiple Social Media Platforms. *Journal of Medical Internet Research*, *19*(1), e24. doi:10.2196/jmir.5780 PMID:28108428

Zhang, X., Yu, Y., Li, H., & Lin, Z. (2016). Sentimental interplay between structured and unstructured user-generated contents. *Online Information Review*, *40*(1), 119–145. doi:10.1108/OIR-04-2015-0101

Zhang, Z., Ye, Q., Song, H., & Liu, T. (2015). The structure of customer satisfaction with cruise-line services: An empirical investigation based on online word of mouth. *Current Issues in Tourism*, *18*(5), 450–464. doi:10.1080/13683500.2013.776020

Zheng, X., Cheung, C. M. K., Lee, M. K. O., & Liang, L. (2015). Building brand loyalty through user engagement in online brand communities in social networking sites. *Information Technology & People*, *28*(1), 90–106. doi:10.1108/ITP-08-2013-0144

Zhou, W., & Duan, W. (2015). An empirical study of how third-party websites influence the feedback mechanism between online Word-of-Mouth and retail sales. *Decision Support Systems*, *76*, 14–23. doi:10.1016/j.dss.2015.03.010

KEY TERMS AND DEFINITIONS

Brand-Oriented UGC: Brand-oriented UGC is any content related to a brand and created by a user with the purpose of sharing content with others using social media tools.

Consumer Buying Behavior: The total buying behavior of the ultimate consumer when purchasing a product or service.

Consumer Engagement: Consumer engagement is an action-oriented relationship and commitment that extends beyond purchasing.

Customer Trust: A belief in the given content of a social commerce organisation that enhances e-word-of-mouth and the purchase intentions of customers. Customers are more likely to buy from people they trust or purchase a product or service that performs what it claims.

E-Word-of-Mouth: E-word-of-mouth can be described as a deliberate influencer of customer-to-customer interactions using online social networking tools. Consumers can generate online content and share such content with their online networks with the purpose of creating word-of-mouth reviews for brands.

Social Media Networks/Platforms: Groups of internet-based applications that facilitate the creation and exchange of personal information or contents or participating in a social networking User-Generated Content

User-Generated Content: UGC is any form of digital content users generated and shared online with other users. These contents produced can be viewed and shared by other users of the service or websites.

Chapter 19
Best Practices of News and Media Web Design:
An Analysis of Content Structure, Multimedia, Social Sharing, and Advertising placements

Sonya Zhang
California State Polytechnic University, Pomona, USA

Hannah Morgia
California State Polytechnic University, Pomona, USA

Samuel Lee
California State Polytechnic University, Pomona, USA

Kelli Lawrence
California State Polytechnic University, Pomona, USA

Karen Hovsepian
California State Polytechnic University, Pomona, USA

Natalie Lawrence
California State Polytechnic University, Pomona, USA

Ashish Hingle
California State Polytechnic University, Pomona, USA

ABSTRACT

As more print media move to online, news and media websites have evolved with increasing complexity in content, design, and monetization strategies. In this article, the authors examined and reported the web design patterns of 150 leading news and media websites in six different categories: TV news, online newspapers, online magazines, and technology news, sports news, and business news, using 28 analytics metrics in four dimensions: content structure, multimedia, social sharing, and advertising placements.

DOI: 10.4018/978-1-6684-6287-4.ch019

INTRODUCTION

Print media like magazines and newspapers have been declining significantly over the years, and forced to adapt to increasing Internet readership and online competition by creating their own online websites and apps in addition to physical products (News Media Alliance, n.d.; State of the Media, 2010). As with many substantial businesses that dominate the Internet today, these news delivering and media websites evolve to become more like lifestyle brand businesses.

Simply adding an online platform isn't panacea for saving traditional news and media businesses - online news and media industry have grown significantly and become one of the most competitive ones (Pew Project for Excellence in Journalism, 2013). WordPress, the most popular open source Content Management System (CMS) powers 75 million websites, about 18% of all, and it provides even small and niche businesses the opportunity to create an impact with a modern and professional-looking website optimized for search engines and accessible to online readers worldwide. From year 2000 to 2017 the global Internet users have jumped from 400 million to 3.7 billion. In 2017, every minute of the day, Google receives 3.6 million search queries, YouTube users watch over 4 million videos, Facebook users share 2.46 million pieces of content, Instagram users post 46,740 new photos, Twitter users send over 456,000 tweets (Domo, 2017). The more content that is published, the more difficult it becomes to attract traffic, which is the lifeline to online news and media businesses. While top news and media brands like CNN.com and Huffington Post dominate the organic search results, others suffer from low visibility. Majority of content published on the Internet is of poor quality or redundant, very few of them received social shares or interaction, and even fewer had backlinks or outbound links (Buzzsumo, 2015). It is more critical now than ever to not only create compelling content but also deliver them via an effective web design.

Our study focuses on the best practices of leading news and media websites, in particular, their web design strategies in content structure, multimedia, social sharing, and advertisement placement. Novice news and media websites without much web design or analytics resources could benefit from adopting these best practices, thus improve search engine optimization (SEO), user experience, and monetization effectively.

LITERATURE REVIEW

Previous studies on content and media web design were either conceptual (Hasan & Abuelrub, 2011) or case studies of a single website (Singh et al., 2014). This limitation is probably due to the difficulty of gaining access to the internal analytics data. In this study we focus on the web design practice of reputable and popular websites across six categories. Since we do not have access to the internal analytics data such as visitor traffic, page views, or ad revenue, we focus on four predominant dimensions that we are able to collect from the user interfaces: content structure, multimedia, social sharing, and ad placements.

Content Structure

Search engines like Google covered a list of common areas for webmasters to optimize platform and delivery of their content, and specially emphasized the importance of SEO friendly content structure, such as using keywords reinforced page title and meta tags, headlines, image alt attributes, self-documenting semantic URLs, well-selected internal and external links, effective navigation, as well as well-structured articles, including attractive article title, appropriate excerpt and length. When strategically designed, these elements can further signal relevance and significance of content topics to the search engines thereby help reinforce search rankings and increase traffic (Zhang & Cabage, 2016).

Internal links are hyperlinks on a website pointing to other pages on the same site. Internal links are important to the success and integrity of the website because they give visitors more ways to move through the website and access the content they are looking for (Bourne, 2013). External links on the other hand refer to links added to original website that connect to other sites. External links may help build up inbound links or backlinks that come from relevant and authoritative websites help drive up source website's search engine rankings (Bourne, 2013). Both internal and external links are a critical part of strategic SEO plan that makes a news and media website successful.

Both page title and meta descriptions are useful because they often dictate how the pages are shown in search results. The most effective page titles are about 10-70 characters long, including spaces. For optimum effectiveness, meta descriptions should be 160-300 characters long. Page titles and meta descriptions should be concise and contain the best keywords. Each page of the website should have its own exclusive title and meta description (SEOQuake, n.d.).

Article structure influence readership. Article titles should be short and attention grabbing, "as a stylistic and narrative luring device trying to induce anticipation and curiosity so the readers click (or tap on) the headline and read on" (Blom & Hansen, 2015). The length of an article has become part of the new publishing strategy as well. The world's largest independent news organization, the Associated Press, has told its journalists to keep their stories between 300 and 500 words, with only exceptions in the top one or two stories (between 500 and 700 words), the top global stories of the day (700-plus words), and the investigative units (Farhi, 2014).

A few popular news websites like LA Times in 2015 and Fox News in 2016 have started using infinite page on their websites. The basic functionality of infinite page, some called long scrolling page, is that as the user scrolls through content, more content is loaded automatically. Infinite scrolling offers an efficient way to browse massive amounts of data in real time without having to wait for pages to preload (Ahuvia, 2013). However not all the websites have joined the trend, concerning the drawbacks such as users feeling overwhelmed, disoriented or lack of control as they travel down a page that seemingly never ends.

Multimedia

Multimedia such as images and videos help effectively communicate content to readers and create a better user experience than plain text. High-quality photographs of products and well-chosen images generate consumer confidence (Wang & Emurian, 2005). Main images play an important role in shaping user aesthetic reactions to a homepage (Djamasbi, Siegel, & Tullis, 2014). The more a page is visually appealing, the more users trust its informational content (Djamasbi et al., 2010). From design aspect, images and colors, and text should be appropriately balanced on each web page to create positive user experience (Hasan & Abuelrub, 2011).

Videos on websites have a similar effect with images. Videos should complement stories, rather than repeating the offerings of streamed news or the content of an accompanying text story (Hermida, 2007). The trend of using large, full-screen background videos in web design has been growing to enrich user experience, such as videos showing happy customers enjoying the product or service, or the process of creating a high-tech and complex product (Wolter, 2015). However, large size of image, sound or video on page should also be avoided because they cause choppy or slow connections and leave visitors a poor first impression (Signore, 2005).

Sliders and carousels are becoming more and more popular way to display images and videos in modern web designs (Cronin, 2009). With slider or carousel navigations, the content rotates vertically or horizontally. The user clicks on one of two toggle elements (usually a left/right or up/down arrow) and the content (can be static images or image links to videos) is rotated in the desired direction. Sliders and carousel is an excellent way to display information such as images and videos in an organized and compact manner, and more importantly, it allows publishers expand the usage of limited screen space.

Social Sharing

As people are spending more time socializing online, businesses leverage social media management and mining to engage customers, influence brand awareness and brand reputation, accelerating viral marketing, and build core business competencies of strategy development (Gupta & Gupta, 2016; Montalvo, 2016). In light of that, social media has transformed the speed and magnitude of information transfer for the world of news and media (Hermida et al., 2012; Ju et al., 2013). In addition to establishing and managing social presence such as Facebook page and Twitter account, news and media websites have been gradually moving reader conversation from traditional comments or discussion forums to social media over the years. There are multiple motivations behind the popular social sharing and decline of comments:

- **Cost:** It gets more expensive to monitor and moderate the more comments that are posted. For example, in some months comment moderation has cost NPR twice what was budgeted although it is serving a very small slice of its overall audience (Jensen, 2016).
- **Social Network Effect:** Users are not only getting news from news publishers and journalists, but also from people and organizations they follow on social media like Facebook and Twitter. Social media helps amplify content more than traditional reader comments. With a single click, a person can share their current readings with family, friends, and public, who can see, respond, or share further. For example, 5 million people each month engage with NPR on Twitter, compared to just a fraction of that number in the NPR.org comments (Jensen, 2016). Also, discussions via social media tend to be more civil, most likely because users are required to use their own names (not that fake accounts don't get through, but there seem to be far fewer than the predominantly fake names that traditional commenters currently rely on).
- **More Monetization Incentive for Publishers:** Online news and media publishers constantly experiment to find out which types of articles (e.g., topics, word counts, and titles) attract more readership and social sharing. The incentive is clear: the number of times an article is shared via social media is usually strongly correlated with page views, and page views are highly correlated with ad revenue for the publishers.
- **Less SEO Motivation for Commenters:** Search engines like Google stopped accounting links posted in the comments, or may even penalize those who constantly build such backlinks for SEO purpose, considering them as deceptive or manipulative link schemes.
- **User-Interest Centered Design:** While search engine retrieves the ranking results based on query keywords, it pays little attention in incorporating user interest, which may impact retrieving qual-

ity data that meet the user's information need (Sethi, 2017). Inheritably representing user interest, social shared content helps disseminating the content to the audience who need or value them.

Ad Placements

In 2010 online news giant Huffington Post generated $30 million revenue, almost all of which was from display advertising. This revenue was generated on roughly 4.8 billion page views, which means the average page view was worth a little more than six-tenths of a cent, or that 1,000 page views were worth about $6.25 (Silver, 2011). In 2014 Huffington Post reached $146 million in revenue. Display ads take forms of banners and pop-ups, and vary in sizes, shapes (vertical, horizontal, square, rectangle) and locations on the page. Google's search engine results page (SERP) and industry heat map results suggest that ad placements above the fold between the top navigation and rich content as well as on the right-hand column or margin are most popular and effective in click-through rate.

While the concept of display advertisements was initially appealing to both businesses and advertisers, early implementation strategies lacked scalability, as the exchanges between companies weren't necessarily rooted in context, meaning that the advertisement often had little to do with the content on the page. This led website visitors to become skeptical of the ads they were seeing, and ultimately resulted in what we know today as "banner blindness" (Hubspot, 2015). In addition, even though contextually relevant banners induce more favorable evaluation and a greater purchase intention toward advertised products than contextually irrelevant counterpart (Jeong, 2010), display ads often stand out from the original website design, and appear annoying to users and causing site abandonment (Goldstein, 2014). Consequently, the existential threat of ad blocking has become a pressing issue to publishers across the world. According to PageFair's 2015 global report on ad blocking, ad blocking grew shockingly by 41% globally to reach 198 million active ad block users, among them US ad blocking grew by 48% to reach 45 million active users, in 12 months up to June 2015. Ad blocking estimated to cost publishers nearly $22 billion during 2015.

These challenges of traditional display ads have driven more and more news and media websites, including Upworthy, Quartz, Complex Media, and Huffington Post, towards native-ads. At the Huffington Post, 30% of revenue comes from native advertising and branded content, according to Chief Executive Jimmy Maymann, while two years ago all of it came from traditional display ads (Wall Street Journal, 2015a). New breed of digital publishers like BuzzFeed and Refinery 29 choose not to curate programmatic (i.e., automated real-time digital ad buying using software) and third-party ads, instead they focus on attracting users with "the deeply engaging content and experiences" (Wall Street Journal 2, 2015b).

Unlike display ads, native ads in digital media offer additional and relevant quality content of paid clients with a more aesthetically pleasing, natural, and non-intrusive method by resembling the design, style, and functionality of the media in which they are disseminated (Federal Trade Commission, n.d.). Therefore, native advertising is seen as a more superior alternative to traditional online banner and pop-up advertorials (Ming & Yazdanifard, 2014).

Native advertising are mostly third party paid advertisements; such as a CNN.com article link "10 Unconventional Ways to Cope with Pain" that re-directs readers to the original full article on Health-Grades.com. Native advertising can also be in-house advertisements, such as a FoxNews.com article link "Peter Thiel: The Insiders Have Been Getting It Wrong" that re-directs readers to the original full article on FoxBusiness.com. Many websites in our study use online content discovery platforms such as OutBrain and Taboola, which specialize in content recommendations and present sponsored website links. Under Federal Trade Commission (FTC) law, advertisers cannot use "deceptive door openers" to induce consumers to view advertising content. Thus, advertisers are responsible for ensuring that native ads are identifiable as advertising before consumers arrive at the main advertising page. In addition, no matter how consumers arrive at advertising content, it must not mislead them about its commercial nature (FTC, n.d.).

METHODOLOGY

Our study focuses on the web design practices of leading news and media. Using Alexa.com, a reputable Amazon-owned web traffic data and analytics company, we selected 150 top websites in six categories: online extension of television news (e.g., CNN.com), online newspapers (e.g., LATimes.com), online magazines (e.g., Wired.com), technology news (e.g., TechCrunch.com), sports news (e.g. ESPN.com), and business news (e.g. Forbes.com). To minimize culture impact, all the websites selected are based in native English-speaking countries, including United States (majority), UK, Canada, and Australia. We then collected data from these websites, specifically from three types of web pages for each website: the homepage (e.g.), a category page (e.g.), and a headline article page (e.g.,). Data was collected using 28 metrics in four dimensions: content structure, multimedia, social sharing, and advertisement placement. Finally, we analyzed the data, explored the patterns, and generalized the best practices in each category and across all categories of news and media websites. Figure 1 shows our research methodology.

Figure 1. Research Methodology

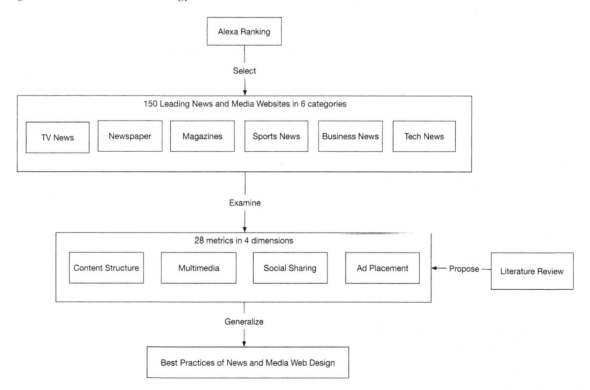

As mentioned above, we developed 28 metrics in 4 dimensions based upon previous studies in the literature review section. They are:

Content structure:
- # of internal links
- # of external links
- # of words in headline article title
- # of words in full article on the article page i.e. length of article
- # of words in article excerpt
- # of characters in page title
- # of characters in meta description
- Key phrases used in page title – yes or no
  ◦ e.g. Key phrases like "Technology" and "News" are used in the page title of TechCrunch.com (Technology News category) home page.
- Key phrases used in meta description – yes or no
- Frequency of top stories - hourly, daily, weekly, monthly
- Infinite page - yes or no

Multimedia:
- # of images
- # of videos
- # of sliders or carousel
- # of images/videos per slider
- Location of feature image
  ◦ Use 3x3 grid, choose one or multiple from Top Left, Top Middle, Top Right, Middle Left, Middle Middle, Middle Right, Bottom Left, Bottom Middle, Bottom Right.

Social Sharing:
- Types of social presence of the website itself
  ◦ e.g. CNN Facebook, CNN Twitter
- Types of social sharing options
  ◦ e.g. Facebook like, Facebook share, Twitter tweet
- Types of social interaction options
  ◦ Comment, discussion forums

Ad Placements:
- # of display ads
- # of video ads
- # of pop-up ads
- Location of the display ads
- Size of the display ads - vertical banner, horizontal banner, or square (other)
- Context relevant display ads
- # of native ads
- Location of the native ads

- # of images used for native ads

Collecting data from multiple news and media websites was complicated and challenging because each website applied different styles, which also kept changing over time. In addition, it was a great amount of content and elements to be parsed, categorized, and counted. We used a combination of software tools such as SEOquake and Mozbars and manual processing.

RESULT ANALYSIS AND DISCUSSION

Content Structure

As Table 1 shows, we find many common patterns (i.e., no statistically significance) across all six categories in regard to Content Structure. Figure 2 shows internal and external links usage across different types of web pages and categories. We find that there are generally about three to four times more internal links than external links on any news and media web page. As discussed in the literature review, internal links is good SEO practice and helps retain readers. External links may help generate inbound links or backlinks sometimes however the tradeoff is by clicking the external link, the reader leaves the original website. We also notice that there are usually more links on home pages than category pages, and more on category page than article page on any website.

We find that the headline article title is usually about 10-12 words long, and the length of a headline article ranges from 500 to 700 words for websites in most categories except Online Magazine and Technology News categories, which are around 1,000 words. According to Burch (2001), "a magazine is different than a newspaper in content and style, because of the way in which it is produced and who it is produced for. Because people who subscribe to magazines usually are on a break, or plan on spending some time reading the magazine at their leisure, (therefore, having plenty of time to browse) an article can be longer than it ordinarily would be in a newspaper." Interestingly the average length of article excerpts for online newspaper articles in our study is noticeably larger than the ones for online magazine articles. In addition, subscription is required to all online newspapers and magazines in order to read the full length of articles, so the online version may not fully represent their print version. We didn't find studies on the length of technology news articles, but we propose that they may need to be more detailed hence longer than other types of news articles due to the complex nature of technology topics.

Key phrases are used in both page title and meta description of all websites to optimize SEO. In regards to length, meta description runs longer than page title. Take Economist.com in Business News category for example, its title tag is <title data-react-helmet="true">The Economist - World News, Politics, Economics, Business &amp, Finance</title>, and its meta description is "<meta data-react-helmet="true" name="description" content="The Economist offers authoritative insight and opinion on international news, politics, business, finance, science, technology and the connections between them."/>. Fresh content helps attract readers to come back visit often. Most websites publish their top stories hourly on home page and daily on category and article page. Websites in Online TV news and Newspaper categories publish more often than websites in other categories, mostly due to a larger number of journalists and reporters working for TV news and newspaper organizations. We did not measure the amount of content in this study but we noticed home page of websites in Online TV and Newspaper categories seem publish more content as well, maybe due to the same reason.

Table 1. Best Practice in Content Structure

Category	# of internal links	# of external links	# of words in headline article title	# of words in full article on the article page	# of words in article excerpt	# of characters in page title	Key phrases used in page title	# of characters in meta description	Key phrases used in meta description	Frequency of top stories	Infinite page
TV News Home Page	205	53	n/a	n/a	15	55	Yes	150	Yes	hourly	No
TV News Category Page	152	38	n/a	n/a	21	45	Yes	101	Yes	daily	No
TV News Article Page	112	45	11	629	15	109	Yes	182	Yes	hourly	No
Newspaper Home Page	260	72	n/a	n/a	24	92	Yes	158	Yes	hourly	No
Newspaper Category Page	198	68	n/a	n/a	19	75	Yes	133	Yes	daily	No
Newspaper Article Page	160	72	12	669	18	131	Yes	190	Yes	hourly	No
Magazine Home Page	187	55	n/a	n/a	10	116	Yes	139	Yes	hourly	No
Magazine Category Page	111	34	n/a	n/a	17	120	Yes	107	Yes	daily	No
Magazine Article Page	95	49	10	1005	6	157	Yes	137	Yes	daily	No
Sports Home Page	243	88	n/a	n/a	18	58	Yes	135	Yes	hourly	No
Sports Category Page	206	82	n/a	n/a	19	46	Yes	78	Yes	daily	No
Sports Article Page	169	60	22	514	15	61	Yes	123	Yes	daily	No
Tech News Home Page	157	64	n/a	n/a	20	49	Yes	132	Yes	hourly	No
Tech News Category Page	132	38	n/a	n/a	20	41	Yes	76	Yes	hourly	No
Tech News Article Page	98	56	10	1971	18	68	Yes	177	Yes	daily	No
Business News Home Page	182	61	n/a	n/a	15	32	Yes	133	Yes	hourly	No
Business News Category Page	140	58	n/a	n/a	17	43	Yes	100	Yes	daily	No
Business News Article Page	100	74	11	664	18	50	Yes	120	Yes	daily	No

* All the numeric metrics use average. For example, on average the homepage of a leading TV News website has 205 internal links.

* All the non-numeric metrics use only the values/modes that occurred most than 50% of the time. For example, more than 50% of the homepage of a leading news and media website is updated hourly, or more than 50% of the websites are not infinite page.

Multimedia

Table 2 shows the results of Multimedia. Figure 3 shows images and videos across different types of web pages and categories. We find that there are about four to ten times more images than videos on any news and media web page. Interestingly, online newspapers such as LATimes.com and NYTimes.com lead in the number of images published per page, while online extension of television news such as CNN.com and BBC.com lead in the number of videos published per page, indicating the media origination of the publishers may influence their website design strategy. We also noticed that Tech News websites have the highest number of images than other categories, coordinating with that they also have the longest headline articles in Content Structure. Perhaps they find images help ease and entertain complex technical topics. In addition, there are usually more images and videos on home pages than category pages, and more on category page than article page on most websites, except for the ones in Online Magazine category, which has more on article page than category page.

Sliders or carousels that contain multiple images or videos are seen on some websites in Online TV News category and Online Newspaper category (15-17 images in one slider or carousel), however they are not popular in other categories. Sliders and carousels allow publishers expand the usage of limited screen space, so they can be more useful for TV news and Newspaper websites which tend to have more content.

For most websites, feature image is mostly located on the top left or top middle, accompanying the linked title and excerpt of the feature article. Such locations correspond to the Google SERP and heat map results to attract readership.

Figure 2. Internal & External Links Across Page and Categories

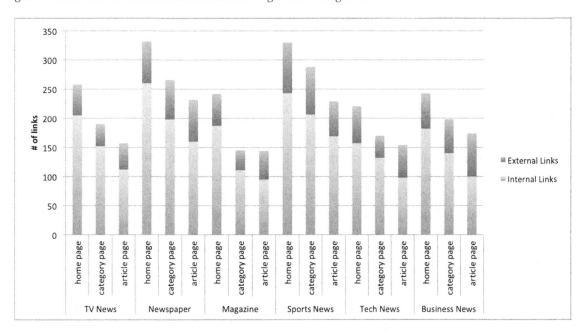

Table 2. Best Practice in Multimedia

Category	# of images per page	# of videos per page	# of sliders or carousels	# of images/ videos per slider	Location of feature image
TV News Home Page	37	9	1	5	Top Left
TV News Category Page	29	8	0	0	Top Left, Top Middle
TV News Article Page	22	5	0	0	Top Left, Top Middle
Newspaper Home Page	47	3	1	17	Top Middle
Newspaper Category Page	34	1	0	0	Top Middle
Newspaper Article Page	18	1	1	15	Top Middle
Magazine Home Page	34	3	0	0	Top Middle
Magazine Category Page	22	1	0	0	Top Middle
Magazine Article Page	34	2	0	0	Top Middle
Sports Home Page	48	8	0	0	Top Middle, Middle Middle
Sports Category Page	41	6	0	0	Top Middle, Middle Middle
Sports Article Page	27	4	0	0	Top Middle, Middle Middle
Tech News Home Page	58	1	0	0	Top Left
Tech News Category Page	39	1	0	0	Top Middle
Tech News Article Page	38	2	0	0	Top Middle
Business News Home Page	47	1	0	0	Top Left
Business News Category Page	36	1	0	0	Top Left
Business News Article Page	32	1	0	0	Top Middle

* All the numeric metrics use average. For example, on average the homepage of a leading TV News website has 37 images and 9 videos.

* All the non-numeric metrics use only the values/modes that occurred most than 50% of the time. For example, more than 50% of the homepage of a leading TV News website places the feature image on top left.

* The value 0 is mostly rounded result for an average that is less than 0.5. For example, the average # of slider would be 0.36 for 9 instances on the category page of 25 TV news websites.

* Outliers will also be taken out to prevent skewing the results. For example, ESPN's infinite pages would skew average image and video count.

Social Sharing

Table 3 shows the results of Social Presence, Social Sharing, and Social Interaction. We find that all the websites have social presence in Facebook and Twitter, and their social presence buttons are mostly located in the footer of every web page. Some popular journalists also have their own Facebook and Twitter presence provided right next to their name under the article they wrote.

Figure 3 shows the types and usage of social sharing options in all 150 websites. All the websites keenly implement social sharing buttons, reader comments, and personalized content to create new and retain current users. In particular, we find a significant number of social sharing options on the article page for most the websites in all categories. Figure 3 shows the types and usage of social sharing options in total of 150 websites. Popular social sharing options include Facebook (used in 145 or 96.7% of websites), Twitter (53 or 35.3%), Google+ (53 or 35.3%), LinkedIn (53 or 35.3%), Pinterest (42 or 28%), and Reddit (36 or 24%). Among all categories, Online Magazine websites boast the most (12) social sharing options: Facebook, Twitter, Google+, LinkedIn, Pinterest, Reddit, Tumblr, Instagram, Stumpleupon, Flipboard, Snapchat, and Youtube.

Table 3. Best Practice in Social Presence, Social Sharing, and Social Interaction

Category	Types of social media presence of the original website	Types of social sharing options of articles	Types of social interaction options
TV News Home Page	Facebook, Twitter	n/a	n/a
TV News Category Page	Facebook, Twitter	n/a	n/a
TV News Article Page	Facebook, Twitter	Facebook, Twitter	n/a
Newspaper Home Page	Facebook, Twitter	n/a	n/a
Newspaper Category Page	Facebook, Twitter	n/a	n/a
Newspaper Article Page	Facebook, Twitter	Facebook, Twitter, Google+, LinkedIn	Comments
Magazine Home Page	Facebook, Twitter, Instagram	n/a	n/a
Magazine Category Page	Facebook, Twitter, Instagram	n/a	n/a
Magazine Article Page	Facebook, Twitter, Instagram	Facebook, Twitter	n/a
Sports Home Page	Facebook, Twitter	Facebook	n/a
Sports Category Page	Facebook, Twitter	Facebook	n/a
Sports Article Page	Facebook, Twitter	Facebook	n/a
Tech News Home Page	Facebook, Twitter	n/a	n/a
Tech News Category Page	Facebook, Twitter	n/a	n/a
Tech News Article Page	Facebook, Twitter	Facebook, Twitter	Comments
Business News Home Page	Facebook, Twitter	n/a	n/a
Business News Category Page	Facebook, Twitter	n/a	n/a
Business News Article Page	Facebook, Twitter	Facebook, Twitter	n/a

* All the non-numeric metrics use only the values/modes that occurred most than 50% of the time. For example, more than 50% of the article page of a leading news and media website has Facebook as a social sharing option.

Figure 3. Images & Videos Across Page and Categories

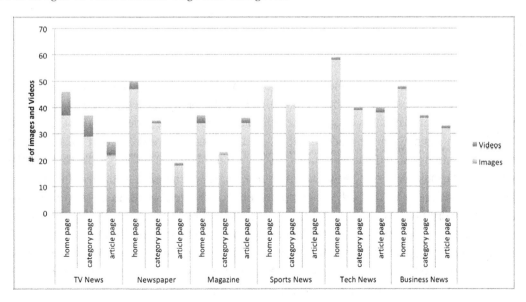

On article pages, social sharing options such as Facebook like, Facebook share, and Twitter tweets also significantly exceed traditional social interacting options such as commenting systems or discussion forums. CNN.com had replaced comments and forums with social sharing only. Among those websites that have kept the comments feature, NYTimes.com opens only 10 percent of its articles for comments, and keeps the comment threads open for just one week. Unlike article pages, which provide detailed content that can be shared, home pages and category pages usually provide only excerpts, headlines, and links to full content, so they rarely present any comments or social sharing options. Figure 4 shows the types and usage of social sharing.

Figure 4. Types & Usage of Social Sharing

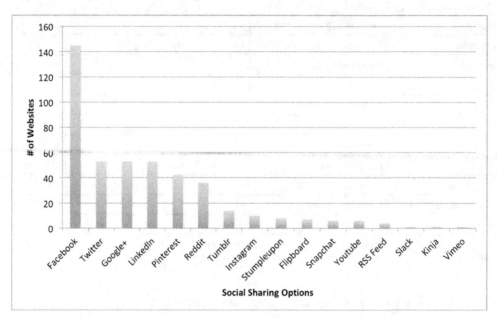

Ad Placements

Table 2 shows the results of Ad Placement. Figure 5 shows display and native ads across different types of web pages and categories. The number of display ads significantly exceeds video ads and popup ads. This may be due to performance concerns – as discussed previously, video ads can slow down page display, and popup ads may annoy readers. Although display ads are required by FTC to be labeled as "Advertisement", almost all of them use smaller font size and subtle font color as close to the background as possible. Display ads are consistently placed on top middle of the page as horizontal banner ad and on the top left as square or vertical ad – as discussed previously these areas are most frequently visited and clicked by general readers.

As discussed previously, display ads that are contextually relevant to the content are more effective. Interestingly, display ads on websites with special topics such as Sports News, Technology News, and Business News are mostly contextually relevant. For examples, Economist.com in the Business News category displays Ernst & Young's ad, TechCrunch.com in the Technology News category displays an ad of a private investment company, SharesPost, and ESPN.com in the Sports News category displays

Capital One credit card ad that features a national championship. Other news and media websites that cover a variety of topics such as TV news, newspaper and magazine just display mostly Google ads targeting audience interests although irrelevant to the website content.

Native ads are known to help create better user experience and generate ad revenue more effectively. While more than half of the websites in our study did not deploy any native ads, those who did actually published a significant amount of native ads throughout the website. For example, CNN.com has 34 on home page, 13 on category page, and an astonishing 45 native ads on its article page. These native ads are usually placed on the bottom of a web page (true to all websites in this study that use native ads), in blocks or groups of 4-5 ad links, with each block below an image, with similar look and feel with the original website. These native ads are also required by FTC to be labeled such as "Paid Content", "Paid Partner Content", "Sponsored", or "Recommended by Outbrain". Outbrain is an online advertiser specializing in presenting sponsored website links. Table 4 shows the best practices in ad placement.

With the above result analysis and discussion, we can provide design recommendations to a novice news and media website in a specific category. For example: The best design for the homepage of a tech news website should have about 157 Internal links, 64 external links, 10 words in the article title, 1980 words in the full article, 20 words in the article excerpt. 49 characters in the page title, 132 characters in meta description, key phrased enforced title and meta tags, and hourly update on top stories. The homepage should use 58 images, 1 video, no slideshows, no infinite scrolling, with banner locations on the Top Middle, Top Right, & Middle Right, and feature image location on the top left. For social media, there should be Facebook and Twitter social presence buttons on the homepage. Social sharing options on home page are not needed, only on article page instead. For advertisement, there should be 5 display ads, no video or pop ads, with location of display ads on Top Middle, Top Right, and Middle Right, in a mix of horizontal banner ads and squared ads. If the website decide to use native ads, the ideal amount should be 4 ad links, each should have an image on top.

Figure 5. Display & Native Ads Across Page and Categories

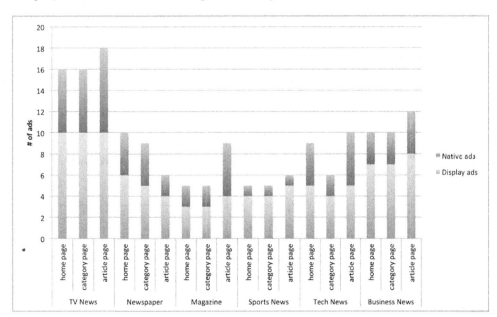

Table 4. Best Practices in Ad Placement

Category	Advertisement								
	# of display ads	# of video ads	# of pop-up ads	Location of the display ads	Size of the display ads	Context relevant display ads	# of native ads	Location of the native ads	# of images used for native ads
TV News Home Page	10	0	0	Top Middle, Top Right	Horizontal, Square	No	6	Bottom Middle	4
TV News Category Page	10	0	0	Top Middle, Top Right	Horizontal, Square	No	6	Bottom Middle	4
TV News Article Page	10	0	0	Top Middle, Top Right	Horizontal, Square	No	8	Middle Middle, Middle Left, Bottom Left, Bottom Middle	5
Newspaper Home Page	6	0	0	Top Middle, Top Right, Middle Right, Bottom Middle	Horizontal, Vertical	No	4	Bottom Middle	2
Newspaper Category Page	5	0	0	Top Middle, Top Right, Middle Right, Bottom Middle	Horizontal, Vertical	No	4	Bottom Middle	1
Newspaper Article Page	4	0	0	Top Middle, Top Right, Middle Right	Horizontal, Vertical	No	2	Bottom Left, Bottom Middle	3
Magazine Home Page	3	0	0	Top Middle	Horizontal	No	2	Bottom Middle	1
Magazine Category Page	3	0	0	Top Middle, Bottom Middle	Horizontal, Square	No	2	Bottom Middle	1
Magazine Article Page	4	0	0	Top Middle	Horizontal, Square	No	5	Bottom Middle	5
Sports Home Page	4	0	0	Top Middle	Horizontal	Yes	1	n/a	n/a
Sports Category Page	4	0	0	Top Middle	Horizontal	Yes	1	n/a	n/a
Sports Article Page	5	0	0	Top Middle	Horizontal	Yes	1	n/a	n/a
Tech News Home Page	5	0	0	Top Middle, Top Right, Middle Right	Horizontal, Square	Yes	4	Bottom Middle	1
Tech News Category Page	4	0	0	Top Middle, Top Right, Middle Right)	Horizontal, Square	Yes	2	Bottom Middle	1
Tech News Article Page	5	0	0	Top Middle, Top Right, Middle Right	Horizontal, Square	Yes	5	Bottom Middle	4
Business News Home Page	7	0	0	Top Middle, Top Right	Horizontal, Square	Yes	3	n/a	n/a
Business News Category Page	7	0	0	Top Middle, Top Right	Horizontal, Square	Yes	3	n/a	n/a
Business News Article Page*	8	0	0	Top Middle, Top Right	Horizontal, Square	Yes	4	n/a	n/a

* All the numeric metrics use average. For example, on average the homepage of a leading TV News website has 7 display ads.
* All the non-numeric metrics use only the values/modes that occurred most than 50% of the time. For example, ads on more than 50% of the homepage of a leading TV News website are horizontal and square.
* The value 0 is mostly rounded result for an average that is less than 0.5. For example, the average # of video ads would be 0.4 for 10 instances on the home page of 25 TV news website.

LIMITATION AND FUTURE STUDY

Due to the various and complicate design of the websites in our study, we had to rely a lot on the manual data collection. As the result, it is likely that we had miscounted a number of elements. In addition, websites change design all the time, every day, even minute, even at the same moment, various version may be delivered to the audience as A/B testing or multi-variant experiment for the purpose of optimization. Lastly, the more data we collect the more accurate we would see the results. For future study we would like to collect data of more pages from more websites.

CONCLUSION

News and media websites are continuing to evolve for better. There's a lot to consider when planning a user friendly and conversion effective web design. Industry leaders like the 150 websites in our study learn and optimize through constant and diligent experiments and analytics with the help of industry experts. Examining and learning their best practices will help many online news and media publishers improve their design strategies. Our study finds that a large number of internal links, images, as well as social sharing options are used on the leading news and media websites to attract readership and enhance user experience. The placement of click-through effective display ads and native ads are usually well integrated with original content. The trend of news and media website design will continue evolving to improve user experience, thereby attract traffic, optimize monetization and obtain market share.

REFERENCES

W3Schools. (2018). *Browser display statistics*. Retrieved from https://www.w3schools.com/browsers/browsers_display.asp

Ahuvia, Y. (2013, May 3). Infinite scrolling: Let's get to the bottom of this. *Smashingmagazine*. Retrieved from https://www.smashingmagazine.com/2013/05/infinite-scrolling-lets-get-to-the-bottom-of-this/

Blom, J. N., & Hansen, K. R. (2015). Click bait: Forward-reference as lure in online news headlines. *Journal of Pragmatics*, *76*(1), 87–100. doi:10.1016/j.pragma.2014.11.010

Borun, J. (2013, October 25). Inbound, outbound, and internal website links. *Bourncreative*. Retrieved from https://www.bourncreative.com/the-real-story-about-inbound-outbound-and-internal-website-links/

Burch, C. (2001, November 1). Newspaper vs. magazine: Which kind of writer are you? *Writerswrite*. Retrieved from https://www.writerswrite.com/journal/nov01/newspaper-vs-magazine-which-kind-of-writer-are-you-11015

Buzzsumo. (2015). *Content, shares and links: What we learnt from 1m posts*. Retrieved from http://marketing.buzzsumo.com/link-study/

Cronin, M. (2009). Sliders in web design: When and how to use them. *Smashingmagazine*. Retrieved from https://www.smashingmagazine.com/2009/03/sliders-in-web-design-when-and-how-to-use-them/

Djamasbi, S., Siegel, M., Tulli, T., & Dai, R. (2010). Efficiency, trust, and visual appeal: usability testing through eye tracking. In *Proceedings from HICSS '10: The 43rd Hawaii International Conference on System Sciences*, Honolulu, HI. 10.1109/HICSS.2010.171

Djamasbi, S., Siegel, M., & Tullis, T. (2014). Can fixation on main images predict visual appeal of homepages? In *Proceedings from HICCS '14: The 47th Annual Hawaii International Conference on System Sciences*, Waikoloa, HI. 10.1109/HICSS.2014.54

Domo. (2017). *Data never sleeps 5.0*. Retrieved from https://www.domo.com/blog/data-never-sleeps-5/

Farhi, P. (2014). New Associate Press guidelines: Keep it brief. *Washington Post*. Retrieved from https://www.washingtonpost.com/lifestyle/style/new-ap-guidelines-keep-it-brief/2014/05/12/f220f902-d9ff-11e3-bda1-9b46b2066796_story.html?utm_term=.7f6eef86a5dc

Federal Trade Committee (FTC). (n.d.). *Native advertising: A guide for businesses*. Retrieved from https://www.ftc.gov/tips-advice/business-center/guidance/native-advertising-guide-businesses

Goldstein, D. G., Suri, S., McAfee, R. P., Ekstrand-Abueg, M., & Diaz, F. (2014). The economic and cognitive costs of annoying display advertisements. *JMR, Journal of Marketing Research*, *51*(6), 742–752. doi:10.1509/jmr.13.0439

Gupta, V., & Gupta, M. (2016). Social media mining: A new framework and literature review. *International Journal of Business Analytics*, *3*(1), 11–16. doi:10.4018/IJBAN.2016010104

Hasan, L., & Abuelrub, E. (2011). Assessing the quality of web sites. *Applied Computing and Informatics*, *9*(1), 11–29. doi:10.1016/j.aci.2009.03.001

Hermida, A. (2007). How the BBC is experimenting with online video. *Reportr*. Retrieved from http://reportr.net/2007/07/06/how-the-bbc-is-experimenting-with-online-video/

Hermida, A., Fletcher, F., Korell, D., & Logan, D. (2012). Share, like, recommend: Decoding the social media news consumer. *Journalism Studies*, *13*(5), 815–824. doi:10.1080/1461670X.2012.664430

HubSpot. (2015). 20 Display advertising stats that demonstrate digital advertising's evolution. Retrieved from http://blog.hubspot.com/marketing/horrifying-display-advertising-stats

Jensen, E. (2016). NPR website to get rid of comments. *NPR*. Retrieved from http://www.npr.org/sections/ombudsman/2016/08/17/489516952/npr-website-to-get-rid-of-comments

Jeong, Y., & King, C. M. (2010). Impacts of website context relevance on banner advertisement effectiveness. *Journal of Promotion Management*, *16*(3), 247–264. doi:10.1080/10496490903281395

Ju, A., Jeong, S. H., & Chyi, H. I. (2014). Will social media save newspapers? Examining the effectiveness of Facebook and Twitter as news platforms. *Journalism Practice*, *8*(1), 1–17. doi:10.1080/17512786.2013.794022

Ming, W. Q., & Yazdanifard, R. (2014). Native Advertising and Its Effects on Online Advertising. *Global Journal of Human-Social Science: Economics*, *14*(8), 1–5.

Montalvo, R. E. (2016). Social Media Management. *International Journal of Management & Information Systems*, *20*(2), 45–50.

News Media Alliance. (n.d.). *Newspaper circulation volume: Report by the Newspaper Association of America*. Retrieved from http://www.naa.org/Trends-and-Numbers/Circulation-Volume/Newspaper-Circulation-Volume.aspx

PageFair. (2015). *The 2015 ad blocking report*. Retrieved from https://pagefair.com/blog/2015/ad-blocking-report/

Sethi, S., & Dixit, A. (2017). An automatic user interest mining technique for retrieving quality data. *International Journal of Business Analytics*, *4*(2), 18–25. doi:10.4018/IJBAN.2017040104

Signore, O. (2005). A comprehensive model for web sites quality. In *Proceedings from WSE'05: The Seventh IEEE International Symposium on Web Site Evolution*, Budapest, Hungary. 10.1109/WSE.2005.1

Silver, N. (2011, Feb 12). *The economics of blogging and the Huffington Post*. Retrieved from http://fivethirtyeight.blogs.nytimes.com/2011/02/12/the-economics-of-blogging-and-the-huffington-post/

Singh, K. K., Kumar, P., & Mathur, J. (2014). Implementation of a model for websites quality evaluation – DU Website. *International Journal of Innovations & Advancement in Computer Science*, *3*(1), 27–37.

State of the Media. (2010). *The state of the news media: An annual report on American journalism*. Retrieved from http://www.stateofthemedia.org/2010/index.php

Wall Street Journal. (2015a). *BuzzFeed nails the 'Listicle'; What happens next?* Retrieved from http://www.wsj.com/articles/buzzfeed-nails-the-listicle-what-happens-next-1422556723

Wall Street Journal. (2015b). *New breed of digital publishers just say no to ad tech*. Retrieved from http://blogs.wsj.com/cmo/2015/07/28/new-breed-of-digital-publishers-just-say-no-to-ad-tech/

Wang, Y. D., & Emurian, H. H. (2015). An overview of online trust: Concepts, elements, and implications. *Computers in Human Behavior*, *21*(1), 105–125. doi:10.1016/j.chb.2003.11.008

Wolter, A. (2015). *Dos and don'ts for using background videos on your website*. Retrieved from https://undullify.com/dos-and-donts-for-using-background-videos-on-your-website/

Zhang, S., & Cabage, N. (2016). Search engine optimization: Comparison of link building and social sharing. *Journal of Computer Information Systems*, *57*(2), 148–159. doi:10.1080/08874417.2016.1183447

This research was previously published in the International Journal of Business Analytics (IJBAN), 5(4); pages 43-60, copyright year 2018 by IGI Publishing (an imprint of IGI Global).

Chapter 20
Searching the Effects of Viral Marketing via Customer-Based Brand Equity on Purchase Intentions

Asmat Nizam Abdul-Talib

(iD) https://orcid.org/0000-0001-6820-2918

Universiti Utara Malaysia, Malaysia

Sana Arshad

Universiti Utara Malaysia, Malaysia

ABSTRACT

The internet has presented marketers with diverse methods to interact with their target market, and viral marketing is one of those low-cost methods. The purpose of this study is to explore how viral marketing impacts purchase intentions through customer-based brand equity (CBBE) on the basis of models proposed by Aaker and Keller. Social media is one of the essential indicators that influence customers to purchase intensions. However, brand loyalty, one of the important components of CBBE, is studied in terms of customers' purchase intentions. This study focuses on identifying the role of viral marketing in developing positive brand equity in customers' mindsets. A comparison of previous and present CBBE models are also presented in this study.

INTRODUCTION

Viral marketing is marked as an important term in marketing theory. The word viral is derived from the word virus, spreading and multiplying quickly from person to person. According to the past studies of Cobb-Walgren, Ruble and Donthu (1995), Christodoulides and Chernatony (2015), Petrescu, Korgaonkar and Gironda, (2015), Hayes, King, and Ramirez (2016) viral marketing is a strong tool that enables to create curiosity in the possible sales, hence increasing its brand equity. The present study seeks to find

DOI: 10.4018/978-1-6684-6287-4.ch020

out if there is any link between viral marketing and brand equity. Whereas it has been observed that marketing needs are required to be more financially accountable. Owing to this fact there is a need to study the brand's equity's influence on consumers' purchase intention. Consequently, the relation between viral marketing and purchase intention will also be studied.

With internet usage of about 460 million people, Asia ranks the highest in the world. Highest internet penetrations are reflected in developed areas such as North America, Europe, and Australia (Miniwatts Marketing Group, 2017). This indicates that viral marketing has strongly impacted in these parts of the world whereas growth level has shown increased internet usage trends in less developed areas such as Africa and Latin America. Africa has reflected about 900% growth which shows users' acceptance towards attractive marketing activities (Miniwatts Marketing Group, 2017). Viral marketing has provoked innovative methods of low cost and effective advertising. Eventually increasing the target audience widely and broadly but at a very low cost (Gallaugher,1999).

This paper aims to discuss and give a more comprehensive understanding of the viral marketing concept and its impact on the brand equity of the firms with strategies of new product offerings in the market. The core focus is to discuss the significance to evaluate the impact of viral marketing on purchasing intensions and patterns through customer-based brand equity for a firm that wants to achieve a competitive advantage.

By doing so, this research intends to answer the following questions;

RQ1- Is there any relationship between Viral marketing and CBBE?
RQ2- How Viral Marketing in firms can create an impact on consumers' purchase intentions (brand loyalty)?

By providing the relationship between viral marketing and consumer-based brand equity it would empirically examine the relationship between consumers' perception of brand equity towards the intentions to purchase.

Various research scholars have presented their definitions; however, Helms's, (2000) viral marketing approach defines as a piece of information communicated and transmitted via emails to potential users in the social circle (Zakaria & Abdul-Talib, 2011). Viral marketing is key to online advertising, as it stimulates purchase intention. Viral marketing is a predominantly exciting part of research as, even with its global usage, it is a novel unexplored area of marketing. Hotmail, Burger King, Holiday Corporation, and The Blair Witch Project are successful marketing campaigns. Therefore, it is concluded that viral marketing can be used for marketing various industries starting from entertainment to information. Some of the evidence also suggested that viral marketing campaigns work well when it is precise and free. These campaigns are based on three models such as the promotions model, the incentive-based model, and the loyalty-based model. Viral marketing is a two-edged sword, as it can be negative or positive contingent on the circumstances. Although viral marketing is considered to be low-cost methods when it comes to digital marketing the tracking results are costly. In this digital era, though spreading the words to millions around the world through consumers is possible, however, companies who opt for this approach, of course, should remember the ills of marketing too. It provides supports to various marketing activities at its best yet this bug has its worst side too.

Keller (1991) suggested that the role of the mediator is strongly acted by Brand equity for viral marketing and consumer purchase intentions. Primarily it helps in firming the advertising-purchase intention association in two of the factors of viral marketing. Furthermore, the negative effects of viral marketing are also decreased if received by consumers. However, according to Christodoulides and De Chernatony (2010), brand equity can be studied from diverse perspectives such as of the company(firm's), manager and consumer. In this study, the customers' perspective would be studied to determine the effect of viral marketing on customer-based brand equity, and its influence on consumers' purchase intentions.

CONCEPT OF VIRAL MARKETING

Viral marketing or Word of Mouth (WOM) gets its origins since ages in the unavailability of media and internet where the message was spread by the people just like a virus multiplies. The tools positively used these days are the internet and social media. Today social media marketing is more efficient than before where it was spread orally. As it spreads the message over to 1 million people, and the message might stay for several years. But unfortunately, viral marketing influence is decreased, because of the reason that people have seen it all. This is the reason why the message should have a unique selling proposition (USP) and should create a differentiation than that of a competitor. To get competent viral marketing, a brand needs to be fascinating, the marketing must be effectively timely targeted (Abdul-Latif & Abdul-Talib, 2017; Abdul-Talib & Abdul-Latif, 2015; Salmenkivi & Nyman, 2007).

Advertisements such as (billboards, ads, commercials, discounts, promotions) create excitements for customers, if the reactions are extremely strong (positive/negative), customer habitually desires to share this with others via online through social media. This is termed as viral marketing phenomena. High valence and high arousal fuel up the emotions are also observed due to controversial viral marketing content. Fortunately, the advertising is going viral and the brand is free marketing through it (Coker, 2016).

Brand Equity And Value Creation

According to Aaker (1991), a customer-based perspective suggests brand equity as a "value provided by a brand linking to its products or services, believing in closeness level between the brand and the customer". However, the creation of value can be grouped into the components of CBBE and utilitarian values such as perceived quality and proprietary assets.

Brand equity is undoubtedly the most valued intangible assets of an organization (Veloutsou and Guzman, 2017). Higher the brand equity higher are the outcomes from a customer to validate several brand advocacy behaviors, such as WOM, endorsement, willingness to sacrifice and satisfaction to pay premiums, (Abu Bakar & Abdul-Talib, 2013; Veloutsou et al., 2013). It can be theoretically measured by marketing(value) or monetary perspectives(premiums) (Kimpakorn and Tocquer,2010). Brand equity from marketing or customer perspective means that it can be measured based on the customer's insights, whereas from a monetary perspective, it means that it can be measured by the satisfaction to pay the premium price. Brand equity can be consumer-based /firm-based (Christodoulides et al., 2015) or sales-based (Datta et al., 2017). Due to various concepts, the exact consensus on how it can be measured has not been reached until now (Çifcietal.,2016).

Comparison Of Consumer Based Brand Equity (Cbbe) Past And Present Models

In the past 20 years, Brand equity models are based on consumer perception, its constructs have been extensively studied because of their disagreement with respect to the components, the number of components and the concept of brand equity itself. Keller (1993) defines CBBE as an understanding of consumers' positive experiences such as (thoughts, feelings, and perceptions about the value provided by the product/services). Model Keller infers brand equity into 6 parts, namely brand performances, brand salience, brand imagery, brand feelings, brand judgments, and brand relationships.

According to Mittal & Sharma (1995) concept of the brand, equity is based on five factors, which are social image, value, performance, trustworthiness, and attachment. However, Aaker & Joachimsthaler (2000) perspective there are only four dimensions of brand equity, that is brand awareness, brand associations, brand loyalty, and perceived quality.

Likely Yoo & Donthu (2001) opinioned consumer-based brand equity in three components, namely marketing, marketing activity (price deals, image, supply, and promotions), brand equity dimensions (perceived product quality, brand loyalty, and brand awareness/associations) and overall brand equity. Whereas Wang & Finn (2013) proposed seven dimensions of (CBBE) such as past brand loyalty, customer brand awareness, customer brand association, current perceived quality, current perceived value, uniqueness and brand emotions spreading into two factors namely future brand loyalty and premium future prices.

Viral Marketing And How It Affects Cbbe

Numerous studies support the growth of CBBE through the social media content (Baalbaki & Guzman, 2016; Christodoulides & Chernatony, 2010; Pappu, Quester, & Cooksey, 2005; Yoo & Donthu, 2001). However, it has also been stated that consumer-based brand equity gives a firm a competitive advantage, which makes it necessary for consumers to identify a brand and be aware of a brand name with a differentiated brand association in mind (Keller 1993; Christodoulides et al., 2015). Therefore the majority of CBBE studies in this context are proposed the Aaker (1991) and Keller (1993) conceptual model for measuring CBBE (Bakshi & Mishra, 2016; Christodoulides, Jevons, & Bonhomme, 2012; Karpinska-Krakowiak, 2016; Kim & Ko, 2012; Langaro, Rita, & de Fatima Salgueiro, 2015; Yazdanparast et al., 2016).

Past studies show that viral marketing impacts positive effects on brand equity and consumer purchase intentions termed as brand loyalty. Moreover, brand equity also positively influences purchase intentions. Viral marketing effects brand equity through various mechanisms and ways. The message content that is interesting and informative impacts positively on brand awareness, quality and value, while the purchase intensions are also affected by offensive content yet they also show significant positive effects. However, measuring CBBE refers to positioning the whole thing that is present in consumers' minds such as (emotional state, pre and post experiences, opinions, values) with regard to a brand. (Keller, 2001).

Hypothesis One: There is a positive connotation between viral marketing and CBBE.

Viral Marketing And Brand Awareness

Viral Marketing has shown massive strength owing to its low-cost, high-conversion nature, it's crucial that you entirely realize its requirements, accomplishments, and to be used for self-benefits through social media marketing (Akbaba, 2006). It provides the advantage to replicate the marketing communications activities to all users around the world where the internet is boundless by time and geographic zone (Akehurst, 2009; Zamani, Abdul-Talib & Ashari, 2016). Social media has the potential to develop trust but it also strengthens relationships amongst corporations and societies. It promotes increasing the company's brand awareness; it also contributes to building success and competence of a company in creating brand awareness. Brand awareness is thought to be one instrument that can affect consumers in making purchasing decisions. Consumers probably decide to buy a product whose brand is familiar, safe and tested to it than a product with a lesser-known or even unknown brand name (Abdul-Talib & Mohd Adnan, 2017; Akbaba, 2006).

Hypothesis Two: There is an influence of viral marketing towards the development of brand awareness.

Viral Marketing And Brand Quality

Perceived quality is defined as consumers' judgment of products' complete performance (Zeithaml, 1988). However, Aaker (1991) opinioned that its consumer's observation of brands to other competitive brands. Likewise, Anselmsson et al., (2014) argued that higher perceived quality brand is can result in charging premium prices compared to competitive brands. Therefore, it is a significant determinant of brand equity developed through WOM. This signifies that perceived quality differentiates brands and provides them a competitive edge over other brands (Aaker 1991; Christodoulides et al., 2015).

Hypothesis Three: WOM influences consumers' perceptions of brand quality.

Viral Marketing And Brand Association

Brand association is the essential dimension of CBBE (Aaker 1991; Christodoulides & de Chernatony, 2010; Keller, 1993). It is the strength of the brand to what extent it can develop a positive feeling of the consumer (Lassar, Mittal & Arun, 1998). According to Keller (1993), brand association to a consumer is reflected through attitude (customer's delightfulness), benefit (perceived value of product or services) and attribute (quality, a frame of mind, understanding, and satisfaction attributed by a brand). Sales promotions, discounts are also some of the ways to keep the consumer associated with the brands. Likewise, Hudson, Huang, Roth & Madden (2015) argued that social media marketing positively influences the customer-brand association. Whereas, Godey et al., (2016) also suggested that brand equity created through social media activities has a constructive (positive) influence on consumer behavior and their association with brand ultimately developing brand loyalty.

Hypothesis Four: WOM positively influences brand associations leading to brand loyalty.

Viral Marketing And Purchase Intentions (Brand Loyalty)

Buying intent refers to the intentions of the customer to purchase a product or service. According to Fishbein and Azjen (1975), it is the sole precise analyst of genuine purchase behavior. Basically, viral marketing could be regarded as a service offered to potential customers by the companies. Conceptually, brand loyalty is a behavioral outcome of brand equity and not as a dimension (Chaundry & Holbrook, 2001). Nam et al., (2011) also argued that quality(physical), work behavior of staff, self-congruence, brand recognition, and lifestyle congruence, brand satisfaction are dimensions of brand equity reflecting in association with brand loyalty. Brand loyalty is argued to be a dimension of consumer-based brand equity (Aaker, 1991; Keller 1993, Abdul-Talib & Japari, 2020; Christodoulides, 2015). In contrast to Nam et al. (2011), brand loyalty is argued to be a behavioral component and an outcome of consumer-based brand equity. Choi, Kim & Mattila (2015) studying fashion sports brands initiated a significant positive relationship between the perceived quality of a brand and brand loyalty. Pappu & Quester (2016) posited that brand trust, brand attitude, satisfaction, and value for money positively influence the brand. Godey et al., (2016) found a strong relationship between CBBE and consumer responses where brand loyalty is considered as a dimension of consumer responses from various marketing activities. Buil, Chernatony, and Martinez (2013) also argued that brand associations, brand awareness, perceived quality, and brand association positively influence brand loyalty.

Hypothesis Five: There is a positive relationship between viral marketing and purchase intentions.

IMPLICATIONS OF STUDY

Viral Marketing through social media marketing if advertised positively and with favorable content, would help in building positive consumer perceptions. (Chi, 2011; Okazaki & Taylor, 2013). It also suggests a positive implication between promotions and CBBE, which is interpreted through the information spread through social media platforms. Specifically, marketing activities such as promotions, product trials, gifts, reductions, and vouchers, show acceptance of brands positively. However, few past studies confirmed a negative connotation has also been identified between sales promotion and brand equity (Valette Florence, Guizani, & Merunka, 2011; Winer, 1986; Yoo et al., 2000).

Practically, this conceptual paper provides understandings for brand executives and owners, particularly handling automotive brands, on by what means to progress; also improve their brand equities and increase the association of their brands. The stated vital components of CBBE proposed by (Aaker and Keller) are brand awareness, brand association, and brand loyalty. Therefore, brand managers can alter their branding and marketing activities (WOM) in order to improve the acceptance and selection of their brands. Furthermore, CBBE models are measures of purchasers' attitudes and insights (Keller, 1993). Henceforth, the practical implication of any CBBE model is a positive indication for executives on how to capture consumers' by catching their minds.

LIMITATIONS OF RESEARCH

This research paper discussed a few dimensions of the CBBE model based on Aaker and Keller and also discussed its influence on purchase intention. Other dimensions of CBBE provided by various scholars such as brand loyalty, perceived quality, brand assets and brand experience that can be adopted in future studies. This research paper also discusses the relationship between WOM and CBBE revealing positive effects. Negative effects of WOM through viral marketing are also one of the important directions which can be explored. This work can be studied empirically after certain statistical tests where this research as the above discussion is totally based on past & modern theoretical Literature. The empirical research will allow the researcher to develop an understanding of the current situation of the marketplace on certain assumptions that may be tested with statistical tools. Future study should delve into facet of consumer behavior in the digital economy is deemed necessary (Ling Chang, Ling Tam, & Suki, 2016; Nathan, Fook Chiun, & Suki, 2016; Suki, 2013a; 2013b; Suki, 2016; Suki & Abang Sulaiman, 2016).

CONCLUSION

This paper put forward that organizations generate brand-related content on social media websites with diverse marketing mix activities, such as viral marketing, publicity, sales promotions, and interactive marketing. Advertising such as sales promotions through social media has shown significant relationships with CBBE and the response of the consumers. Hence, the past studies validate that social media influences users' perceptions, behaviors, and responses which ultimately helps to develop CBBE. Hamid, Romiza, & Cheng (2013); Tsai & Me (2013).This study critically reviewed in both past and present studies, revealing that viral marketing through social media such as Youtube, Twitter, and Facebook are strategic channels for market stimuli and responsible for triggering positive insights of products in customers' mindsets (Kotler & Keller, 2012).

REFERENCES

Aaker, D. A. (1991). *Managing brand equity. Capitalizing on the value of the brand name*. The Free Press.

Aaker, D. A., & Equity, M. B. (1991). Capitalizing on the Value of a Brand Name (Vol. 28). Academic Press.

Aaker, D. A., & Joachimsthaler, E. (2000). *Brand leadership*. Free Press.

Abdul-Latif, S. A., & Abdul-Talib, A. N. (2017). Consumer racism: A scale modification. *Asia Pacific Journal of Marketing and Logistics*, 29(3), 616–633. doi:10.1108/APJML-02-2016-0026

Abdul-Talib, A. N., & Abdul-Latif, S. A. (2015). Antecedents to willingness to Boycotts among Malaysian muslims. In *Emerging Research on Islamic Marketing and Tourism in the Global Economy* (pp. 70–106). IGI Global. doi:10.4018/978-1-4666-6272-8.ch004

Abdul-Talib, A. N., & Japari, N. (2020). Brand Consciousness and Brand Loyalty: A Study on Foreign Brand Beauty and Skin Care Products. In Economic, Educational, and Touristic Development in Asia (pp. 106-126). IGI Global. doi:10.4018/978-1-7998-2239-4.ch006

Abdul-Talib, A. N., & Mohd Adnan, M. M. (2017). Determinants of consumer's willingness to boycott surrogate products. *Journal of Islamic Marketing*, 8(3), 345–360. doi:10.1108/JIMA-08-2015-0065

Abu Bakar, A. R., & Abdul-Talib, A. N. (2013). A case study of an internationalization process of a private higher education institution in Malaysia. *Gadjah Mada International Journal of Business, 15*(3).

Akbaba, A. (2006). Measuring service quality in the hotel industry: A study in a business hotel in Turkey. *International Journal of Hospitality Management*, 25(2), 170–192. doi:10.1016/j.ijhm.2005.08.006

Akehurst, G. (2009). User-generated content: The use of blogs for tourism organizations and tourism consumers. *Service Business*, 3(1), 51–61. doi:10.100711628-008-0054-2

Anselmsson, J., Vestman Bondesson, N., & Johansson, U. (2014). Brand image and customers' willingness to pay a price premium for food brands. *Journal of Product and Brand Management*, 23(2), 90–102. doi:10.1108/JPBM-10-2013-0414

Baalbaki, S., & Guzman, F. (2016). A consumer-perceived consumer-based brand equity scale. *Journal of Brand Management*, 23(3), 229–251. doi:10.1057/bm.2016.11

Buil, I., De Chernatony, L., & Martinez, E. (2013). Examining the role of advertising and sales promotions in brand equity creation. *Journal of Business Research*, 66(1), 115–122. doi:10.1016/j.jbusres.2011.07.030

Chang, L.D.M., Ling Tam, A.Y., & Suki, N.M. (2016). Moderating effect of races towards consumers' feeling of TCM usage. In N.M. Suki (Ed.), Handbook of research on leveraging consumer psychology for effective customer engagement (pp. 306-323). Hershey, PA: IGI Global.

Chaudhuri, A., & Holbrook, M. B. (2001). The chain of effects from brand trust and brand affect to brand performance: The role of brand loyalty. *Journal of Marketing*, 65(2), 81–93. doi:10.1509/jmkg.65.2.81.18255

Christodoulides, G., Cadogan, J. W., & Veloutsou, C. (2015). Consumer-based brand equity measurement: Lessons learned from an international study. *International Marketing Review*, 32(3/4), 307–328. doi:10.1108/IMR-10-2013-0242

Christodoulides, G., & De Chernatony, L. (2010). Consumer-based brand equity conceptualization and measurement: A literature review. *International Journal of Research in Marketing*, 52(1), 43–52.

Cifi, S., Ekinci, Y., Whyatt, G., Japutra, A., Molinillo, S., & Siala, H. (2016). Cross-Validation of customer-based brand equity models: Driving customer equity in retail brands. *Journal of Business Research*, 69(9), 3740–3747. doi:10.1016/j.jbusres.2015.12.066

Cobb-Walgren, C. J., Ruble, C. A., & Donthu, N. (1995). Brand equity, brand preference, and purchase intent. *Journal of Advertising*, 24(3), 25–40. doi:10.1080/00913367.1995.10673481

Coker, B. (2016). *Going Viral, The 9 Secrets of irresistible marketing*. Academic Press.

Coleman, D. A., de Chernatony, L., & Christodoulides, G. (2015). B2B service brand identity and brand performance: An empirical investigation in the UK's B2B IT services sector. *European Journal of Marketing*, *49*(7/8), 1139–1162. doi:10.1108/EJM-03-2013-0154

Davcik, N. S., Vinhas da Silva, R., & Hair, J. F. (2015). Towards a unified theory of brand equity: Conceptualizations, taxonomy, and avenues for future research. *Journal of Product and Brand Management*, *24*(1), 3–5. doi:10.1108/JPBM-06-2014-0639

Fishbein, M., & Ajzen, I. (1975). *Belief, attitude, intention, and behavior*. Addison-Wesley.

Gallaugher, J. (1999). Challenging the new conventional wisdom of net commerce strategies. *Communications of the ACM*, *42*(7), 27–29. doi:10.1145/306549.306558

Hayes, J. L., King, K. W., & Ramirez, A. Jr. (2016). Brands, friends, and viral advertising: A social exchange perspective on the ad referral processes. *Journal of Interactive Marketing*, *36*, 31–45. doi:10.1016/j.intmar.2016.04.001

Helm, S. (2000). Viral marketing: Establishing customer relationships by 'word-of-mouse'. *Electronic Markets*, *10*(3), 158–161. doi:10.1080/10196780050177053

Hudson, S., Huang, L., Roth, M. S., & Madden, T. J. (2016). The influence of social media interactions on consumer-brand relationships: A three-country study of brand perceptions and marketing behaviors. *International Journal of Research in Marketing*, *33*(1), 27–41. doi:10.1016/j.ijresmar.2015.06.004

Keller, K. L. (2001). Building customer-based brand equity: A blueprint for creating strong brands building customer-based brand equity. *Journal of Marketing Communications*, *15*(2–3), 139–155. doi:10.1080/13527260902757530

Lassar, W., Mittal, B., & Sharma, A. (1995). Measuring customer-based brand equity. *Journal of Consumer Marketing*, *12*(4), 11–19. doi:10.1108/07363769510095270

Liu, H. H., & Wang, N. Y. (2019). Interrelationships between Viral Marketing and Purchase Intention via Customer-Based Brand Equity. *Journal of Business and Management Sciences*, *7*(2), 72–83. doi:10.12691/jbms-7-2-3

Miniwatts Marketing Group. (2017). *Taiwan Internet Usage Stats and Marketing Report*. Retrieved from the World Wide Web: http://www.internetworldstats.com/asia/tw.htm

Nathan, R. J., Fook Chiun, D. C., & Suki, N. M. (2016). An online marketing strategies assessment for companies in airlines and entertainment industries in Malaysia. In N. M. Suki (Ed.), *Handbook of research on leveraging consumer psychology for effective customer engagement* (pp. 1–15). IGI Global.

Okazaki, S., & Taylor, C. R. (2013). Social media and international advertising: Theoretical challenges and future directions. *International Marketing Review*, *30*(1), 56–71. doi:10.1108/02651331311298573

Pappu, R., & Quester, P. G. (2016). How does brand innovativeness affect brand loyalty? *European Journal of Marketing*, *50*(1/2), 2–28. doi:10.1108/EJM-01-2014-0020

Petrescu, M., Korgaonkar, P., & Gironda, J. (2015). Viral advertising: A field experiment on viral intentions and purchase intentions. *Journal of Internet Commerce, 14*(3), 384–405. doi:10.1080/15332861. 2015.1080057

Raji, R. A., Rashid, S. M., Ishak, S. M., & Mohamad, B. (2019). Do Firm-Created Contents on Social Media Enhance Brand Equity and Consumer Response Among Consumers of Automotive Brands. *Journal of Promotion Management.* Advance online publication. doi:10.1080/10496491.2019.1612490

Salmenkivi, S. & Nyman, N. (2007). *Yhteisöllinen media ja muuttuva markkinointi 2.0.* Academic Press.

Suki, N. M. (2013a). Students' demand for smartphones: Structural relationships of product features, brand name, product price and social influence. *Campus-Wide Information System Journal, 30*(4), 236–248. doi:10.1108/CWIS-03-2013-0013

Suki, N. M. (2013b). Consumer shopping behaviour on the Internet: Insights from Malaysia. *Electronic Commerce Research, 13*(4), 477–491. doi:10.100710660-013-9131-2

Suki, N. M. (2016). *Handbook of research on leveraging consumer psychology for effective customer engagement.* IGI Global. Retrieved from http://www.igi-global.com/book/handbook-research-leveraging-consumer-psychology/149284

Suki, N. M., & Abang Sulaiman, A. S. (2016). Does halal image strengthen consumer intention to patronize halal stores? some insights from Malaysia. *Journal of Islamic Marketing, 7*(1), 120–132. doi:10.1108/JIMA-12-2014-0079

Valette-Florence, P., Guizani, H., & Merunka, D. (2011). The impact of brand personality and sales promotions on brand equity. *Journal of Business Research, 64*(1), 24–28. doi:10.1016/j.jbusres.2009.09.015

van Doorn, J., Lemon, K. N., Mittal, V., Nass, S., Pick, D., Pirner, P., & Verhoef, P. C. (2010). Customer engagement behavior: Theoretical foundations and research directions. *J. Serv. Res., 13*(3), 253–266. doi:10.1177/1094670510375599

Veloutsou, C., Christodoulides, G., & Chernatony, L. (2013). A taxonomy of measure for consumer-based brand equity: Drawing on the views of managers in Europe. *Journal of Product and Brand Management, 22*(3), 238–248. doi:10.1108/JPBM-02-2013-0256

Veloutsou, C., & Guzman, F. (2017). The evolution of brand management thinking over the last 25 years are recorded in the Journal of Product and Brand Management. *Journal of Product and Brand Management, 26*(1), 2–12. doi:10.1108/JPBM-01-2017-1398

Wang, L., & Finn, A (2013). Heterogeneous sources of customer-based brand equity within a product category. *Marketing Intelligence & Planning, 31*(6), 674–696. doi:10.1108/MIP-01-2013-0012

Yoo, B., & Donthu, N. (2001). Developing and validating a multidimensional consumer-based brand equity scale. *Journal of Business Research, 52*(1), 1–14. doi:10.1016/S0148-2963(99)00098-3

Zakaria, N., & Talib, A. N. A. (2011). What did you say? A cross-cultural analysis of the distributive communicative behaviors of global virtual teams. In *2011 International Conference on Computational Aspects of Social Networks (CASoN)* (pp. 7-12). IEEE. 10.1109/CASON.2011.6085910

Zamani, S. N. M., Abdul-Talib, A. N., & Ashari, H. (2016). Strategic orientations and new product success: The mediating impact of innovation speed. International Information Institute (Tokyo) Information, 19(7B), 2785-2790.

Zeithaml, V. A. (1988). Consumer perceptions of price, quality, and value: A means-end model and synthesis of evidence. *Journal of Marketing*, *52*(3), 2–22. doi:10.1177/002224298805200302

This research was previously published in the Handbook of Research on Technology Applications for Effective Customer Engagement; pages 66-75, copyright year 2021 by Business Science Reference (an imprint of IGI Global).

Chapter 21

Postmodern Discourse in Digital Advertising:
A Study on "Deneysel Bankacilik" Advertising Series

Mehmet Yakin
https://orcid.org/0000-0002-2603-5741
Istanbul Arel University, Turkey

ABSTRACT

In the postmodern world, ads try to establish an emotional bond between the consumer and the storytelling instead of a classic "Buy it!" expression. One of the most used methods of storytelling in terms of advertising in social media is viral advertising. Viral advertising makes an effort to attract attention to the brand in social media, sometimes by showing the brand, sometimes with an implicit expression. In this study, the process of advertising taking place in the digitalized world and the transition from modern marketing to postmodern marketing will be examined. In the case of "Deneysel bankacılık," the use of postmodern marketing in digital advertising will be evaluated.

INTRODUCTION

In parallel with technological developments, advertisements are in an effort to show the brand in every field that the potential audience is located. In the postmodern world, advertisements try to establish an emotional bond between the consumer and the storytelling, instead of classic "Buy it!" expression. One of the most used methods of storytelling in terms of advertising in social media is viral advertising. Viral advertising makes an effort to attract attention to the brand in social media, sometimes by showing the brand, sometimes with an implicit expression. Viral advertising that gets its name from its spread to the consumer like a virus, can also be considered as successful advertising because the advertising costs are significantly reduced, the spread expands implicitly and the consumer sees them with a trust that it comes from their acquaintance rather than being aware of the fact that it is an advertisement. As a result

DOI: 10.4018/978-1-6684-6287-4.ch021

of the same postmodern marketing, viral advertising stands out as an alternative way for the advertising sector to capture the fleeing target audience.

Sözer defines postmodern marketing communication as "The whole of the activities planned and carried out for the delivery of creative, consistent and continuous messages through selected communication channels in line with the needs and market characteristics of the target audience in order to create consumer-based brand value" (2009, p. 28). The transition from the tangible to abstract has manifested itself in the brand, marketing communication and, of course, advertising in the postmodern era. Advertisements are now more than just convincing the consumer that the branded product meets the need in a concrete way, they have become a means of reflecting the personality of the brand and the impersonation of the brand that stays with target audience on the good and bad day. In this context, through advertisements, brands try to act on a communication frequency that is more natural and sincere with the target audience.

Advertising is moved from information-loaded property to a meaningful dimension. As one of the advertising creators, Larry Light says, today's advertising does not aim to create a sales proposal, but a unique brand personality and image. Advertising can be defined as a form of cultural communication that gives personality to products, idealizes consumers' self-images and lifestyles and offers suggestions. The way of effective advertising is to create brands that offer the opportunity to produce cultural and symbolic meanings and to offer consumers the opportunity to express themselves (Stutts and Barker, 1999, p.209). According to Kayaman and Armutlu, the postmodern consumer prefers to go beyond the narratives of modernism and prefers to be happy in separate and different moments instead of looking for centralized, unified moments. As a result of this situation, the market has become a center where moments of fragmented self and pleasures take place. In other words, the market builds on many consumers and products and presents a structure in which all relations are temporary and the consumer does not need to establish a comprehensive relationship for each change (Kayaman and Armutlu, 2003, p.8).

The "Deneysel Bankacılık" series, prepared by the Kompüter advertising agency for Garanti Bank, was featured on social media with 37 content videos over 3 years period. Reaching 16,000 subscribers on Youtube alone, the ad series achieved a total of approximately 50 million views on Youtube. "Deneysel Bankacılık" series described the pathetic story of an attempt who chooses Garanti Bank as a competitor while introducing Garanti Bank's corporate identity and services using ironic storytelling. In this series of advertisements prepared for the Bank, Garanti Bank was positioned as a competitor brand and "Deneysel Bankacılık" employees, who strive to exist against this brand and their tragicomic story brought to the screens. Garanti Bank has a modern image that has been established in the minds of consumers with its corporate structure, adaptation to technology and experience in the banking sector through marketing communication efforts since its establishment in 1946. The reproduction and re-presentation of this image in the postmodern structure is far from remarkable for the consumer. Therefore, the brand tries to draw a natural and sincere image in the perception of the target audience by creating an incompetent competitor in postmodern time and criticizing itself through this competitor. Through an imaginary opponent's tragicomedy, the bank's corporate look and structure were affirmed and by demonstrating an alternative approach to banking and bank image allows forming a communication language that involves postmodernism's "anti-institutionalism". In this study, the process of advertising taking place in the digitalized world and the transition from modern marketing to postmodern marketing will be examined. In the case of "Deneysel Bankacılık", the use of postmodern marketing in digital advertising will be evaluated.

TRANSFORMATION OF ADVERTISING FROM MODERN MARKETING TO POSTMODERN MARKETING

Postmodernism which points to a new social order; expresses the development of a new epistemology that responds to the contemporary situations of knowledge. As a concept that symbolizes the dominance of new cultural values and processes; postmodernism accepts information and communication technologies and scientific knowledge as a reflection of postmodern society. In this context, postmodernism can be considered unattached to modernism and described as "modernism that continues but inconclusive" (Lyotard, 1984, p.3). Postmodernism defines a new state that encompasses all fields of culture and thought. As a contemporary movement of thought, postmodernism points to a new phase in the process of social development and, according to its discourse, it means the dominance of different forms and tendencies compared to the past. Postmodern dynamics that gain strength parallel to the process of postmodernism; mediates the change of concept, value, and phenomena. According to George Ritzer, it is important to remember that the biggest importances of postmodern social theory are its emphasis on fascination, the absence of fascination in the modern world and the need for ongoing fascination (2000, p.101).

Jean Baudrillard claims that computerized social organization replaces production and we are in a new age of simulation. If modernity is the era of production that codes and models are controlled by the industrial bourgeoisie, on the contrary, the era of post-modern simulations is the era of models, codes, and information and signs ruled by cybernetics. In this media environment, the boundary between information, entertainment, image, and politics explodes, and the entropy created by the information bombardment causes the masses to become silent masses (1991, p.22). Baudrillard emphasizes that social production is replaced with production and Alvin Toffler also examines that argument in terms of production processes. Futurologist Toffler, in his book The Third Wave which he wrote in the 80s and foresighted the future, emphasizes that the customer is approaching the production process with constant change. According to Toffler, in some organizations, the customer can directly adjust the properties of the product he wants through the company's communication ties. Thus, in the production process, it will become indistinguishable from who is the customer and who is the manufacturer. In this study, not only the production processes but also the importance of the consumer in marketing and advertising processes draw attention. As it will be emphasized in the research section of the study, consumers played an active role both in distancing the classical understanding of advertising messages within the postmodern structure and shaping the duration and content of the campaign designed for a certain period from a modern perspective.

Zygmunt Bauman defended the opinion that postmodern theory focuses on a style of perception as "a life under permanent and irreplaceable conditions of uncertainty; claims cannot be proven that historically robust than its shaped customs and binders based on a floor, with its own, there are an unlimited number of life forms in a race" (1996, p.145). He states that the postmodern view embraces all forms of view because modernism cannot reach full stability as initially, it seemed as disengagement from the past.

In his book "Postmodern Marketing", Stephen Brown talks about the seven elements of postmodern social structure that characterize postmodern marketing. These elements can be summarized as follows;

- **Fragmentation:** Politics, economy, and thaw in the market.
- **Hyper-Reality:** Fantasy world of virtual reality.
- **De- Differentiation:** Blurring of traditional borders and erosion and destruction of hierarchical structures.

- **Chronology:** Historical interests, aspirations.
- **Pastiche:** Mixture of literature, music and architecture styles.
- **Anti- Foundationalism:** Antipathy towards Orthodox structure and universal reality.
- **Pluralism:** This element is not a separate category but the other six elements can be combined and it shows postmodern structure is open and tolerant of differences.

The brand and the product represent two different dimensions as abstract and concrete. While the modern period focuses on the concrete and therefore the product, the abstract has come to the forefront in the postmodern period. During this period in which the brand image began to be discussed, the products were located in a position to create personalities and to establish an emotional connection like a human being, having a certain lifestyle. On the other hand, due to the impact of technological developments in production processes, production by different manufacturers in the same product segment made the distinction difficult due to the high quality and similar price of the products.

The reflection of the differences between modern and postmodern marketing in advertising has necessitated the emergence of new approaches in addition to the modern way of advertising, and a new paradigm regarding the functioning of advertising has come up in the postmodern environment.

The postmodern individual is an individual who attaches importance to language games and seeks satisfaction through experience. Therefore, it is inevitable to place these features in the advertising and communication model. Virtual reality offers consumers a world of visual images, enabling them to participate in some products as if they were the real world experience. Although modernist advertisements use traditional communication techniques to reflect the truth as much as possible using metaphor; the confusion of reality and artificial in postmodern advertising and the emergence of "virtual reality" that expresses being real, create different consumer reaction. The emergence of new forms created in images with the help of technology has facilitated the creation of new simulations (Odabaşı, 2004, p.181).

It is seen that communication tools are diversified with the inclusion of virtual technologies and interactive technologies besides mass media and it is now difficult to transmit the same message to all individuals through a single channel. It is seen that the message delivered to the individual through different channels is now used more intensively to attract the attention of the individual who is more effective in expressing himself by standing out from the mass. Another important element that needs to be examined in this paradigm that affects advertising in the postmodern structure is the change in advertising texts.

Postmodern advertisements provide little information about the use and characteristics of products, and stand out their focus on symbolic relationships that are more connected with consumption. Therefore, it is very difficult to speak of a single style. Any style is valid (Odabaşı, 2004, p.183).

The advertising text that can be seen in any kind of structure that contributes to the image can sometimes give no idea about the product in the structure which we can call as teaser and may only be aimed at stimulating the sense of curiosity, on the other hand, the product may be presented within the consumer's experience of use, especially in advertisements. As we have seen in the use, the display of the user experience of a celebrity may be more important than the functional characteristics of the product. Therefore, it is difficult to talk about consistency in advertising messages and advertising messages can be constantly differentiated depending on the wishes, expectations, and agenda of the consumer.

In today's society, it is important that individuals have fun and be happy at the moment. While the individual determines both his / her perception and consumption behavior in this context, it is impossible for advertising messages not to be affected by this wind. Especially with the internet, the individual is now able to produce advertisements and publish advertisements to carry more entertaining and curious elements such as viral advertising applications to reach more people. Focusing on creating an emotional bond between the consumer and the product rather than providing information about the product allows non-rational presentations becoming widespread.

The collapse of linear discourse, which is one of the distinctive elements of the postmodern era, reveals itself as the increasing importance of visuality and cynicism in advertisements. In the past, advertising messages, which have established the serious tone of the relationship with the consumer, are respectful to the consumer and designed to affirm the brand image, have left their place to the concept of advertising that teases itself and its messages and tried to spoil the serious message tone as much as possible. In order to be sincere with the consumer and gain the sympathy of the consumer, advertising messages are structured through sincere and honest discourses instead of linear discourses.

FROM ADVERTISING TO DIGITAL ADVERTISING

In his book "Crystallizing Public Opinion", Edward Bernays states that the mental equipment of the average individuals is collective judgments on many issues that touch their daily physical or mental life (1961, p.62). The actions of the individual are influenced by the social implications of people's thoughts, behaviors, and attitudes. Bernays calls this "consensus" and states that this creates a common public mind (1961, p.69). The main purpose of the brands is to provide information about brand value to create a lifestyle and to create a consumer society.

In the advertising sector, the use of the Internet to have a better connection with consumers began in the 1990s. Internet use continues to increase every day, and the user age is gradually decreasing. The Internet is also widely used as a line of communication worldwide. When media and the Internet are merged, new media is created and the new media network initiates more interactive process than mass media. Social media exemplifies this formation with platforms such as Facebook, YouTube, and Twitter. The social media network offers these opportunities by serving people in the network. The transformation of the social structure has initiated a new form of social organization in society and this form continues to evolve day by day. In this context, Castells concluded that "the network as a social form is free or neutral" (2000, p.16). Advertisers provide brand new and different ideas to strengthen interaction using video and visual aided social media tools. In this context, it is possible to see the ideas of network advertising in viral advertising.

Viral marketing was first introduced by Douglas Rushkoff (1994), and in 1996 it was more theorized by Jeffrey Rayport. The message of communication is spread like a virus among humans. Seth Godin (2000, p.13) said: "we live in a world where consumers resist active marketing. Therefore, it has become imperative to stop marketing noticeably to consumers. The idea is to create an environment where consumers can market to each other." The main purpose of viral advertising is to create a new way in which people communicate, inform, disseminate information and entertain. As a result, viral marketing works to effectively capture the attention of consumers and build brand awareness.

The process of digitalization radically changed the forms of communication, perception, and comprehension, in short, people's lifestyle. But change is not only that. Internet-based applications and devices have changed the rules, balance, time, and space concepts (Karahasan, 2012, p.18); differentiated our ways of recognition, acting and experiencing (Cooper, 2002, p.160). Developments in the Internet, electronic messaging, online search, social media, mobile communication and gaming environments have led to digital advertising (Özkındakçı, 2012, p.156). There has been a change in consumers who are in a passive position in traditional advertising and receive as much information as presented, to digital advertising applications that offer as much information as consumers want (Lombard and Duch, 2017, p.169).

At the same time, digitalization allows the integrated use of all communication tools and the emergence of digital creative ideas. However, the realization of digitalization in the field of communication and the area where the greatest impact experienced is the positioning of advertising in virtual space (Doğan, 2015, p.14). Digital advertising is defined as a form of promotion using the Internet and digital technology to send marketing messages. Digital advertising can be considered as a rapidly growing phenomenon that began in 1994. On the other hand, the Internet is the fastest growing medium of recent years and is the most nourishing digital advertising sector (Öztürk, 2016, p.349).

Basically, the story consists of all the depicted events. The plot is the causal chain that these events are somehow linked and therefore need to be depicted in relation to each other. The narrative is the mode chosen to show or pronounce these events and to make it happen (Cobley, 2001, p.5). The concept of narrative is defined as transferring two or more events (or a situation and an event) that are brought together as a whole to a logically interconnected, happened in a specific time and coherent (Mutlu, 2004, pp.28-29). Not every literary text is a narrative, but with the same logic, not every narrative may have a literary content. There are two approaches to the definition of narrative; while the first one only accepts texts that transferred orally, the second one sees all kinds of texts as narratives (Jahn, 2012, pp.48-51).

People can easily perceive and store the information when it is organized and presented in the narrative structure as they are transmitted through stories (Lien and Chen, 2013, p.517). In today's world that where competition is increasing, consumers are exposed to intense advertising messages, and brands need to use different and creative methods to attract consumers' attention. The advertisements are communicated with the target audience using easily recognizable narrative patterns (Hollebeek, 2011, p.559).

With narrative content, instead of real benefits and rational questions, the consumer is expected to develop an emotion, attitude and ultimately behavior towards the product around a story. In the narrative process, especially with the stories described, it aimed to understand a number of events that the consumer can relate to consumption of the product or make an imagination about these events (Adaval & Wyer, 1998, p.214).

By wrapping up product value with a good story, the story automatically becomes the driving force behind brand values and thus separates them from similar products (Kaliszewski, 2013, p.9). According to Sutherland, there are three main mechanisms in which humorous ads are more effective than plain ads:

1. Humorous ads are more powerful.
2. Humorous advertising appears to have less discussion and the audience opts for entertainment rather than accurate evaluation.
3. The likelihood of being more influential and acclaimed is increased.

Turkish Language Institution defines parody as "A genre that teases a piece considered seriously while not corrupting its form, giving it a completely different feature and constructing a humorous effect from this distinction of its essence and form." Simon Dentith (2000, p.9) defines parody as "any cultural practice that critically or alluringly imitates another cultural product or practice". Attempts to define parody have gained a new dimension within postmodernism. According to some research, parody is the most popular technique of postmodernism (Cebeci, 2008, p.144). From a traditional point of view, parodies in ads are a way to deliver fun advertising messages. The main purpose of parody in entertaining advertisements is to ensure brand development (positive behavior), remind, create recognition and similar situations (Jean, 2009, p.19).

ANTI-INSTITUTIONALISM IN DIGITAL ADVERTISING: A STUDY ON "DENEYSEL BANKACILIK" VIRAL ADVERTISING SERIES

Casting doubt on the "great narratives" produced by the Cartesian mind with postmodernism has led to doubts about the absoluteness and universality of knowledge, and thus, Cartesian mind's pointing to the absolute truth has been replaced by electoral, reflexivity, randomness and fragmentation (Sarup, 2010, p.168).

In this part of the study, "Deneysel Bankacılık" viral advertising series prepared by Kompüter Advertising Agency for Garanti Bank will be examined in the context of postmodern marketing and digital advertising. To give a brief before the case study about Garanti Bank, Turkey Garanti Bankası A.Ş. was established on 11 April 1946 with the status of the private capital bank. Garanti Bank's head office is located in Istanbul. As of 31 March 2019, the Bank has 922 domestic and 8 foreign branches and 2 representative offices. BBVA is the main partner that has a 49.85% share of Garanti Bank. BBVA is a global group of 72 million retail and commercial customers offering a wide range of financial and non-financial products and is headquartered in Spain. The BBVA Group, which operates in 35 countries, has more than 130,000 employees (KPMG, 2019).

METHODOLOGY

The case study is a qualitative method based on definition, understanding, and explanation (Tellis, p.2000). According to Gillham, a case study is a study that addresses specific questions from answers, organizes and examines the different evidence obtained from the case, gives the best possible answers to the research questions, summarizes and blends them. With the weaknesses or difficulties, extracting and using a large number of sources from the evidence is the main feature of the case study (2000, p.2). It is possible to diversify the case study according to the size of interest. According to Yin, it is possible to mention two different types of case studies as singular and multiple. Single case studies work on a single theory and focus on a specific event and multiple case studies focus on recurrent and interrelated events (Yin, 1993). In light of these definitions and considering the suitability of "Deneysel Bankacılık" on post-modern marketing anti-institutionalism, the case study was chosen as the methodological method of the research. A single case study will put into practice based on the definitions of Yin. After the postmodern marketing concept and case study mentioned in the literature section of the study, the overlapping points of the literature and the research section will be presented in the conclusion section.

FINDINGS

"Deneysel Bankacılık" (Experimental Banking) is a digital project published by Garanti Bank on various social media channels, particularly YouTube, in 4 seasons between 2014-2017. This project is an absurd comedy series about a man has the ambition to work better that starts to work in a "known bank"

(Garanti Bank) making inventions to create their alternative products. This man is the brother of *"Erdal Bakkal"* played by theater and cinema artist Cengiz Bozkurt's character in one of the favorite series of the period *Leyla and Mecnun*. In order to prove its superiority against his brother in the competition, the main character invented 5 new products in the project in the first season and this products represent 5 existing products that Garanti Bank would like to promote: as a rival to Mobile Banking "Full Body Branch", to Internet Banking "Ro-Banking" to e-Savings Account "Nö –Vadeli" to Net Account "Artificial Accumulations" and to Golden Account "Organic Gold Account" (Öner, 2017).

The project continued in 2015 with Season 2. The first part of the season meets with the audience in the form of a song that will increase the viral impact of the project, and in the following chapter, it continues to compete with Garanti Bank with its "Deneysel Bankacılık" personnel and the first branch. In 2016, Garanti Bank was asked their customers to share the answer the question "Why does *Deneysel Bankacılık* have to come back?" via social media, and video responses from followers provided important and positive contributions to the realization of bank-customer interaction through social media channels.

Ipsos' article named *'0 golden rule' of interaction in the digital world* stated that making users feel their impacts on the digital platforms instantly makes them proud to be on this platform and also encourages them to have a goal to contribute to this platform (IPSOS, 2018).

Even in the third season, the support of the followers is a concrete indicator of the bond they establish with the brand through the project and can be regarded as an example of Garanti's effective communication strategy. Ensuring the continuity of the project with a different innovation each season, Garanti Bank aimed to reach a wide audience in the 4th season with the participation of different celebrities in "Deneysel Bankacılık" films. "Deneysel Bankacılık" has reached millions of followers on social media since 2014 with the slogan *Another Wish!*, which rivals Garanti Bank's innovative technology and products with fun alternatives, and says goodbye to its fans with its latest film "The End".

"Deneysel Bankacılık" tells the adventures of Tanju and Şafak characters in which Cengiz Bozkurt and Şafak Sezgin gave life. Since 2014, 37 short films have been published in four different series. While the films produced by Kompüter Advertising Agency have reached over 100 million views to date, it has won many awards in national and international platforms, especially Crystal Apple, the most important organization in the advertising and marketing world (Ahmed, 2017). Garanti Bank's "Deneysel Bankacılık" project (Garanti, 2016) won;

- 26th Crystal Apple Creativity Festival; "Best Film in Banking Sector", "Best Digital Campaign", 3 Crystal Apples in "Best Online Video" categories, Special Jury Award in "Film, TV and Cinema" category, "Silver Apple" in Viral Project Service Category, "Most Creative Social Media Communication Service" category "Bronze Apple"
- Mixx Awards in 2014 Turkey Awards; " Viral category" Gold Mixx, "Branded Content category" Silver Mixx,
- Four awards in the "Best Viral Campaign", Best Video, Best Web Campaign and Best Branded Content Usage categories in the "Digital" section of Mediacat Felis 2014 Awards,
- 28th Crystal Apple Festival, Two Crystal Apples "Campaign / Service" and "Online Film / Service" of the digital ads category; "Online Film / Service" and "Social Media / Co-Creation and User-Generated Content".

Turkey IAB Mixx Awards Success Stories in the Library (https://www.iabturkiye.org/deneysel-bankacilik) the main headings of the campaign are summarized as follows;

- **Marketing Objective:** Watching films prepared within the scope of the campaign and creating positive dialogue on social media.
- **The Purpose of the Campaign:** Making films that will explain Garanti Bank's banking products without annoying internet users.
- **Target Audience:** Target audience was internet users of all ages and socioeconomic groups who used or were candidates for banking products .
- **Creative Strategy:** The story of a man whose brother started to work at Garanti Bank was ambitioned to start "Deneysel Bankacılık" and via that story, the ad narrated Garanti products.
- **Practice:** "Deneysel Bankacılık" communicated through its own social media channels, thus positioning itself as a competitor to Garanti Bank. He interacted with people through his Facebook page, Twitter account, video channels (YouTube, Dailymotion, İzlesene).
- **Conclusion:** Films have been shared tens of thousands of times, seen more than 8 million times. More than 26,000 users liked Facebook page of "Deneysel Bankacılık". Moreover, without ever seeing 'like' ads, they like the page only because they really wanted to. The campaign was the most positive commented campaign of Garanti Bank to this date in the banking sector where it was very difficult to produce positive comments.

In the interview conducted by Yiğit Kaytmaz for Campaign magazine, Burcu Tokcan, Marketing Communication and Media Manager of Garanti Bank uses the following statements about the development of the series;

... We have already seen that the digital world is growing rapidly, we were doing a lot of different projects and their results we were getting very clear. We had this fact one hand. On the other hand, we had many products and services in the world that we wanted to share with digital customers. We thought we'd put them under one roof. We started, then we placed it on a brief. This brief had important criteria. First of all, it had to be a very strong viral. We wanted something different because there is too much video work and it needs to be differentiated in that area. Therefore, we have prepared a stylish, difficult brief. Three agencies have arrived. One was Kompüter. We were very impressed while listening to Kompüter. They made a great presentation. They told us something strategically close to the world we wanted. We have listened to scenarios with tears. It wasn't just funny but also there was a clever comedy.

Normally this is an advertisement of Garanti, but we did not keep it in Garanti Bank's social media accounts. As a strategy, we saw it as a competitor and opened separate accounts and made him speak separately. It has 50,000 followers.

It received 7-8 awards. We are very pleased, of course, it is very difficult to get a positive response on social media in the financial advertisement area. In this first phase, there is a total of 97 percent positive and neutral reflections. That's a huge number. Over 90 percent in the second phase.

Table 1. "Deneysel Bankacılık" advertising series films

The name of the movie	Release date	Views Number	Likes	Dislikes
Tüm Vücut Şubesi	December 25, 2014	383.334	548	53
Ro Bankacılık	December 25, 2014	116.156	460	17
Yapay Birikim	December 25, 2014	61.141	209	15
Nö Vadeli	December 25, 2014	78.101	271	18
Organik Altın Hesabı	December 25, 2014	96.910	281	32
Deneyerek Geliyoruz	December 25, 2014	30.183	144	13
Çalışma Ortamı	January 7, 2015	553.617	396	46
Deneysel Mortgage	January 7, 2015	2.955.930	381	98
Holo 3000	January 7, 2015	2.851.310	885	123
Şarkı	January 7, 2015	4.462.059	2.900	304
Deneysel Bankacılık Neden Geri Dönmeli?	February 1, 2016	70.821	234	46
Geri Dönüş	February 5, 2016	2.088.284	434	35
Yüksek Teknoloji	February 6, 2016	3.552.798	448	84
Üstün Hizmet	February 7, 2016	2.827.043	337	48
Deneysel'e sor!	April 25, 2016	7.099	116	5
Kazaklarımızı giydik geliyoruz	February 17, 2017	553.630	289	29
Şarkılı Şiir Saati: Eye Recognition (Dinletemedim)	February 20, 2017	1.049.170	791	283
Deneysel Hız	February 27, 2017	1.121.671	752	338
Hadi Ordan	March 10, 2017	1.169.776	393	34
Deneysel Sohbetler – Saba Tümer	March 15, 2017	820.085	316	47
Şarkılı Şiir Saati: Renkli Misketler	March 21, 2017	2.057.140	541	41
Deneysel Güç	March 28, 2017	1.937.351	276	31
Gülünç Olma Ugi	April 28, 2017	919.640	158	46
Deneysel Sohbetler – Ceza	May 4, 2017	1.312.040	427	30
Hadi Ordan (2.Bölüm)	May 12, 2017	1.286.213	245	11
Deneysel Sunar: Bilinçli Tagleyiniz	May 18, 2017	1.334.869	113	5
Deneysel – IIP Sertifikası	May 26, 2017	423.208	177	14
Deneysel Aşk	June 6, 2017	186.581	104	1
Bir Fotoğraf, Bir Anı	June 6, 2017	1.827.888	218	23
Deneysel Basket	June 15, 2017	1.066.310	312	34
Deneysel Caz	July 6, 2017	1.302.817	201	17
Deneysel Altın Hesabı	July 24, 2017	1.427.071	159	22
Deneysel Sohbetler – Seyithan Özdemir	August 3, 2017	1.540.536	434	35
Şarkılı Şiir Saati – Garanti Cep	August 17, 2017	1.756.690	389	40
Hadi Ordan (3.bölüm)	September 6, 2017	1.521.692	270	11th
Deneysel Genç	September 29, 2017	2.365.309	254	40
The End	November 9, 2017	2.552.856	742	43

According to Berent Baytekin, partner of Autonomy Film, who produced the "Deneysel Bankacılık" commercial series;

The consumer's expectation from a brand is no longer limited to the product. It is very important for brands to support social responsibility projects in the recent period without giving any image of trying to market any products that remind both the days that are important for our history and the international special days. We are very pleased to be involved in such projects. Such campaigns enable many brands to respond very quickly in terms of brand communication through social media, and the advertising agencies to engage in a creative race to produce the most prominent project. Therefore, more and more creative films are produced every year.

Uçar uses the following consumer statements about "Deneysel Bankacılık" which is discussed in his article where he examines the attitudes of consumers towards advertisements through qualitative research;

.... some ads are linked to the series and you know people love these ads like watching series. There was advertising named "Deneysel Bankacılık". We can sit and watch it with friends, also one of my friends is an advertiser because this ad has a subject and actors and everything. (Uçar, 2017, p.218)

According to these three views, it is possible to say that advertising adopts a postmodern discourse, especially in digital environments. In Turkey, especially the Turkcell brand for young people gencturkcell has this type of postmodern take in their advertising campaigns through this rhetoric. "Deneysel Bankacılık" advertising series designed by Kompüter advertising agency for Garanti Bank differed from the understanding of modern advertising with its rhetoric and structure. This differentiation ensures that the communication between Garanti Bank and the consumer works successfully in the postmodern structure, while it also strikingly positively affects the brand's image. The evolution of modern discourses of advertising into a postmodern discourse within the postmodern structure of today's society, facilitates the efficient existence of brands within the postmodern structure as well as the modern structure. At the same time, such expansions help to create a flexible basis for advertising activities on a wider scale.

FUTURE RESEARCH DIRECTIONS

Today, social media affects lifestyles and consumption habits. The effects of different marketing communication campaigns (such as advertising, public relations) should be investigated. The effects of digital advertising on different age groups, cultures and genders should be compared. Research on the impact of postmodern discourse on advertising will make it easier to understand the consumption habits of today's society.

CONCLUSION

Marketing is an area that shapes people's needs, makes them fancy the brands and enables them to buy. Advertising is a powerful marketing method that allows you to express the product or service that basically affects people's emotions. In this context, emotions are a factor that drives sharing for viral advertising. In viral advertising, creativity means making emotional connections with internet users. Humor encourages us to share like any emotion that arouses excitement, anger, and worry in consumers.

Creativity in art has a different concept compared to advertising. In general, art is regarded as the expression of self. In other words, creativity depends on the artist's experience, talent, and preference. On the other hand, creativity in advertising is based on the purpose of the brand and the characteristics of the product. Creativity is not necessary for advertising, but it is necessary to achieve the purpose of advertising; because advertising is the promotion of a brand, product or service, and a way of expressing product use.

In traditional advertising and viral advertising, there are some differences in practice in terms of creativity, target audience, story, time, etc. However, ultimately the purpose and scope are to create a common language between consumers and society.

Post-modern period's distinctive conditions (surreality, fragmentation, elimination of differentiation, chronology, pastiche, anti-institutionalism, pluralism, the displacement of production and consumption, the decentralization of the subject, paradoxical merger / contrasts-antithesis) dominantly makes its presence felt and the individual's passive position led to a role that likes to be active and constantly in contact with the brand. Befittingly to this role, also as a result of the change in information communication technologies, the Internet gained importance as well as mass media and these seem as the striking elements of the change of advertising.

The complex and chaotic structure of the postmodern structure is often seen in today's advertising applications. As a result of the changing characteristics of the consumer, postmodern discourses and visual design applications have a wide place in today's advertising approach. Thus, the target audience is tried to be reached through the language and perception of the consumer, which differs from the modern era.

"Deneysel Bankacılık" series, which was scripted by Kompüter Advertising Agency between 2014 and 2017 and supported on both traditional and other social media channels and published on Youtube as the main channel for Garanti BBVA, draws attention as a case study prepared by following the postmodern marketing approach. In the modern advertising approach, the institutions are glorified, the one-way communication model was adapted and concrete messages are presented. Unlike modern advertising, postmodern advertising is opposed to the uplifting of institutions. Because consumers have learned the modern advertising concept over time and they closed their minds against these advertisements. For brands to gain a place in the consumer's mind, it has become obligatory for them to go through an evolutionary process, such as the awareness of the consumer about anti-advertising. In the case of Deneysel Bankacılık, it is seen that brands have fun with modern systems and structures including their institutions as a result of postmodern conditions.

In the end, while this advertisement criticizes the banking structure and the advertisements of the bank, it tries to put the importance of the fact that institutions take this business seriously to consumers' minds. Although we continue our lives with a postmodern mind structure, we still exist within a modern system. Money is one of the most important tools of change in this system and we have to use the banking system to protect and increase our assets. The modern system supports this requirement. However, even if the individual continues to exist within this modern structure, with criticizing, maintains his attitude towards this structure from an ironic point of view. "Deneysel Bankacılık" series conveys this ambivalent situation through humor.

While the "Deneysel Bankacılık" series was designed only for 2014 and consisted only a couple of video works, the intense interest of the target audience, the frequent sharing of the target audience on social media and the winning of many advertising awards ensured the continuity of the work. The series lasted for about three years, but inevitably the template becomes recognizable and thus lost its entertainment factor. As an advertiser, Garanti BBVA recognizes the positive impact of this work on both its corporate reputation and the image of the brand. For this reason, entertainment and postmodern discourse content continue with new "postmodern" advertising efforts. Today, the brand continues its "postmodern" efforts with the content prepared by two comedians known as "Megateknoforce" which draws attention to the people's problems with technology and the dilemma experienced by the individual in the modern world.

REFERENCES

Adaval, R., & Wyer, S. R. Jr. (1998). The Role of Narratives in Consumer Information Processing. *Journal of Consumer Psychology, 7*(3), 207–245. doi:10.120715327663jcp0703_01

Ahmed, S. (2017). *Deneysel Bankacılık Pes Ederek Dünyayı Terk Etti*. https://www.campaigntr.com/deneysel-bankacilik-pes-etti/

Baudrillard, J. (1991). *Sessiz Yığınların Gölgesinde ya da Toplumsalın Sonu*. Ayrıntı Yayınları.

Bauman, Z. (1996). *Yasa Koyucular ve Yorumcular, Çev. Kemal Akatay*. Metis Yayınları.

Bernays, E. (1961). *Crystallizing Public Opinion*. Liveright Publishing Corporation.

Caldiero, C. (2016). *Neo-PR: Public Relations in a Postmodern World*. Peter Lang. doi:10.3726/978-1-4539-1660-5

Castells, M. (2000). Materials for an Exploratory Theory of the Network Society. *The British Journal of Sociology, 51*(1), 5–24. doi:10.1080/000713100358408

Cebeci, O. (2008). *Komik Edebi Türler*. İthaki Yayınları.

Cobley, P. (2001). *Narrative*. Routledge.

Cooper, S. (2002). *Techno Culture and Critical Theory*. Routledge.

Dentith, S. (2000). *Parody*. Routledge.

Doğan, B. Ö. (2015). *Online Reklamcılık*. Köprü Kitapları.

Estanyol, E. (2012). Marketing, Public Relations, and how Web 2.0 is Changing Their Relationship. *PR Review, 38*, 831–837.

Firat, A. F. (1991). The Consumer in Postmodernity. In Advances in Consumer Research. Association for Consumer Research.

Gabardi, W. (2001). *Negotiating Postmodernism*. University of Minnesota Press.

Godin, S. (2000). *Unleashing the Ideavirus*. Do You Zoom.

Hollebeek, L. (2011). Exploring Customer Brand Engagement: Definition and Themes. *Journal of Strategic Marketing, 19*(7), 555–573. doi:10.1080/0965254X.2011.599493

Jahn, M. (2012). *Anlatıbilim*. Dergâh Yayınları.

Kaliszewski, S. (2013). *Through a Narratalogical Lens: An Analysis of the Storytelling Elements in Award-Winning Advertisements*. The University of Warwick.

Karahasan, F. (2012). *Taşlar Yerinden Oynarken: Dijital Pazarlamanın Kuralları*. Doğan.

KPMG. (2019). T. *Garanti Bankası Anonim Şirketi ve Finansal Kuruluşları 31 Mart 2019 Hesap Dönemine Ait Kamuya Açıklanacak Konsolide Finansal Tablolar, Bunlara İlişkin Açıklama ve Dipnotlar ile Sınırlı Denetim Raporu*. https://www.garantiinvestorrelations.com/tr/images/pdf/BDDK_Konsolide_TR_rapor.pdf

Lien, N.-H., & Chen, Y.-L. (2013). Narrative Ads: The Effect of Argument Strength and Story Format. *Journal of Business Research, 66*(4), 516–522. doi:10.1016/j.jbusres.2011.12.016

Lombard, M., & Synder-Duch, J. (2017). Digital Advertising in the Digital Age: The Power of (Tele) Presence. In Digital Advertising Theory and Research (pp.169-188). New York: Routledge.

Lyotard, J. F. (1984). *The Postmodern Condition*. Minneapolis University of Press.

Mutlu, E. (2004). *İletişim Sözlüğü*. Ankara: Bilim ve Sanat Yayınları.

Odabaşı, Y. (2004). *Postmodern Pazarlama*. Kapital Medya Hizmetleri A.Ş.

Özkundakçı, M. (2012). *Üçü Bir Arada*. İstanbul: Hayat Yayıncılık.

Öztürk, R. G. (2016). Türkiye'de Dijital Reklamın Tarihi. In E. Çağlak (Ed.), *Bu Toprakların İletişim Tarihi* (pp. 347–364). İstanbul: Nobel.

Ritzer, G. (2000). *Büyüsü Bozulmuş Dünyayı Büyülemek*. Ayrıntı Yayınları.

Sarup, M. (2010). *Post-Yapısalcılık ve Postmodernizm-Eleştirel Bir Giriş*. Kırkgece Yayınları.

Sutherland, M., & Sylvester, A. K. (2004). *Reklam ve Tüketici Zihni*. İstanbul: Mediacat.

Tellis, W. M. (1997). Introduction to Case Study. *Qualitative Report, 3*(2), 1–14. https://nsuworks.nova.edu/tqr/vol3/iss2/4 PMID:9035020

Toffler, A. (2008). *Üçüncü Dalga: Bir Fütürist Analizi Klasiği*. Koridor Yayıncılık.

Uçar, F. (2017). Tüketicilerin reklamcılığa yönelik genel tutumları. Global Media Journal Turkish Edition, 7(14), 203-222.

Yin, R. (1993). *Applications of case study research*. Sage Publishing.

ADDITIONAL READING

Caldiero, C. (2016). *Neo-PR: Public Relations in a Postmodern World*. Peter Lang. doi:10.3726/978-1-4539-1660-5

Estanyol, E. (2012). Marketing, Public Relations, and how Web 2.0 is Changing Their Relationship. *PR Review*, *38*, 831–837.

Gabardi, W. (2001). *Negotiating Postmodernism*. University of Minnesota Press.

KEY TERMS AND DEFINITIONS

Advertising: One of sales persuasion efforts for target audience.

Consumption: The action of buying or using a product.

Digital Advertising: All kinds of advertising activities in social media and also in internet.

Postmodern Marketing: Postmodern marketing takes same philosophical perspective and applies it to the way advertising initiatives are handled in the current post-World War II era. Postmodern marketing is approaching or has passed through a new era in advertising, branding, and strategic brand thinking.

Postmodernism: Postmodernism has many different meanings and contexts, mostly indicating some dramatic change from modernity – the way that things used to be. Postmodernism itself would deny there is a single right definition.

This research was previously published in the Handbook of Research on New Media Applications in Public Relations and Advertising; pages 180-194, copyright year 2021 by Information Science Reference (an imprint of IGI Global).

Chapter 22
Social Media–Based Visual Strategies in Tourism Marketing

Jing Ge
University of California, Berkeley, USA

Ulrike Gretzel
University of Southern California, Los Angeles, USA

ABSTRACT

Social media-based visual strategies are quintessential elements of tourism and social media marketing; yet, very little is known about how firms formulate and implement such strategies in a technologically advanced and consumer-driven communication context. Drawing on rhetorical structure theory, and marketing, tourism and social media marketing literature, this research examines and dissects the structure of social media-based visual strategies implemented by tourism marketers. 250 Weibo posts initiated by 5 Chinese provincial destination marketing organizations were collected and analyzed. The results show a diversity of social media-afforded visual modalities, a variety of visual content and marketing goals, and different rhetorical relations between visuals and their accompanying text. This research advances social media marketing and tourism literature by exploring essential structural aspects of social media-based visual rhetoric and offers firms a holistic overview of possible visual strategies.

1. INTRODUCTION

Social media accentuate the significance of visual strategies, especially in tourism (Gretzel, 2017). As Burns, Palmer and Lester (2010 p.xv) argue, "tourism is an essentially visual experience". The adoption of visual strategies helps firms effectively reach potential and existing customers, develop a highly engaged consumer base, perpetuate a desirable destination image, and stimulate value co-creation activities (Bennett, 2013; Leung et al., 2017; Stepchenkova & Zhan, 2013; Swani et al., 2017). Yet, social media-based visual strategies are more complex and dynamic than those deployed in traditional media and therefore raise challenges for theoretical and practical understandings of their formulation and implementation. A recent report (Social Media Examiner, 2017) suggests that, although firms increasingly adopt visu-

DOI: 10.4018/978-1-6684-6287-4.ch022

als in their attempts to achieve marketing success, they still struggle to create visual strategies that are engaging and rewarding to consumers.

Marketing and tourism studies conceptualize visual strategies along three dimensions, i.e. marketing goals, message content and format (Taylor, 1999), and ignore the multimodal message formats available in computer-mediated communication (CMC) (e.g. co-occurrence of text and video) (Herring, 2015). Moreover, social media marketing literature mainly focuses on the effectiveness of specific visual formats (e.g. video, photograph) in engaging consumers while neglecting other essential dimensions and their embeddedness in social media posts. Noteworthy is that the most typical format of tourism marketing materials is the combination of photographs and text (Decrop, 2007). Ge and Gretzel (2018b) confirm that social media posts by tourism firms commonly comprise images and text. This emphasizes the need to examine and conceptualize social media-based visual strategies in tourism by considering the logical and rhetorical relations between visuals and text because understanding such relations underlines the creation of persuasive multimodal message formats (Taboada & Habel, 2013). Yet, the structural dimensions of social media-based visual strategies remain underexplored.

Focusing on China, and in particular Sina Weibo, this paper systematically examines firm-formulated visual strategies by identifying their message content, message format, marketing goals, and the relations between image and text in these messages. Sina Weibo – the most prominent microblogging platform in China – has been identified as a platform where the adoption of visuals for marketing and communication purposes is a common practice (China Internet Watch, 2017). Further, a focus on China, a culture with an especially high use of visual communication, can advance the visual communication, tourism and social media marketing literatures and provide new insights for marketing practice by concentrating on lead users.

2. BACKGROUND

2.1. Visual Communication

Marketing and communication literatures focus on visual communication, i.e. the conveyance of information using a broad spectrum of images (Smith, 2005), primarily in the context of traditional media. The common consensus is that visual advertising can draw consumers' attention, motivate them to process the information, and influence their purchase intentions (Khachatryan, et al., 2018). This line of research examines the visual structure of print and TV advertising, focusing on complexity (i.e. visual details and variations such as color and luminance), design complexity (i.e. visual layout), format of presentation and meaning production (Bulmer & Buchanan-Oliver, 2006; Pilelienė & Grigaliūnaitė, 2016; Pieters, Wedel, & Batra, 2010). Specifically, identified visual modalities facilitated by print and TV include pictures, photographs, and video. They are adopted by firms to convey literal meanings (i.e. factual information) and assigned meanings (e.g. using a photo of a beach to signify freedom), or to represent abstract concepts (e.g. social status) (Bulmer & Buchanan-Oliver, 2006; Moriarty, 1987; Ritson & Elliott, 1999). Research on visual rhetoric in advertising mainly focuses on the relations of visuals with the products they represent or on the relations among visual elements (Maes & Shilperoord, 2008; Gkiouzepas & Hogg, 2011). The seminal work by Phillips and McQuarrie (2004) reveals three ways in which images relate to each other: juxtaposition (images are presented side-by-side), fusion (the images are combined) and replacement (the present image points to an absent one).

The communication literature categorizes visual-text relationships based on the extent to which visuals relate to the text, including functions expressing little relation to the text (e.g. decorate, elicit emotion), functions expressing close relation to the text (e.g. explain, organize), and functions going beyond the text (e.g. interpret, transform) (Marsh & White, 2003). Moreover, existing literature reveals five main functions of visual message elements: 1) conveying additional information; 2) clarifying and illustrating the propositions presented in the text; 3) elevating the trustworthiness of the claims; 4) enticing consumers to consume the message, and 5) creating a favorable impression of the product (Taboada & Habel, 2013; Belch & Belch, 2007; Jaeger & MacFie, 2001). Importantly, past studies emphasize that visuals mixed with text are more effective than visual- or text-only messages (Jaeger & MacFie, 2001; Li, Huang, & Christianson, 2016). Luarn, Lin and Chiu (2015) also point out that an image mixed with text is an optimal message format – consumers can gain product impressions from the image and obtain product descriptions from the text. Yet, the exact way in which visuals relate to the text they accompany is unclear, and this poses critical challenges to communication professionals (Harrison, 2003).

2.2. Visual Communication in Tourism Marketing

Visual techniques represent an important dimension of the language of tourism (Dann 1996), and especially of tourism marketing (Decrop, 2007). Campelo, Aitken and Gnoth (2011) also stress the importance of visual rhetoric for destination branding and place-making. Marketing visuals have traditionally initiated an important circle of representation in tourism that shapes tourism experiences (Jenkins, 2003). Moreover, visual communication has been identified as critical for tourism-related social media marketing (Gretzel & Yoo, 2013). However, the tourism literature currently focuses predominantly on visual content, largely ignoring other dimensions of visual communication.

2.3. Marketing Communication on Social Media

Drawing on specific social media affordances, i.e. visibility, association and message format, (Herring, 2015; Treem & Leonardi, 2012), this research postulates that social media-based communication entails distinct characteristics that facilitate a variety of marketing goals. Social media support multiple message formats (such as video, photograph, text) that permit marketers to convey marketing messages in engaging ways (Ge, Gretzel, & Clarke, 2014). In addition, marketing communication on social media is accessible to all social media users who view a firm's newsfeed, not only those who were targeted (Rice et al., 2017). However, such high visibility requires firms to formulate visual strategies that resonate with both target and general consumers. Moreover, association with content occurs via user-to-user and user-to-content connections (Oostervink et al., 2016). The first refers to social ties and can be realized through tagging, following and acquiring followers. The second concerns acknowledging/responding to posts through likes, comments and reposts/shares (Treem & Leonardi, 2012). Both forms of association permit firm-initiated visual communication to achieve an extended reach and enhanced interactivity (Boyd, Golder, & Lotan, 2010).

2.4. Visual Social Media Marketing

Social media accommodate a wide range of visual modalities (Herring, 2015), thus, supporting visual complexity. Furthermore, social media culture encourages creativity (Highfield & Leaver, 2016). Shifman

(2012) points out that innovative visual content use manifests most prominently in the creation and use of memes. To seize the potential of visuals in social media marketing, firms need to develop comprehensive visual strategies that take into account the complexity and embeddedness of visual communication (Gretzel, 2017). Yet, the literature primarily focuses on visual modalities per se and simply compares their effectiveness in driving consumer engagement. It finds that visuals are more effective than text in stimulating consumer responses due to their capability of increasing the vividness of online content and of exhibiting high information richness (Hsieh & Tseng, 2017; Sabate et al., 2014). What formats of visuals are most able to drive consumer engagement is however not clear. While some studies show that the use of photographs and pictures can generate more consumer responses than video (e.g. Kwok & Yu, 2013; Kwok, et al., 2015; Leung, Bai, & Erdem, 2017; Sabate et al., 2014), Tafesse (2015)'s work provides contradictory results. This suggests that there is a great need for systematic research on visual social media-based marketing strategies.

3. CONCEPTUAL FRAMEWORK

The above discussion indicates that a structural understanding of social media-based visual strategies plays an important role in enhancing firms' marketing and communication efforts. However, critical questions related to visual strategy formulation and implementation by firms have yet to be answered. This section of the paper seeks to conceptualize important structural dimensions of such visual strategies to inform social media marketing decisions.

3.1. Social Media-Based Visual Strategies

Focusing on traditional advertising, Taylor (1999, p. 7) defines message strategy as "a guiding approach to a company's promotional communication efforts for its products, its services, or itself". It refers to both textual and visual strategy and constitutes message content (e.g. product price and features) and message format (e.g. using of pictures, text) (Laskey et al., 1989). This dated conceptualization is limited in its applicability to examining social media-based visual strategies in tourism. It only focuses on advertising without considering other marketing goals and ignores the most typical format of tourism marketing materials, i.e. combinations of image and text and relations between these two components (Decrop, 2007). Furthermore, message format is too limited to capture multimodal message formats in CMC on "Web 2.0 platforms that support a convergence of channels or "modes" (text, audio, video, images)" for facilitating user interactions (Herring, 2015, p. 1). In light of these limitations, this paper generally defines social media-based visual strategy as an overarching approach to a firm's social media marketing and communication efforts. It compasses four dimensions: marketing goals, message content, social media-afforded message formats, and logic/rhetorical relations between an image and its accompanying text.

3.2. Marketing and Communication Goals

Visuals can assist firms to achieve their marketing and communication goals. It is well recognized that firms adopt different forms of visuals (e.g. video, photo) to promote and advertise their products, for example, to convey product image, features, benefits and qualities (Phillips & McQuarrie, 2004; Swani et al., 2017). In the social media context, firms adopt visuals to fulfill broader communication goals that go beyond the traditional marketing mix. Scholars find that firms adopt images to show their appreciation, publish community activities and entertain consumers (Coursaris, Van Osch & Balogh, 2013; Kwok & Yu, 2013; Kwok et al., 2015; Leung et al., 2017). Social media marketing requires firms to broadly focus on engagement due to its essential role in building customer relationships and in shaping value co-creation activities (Ge & Gretzel, 2018a; Gretzel & Yoo, 2013). This research therefore adopts the following conceptual categories: product description, promotion, advertising, public relations, sales, customer service, and engagement (Coursaris et al., 2013; Jensen & Jepsen, 2008; Laskey, Day, & Crask, 1989; Leung et al., 2017).

3.3. Visual Content

Firms adopt visuals to depict diverse types of content. Content is defined as the appearances or signs presented in a visual in their totality (Albers & James, 1988). Albers and James (1988) posit that visual content can be conveyed through a metonymic or a metaphoric perspective. The first refers to all image attributes representing themselves and should be described based on appearances, whereas the second treats visuals as symbols and examines what an image signifies beyond mere appearances. This research focuses on the metonymic perspective. It thus aligns with literal visual analysis, that is, describing and reporting what is presented in visuals (Moriarty, 1987). For example, backpackers are coded as people rather than as a travel style. Existing tourism marketing metonymic content classifications typically include architecture and buildings, nature and wildlife, local people, cultural tradition, and local cuisine (Burns, Palmer, & Lester, 2010; Schmallegger, Carson, & Jacobsen, 2009). This paper is guided by the following categories proposed by Stepchenkova and Zhan (2013): nature and landscape, people, architecture and buildings, way of life, traditional clothing, food, animal, leisure activities, wild life, art objects, tourism facilities, festivals and events.

3.4. Visual Message Format

Message format, i.e. communication morphology or a means of composing messages (Herring, 2015), has expanded its spectrum on social media. Traditionally, words and static images (e.g. signs, photos) occur in print materials, while spoken text and moving images (e.g. videos) take place in TV. In sharp contrast, social media accommodate multimodal message formats (Herring, 2015). It has been adopted to examine how social media users deploy images and text to deliver vivid information and to stimulate user interactions (Xie, 2008). Building on previous research, this study defines visual message format as involving a variety of image-based communication morphologies. In this paper, social media posts are conceptualized as including text and visual components (Figure 1) as text-only and image-only posts are rare in tourism marketing contexts (Ge & Gretzel, 2018b).

The following visual formats are identified: picture, photo, GIF, video, infographic, and text-based image (Herring, 2004; Kwok & Yu, 2013; Leung et al., 2017). Importantly, emojis, emoticons and stickers are not considered as separate categories but would be considered as part of the text component if embedded there or as a form of picture if added as a separate visual component.

Figure 1. Multimodal structure of social media post (Source: Screenshot of the Author's Sina Weibo Post)

3.5. Rhetorical Structure Theory

Rhetorical Structural Theory (RST) aims at identifying how textual units relate to each other logically and rhetorically (Mann & Thompson, 1988). Its primary focus has been on written discourse (Mann, Matthiessen & Thompson, 1992), but it has also been applied to spoken dialogue and multimedia discourse (Taboada & Mann, 2006). By adopting the list of rhetorical relations from RST, this study treats the visual component of a social media post and its accompanying textual component as separate units and identifies the rhetorical relation between them. The advantages of using RST relations are that they are well-defined and have been tested extensively for textual materials and multimodal documents such as text and figures (e.g. Taboada & Habel, 2013), although this is the first study to apply them to analyze social media-based visual strategies. The list of rhetorical relations adopted for this research consists of: circumstance, solutionhood, elaboration, background, enablement, motivation, evidence, result, justification, volitional cause, non-volitional cause, volitional result, non-volitional result, purpose, antithesis, concession, condition, otherwise (i.e. a hypothetical or unreal situation), interpretation, evaluation, restatement, summary, sequence, and contrast (Mann & Thompson, 1988).

Figure 2 summarizes the dimensions of social media-based visual strategies this paper conceptualizes for social media-based tourism marketing. It assumes that firms have different choices to make when encoding information and meanings for marketing purposes on social media. The encoding process leads to messages that are delivered through a combination of text with different visual formats that depict various categories of visual content. The visual and textual components are put into specific relations to each other in order to support the particular marketing communication goal the firm hopes to achieve with the social media post.

Figure 2. Conceptual framework

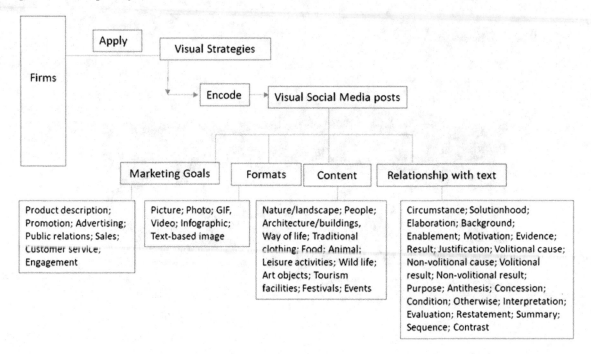

The literature review suggests that crafting successful social media-based visual strategies involves decisions across multiple structural dimensions. The conceptual model identified four dimensions as essential building blocks. Accordingly, the empirical research based on this conceptual model addresses four specific research questions:

RQ1: What marketing goals are communicated in firm-published social media posts?
RQ2: What types of visual content are depicted in these posts?
RQ3: What types of visual format are adopted by tourism firms to convey these posts?
RQ4: How do visuals relate to the text they accompany?

4. METHODOLOGY

4.1. Data

The data are Sina Weibo posts that contain text and image components (as shown in Figure 1 above). Because social media-based visual strategies in tourism is a new line of inquiry, this paper sought information-rich samples to capture the phenomenon it is interested in (Bauer & Gaskell, 2000); this led to sampling visual social media posts used by Destination Marketing Organizations (DMOs). They are not only active social media users but proficient visual marketers who fully leverage diverse visual forms (e.g. videos, photos) to initiate social media conversations (Ge & Gretzel, 2018b). They can be conceptualized as lead users (Hippel, 1989) in tourism and thus can be considered as particularly important in informing the understanding of visual strategy formulation and implementation. This paper conducted a pretest and selected 5 sample DMOs (Shandong, Henan, Sichuan, Jinagxi and Zhejiang DMOs) because of their high frequency of visual posts.

Firm-consumer conversations on Chinese social media are often conveyed through multimodal message formats and through creative language (e.g. humour) (Ge & Gretzel, 2018b). Analyzing such language is still a critical challenge for automatic coding (Anderson, 2016). Thus, the use of manual methods of analysis and the exploratory nature of this study, both of which call for close, iterative analysis, limited the amount of data that could be analyzed (Bauer & Gaskell, 2000). With this in mind, this study used a manual data collection approach to obtain rich data (Bauer & Gaskell, 2000) and collected the first 50 DMOs' Sina Weibo posts from 10 September 2014 to 10 October 2014 based on the following criteria: 1) they are sample DMO-initiated posts rather than reposts of other users' posts; 2) none of the images are repetitive; and, 3) the subsequent 10 images are similar to these 50 posts (e.g. landscape/nature). A high-level tourism firm-consumer interaction was found in this one-month time window due to the occurrence of the mid-Autumn festival and National Day (China Internet Watch, 2013). A total of 250 DMO posts – considered as an effective size for a manual coding study (Kolbe & Burnett, 1991) – were collected.

4.2. Analysis Methods

A working premise of this research is that visual strategies applied in encoding social media posts encompass marketing goals, message format(s) and content, and rhetorical relations with the text. Computer-mediated discourse analysis, a language-focused approach that adapts methods from linguistics and related fields to analyze digital discourse, is adopted (Herring, 2004). Specifically, this study employs two complementary discourse-based methods: Text analysis is used to identify marketing goals, visual content, and format; pragmatics, specifically rhetorical structure analysis, is deployed to analyze rhetorical relations between the visual and the text component. A sample set comprising 50 posts was coded by one of the authors as well as a Chinese visiting scholar. The Cohen's Kappa for coding content was 0.83, indicating a solid agreement (Cohen, 1960). The kappa value derived from coding rhetorical relations was 0.62. This represents 'substantial' agreement according to Landis and Koch (1977). The first author, a native Chinese speaker and a visual communication researcher, coded the remainder of the posts; the second author, a social media marketing and tourism researcher, coded a large amount of the data together with the first author until consensus on the most likely interpretation of each visual Weibo posts in context was reached.

This research analyzed visual strategies based on the conceptual framework depicted in Figure 2 using iterative coding. Text-based images (n=9) were omitted from coding visual content, because they are images of words rather than true visuals (Marsh & White, 2003). The coding of visual content was guided by: 1) considering each image as a single unit of content; and, 2) coding essential attributes within the visual based on size and location within the visual. Leftover data for all dimensions was subjected to inductive coding, which identified several emerging categories.

5. RESULTS

5.1. Marketing Goals

DMOs adopted visuals to communicate both product- and non-product-related marketing goals, all of which pertain to the social media marketing paradigm (Gretzel & Yoo, 2013). Overall, product description and engagement are the most prominent marketing goals (Table 1). While the first focuses on introducing facts about the local cuisine, culture, and tourism attractions at the destination, the second departs from the realm of the destination. Surprisingly, the sample DMOs preferred to use non-tourism engagement (e.g. advice on developing one's virtue such as humbleness and understanding true happiness and love) more than tourism-related engagement (e.g. travel tips). In contrast, public relation, promotion and sales are little-adopted marketing goals. The reason could be that DMOs try to avoid hard advertising and direct selling in social media marketing. Moreover, data analysis did not find the evidence that they use visuals to achieve customer service.

Table 1. Visual-conveyed marketing goals: Descriptions and frequency distribution

Categories	Descriptions	Numbers	Percentage
Product description	Information about destination, including local cuisine, restaurants and cafes, hotels, tourist attractions, events/festivals, tours, architecture, etc.	123	49.2%
Non-tourism engagement	Entertainment (e.g. jokes, movies), life philosophy, and advice on health, family and social relationship management.	85	34%
Tourism-related engagement	Non-destination specific travel tips, travel information about and recommendations of foreign destinations.	28	11.2%
Public relation	Destination information published by media.	9	3.6%
Promotion	Special offers and discounts.	3	1.2%
Sales	Sales of tickets to tourism attractions or tour packages.	2	0.8%
Total		**250**	**100%**

5.2. Visual Content

The DMOs in our dataset used visuals to depict 9 out of 13 content categories identified in the conceptual framework (Figure 2). Landscape and nature are most prevalent (Table 2), followed by food, people and architecture/buildings. Festivals, art objects and animals are least frequently used. Interestingly, landscape/nature and architecture/buildings visuals can be destination and non-destination-specific (e.g. the Eiffel Tower). Similarly, people depicted in images include not only locals and tourists but also people in general. While food mainly involves local cuisine, objects are general material things that are relevant to consumers' travel or daily life (e.g. umbrella, calendar).

Table 2. Visual content: Descriptions and frequency distribution

Categories	Descriptions	Numbers	Percentage
Landscape/Nature	Pristine nature, archeological sites and natural attractions without or with minor human- and animal-related elements, e.g. deserts, forests, jungles, rivers, lakes, beaches, caves, and mountains.	68	27.1%
Food	Local cuisine and food in general as focus of the image.	47	19.2%
People	Locals, tourists, or people in general depicted in the center of the image.	47	19.2%
Architecture/ Buildings	Interior or exterior of traditional and modern architecture without or with minor human-related elements, e.g. public buildings, museums.	30	12.4%
Objects	Material things, e.g. calendar, luggage.	19	8%
Leisure activities	Depictions of active life style free from compulsory activities such as working or doing housework, e.g. outdoor activities such as boating, hiking.	10	4.4%
Art objects	Traditional and modern Chinese art and western art.	8	3.6%
Animals	Local animals and animals in general in the center of the image.	8	3.6%
Festivals	Depictions of local and traditional events.	4	2.5%
Total		**241***	**100%**

5.3. Visual Message Formats

The results show that Chinese DMOs adopted all the Weibo-afforded message formats, including text, static images (e.g. picture) and animated images (e.g. video, GIF) (Ge et al., 2014), and delivered posts with single, multiple and composite modalities. Composite photographs account for the largest percentage (Table 3; Figure 3), followed by photograph and composite photographs with superimposed text. They prefer to use these three categories to introduce landscape/nature, local food, and architecture/buildings

Conversely, text-based image, infographic, video and GIF are little-utilized categories. The reason might be that as opposed to other prevalent visual modalities, text-based image and infographic are less visually appealing, and video and GIF require more production efforts. Moreover, compared to the other identified modalities, a composite photograph that includes text-based images is most visually complex and information-laden.

5.4. Rhetorical Relations

The rhetorical structure analysis revealed only seven ways in which visuals relate to the text component, with decoration being a relation not currently acknowledged in the literature. Overall, the elaboration function of visuals is most prevalent, followed by restatement, evidence and decoration. The sample DMOs prefer to use images for providing details that relate to the text. This might be seen as an optimal way to overcome the 140-character message limit on Weibo. Moreover, they also deploy visual to repeat the information presented in the text. This practice might help DMOs emphasize the specific textual information they intend to convey. Preparation was also used in several cases to introduce/mention the topic presented in the text. In contrast, DMOs rarely adopted motivation and enablement to encourage consumers to perform the action described in the text component (Table 4; Figure 4).

Table 3. Visual modalities: Descriptions and frequency distribution

Categories	Descriptions	Numbers	Percentage
Composite photograph	Two or more photographs combined.	71	28.4%
Photograph	Single photograph.	67	26.8%
Composite of photographs mixed with text	Combination of two or more photographs with superimposed text.	41	16.4%
Picture	Single picture.	17	6.8%
Composite picture mixed with text	Combination of two or more pictures with superimposed text.	10	4%
Photograph mixed with text	Photograph with superimposed text.	8	3.2%
Text-based image	Image depicting words/characters.	8	3.2%
Composite picture	Two or more pictures combined.	6	2.4%
Picture mixed with text	Picture with superimposed text.	5	2%
Video	Weibo short video format.	4	1.6%
GIF	Graphics Interchange Format.	4	1.6%
Infographic	Visual representations of information.	3	1.2%
Composite infographic	Combination of two or more infographics.	2	0.8%
Composite of photograph and text-based image	Combination of two or more components with at least one being a text-based image and one being a photograph.	2	0.8%
Composite of text-based images	Two or more text-based images.	1	0.4%
Composite of photograph mixed with text and text-based image.	Combination of two or more components with at least one being a text-based image and one being a photograph with superimposed text.	1	0.4%
Total		**250**	**100%**

*Figure 3. Composite photograph (Source: Henan DMO-Published Sina Weibo Post) *Text-only images (n=9) were excluded*

Table 4. Rhetorical relationship categories: Descriptions and frequency distribution

Categories	Descriptions	Numbers	Percentage
Elaboration	Visual provides further details that relate to the text.	92	36.8%
Restatement	Repeats the information presented in the text.	50	20%
Evidence	Justification for the claim presented in the text.	41	16.4%
Decoration	Visually appealing photo/picture to beautify the text.	37	14.8%
Preparation	Visuals introduce/mention the topic presented in the text	18	7.2%
Enablement	Presents specific details that facilitate performing the action described in the text.	8	3.2%
Motivation	Presents a reason for performing the action described in the text	4	1.6%
Total		**250**	**100%**

Figure 4. Example of visual used as decoration (Source: Shandong DMO-Published Sina Weibo Post)

一颗善良的心会让你拥有有爱。不要悲观的认为你很不幸。实在比你不幸的人还很多。敢于面对困境的人，生命如此坚强。

Note: The loose translation of the text: "Having a kind heart allows you to have friendship. Don't pessimistically feel you are unlucky. There are many people who are more unfortunate than you. People who are resilient can face setbacks without fear."

6. CONCLUSION AND DISCUSSION

6.1. Research Questions Revisited

Overall, the analysis confirmed the applicability of the conceptual framework but also identified new categories within the visual strategy dimensions. The results sanction the postulation of this research –

social-media based visual strategies vary across multiple dimensions. The results of the first research question – what marketing goals are communicated in firm-published social media post – show the prominent adoption of product description and engagement as well as the rare use of promotion and sales. These results align with the findings derived from the second research question about the visual content depicted in these visual posts, that is, the identification of both destination- and non-destination-related content. This finding underlines that destination marketing on social media adopts a fundamentally different approach (Gretzel & Yoo, 2013). Extent marketing literature focuses on the use of visual communication for product promotion and advertising. However, this research reveals the prevalence of visuals to provide product information, endorsing the idea that firms should avoid direct advertising and hard selling on social media (Ge & Gretzel, 2018b). The non-destination-related engagement goals (i.e. entertainment, life philosophy) respond to the statement that on social media, firms need to treat themselves as invited guests, 'bring wine', and talk about interesting things of relevance to their followers (Russel, 2009). They allow for enhancing brand community experiences and help firms build long-term consumer relationships (Martínez-López, et. al., 2017).

The results relating to the third research question – what types of message modalities are adopted by tourism firms – show that firms have a large array of visual modalities at their disposal. Multimodal forms of visuals (e.g. photograph mixed with text) can help firms not only overcome word constraints imposed by social media platforms but also deliver more vivid and information rich messages (Luarn, Lin, & Chiu, 2015). However, not all forms are necessarily used to their full potential. While previous research highlights video as generating higher consumer responses on social media due to its higher level of vividness (Swani, et. al., 2017), this research found it is a little-utilized format in DMOs' visual strategies.

The results of the fourth research question – how visuals relate to the text they accompany – support the assumption that visuals can form strong rhetorical relations with the text. However, the analysis also identified simple decoration relations. Decoration sheds light on the importance of the 'attention economy' on social media – the most valuable resource in the information era is not information, but the attention people pay to it (Shifman, 2012), and compelling visuals are known to grab attention. The most used category, i.e., elaboration, is unsurprising. It aligns with previous studies – firms often adopt visuals to convey additional information or clarify the propositions presented in the text (Belch & Belch, 2007; Jaeger & MacFie, 2001). Moreover, the second-most dominant category, i.e. restatement, suggests that the visually appealing images can not only repeat but also amplify items presented in the text. The adoption of visuals to provide evidence supports the idea that they can elevate the trustworthiness of the claims presented in the text (Decrop, 2007). In contrast, the little-utilized categories (i.e. enablement, motivation) suggest Chinese DMOs do not fully leverage the potential of visuals to initiate social media interactions, given that they can be used to facilitate and entice actions beyond what is presented in the text.

6.2. Theoretical Contributions

First, the study broadens general marketing literature, and specifically the tourism and social media marketing literatures by systematically examining and identifying social media-based visual strategies in light of four dimensions: marketing goals, content, format, and rhetorical relations between an image and its accompanying text. As the literature review showed, previous conceptualizations of visual strategy focused only on marketing goals, message content, and message format. Second, this study contributes to the tourism literature by not only illustrating the complexity of its most typical message format (i.e.

combinations of images and text) but identifying a variety of relations between visual and textual message components. Third, while the literature on social media marketing already acknowledges visual formats and their effectiveness in generating consumer responses, this study goes beyond existing literature by dissecting and highlighting the structural building blocks of social media-based visual communication strategies. Fourth, this study advances RST by applying and adapting it to the social media context. Finally, the results can inform future research aimed at further understanding the immensely complex and dynamic domain of consumer engagement on social media.

6.3. Practical Implications

First, this research provides tourism firms with guidance on what structural dimensions to consider when formulating visual communication strategies on social media. Second, it sheds light on ways to engage with potential and existing customers on social media, and especially Weibo. The prominent adoption of engagement-based marketing goals and non-destination-related visual content shows how important relational capital is for social media conversations on Weibo (Stark & Crawford, 2015). Third, the uncovered rhetorical relations challenge tourism marketers to carefully consider their use of visuals in relation to the textual components of their social media messages. The way in which the visual strategies are formulated further offers implications for social media platforms in terms of designing and optimizing the technological basis of their system to facilitate marketing communication, e.g. through the support of composite visuals. In addition, the prominence and complexity of visual use (especially text-based images) suggests a pressing need for automated social media listening/sentiment analysis tools that can process visual messages.

6.4. Limitations and Future Research

As the first attempt at conceptualizing social media-based visual tourism marketing strategies, this research of course has its limitations and suggests fruitful directions for future work. First, the data were primarily coded by one person. While discussions with social media and marketing experts and confirmation of the coding schemes with others added reliability, such a one-person approach is limited in terms of objectivity and incorporating multiple perspectives. However, this process allowed for consistency in the method (Fereday & Muir-Cochrane, 2006). Further, the coding to identify marketing goals and the intricate rhetorical relations went beyond following a rigid coding scheme. It required a deep reading of the selected text and called for the skills, insights and analytic abilities of a researcher with elaborate domain expertise (Elo & Kyngäs, 2008). Second, this research only analyzed DMO-formulated visual strategies on Sina Weibo; however, it is the most influential platform in terms of firm-consumer interactions and visual communication and, thus, can be seen as a best practice case. Third, to conduct in-depth analysis, this research only focused on destination marketing in China as a specific context. Although China and destination marketing provide ideal contexts due to their high level of social media engagement between consumers and firms, further applications of the conceptual categories derived from this research in other national and tourism marketing contexts will allow for additional testing of the conceptual model. Finally, the focus of this research was on the rhetorical structure analysis of relations between visuals and their accompanying text, rather than on multimodal discourse analysis that captures the complexities of images involving text, such as colors, layout and angles. Nevertheless, the results derived from this research address how images relate to the text in a logical and coherent way, which is fundamental to understanding multimodal communication (Taboada & Habel, 2013).

Despite these limitations, the findings of this research provide convincing evidence of the structural complexity of social media-based visual marketing strategies, which needs to be further explored in future research. Further, the methodological approach is transferable, which means it can be applied to study visual communication in other marketing contexts. To further extend the research, visual strategies on different social media platforms could be the focus and would shed light on the impact of the affordances and use culture of the platform. Another branch of research may tap into the social semiotic paradigm, and examine interactional, representational and compositional meanings formulated in social media messages. Specifically, coding of the visuals in terms of representational categories of particular relevance to social media contents (e.g. design complexity and filters) could also add insights beyond rhetorical structure. The current research helped define and describe the domain of social media-based visual communication strategies. Future research can build on its findings in important ways, for instance by examining consumer responses to the different types of visual content and image-text relations identified or by developing algorithms to support machine learning in this context.

REFERENCES

Albers, P. C., & James, W. R. (1988). Travel photography: A methodological approach. *Annals of Tourism Research*, *15*(1), 134–158. doi:10.1016/0160-7383(88)90076-X

Anderson, M. (2016). *Why sarcasm is such a problem in artificial intelligence*. Retrieved from https://thestack.com/cloud/2016/02/11/why-sarcasm-is-such-a-problem-in-artificial-intelligence/

Bauer, M. W., & Gaskell, G. (2000). *Qualitative researching with text, image and sound*. London: SAGE Publications Ltd. doi:10.4135/9781849209731

Belch, G. E., & Belch, M. A. (2007). *Advertising and promotion: An integrated marketing communications perspective*. New York: McGraw-Hill.

Bennett, S. (2013). What is visual social media marketing (and how does it raise engagement)? *Adweek*. Retrieved from http://www.adweek.com/socialtimes/visual-social-marketing/479112

Boyd, D., Golder, S., & Lotan, G. (2010). Tweet, tweet, retweet: Conversational aspects of retweeting on Twitter. In *Proceedings of the 43rd Hawaii International Conference on System Science,* Honolulu, HI (pp. 1–10). IEEE. 10.1109/HICSS.2010.412

Bulmer, S., & Buchanan-Oliver, M. (2006). Advertising across cultures: Interpretations of visually complex advertising. *Journal of Current Issues and Research in Advertising*, *28*(1), 57–71. doi:10.108 0/10641734.2006.10505191

Burns, P. M., Palmer, C., & Lester, J. A. (Eds.). (2010). *Tourism and visual culture: Theories and concepts* (Vol. 1). London: CABI. doi:10.1079/9781845936099.0000

Campelo, A., Aitken, R., & Gnoth, J. (2011). Visual rhetoric and ethics in marketing of destinations. *Journal of Travel Research*, *50*(1), 3–14. doi:10.1177/0047287510362777

China Internet Watch. (2013). *Chinese spending more on gifts for Mid-Autumn and National Day.* Retrieved from http://www.chinainternetwatch.com/4017/gift-price-on-mid-autumn-festival-national-day/#ixzz3c38vXJJZ

China Internet Watch. (2017). *Weibo has become the most important marketing platform for video contents.* Retrieved from https://www.chinainternetwatch.com/22871/weibo-top-video-promotion-platform/

Cohen, J. (1960). A coefficient of agreement for nominal scales. *Educational and Psychological Measurement, 20*(1), 37–46. doi:10.1177/001316446002000104

Coursaris, C. K., Van Osch, W., & Balogh, B. A. (2013). A social media marketing typology: Classifying brand facebook page messages for strategic consumer engagement. In *Proceedings of ECIS.* AIS Electronic Library (AISeL).

Danesi, M. (2016). *The semiotics of emoji: The rise of visual language in the age of the Internet.* UK: Bloomsbury Publishing.

Dann, G. M. (1996). *The language of tourism: a sociolinguistic perspective.* UK: Cab International.

Decrop, A. (2007). The influence of message format on the effectiveness of print advertisements for tourism destinations. *International Journal of Advertising, 26*(4), 505–525. doi:10.1080/02650487.2007.11073030

Elo, S., & Kyngäs, H. (2008). The qualitative content analysis process. *Journal of Advanced Nursing, 62*(1), 107–115. doi:10.1111/j.1365-2648.2007.04569.x

Fereday, J., & Muir-Cochrane, E. (2006). Demonstrating rigor using thematic analysis: A hybrid approach of inductive and deductive coding and theme development. *International Journal of Qualitative Methods, 5*(1), 80–92. doi:10.1177/160940690600500107

Ge, J., & Gretzel, U. (2018a). A taxonomy of value co-creation on Weibo–a communication perspective. *International Journal of Contemporary Hospitality Management, 30*(4), 2075–2092. doi:10.1108/IJCHM-09-2016-0557

Ge, J., & Gretzel, U. (2018b). Impact of humour on firm-initiated social media conversations. *Information Technology & Tourism, 18*(1-4), 61–83. doi:10.100740558-017-0097-0

Ge, J., Gretzel, U., & Clarke, R. J. (2014). Strategic use of social media affordances for marketing: a case study of Chinese DMOs. In *Proceedings of Information and Communication Technologies in Tourism* (pp. 159–173). Cham, Switzerland: Springer.

Gkiouzepas, L., & Hogg, M. K. (2011). Articulating a new framework for visual rhetoric in advertising: A structural, conceptual and pragmatic investigation. *Journal of Advertising, 40*(1), 103–120. doi:10.2753/JOA0091-3367400107

Gretzel, U. (2017). The visual turn in social media marketing. *Tourismos, 12*(3), 1–18.

Gretzel, U., & Yoo, K. H. (2013). Premises and Promises of Social Media Marketing in Tourism. In McCabe, S. (Eds,), The Routledge Handbook of Tourism Marketing (pp. 491-504). New York: Routledge.

Harrison, C. (2003). Visual social semiotics: Understanding how still images make meaning. *Technical Communication (Washington)*, *50*(1), 46–60.

Herring, S. C. (2004). Computer-mediated discourse analysis: An approach to researching online behavior. In A. Sasha, R. K. Barab, & J. H. Gray (Eds.), *Designing for Virtual Communities in the Service of Learning* (pp. 338–376). New York: Cambridge University Press. doi:10.1017/CBO9780511805080.016

Herring, S. C. (2015). New frontiers in interactive multimodal communication. In A. Georgapoulou & T. Spilloti (Eds.), *The Routledge handbook of language and digital communication* (pp. 398–402). London: Routledge.

Highfield, T., & Leaver, T. (2016). Instagrammatics and digital methods: Studying visual social media, from selfies and GIFs to memes and emoji. *Communication Research and Practice*, *2*(1), 47–62. doi: 10.1080/22041451.2016.1155332

Hippel, E. V. (1989). New product ideas from 'lead users.' *Research Technology Management*, *32*(3), 24–27. doi:10.1080/08956308.1989.11670596

Hsieh, S. H., & Tseng, T. H. (2017). Playfulness in mobile instant messaging: Examining the influence of emoticons and text messaging on social interaction. *Computers in Human Behavior*, *69*(April), 405–414. doi:10.1016/j.chb.2016.12.052

Jaeger, S. R., & MacFie, H. J. H. (2001). The effect of advertising format and mean-end information on consumer expectations for apples. *Food Quality and Preference*, *12*(3), 189–205. doi:10.1016/S0950-3293(00)00044-6

Jenkins, O. H. (2003). Photography and travel brochures: The circle of representation. *Tourism Geographies*, *5*(3), 305–328. doi:10.1080/14616680309715

Jensen, M. B., & Jepsen, A. L. (2008). Online marketing communications: Need for a new typology for IMC? *Journal of Website Promotion*, *2*(1-2), 19–35. doi:10.1080/15533610802104083

Khachatryan, H., Rihn, A., Behe, B., Hall, C., Campbell, B., Dennis, J., & Yue, C. (2018). Visual attention, buying impulsiveness, and consumer behavior. *Marketing Letters*, *29*(1), 23–35. doi:10.100711002-018-9446-9

Kolbe, R. H., & Burnett, M. S. (1991). Content-analysis research: An examination of applications with directives for improving research reliability and objectivity. *The Journal of Consumer Research*, *18*(2), 243–250. doi:10.1086/209256

Kwok, L., & Yu, B. (2013). Spreading social media messages on Facebook an analysis of restaurant business-to-consumer communications. *Cornell Hospitality Quarterly*, *54*(1), 84–94. doi:10.1177/1938965512458360

Kwok, L., Zhang, F., Huang, Y. K., Yu, B., Maharabhushanam, P., & Rangan, K. (2015). Documenting business-to-consumer (B2C) communications on Facebook: What have changed among restaurants and consumers? *Worldwide Hospitality and Tourism Themes*, *7*(3), 283–294. doi:10.1108/WHATT-03-2015-0018

Landis, J. R., & Koch, G. G. (1977). The measurement of observer agreement for categorical data. *Biometrics*, *33*(1), 159–174. doi:10.2307/2529310

Laskey, H. A., Day, E., & Crask, M. R. (1989). Typology of main message strategies for television commercials. *Journal of Advertising*, *18*(1), 36–41. doi:10.1080/00913367.1989.10673141

Leung, X. Y., Bai, B., & Erdem, M. (2017). Hotel social media marketing: A study on message strategy and its effectiveness. *Journal of Hospitality and Tourism Technology*, *8*(2), 239–255. doi:10.1108/JHTT-02-2017-0012

Li, Q., Huang, Z. J., & Christianson, K. (2016). Visual attention toward tourism photographs with text: An eye-tracking study. *Tourism Management*, *54*(June), 243–258. doi:10.1016/j.tourman.2015.11.017

Luarn, P., Lin, Y.-F., & Chiu, Y.-P. (2015). Influence of Facebook brand-page posts on online engagement. *Online Information Review*, *39*(4), 505–519. doi:10.1108/OIR-01-2015-0029

Maes, A., & Shilperoord, J. (2008). Classifying visual rhetoric. Conceptual and structural heuristics. In E. F. McQuarrie & B. J. Phillips (Eds.), *Go Figure! New Directions in Advertising Rhetoric* (pp. 227–253). NY: M.E. Sharpe Inc.

Mann, W. C., Matthiessen, C. M. I. M., & Thompson, S. A. (1992). Rhetorical structure theory and text analysis. In W. C. Mann & S. A. Thompson (Eds.), *Discourse description: Diverse linguistic analyses of a fund-raising text* (pp. 39–78). Amsterdam: John Benjamins Publishing Company. doi:10.1075/pbns.16.04man

Mann, W. C., & Thompson, S. A. (1988). Rhetorical structure theory: Toward a functional theory of text organization. *Text-Interdisciplinary Journal for the Study of Discourse*, *8*(3), 243–281. doi:10.1515/text.1.1988.8.3.243

Marsh, E. E., & Domas White, M. (2003). A taxonomy of relationships between images and text. *The Journal of Documentation*, *59*(6), 647–672. doi:10.1108/00220410310506303

Martínez-López, F. J., Anaya-Sánchez, R., Molinillo, S., Aguilar-Illescas, R., & Esteban-Millat, I. (2017). Consumer engagement in an online brand community. *Electronic Commerce Research and Applications*, *23*(May-June), 24–37. doi:10.1016/j.elerap.2017.04.002

Michaelidou, N., Siamagka, N. T., Moraes, C., & Micevski, M. (2013). Do marketers use visual representations of destinations that tourists value? Comparing visitors' image of a destination with marketer-controlled images online. *Journal of Travel Research*, *52*(6), 789–804. doi:10.1177/0047287513481272

Moriarty, S. E. (1987). A content analysis of visuals used in print media advertising. *The Journalism Quarterly*, *64*(2-3), 550–554. doi:10.1177/107769908706400238

Oostervink, N., Agterberg, M., & Huysman, M. (2016). Knowledge sharing on enterprise social media: Practices to cope with institutional complexity. *Journal of Computer-Mediated Communication*, *21*(2), 156–176. doi:10.1111/jcc4.12153

Phillips, B. J., & McQuarrie, E. F. (2004). Beyond visual metaphor: A new typology of visual rhetoric in advertising. *Marketing Theory*, *4*(1-2), 113–136. doi:10.1177/1470593104044089

Pieters, R., Wedel, M., & Batra, R. (2010). The stopping power of advertising: Measures and effects of visual complexity. *Journal of Marketing*, *74*(5), 48–60. doi:10.1509/jmkg.74.5.48

Pilelienė, L., & Viktorija, G. (2016). Effect of visual advertising complexity on consumers' attention. *International Journal of Management. Accounting and Economics*, *3*(8), 489–501.

Rice, R. E., Evans, S. K., Pearce, K. E., Sivunen, A., Vitak, J., & Treem, J. W. (2017). Organizational media affordances: Operationalization and associations with media use. *Journal of Communication*, *67*(1), 106–130. doi:10.1111/jcom.12273

Ritson, M., & Elliott, R. (1999). The social uses of advertising: An ethnographic study of adolescent advertising audiences. *The Journal of Consumer Research*, *26*(3), 260–277. doi:10.1086/209562

Russell, M. G. (2009). A call for creativity in new metrics for liquid media. *Journal of Interactive Advertising*, *9*(2), 44–61.

Sabate, F., Berbegal-Mirabent, J., Cañabate, A., & Lebherz, P. R. (2014). Factors influencing popularity of branded content in Facebook fan pages. *European Management Journal*, *32*(6), 1001–1011. doi:10.1016/j.emj.2014.05.001

Schmallegger, D., Carson, D., & Jacobsen, D. (2009). The Use of Photographs on Consumer Generated Content Websites: Practical Implications for Destination Image Analysis. In N. Sharda (Ed.), *Tourism Informatics: Visual Travel Recommender Systems, Social Communities, and User Interface Design* (pp. 243–257). Hershey, PA: IGI Global.

Shifman, L. (2012). An anatomy of a YouTube meme. *New Media & Society*, *14*(2), 187–203. doi:10.1177/1461444811412160

Smith, K. L. (2005). Perception and the Newspaper Page. In K. L. Smith, S. Moriarty, K. Kenney, & G. Barbatsis (Eds.), *Handbook of Visual Communication: Theory, Methods, and Media (pp.81-p.98)*. NY: Routledge.

Social Media Examiner. (2017). *Visual content and social media marketing: New research*. Retrieved from https://www.socialmediaexaminer.com/visual-content-and-social-media-marketing-new-research/

Stark, L., & Crawford, K. (2015). The conservatism of emoji: Work, affect, and communication. *Social Media and Society*, *1*(2), 1–11.

Stepchenkova, S., & Zhan, F. (2013). Visual destination images of Peru: Comparative content analysis of DMO and user-generated photography. *Tourism Management*, *36*(June), 590–601. doi:10.1016/j.tourman.2012.08.006

Swani, K., Milne, G. R., Brown, B. P., Assaf, A. G., & Donthu, N. (2017). What messages to post? Evaluating the popularity of social media communications in business versus consumer markets. *Industrial Marketing Management*, *62*(April), 77–87. doi:10.1016/j.indmarman.2016.07.006

Taboada, M., & Habel, C. (2013). Rhetorical relations in multimodal documents. *Discourse Studies*, *15*(1), 65–89. doi:10.1177/1461445612466468

Taboada, M., & Mann, W. C. (2006). Applications of rhetorical structure theory. *Discourse Studies*, *8*(4), 567–588. doi:10.1177/1461445606064836

Tafesse, W. (2015). Content strategies and audience response on Facebook brand pages. *Marketing Intelligence & Planning, 33*(6), 927–943. doi:10.1108/MIP-07-2014-0135

Taylor, R. E. (1999). A six-segment message strategy wheel. *Journal of Advertising Research, 39*(6), 7–7.

Treem, J. W., & Leonardi, P. M. (2012). Social media use in organizations: Exploring the affordances of visibility, editability, persistence, and association. *Annals of the International Communication Association, 36*(1), 143–189. doi:10.1080/23808985.2013.11679130

Xie, B. (2008). Multimodal computer-mediated communication and social support among older Chinese internet users. *Journal of Computer-Mediated Communication, 13*(3), 728–750. doi:10.1111/j.1083-6101.2008.00417.x

This research was previously published in the International Journal of Semiotics and Visual Rhetoric (IJSVR), 2(2); pages 23-40, copyright year 2018 by IGI Publishing (an imprint of IGI Global).

Chapter 23
Drivers of Social Media Content Marketing in the Banking Sector:
A Literature Review

Aastha Sawhney

Amity Business School, Amity University, Noida, India

Vandana Ahuja

iD https://orcid.org/0000-0002-4512-7203

Amity Business School, Amity University, Noida, India

ABSTRACT

Due to technological advancement, the economy is shifting from market-driven stature to a network-oriented economy, and social media has captured prime IT trends of the technology world. The banking sector has also been trapped in the digital wave, and the banks are compelled to focus and redefine their digitalisation processes as they witness a rapid change in consumer behaviour and buying habits. Digital marketing and other social media platforms have enabled banks to become an influential tool in not only acquiring the target prospects but also for facilitating their businesses. Content marketing is a crucial ingredient to the overall digital marketing strategy to measure the effectiveness and success of an organization's online communication. Apart from the quality of the content, marketers should be conscious and must introspect their respective target audiences while delivering and promoting the content. This research paper is based on an extensive literature review that outlines the concept of social media content marketing while highlighting the various benefits it offers to the banking sector, thereby defining multiple digital media content marketing strategies that enable banks to accomplish their objectives.

DOI: 10.4018/978-1-6684-6287-4.ch023

1. INTRODUCTION

According to (Bruhn, Schoenmueller & Schäfer, 2012), due to digitalization waves in the marketplace, traditional marketing has considerably been taken over by various social networks. It has a favourable impact not only on consumers at large but also acting as a critical tool for businesses to rethink and re-define their marketing strategies. These technological changes have opened the economy for global players, enhanced competition changed the consumption patterns & consumer buying behavior and has further altered the environment in the manner in which the organizations are conversing with their target audience (Njeri, 2014; Siamagka et al., 2015). Nowadays, organizations across the industries are shifting to digital platforms to sustain in the marketplace and enhance their performance by attracting the target audience (Dodokh, 2017). Moreover, organizations are compelled to devise strategies in proficient ways to attain competitive advantage (Franco et al., 2016). One of the primary tools that are adopted by the organizations is the usage of social Media (Akmese et al., 2016).

Various studies conducted by the researchers on social media usage has been reflecting an increasing trend across sectors and has become a vital ingredient in marketing and evolving the brand in the marketplace (Hanna, Rohn, & Crittenden, 2011). Thus, an ideal social media strategy enables brands to increase their visibility (Shen & Bissel, 2013) and sustain long term relationships (Yan, 2011), which facilities brands to develop conversations with their clients and interact with them effectively.

Thus, social media marketing has taken over an edge over others. It has provided marketers with a platform to acquire, engage, communicate, connect, and create long term relationships with their target audience (Chikandiwa, Contogiannis, & Jembere, 2013). Moreover, various organizations are massively investing and tapping in diverse social media marketing strategies due to the vast opportunities prevalent in the marketplace (Mitic & Kapoulas, 2012). As stated by (Ansari, Ghori, & Kazi, 2019), with a full range of benefits, social media marketing majorly caters to three advantages entailing fundamentally free, customized as well as societally acknowledged. Adding to this (Parusheva, 2017) stated that it not only permits organizations to enjoy cost benefits but unlocks new market segments effectively. Various scholars (Coulter, Bruhn, Schoenmueller & Schäfer, 2012), have cited that the new age social media techniques are widely accepted and implemented in the commercial arena. As per the latest "Social Media Statistics in India report" (Nandita Mathur, 2019), the number of social media users in India has grown from 326.1 million in 2018 to 351.4 million in 2019. Also, the reports quantified that in India, on average, users spend 2.4 hours on social media in a day, and out of the entire Indian population, 493 million are regular users of the internet.

Bhattacharya et al., (2000) has started his work on banking sector automation where various reforms have been cited, which is further trailed by Narsimhan Committee. The existing marketing methods are now augmented by information technology with significant emphasis on the usage of the internet (Urban, 2004). Also study conducted by (Rajshekhara, 2004) has examined and concluded that the role of information technology in the Indian banking sector will bring a drastic change over a while. Moreover, digital marketing can be referred to as a process of developing cohesive communication patterns with the target audience via digital platforms and technology (Smith, 2015).

In the present scenario (Zomorodian and Lu, 2017), cited that the banking sector is massively clutched in digital wave and hence banking & other financial institutions are considering social media & content marketing as a vital ingredient for creating banks awareness, acquiring new prospects, creating brand perceptibility, equity, status, disseminating knowledge, ensuring brand recall and fostering long term relationships with customers. Banks understand the need for social media and consider using social platforms to curb the mounting financial needs of the target audience through customization and delivering value to them (Mitic & Kapoulas, 2012). These technological innovations have fostered the process of information transmission and processing. Banks today adopt social media practices to market their financial products, create awareness, and provide extended customer services, which in turn enhance the customer service experience and relation (Ibrahim, Abdallahamed & Adam, 2018). Therefore, it can be concluded that information technology enhancement has transmuted the financial product range, service networks, and nature & packaging of the banking products & services. (Campanella et al., 2013).

Social Media Content Marketing is one such strategy that has attracted a lot of attention with the rise in technological advancement in the banking sector over the last few years. Thus, the essence of effective content marketing lies in the adoption of a well-defined and quality content strategy, i.e., appropriate usage of words (Gajanova, 2018). Thus, the instructive, informative, or engaging content attracts the attention of the target audience and help in building conversations with them (Muller & Christandl, 2019). However, banks need to analyze that the existing marketing strategies should be well integrated with the evolution of globalization, technical advancement, and changes in customer requirements. As per the latest studies, the approach of incorporating videos with infographics is 96% successful for enriching the content (Krizanova et al., 2013). Presently various social networking sites, including Facebook, engage their audience through videos, which in turn amounts to 55% of the internet users (Achen et al., 2018). Also, Thus, there is a vital need to formulate content not only thematically but also formally.

Therefore, understanding the various drivers of social media content marketing is crucial for both academicians and managers (Schultz & Peltier, 2013; Kumar, Bezawada, Rishika, Janakiraman, & Kannan, 2016). According to the existing literature, various studies have been conducted on specific issues such as consumption behavior (Chang, Yu, & Lu, 2015; Relling, Schnittka, Sattler, & Johnen, 2016), CRM (Trainor, Andzulis, Rapp, & Agnihotri, 2014), product management (Asmussen, Harridge-March, Occhiocupo, & Farquhar, 2013), innovation management (Gebauer, Füller, & Pezzei, 2013). Though these studies provide a detailed progression in specific industries, however, the existing literature does not reflect much on the drivers of social media content marketing specifically to the banking domain.

The present study focuses on addressing this research gap by aiming at the following objectives:

- To study the existing literature published in the domain of Social Media Content Marketing
- To develop a social media content marketing conceptual model for the banking sector

The structure of the paper includes a literature review followed by proposed digital marketing strategies, further leading to the implications and conclusions based on findings.

2. LITERATURE REVIEW

2.1 Social Media

As defined by (Pan & Crotts, 2012), social media can be defined as a collection of online communication networks related to a particular group-based input where people interact, share content and develop associations & partnerships. This may further include various online applications & web portals that facilitate sharing content with the target audiences in a shorter period effectively and appropriately (Wahi, Medury & Misra, 2014).

2.2 Content Marketing

Content Marketing Institute (2015), defines the term "Content Marketing refers to a phenomena of formulating and dispensing the content to the target segment to create interest in the mindsets of the audience, acquire and absorb the prospects to generate profits. Also, the Content Marketing Institute shows the perspective of various experts who have defined content marketing.

Thus, "content marketing is circulating the content to the target segment who are probing for the same information at various channels. Hence, it is a comprehensive tool to design, organize and conglomerate content," as stated by Michael Brenner (Content Marketing Institute, 2015).

Similarly, Sam Decker, CEO of Mass Relevance (the SaaS leader in social integration), proposes content marketing as a strategy to formulate and organize content into various typologies, be it for creating awareness, educational, emotional or entertaining & so on and after that furnishing the same content on different platforms to seek customer attention, provide a fundamental solution and to attract them to learn and experience more about the brand (Content Marketing Institute, 2015).

In a nutshell, "content marketing as a concept refers to the method or the way the brands narrate an authentic story about their product/service, its values & culture and what they are" (Denning, 2011). Also, to gain insights about a company & its product line, consumers seek information about the company they wish to associate with and introspect how customer-centric their solutions are to meet the customer's needs (Denning, 2011).

2.3 Social Media Content Marketing

In context to the past studies, social media platforms act as an influential tool in building brand image (Bruhn, Schoenmueller & Schäfer, 2012). With extensive & appropriate usage of social platforms, banks tap & build their goodwill & equity in the eyes of the target audience by differentiating their products & influence consumer's mindsets by developing long term relationships with the brand.

Rowley (2008), social media content marketing provides a platform where social media and content marketing intersects. Due to the shift of consumers to the online platforms, the attention towards understanding & implementing social media content marketing strategies have taken an edge. Moreover, social media content marketing is not just limited to sharing content on social platforms. Still, it also deals with connecting social business to these social sites, collaboration, newsroom techniques, and principles to content marketing (GÜMÜŞ, 2017). As cited by (Merholz, 2002), the significant implications of social media content marketing can be enlisted as:

- Increasing interaction with the target audience and creating brand awareness among the prospects
- Promoting two-way communication channel between banks & their clients
- Acquiring instant and accurate feedback
- Assisting in advertising or creating publicity among the masses

2.4 The Most Popular Social Media Tools and Applications

The concept of "weblog" came into existence in 1997 by Jorn Barger (Wortham, 2007). Adding to this, (Merholz, 2002) infringed the word "weblog" into "wee" and "blog" and invented the expression "blog" in 1999.

According to Baker and More (2008) blogs can be identified as personal web pages where one can post details, information & share knowledge about various topics which can further be modified from time to time (Baker & Moore, 2008). As reflected by (Baggetun & Wasson, 2006) also states, "weblog as a web page that serves as a publicly accessible personal or group journal for an individual or a group." Even (Williams & Jacobs, 2004) referred to blogs as a convenient method of micro-publishing, offering the prospect for interactive activity and brainstorming. Bloggers can establish a secure connection with their readers by tagging and & categorically organising the content to share ideas, opinions, and thoughts. This further facilitates the readers to share viewpoints on different blogs, and the most appealing part of it is that the blogger remains open to communication. Laying down emphasis on the massive influence of blogs in the present scenario (Eide & Eide, 2005) cited blogs to be a very significate tool which has a sociocultural force.

2.4.1 Wikis

To an extent, it can be stated that wikis often resemble blogs. (Mattison, 2003) opposes that both of them, i.e., blogs & wikis, are perfect examples of cooperative & combined efforts of groupware. However, we can refer a wiki as a blog, but it is not the vice versa. Moreover (Leuf & Cunningham, 2001), who coined & discovered the concept of wikis, stated that wikis are an assortment of freely expandable intertwined pages of the web which are connected by a hypertext loading phenomena for uploading and amending data or material into a a database which can be further edited by users. It has also been stated that Wikis are far more open platforms to communicate than blogs, and are very user friendly since they allow their users to change/edit information written by them.

In other words, wikis showcase the positive attributes of a blog. Financial institutions consider wikis as shared knowledge repositories that enable in enhancing knowledge base (Godwin-Jones, 2003). About (Kokkinaki, 2009), wikis facilitate collaborative efforts of team members & portray their skills, critical thinking, and social skills and thereby facilitating better understanding and analysis of the content in the minds of the target audience. Adding to the same, wikis are considered as a useful tool for sharing problems and acquiring speedy feedback in the digital arena.

2.4.2 Multimedia Sharing and Social Networking Sites (SNSs)

Anderson (2007), shared his viewpoint based on serving Web 2.0, which reflects that there is a phenomenal change in individual creation and user-developed content through personalisation while sharing the same on social networking sites entailing YouTube, Twitter, Myspace, Facebook, etc.

Considering the statistical data cited on Facebook Press Room (Facebook, 2010), it reflects that today out of 500 million Facebook users, half of them are consistent users. Also, it is being cited by researchers that an average user has minimum 130 friends. Since the user is connected with various groups, blogs, posts, pages or events which in turn creates 30 billion pieces of content that is shared on social platforms and networking sites.

Evans (2010) mentioned that seventy-five million Twitter users consists of more than four billion images as per February 2019 data. Also, it has been reported that total number of twitter accounts has increased over a period of time (Bianchi, 2010).

Metekohy (2010), stated that that two billion items of videotapes are consistently viewed by YouTube users whose average visit time is minimum 15 minutes and every minute users are uploading videos

& content on YouTube. Evans (2010) stated that LinkedIn has 50,000.000 members and the number is increasing with passage of time. Moreover, in the present scenario, the concept of social tagging is becoming a major trend on the social media networking sites and social bookmarking, tag clouds, folksonomy, and collabulary are attracting a huge traffic on their portals (Anderson, 2007).

2.5 Outline of Indian Banking Sector

As cited by (Mitic & Kapoulas, 2012) and Reserve Bank of India (RBI), the Indian Banking sector is well structured and sufficiently capitalized. Even the condition relating to the economic & financial perspective is showing a positive indication for the overall development. According to (Özeltürkay, Yaşa, & Mucan, 2014), the credit markets and liquidity risk studies reflect that the banks are performing well and can survive effectively in a global depression. The digital payment system, which has progressed in 25 countries across the globe, the Indian Immediate Payment Service (IMPS), occupies the position at a level 5 in the Faster Payments Innovation Index.

In context to (Matkovic, Sakal, & Tumbas, 2011), Indian's banking sector is one of the largest service sectors in the country, and the availability of quality services becomes an essential ingredient in regulating the overall industry (Ishola & Olusoji, 2020). Today, with advent of digitalization in the banking domain, bank orientation has primarily changed from customer acquisition to customer retention wherein banks are focusing on creating long term relationships and sustain them effectively (Jain & Bhatnagar, 2016). Moreover, banks are offering various consumer friendly digital products and services which have enabled customer is carrying out transactions without a hassle like Internet Banking, ATM services, etc. Thus, by stressing on the significance of social media, content marketing has facilitated banks in promoting, supporting, enhancing, and monitoring a wide range of activities (Sharma & Sharma, 2014).

2.6 Consumer Behavior in Indian Banking Sector

In the present banking arena, consumers look for various convenient ways of interaction with their respective banks, whether interacting through visiting the branch & interacting verbally, or through virtual platforms like bank's website, emails, or through mobile banking services which bank's offers (Parusheva, 2017). Thus, for communicating with audiences to create more awareness & share information about the financial products & services, banks are exploring & adopting various digital and social media platforms to ensure their presence in the marketplace (Adl & Elfergany, 2020). According to the recent trends & study (Balaram Babu & Mohan Babu, 2018) banking sector has undergone a significant transformation specifically over the last five years. Customer satisfaction has become a fundamental matrix for the successful functioning of the banks, and all branch managers consider this as a critical component in achieving their respective goals & objectives (Favre-Bonte, Elodie & Thevenard-Puthod 2013).

2.7 Four Stages Process - Social Marketing Strategy

Today social media offers lucrative prospects to marketers, but at times, it may not be a sustainable strategy for your target audience. Hence, as a marketer, we need to be cautious in adopting & designing the social marketing strategy depending on the potential benefits it offers to the target segment and should stress on customer engagement.

(Li & Bernoff's, 2008) P.O.S.T. model (an acronym which indicates People, Objectives, Strategy, and Technology) describes the four stages driven social marketing process which focuses on integrating social media with the social marketing strategy. The underlying assumption of this model is that organisations are keen on adopting social media for customer engagement rather than using it as a mere platform for information dissemination.

Figure 1. Stages Social Marketing Strategy

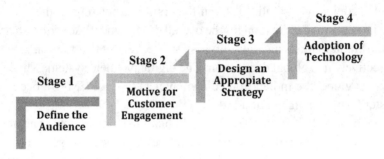

2.7.1 Stage 1

At the first stage, identify and segregate the audience segment, which needs to be tapped for social marketing and social media. For instance, organizations may be targeting working professionals, but as per their working policies, individuals might not have access to social networking sites at their offices; however, they can have access to the same at their home premises. It has also been stated that adults aged 18 to 33 years are more likely to watch videos and use social networking sites compared with people older than 55 years (Zickuhr, 2010). Secondly, be aware of how the target audience is utilizing social media.

- Is the target audience engaged in writing original content and publishing the same on various social networking sites, blogs, and other social platforms?
- Do the audience indulge in reading reviews but never respond in sharing their opinion?
- Are they leaving a comment on another related post?
- Are they active in looking at various activities on social platforms but restrict themselves from giving valuable contributions?

After finding answers to the stated questions, organizations should invest their time, efforts & resources in developing a strategy in line with the target audience preferences & program objectives.

2.7.2 Stage 2

During the second phase, introspect the objective for engaging the target audience. There are five purposes as recommended by (Li & Bernoff, 2010) that depict tactical thinking regarding how to deploy audience interest and expertise to advance products and services.

- The First purpose is to actively listen and pay attention to audience feedback & opinion regarding the organization, its product & services, behaviors, and so on. Social media may also act as a value-added tool to fetch these data without time & geographic constraints (Galli, 2019). Hence, this purpose satisfies the basic principle of social marketing that focuses on the significance of formative research and understanding the consumer before making any programmatic decisions.

- The second purpose is to encourage the audience to develop conversations, i.e., let the audience speak to their family, friends, reference groups, colleagues, and society at large regarding the product & services of the organization. This, in turn, would multiple the existing promotional efforts through word of mouth communication and making the target audience more comfortable in conversating about the same.

- The third purpose facilitates tapping the most appropriate prospects and vocal supporters by inviting them to be the real advocates for the brand. Though the process would be comprehensive and time-consuming but will help in identifying advocates who are more likely to share information, provide recommendations, influence others to take action, and increase demand for products and services (Conroy & Narula, 2010).

- The fourth objective is to facilitate the audience with a channel to assist one another. It focused on extending appropriate customer service by answering queries & questions of the audience at an online forum.

- The fifth objective is to involve your target audience while designing products & services. As interacting with audience while conducting research will enable organizations to know and understand various gaps, information & problems that audiences are facing and also helps in identifying the platform where the audience would like to receive information, what price they are willing to pay and the perceived benefits from the product or service. The organisations can further consolidate audience members for creating appropriate strategies for deploying social media strategies.

2.7.3 Stage 3

This step involves preparing the framework to involve the target audience in order to fulfil the goal ascertained in step 2. As explored by researchers that people tend to remain associated with whom they have significant relationship. Thus, organisations need to expressive in defining the reasons & benefits to its target audience for being connected and establishing a long term bond with the organization. Precisely, the organisations need to tell their audience about the value proposition they are going to offer so that the relationship becomes meaningful and mutually beneficial.

The organization should draft and showcase a blue print regarding the various parameters on which the success of its social media strategy can be evaluated and should also reflect how relationships with its audience will be fostered. Few of the parameters that can be considered for evaluation & measurement can be audience reach, customer engagement, brand likeability, sentiment analysis, etc.

2.7.4 Stage 4

The fourth step relates to the selection of the most optimal technology. Organizations should analyse their target audience preferences regarding the type of social media they use and the way they deploy the same, etc. This will further enable the organization to ascertain the appropriate social media application to use for its audience. Moreover, it is recommended that instead of using new social media applications, organisations should first ascertain traditional & well established groups & communities and should try to be a part of the same. This will result in understanding and exploring the appropriate platform where the target audience is indulging into conversations and the subject matter of the same.

2.8 Antecedents of Digital Content Marketing Strategy

In the context of digitalization, the various attributes to be taken into consideration entails focusing on quality rather than the volume. According to (Baltes, 2015) the content & themes should be in line with the selected target audiences or the prospects (Ionescu, 2015), the inclusion of keywords by deploying the search engine optimization techniques, adoption of various media platforms by advertising (sharing & re-sharing) on different social media engines and engaging audience in developing conversations usually who share and comment on your shared content (Meltwater, 2014).

2.8.1 Content Quality

Rowley (2008), stated digital content as small fragments of objects disseminated to a set of audiences via electronic networks. Content marketing is a phenomenon for formulating and circulating digital content to grab prospects attention, gain market share, and engage the target segment through conversations and drive profitability (Baltes, 2015). Hence, quality content is the key ingredient and should be based on the core values of the organization (Thackeray, Neiger, & Keller; 2012).

2.8.2 Target Audience

As per the model proposed by (Bernoff, 2007), i.e., POST (an acronym for people, objectives, strategy, and technologies) wherein the "People" facet strongly recommends various organizations first to comprehend their clients from multiple elements and then adopt any social media for circulating their content. Similarly, (Safko & Brake, 2009), stated ACCESS which is an acronym for audience, concept, competition, execution, social media, and sales viability also acclaims that only after understanding and defining the audience, organizations need to strategize various ideas & approaches for formulation & designing of content for the target audience.

2.8.3 Search Engine Optimization

According to (Karjaluoto & Leinonen, 2009), the dynamic process of Search Engine Optimization relates to refining the web site's traffic by achieving higher search engine rank in organic search results. Moreover, if the website makes a higher rank during the search engine results pages (SERPs), the opportunity for the target prospects visiting the site increases (Enge et al., 2012). (Baozhen & Shilun, 2010) reflected that the primary purpose of SEO as a content marketing strategy is to apprise the target audience about the products or services available, which in turn acts as a crucial component in enhancing the organization's web visibility.

2.8.4 Variety of Media

Boyd & Ellison, 2008; Singh et al., (2008) variety and classification of social media techniques relates to concreted acceptance of social media among the commercial world as tools entailing blog posts, eBooks, infographics, checklists, audio content, webinars, microblogs, social networks, media sharing content, social bookmarking and voting sites. Also, in context to (Baltes, 2015), a variety of media majorly depends upon the nature of the content to be designed or created.

2.8.5 Advertising Effort

In the present advertising scenario, social media has a significant influence which has forced organizations to be more cautious while advertising specifically in terms of the content that consumers write and should be vigilant in evading any unexpected blunders to prevent a viral consumer criticism on networking sites (Saravanakumar & Lakshmi, 2012). Advertisements designed by brands for social media acts as a powerful weapon in acquiring potential clientele so well as to make the prospects follow their content on social platforms (Hacıefendioğlu, 2011).

2.8.6 Engage With People

According to (Baltes 2015), an organization can boost its market share, enhance its reach, and can effectively connect by engaging with target audience customers through conversations. According to (GÜMÜŞ, 2017) the fusion of social media in the promotion mix is highly significant as it not only facilitates organizations to communicate with their target audience but also promotes in building up customer conversations about the organization's products, services, goals, etc.

Table 1 represents a consolidated view of various papers studied to understand the above cited antecedents of social media content marketing in depth.

Proposed Model

With the advent of digitalization in the banking sector and reference to the above-cited arguments, authors have cited the below-depicted model (Figure 2). This model reflects various digital content marketing strategies that banks can adopt to accomplish their banking marketing goals and objectives.

3. RESEARCH METHODS

An extensive and detailed study has been done to understand the influence of social media content marketing on the marketing strategies of banks. The study is based on secondary sources such as articles, magazines, reports, research papers, and literature related to social media content marketing and marketing strategies of banks. In this context, databases such as EBSCO, ProQuest, ABDC listed journals, and other databases were accessed.

Table 1. Consolidated view of papers reflecting various antecedents of social media content marketing

Paper Name	Author	Year	Publications	Content Quality	Target Audience	Variety of Media	Advertising Efforts	Engage with People	SEO
Impact of Brand Awareness and Social Media Content Marketing on Consumer Purchase Decision.	Ansari, S., Ansari, G., Ghori, M. U., & Kazi, A. G.	2019	Journal of Public Value and Administration Insights, 2(2), 5-10.	✓	✓	✓	×	✓	×
Role and impact of social media on banking industry	Dr. P Balaram Babu and CH Mohan Babu	2018	International Journal of Commerce and Management Research	×	✓	✓	✓	✓	×
The Effects of Social Media Content Marketing Activities of Firms on Consumers' Brand Following Behavior	GÜMÜŞ, N.	2017	Academic Research International, 8(1), 1-8.	✓	✓	×	✓	×	×
Social Media Banking Models: A case study of a practical implementation in banking sector.	Parusheva, S.	2017	Economic Research, (3), 125-141	×	✓	✓	✓	×	×
Elements of strategic social media marketing: A holistic framework.	Felix, R., Rauschnabel, P. A., & Hinsch, C.	2017	Journal of Business Research, 70, 118-126.	✓	✓	✓	✓	✓	✓
How Content Marketing Can Help the Bank Industrial: Experience from Iran	Zomorodian, S., & Lu, Y.	2017	International Conference on Management Science and Engineering Management (pp. 626-633). Springer, Cham.	✓	✓	✓	✓	✓	×
Content marketing - the fundamental tool of digital marketing	Loredana Patruitu Baltes	2015	Bulletin of the Transilvania University of Brașov Series V: Economic Sciences • Vol. 8 (57) No. 2 - 2015	✓	✓	✓	✓	✓	×
The usage of digital marketing channels in SMEs.	Taiminen, H. M., & Karjaluoto, H.	2015	Journal of Small Business and Enterprise Development	✓	✓	✓	✓	✓	✓
How Turkish Banks Benefit from Social Media: Analyzing Banks Formal Links	Özeltürkay, E. Yaşa, and Burcu Mucan	2014	International Journal of Strategic Innovative Marketing 1, no. 2 (2014): 120-129.	✓	×	✓	✓	✓	×
How Turkish Banks Benefit from Social Media: Analyzing Banks Formal Links	Özeltürkay, E. Yaşa, and Burcu Mucan	2014	International Journal of Strategic Innovative Marketing 1, no. 2 (2014): 120-129.	✓	×	✓	✓	✓	×
Overlapping factors in search engine optimization and web accessibility	Moreno, L., & Martinez, P.	2013	Online Information Review.	✓	×	✓	×	×	✓
Integrating Social Media and Social Marketing: A Four-Step Process	Rosemary Thackeray, Brad L. Neiger, and Heidi Keller	2012	Health Promotion Practice March 2012 Vol. 13, No. 2 165–168, DOI:10.1177/1524839911432009 © 2012 Society for Public Health Education	✓	✓	×	×	✓	×

continues on following page

Table 1. Continued

Paper Name	Author	Year	Publications	Content Quality	Target Audience	Variety of Media	Advertising Efforts	Engage with People	SEO
Theoretical Models of Social Media, Marketing Implications, and Future Research Directions	Bing Pan and John C. Crotts	2012	Social media in travel, Tourism, and hospitality: Theory, practice, and cases, 1, 73-86.	✓	×	✓	×	✓	×
Understanding the role of social media in bank marketing	Mitic, M., & Kapoulas, A.	2012	Marketing Intelligence & Planning, 30(7), 668-686.	✓	✓	✓	✓	✓	×
Are social media replacing traditional media in terms of brand equity creation?	Coulter, K. S., Bruhn, M., Schoenmueller, V., & Schäfer, D. B.	2012	Management Research Review	✓	×	✓	✓	✓	×
Web 2.0 Technologies in Internal and External Communications in the Banking Sector	Matkovic, P., Sakal, M., & Tumbas, P.	2011	Theory, Methodology, Practice, 7(2), 87.	✓	✓	✓	×	✓	×
Personalization and sociability of open knowledge management based on social tagging	Baozhen Lee and Shilun Ge	2010	Personalization and sociability of open knowledge management based on social tagging. Online Information Review	✓	×	✓	×	✓	✓
Users' adoption of e-banking services: the Malaysian perspective.	Poon, W. C.	2008	Journal of Business & Industrial Marketing	✓	×	×	✓	×	×
Understanding digital content marketing	Rowley, J	2008	Journal of marketing management, 24(5-6), 517-540	✓	✓	✓	✓	✓	×
Segmentation of bank customers by expected benefits and attitudes	Machauer, A., & Morgner, S.	2001	International Journal of Bank Marketing	×	✓	×	×	×	×

Figure 2. Author's Representation - Drivers of Digital Content Marketing Strategy

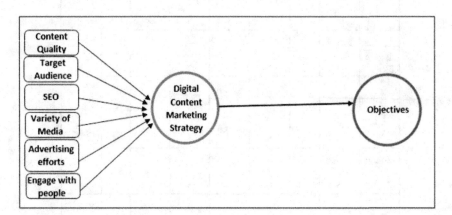

4. DISCUSSION OF FINDINGS

Balaram Babu & Mohan Babu (2018), the present Indian Banking Sector, social media content marketing has become a powerful tool in enhancing and sustaining relationships with consumers. With the advent of various financial institutions and their wide variety of financial products, social media content marketing provides a platform for connecting and developing relationships with the target audience apart from the sales process.

It further enhances the process of analyzing consumer's understanding of the financial services of the banks through advertising to the target audience, providing customized customer services, and an experiential user environment (Souissi, Azouzi, & Jarboui, 2018). It also provides people a platform to share their knowledge & experiences by initiating conversations and therefore reach out to more prospects than the traditional approach. But the social media marketing is still in its infant stage since banks are not utilizing this approach to its optimum level as they have restricted themselves to selling products, conversing with customers & facilitating in carrying out online banking services (Parusheva, 2017).

The value proposition offered by social media content marketing cannot be overruled, especially for the achievement of long-term goals (Kim, Kim, & Lennon, 2018). Banks have already started initiating various practices to curb the challenges regarding privacy and security issues and are trying to mitigate risks involved in carrying out online banking transactions through social media platforms. Further, (Matkovic, Sakal, & Tumbas, 2011), social media content marketing strategies for banks have evolved around return on Investment strategy and enhance are enabling banks to use this platform ranging from Facebook to Instagram to facilitate real-time solutions for the customers and increasing the intangible value associated with different banks.

Mitic & Kapoulas (2012) suggested that in the banking domain, a content marketing strategy can only be beneficial if the banks stress on disseminating quality content. Pan & Crotts (2014), the quality of content will enable banks to ascertain the optimal frequency of promotion through a right social media platform. In the present competitive banking scenario, which is highly dynamic and acquiring potential customers is a significant challenge, the high quality of content facilitates obtaining the right prospects and building trust among the target audience (Zomorodian & Lu, 2017).

Baltes (2015) stated that banks need to conduct a thorough target analysis as it facilitates in ascertaining the appropriate content marketing strategy by determining potential prospects characteristics in terms of their demographics, income, gender, age, areas of interest, preference of specific networking platforms, etc. Adding to the context (Chikandiwa, Contogiannis, & Jembere, 2013) stated that the first motive for banks should be introspecting the purpose for deploying social media in serving their target audience rather than just focusing on the tools to be used on social platforms.

The banking sector can, therefore, adopt the SEO techniques to build up accessibility to their website. Also, web accessibility is fundamentally related to the content shared on the webpages; thus, the availability of a webpage can be drastically enhanced with SEO practices (Moreno & Martinez, 2013).

As cited by Mangold and Faulds (2009), in context to the present banking scenario, due to augmentation of complexities in the bank services, there is an abrupt need to disseminate knowledge to the prospects to create value for their services. According to (Hanna et al., 2011), prerequisites for implementing social media strategies that assimilate social media with marketing communication have become inevitable to sustain customer relations with the banks.

Zomorodian and Lu, (2017), with the advent of industrialization in the Indian banking sector, banks use social media as a platform to enhance their market share by acting as a catalyst in igniting communication channel with its customers, facilitating brand equity and developing trust among its target audience. Moreover, as stated by (Poon, 2008), there is a significant rise in public awareness about various e-banking services offered by banks, which in turn has facilitated to adoption of technology applications.

The content shared by banks through their social media campaigns facilitates specific vital points that motivate the target audience to initiate conversation and engage them in strengthening customer relationships, obtaining relevant feedback and influence them with online content (Murdough, 2009). Further adding to this, (Keller, 2009) explained that these critical points entailing views, feelings, opinions, judgments, insights, knowledge, and experiences help in developing brand association in the consumer mindsets.

Therefore, results of this study also sheds light on various benefits that social media content marketing strategy provides to the banking sector through Figure 3:

Figure 3. Benefits of Social Media Content Marketing

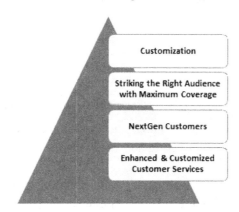

- Customization

A coordinate relationship can be established between the banks & the prospects, and the banks can cater to new potentialities while focusing on customizing their messages regarding their financial products & services with their clients.

- Striking The Right Audience with Maximum Coverage

Social media has enabled banks to enhance their market reach by adopting various social media marketing strategies. It has helped banks in enhancing sales figures, advertising the right content to the audiences, deepening partnerships, and enabling 24x7 anywhere anytime banking to customers across the world, thus eliminating geographical constraints.

- NextGen Customers

The youth today (18-30 years) doesn't want to approach bank branch or relationship managers to gain financial insights about the products & services, investment choices & so on. They look forward to all information online and in a user-friendly manner. Hence social media content marketing enables to overcome this barrier by sharing relevant and appropriate content & information through social media content marketing strategies. This further emphasis on the need for creating a strong social presence & effective social media content strategy in order to communicate with their target audience.

Banks can further leverage this young generation for cross-selling products by deepening their knowledge while promoting the right content on social media platforms.

- Enhanced and Customized Customer Services

Social media content marketing strategies is providing multifold benefits to banks for delivering client support. This can further develop stronger relationships with existing as well as new prospects while improving the reaction time. Customer knowledge can also be upgraded on the social platforms for activities like user authentication & credit grading, which empowers banks to provide better support to customers.

5. CONCLUSION

Today Social media is universal and pervasive and increasingly gaining significance as it facilitates organizations to create and sustain long term relationships with their target audience. Thus, banks need to analyze and adopt various digital marketing and social media content marketing strategies as a part of their overall marketing strategy.

In the present scenario, banks need to strategize well according to the current demands of their customers to gain retention. The behavior towards the banking sector of the coming new generation as well as the actual young age is very different than that of the old one. Thus banking sectors, as well as all the financial institutions, are into social media marketing to stay connected with their customers and also to get the work done easier through social media marketing.

Social media content marketing is a trending strategy of digital marketing and, apparently, for the overall marketing strategy required in the banking domain. Thus, to have a sound digital marketing strategy, banks should focus on delivering high content quality on the social platforms to their target audience. Further, to deploy an effective & quality content strategy, marketers should define their audiences aptly, understand their motives & interests for engaging the customer on social platforms, and accordingly should design an appropriate plan. The main aim for deputing a content strategy by banks to aware, inform, and educate target audiences by the financial products and services and further mature the customer relationship by building trust and loyalty among the target audience.

In a nutshell, social media content marketing has become an important strategy of digital marketing and will prevail in the future digital marketing arena. Moreover, in order to deploy an effective digital marketing strategy & accomplish organizational objectives, marketers need to focus on quality content marketing. Also, organizations should carry out extensive research in order to customize their social media content marketing strategies so as to meet the needs & expectations of their target audience. Therefore, social media content marketing strategies play a vital role in apprising and informing their target audience and upsurge brand loyalty by fostering long term relationships.

To be successful in creating a social media content strategy, banks need to focus on various strategies digital content strategies entailing content quality, understanding the target audience, utilizing multiple search engine optimization techniques, focusing on the advertising efforts & engaging the audience in developing conversation while using various social media platforms to meet their stated goals & objectives.

6. MANAGERIAL IMPLICATIONS

Content marketing is still being in the infant stage, and a lot needs to be explored in the stated domain. Banks, while formulating their overall marketing strategy, should consider and emphasize on adopting various digital content marketing strategies. These digital content strategies offer an array of opportunities to banks to boost their market share, enhance their reach, and can effectively connect by engaging with target audience customers through conversations.

The implications of this research will serve to provide inputs to the banking sector regarding the most productive social media content strategy. Further, we can conduct a comprehensive analysis on various social media content typology that can be utilized in the banking sector and can also study the impact of different social media content typologies on consumer brand engagement and consumer-brand relationships.

Bank managers can help in creating specific social media content that is directed towards their particular short term & long term objectives and goals. Well-directed special media campaigns can help in building strong consumer-brand relationships and convey the thoughts & ideas of the bank managers to the consumers. This can create an ecosystem of trust & harmony between all the stakeholders.

REFERENCES

Achen, R. M., Kaczorovski, J., Horsmann, T., & Ketzler, A. (2018). Exploring Off-Season Content and Interaction on Facebook: A Comparison of U.S. Professional Sport Leagues. *International Journal of Sport Communication*, *11*(3), 389–413. doi:10.1123/ijsc.2018-0013

Adl, A., & Elfergany, A. K. (2020). Tracking How a Change in a Telecom Service Affects Its Customers Using Sentiment Analysis and Personality Insight. *International Journal of Service Science, Management, Engineering, and Technology, 11*(3), 33–46. doi:10.4018/IJSSMET.2020070103

Akmese, H., Aras, S., & Akmese, K. (2016). Financial performance and social media: A research on tourism enterprises quoted in Istanbul stock exchange (BIST). *Procedia Economics and Finance, 39*, 705–710. doi:10.1016/S2212-5671(16)30281-7

Anderson, P. (2007, February). *What is Web 2.0? Ideas, technologies, and implications for education.* Retrieved September 2, 2010, from CiteSeeRx: http://citeseerx.ist.psu.edu/viewdoc/download?doi=10.1.1.108.9995&rep=rep1&type=pdf

Angelini, A., Ferretti, P., Ferrante, G., & Graziani, P. (2017). Social media development paths in banks. *Journal of Promotion Management, 23*(3), 345–358. doi:10.1080/10496491.2017.1294868

Ansari, S., Ansari, G., Ghori, M. U., & Kazi, A. G. (2019). Impact of Brand Awareness and Social Media Content Marketing on Consumer Purchase Decision. *Journal of Public Value and Administration Insights, 2*(2), 5–10. doi:10.31580/jpvai.v2i2.896

Asmussen, B., Harridge-March, S., Occhiocupo, N., & Farquhar, J. (2013). The multi-layered nature of the internet-based democratization of brand management. *Journal of Business Research, 66*(9), 1473–1483. doi:10.1016/j.jbusres.2012.09.010

Baggetun, R., & Wasson, B. (2006). Self-Regulated Learning and Open Writing. *European Journal of Education, 41*(3-4), 453–472.

Baker, J., & Moore, S. (2008). Distress, Coping, and Blogging: Comparing New Myspace Users by Their Intention to Blog. *Cyberpsychology & Behavior, 11*(1).

Baltes, L. P. (2015). Content marketing- the fundamental tool of digital marketing. Bulletin of the Transilvania University of Brasov. *Economic Sciences. Series V, 8*(2), 111.

Sharma & Sharma. (n.d.). *Banking Sector in India: An overview.* Gurukul Kangri University.

Barreda, A. A., Bilgihan, A., Nusair, K., & Okumus, F. (2015). Generating brand awareness in online social networks. *Computers in Human Behavior, 50*, 600–609. doi:10.1016/j.chb.2015.03.023

Bernoff, J. (2007). The POST method: a systematic approach to social strategy. *Forester.* Available at: https://forrester.typepad.com/groundswell/2007/12/the-postmethod.html

Bhattacharya & Bolton. (2000). Relationship marketing in mass markets. Handbook of Relationship Marketing.

Bianchi, L. (2010, May 10). *Twitter Facts & Figures.* Retrieved September 25, 2010, from Viral Blog: https://www.viralblog.com/research/twitter-facts-figures/

Boyd, D. M., & Ellison, N. B. (2008). Social network sites: Definition, history, and scholarship. *Journal of Computer-Mediated Communication, 13*(1), 210–230. doi:10.1111/j.1083-6101.2007.00393.x

Brand, F. (2011a, March 7). *Financial Brand: Marketing Insights for Banks & Credit Unions.* Retrieved January 15, 2012, from How Many Facebook Fans Can Financial Institutions Expect: https://thefinancialbrand.com/17424/facebook-page-fans-likes-for-banks-credit-unions/

Bruhn, M., Schoenmueller, V. & Schäfer, D. (2012). Are social media replacing traditional media in terms of brand equity creation. *Management Research Review, 35*(9), 770 - 790.

Campanella, F., Del Giudice, M., & Della Peruta, M. R. (2013). The role of information in the credit relationship. *Journal of Innovation and Entrepreneurship, 2*(1), 1–16. doi:10.1186/2192-5372-2-17

Campanella, F., Della Peruta, M. R., & Del Giudice, M. (2017). The effects of technological innovation on the banking sector. *Journal of the Knowledge Economy, 8*(1), 356–368. doi:10.100713132-015-0326-8

Carr, J. D., Lucie, Q., Rojas, W., Rossochacki, B., Yang, T., & Wen, Y. (2015). Social media in product development. *Food Quality and Preference, 40*, 354–364. doi:10.1016/j.foodqual.2014.04.001

Chang, Y. T., Yu, H., & Lu, H. P. (2015). Persuasive messages, popularity cohesion, and message diffusion in social media marketing. *Journal of Business Research, 68*(4), 777–782. doi:10.1016/j.jbusres.2014.11.027

Chikandiwa, S. T., Contogiannis, E., & Jembere, E. (2013). The adoption of social media marketing in South African banks. *European Business Review, 25*(4), 365–381. doi:10.1108/EBR-02-2013-0013

Coulter, K. S., Bruhn, M., Schoenmueller, V., & Schäfer, D. B. (2012). Are social media replacing traditional media in terms of brand equity creation. *Management Research Review.*

Dodokh, A. M. I. (2017). *The Impact of Social Media Usage on Organizational Performance: A Field Study on Dead Sea Products Companies in Jordan.* Middle East University Faculty of Business.

Eide, F., & Eide, B. (2005, March 2). *Brain of the Blogger.* Retrieved November 7, 2010, from Eide Neurolearning Blog: https://eideneurolearningblog.blogspot.com/2005/03/brain-of-blogger.html

Enge, E., Spencer, S., Stricchiola, J., & Fishkin, R. (2012). *The art of SEO.* O'Reilly Media, Inc.

Evans, M. (2010, January 26). *75M Twitter Users but Growth Slowing.* Retrieved May 6, 2010, from ME Mark Evans: http://www.twitterrati.com/2010/01/26/75m-twitter-users-but-growth-slowing/

Facebook. (n.d.). *Statistics.* Retrieved 10 11, 2010, from Facebook: https://www.facebook.com/press/info.php?statistics

Favre-Bonte, V., Elodie, G., & Thevenard-Puthod, C. (2013). Identifying different forms of innovation in retail banking *International Journal of Service Science, Management, Engineering, and Technology, 4*(4), 43–57.

Felix, R., Rauschnabel, P. A., & Hinsch, C. (2016). Elements of strategic social media marketing: A holistic framework. *Journal of Business Research.*

Felix, R., Rauschnabel, P. A., & Hinsch, C. (2017). Elements of strategic social media marketing: A holistic framework. *Journal of Business Research, 70*, 118–126. doi:10.1016/j.jbusres.2016.05.001

Franco, M., Tursunbayeva, A., & Pagliari, C. (2016). Social Media for e-Government in the Public Health Sector: Protocol for a Systematic Review. *JMIR Research Protocols*, 5(1), 1–10. doi:10.2196/resprot.5421 PMID:26969199

Gajanová, Ľ. (2018). Strategy of Online Content Marketing Based the Demographic and Psychographic Segmentation. *Marketing Identity*, 6(1/1), 303-314.

Galli, B. J. (2019). The Value of Marketing in Project Environments from Three Key Perspectives. *International Journal of Service Science, Management, Engineering, and Technology*, 10(1), 1–18. doi:10.4018/IJSSMET.2019010101

García-Peñalvo, F. J., de Figuerola, C. G., Merlo, J. A., Lee, B., & Ge, S. (2010). Personalisation and sociability of open knowledge management based on social tagging. *Online Information Review*.

Gebauer, J., Füller, J., & Pezzei, R. (2013). The dark and the bright side of co-creation: Triggers of member behavior in online innovation communities. *Journal of Business Research*, 66(9), 1516–1527. doi:10.1016/j.jbusres.2012.09.013

Godwin-Jones, R. (2003, May). Blogs and Wikis: Environments for On-line Collaboration. *Language Learning & Technology*, 7(2), 12–16.

Gümüş, N. (2017). The Effects of Social Media Content Marketing Activities of Firms on Consumers' Brand Following Behavior. *Academic Research International*, 8(1), 1–8.

Hacıefendioğlu, Ş. (2011). Reklam ortamı olarak sosyal paylaşım siteleri ve bir araştırma. *The Journal of Knowledge Economy & Knowledge Management*, 6.

Hanna, R., Rohn, A., & Crittenden, V. (2011). We're all connected: The power of the social ecosystem. *Business Horizons*, 54(3), 265–273. doi:10.1016/j.bushor.2011.01.007

Hines. (2017). *4 Ways to Measure Brand Awareness*. Available at: https://www.fronetics.com/4-ways-measure-brand-awareness/

Hudson, S., Huang, L. R. S., Madden, M., & Thomas, J. (2015). The influence of social media interactions on consumer-brand relationships: A three-country study of brand perceptions and marketing behaviors. *International Journal of Research in Marketing*, xx, xxx–xxx. doi:10.1016/j.ijresmar.2015.06.004

Hutter, K., Hautz, J., Dennhardt, S., & Fuller, J. (2018). The impact of user interactions in social media on brand awareness and purchase intention: The case of MINI on Facebook. *Journal of Product and Brand Management*, 22(5/6), 342–351. doi:10.1108/JPBM-05-2013-0299

Ibrahim, M., Abdallahamed, S., & Adam, D. R. (2018). Service Recovery, Perceived Fairness, and Customer Satisfaction in the Telecoms Sector in Ghana. *International Journal of Service Science, Management, Engineering, and Technology*, 9(4), 73–89. doi:10.4018/IJSSMET.2018100105

Incite, N. M. (2012). *State of Social Customer Service Report 2012*. Available from: https://soulofbrands.files.wordpress.com/2012/11/nm-incite-report-the-state-of-social-customer-service-2012.pdf

Ishola, O. A., & Olusoji, M. O. (2020). Service Sector Performance, Industry and Growth in Nigeria. *International Journal of Service Science, Management, Engineering, and Technology, 11*(1), 31–45. doi:10.4018/IJSSMET.2020010103

Jain, A., & Bhatnagar, V. (2016). Analysis of grievances in the banking sector through big data. *International Journal of Service Science, Management, Engineering, and Technology, 7*(4), 21–36. doi:10.4018/IJSSMET.2016100102

Jenkins, H. (2006). *Fans, Bloggers, and Gamers*. New York University Press.

Karjaluoto, H., & Leinonen, H. (2009). Advertisers' perceptions of search engine marketing. *International Journal of Internet Marketing and Advertising, 5*(1/2), 95–105. doi:10.1504/IJIMA.2009.021952

Keller, K. L. (2009). Building strong brands in a modern marketing communications environment. *Journal of Marketing Communications, 15*(2-3), 139–155. doi:10.1080/13527260902757530

Kim, J. H., Kim, M., & Lennon, S. J. (2018). E-service performance of apparel e-retailing websites: A longitudinal assessment. *International Journal of Service Science, Management, Engineering, and Technology, 9*(1), 24–40. doi:10.4018/IJSSMET.2018010103

Kokkinaki, A. D. (2009). The potential use of Wikis as a tool that supports collaborative learning in the context of Higher Education. In *m-ICTE2009 V International Conference on Multimedia and ICT in Education* (pp. 1119-1123). Badajoz: FORMATEX.

Križanová, A., Majerová, J., Klieštik, T., & Majerčák, P. (2013). Theoretical aspects of brand building in seafood industry. *NAŠE MORE: znanstveno-stručni časopis za more i pomorstvo, 60*(5-6), 105-112.

Kumar, A., Bezawada, R., Rishika, R., Janakiraman, R., & Kannan, P. K. (2016). From social to sale: The effects of firm-generated content in social media on consumer behavior. *Journal of Marketing, 80*(1), 7–25. doi:10.1509/jm.14.0249

Leuf, B., & Cunningham, W. (2001). The Wiki way. Boston, MA: Addison-Wesley Professional.

Machauer, A., & Morgner, S. (2001). Segmentation of bank customers by expected benefits and attitudes. *International Journal of Bank Marketing, 19*(1), 6–18. doi:10.1108/02652320110366472

Mahboub, R. M. (2018). *The impact of social media usage on performance of the banking sector in Middle East and North Africa countries*. Academic Press.

Mathur, N. (2019). *Social Media Statistics in India*. https://www.talkwalker.com/blog/social-media-statistics-in-india

Matkovic, P., Sakal, M., & Tumbas, P. (2011). Web 2.0 technologies in internal and external communications in the banking sector. *Theory, Methodology, Practice, 7*(2), 87.

Mattison, D. (2003, April). *Quickiwiki, Swiki, Twiki, Zwiki, and the Plone Wars Wiki as a PIM and Collaborative Content Tool*. Retrieved July 15, 2010, from Information Today: https://www.infotoday.com/searcher/apr03/mattison.shtml

Merholz, P. (2002, May 17). *Play with Your Words*. Retrieved October 17, 2010, from peterme.com: https://www.peterme.com/archives/00000205.html

Metekohy, M. (2010, May 17). *YouTube Statistics*. Retrieved September 25, 2010, from Viral Blog: https://www.viralblog.com/research/youtube-statistics/

Mitic, M., & Kapoulas, A. (2012). Understanding the role of social media in bank marketing. *Marketing Intelligence & Planning*, *30*(7), 668 - 686.

Mitic, M., & Kapoulas, A. (2012). Understanding the role of social media in bank marketing. *Marketing Intelligence & Planning*, *30*(7), 668–686. doi:10.1108/02634501211273797

Moreno, L., & Martinez, P. (2013). Overlapping factors in search engine optimization and web accessibility. *Online Information Review*, *37*(4), 564–580. doi:10.1108/OIR-04-2012-0063

Muller, J., & Christandl, F. (2019). Content is king – But who is the kon of kings? The effect of content marketing, sponsored content & user – generated content on brands responses. *Computers in Human Behavior*, *96*, 46–55. doi:10.1016/j.chb.2019.02.006

Murdough, C. (2009). Social media measurement: It's not impossible. *Journal of Interactive Advertising*, *10*(1), 94–99. doi:10.1080/15252019.2009.10722165

Njeri, M. W. (2014). *Effect of Social Media Interactions on Financial Performance of Commercial Banks in Kenya* (Master Thesis). School of Business, Department of Finance, University of Nairobi.

Özeltürkay, E. Y., & Mucan, B. (2014). How Turkish Banks Benefit from Social Media: Analyzing Banks Formal Links. *International Journal of Strategic Innovative Marketing*, *1*(2), 120–129.

Pan, B., & Crotts, J. C. (2012). Theoretical models of social media, marketing implications, and future research directions. *Social Media in Travel, Tourism, and Hospitality: Theory, Practice, and Cases, 1*, 73-86.

Parusheva, S. (2017). Social Media Banking Models: A case study of a practical implementation in banking sector. *Икономически изследвания*, (3), 125-141.

Patrutiu Baltes, L. (2015). Content marketing-the the fundamental tool of digital marketing. *Bulletin of the Transilvania University of Brasov. Series V, Economic Sciences*, *8*(2), 111–118.

Poon, W. C. (2008). Users' adoption of e-banking services: The Malaysian perspective. *Journal of Business and Industrial Marketing*.

Poradova, M. (2020). Content marketing strategy and its impact on customers under the global market conditions. In *SHS Web of Conferences* (Vol. 74, p. 01027). EDP Sciences. 10.1051hsconf/20207401027

Rajashekhara, K. S. (2004, July 4). Application of IT in Banking. *Yojana*.

Relling, M., Schnittka, O., Sattler, H., & Johnen, M. (2016). Each can help or hurt: Negative and positive word of mouth in social network brand communities. *International Journal of Research in Marketing*, *33*(1), 42–58. doi:10.1016/j.ijresmar.2015.11.001

Rowley, J. (2008). Understanding digital content marketing. *Journal of Marketing Management*, *24*(5-6), 517–540. doi:10.1362/026725708X325977

Safko, L., & Brake, D. K. (2009). *The Social Media Bible: Tactics, Tools, and Strategies for Business Success*. Wiley.

Schultz, D. E., & Peltier, J. (2013). Social media's slippery slope: Challenges, opportunities and future research directions. *Journal of Research in Interactive Marketing*, 7(2), 86–99. doi:10.1108/JRIM-12-2012-0054

Shankar, R., & Khan, S. (2012). *The Next Generation Social Banking Ecosystem: A Road Map for Banks*. Happiest Minds Technologies. Available from https://www.happiestminds.com/whitepapers/The-Next-Generation-Social-Banking-Ecosystem--A-Road-Map-for-Banks.pdf

Shen, B., & Bissell, K. (2013). Social media, social me: A content analysis of beauty companies' use of Facebook in marketing and branding. *Journal of Promotion Management*, 19(5), 629–651. doi:10.1 080/10496491.2013.829160

Singh, C. (n.d.). *Role of digital marketing initiatives on demographic profile in improving sales with special reference to HDFC bank*. Academic Press.

Singh, T., Veron-Jackson, L., & Cullinane, J. (2008). Blogging: A new play in your marketing game plan. *Business Horizons*, 51(4), 281–292. doi:10.1016/j.bushor.2008.02.002

Smith, K. T., Blazovich, J. L., & Smith, L. M. (2015). Social Media Adoption by Corporations: An Examination by Platform, Industry, Size, and Financial Performance. *Academy of Marketing Studies Journal*, 19(2), 1–18.

Souissi, Y., Azouzi, M. A., & Jarboui, A. (2018). The Bank's Regional Director's Emotional Bias and the Bank's Performance. *International Journal of Service Science, Management, Engineering, and Technology*, 9(3), 30–47. doi:10.4018/IJSSMET.2018070103

Taiminen, H. M., & Karjaluoto, H. (2015). The usage of digital marketing channels in SMEs. *Journal of Small Business and Enterprise Development*, 22(4), 633–651. doi:10.1108/JSBED-05-2013-0073

Thackeray, R., Neiger, B. L., & Keller, H. (2012). Integrating social media and social marketing: A four-step process. *Health Promotion Practice*, 13(2), 165–168. doi:10.1177/1524839911432009 PMID:22382492

Thomas, M. (2011). Social media in finance: Users want tangible benefits, not friendship, Deutsche Bank Research. *E-Banking Snapshot, 37*, 1-4. Available from: http://www.dbresearch.com/PROD/DBR_INTERNET_EN-PROD/PROD0000000000273185.pdf

Trainor, K. J., Andzulis, J. M., Rapp, A., & Agnihotri, R. (2014). Social media technology usage and customer relationship performance: A capabilities-based examination of social CRM. *Journal of Business Research*, 67(6), 1201–1208. doi:10.1016/j.jbusres.2013.05.002

Urban, G. L. (2004). *Digital Marketing Strategy: Text and Cases*. Person Prentice Hall.

Wahi, A. K., Medury, Y., & Misra, R. K. (2014). Social Media: The core of enterprise 2.0. *International Journal of Service Science, Management, Engineering, and Technology*, 5(3), 1–15. doi:10.4018/ijssmet.2014070101

Williams, B. J., & Jacobs, J. J. (2004). Exploring the use of blogs as learning spaces in the higher education sector. *Australasian Journal of Educational Technology*, *20*(2), 232–274.

Wortham, J. (2007, December 17). *After 10 Years of Blogs, the Future's Brighter Than Ever*. Retrieved November 1, 2010, from Wired: https://www.wired.com/entertainment/theweb/news/2007/12/blog_anniversary

Yan, J. (2011). Social media in branding: Fulfilling a need. *Journal of Brand Management*, *18*(9), 688–696. doi:10.1057/bm.2011.19

Zomorodian, S., & Lu, Y. (2017, July). How Content Marketing Can Help the Bank Industrial: Experience from Iran. In *International Conference on Management Science and Engineering Management* (pp. 626-633). Springer.

This research was previously published in the International Journal of Service Science, Management, Engineering, and Technology (IJSSMET), 12(3); pages 54-72, copyright year 2021 by IGI Publishing (an imprint of IGI Global).

Chapter 24
What Attracts Followers?
Exploring Factors Contributing to
Brand Twitter Follower Counts

Yu-Qian Zhu

Department of Information Management, National Taiwan University of Science and Technology, Taiwan

Bo Hsiao

iD https://orcid.org/0000-0002-2894-9678

Department of Information Management, Chang Jung Christian University, Taiwan

ABSTRACT

Although business and researchers acknowledge the importance of social media, little research has been conducted to explore what attracts people to follow brand Twitter accounts. This research attempts to achieve an analytical understanding of the factors that contribute to brand Twitter follower count based on social network and communication theories. Using data from 346 Twitter accounts spanning 48 industries and 31 countries, the authors found that the quality and quantity of tweets, as well as social learning of brand Twitter accounts are positively related to brand Twitter account followers; contrary to popular belief, the use of hashtags and links and interactivity with users are not positively related to brand Twitter account followers. The study is among the first to investigate what attracts brand Twitter account followers, which offers important strategic recommendations for brand social media managers on how to manage their social media accounts.

INTRODUCTION

The era of social media has afforded new communication channels for businesses in attracting, developing, and maintaining customers (Li, Berens, & Maertelaere, 2013; Wamba, Akter, Bhattacharyya & Aditya; 2016). Social media, i.e., the Internet-based applications that allow the creation and exchange of user-generated content (Kaplan & Haenlein, 2010) has gained strategic importance as a powerful new form of electronic word of mouth, reported being approximately twenty times more effective than

DOI: 10.4018/978-1-6684-6287-4.ch024

marketing events and thirty times more effective than media appearances (Trusov, Bucklin & Pauwels, 2009). Research found that followers of brand on social media have higher trust and brand identification (Kim, Sung, & Kang, 2014; Maldonado & Sierra; 2016; Díaz-Díaz & Pérez-González; 2016), are more loyal to the brand (Laroche, Habibi, Richard & Sankaranarayanan, 2012; Laroche, Habibi & Richard, 2013), have higher customer purchase intentions (Goh, Heng & Lin, 2014; Kim & Ko, 2012), buy more frequently, and are more profitable (Rishika, Kumar, Janakiraman & Bezawada, 2013). Social media engagements also enhance brand equity, relationship equity, and value equity (Kim & Ko, 2012; Yu, Duan & Cao, 2013). Twitter, a microblogging and social networking service, in particular, is noteworthy. Launched in 2007, Twitter now has 330 million monthly active users, 500 million tweets per day, and 80% users on mobile (as of September 2019). Twitter has become the social platform of choice for brands' customer engagement, with 413 companies (83%) of the Fortune 500 active on Twitter (Barnes & Andonian, 2014).

Although business and researchers acknowledge the strategic importance of social media, little research has been conducted to explore what attracts people to follow brands' twitter accounts. Follower count is a key metric for social media marketing as it is Twitter's most basic currency (Hutto, Yardi, & Gilbert; 2013). The followers form an audience to the brand and provide the brand access to a network of social ties, resources, and influence (Hutto et al., 2013). Most prior research has addressed brands' Twitter followers from either the brand relationship or the need satisfaction perspective. Research reported that users follow a brand on Twitter to engage in the brand community (Phua, Jin & Kim; 2017), or as a result of brand attachment (Chu, Chen, & Sung; 2016). Yang (2011) argued that by following a brand's Twitter account, individuals fulfill the sense of belonging and citizenship. Zhu & Chen (2015) thought that individuals seek self-esteem and relatedness by following brands on Twitter. However, these researches are from a follower's perspective, i.e., what followers need and want. Most of them have used psychological measures as the dependent variable, rather than actual follower counts. Furthermore, little research has explored the features of brand activities (e.g., interaction, frequency of posting) and their impact on follower counts.

A few scholarly works have revealed some preliminary findings regarding follower count from the account activity perspective. Hutto et al. (2013) reported that message content, social behavior, and network structure could predict follower counts for Twitter accounts. Unfortunately, the research was only geared toward individual Twitter accounts, not business or brand accounts, with no brand-related variables in the model. Levine, Mann & Mannor (2015) found that learning actively online can provide deeper insights into how to attract followers. Stevanovich (2012) argued that engaging users, developing relationships and compelling content are key components of success in social media discourse. Mueller & Stumme (2017) explored how user profiles on Twitter affect follower counts. Despite these pioneer works, no comprehensive research that integrates both the communication perspective and social network perspective has been conducted specifically on business Twitter accounts. This paper attempts to achieve an analytical understanding of the factors that contribute to the number of followers for brands on Twitter based on an integrative model encompassing both the communication perspective and social network perspective with a comprehensive set of variables selected based on sound theoretical framework. Specifically, we seek to examine how Grice's Maxims of communication, social learning and social interactivity contribute to brands' twitter follower counts and present strategic recommendations for social media marketing managers. Our results highlight the importance of quality of the tweets, tweet presentation, tweet frequency and social learning to follower counts.

This research contributes to the literature in two ways. First, for practitioners, the number of followers has long been used as a main performance index for social media metrics (Adweek, 2011). However, most of the results are from trade journals or bloggers, while academic research that is based on theory and empirically tested is little. Thus, this research helps to clarify the question of how to attract Twitter followers for brands managing their Twitter accounts, and gives a clear picture to brand social media managers about what to do based on a theory-guided, and empirically validated research. Second, theoretically, this research contributes by integrating research from both the communication perspective and the social network perspective to develop and test a theoretically and empirically driven model of contributing to brands' Twitter follower counts. By grounding our model in theories of communication and social networks, we highlight the significant role of quality and quantity of Tweets, the presentation of Tweets from the communications perspective, and social learning from the social networks perspective as key drivers of Twitter follower counts.

In the following sections, we will first give an overview of brands' Twitter accounts and an explanation of the ways in which brands' Twitter accounts operate. We will next describe the nature of the Twitter data we use for our exploratory analyses, offer basic descriptive results, and develop our hypotheses. Then, the paper will provide a few in-depth analyses of the variables linked to brand twitter follower counts.

BRAND TWITTER ACCOUNT ACTIVITIES

Twitter allows corporations to build brand pages with customizable logos and features. Brands are able to build a profile that consists of their user name, photo, bio, as well as their website on Twitter, which people, as well as other brands, can follow to see all the postings by the brand. Brands post Tweets, short messages that are up to 280-characters in length, which are visible to all users and updated in their followers' timelines. Users can choose to retweet original messages from other accounts. Retweets enable users to spread information of their choice beyond the reach of the original tweet account's followers. Users can also express their love for a certain Tweet by marking it as a "Favorite", which is a small star icon at the bottom of the Tweet. Twitter designed the Favorite mechanism to allow users a virtual way of saying them like it enough to mark it.

Twitter offers some tools to organize users' posting. For example, you can add categories to your tweet by using "hashtag", i.e., the # symbol (e.g. #BlackFriday) either as they appear in a sentence, e.g., "Find the Best #BlackFriday Deals" or appended to it like "Find the Best Black Friday Deals. #BlackFriday". A hashtag allows grouping of similarly tagged messages, as well as allowing a keyword search to return all messages that contain it. The hashtag function has been implemented across different social platforms besides Twitter, such as Facebook, Pinterest, and Instagram, to allow for easy searching and content-categorization. You can also mention other users in tweets to direct it towards them by using the @ symbol (e.g. @twitter). The users that are mentioned in the tweets will be able to see the message at their timeline and respond to it. Figure 1(a) below shows how we can use the @ symbol to direct the conversation.

Although Twitter has a 280 characters limit, you can embed links to your tweets to direct users to more details. If the link points to a picture, the picture will automatically be displayed in non-mobile browsers. Figure 1b below shows on embedded links look like in tweets. As tweets are a blend of messages and symbols such as # and links to other resources, the presentations of tweets can vary from easily readable to needing efforts to decipher. For example, This Tweet from IBM, "RT @ IBMWatson: #ChefWatson can create hundreds of new recipes to suit your <u>tastes.cnnmon.ie/</u> 1DyjIrC via@CNNMoney http://t.co/ JLB Pcyc..." takes more processing to understand than plain English does. Figure 1c shows an example of complex tweets with hashtags and links.

Figure 1.

THEORETICAL BACKGROUND AND HYPOTHESES

Although no prior research has directly addressed factors contributing to brands' Twitter followers count, there have been some related pioneer work in this field. Hutto et al. (2013) selected a total of 22 variables based on various theories and reported that for individual accounts on Twitter, informational content, the burstiness of tweeting, and profile elements (i.e., length of description, URL, and location) emerged as significant positive predictors of follower growth. Broadcast content (e.g., content not addressed to a specific recipient) and negative sentiments in Tweets are negatively related to follower growth. The number of followers and network overlap also contributes to follower growth. Levin et al. (2015) designed a mechanism for online agents to manage Twitter accounts via learning from its own history. Their result found that learning actively is an effective way to attract followers. Stevanovich (2012) emphasized the similarities of Twitter and other communication media and approached Twitter from a communication theory perspective. Through rhetorical analysis, the research showed that brands can achieve success in social media by engaging users, developing relationships and providing compelling content (Stevanovich, 2012). Mueller & Stumme (2017) proposed a classifier that labels users who will increase their followers based on different types of profile names and profile features such as whether there is a description or URL.

Twitter, as a new form of computer-mediated media, combines both social interaction/social networks and news media (Fischer & Reuber, 2011; Kwak, Chun & Moon; 2011). Indeed, as Stevanovich (2012) observed, social media is like other communication vehicle that demands the use of sound rhetoric and communication theories and applications. Twitter is used as a source of information (Westerman, Spence & van der Heide; 2012) as well as a social network platform (Lee & Kim, 2014). Thus, it is helpful to examine Twitter from both the communication perspective and the social network perspective.

Reeves & Nass (1996) observed that people tend to treat computers and new media as if they were either real people and respond to them naturally and socially, as they would either to another person, such as by being polite, cooperative, attributing personality characteristics such as aggressiveness, humor, expertise, and even gender. This observation broadens the application of some communication theories to the realm of human-computer interaction, of which Grice's Maxims (Grice, 1975) is one. Grice argued that people generally feel that conversations should be guided by four basic principles: quality, quantity, relevance, and manner (Grice, 1975). First, the maxim of quantity requires that the communicator to be as informative as one possibly can, and gives as much information as is needed, and no more. Second, the maxim of quality asks for truthful and evidence-based content. Third, the maxim of relevance seeks relevant and pertinent content. Finally, the maxim of manner demands clear, brief, and orderly communication without obscurity and ambiguity.

Grice's Maxims (Grice, 1975) have been widely used not only in face-to-face communication but also in computer-mediated communications (Baratgin, Jacquet & Cergy.;2019; Berendt, Günther & Spiekermann; 2005; Herring, 1999). Herring (1999) applied the Maxim of relevance and examined online interaction coherence. Baratgin et al. (2019) applied Grice's Maxims in chatbot and found that these maxims had a particularly important impact on response times and the perceived humanness of a conversation partner. Berendt et al. (2005) found Grice's Maxims as a popular guideline in on-line agent communication design.

Based on Grice's Maxims (Grice, 1975) and the unique features of social networks, this research proposes a research framework that encompasses both the communication perspective and the social network perspective to account for the factors contributing to brand Twitter accounts' follower numbers. The research framework is depicted in Figure 2 below.

Figure 2. Research framework

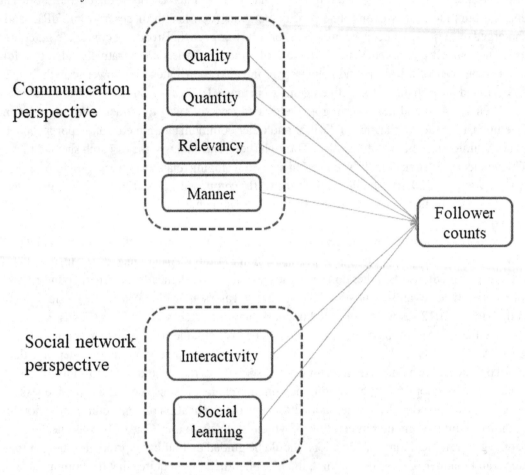

The Communication Perspective

For the communication perspective, this research adopts Grice's Maxims as a guiding theory, which provides four principles to achieve effective communication. As the Maxims were designed for human conversation, when applying it to the Twitter context, some adaptions are necessary. We modified some of the content of the maxims below for our research:

1. **Maxims of Quality:** Tweet content should be true and of good quality. This can be gauged by the percentage of content that is favorited by users.
2. **Maxims of Quantity:** The numbers of Tweets should suffice to convey enough information for the brand. The quantity of communication can be measured by the frequency of tweeting by brands.

3. **Maxim of Relevance:** Tweet content should be relevant. On Twitter, relevance is defined as the match between the follower's information needs and the information corporation accounts provide. As Nielson's (2013) Twitter Consumer Survey showed, most people following brand want to get information concerning the brand itself: promotions, offers, brand news, etc. It seems that the relevance of the brand's twitter account is about the brand itself: original messages from, and about the brand. The relevance of content can be measured by the percentage of original content in Tweets.

4. **Maxims of Manner:** Tweets should have a clear, easy-to-understand presentation. The manner on Twitter can be measured by the percentage of tweets with a clean and neat presentation, without the use of complex symbols and links.

Quality

The first maxim is about the quality of the messages. Gallup's research reported that to follow trends and find information is one of the main reasons for people to use social media (Gallup, 2014). Users actively engage in social media to fulfill their informational needs (Phua et al., 2017). Hutto et al. (2013) found that the percentage of informational content is a top predictor of individual Twitter follower counts. As users go on twitter to find information, the quality of the messages (informative vs. un-informative) from brand Twitter accounts will be positively associated with follower counts. Users typically will unfollow an account due to low-quality content (Kwak et al., 2011). Accounts offer high-quality content that is informative, on the contrary, will attract more users than accounts that do not. Therefore,

H1: The quality of messages from brands' Twitter accounts is positively related to brand Twitter follower counts.

Quantity

The maxim of quantity states that you should provide enough messages to explain yourself, but also do not make your contribution more informative than is required (Grice, 1975). On Twitter, if you rarely send out tweets, it is unlikely that you'll have many followers. But if you send out tweets too frequently, followers flooded by your tweets are also likely to abandon you as well. Mueller & Stumme (2017) reported a negative relationship between inactive days of accounts and the number of followers for Twitter accounts. On the one hand, consistent tweeting frequency is important for attracting and keeping followers (Thoring, 2011). On the other hand, too much tweeting may lead to information overload and less social media engagement (Bontcheva et al., 2013). Thus, we should expect to see a curvilinear relationship between tweets per day and follower counts.

H2: There is an inverted U-shape relationship between tweets per day and follower counts.

Relevance

Relevance refers to the relationship between an information object and an information need (Bradford, 1934). Twitter Consumer Survey of Nielson (2013) shows that 53% of people following brand want to be notified of special offers and promotions; 51% hope to stay up to date with brand news, 44% desire to learn about new products and services, and 30% like to have access to exclusive content. Thus, relevance in Twitter means meeting follower's information needs by providing them with the content they're looking for. Relevant information leads to higher levels of perceived usefulness and ease of use, and higher user satisfaction, and ultimately, intentions to use the system (Hong et al., 2002). Therefore, relevant information could not only help retain current followers, but also contribute to follower growth. Hence, the more relevant the information, the more followers you'll have.

H3: Tweets' relevance is positively related to brands' Twitter account's follower counts.

Manner

The Maxims of manner requires messages to be clearly expressed or presented. Obscurity of expression and ambiguity should be avoided. Messages should be brief and orderly (Grice, 1975). In twitter, the Maxim of manner could be applied to the appearance of tweets. As tweets are a blend of messages and symbols such as #, and links to other resources, the presentations of tweets can vary from easily readable to needing efforts to decipher. Although hashtags and links offer great benefits such as easy categorization and discoverability, usage of these tools amongst Tweet contents also makes the presentation of the tweets less clean and tidy. Hutto et al. (2013) conducted research over 522,368 tweets and found that on average, hashtags were used in about 26% of total tweets and there was a strong negative relationship between hashtag ratio and number of followers, confirming the importance of Tweet presentation to attract followers. Therefore,

H4: The use of hashtags and links is negatively related to brands' twitter account followers.

The Social Network Perspective

Interactivity

From a social network perspective, two factors are examined for their influences on brand twitter account followers. The first one is interactivity with followers. Twitter provides organizations the ability to engage with the public and relationship-building communication channel that has been missing from websites. Kaplan and Haenlein (2010) viewed social media as "all about sharing and interaction" and urged business to ensure that "you engage in discussions with your customers". Lovejoy, Waters & Saxton (2012) suggested that Twitter's interactive messages like replies and mentions can assist organizations in communicating with other users. Saffer, Sommerfeldt & Taylor (2013) found that high organizational Twitter interactivity positively affects the perceived organization–public relationship of individuals. On Twitter, there are two commonly used methods of interacting with followers: user mention and reply. Therefore, higher interactivity in the forms of replies and mentions on Twitter by brands should be positively related to their follower counts.

H5: High interactivity in the forms of replies and mentions are positively related to brands' Twitter account's follower counts.

Social Learning

Learning is important to gain new followers. Levin et al. (2015) found that actively learning from past account history is an effective way to attract followers. However, learning is not restricted to learning from one's own history. On Twitter, brand Twitter accounts can not only broadcast messages to their followers, but also follow other brands of interest, such as suppliers or competitors, celebrities, news agencies, and opinion leaders, etc. By following other accounts, businesses form social networks via outbound connections that facilitate information sharing (Quercia, Capra & Crowcroft; 2012) Businesses often want to find groups of related or similar social entities to follow. Twitter and other social media have become important new resources for social learning (Greenhow & Robelia, 2009). Walmart, for example, followed Cover Girl, Huggies, Oral-B, Bounty, and a number of other suppliers. By following each other, brands form a social network on Twitter and are kept abreast of the updates and trends from the accounts they follow. The social learning theory (Bandura, 1977) states that people can acquire new patterns of behavior by observing the behavior of others. Through observational learning, individual behaviors can spread across the population through a diffusion chain. Similarly, Bikhchandani, Hirshleifer & Welch (1998) argue that social learning leads to conformity, the rise of fads and information cascade. People learn by observing each other for several possible reasons: 1) positive payoff externalities, which lead to conventions such as driving on the right or left side of the road; 2) preference interactions, as with everyone desiring to wear "fashionable" clothing as determined by what others are wearing; and 3) sanctions upon deviants, as with a dictator punishing opposition behavior (Bikhchandani et al., 1998). On Twitter, social learning could be achieved and gauged by following and observing what others do and adjust one's twitting behaviors accordingly. The more accounts one follows, the more information one is exposed to, and the easier it is to get the latest trends and topics.

H6: Social learning by brand twitter accounts is positively related to brands' Twitter account's follower counts.

METHODS

Data Collection

We adopted a mix data collection approach as our required data came from different sources. First, for Twitter-related data, we directly collected the data for this study using Twitter.com and Twitonomy. com, an online Twitter analytics website. Second, we also relied on secondary data as we studied the verified brand Twitter accounts for Global 500 Brand from Brand Finance (www.brandirectory.com), an independent brand valuation and strategy consultancy headquartered in London, with presence in over 20 countries. We chose Global 500 Brand as it allows us to control for brand equity's influence on Twitter followers. These brands span across 49 industries and include companies such as Coca Cola, BP, Google, Volvo, and Accenture. For brands with multiple Twitter accounts (for example, Walmart, Walmart Labs, Walmart Newsroom), we chose the official and general-purpose one (Walmart). Of the 500 brands listed, excluding those without a verified English Twitter account, we had a final usable sample of 346 Twitter accounts spanning 48 industries from 31 countries. For robust results, we collected follower counts twice, once in 2014 and once in 2015, to purposefully examine the longitudinal effects of Twitter activities. By tracking follower counts at the time of the data collection and one year later, we were able to derive a causal relationship between Twitter activities and follower counts.

We collected brand value in 2014, brand industry and country data from Brand Finance. Brand Finance calculated brand values using the Royalty Relief methodology which determines the value a company would be willing to pay to license its brand as if it did not own it. Brand Twitter follower counts were collected twice, once in March 2014 and one year later, March 2015 from Twitter.com. The number of accounts followed in March 2014 was also collected from Twitter. Finally, Twitter activity data for the most recent 3200 Tweets up till March 2014 were collected from Twitonomy.com and included tweets per day, percentage of tweets that are re-tweets of others contents (i.e., non-original contents), average numbers of user mentions per tweet, percentage of replies in the total analyzed tweets, average number of links per tweet, average number of hashtags per tweet, and percentage of tweets favorite by others.

Variables

We operationalized the variables using the data discussed above. The dependent variable is follower count, both in March 2014 (afterward, FC_{2014} is used to represent the follower count in March 2014) and one year later in March 2015 (FC_{2015} is used to represent follower count in March 2015). Following Kwak et al. (2011), the quality of Tweets (quality) was assessed by the percentage of Tweets that receive "Favorite" from followers, as the number of "Favorite" (notation; FAV) indicates liking and approval of the content from users. Quantity of Tweets was measured by the average number of tweets brand Twitter accounts send out per day (notation; TPD). As Hypothesis 2 proposes a curvilinear relationship between quantity of Tweets and follower count, we included both quantity and quantity square in the model. Relevance was gauged by the percentage of original tweets, which is obtained by deducting the percentage of tweets that are re-tweets of others' contents from 100% (notation; $1-RET$). We used two indices for manner: average number of links per tweet (notation; LPT) and average number of hashtags per tweet (notation; HPT), as these two have great influences on the presentation of tweets.

There are two social network-related constructs: interactivity and social learning. Average numbers of user mention per tweet (notation; MPT) and percentage of replies (notation; RP) in the total analyzed tweets were used to measure interactivity (notation; ZS). Since these two are highly correlated (0.74), we averaged the z scores of these two as an index of interactivity. Social learning was measured by the number of other accounts the brand corporate accounts follow (notation; FO).

For control variables, we included brand value (notation; BV) in 2014 as a control variable in the model since the more value a brand has, the more likely people are willing to follow it. Controlling for brand value would enable us to discover unique activities on Twitter that lead to more followers. We also controlled for industry and used 5 dummy variables for 6 industries (Finance and insurance (notation; I_1), manufacturing (notation; I_2), information (notation; I; information industry was the baseline for the 5 dummy variables [0,0,0,0,0]), services (notation; I_4), transportation and warehousing (notation; I_5), others (notation; I_3)) according to U.S. census industry categorization guidelines. Geographic locations of the companies (Africa (notation; A_1), America (notation; A_2), Asia (notation; A), Europe (notation; A_3) and Oceania (notation; A_4)) were also included in our analysis as control. Here, the 4 area dummy variables will be used for 5 areas and Asia was set as [0,0,0,0].

5. ANALYSIS AND RESULTS

Table 1 and Table 2 summarized the descriptive statistics of all the variables and their correlation matrix.

The average brand value for the 346 brands was around 8000 million U.S. dollars. The average follower count was around 400,000 for 2014, and 600,000 a year later. Brands on average followed 6,188 other Twitter accounts, sent out 16 tweets a day, and averaged 0.62 user mentions, 0.56 hashtag, and 0.39 link per tweet. 35.6% of the tweets were replies, and average, 36% of tweets were favorited.

Table 1. Descriptive statistics

	N	Mean	Std. Deviation	Median	Skewness	Kurtosis
Follower count 2015 (FC_{2015})	346	594398.84	1776670.62	97180.00	5.76	40.36
Follower count 2014 (FC_{2014})	346	397456.27	1296879.50	51393.00	6.30	48.06
Following (*FO*)	346	6188.73	32153.40	768.50	14.29	231.40
Brand value (*BV*; in millions of USD)	346	7956.47	7985.60	4659.00	2.87	10.38
Tweets per day (*TPD*)	346	16.42	43.19	4.38	6.93	66.06
User mentions per tweet (*MPT*)	346	0.62	0.33	0.64	0.07	-0.08
Replies % (*RP*)	346	35.61	32.80	23.36	0.63	-1.06
Links per tweet (*LPT*)	346	0.39	0.24	0.04	0.42	-0.61
Hashtags per tweet (*HPT*)	346	0.56	0.46	0.47	1.69	4.96
Retweets % (*REP*)	346	11.07	11.84	7.93	1.80	4.54
Favorited % (*FAV*)	346	36.00	22.43	32.97	0.60	-0.27
Industry		Percentages				
Finance and Insurance	59	17.05%				
Information	62	17.92%				
Manufacturing	116	33.53%				
Services	29	8.38%				
Transportation and Warehousing	22	6.36%				
Others	58	16.76%				
Area						
Africa	1	0.29%				
America	182	52.60%				
Asia	48	13.87%				
Europe	109	31.05%				
Oceania	6	1.73%				

Table 2. Correlations among variables

	FC_2015	FC_2014	FO	BV	TPD	MPT	RP	LP	HP	REP	FAV	I_1	I_2	I_3	I_4	I_5	A_1	A_2	A_3	A_4
FC_2014	.97**																			
FO	.16**	.19**																		
BV	.16**	.16**	.02																	
TPD	.11*	.12*	.26**	.04																
MPT	.04	.04	.19**	.07	.35**															
RP	.02	.03	.20**	.04	.46**	.76**														
LP	-.07	-.08	-.14*	.00	-.21**	-.35**	-.58**													
HP	-.08	-.09	-.08	.02	-.21**	-.18**	-.39**	.30**												
REP	.23**	.22**	-.05	.10	-.30**	-.30**	-.58**	.60**	.38**											
FAV	.44**	.42**	.08	.20**	-.09	.02	-.17**	.28**	.27**	.78**										
I_1	-.11*	-.11*	-.06	.03	-.10	-.13*	-.04	.08	-.09	-.08	-.19**									
I_2	-.08	-.08	.06	-.09	-.05	.01	.01	-.14**	.03	.05	.02	-.32**								
I_3	.03	.03	.00	.00	.04	.08	.16**	-.06	-.01	-.01	.07	-.20**	-.32**							
I_4	-.02	-.03	-.04	.00	-.03	.04	-.05	.12*	.15*	.09	.09	-.14*	-.21**	-.14*						
I_5	-.07	-.06	-.03	-.02	.08	-.04	-.04	-.02	-.02	-.07	-.10	-.12*	-.19**	-.12*	-.08					
A_1	-.01	-.01	-.01	-.02	.00	.03	.03	-.05	-.03	-.02	-.03	-.02	-.04	-.02	-.02	-.01				
A_2	.13*	.14**	.08	.05	.06	.20**	.09	.01	-.02	.13*	.23**	-.03	-.15**	.07	.04	.01	-.06			
A_3	-.08	-.09	-.04	-.04	-.01	-.14**	-.09	.12*	.12*	.05	-.06	.09	.10	-.02	-.03	-.07	-.04	-.71**		
A_4	-.04	-.04	-.01	-.05	.06	.13*	.20**	-.14*	-.14*	-.20**	-.14**	.18**	-.09	.00	-.04	-.03	-.01	-.14**	-.09	

PS1: **: Correlation is significant at the 0.01 level (2-tailed) and at the 0.05 level (2-tailed). N=346

PS2: *LP*= Links %; *HP*=Hashtags %

Multiple regression was used to analyze the relationships between variables with SPSS. SPSS is one of the most popular software packages geared towards statistical analysis and data mining (Verma, 2012). Since regression analysis is based on the minimization of squared error, a few extreme observations can exert a disproportionate influence on parameter estimates. Our data set, unfortunately, has strongly skewed distributions (i.e. the absolute value of skewness and kurtosis greater than 2), for follower counts, following, brand value, tweets per day, average hashtags and retweets percentage. Thus, we performed a log ten transformation of these variables to achieve normality and homoscedasticity (Hair et al., 2006) and reran the analysis. We performed hierarchical multiple regression analyses so that the contribution of each set of variables to the dependent variable can be seen and model comparison can be achieved. For the i-th company ($i=1,\ldots,346$) in the k-th period (e.g., $k\in(2014,2015)$), we tested a total of five models: Model 0 (baseline model) included only the control variables, while Model 1 to Model 4 had a mix of combination of the proposed variables and control variables. Model 1 included only the variables from our hypotheses (the mathematics equation can be found in Model (1)); we added brand equity along with our research variables in Model 2; in Model 3, industry information was additionally controlled for; finally, in the Model 4, geographic area info was introduced besides all the other variables. The results are reported in Table 3 and Table 4 below:

$$
\begin{aligned}
\log(FC_{k,i}) = {} & \beta_{0,k} + \beta_{9,k}(BV_i) + \beta_{10,k}(I_{1,i}) + \beta_{11,k}(I_{2,i}) + \beta_{12,k}(I_{3,i}) + \beta_{13,k}(I_{4,i}) \\
& + \beta_{14,k}(I_{5,i}) + \beta_{15,k}(A_{1,i}) + \beta_{16,k}(A_{2,i}) + \beta_{17,k}(A_{3,i}) + \beta_{18,k}(A_{4,i}) + \varepsilon_i
\end{aligned}
\tag{0}
$$

$$
\begin{aligned}
\log(FC_{k,i}) = {} & \beta_{0,k} + \beta_{1,k}\log(FO_i) + \beta_{2,k}\log(TPD_i) + \beta_{3,k}TPD_i^2 + \beta_{4,k}LPT_i \\
& + \beta_{5,k}HPT_i + \beta_{6,k}FAV_i + \beta_{7,k}\log(1-RET_i) + \beta_{8,k}(ZS_i) + \varepsilon_i
\end{aligned}
\tag{1}
$$

$$
\begin{aligned}
\log(FC_{k,i}) = {} & \beta_{0,k} + \beta_{1,k}\log(FO_i) + \beta_{2,k}\log(TPD_i) + \beta_{3,k}TPD_i^2 + \beta_{4,k}LPT_i \\
& + \beta_{5,k}HPT_i + \beta_{6,k}FAV_i + \beta_{7,k}\log(1-RET_i) + \beta_{8,k}(ZS_i) + + \beta_{9,k}(BV_i) + \varepsilon_i
\end{aligned}
\tag{2}
$$

$$
\begin{aligned}
\log(FC_{k,i}) = {} & \beta_{0,K} + \beta_{1,K}\log(FO_i) + \beta_{2,K}\log(TPD_i) + \beta_{3,K}TPD_i^2 \\
& + \beta_{4,K}LPT_i + \beta_{5,K}HPT_i + \beta_{6,K}FAV_i + \beta_{7,K}\log(1-RET_i) + \beta_{8,K}(ZS_i) \\
& + \beta_{9,K}(BV_i) + \beta_{10,K}(I_{1,i}) + \beta_{11,K}(I_{2,i}) + \beta_{12,K}(I_{3,i}) + \beta_{13,K}(I_{4,i}) + \beta_{14,K}(I_{5,i}) + \varepsilon_i
\end{aligned}
\tag{3}
$$

$$
\begin{aligned}
\log(FC_{k,i}) = {} & \beta_{0,k} + \beta_{1,K}\log(FO_i) + \beta_{2,k}\log(TPD_i) + \beta_{3,k}TPD_i^2 + \beta_{4,k}LPT_i \\
& + \beta_{5,k}HPT_i + \beta_{6,k}FAV_i + \beta_{7,k}\log(1-RET_i) + \beta_{8,k}(ZS_i) + \beta_{9,k}(BV_i) \\
& + \beta_{10,k}(I_{1,i}) + \beta_{11,k}(I_{2,i}) + \beta_{12,k}(I_{3,i}) + \beta_{13,k}(I_{4,i}) + \beta_{14,k}(I_{5,i}) + \beta_{15,k}(A_{1,i}) \\
& + \beta_{16,k}(A_{2,i}) + \beta_{17,k}(A_{3,i}) + \beta_{18,k}(A_{4,i}) + \varepsilon_i
\end{aligned}
\tag{4}
$$

Overall, the baseline model (Model 0) has an R squared of 24%, meaning that our control variables, i.e., brand value, geographic location, and industry together explained 24% of total variances in follower counts. The proposed model (Model 4) has an R squared of 0.76, meaning that 76% of variances in follower counts could be explained by our model, indicating a good model fit. The hypotheses-only model (Model 1) without all the control variables along explained about 74% of total variances. Geographic locations did not seem to impact the number of followers in the final model while being in certain industries (such as manufacturing and finance) attracts fewer followers than the benchmark industry (information technology). Brand value, as expected, was positively related to follower counts.

The results supported H1, with quality of tweets measured by percentage of tweets favorited significantly related to both follower counts in 2014, and a year later in 2015, highlighting the importance of quality of content in brand Twitter accounts.

H2 argued a curvilinear relationship between tweets per day and follower counts. The results indicated that tweets per day was positively related to follower counts, and tweets per day squared was negatively related to follower counts (b= -0.17 and -0.21 for 2014 and 2015 follower counts). We plotted a graph to clarify the pattern of such a curvilinear relationship for the original data in 2014 (see Figure 3). The graph shows that as the number of tweets per day increases, follower counts decrease for the original data set. Thus, H2 received support.

H3 posited that tweets' relevance measured by the percentage of original content is positively related to brand Twitter account's follower counts. This hypothesis was not substantiated.

H4 argued that the use of hashtags and links could be negatively related to follower counts. The results supported this hypothesis, with a significant negative relationship between manners and follower counts in both years.

For H5, interactivity with followers in the forms of replies and mentions is not significantly related to brands' Twitter account's follower counts. Thus, H5 was not supported.

Finally, H6 received support. Social learning measured by the number of accounts followed is positively related to brands' Twitter account's follower counts. However, the effects of social learning seem to wear out within a year: it was only significant for 2014 (b=0.10) but was no longer effective a year later in 2015.

DISCUSSION AND CONCLUSION

Summary of Findings

Although the importance of social media has been increasingly recognized, little research has been conducted to explore what attracts people to follow brand twitter accounts. The current research addressed this gap in the literature and the results show that the frequency and quality of the tweets, Tweeting manner, as well as social learning all contributed to follower counts. Specifically, the quality of tweets is the most important factor leading to follower counts, followed by the frequency of tweets. Lack of manners in tweets with too many hashtags and links could lead to negative impacts in follower counts, while social learning through following others could facilitate follower growth in the short run.

Table 3. Hierarchical multiple regression results with log ten transformed data 2014

Independent	Dependent Variable: $\log(FC_{2014})$				
	Model 0	Model 1	Model 2	Model3	Model 4
Intercept	1.13(0.59)	5.26***(0.80)	3.91***(0.88)	4.34***(0.89)	4.24***(0.90)
Brand Value					
$\log(BV)$	0.29***(0.15)		0.10***(0.29)	0.09***(0.09)	0.09***(0.09)
Industry					
I_1	-0.34***(0.15)			-0.10***(0.09)	-0.10***(0.09)
I_2	-0.16**(0.13)			-0.12***(0.08)	-0.12***(0.08)
I_3	-0.07(0.15)			-0.03(0.09)	-0.04*0.09)
I_4	-0.09(0.19)			-0.07**(0.11)	-0.08**(0.11)
I_5	-0.15***(0.21)			-0.05(0.12)	-0.05(0.12)
Country					
A_1	0.02(0.85)				0.00(0.48)
A_2	0.40***(0.14)				0.01(0.08)
A_3	0.24***(0.15)				0.04(0.09)
A_4	0.08(0.37)				-0.02(0.22)
Social learning					
$\log(FO)$		0.12***(0.03)	0.11***(0.03)	0.10***(0.03)	0.11***(0.03)
Quantity					
$\log(TPD)$		0.34***(0.06)	0.33***(0.06)	0.29***(0.06)	0.29***(0.06)
TPD^2		0.04(0.00)	0.04(0.00)	0.05(0.00)	0.05(0.00)
Manner					
LPT		-0.11***(0.14)	-0.11***(0.14)	-0.10***(0.14)	-0.11***(0.14)
HPT		-0.13***(0.06)	-0.13***(0.06)	-0.12***(0.06)	-0.13***(0.06)
Quality					
FAV		0.70***(0.00)	0.68***(0.00)	0.68***(0.00)	0.68***(0.00)
Relevance					
$\log(1-RET)$		-0.08**(0.42)	-0.06**(0.42)	-0.07**(0.42)	-0.07**(0.42)
Interactivity					
ZC		0.01(0.03)	0.01(0.03)	0.03(0.03)	0.03(0.03)
R square	0.24	0.74	0.75	0.76	0.76
Adjusted R square	0.22	0.74	0.74	0.75	0.75

PS: ** is significant at the 0.01 level (2-tailed) and ** is significant at the 0.05 level (2-tailed).

Table 4. Hierarchical multiple regression results with logten transformed data 2015

	Dependent Variable: $\log(FC_{2015})$				
	Model 0	**Model 1**	**Model 2**	**Model3**	**Model 4**
Intercept	1.16**(0.60)	5.63(0.79)	4.12(0.87)	4.54(0.88)	4.50(0.90)
Brand Value					
$\log(BV)$	0.30***(0.30)		0.11***(0.09)	0.10***(0.09)	0.10***(0.09)
Industry					
I_1	-0.30***(0.16)			-0.05(0.09)	-0.05(0.09)
I_2	-0.11(0.14)			-0.06(0.08)	-0.07(0.08)
I_3	-0.04(0.16)			-0.01(0.09)	-0.01(0.09)
I_4	-0.09(0.19)			-0.08***(0.11)	-0.08***(0.11)
I_5	-0.14***(0.21)			-0.04(0.12)	-0.04(0.12)
Country					
A_1	0.04(0.86)				0.01(0.47)
A_2	0.38***(0.14)				0.00(0.08)
A_3	0.22***(0.15)				0.02I(0.09)
A_4	0.08(0.38)				-0.02(0.21)
Social learning					
$\log(FO)$		0.05(0.03)	0.04(0.03)	0.04(0.03)	0.04(0.03)
Quantity					
$\log(TPD)$		0.37***(0.06)	0.37***(0.06)	0.35***(0.06)	0.35***(0.06)
TPD^2		-0.05(0.00)	-0.05(0.00)	-0.05(0.00)	-0.05(0.00)
Manner					
LPT		-0.15***(0.14)	-0.14***(0.14)	-0.14***(0.14)	-0.14***(0.14)
HPT		-0.10***(0.06)	-0.10***(0.06)	-0.09***(0.06)	-0.09***(0.06)
Quality					
FAV		0.72***(0.42)	0.70***(0.00)	0.70***(0.00)	0.70***(0.00)
Relevance					
$\log(1-RET)$		-0.07**(0.42)	-0.06*(0.41)	-0.07**(0.42)	-0.07**(0.42)
Interactivity					
ZC		0.02(0.03)	0.01(0.03)	0.03(0.03)	0.03(0.03)
R square	0.23	0.75	0.76	0.76	0.76
Adjusted R square	0.20	0.74	0.75	0.75	0.75

PS: ** is significant at the 0.01 level (2-tailed) and ** is significant at the 0.05 level (2-tailed).

Figure 3. Pattern of curvilinear relationship between tweets per day and follower counts

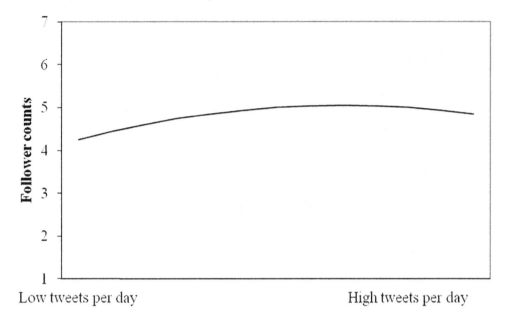

Discussion

First, the results highlighted the importance of quality content in attracting followers on Twitter. This echoes with prior research that identified Twitter as a media more than a social network. Kwak et al. (2010) obtained 41.7 million user profiles, 1.47 billion social relations, 4,262 trending topics, and 106 million tweets by crawling Twitter and found that the majority (over 85%) of topics are headline news or persistent news in nature. Thus, it is quality content, rather than social interactions, that are the backbone of Twitter, and the key driver for follower counts. With this insight in mind, the finding that interactivity is not positively related to follower counts is understandable, as most followers treat Twitter as a source of news and information, rather than means of interaction and networking with brands. Thus, high interactivity of brands published on brands' timelines actually distracts and drives followers away, as reading interactions between the brand and its followers may not usually be considered as quality content.

Another interesting finding is that followers don't seem to care whether the tweet is from the brand or retweeted content, as relevance is not positively related to follower counts. Possibly it is because they care more about the quality of the content. Even if it's a retweet, as long as it's interesting, they do not turn away.

Quantity of tweets has a curvilinear relationship with follower counts. This confirms the maxim of quantity: you should provide enough messages to explain yourself, but also do not make your contribution more informative than is required. Therefore, there is this intricate balance of providing enough messages, but not too many messages.

Finally, contrary to public belief that hashtags help your tweets get discovered and are thus beneficial for your follower counts, the results showed that hashtags and links are both negatively related to follower counts. Although hashtags and links add a wealth of information to tweets and expand the limits of the 280 characters count, it seems that they also add difficulty in reading tweets and drive followers away.

Looking at both data sets with both 2014 and 2015 follower data, we could see that the results are quite consistent for the year sampled, and one year later, even though the average follower count had a 50% increase over the year. This may be due to the consistency in the style of operation for brand Twitter accounts, but it also may signal the unique feature of social network: quality content is shared by one follower to his or her network, then someone in that network likes it and share again...and the sharing goes on and on as time goes by. Thus, a good tweet goes a long way on Twitter. The influence of tweets extends beyond the hour and the day it was published, but rather lives as long as it is being shared, favorited, and commented on.

Theoretical Contribution

This study aims to contribute to social media regarding brands' Twitter activities. Compared with other research on Twitter follower counts (e.g., Hutto et al., 2013; Mueller & Stumme; 2017), we have several advantages. First, we specifically examined brands' Twitter activities, while the other studies focused on Twitter accounts in general. Second, we offer a parsimonious model (with only 6 key variables, compared with over 20 variables in other research) that explained a high percentage of variances in the dependent variable. We contribute to Twitter research in several ways. First, by building on the foundation of Grice's Maxims (Grice, 1975) and features of social networks, this research provided a theoretical framework to understand the context of brands' Twitter accounts. It clarified what factors contribute to follower counts in the context of high-value brands. The results showed that the quality and frequency of the tweets, the Tweeting manner, as well as social learning all play a role in follower counts.

Second, the proposed model has established the importance of the communication perspective on Twitter in attracting followers. Twitter, with its dual nature that combines both social interaction/social networks and news media (Fischer& Reuber, 2011; Kwak et al., 2010), sometimes causes confusion to corporations as to whether to treat it as a media or a social network. This research confirmed prior findings that Twitter is, by and large, a news media. Whereas most prior research has focused on the social network nature of Twitter, the results of this research indicated that the communication perspective of Twitter also warrants attention.

Finally, this study clarified some of the myths about Twitter follower counts on the internet with theory-guided tests. The results showed that contrary to popular belief, hashtags and links may not always work in your favor. Additionally, interactivity with some followers published on timelines can drive other followers away. The findings help provide a systematic overview that enriches extant social media literature while providing insights into the important factors contributing to Twitter follower counts.

Practical Implication

The findings of this study can help brand Twitter managers gain a better understanding of how to attract followers on Twitter. Based on the findings, we offer the following recommendations for practice.

First, Focus on the quality of content. The results indicated that of all the factors, the quality of the content has the highest impact on follower counts. Thus, brand Twitter managers should focus on providing quality content to their followers. They can examine their history and find out what type of tweets are most liked and shared, and provide more similar content. In addition, they can also learn from others: studying their competitors and see their most shared and liked contents, and derive insights from there as well.

Second, don't publish every interaction with customers. Although Twitter is often used for interacting with customers, it may not always be necessary to publish every interaction on the brands' Twitter timeline and let everybody see it. If possible, interaction with specific customers can take the form of private messaging, so that only those involved will see the reply, without bombarding other followers with conversational tweets. Some companies separate customer service with general-purpose Twitter accounts, for example, Bank of America news, and Bank of America customer service. This may also be a sensible way to manage a brand's Twitter account.

Third, Tweet often, but not too much. The results indicated an inverted U shape relationship between tweets per day and follower counts. Thus, as tweets per day increase, brand twitter accounts gain more followers at first, and then, as the number of tweets keeps increasing, followers begin to leave. There is an intricate balance to keep in tweets per day. The majority of brands' Twitter accounts send out less than 10 tweets per day, which could be a good range to start with.

Fourth, use hashtags and links wisely. Hashtags and links help increase discoverability and information content, but they also render the content of tweets less readable. Therefore, brand Twitter managers should use caution when use hashtags and links. It would be helpful if the hashtags and links are not mixed along with the content, but rather, put at the end of the tweets so that the readability of the tweets is improved.

Finally, learn from the leaders. The findings indicated that the more accounts a brand follows, the more followers it gains. Following other accounts keep brand Twitter managers up with the latest development, popular trends, and hot topics. Thus, managers need to embrace the opportunity of learning from others by following other accounts on Twitter that are relevant to their brand or industry.

Limitation and Future Research

There are several limitations in this research that present opportunities for future research. First, although the sample of 346 companies from the Global 500 Brand, each with up to 3200 tweets is sufficiently diverse to support the findings, the results are not tested against companies with small and medium brand value. We expect the model to still hold for all kinds of companies. Future studies could sample a larger set of companies to include small and medium-sized brands. Second, the generalizability of our findings is limited to Twitter accounts that operate in English, catering to the English speaking audience. Future research could explore Twitter accounts that use languages other than English, and explore the role of culture in Twitter follower counts. A third limitation is that our measures for quality, relevance, manner and social learning are quantitative surrogates and not direct measures of these constructs. Although using data from Twitter and Twitter analytics site has the advantage of providing an objective, data-driven approach, direct measuring of the constructs can give us richer information and dimensional knowledge about the constructs. Thus, future research could benefit from user surveys to further understand the question.

CONCLUSION

Practitioners and researchers increasingly recognize the important role social media plays in building brands and communicating with customers. This study is one of the first attempts to develop a theory on brands' Twitter followers by adopting both the communication and social network perspectives in the context of brand Twitter account. Our results revealed that the quality and frequency of tweets, presentation manner, and social learning all contributed to follower counts. With an understanding of the major contributing factors to Twitter follower counts, these results serve as a basis for future theoretical development in the area of social media marketing, which in turn, could also yield valuable insights that guide practice.

REFERENCES

Adweek. (2011). *5 Twitter Metrics Beyond Follower Count.* http://www.adweek.com/socialtimes/5-twitter-metrics-beyond-follower-count/445796

Bandura, A. (1977). *Social Learning Theory.* Prentice Hall.

Baratgin, J., Jacquet, B., & Cergy, F. (2019). Cooperation in Online Conversations: The Response Times as a Window Into the Cognition of Language Processing. *Frontiers in Psychology, 10,* 727. doi:10.3389/fpsyg.2019.00727 PMID:31024385

Barnes, N. G., & Andonian, J. (2014). *The 2014 Fortune 500 and social media.* University of Massachusetts Dartmouth. http://www.umassd.edu/cmr/socialmediaresearch/2014fortune500andsocialmedia/

Berendt, B., Günther, O., & Spiekermann, S. (2005). Privacy in e-commerce: Stated preferences vs. actual behavior. *Communications of the ACM, 48*(4), 101–106. doi:10.1145/1053291.1053295

Bikhchandani, S., Hirshleifer, D., & Welch, I. (1998). Learning from the Behavior of Others: Conformity, Fads, and Informational Cascades. *The Journal of Economic Perspectives, 12*(3), 151–170.

Bontcheva, K., Gorrell, G., & Wessels, B. (2013). *Social media and information overload: Survey results.* arXiv preprint arXiv:1306.0813

Bradford, S. C. (1934). Sources of information on specific subjects. Engineering, 137, 85-86. Reprint (1985). *Journal of Information Science, 10*(4), 176–180.

Chu, S. C., Chen, H. T., & Sung, Y. (2016). Following brands on Twitter: An extension of theory of planned behavior. *International Journal of Advertising, 35*(3), 421–437. doi:10.1080/02650487.2015.1037708

Díaz-Díaz, R., & Pérez-González, D. (2016). Implementation of Social Media Concepts for e-Government: Case Study of a Social Media Tool for Value Co-Creation and Citizen Participation. *Journal of Organizational and End User Computing, 28*(3), 104–121. doi:10.4018/JOEUC.2016070107

Fischer, E., & Reuber, A. R. (2011). Social interaction via new social media: (How) can interactions on twitter affect effectual thinking and behavior. *Journal of Business Venturing, 26*(1), 1–18. doi:10.1016/j.jbusvent.2010.09.002

Gallup. (2014). *The Myth of Social Media.* Retrieved July 3, 2014, from http://online.wsj.com/public/resources/documents/sac_report_11_socialmedia_061114.pdf

Goh, K. Y., Heng, C. S., & Lin, Z. (2013). Social Media Brand Community and Consumer Behavior: Quantifying the Relative Impact of User- and Marketer-Generated Content. *Information Systems Research*, *24*(1), 88–107. doi:10.1287/isre.1120.0469

Greenhow, C., & Robelia, B. (2009). Old communication, new literacies: Social network sites as social learning resources. *Journal of Computer-Mediated Communication*, *14*(4), 1130–1161. doi:10.1111/j.1083-6101.2009.01484.x

Grice, H. P. (1975). Logic and Conversation. In P. Cole & J. L. Morgan (Eds.), Syntax and Semantics: Vol. III. *Speech Acts* (pp. 41–58). Academic Press. doi:10.1163/9789004368811_003

Hair, J. F. Jr, Black, W. C., Babin, B. J., Anderson, R. E., & Tatham, R. L. (2006). *Multivariate Data Analysis* (6th ed.). Pearson Prentice Hall.

Herring, S. (1999). Interactional coherence in CMC. *Journal of Computer-Mediated Communication*, *4*(4).

Hong, W., Thong, J. Y., Wong, W. M., & Tam, K. Y. (2002). Determinants of user acceptance of digital libraries: An empirical examination of individual differences and system characteristics. *Journal of Management Information Systems*, *18*(3), 97–124. doi:10.1080/07421222.2002.11045692

Hutto, C. J., Yardi, S., & Gilbert, E. (2013, April). A longitudinal study of follow predictors on twitter. In *Proceedings of the sigchi conference on human factors in computing systems* (pp. 821-830). ACM. 10.1145/2470654.2470771

Kaplan, A. M., & Haenlein, M. (2010). Users of the world, unite! The challenges and opportunities of Social Media. *Business Horizons*, *53*(1), 59–68. doi:10.1016/j.bushor.2009.09.003

Kim, A.J., & Ko, E. (2012). Do social media marketing activities enhance customer equity? An empirical study of luxury fashion brand. *Journal of Business Research*, 65(10),1480,1486.

Kim, E., Sung, Y., & Kang, H. (2014). Brand followers' retweeting behavior on Twitter: How brand relationships influence brand electronic word-of-mouth. *Computers in Human Behavior*, *37*, 18–25. doi:10.1016/j.chb.2014.04.020

Kwak, H., Chun, H., & Moon, S. (2011). Fragile online relationship: A first look at unfollow dynamics in Twitter. In *Proceedings of the 2011* (pp. 1091–1100). Annual Conference on Human Factors in Computing Systems. doi:10.1145/1978942.1979104

Laroche, M., Mohammad, R. H., Richard, M.-O., & Sankaranarayanan, R. (2012). The effects of social media based brand communities on brand community markers, value creation practices, brand trust and brand loyalty. *Computers in Human Behavior*, *28*(5), 1755–1767.

Laroche, M., Mohammad, R. H., & Richard, M.-O. (2013). To be or not to be in social media: How brand loyalty is affected by social media? *International Journal of Information Management*, *33*(1), 76–82. doi:10.1016/j.ijinfomgt.2012.07.003

Lee, E.-J., & Kim, Y. W. (2014). How social is Twitter use? Affiliative tendency and communication competence as predictors. *Computers in Human Behavior*, *39*, 296–305. doi:10.1016/j.chb.2014.07.034

Leung, C. K. S., & Jiang, F. (2015, September). Big data analytics of social networks for the discovery of "following" patterns. In *International Conference on Big Data Analytics and Knowledge Discovery* (pp. 123-135). Springer. 10.1007/978-3-319-22729-0_10

Levine, N., Mann, T. A., & Mannor, S. (2015). *Actively learning to attract followers on Twitter*. arXiv preprint arXiv:1504.04114

Li, T., Berens, G., & de Maertelaere, M. (2014). Corporate Twitter Channels: The Impact of Engagement and Informedness on Corporate Reputation. *International Journal of Electronic Commerce, 18*(2), 97–125. doi:10.2753/JEC1086-4415180204

Lovejoy, K., Waters, R. D., & Saxton, G. D. (2012). Engaging stakeholders through Twitter: How nonprofit organizations are getting more out of 140 characters or less. *Public Relations Review, 38*(2), 313–318. doi:10.1016/j.pubrev.2012.01.005

Maldonado, M., & Sierra, V. (2016). Twitter Predicting the 2012 US Presidential Election?: Lessons Learned from an Unconscious Value Co-Creation Platform. *Journal of Organizational and End User Computing, 28*(3), 10–30. doi:10.4018/JOEUC.2016070102

Mueller, J., & Stumme, G. (2017). Predicting rising follower counts on Twitter using profile information. In *Proceedings of the 2017 ACM on Web Science Conference* (pp. 121-130). ACM. 10.1145/3091478.3091490

Nielson. (2013). *Twitter Consumer Survey*. Nielson Holdings.

Phua, J., Jin, S. V., & Kim, J. J. (2017). Gratifications of using Facebook, Twitter, Instagram, or Snapchat to follow brands: The moderating effect of social comparison, trust, tie strength, and network homophily on brand identification, brand engagement, brand commitment, and membership intention. *Telematics and Informatics, 34*(1), 412–424. doi:10.1016/j.tele.2016.06.004

Quercia, D., Capra, L., & Crowcroft, J. (2012). The social world of twitter: Topics, geography, and emotions. *Sixth International AAAI Conference on Weblogs and Social Media*.

Reeves, B., & Nass, C. (1996). *The Media Equation: How People Treat Computers, Television, and New Media Like Real People and Places. Chicago, IL: Center for the Study of Language and Information*, Cambridge University Press.

Rishika, R., Kumar, A., Janakiraman, R., & Bezawada, R. (2013). The Effect of Customers' Social Media Participation on Customer Visit Frequency and Profitability: An Empirical Investigation. *Information Systems Research, 24*(1), 108–127. doi:10.1287/isre.1120.0460

Saffer, A. J., Sommerfeldt, E. J., & Taylor, M. (2013). The effects of organizational twitter interactivity on organization–public relationships. *Public Relations Review, 39*(3), 213–215. doi:10.1016/j.pubrev.2013.02.005

Stevanovich, M. (2012). *Rhetorical Analysis of Successful Brands in Social Media Discourse*. Gonzaga University.

Thoring, A. (2011). Corporate tweeting: Analysing the use of Twitter as a marketing tool by UK trade publishers. *Publishing Research Quarterly, 27*(2), 141–158. doi:10.100712109-011-9214-7

Trusov, M., Bucklin, R. E., & Pauwels, K. (2009). Effects of word-of-mouth versus traditional marketing: Findings from an Internet social networking site. *Journal of Marketing*, *73*(5), 90–102. doi:10.1509/jmkg.73.5.90

Verma, J. P. (2012). *Data analysis in management with SPSS software*. Springer Science & Business Media.

Wamba, S.F., Akter, S., & Bhattacharyya, M & Aditya. (. (2016). How does Social Media Analytics Create Value? *Journal of Organizational and End User Computing*, *28*(3), 1–9. doi:10.4018/JOEUC.2016040101

Westerman, D., Spence, P. R., & Van Der Heide, B. (2012). A social network as information: The effect of system generated reports of connectedness on credibility on Twitter. *Computers in Human Behavior*, *28*(1), 199–206. doi:10.1016/j.chb.2011.09.001

Yang, J. (2011), Endeavour to open a new horizon of public diplomacy with Chinese characteristics, retrieved 28.9.18, http://ye.chineseembassy.org/eng/m1/t805868.htm

Yu, Y., Duan, W., & Cao, Q. (2013). The impact of social and conventional media on firm equity value: A sentiment analysis approach. *Decision Support Systems*, *55*(4), 919–926. doi:10.1016/j.dss.2012.12.028

Zhu, Y. Q., & Chen, H. G. (2015). Social media and human need satisfaction: Implications for social media marketing. *Business Horizons*, *58*(3), 335–345.

This research was previously published in the Journal of Organizational and End User Computing (JOEUC), 33(1); pages 71-91, copyright year 2021 by IGI Publishing (an imprint of IGI Global).

Chapter 25
Enhanced Event Detection in Twitter Through Feature Analysis

Dharini Ramachandran.

Vellore Institute of Technology, Chennai, India

Parvathi R.

Vellore Institute of Technology, Chennai, India

ABSTRACT

The Digital era has the benefits in unearthing a large amount of imperative material. One such digital document is social media data, which when processed can give rise to information which can be helpful to our society. One of the many things that we can unearth from social media is events. Twitter is a very popular microblog that encompasses fruitful and rich information on real world events and popular topics. Event detection in view of situational awareness for crisis response is an important need of the current world. The identification of tweets comprising information that may assist in help and rescue operation is crucial. Most pertinent features for this process of identification are studied and the inferences are given in this article. The efficiency and practicality of the features are discussed here. This article also presents the results of experimentation carried out to assess the most relevant combination of features for improved performance in event detection from Twitter.

1. INTRODUCTION

Social media enables people to stay connected. Posting every episode and incident in Social media has become a natural customary behavior among people. These episodes range from day to day activities to critical topics/events. Hence, anything including a new or a trending event/topic will be surely posted on social media. This contributes to a humongous amount of data. Analytics on such data help us in understanding the behavioral patterns, trends, human understanding on a topic, their opinions on the same and much more. Event Detection concentrates on bringing events to light from this large clutter

DOI: 10.4018/978-1-6684-6287-4.ch025

of raw social media data. The events may be either a physical event or a popular topic being discussed in the media. Events can be small scale or large scale, ranging from localized birthday parties to global election predictions.

1.1. Social Media Text Analytics

Nowadays the use of Social media is widespread, to an extent where people first post it on social media platform and only then start discussing it personally. Situations have changed wherein people will find out about the happenings from news and then post their discussions about it on social media, whereas now happenings are posted first on social media and then broadcasted in news channels. The proficiency in getting information about the world and the ease in sharing the experiences, views, ideas are the predominant merits of social media.

The happenings around the world posted in social media can benefit in revealing countless valuable information if processed properly. Also, the raw data serve as a hub of details of a happening from the user point of view. The main challenge in handling this raw data is that it contains noise and it is unstructured. This warrants new kind of data analysis and mining techniques to uncover extensive information such as Opinions, Sentiments, News, Events, Popular Topics, User groups, Document groups, Trends, Characteristics of Users. In social media, major analytics is performed in the areas of Event Detection, Opinion Mining, Recommendation System, Sentiment Analysis, Trend Analysis, Question Answering System and Community Detection.

1.2. Why Twitter

Twitter is a fast-growing microblogging service that allows users to post messages (Tweets) with the number of characters not exceeding 280. Twitter satisfies the curiosity of people by letting users post "What's happening?" around them and know "What's happening" around the globe. The short text property of Twitter makes it effortless to share information instantly. A "Tweet" in twitter is the message that users post on Twitter with a limit of 280 characters (Twitter Support, 2017). A "Retweet" is a tweet forwarded by a user which he/she got from another user- something that the user likes to share. An '@' symbol represents the Username of the twitter account and it is used to call out the user in tweets. A "#" symbol represents the 'Hashtag' which depicts the topic of the tweet. Users can "Follow" other users and those who do will receive the tweets sent by latter.

The willingness of Twitter to share its publicly available tweets is highly welcomed by the research community. Twitter provides Application Programming Interface (API) to enable an application or website to connect to the worldwide conversation happening on Twitter. Another main reason for opting twitter is the availability of crisp yet rich information from all over the world on Celebrities, News channels, Government agencies, Political parties, Private organizations, individuals and much more.

1.3. Situational Awareness

During disastrous situations involving danger to people or property, Social Media helps in providing an immeasurable amount of relevant information. The situational information is most needed for identifying exactly where help is needed and also what kind of help is needed. Those who are affected or bystanders know this information more clearly. And the fastest way of making this information publicly available is by posting them in social media. Twitter is one such platform where users give and receive firsthand information about events. Users, either victims or spectators, in both case act as rich source of data and intelligence with their posts enabling us to know what really happened in a particular place. Situational Awareness deals with two major areas such as Help & Rescue, Summarization & analysis.

The long-term objective of our work is to present a model that analyses the tweets posted during disasters in real-time and uncover the tweets in accordance to the two major categories mentioned above. As a starting point, classification of tweets into Disaster Oriented and Non-Disaster Oriented categories is carried out. The main aim of the experimentation is to analyze the performance of the classification based on the features used. Generally, the utilization of correct features increases the chance of getting high accuracy in classification.

1.4. Challenges

The challenges prevalent in the typical text analysis is also prevalent in Social media data. The nature of twitter data is highly different ranging from formal announcements to informal colloquial texts. The complexity is further intensified with the arduous nature of data comprising of the messages that originate directly from people showcasing everything from their day-to-day activities to their experiences. The informal nature, slangs, abbreviations, acronyms in the messages, text highly dependent on the person's writing style, text with ungrammatical structure and spelling errors account for the complexity in analysis of those messages. The limited number of characters makes it difficult to identify the context and nature of the shared information within such short text. These challenges warrant different kind of analytics rather than the techniques used for traditional and formal texts.

2. RELATED WORK

Event detection is an emerging research field and many commendable works have been done to effectively identify the events. The theme of the paper is to understand the features used in the detection process. Hence the literature survey has been confined to focus on the features used. The most commonly used feature is the Term Vector (the vector representation of the word in a tweet) as in (Elsawy et al., 2014; Löchtefeld et al., 2015). TwitterStand (Sankaranarayanan et al., 2009) is a news detection system that utilizes the Term Vector for the event detection process along with other metadata. This term vector is obtained after the preprocessing. While the work in (Gu et al., 2011) uses Term vector, n-gram models are also utilized to identify and model the events. Authors in the work (Weng and Lee, 2011) uses individual word in the process of detecting events. The approach given in (Saravanou et al., 2015) adopted a flood-based lexicon along with the word vectors. The lexicon is compared with the tweets and the final list of words are prepared. The authors of the work presented in (Tan et al., 2014) utilize the tweet words to identify the hot topics in a community. The word vectors are used to identify topic distribution and community distribution. A system to identify situational information during a disaster (Rogstadius et al., 2013) is proposed, where the keywords are tracked automatically. Similar tweets are clustered and the users are provisioned to verify and analyze the scores using crowdsourcing techniques. The similarity between Word vectors of tweets are identified using cosine similarity metric. The similar tweets are clustered to form stories about certain event using an extended version of the Locality-sensitive hashing algorithm.

In the process of identifying events, work has been done to estimate the spatial and temporal aspects of the events. A program called Jasmine (Watanabe, Ochi, Okabe et al., 2011) examines the tweet content to identify an event and also estimate the location of the event. A Place Name database is used to match the locations mentioned in the tweet to the physical location, the feature used here is the actual tweet word. The work presented in (Tzeng et al., 2012) focuses on determining the duration of an event using aging theory. Here the collected tweets are transformed into energy domain and hence events are considered as organisms and their death is predicted to detect the end of an event. The features used are of two kinds, Author features such as number of tweets posted and Textual features such as length of the tweet, frequency and position of the event related words. To identify events in correspondence to locations, the approach used in (Unankard et al., 2015) uses locations from the tweet, from Geo-tagged location and from IP address. The features used from tweets are the words after slang conversion. These processed words are transformed to vectors using TFIDF Score.

The work in (Popescu et al., 2011) utilizes the Part-Of-Speech tags and regular expressions to identify an event and its descriptions. Eventweet (Abdelhaq et al., 2013) takes the keywords (from a tweet) into consideration when identifying an event. If a keyword burst occurs, the tweets containing the keywords are clustered.

The proposed work in (Weiler et al., 2013) detects events based on the tweets based on the geographical and temporal dimensions. The features taken into account are the event term and the co-occurring terms. Twevent (Li et al., 2012) is a system that considers a segment of the tweet as a feature. The system takes both unigrams and multigrams of words as segments. Bursty segments are identified and processed to detect events. In another work focusing on real-time detection of traffic status (D'Andrea et al., 2015) the authors use the tweet words as a feature. But then, this feature is not used directly. The tweets are subjected to preprocessing such as tokenization, stopword removal and stemming. The terms are represented as vectors using IDF score. The feature selection process named Information Gain is used to filter out the most important vectors. Those vectors with positive Information Gain value are only considered as features to the system.

A specific work on detecting suicidality on Twitter (O'Dea et al., 2015) is done using frequency of the tweet words and the TFIDF score of the same. Machine learning using SVM is performed on the features to find suicidal messages posted on twitter. An approach for identifying the relatedness among the events is given (Laylavi et al., 2017) where the features used are the tweet words. The content of the tweet is preprocessed by removing the stopwords. This feature is used to build term classes which again is a set of specific words. For the real-time analysis of twitter data, a framework is proposed in (Gaglio et al., 2016). The features used are the actual terms (tweet words) occurring in the tweets. A set of co-occurring terms are identified whose likelihood ratio with a reference corpus is calculated. Also the TFIDF value of the terms is calculated. The information on whether a term can be recognized by Named Entity Recognition (NER) is stored in a variable. These three (co-occurring terms, TFIDF Value, NER information) are used as features for the term selection process which is dynamic in nature to adapt to the real-time processing.

3. FEATURE COMPONENTS UNDER ANALYSIS

The employed model need not be a complex one to get better results. A better set of features can give the best result even with a simpler model. For any classification or clustering problem, the handled features influence the performance. Fine tuning the number of features and the amount of data fed are crucial to obtain the desired level of accuracy. The raw data should be precisely reconstructed into features which exemplifies the problem so that the model can deliver accurate results. The algorithms used in our experiment are Naive Bayes and Decision Tree. Though there are different other state of the art algorithms, we have tried to assess the features based on these two basic yet powerful algorithms. It can be seen that, the same algorithms give varied results with different combination of features. The results obtained from this experimentation demonstrate that better results can be achieved with the better combination of features.

The objective of the study is to analyze the impact of features on the performance of event detection. The intention is to narrow down to a feature or combination of features that escalates the event detection performance which can be used along with other influential tweet metadata to uncover events in a much better way. The features studied in the experimentation are

- Tweet Word
- POS (Part-Of-Speech) Tag
- TFIDF (Term Frequency Inverse Document Frequency) Score

In case of textual data, the most important feature is the actual word. The word carries the essence of the document. The words in the tweet hold the nature of communication by the person and it needs to be included in the analysis.

Also, just using words without their placement in the sentence loses the significance of the word. For this purpose, Part-Of-Speech word tags are used. The Part-Of-Speech tag for tweet text is slightly different from traditional text due to the challenges as discussed in 'Section 1.4 Challenges', such as the nature of twitter data, informal colloquial texts, slangs, abbreviations in it. Hence, it makes the placement of tags much more complex yet much more useful. The importance of POS tag is immense in natural language processing. In our experiment, the learning and understanding about the disaster events is being performed from a bulk of raw tweets. The words are the building blocks of such understanding. To know the importance of a word in a sentence, it is vital to know the word's placement information in the same. The placement of a word in the sentence, helps us understand the word sense. The POS tag encloses such vital information in it. Providing it as a feature, to a machine learning algorithm, helps us in getting better results

The main theme of a document can be identified using the TFIDF score. The TFIDF - Term Frequency Inverse Document Frequency shows the most significant occurring word in the document. Common words that occur very frequently and words that occur very rarely, may not give much impact to the theme of the document and gets a lower score. The remaining significant words which may give high impact towards the theme of the document gets a high score. The TFIDF score identifies the important words in a tweet by taking into account its commonness and rarity. A very rare or very common word in the whole corpus gets lower importance than the rest. TFIDF weight is a vital feature which gives much better results during classification.

4. ARCHITECTURE OF THE EVENT DETECTION SYSTEM

The main aim of the work is to identify the best set of features that can help in better event detection process. The features fed to a model have greater influence on the performance of the model. Creation of features from the large clutter of raw data is an important step in solving a machine learning problem. The features aid in representing the useful attributes of raw data, in a way that can be utilized well by the machine learning algorithm. These representations of raw data in the form of features play a vital role in enhancing the performance of the model. Hence, the identification of a better set of feature combination is undertaken in this work. This analysis benefits in aiding us achieve much better performance in event detection process. The features studied are the actual word in a tweet, the POS tag and the TFIDF score. To encompass the actual essence of communication of social media data, the actual word is included in the analysis. Also, the words are included in both the text form and also in the vectorized form. To carry the importance of each and every word in the sentence, POS tag is included. The TFIDF score encompasses the importance of a word in the whole corpus. Two powerful algorithms - a probabilistic model (naive bayes) and a tree-based model (decision tree) are utilized for assessing the features.

Figure 1. Architecture of the system

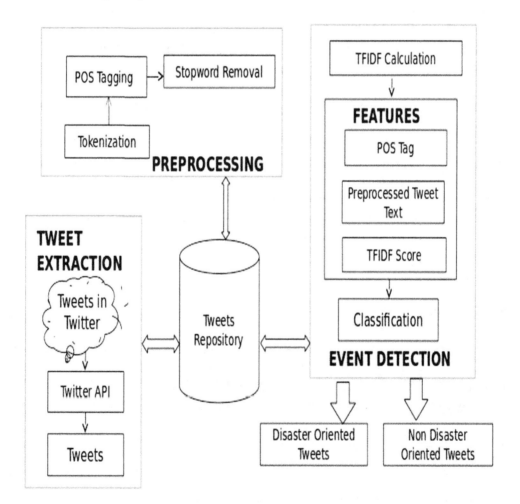

The architecture of the system is given in Figure 1. The main components of the system are Tweet Extraction, Preprocessing, TFIDF Scoring and Event Detection using classification. The aim of the experiment is to identify the best feature/combination of features for the event detection process. The tweets fed into the system are extracted using Twitter API which forms the first step of the experiment. The next step is to preprocess the obtained raw data which includes cleaning the data and identifying the POS Tags. Calculating the TFIDF score for each word is the next step. Now the features are ready and are fed to the classification algorithms to categorize the tweets into Disaster and Non-Disaster Oriented tweets.

4.1. Tweets Extraction

Twitter provides Application Programming Interface to enable the extraction of tweets that are publicly available. Twitter offers two kinds of API (Twitter, 2017) namely REST API and Streaming API. The Streaming API allows real-time monitoring and processing of Tweets whereas REST API enables access to read and write Twitter Data. The Tweet IDs (Tweet Identifier) of the disaster-oriented tweets from (Rudra et al., 2015) are utilized for the disaster class. The Tweet IDs correspond to tweets collected during five disaster events corresponding to a Blast in Hyderabad, India (February 2013), a Shootout in Sandy Hook elementary school, USA (December 2012), a Flood in Uttarakhand, India (June 2013), a Typhoon in Hagupit, Philippines (December 2014), an Earthquake in Nepal (April 2015), a Train Derailment in Harda, India (August 2015). The non-disaster Tweet IDs are collected from (Politecnico di Torino, 2017) posted during Paralympics event held at London in 2012 and a music concert by Madonna, an American singer, song writer, in September 6, 2012.

The tweets are extracted using Twitter REST API by utilizing the corresponding Tweet ID for each Tweet, OAuth and Tweepy (python library for accessing Twitter data). The extracted tweets are in JSON format consisting of the tweet's text along with the tweet's metadata such as user information, retweet information, geographic location etc. These tweets are used as the training dataset. The obtained JSON format data is fed into MongoDB as Collection. The text of the tweets is extracted from the MongoDB Collection and employed for further processing.

4.2. Preprocessing

4.2.1. POS Tagging

Tokenization is the process of separating the words in a sentence. The extracted tweets are tokenized into individual words. The Part-Of-Speech tags for the words are identified and placed along the words. The Tokenization and POS tagging are performed using Tweet NLP (Gimpel et al., 2011) . This twitter specific POS tagger includes some tags specific to tweets such as # for Hashtag, @ for username, U for URL etc.

4.2.2. Stopword Removal

The most common words in the language which may be of less significance in terms of the analysis are called Stopwords. These words may occur very frequently in texts but provide almost no help in categorization. Examples are a, an, and, are, of, the, etc. These common words arise very often in both formal and informal texts. Hence, the stopwords are removed from the tweet words in the next step. The following sections of the tweet are eliminated as they benefit very little in the analysis.

- stopwords
- Usernames - @, Retweet tag – RT, URLs
- Punctuations, Emoticons, Numerals

The example in Figure 2 shows a tweet before and after preprocessing.

Figure 2. An example of preprocessing

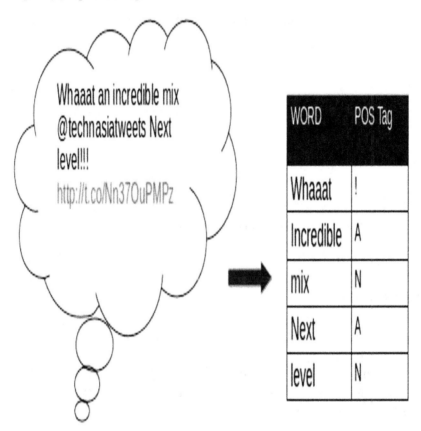

4.2.3. Vector Representation

A text representation using the classic Bag-of-words technique presents a high dimensional feature set as a result of the variety of words being involved. To simplify these dimensions, a sparse representation can be followed. The tweets are messages which are short in length and hence a sparse representation will be suitable and practically convenient. With the Dictionary Vectorizer, features (tweet words and POS tags) are represented as a sparse matrix with the value '1' in the presence of the feature in the document and the absent features are not stored.

4.3. TFIDF Scoring

The TFIDF (Term Frequency - Inverse Document Frequency) is calculated for the tweet words. Not all tweet words are important in a tweet. The TFIDF score indicates how important a tweet word is, to a tweet, in the whole collection. A tweet word occurring many times within a small number of tweets gets the highest score. A tweet word occurring fewer times in a tweet or occurring in many tweets gets a relatively lower score. A tweet word occurring in virtually all tweets gets the lowest score.

$tf_{w,t}$ -Term Frequency
df_w - Document Frequency
idf_w - Inverse Document Frequency
The TF-IDF score is calculated with the following formula

$$tfidf_{w,t} = tf_{w,t} \times idf_w \tag{1}$$

$$idf_w = \log(n/df_w) \tag{2}$$

where

n = total number of tweets in the collection

$tf_{w,t}$ = no. of occurrences of tweet word w in a tweet t

df_w = no. of tweets t in the collection that contains tweet word w

Using the equation 1 the TFIDF Score is calculated for each and every tweet word in the collection.

4.4. Dataset Preparation

After the completion of all the preprocessing and TFIDF Scoring, the dataset is prepared to include all tweet words and its corresponding Vector representation, POS Tags, TFIDF score, Label. Labels are named TRUE for disaster-oriented tweets and FALSE for non-disaster tweets. The final dataset consisted of 398818 tweet words (including disaster and non-disaster dataset) and their corresponding POS Tag, TFIDF Score and Vector representation.

4.5. Classification of Tweets

Learning is achieved using the supervised learning mechanism. In training phase of classification, the algorithm is given a set of data with the corresponding label to learn. In the testing phase, the algorithm will assign a label to another set of given data based on the learning achieved in the training phase. With the Naive Bayes and Decision Tree algorithms in experimentation, the classification is performed with two kinds of input, one with the Vector representation of the tweet words and one with the textual representation of tweet words.

5. EXPERIMENTAL EVALUATION

5.1. Machine Learning Models Employed

Two machine learning models are employed for the analysis of the features – Naive Bayes and Decision Tree. The reason for choosing Naive Bayes is that it is a generative model. The classifier is based on the Naive Bayes algorithm. The algorithm uses the Bayes rule to express P(label |features) in terms of P(label) and P(features |label). Also, there is an assumption that all features are independent given a label. The Decision Tree classifier decides the label to assign based on the tree structure. The branches of the tree are the conditions or questions on feature values that branches out according to the answers and leaves have the label assignments.

5.2. Experimental Results

The results of the experiments are given in Tables 1 and 2. The performance of the event detection by using the three features and its combinations are studied during the experimentation. The aim of the experiment is to classify tweets into two classes - Disaster Oriented and Non-Disaster Oriented. The features are evaluated under the metrics Accuracy, Precision, Recall, F-Measure

Table 1. Accuracy

	WORD	TFIDF	WORD + POS	WORD + TFIDF	WORD + POS +TFIDF
NAIVE BAYES	93.064	89.65	92.732	94.542	94.318
NAIVE BAYES -Vector	93.046	89.645	92.793	94.313	94.147
DECISION TREE	93.077	89.65	93.326	94.542	94.318
DECISION TREE – Vector	93.077	89.653	93.327	97.058	**97.211**

Accuracy of the performance gives us the fraction of the classifications that are correctly classified and is calculated using the formula given in the Equation 3 (Manning et al., 2008).

$$Accuracy = (TP + TN)=(TP + FP + FN + T N) \tag{3}$$

Where

T P = Relevant items correctly identified as relevant

T N = Irrelevant items correctly identified as irrelevant

F P = Irrelevant items incorrectly identified as relevant

F N = Relevant items incorrectly identified as irrelevant

Precision and Recall are the measures used to understand the performance of the system in terms of the retrieved relevant documents and the actual relevant documents.

Precision(P) = (no: of relevant items retrieved) /(no: of retrieved items)

Recall(R) = (no: of relevant items retrieved) / (no: of relevant items)

Precision, Recall and F-measure are calculated using the formulas given in Equations 4, 5 and 6 respectively

$$P = TP/(TP + FP) \tag{4}$$

$$R = TP/(TP + FN) \tag{5}$$

$$F = 2PR/(P + R) \tag{6}$$

Table 2. Precision, Recall and F-Measure

Algorithm	Measures	Word	TFIDF	WORD + POS	WORD + TFIDF	WORD+ POS + TFIDF
Naive Bayes	Precision	0.945	0.905	0.952	0.968	0.971
	Recall	0.967	0.968	0.954	0.96	0.955
	F-Measure	0.956	0.935	0.953	0.964	0.963
Naive Bayes – Vector	Precision	0.943	0.908	0.95	0.966	0.968
	Recall	0.968	0.964	0.957	0.96	0.955
	F-Measure	0.955	0.935	0.953	0.943	0.962
Decision Tree	Precision	0.948	0.905	0.951	0.974	0.978
	Recall	0.963	0.967	0.963	0.988	0.986
	F-Measure	0.955	0.935	0.957	0.981	0.982
Decision Tree – Vector	Precision	0.949	0.908	0.952	0.98	0.981
	Recall	0.962	0.962	0.962	0.981	0.983
	F-Measure	0.955	0.935	0.957	0.981	0.982

6. ANALYSIS AND DISCUSSION

The objective of the experimentation is to narrow down the best feature or feature combinations for better event detection from Twitter. Various feature combinations have been experimented and the performances are compared. The combinations taken into consideration are

- Word (Textual representation and Vector Representation),
- TFIDF Score,
- Word and POS,

- Word and TFIDF
- Word and POS and TFIDF,

on two algorithms - Naive Bayes and Decision Tree. The accuracy of the results is measured with both single fold cross validation and 10-fold cross validation. A training and testing split of 70% and 30% respectively is utilized for the validation of the dataset. The results discussed in this paper are from single fold validation.

Figure 3. Comparison of accuracies

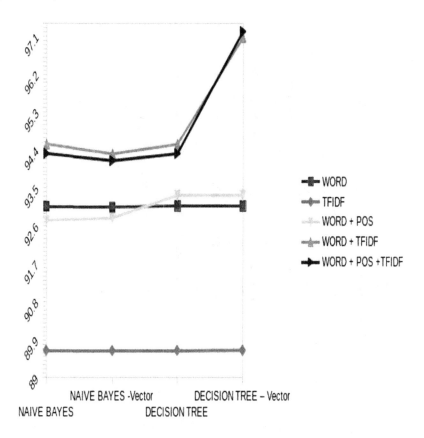

Figure 3 shows the comparison of the accuracies observed in the experimental results. From the graph, it is evident that the maximum accuracy is obtained for the combination of all the three features. Also, the least is observed when the TFIDF feature alone is used.

The algorithms gave a lower performance when using only TFIDF Score of the tweet word. The TFIDF score without the actual word gives lesser performance compared to the one with the actual tweet word, which gives us a clear conclusion that the significance of TFIDF increases with the inclusion of actual word. Using the Tweet word feature alone gives better performance than the other two features. The combination of the three features gives a better accuracy. The best performance is obtained with the vector representation of the tweet word along with the other two features.

Figure 4 depicts the comparison of the Precision and Recall measures noted in the experimentation. It can be seen that the combination of tweet word and TFIDF gives the best performance in terms of all the three metrics when subjected to Decision Tree-Textual representation. The next best performance can be seen in the combination of all the three features under the Decision Tree - Numerical representation. While the lowest performance can be seen in terms of Precision using TFIDF alone but the recall value for the same is similar to all the other recall values.

Figure 4. Comparison of precision, recall, and F-Measure

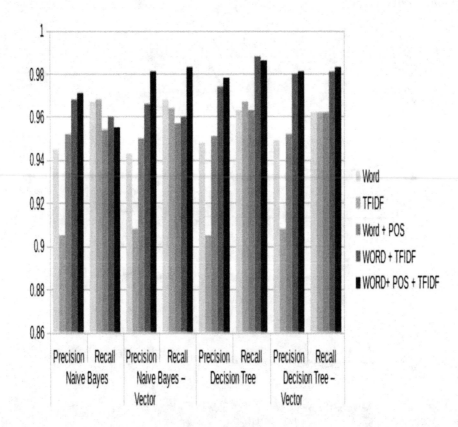

Looking at the F-Measure, it is evident that the combination of all the features gives unmistakably good results comparing to all the other results. With regard to the Recall metric, the best is obtained with the combination of tweet word and TFIDF score with Decision Tree algorithm. Whereas, in terms of Precision, the best is observed in the combination of all the three features.

Comparing the two algorithms, the Decision tree gives best performance but at the cost of time. The time taken by decision tree algorithm in our experimentation is more than twice the time taken by Naive Bayes algorithm. Though Naive Bayes gives a comparably lower performance, the time taken is considerably less. Consequently, the experimentation gives us a concluding result that the combination of all the three features gives commendable performance.

In the Decision Tree algorithm (Word Representation), though the F-measure for WORD+TFIDF (0.981) is competent with that of the WORD+TFIDF+POS (0.982) combination, there is an increase in the Precision measure (0.978) of the latter. With an increase in the precision measure, the inclusion of POS tag shows it increases the ability of retrieving relevant instances by the algorithm.

In the Decision Tree Algorithm (Vector representation) also, the combination WORD+TFIDF has given a F-measure of 0.981 while WORD+TFIDF+POS has given 0.982. With the latter combination, there is an increase in the recall measure (0.983) that shows better sensitivity. Likewise, there is an increase in precision (0.981).

Though the combination of WORD+TFIDF (94.542) has succeeded WORD+TFIDF+POS (94.318), in accuracy in the Decision Tree algorithm (Word Representation), the increase in recall and precision measures can be seen with the inclusion of POS tag. For this test case, this increased value seems minimal, but, as the impact is demonstrated in two most important metrics - Precision and Recall, it evidently shows the advantage in including the POS tag.

As already included in 'Section 2 Background', the works in the literature have used some of the features studied in this experimentation for different applications. To the best of our knowledge, there was no work that concentrates on assessing the features for the event detection process. Also, the various works that have been carried were performed on different datasets, that were not made public. Since we could not obtain the tweet IDs, it was not possible for us to compare our results. And from the paper cited as (Rudra et al., 2015), from where we have obtained the tweet IDs for our experimentation, the methodology and application of the work is entirely different thus making it not possible for us to compare the results. To understand the features and their importance, to understand our analysis, we tried out different combination of features in different algorithms and compared the results

7. CONCLUSION AND FUTURE WORK

Event detection from social media in view of situational awareness during any disaster event aids in obtaining firsthand information. The experiment carried out to identify disaster-oriented tweets is explained in this paper. The features employed in a model have a direct impact on the results achieved. Thence the intention of this work is to identify the best combination of features for the event detection process. The results show that the combination of the three features Tweet word, POS Tag and TFIDF score gives best result compared to the individual features and their other combinations. Using this combination of textual features of the tweet messages along with other features obtained from a tweet's metadata can undeniably render improvement in performance of the event detection process.

Building a system that can analyze tweets in near real-time and identify those that can help in Rescue measures from emergency responders during disaster event is our future work. A lexicon that works for disaster-oriented tweets will definitely help in the event detection process. A lexicon and similarity of tweet words with the lexicon, weightage based on that similarity are to be included in our future work. A model that includes weightage based on the hashtag, metadata like author's information will enhance the credibility of the detection process. In future work, we will include the credibility analysis and weightage-based enhancements to the event detection process.

REFERENCES

Abdelhaq, H., Sengstock, C., & Gertz, M. (2013). Eventweet: Online localized event detection from twitter. *Proceedings of the VLDB Endowment International Conference on Very Large Data Bases*, *6*(12), 1326–1329. doi:10.14778/2536274.2536307

Baralis, E., Cerquitelli, T., Chiusano, S., Grimaudo, L., & Xiao, X. (2013). Analysis of twitter data using a multiple-level clustering strategy, In International Conference on Model and Data Engineering, Springer,13-24.

D'Andrea, E., Ducange, P., Lazzerini, B., & Marcelloni, F. (2015). Real-time detection of traffic from twitter stream analysis. *IEEE Transactions on Intelligent Transportation Systems*, *16*(4), 2269–2283. doi:10.1109/TITS.2015.2404431

Elsawy, E., Mokhtar, M., & Magdy, W. (2014). Tweetmogaz v2: Identifying news stories in social media. In *Proceedings of the 23rd ACM International Conference on Conference on Information and Knowledge Management* (pp. 2042–2044). 10.1145/2661829.2661843

Gaglio, S., Re, G. L., & Morana, M. (2016). A framework for real-time twitter data analysis. *Computer Communications*, *73*, 236–242. doi:10.1016/j.comcom.2015.09.021

Gimpel, K., Schneider, N., O'Connor, B., Das, D., Mills, D., Eisenstein, J., . . . Smith, N. A. (2011). Part-of-speech tagging for twitter: Annotation, features, and experiments. In *Proceedings of the 49th Annual Meeting of the Association for Computational Linguistics: Human Language Technologies* (pp. 42–47).

Gu, H., Xie, X., Lv, Q., Ruan, Y., & Shang, L. (2011). Etree: Effective and efficient event modeling for real-time online social media networks. In *Proceedings of 2011 IEEE/WIC/ACM* Web Intelligence and Intelligent Agent Technology (WI-IAT) (Vol. 1, pp. 300–307).

Laylavi, F., Rajabifard, A., & Kalantari, M. (2017). Event related-ness assessment of twitter messages for emergency response. *Information Processing & Management*, *53*(1), 266–280. doi:10.1016/j.ipm.2016.09.002

Li, C., Sun, A., & Datta, A. (2012). Twevent: segment-based event detection from tweets. In *Proceedings of the 21st ACM international conference on Information and knowledge management* (pp. 155-164).

Löchtefeld, M., Jäckel, C., & Krüger, A. (2015). Twitsoccer: knowledge-based crowd-sourcing of live soccer events. In *Proceedings of the 14th International Conference on Mobile and Ubiquitous Multimedia* (pp. 148–151). ACM. 10.1145/2836041.2836055

Manning, C. D., Raghavan, P., & Schütze, H. (2008). *Introduction to information retrieval* (Vol. 1). Cambridge: Cambridge University Press. doi:10.1017/CBO9780511809071

O'Dea, B., Wan, S., Batterham, P. J., Calear, A. L., Paris, C., & Christensen, H. (2015). Detecting suicidality on twitter. *Internet Interventions*, *2*(2), 183–188. doi:10.1016/j.invent.2015.03.005

Popescu, A. M., Pennacchiotti, M., & Paranjpe, D. (2011). Extracting events and event descriptions from twitter. In *Proceedings of the 20th international conference companion on World wide web* (pp. 105–106). 10.1145/1963192.1963246

Rogstadius, J., Vukovic, M., Teixeira, C., Kostakos, V., Karapanos, E., & Laredo, J. A. (2013). Crisistracker: Crowdsourced social media curation for disaster awareness. *IBM Journal of Research and Development*, *57*(5), 4–1. doi:10.1147/JRD.2013.2260692

Rudra, K., Ghosh, S., Ganguly, N., Goyal, P., & Ghosh, S. (2015). Extracting situational information from microblogs during disaster events: a classification-summarization approach. In *Proceedings of the 24th ACM International on Conference on Information and Knowledge Management* (pp. 583–592). 10.1145/2806416.2806485

Sankaranarayanan, J., Samet, H., Teitler, B. E., Lieberman, M. D., & Sperling, J. (2009). Twitterstand: news in tweets. In *Proceedings of the 17th ACM SIGSPATIAL international conference on advances in geographic information systems* (pp. 42–51).

Saravanou, A., Valkanas, G., Gunopulos, D., & Andrienko, G. (2015). Twitter floods when it rains: A case study of the UK floods in early 2014. In *Proceedings of the 24th International Conference on World Wide Web* (pp. 1233–1238). 10.1145/2740908.2741730

Tan, Z., Zhang, P., Tan, J., & Guo, L. (2014). A multi-layer event detection algorithm for detecting global and local hot events in social networks. *In Proceedings of the 14th International Conference on Computational Science. Procedia Computer Science*, *29*, 2080–2089. doi:10.1016/j.procs.2014.05.192

Twitter. (2017). Retrieved from https://dev.twitter.com/docs

Twitter Support. (2017). Retrieved from https://support.twitter.com

Tzeng, Y. S., Jiang, J. Y., & Cheng, P. J. (2012). Event duration detection on microblogging. In *Proceedings of the 2012 IEEE/WIC/ACM International Joint Conferences on Web Intelligence and Intelligent Agent Technology* (Vol. 1, pp. 16–23).

Unankard, S., Li, X., & Sharaf, M. A. (2015). Emerging event detection in social networks with location sensitivity. *World Wide Web (Bussum)*, *18*(5), 1393–1417. doi:10.100711280-014-0291-3

Watanabe, K., Ochi, M., Okabe, M., & Onai, R. (2011). Jasmine: a real-time local-event detection system based on geolocation information propagated to microblogs. In *Proceedings of the 20th ACM international conference on Information and knowledge management* (pp. 2541–2544). 10.1145/2063576.2064014

Weiler, A., Scholl, M. H., Wanner, F., & Rohrdantz, C. (2013). Event identification for local areas using social media streaming data. In *Proceedings of the ACM SIGMOD Workshop on Databases and Social Networks* (pp. 1–6). 10.1145/2484702.2484703

Weng, J., & Lee, B. S. (2011). Event detection in twitter. In *Proceedings of the Fifth International AAAI Conference on Weblogs and Social Media (ICWSM)* (pp. 401–408).

This research was previously published in the International Journal of Information Technology and Web Engineering (IJITWE), 14(3); pages 1-15, copyright year 2019 by IGI Publishing (an imprint of IGI Global).

Chapter 26
Tactics for Influencing the Consumer Purchase Decision Process Using Instagram Stories:
Examples From Around the World

Hale Fulya Yüksel
 https://orcid.org/0000-0003-2953-5212
Afyon Kocatepe University, Turkey

Erkan Akar
Afyon Kocatepe University, Turkey

ABSTRACT

The purpose of this study is to put forth tactics to influence the consumer purchase decision process by using Instagram Stories tools. The tactics are handled with successful examples from around the world. Analysis of the examples reveal that many powerful tools of Instagram Stories such as different camera modes, face filters, stickers, live video, "see more" links, shopping stickers, hashtags, etc. can be used to accomplish business goals like driving online and in-store sales, promoting apps, raising brand awareness, generating leads, gathering follower feedback, and retaining customers by influencing consumers at every stage of the purchase decision process.

INTRODUCTION

Traditional commerce has become electronic with the rise of the Internet, and it has transformed almost everything about consumers' lives such as the ways of communicating and gathering information about product offerings or how to make purchases (Darley, Blankson & Luethge, 2010). Because of the particular impact of the digital revolution on consumer purchase decision-making, today's consumers

DOI: 10.4018/978-1-6684-6287-4.ch026

are not limited to offline shopping; instead they now have access to product information anywhere (at home, at the workplace, or at any other place with the use of mobile devices) (Charlesworth, 2009: 16) and anytime.

According to the "Digital in 2018" report, the number of internet users is 4.021 billion, the number of social media users is 3.196 billion and the number of mobile phone users is 5.135 billion. Moreover, almost 1.8 billion people around the world are making online purchases (Kemp, 2018) and this number is expected to be over 2.14 billion in 2021 (Statista, 2019a). According to the "Social Commerce Revisited 2018" report, all social media platforms influence consumers' shopping journeys and as the report reveals, 58% of respondents say that social media influence a purchasing decision (SUMO Heavy Industries, 2018).

Looking at the literature on this subject, Djafarova and Rushworth (2017) investigated how different types of celebrities on Instagram affect consumer buying intention. Veirman, Cauberghe and Hudders (2017) explored Instagram influencers' impact on brand attitude. Casalo, Flavian and Ibanez-Sanchez (2020) examined influencers on Instagram, and identified some key antecedents and consequences of opinion leadership. This study theoretically contributes to the literature on both digital content marketing and online consumer behavior, by explaining the use of Instagram Stories tools in influencing the consumer purchase process. Therefore, it is one of the first studies in this field.

CONSUMER PURCHASE PROCESS IN THE DIGITAL ERA

The traditional consumer purchase process consists of five stages including problem/need recognition, information search, evaluation of alternatives, purchase decision and post purchase evaluation (Engel, Blackwell & Miniard, 1990; Butler & Peppard, 1998; Tco & Yeong, 2003; Park & Cho, 2012; Wolny & Charoensuksai, 2014). The effects of the digital revolution on these stages may be summarized as shown in Table 1.

CONTENT MARKETING IN THE DIGITAL ERA

Content marketing is not a new phenomenon, but the emergence of the Internet and digital channels including social media has facilitated companies to take advantage of content to attract current and potential customers (Lieb, 2012: 2).

Content marketing can be defined as attracting, engaging and inspiring customers to buy and share via content that relates to the interests and behaviors of the customers' buying cycle (Odden, 2012: 99). The growth of the social and mobile Web has changed communication methods (Rose & Pulizzi, 2011) and digitalized content marketing. Rowley (2008) defines digital content marketing as:

The management process responsible for identifying, anticipating, and satisfying customer requirements profitably in the context of digital content, or bit-based objects distributed through electronic channels.

A research study by the Content Marketing Institute (2017) reveals that digital channels are highly used to distribute content as shown in Figure 1.

According to the same research, content marketing tactic usage is listed in Figure 2.

Table 1. Effects of "digital" on the consumer purchase decision process

Consumer Purchase Process Stage	Effects of "Digital"
1. Problem/Need Recognition	• Stimuli from both offline and online sources may trigger identification of a need (Jayawardhena, Wright & Masterson, 2003). • Routine daily online interactions such as exposure to friends' interactions on online social networks about new products, engagement with or observation of editorial content, and exposure to formal marketing communications trigger need recognition (Ashman, Solomon & Wolny, 2015).
2. Information Search	• For today's consumers, online social network communities may serve as a place to share and gather shopping information (Park & Cho, 2012). • Before making a purchase, information can be collected from online sources such as search engines, web sites or comparison sites (Wolny & Charoensuksai, 2014).
3. Evaluation of Alternatives	• Virtual communities and user groups' endorsements, simulation and testing opportunities help in evaluating the alternatives in the marketspace (Butler & Peppard, 1998). • The decision aids can be classified as: Passive (collaborative filtering methods, expert or peer evaluation listings, etc.) and active (software tools such as comparison matrices, recommendation agents, and ordering and ranking tools) (Breugelmans et al., 2012).
4. Purchase Decision	• In the marketspace, the factors that influence an actual purchase decision are ease of ordering and delivery; payment; security and conditions (Butler & Peppard, 1998). • Social networks that use Web and mobile technologies have created an opportunity for people to be involved in online and social commerce activities such as online shopping and purchases (Sharma & Crossler, 2014). • People use social network sites and other social platforms when they purchase a product because they get informational and emotional support from other members of these communities. This supportive information can affect purchase decisions because they can be related to direct or indirect experiences about the products (Hajli, 2014).
5. Post Purchase Evaluation	• The satisfaction value of a purchase depends on both the satisfaction of the purchaser and the satisfaction of others, virtually expressed as likes, comments and shares, etc. (Ashman, Solomon & Wolny, 2015). • Post purchase experiences are shared by customers who are motivated by the variety of digital channels. Over these channels, customers express their satisfaction or dissatisfaction and recommend digital content to others (Dahiya & Gayatri, 2018).

Figure 1. Channels that B2C marketers use to distribute content (Content Marketing Institute, 2017)

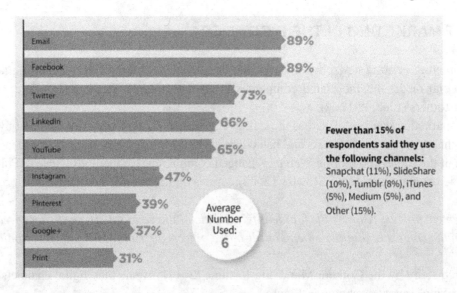

Figure 2. B2C marketers' content marketing tactic usage (Content Marketing Institute, 2017)

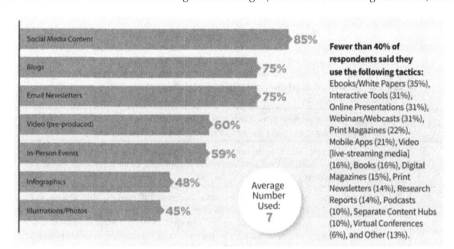

According to the research by the Content Marketing Institute (2018) the top three most effective types of content that are used for content marketing purposes are shown in Figure 3.

Figure 3. The top 3 most effective types of content that B2C marketers use for content marketing purposes (Content Marketing Institute, 2018)

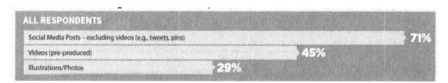

MAJOR DIGITAL CONTENT CHANNELS

Digital channels can be considered as tools for delivering content. Major types of digital channels (Lieb, 2012), their role in the online consumer purchase process and the types of content that are shared on these channels are listed in Table 2.

CLASSIFICATION OF SOCIAL MEDIA CONTENT

There is limited literature on the classification of social media content. In one of these studies, Keefe (2017) classifies social media content in terms of privacy controls as public, private or ephemeral content. Public social media content has no privacy and is accessible to any person who wishes to view the user's account on a social media platform. Private social media content refers to content where users give limited access to a specific group of people to view the posted content. Ephemeral social media content, which has a temporary nature, enables users to share more personal information and better reflects users' feelings, personalities, and everyday life (Keefe, 2017).

Table 2. Digital content channels

Channel	Role in the Online Consumer Purchase Process	Types of Content
Social Networks	User comments on social network sites provide valuable information for both participants and companies such as information about tastes, desires and needs of social network users; their usage, consumption behavior and origin; and the levels of satisfaction/dissatisfaction with the products and services (Curras-Perez, Ruiz Mafe & Sanz-Blas, 2013).	• text • audio • picture • video
Geo-social Networks	Being one of the most popular geo-social network platforms, Foursquare encourages users to interact with other users and share their experiences (Bozanta & Kutlu, 2018).	• text • picture
Location-based Content	Location-based content, which works only on smartphones and tablet computers, includes offering information, guidance, rewards, incentives to purchase, or answers to questions and it has an immediate contextual relevance (Lieb, 2012).	• text • picture
Online Directories	Customers can acquire new product information or company information from a business's online directory and online directories have an important role in facilitating Web browsing and decision-making. Yahoo and DMOZ are two examples of general Web directories and the labels and categorization of directories help users to find information in less time and to have a better Web navigation experience (Chung, 2012).	• text
E-mail	Marketers may keep customers interested in the brand using regular e-mail communication which provides varying content that customers desire (Merisavo & Raulas, 2004).	• text • audio • picture • video
Social Bookmarking	Using social bookmarking, Internet users can save, categorize or share online content (Weisgerber & Butler, 2015). Social tagging has the benefit of capturing information from various resources about specific content from users and communities in terms of their preferences, interests or chosen categories (Rangiha, Comuzzi & Karakostas, 2016).	• text (link)
Blogs	Blogs can be considered as important digital information sources in Web 2.0 because of the rich digital content they include. Especially, popular blogs are important information sources that consumers browse, adopt and trust; hence they frequently influence purchase behavior (Ho et al., 2015).	• text • audio • picture • video
Podcasts	Podcasts are a good medium to publish authentic content and create a genuine relationship with consumers. In addition, more consumers are turning to their favorite podcasts every day and marketers may use this tool to adjust consumers' needs (Kareh, 2017).	• audio • video
Webinar	Using both broadly appealing webinars to create awareness and leads, and smaller webinars to attract a more qualified base of prospects (Handley & Chapman, 2010), companies may influence consumer decision-making.	• video
Apps and Widgets	App adoption and continued use of the branded app influences purchase behavior and increases future spending. Moreover, apps that provide portable, convenient, and interactive engagement opportunities allow customers to interact with the brand on a habitual basis (Kim, Wang & Malthouse, 2015).	• text • audio • picture • video
Online Video, Long-form Publishing (e-books, white papers, digital magazines)	Offering a report, white paper or video for free may encourage customers to decide to purchase (Allen, 2016).	• text • audio • picture • video
Microblogging	According to Zhang and Peng (2015), microblogging sites enable users to access information sources and create real-time communication with other users as well as empower them to participate in the diffusion of advertising messages. Mirkovski et al. (2018) summarize the motivations of microblog use from the findings of two prior studies: keeping in touch with friends and colleagues, increasing the visibility of interesting events/activities to one's social networks, gathering useful information for one's profession or other personal interests, seeking help and opinions, releasing emotional stress, talking about daily activities, and sharing information.	• text • picture • video

continues on following page

Table 2. Continued

Channel	Role in the Online Consumer Purchase Process	Types of Content
E-Learning/ Online Training	Online consumer learning, which is usually presented in the form of tutorials or similar step-by-step instructions, helps consumers to gain knowledge and reduce cognitive effort; therefore, it affects decision-making and product adoption (Steils, Crie & Decrop, 2019).	• text • audio • picture • video
Online Community	According to Martinez-Lopez et al. (2017), consumers use online brand communities for creating relationships with other consumers, searching information and defining their personalities. Consumers visit online communities to gain information about products and user-generated contents in these communities may influence consumers' purchase decisions (Li, Wang & Lin, 2018).	• text • picture • video
Wikis	Wikis are open systems that enable users to collaboratively contribute content (Wu et al., 2013). Companies that provide products or services may influence consumer decision-making by focusing on a company or brand's presence and increasing visibility of their content on wikis such as Wikipedia.	• text • picture
Digital Media Center/ Press Room; Case Studies; Articles and Columns; Visual Information (Charts, Diagrams, Infographics, Maps)	Digital media centers/press rooms supply the high demand for transparency and easy access to information; case studies build credibility and trust; articles and columns that company executives contribute demonstrate depth and breadth of knowledge, trends, or new technologies; visual information capture attention and interest, and because they are also shareable they help in the dissemination of storytelling (Lieb, 2012). As a result, all these channels may directly or indirectly help companies to influence consumer decision-making.	• text • picture • video

On the other hand, Chen and Cheung (2019) mention two forms of social media content as persistent content or ephemeral content. Persistent content is a typical form of social media content which is displayed permanently and publicly on users' profiles. This type of persistent content can cause some concerns in users such as privacy, disclosure and outcomes of use. Based on these concerns, the use of ephemeral content increased notably and it is now a prominent component of user experience in the social media ecosystem (Chen & Cheung, 2019).

EPHEMERAL CONTENT

The word "ephemeral" is derived from the Greek word "ephémeros" which means "lasting one day" and today it is used to define the fast-moving and short-lived nature of content and media (Kavanagh, 2018). Ephemerality is not only related to contents that are consumed in a very short time, but it is also related to contents that can only be viewed for a limited amount of time or a certain number of times (Vázquez-Herrero et al., 2019). Chen and Cheung (2019) define ephemeral content as:

Communication artifacts, including text, pictures, and videos, that will be erased after being displaying for a limited period of time.

Ephemeral content is a type of short-lived content which lasts 24 hours at most and then disappears forever (Sheetrit, 2017). Ephemerality of content affects users' content composition, self-presentation, and online communication behavior (Villaespesa & Wowkowych, 2020). The reasons for the growth of ephemeral content can be (Beaulac, 2019):

- Suitability for mobiles
- Authenticity
- Preventing the main feed from clogging up with content

In a marketing perspective, there are several benefits of using ephemeral content; some of which can be listed as the following (Sheetrit, 2017):

- Unlike long-lasting sponsored ads or spammy posts that push customers to make purchases, ephemeral content is thought to be more authentic.
- Fear of missing out (FOMO) is triggered by content that is lost within hours; therefore, this type of content makes audiences take fast action.
- QR codes can facilitate access to content.
- Ephemeral content may grab potential customers' attention which is very important.

Today's popular social media platforms that provide ephemeral content can be listed as Snapchat, Facebook, Instagram, and WhatsApp.

Brief explanations of these social media platforms that provide ephemeral content are as follows (Mialki, 2019):

- Snapchat is likely the first app that comes to mind when people think of ephemeral content; and using Snapchat advertising, users can both send ephemeral content to individuals or groups, and post on public "Stories".
- Facebook Stories of a user can be reached by tapping the profile picture of that user. Moreover, it appears automatically at the top of the user's News Feeds.
- Instagram's ephemeral content feature, which is called "Stories", functions in a similar way to Facebook Stories.
- WhatsApp Status feature, which is inspired by Snapchat, uses photos, text, emojis and sketches (Cipriani, 2017).

INSTAGRAM STORIES AND ITS POWERFUL TOOLS FOR MARKETING

Instagram launched "Instagram Stories" in August 2016 which enabled users to post photo and video slideshows that disappeared after 24 hours (Gallagher, 2018), and this addition to Instagram became one of the biggest game-changers for the platform (Scholl, 2018a). Instagram Stories offer a visual ephemeral microformat which has portrait orientation with horizontal navigation and it affected the media production models that are used on mobile devices for news consumption (Vázquez-Herrero et al., 2019).

Today, Instagram has over 1 billion active monthly users and more than 500 million of them actively use Stories on a daily basis (Instagram, 2019a). More than 25 million company profiles are active on Instagram and more than 2 million companies use Instagram advertisements to reach customers per month. At the same time, over 200 million Instagram users visit at least one company profile daily (Instagram, 2019b). One out of three of the most viewed Stories are from business profiles and 50% of business profiles on Instagram worldwide create at least one story during a typical month (Instagram, 2019c).

Aside from Instagram's main features, Stories has many unique benefits that offer a lot of potential for marketers. The reasons for this are as follows (Scholl, 2018a):

- Stories appear in small circles along the top of a feed, and this place separated from other content draws a lot more attention and increases engagement.
- Stories resemble various forms of live content.

Instagram Stories has a lot of tools for marketers to explore which are described in Table 3.

Table 3. Instagram stories tools and their descriptions

Tool	Description
Boomerang	Boomerang mode creates a mini video that plays forward and backward.
Mention	A user can be mentioned in a story by typing "@" followed by the username. If people tap on "mention" they see a pop-up that takes them to that profile. The user who is mentioned in a story is informed by a notification. Mention stickers are also available for the same purpose.
Hashtag	Users can include hashtags starting with "#" and people watching the story can tap on the hashtag to visit the hashtag page and explore related posts. Type mode and hashtag stickers can be used for this purpose.
Type	Type mode enables users to share texts with creative styles and backgrounds without a need for a photo or video. In addition, text messages can be added to picture or video stories.
Drawing	A drawing tool helps users to draw, highlight, color or erase.
"See More" Links	Verified accounts or accounts with more than 10,000 followers can add links to their stories to share more information. If users tap "See More" or swipe up, they can view the link right inside the app.
Live Video	Live mode enables users to share live videos for up to one hour. A notification is sent to the users' followers to invite them to watch it. Users can choose to receive or turn off comments while they're live. Moreover, the users can choose to add a replay of the live video for 24 hours or else it will disappear after the live session ends. Users can also add a guest while broadcasting. In this case, the screen splits into two and the live session continues with two users at the same time.
Stickers	Tapping the stickers button, users can add customizable stickers to their story such as the weather, the current time and day, location, etc. For a location sticker, people watching the story can tap the sticker to learn more about the location. Other sticker types include geosticker; special emoji stickers; country-specific, special occasion or holiday stickers; selfie sticker; GIF stickers; poll sticker; countdown sticker; questions sticker; emoji slider sticker; mention and hashtag stickers; etc.
Hands-Free	"Hands-Free" mode in the format picker lets users start recording a video with just one tap and continue recording several stories until the user taps again and stops it.
Face Filters	Face filters help the user to transform into a variety of characters. To use face filters, users should open the camera and tap the face icon in the bottom right-hand corner.
Rewind	Rewind camera mode allows users to make videos that play in reverse.
Reply	While watching a story, users can reply to the story with a text, a picture or a video. Creative tools can also be used in replies, including face filters, stickers and rewind. A sticker of the story is included in the reply which users can move around and resize.
Focus	Focus camera mode enables users to take portraits of themselves or friends while focusing on the person and softly blurring the background.
Superzoom	Superzoom camera mode can be used to create a story that automatically zooms in on a subject with dramatic sound effects.
Sharing to Stories	Users can tap the share button of different apps and share the content from that app in their stories.

continues on following page

Table 3. Continued

Tool	Description
Sharing Feed Posts to Stories	A feed post can be shared in stories such as a sticker with a customized background by tapping the paper airplane button below the post. The posts shared to stories display the original poster's username and tapping on the picture takes users to the original post.
Shopping Tags	Tapping on the sticker that includes a shopping bag icon, users can see more details about the product and start shopping. Companies must be approved for shopping on Instagram and finish the setup, before being able to add product stickers to their stories. As Gollin (2020) points out, the new addition of Instagram enables influencers, celebrities and other public figures to add shopping tags which increases the importance of influencer marketing for companies.
Source: (Instagram, 2019a)	
Create	Create mode in the camera lets users to share without using a photo or video. Interactive stickers such as question, poll or countdown stickers are available in this create mode. Moreover, GIFs can be attached to the Stories and "On This Day" button can be used to include content from previous years.
Close Friends List	Users can add people to the close friends list and share Stories that are only visible to the list members. These Stories usually appear at the beginning of the Stories queue with a green circle.
Donation and Music Stickers	Donation sticker is a new type of sticker which allows nonprofit organizations to collect donation. Users can add music stickers to play music in the background of the Story.
AR Filters	Previously, standard face filters were provided by Instagram and professional creators; but now augmented reality (AR) filters can be created by anyone and they are available for all the users.
Reels	Reels feature allows users to create 15 second video clips with music that can be shared in Stories.
Source: (Gollin, 2020)	

Instagram Stories is originally designed for sharing and consuming ephemeral content but over time a new feature called "Highlights" is introduced which provides a form of permanent content. Highlights feature allows users to save their selected Stories in their profile permanently (Bojkov, 2019). Similar to Highlights, IGTV is also a newer function of Instagram which lets users to share long-form (up to 60 minutes) videos permanently. IGTV videos are sometimes misinterpreted as ephemeral content because the new IGTV icon appears between the main Instagram logo and the direct message icon on the news feed, right above Instagram Stories; but technically IGTV isn't ephemeral content (Beaulac, 2018). Both Highlights and IGTV may offer great value to marketers but since this study is devoted to ephemeral content and Instagram Stories, these two features are not included in the remainder of the study.

BUSINESS GOALS OF USING INSTAGRAM STORIES AND ITS TACTICS

The goals of using Instagram Stories (Instagram, 2019d) and the tactics that can be used by businesses to reach these goals are discussed below.

Drive Online Sales

The "tapping" progression of Instagram is a great way to tell a story, build expectation and promote a sale. Tactics about this can be: Using various photos of a product from different angles, on different people or in different environments; and then offering something to call followers to action (Later & HubSpot, 2018, Boostly, 2018).

Call-to-action tools for driving sales can be the "See More" links or shopping stickers. Shopping stickers enable potential customers to learn more about products and "See More" links take users to the web site which can facilitate online buying.

Example

Waterdrop is a company that produces small cubes containing fruit and plant extracts. These cubes dissolve in water which frees people from buying beverages on the go. The objective of Waterdrop in using Instagram Stories was to promote its bottle set, which includes a reusable glass bottle and assorted Waterdrop 12-packs. Men and women in Austria and Germany between the ages of 20 and 55 were the target audience for this campaign. Emphasizing the company's focus on a healthy lifestyle, they created a video Story showing a Waterdrop bottle being held by a woman as she walks through a city. The link at the bottom of the Story took users directly to the Waterdrop web site. The campaign reached 1.8 million people in 10 days, which is a 6X increase compared to the previous month. It also attracted 8.4X more web site visitors over this period. Moreover, the sales conversion rate increased by 24% compared to the previous month (Instagram, 2019d).

Increase In-Store Sales

One of the great ways to boost in-store sales is using Instagram Stories. Companies can create attractive, funny and exciting Stories using different tools such as stickers, filters or formats like superzoom or boomerang to raise awareness about products and hence increase in-store sales. Countdown stickers can be used to inform customers about limited-time offers. Loyal customers can be added to the Close Friends List and special in-store offers may be presented just for them.

Example

McDonald's Malaysia wanted to increase sales of its McFlurry and McCafé offerings and used animated video ads in Instagram Stories to attract millennials. The company added playful elements to the design of the Stories such as a timing bar to create a sense of urgency and encourage people to watch the ad before it disappears, colorful text overlays that highlighted product features, and animated elements such as coffee beans, hearts and stars to tease and hold viewers' attention. After a 2-month campaign, McDonald's reached 60% of the target audience and tripled in-store sales of the promoted offerings (Instagram, 2019d).

Promote Your App

Instagram offers one of the most cost-effective ways to promote apps which drives downloads and retains users. Instagram Stories is the best way to keep the app in mind without exposing followers to lots of pictures in their feed (App Partner, 2017).

Countdown stickers are also effective in making limited-time offers to encourage users to download the app. "Swipe up" links can be added into the Stories to direct consumers to the download page.

Example

Hatier is a publishing house located in France and one of the most remarkable publications of the company is a French language grammar reference book entitled "Bescherelle". Hatier used Instagram Stories to promote its new mobile app "Mon coach Bescherelle" which was designed to help users improve their spelling and writing skills. The aim of the ads on Stories was to inform Instagram users about the new app and activate them to download it. Hatier's ads targeted people who liked its Facebook page, friends of these people and a 5% lookalike audience. Moreover, considering the B2B market, it used core targeting with interest areas such as "reading", "media" and "recruitment". The ads were designed to look like a regular Instagram Story that could possibly be posted by an account that the user was already following, but at the end of the story a view of "Bescherelle" was placed with a download link. There were 3407 app downloads at the end of the campaign and the cost per acquisition was 0.59 euros (Instagram, 2019d).

Raise Brand Awareness

Instagram Stories can help a brand stand out by capturing the target audience's attention with images and videos, and drive brand awareness (Scholl, 2018b). Tools that add fun to Stories like face filters; camera modes such as boomerang, superzoom, focus, rewind; stickers; drawing features, etc., can be used for creating attractive content which raises awareness.

AR filters can be created for a new product release and they can be used to generate buzz around the brand and drive engagement; background music can be added with music stickers to resonate with target audience and make them feel like the company is in touch with their tastes and interests (Gollin, 2020).

Example

Ted Baker, a British luxury clothing retail company, used Instagram Stories to raise awareness of their new autumn/winter 2018 collection. The company particularly wanted to reach young consumers and this objective directed them to use Instagram Stories ads. They created eight videos for Stories which showed items from the menswear and womenswear collections. Different effects such as split screens or kaleidoscopic visuals were used to attract consumers and to encourage them to visit the company's web site through "swipe up" links in the stories. The campaign increased ad recall by 8.2 points and consideration by 3 points. Moreover, compared to the previous spring/summer 2018 season, the campaign resulted in 22% more web site conversions amongst 18- to 24-year-olds (Instagram, 2019d).

Generate Leads

Instagram Stories provides a fun way to capture more leads and can be used to chat with the audience, arrange contests and create engaging videos. Tactics about this can be (Calus, 2018):

- Customers can be invited to comment on a picture or a video on Instagram and ask their questions. Then the company can create an epic Story in which they answer those questions (all or the most relevant ones). This approach enables engaging the whole audience at once instead of having private one-to-one messaging. Live video option is also a good alternative for answering questions and helps to build trust with the customers in a fantastic way, showing the transparency of the company.

- Contests are a great way to generate engagement. They create a sense of urgency since a Story disappears after 24 hours, and people play along as long as the giveaway is good and relevant to them. Therefore, it will improve engagement and as a result the Instagram algorithm will push the content more.
- A fantastic way to generate more leads is to create how-to videos via IGTV. Another way can be creating Instagram Stories that teach customers about something in a company's niche.
- Companies can invite customers to submit their suggestions via Instagram Stories about anything related to the products or the company itself (like the decision about a new logo, etc.). This creates positive associations with the brand and makes customers feel included and trusted. The suggestions can be collected via Direct Message or a comment on the latest photo.
- Instagram Stories can be used to promote materials on other platforms such as blog posts, or big announcements on the web site by just adding a compelling call to action message to the Story with a link that takes the followers straight to that page.
- It is good for businesses to post a mix of fun, informal content and promotional content in Instagram Stories since this platform is a relaxed place and has lower quality standards. These types of Stories help companies to build a more engaged community (Later & HubSpot, 2018) and provide an opportunity to generate more leads.

Example

Opel automotive company from Germany is one of the largest automakers in Europe. In 2018, between March 26 and April 9, the company used Instagram Stories to promote its ADAM model and generate leads for a contest to win one of the ADAM model cars. Opel used carousel format ads for sharing the stories about the new line, in each carousel card, there was a different ADAM car with a different animated emoji. At the end of the carousel, the viewers were asked to take a test to find out which ADAM model they were. After completing the test, the viewers could enter the contest to win an Opel ADAM and sign up for a newsletter about the new line. During the campaign period, there was a 2.5X increase in contest registrations which meant 1887 completed forms. In addition, the cost per registration was decreased to 2.04 euros (Instagram, 2019d).

Gather Follower Feedback

Interactive poll stickers on Instagram Stories enable businesses to ask questions and obtain results from the votes of followers including their interests, likes, dislikes, etc. Companies can collect feedback on the products, crowdsource ideas, or simply entertain the followers with poll stickers. It offers an entirely new way to engage with the audience (Later & HubSpot, 2018).

The emoji slider sticker is a new audience feedback sticker. It polls the viewers on a rating scale using any emoji (Hatmaker 2018). Furthermore, question stickers can be used for crowdsourcing ideas, collecting testimonials, or learning what content people want to see more of (Carbone, 2018).

Example

Jen Atkins, a celebrity hairstylist, collaborated with Calpak to create her own luggage collection. Jen Atkins used Instagram Stories polls to gather feedback from followers about the features of the luggage and shared the results of the polls while promoting the launch of the collection. She showed how her followers helped to create the collection. The followers are likely to continue interacting with the Stories if they know that they're being heard and their feedback makes a difference (Carbone, 2019).

Retain Customers

An Instagram takeover is defined as (Lua, 2018):

The process of taking over someone else's Instagram account temporarily and sharing content with their audience.

The difference between Instagram Stories takeovers and regular Instagram takeovers is that Instagram Stories doesn't appear in the feed and since the content in Stories disappears after 24 hours, Stories takeovers are time-sensitive (Fitzpatrick 2017). Doing regular takeovers is a great way to bring variety and consistency to using Instagram Stories. This approach can help vary the content and keep customers returning for more (Later & HubSpot, 2018). Tactics for effective Instagram Stories takeovers can be (Talbot, 2018):

- Promoting the takeover (posting a descriptive photo or video in the feed, using live video to inform about the upcoming event, direct messaging to followers including a link to the brand page, cross-promoting on other social channels, etc.)
- Showing the day (properly introducing yourself, providing elements that are memorable such as interviews, tips that show expertise and question and answer sessions).
- Providing a unique experience (standing out from the crowd of content to have viewers checking in for more).
- Using the Instagram capabilities (increasing reach by adding location tags or popular hashtags, adding creativity and fun by using face filters or emojis, and asking viewers to vote in a poll to guide the day in the Stories).
- Ending Strong (ending the story with a strong call-to-action statement such as including a swipe up link that goes to content).

In addition to takeovers, live videos can be utilized for giving information to customers about product use, and question or poll stickers can be used to continue engagement and retain customers. Gollin (2020) suggests using the Close Friends List for VIP customers to provide sneak peeks, product updates and special discounts.

Example

Victoria's Secret collaborated with the model Stella Maxwell and yoga teacher Beth Cooke to take over the company's Instagram Stories. They invited customers to join their yoga session to #trainlikeanangel.

Stella Maxwell had more than 3.3 million followers at that time and it is likely that the takeover helped Victoria's Secret to increase followers. In addition, Victoria's Secret called to action on three levels in the story by: 1) swiping up the link to join the yoga class, 2) practically doing yoga at home, and 3) swiping up the link to shop the yoga outfit (Ehrhardt, 2017).

CONCLUSION

As of April 2019, approximately half of more than 1 billion Instagram users actively use Stories every day (Instagram, 2019a). The number of daily active Instagram Stories users increased from 400 million in June 2018 (Constine, 2019) to more than 500 million in April 2019 (Instagram, 2019a). This increase in the number of users offers a potential for marketers. It facilitates the possibility to reach more users and achieve marketing objectives.

Furthermore, the majority of Instagram users are young people. According to a study by Statista on worldwide Instagram users, 32% of them are aged between 18 and 24 and 33% of them are aged between 25 and 34 (Statista, 2019b). Ting, Run and Liew (2016) state that young mobile users like to take photos and share them with others right away, and hence they spend more time on Instagram than other sites.

Instagram Stories is one of the primary channels for daily ephemera which provides a space for users to spontaneously share photos and harmlessly eccentric videos (Ceres, 2018). From a marketing perspective, if companies want to engage with followers, they can't ignore social media stories. Because, the ephemeralness of them forces companies to post fresh content and they encourage interaction for everyone (Hartshorne, 2018). Instagram Stories enables engagement in an easy and entertaining way with its unique and powerful tools such as links to outside content, mentions and hashtags, superior drawing capabilities, etc.

Instagram has business tools that provide insights to learn more about followers and the performance of shared content (such as how specific posts and stories performed and how people engaged with them) (Instagram, 2019e). Instagram Stories tools such as polls, questions and emoji slider stickers can facilitate the tracking and measurement of interactions, and enable effective marketing.

According to a recent study, 53% of people who use stories across the Facebook family of apps—which includes Facebook Stories, Instagram Stories, Messenger Stories and WhatsApp Status—state that using Stories increases their online purchases. In the same study, people said that after seeing a product or service in Stories, they took the following 4 actions: 56% of them browsed the brand's web site to get more information, 50% of them looked for the product or service on web sites where they could buy it, 38% of them talked to someone about the product or service, and 34% of them visited a store to check out the product or service (Facebook, 2018a; Facebook, 2018b).

In the perspective of the consumer purchase process, different Instagram Stories tools can be used in each stage for influencing consumers. For instance, creating interesting and attractive content is important to trigger need recognition, and camera modes such as boomerang, rewind, focus or superzoom as well as tools like face filters, stickers, and hashtags are great for creating such compelling content. Live videos are excellent for giving information about products. Moreover, hashtags or "see more" links can also be used for directing consumers to product or brand information. All Instagram Stories tools that increase the attractiveness of the content and make it stand out may facilitate the evaluation of alternatives. To close a sale or call consumers to action, using shopping stickers and "swipe up" links that take customers to e-commerce web sites are good ways. To collect customer feedback after the purchase, interactive tools such as questions, polls or emoji slider stickers can be used.

FUTURE RESEARCH DIRECTIONS

Further studies on the subject may focus on empirical research about which of the Instagram Stories tools are more effective at different stages of the purchasing process and on the effectiveness of other Stories platforms in achieving marketing goals.

It is very important for marketers to understand consumers' perceptions about Instagram Stories contents and tools that are used to create content. By determining what kinds of content consumers like to encounter in their Instagram Stories feed, it becomes possible to develop effective and attractive digital content strategies at every stage of the purchasing process using the right tools of the platform.

REFERENCES

Allen, K. R. (2016). *Launching new ventures: An entrepreneurial approach* (7th ed.). Cengage Learning.

App Partner. (2017). *11 Instagram marketing tactics to skyrocket app downloads*. Retrieved April 11, 2019, from https://www.apppartner.com/11-instagram-marketing-tactics-skyrocket-app-downloads/

Ashman, R., Solomon, M. R., & Wolny, J. (2015). An old model for a new age: Consumer decision making in participatory digital culture. *Journal of Customer Behaviour*, *14*(2), 127–146. doi:10.1362/147539215X14373846805743

Beaulac, H. (2018). *How to drive ecommerce sales using Instagram Stories and other ephemeral content*. Retrieved March 23, 2020, from https://foundr.com/instagram-ephemeral-content

Beaulac, H. (2019). *The future of ephemeral content on social media*. Retrieved April 9, 2019, from https://www.acquisio.com/blog/agency/the-future-of-ephemeral-content-on-social-media/

Bojkov, N. (2019). *Everything about Instagram Story Highlights*. Retrieved March 23, 2020, from https://embedsocial.com/blog/instagram-highlights/

Boostly. (2018). *The ultimate guide to Instagram for business*. Retrieved April 11, 2019, from https://www.loudpitch.com/wp-content/uploads/2018/08/The-Ultimate-Guide-to-Instagram-for-Business.pdf

Bozanta, A., & Kutlu, B. (2018). Do Twitter phenomena check-in popular venues on Foursquare too? *Information Discovery and Delivery*, *46*(3), 137–146. doi:10.1108/IDD-04-2018-0012

Breugelmans, E., Köhler, C. F., Dellaert, B. G. C., & Ruyter, K. (2012). Promoting interactive decision aids on retail websites: A message framing perspective with new versus traditional focal actions. *Journal of Retailing*, *88*(2), 226–235. doi:10.1016/j.jretai.2011.10.003

Butler, P., & Peppard, J. (1998). Consumer purchasing on the internet: Processes and prospects. *European Management Journal*, *16*(5), 600–610. doi:10.1016/S0263-2373(98)00036-X

Calus, V. (2018). *7 Brilliant ways to use Igtv and Instagram stories for lead generation.* Retrieved April 11, 2019, from https://planable.io/blog/igtv-instagram-stories-lead-generation/

Carbone, L. (2018). *7 Ways to use the new Instagram stories question sticker for your business.* Retrieved April 12, 2019, from https://later.com/blog/instagram-stories-question-sticker/

Carbone, L. (2019). *6 Creative ways to use Instagram stories polls.* Retrieved April 12, 2019, from https://later.com/blog/instagram-stories-polls/

Casalo, L. V., Flavian, C., & Ibanez-Sanchez, S. (2020, September). Influencers on Instagram: Antecedents and consequences of opinion leadership. *Journal of Business Research, 117,* 510–519. doi:10.1016/j.jbusres.2018.07.005

Ceres, P. (2018). *How to supercharge your Instagram stories.* Retrieved April 12, 2019, from https://www.wired.com/story/how-to-use-instagram-stories/

Charlesworth, A. (2009). *The digital revolution.* Dorling Kindersley Limited.

Chen, K. J., & Cheung, H. L. (2019). Unlocking the power of ephemeral content: The roles of motivations, gratification, need for closure, and engagement. *Computers in Human Behavior, 97,* 67–74. doi:10.1016/j.chb.2019.03.007

Cipriani, J. (2017). *WhatsApp status: Everything you need to know about the Snapchat clone.* Retrieved April 15, 2019, from https://www.cnet.com/how-to/how-to-use-whatsapps-new-status-feature/

Chung, W. (2012). Managing web repositories in emerging economies: Case studies of browsing web directories. *International Journal of Information Management, 32*(3), 232–238. doi:10.1016/j.ijinfomgt.2011.11.004

Constine, J. (2019). *Facebook plans new products as Instagram stories hits 500m users/day.* Retrieved April 15, 2019, from https://techcrunch.com/2019/01/30/instagram-stories-500-million/

Content Marketing Institute. (2017). *B2C content marketing: 2017 benchmarks, budgets, and trends—North America.* Retrieved from https://contentmarketinginstitute.com/wp-content/uploads/2016/10/2017_B2C_Research_Final-rev-10-26-16.pdf

Content Marketing Institute. (2018). *B2C content marketing: 2017 benchmarks, budgets, and trends—North America.* Retrieved March 22, 2019, from https://contentmarketinginstitute.com/wp-content/uploads/2017/12/2018_B2C_Research_Final.pdf

Curras-Perez, R., Ruiz-Mafe, C., & Sanz-Blas, S. (2013). Social network loyalty: Evaluating the role of attitude, perceived risk and satisfaction. *Online Information Review, 37*(1), 61–82. doi:10.1108/14684521311311630

Dahiya, R., Gayatri (2018). A research paper on digital marketing communication and consumer buying decision process: An empirical study in the Indian passenger car market. *Journal of Global Marketing, 31*(2), 73–95. doi:10.1080/08911762.2017.1365991

Darley, W. K., Blankson, C., & Luethge, D. J. (2010). Toward an integrated framework for online consumer behavior and decision making process: A review. *Psychology and Marketing*, *27*(2), 94–116. doi:10.1002/mar.20322

Djafarova, E., & Rushworth, C. (2017). Exploring the credibility of online celebrities' Instagram profiles in influencing the purchase decisions of young female users. *Computers in Human Behavior*, *68*, 1–7. doi:10.1016/j.chb.2016.11.009

Ehrhardt, J. (2017). *These 5 brands demonstrate the creative use of Instagram stories*. Retrieved April 12, 2019, from https://blog.influencerdb.com/these-five-brands-demonstrate-the-successful-use-of-instagram-stories/

Engel, J. F., Blackwell, R. D., & Miniard, P. W. (1990). *Consumer behavior* (6th ed.). The Dryden Press.

Facebook. (2018a). *Insights to go*. Retrieved April 15, 2019, from https://www.facebook.com/iq/insights-to-go/53-53-of-people-who-use-stories-across-the-facebooks-family-of-apps-surveyed-say-they-are-making-more-online-purchases-as-a-result-of-using-stories-stories-are-defined-as-photos-and-videos-temporarily-viewed-or-shared-for-24-hours-on-social-media?ref=fbiq_article_stories_sales

Facebook. (2018b). *Why stories is a format that can help marketers promote brands*. Retrieved April 15, 2019, from https://www.facebook.com/business/news/insights/why-stories-is-a-format-that-can-help-marketers-promote-brands#

Fitzpatrick, P. (2017). *How to run an Instagram Story takeover*. Retrieved April 12, 2019, from https://www.socialmediaexaminer.com/how-to-run-instagram-story-takeover/

Gallagher, B. (2018). *How to turn down a billion dollars: The Snapchat story*. Random House.

Gollin, M. (2020). *7 Newest Instagram Stories features (and how marketers can use them)*. Retrieved April 23, 2020, from https://www.falcon.io/insights-hub/industry-updates/social-media-updates/5-new-instagram-stories-features-for-2018-and-how-marketers-can-use-them/

Hajli, M. N. (2014). The role of social support on relationship quality and social commerce. *Technological Forecasting and Social Change*, *87*, 17–27. doi:10.1016/j.techfore.2014.05.012

Handley, A., & Chapman, C. C. (2010). *Content Rules: How to Create Killer Blogs, Podcasts, Videos, Ebooks, Webinars (and More) That Engage Customers and Ignite Your Business*. Wiley.

Hartshorne, D. (2018). *New Instagram features for interacting with your followers and other brands*. Retrieved April 14, 2019, from https://www.sendible.com/insights/instagram-features-for-engagement

Hatmaker, T. (2018). *Instagram adds emoji slider stickers to spice up polls*. Retrieved April 12, 2019, from https://techcrunch.com/2018/05/10/instagram-emoji-poll-stickers/

Ho, C. H., Chiu, K. H., Chen, H., & Papazafeiropoulou, A. (2015). Can Internet blogs be used as an effective advertising tool? The role of product blog type and brand awareness. *Journal of Enterprise Information Management*, *28*(3), 346–362. doi:10.1108/JEIM-03-2014-0021

Jayawardhena, C., Wright, L. T., & Masterson, R. (2003). An investigation of online consumer purchasing. *Qualitative Market Research*, *6*(1), 58–65. doi:10.1108/13522750310457384

Instagram. (2019a). *Our story: A quick walk through our history as a company*. Retrieved April 9, 2019, from https://instagram-press.com/our-story/

Instagram. (2019b). *Why Instagram?* Retrieved April 9, 2019, from https://business.instagram.com/getting-started

Instagram. (2019c). *The rise of stories*. Retrieved April 9, 2019, from https://business.instagram.com/a/stories?ref=igb_carousel

Instagram. (2019d). *Success stories*. Retrieved April 11, 2019, from https://business.instagram.com/success/?case_study_tags[0]=stories-ad

Instagram. (2019e). *About Instagram insights*. Retrieved April 15, 2019, from https://help.instagram.com/788388387972460

Kareh, A. (2017). *How podcasts can lead to better connections with your audience*. Retrieved April 2, 2019, from https://www.forbes.com/sites/forbesagencycouncil/2017/04/11/establish-goodwill-and-credibility-for-a-better-connection-with-your-audiences-by-using-podcasts/#6598039429d4

Katai, R. (2019). *Five of the best Instagram stories ads examples and what we can learn from them*. Retrieved February 27, 2019, from https://nealschaffer.com/instagram-stories-ads-examples/

Kavanagh, D. (2018). *Ephemeral content consumers: 5 things every brand should know*. Retrieved April 9, 2019, from https://blog.globalwebindex.com/trends/ephemeral-content/

Keefe, N. (2017). Dance like no one is watching, post like everyone is: The accessibility of "private" social media content in civil litigation. *Vand. J. Ent. & Tech., 19*, 1027–1055.

Kemp, S. (2018). *Digital in 2018: World's Internet users pass the 4 billion mark*. Retrieved March 14, 2019, from https://wearesocial.com/blog/2018/01/global-digital-report-2018

Kim, S. J., Wang, R. J. H., & Malthouse, E. C. (2015). The effects of adopting and using a brand's mobile application on customers' subsequent purchase behavior. *Journal of Interactive Marketing, 31*, 28–41. doi:10.1016/j.intmar.2015.05.004

Later & HubSpot. (2018). *Instagram for business in 2018: Using Instagram stories, carousels, ads, influencers, and more!* Retrieved April 11, 2019, from https://cdn2.hubspot.net/hubfs/53/Instagram_for_business_in_2018_HubSpot_Later-1.pdf

Li, Q., Wang, Q., & Lin, Z. (2018). Effects of consumer visit to online community and product channel on local sales of large consumer goods: Evidence from real estate industry. *The Journal of Strategic Information Systems, 27*(2), 191–204. doi:10.1016/j.jsis.2017.11.001

Lieb, R. (2012). *Content marketing: Think like a publisher—How to use content to market online and in social media*. Que Publishing.

Lua, A. (2018). *All you need to know about Instagram takeovers: How to host a takeover in 6 simple steps*. Retrieved April 12, 2019, from https://buffer.com/library/instagram-takeover

Martinez-Lopez, F. J., Anaya-Sanchez, R., Molinillo, S., Aguilar-Illescas, R., & Esteban-Millat, I. (2017). Customer engagement in an online brand community. *Electronic Commerce Research and Applications*, *23*, 24–37. doi:10.1016/j.elerap.2017.04.002

Merisavo, M., & Raulas, M. (2004). The impact of e-mail marketing on brand loyalty. *Journal of Product and Brand Management*, *13*(7), 498–505. doi:10.1108/10610420410568435

Mialki, S. (2019). *5 Reasons brands should consider ephemeral content & best practices when creating a strategy*. Retrieved April 9, 2019, from https://instapage.com/blog/ephemeral-content

Mirkovski, K., Jia, Y., Liu, L., & Chen, K. (2018). Understanding microblogging continuance intention: The directed social network perspective. *Information Technology & People*, *31*(1), 215–238. doi:10.1108/ITP-07-2015-0168

Odden, L. (2012). *Optimize: How to attract and engage more customers by integrating SEO, social media, and content marketing*. John Wiley & Sons, Inc.

Park, H., & Cho, H. (2012). Social network online communities: Information sources for apparel shopping. *Journal of Consumer Marketing*, *29*(6), 400–411. doi:10.1108/07363761211259214

Rangiha, M. E., Comuzzi, M., & Karakostas, B. (2016). A framework to capture and reuse process knowledge in business process design and execution using social tagging. *Business Process Management Journal*, *22*(4), 835–859. doi:10.1108/BPMJ-06-2015-0080

Rose, R., & Pulizzi, J. (2011). *Managing content marketing: The real-world guide for creating passionate subscribers to your brand*. CMI Books.

Rowley, J. (2008). Understanding digital content marketing. *Journal of Marketing Management*, *24*(5-6), 517–540. doi:10.1362/026725708X325977

Scholl, H. (2018a). *Profit from Facebook Instagram Stories marketing ads*. Publisher.

Scholl, H. (2018b). *Facebook Instagram Stories Marketing ads: Pictorial training guide*. Publisher.

Sharma, S., & Crossler, R. E. (2014). Disclosing too much? Situational factors affecting information disclosure in social commerce environment. *Electronic Commerce Research and Applications*, *13*(5), 305–319. doi:10.1016/j.elerap.2014.06.007

Sheetrit, G. (2017). *5 social media trends that will have maximum impact in 2018*. Retrieved April 9, 2019, from https://www.adweek.com/digital/guy-sheetrit-over-the-top-seo-guest-post-5-social-media-trends-that-will-have-maximum-impact-in-2018/

Statista. (2019a). *Number of digital buyers worldwide from 2014 to 2021 (in billions)*. Retrieved March 14, 2019, from https://www.statista.com/statistics/251666/number-of-digital-buyers-worldwide/

Statista. (2019b). *Distribution of Instagram users worldwide as of January 2019, by age group*. Retrieved April 15, 2019, from https://www.statista.com/statistics/325587/instagram-global-age-group/

Steils, N., Crie, D., & Decrop, A. (2019). Online consumer learning as a tool for improving product appropriation. *Journal of Retailing and Consumer Services*, *46*, 51–57. doi:10.1016/j.jretconser.2018.04.007

SUMO Heavy Industries. (2018). *The 2018 social commerce survey.* Retrieved March 14, 2019, from https://sumoheavy.lpages.co/2018/

Talbot, K. (2018). *5 tips for an effective Instagram story takeover.* Retrieved April 12, 2019, from https://www. forbes.com/sites/katetalbot/2018/03/19/5-tips-for-an-effective-instagram-story-takeover/#103dac8f282a

Teo, T. S. H., & Yeong, Y. D. (2003). Assessing the consumer decision process in the digital marketplace. *Omega, 31*(5), 349–363. doi:10.1016/S0305-0483(03)00055-0

Ting, H., Run, E. C., & Liew, S. L. (2016). Intention to use Instagram by generation cohorts: The perspective of developing markets. *Global Business and Management Research, 8*(1), 43–55.

Vázquez-Herrero, J., Direito-Rebollal, S., & López-García, X. (2019). Ephemeral journalism: News distribution through Instagram Stories. *Social Media + Society, 5*(4), 1-13.

Veirman, M. D., Cauberghe, V., & Hudders, L. (2017). Marketing through Instagram influencers: The impact of number of followers and product divergence on brand attitude. *International Journal of Advertising, 36*(5), 798–828. doi:10.1080/02650487.2017.1348035

Villaespesa, E. & Wowkowych, S. (2020). Ephemeral storytelling with social media: Snapchat and Instagram Stories at the Brooklyn Museum. *Social Media + Society, 6*(1), 1-13.

Weisgerber, C., & Butler, S. H. (2015). Social media as a professional development tool: Using blogs, microblogs, and social bookmarks to create personal learning networks. In *Teaching Arts and Science with the New Social Media.* Emerald Group Publishing Limited.

Wolny, J., & Charoensuksai, N. (2014). Mapping customer journeys in multichannel decision-making. *Journal of Direct, Data and Digital Marketing Practice, 15*(4), 317–326. doi:10.1057/dddmp.2014.24

Wu, K., Vassileva, J., Zhu, Q., Fang, H., & Tan, X. (2013). Supporting group collaboration in wiki by increasing the awareness of task conflict. *Aslib Proceedings, 65*(6), 581–604. doi:10.1108/AP-05-2013-0046

Zhang, L., & Peng, T. Q. (2015). Breadth, depth, and speed: Diffusion of advertising messages on microblogging sites. *Internet Research, 25*(3), 453–470. doi:10.1108/IntR-01-2014-0021

This research was previously published in the International Journal of Customer Relationship Marketing and Management (IJCRMM), 12(1); pages 84-101, copyright year 2021 by IGI Publishing (an imprint of IGI Global).

Chapter 27
Identifying Key Important Factors Affecting Consumer Purchase Behaviour on Luxury Brand Through the Use of Instagram

Pankarn Panachuenvongsak
Business School, Brunel University London, UK

Olusoyi Richard Ashaye
Business School, Brunel University London, UK & University of Wales Trinity Saint David, UK

ABSTRACT

Purchasing via the internet is one of the most rapidly growing forms of shopping, which has overcome traditional retailing since late 1998. In this chapter, factors related to online and social media shopping and the benefits of using social media will be discussed. Instagram application, tendency of using brand name, online consumer behaviour, and Thai consumer behaviour towards the use of social media will also be illustrated to review what the key factors important in online shopping mentioned in previous research are.

INTRODUCTION

In this chapter, factors related to online and social media shopping, benefits of using social media will be discussed. Instagram application, tendency of using brand name, online consumer behaviour and Thai consumer behaviour towards the use of social media will also be illustrated to review what are the key factors important in online shopping mentioned in previous research.

DOI: 10.4018/978-1-6684-6287-4.ch027

Revision of Factors Toward Online Shopping

Purchasing via the internet is one of the most rapidly growing forms of shopping which overcome the traditional retailing since late 1998 (Ha and Perks, 2005: Lohse *et al.*, 2000). Number of researchers have studied about online shopping service (Jarvenpaa and Todd, 1997; Lohse and Spiller, 1998; Szymanski and Hise, 2000; Liu and Arnett, 2000) and classified the attributes of online shopping into four categories. **Merchandising** refers to product assortment, variety and product information. Szymanski and Hise (2000) proved that rich product assortment can increase customer satisfaction. Furthermore, extensive and higher **quality information** available online leads to better buying decisions and higher levels of consumer satisfaction (Lohse and Spiller, 1998).

For **customer service** such as security, return and payment policy (Jarvenpaa and Todd, 1997; Kolesar and Galbraith, 2000), uninterrupted and beneficial communication are all customers want. (Lohse and Spiller, 1998). Online shopping seems to be pleasurable and satisfying to consumers when an online site is fast, uncluttered, and easy to navigate. Uncluttered and easy to navigate sites shorten shopping time and the effort consumers (Szymanski and Hise, 2000). Most online shopping provides a product search engine, and navigation guidance to help consumers' searching and purchasing. Lastly, consumers are concerned about **privacy and financial information**. While most online shopping sites provides personal information privacy protection policy and guarantee for transaction security (Elliot and Fowell, 2000).

However, Wolfinbarger and Gilly (2001) implied that important factors lead people to shop online are **goal-oriented** and **experiential** which contradicted to the above literature. By way of contrast, goal-oriented motives are more common among online shoppers than experiential motives. Consumers report that shopping online results in an increased sense of freedom and control when compared to traditional shopping. Conversely, many writers still believe that online shopping provide interactivity and personalised experiences to customers (ibid, 2001).

To be more specific, there are several studies mentioned about factors influence consumer for shopping through social network site which will be indicated in the following part.

Rational Benefits

There are a number of previous research expressed that rational benefit is a fundamental for building long-term relationship and satisfaction towards online shop (Ravald and GroÈnroos, 1996; Gwinner *et al.*, 1998; Patterson and Smith, 2001). According to Gwinner *et al.* (1998), a rational benefit can be defined as a benefit to which customers acquire from long-term relationships beyond the core service performance. The researcher also suggests that an important part of a rational benefit is the sense of reduced anxiety, trust, and confidence that customers experience

Overall Satisfaction

Jones and Sasser (2005) pinpointed that a high level of satisfaction can lead to high customer loyalty, and a truly loyal customers are all satisfied customers. In the same way, customer satisfaction can act as a barometer for measuring how well company served its own customers and how well customers like and satisfy their experience on the site (ibid, 2005, p.95).

Purchase Intention

Purchase intention is a mixture of consumers' interest and the possibility of buying a product. Results from many studies pointed out that purchase intention is strongly related to attitude, preference and satisfaction toward a brand or a product (Kim *et al.*, 2010; Kim and Ko, 2010; Kim and Lee, 2009). Therefore, measuring purchase intention assumes consumers' future behavior based on their attitudes. Purchase intention is a variable for measuring customers' future contributions to a brand. On the other hands, customer equity is a behavioral accounting for actual purchasing record. Overall quality of the shopping experience and satisfaction are the key elements for both attitude towards shopping online and intention to buy (Nowlis and McCabe 2000, Novak et al. 2000).

Price Perceptions

Jiang and Rosenbloom (2005) highlighted that satisfaction examined the role of price. When shopping on the internet, customers cannot actually see the product before purchase. So, consumers are forced to rely on price than other elements (Liu and Arnett, 2000).

Unplanned Purchases

Many researchers implied that unplanned purchase or impulse buying is a purchase decision made with no explicit recognition of a need prior to entry the store (Kollat and Willett, 1967; Kollat, 1966; Bellenger *et al.*, 1978). Although Abratt and Goodey (1990) commented that there was a lack of consensus about the meaning of impulse purchase which is difficult to compare findings and accumulated information about the nature of impulse behaviour.

Unplanned purchase can happen through two situations. One is in-store stimuli (E.g., price, light, music) as it acts as a reminder of shopping needs which offer new ways of satisfying needs (Kollat and Willett, 1969). Another one is customer commitment hypothesis. The study of Kollat and Willett in 1967 concluded that unplanned purchasing can be described as a blend of hypotheses such as in-store stimuli and customer commitment.

Shopping Convenience

Overall shopping convenience is defined as time and effort savings in shopping. For instance, a research from (Szymanski and Hise, 2000) revealed that online shopping or shopping via social media seems to be pleasurable and satisfying to consumers when the retailer sites are fast, uncluttered, and easy to navigate. Uncluttered and easy to navigate sites shorten shopping time and the cognitive effort (Szymanski and Hise, 2000).

Numerous shopping motive studies (Stephenson and Willett, 1969; Darden and Ashton, 1975; Williams *et al.*, 1978; Bellenger and Korgaonkar, 1980; Eastlick and Feinberg, 1999) have identified convenience as a distinct motive for store choice in the online setting. Bellenger and Korgaonkar (1980) characterised the convenience shopper as selecting stores based upon time or effort savings.

Recent research (Swaminathan *et al.*, 1999) suggests that convenience is an important factor as a location becomes unnecessary in the online shopping context. The online shoppers are motivated by the convenience of placing orders online at home any time which consistent with past research regarding time and effort savings (Bellenger and Korgaonkar, 1980; Eastlick and Feinberg, 1999). In other words, time and effort savings as a part of the overall shopping convenience construct.

Another literature Jiang and Rosenbloom (2005) emphasised about shopping convenience that shopping convenience was found to have significant, and strong correlation with price perception and the correlation between the two is positive. Generally, customers have a positive perception of price on e-tailers who offer pleasurable shopping convenience. This can be analysed that consumers are more willing to pay for convenience for buying at one e-store.

Reference Group

A reference group is a person or group of people that significantly influences an individual's purchase behaviour. There are an operationalisation of reference groups by Hyman (1942) and additional research (Newcomb 1943; Sherif 1948) claimed that reference group have been used by advertisers in an efforts to persuade consumers to purchase products and brands. Reference groups show up people to behaviour and lifestyles, influence self-concept, contribute to the formation of values and attitudes and generate pressure for conformity to group norms. For instance, a group of celebrities (Bearden and Etzel, 1982).

Self- Expressive

Social class was characterised by the need for psychological association with a person or group and is reflected in the acceptance of positions expressed by others (Bearden and Etzel, 1982). The study of Waterman (1990) proposed that the roots of the concept of self-expressiveness can be traced as " true self ". It refers to the potentiality of people which represents the greatest fulfillment in living of which each is capable include with the unique potential to distinguish the individual from others. In other words, self-expressive reflects the sense of being an excellence and a perfection. In this case, to be accepted by others considered to be one of the benefits derived from true self. Krishnamurthy and Dou (2008) summarised that emotional motives of using social media are a social connection and self-expression. By the same token, Park *et al.* (2009) found four motives for using social networking sites: socialising, entertainment, self-status seeking, and information.

Social Trends

Ward (1974) implied that social trends refer to trends which relate to the social and cultural values also practices within consumer's society or environment at that moment. It reflects ways of people behaviour and the reason why people behave in that way. Social trends are intergenerational. Conversely, few societal trends are only applicable to one specific group, but still it has the power to affect society as a whole.

Social trends are very practical and vital to incorporate into strategy, communication and product development. Shao (2009) proposed that people perform a variety of activities online which are consumption of information and entertainment, participation in social interaction and community development, and production of self-expression and self-actualization.

Shop Commitment

Many researchers emphasised that commitment is a vital component of a successful long-term relationship (Dwyer *et al.*, 1987; Morgan and Hunt, 1994). Commitment has been defined as a desire to maintain a valued relationship (Moorman et al., 1992) or a tendency to resist change (Pritchard *et al.*, 1999). It plays a key mediating role in building consumers' loyalty and future behavioral intention (Garbarino and Johnson, 1999; Morgan and Hunt, 1994; Pritchard et al., 1999). In the service marketing literature, service quality, perceived value, and satisfaction are considered as antecedents of commitment (GroÈn-roos, 1990; Hocutt, 1998; Shemwell *et al.*, 1998).

Security Perception

Assurance of security also plays a crucial role in customer's trust in terms of reducing customer's concerns about personal data abuse and vulnerability of transaction data (Jarvenpaa and Todd, 1997; Ratnashingham, 1998). Consumers want detailed information on how their private and transaction data are secured (Elliot and Fowell, 2000). If the perceived level of security assurance meets consumer's expectations, consumers may willing to disclose their personal information and try to purchase with comfort (Park and Kim, 2003). Consumers are concerned about disclosing their private and financial information. While most online shops provide personal information, privacy protection policy and guarantee for transaction security (Elliot and Fowell, 2000). If a perception of security risk decreases, satisfaction with the information service of online stores is expected to increase.

Shop Awareness

A previous study of Park and Kim (2003) introduced shop awareness as a customer's perception of online shopping store which is based on external information circumstances like advertising or word-of-mouth communication. In addition, shop awareness can be defined as an ability of a buyer to recognise or recall that a site is a member of a certain service category (Aaker, 1991). This assumed to have an impact on the choice of customers such as satisfaction and convenience when service or shop attributes are difficult to evaluate.

Reason for Social Media Engagement

From the literature, Boyd and Ellison (2008) asserted that social media such as Facebook, Twitter or Instagram have emerged into mass use from 2003 onwards. It enables people to share and interact with each others, create and maintain a community of people (Drury, 2008; Heinonen, 2011). Differences between many concepts had been a controversial topic. Many researchers argued about user-generated content is a characteristic of social media. For instance, Kaplan and Haenlein (2010) pointed out that the concepts social media and user-generated content have been used exchangeably (Kaplan and Haenlein, 2010). Different type of social media depending on their type and characteristics have been suggested (Krishnamurthy and Dou, 2008; Shao, 2009).

Indeed, Heinonen (2011) stated that consumer motives in social media engagement demonstrated consumers' activities. As well as Krishnamurthy and Dou (2008) summarised the motivations into two main groups. First is **rational motives**, such as knowledge-sharing and advocacy, and the second one is

emotional motives, such as social connection and self-expression. By the same token, Park *et al.* (2009) found four motives for using social networking sites: socialising, entertainment, self-status seeking, and information.

On the contrary, Shao (2009) argued that people perform a variety of activities online which are information and entertainment consumption, social interaction and community development participation, and production of self-expression and self-actualisation. People often engage in all three activities or a combination of two and that it is not always possible to differentiate clearly between the activities (ibid, 2009).

The Benefits of Shopping Through Social Media

In terms of benefits, the Internet-based commerce enables consumers to search for information and purchase products or services directly with the online store. Hence, consumer purchase behaviour depends on the web-based appearance such as pictures, images, product information and video clips but not the actual experience that customers can touch or smell (Lohse and Spiller, 1998; Kolesar and Galbraith, 2000).

The way of presenting information, guidance or order fulfillment are all essential characteristics which building customer's shop commitment (Alba *et al.*, 1997; Reynolds, 2000). Consumers tend to engage in relational behaviours for achieving the right decision making, reducing information searching process, achieving more cognitive consistency in decisions, and reducing the perceived risks in future (Sheth and Parvatiyar, 1995). Consumer starts feeling safe with the service provider after the first transaction (Ravald and GroÈnroos, 1996). When consumers trusted a company and realised that this company can fulfill their needs and finally, they become committed to the company.

In addition, the online shopping environment enables consumers to reduce their decision-making efforts by providing vast selection, information screening, reliability, and product comparison (Alba *et al.*, 1997).

Instagram Application

Instagram is one of the most popular application for online photo-sharing communities (Daniells, 2012: Bakhshi *et al.*, 2014). It was considered as a new form of communication where users can share their real-time updates by taking and manipulating photos and videos (Protalinski, 2012: Hu *et al.*, 2014). Also, people can interact with other users through comments and 'likes'.This service has seen rapid growth with the impressive pace since it was launched in October 2010 (Protalinski, 2012: Hu *et al.*, 2014: Bakhshi *et al.*, 2014). Nowadays, Instagram reached nearly 100 million users and having every second a new user registered (Daniells, 2012).

Moreover, in 2013, Instagram attracted more than 150 million active users, with an average of 55 million photos uploaded by users per day (Instagram 2013). There is one study performed by Rainie *et al.*, (2012) demonstrated that Instagram is more likely to be used by young adults. Photo-sharing services like Instagram are examples of participatory sensing applications. The sensed data is a picture of a specific place. Users can extract information in many ways (Silva *et al.*, 2013). Those who use Instagram are trying to make their images look more shareable and interesting which is benefitial for people to utilise Istagram as a channel of operating business (Alper, 2013).

The Tendency to Use the Brand Name

Brand name considered as the vital components of branding which verbalised by consumers (Sarabia and Ostrovskaya, 2012) and it is a linkage between what the corporation wants and how consumers perceive in their mind. Aaker and Keller (1990) suggested that brand name should be descriptive, suggestive, distinctive and build associations with the product and company. Therefore, brand name can be related to the perception, expectation and feeling of the customer towards a product. Especially, it reflects the associations that consumers perceive in their minds.

The Brand name used when customers intend to express as a sign of status or quality (Sarabia and Ostrovskaya, 2012) and provides symbolic meanings during decision-making process (Herbig and Milewicz, 1993). The tendency of using brand name has been analysed from the perspective of brand equity (Jung and Sung, 2008), and from a relational benefits focus (Aggarwal, 2004). Furthermore, the tendency of using brand name is due to it acting as a facilitator and transmitter of its image, culture, values and quality (Bnicks *et al.*, 2000).

Bengtsson (2003) observed that frequent engagement with brands can make consumers more dependent. It has been confirmed that the consumer-brand relationship can be seen as a dependent and interdependent relationship (Bradley *et al.*, 2007). To be more specific, Tarka (2008) reaches a similar conclusion by proving that the values of Sense of Belonging and Being Well-Respected are those most associated with the brand name which is similar to self-expressive.

Theory of Online Consumer Behaviour

Changing in businesses and consumers had made a difficulty for all to understand the consumer behaviour especially the behaviour of the consumer on the website. Most of the consumers are now a computer and smartphone user which perform all functions of a traditional one. Similarly, all the physical stores have been transformed into a virtual store. Thus, there is a need to understand and measure online consumer behaviour (Koufaris, 2002). Many researchers studied and built the model of online consumer behaviour. The study have shown that overall quality of the shopping experience is the key element in both attitude towards shopping online and intention to buy (Nowlis and McCabe 2000, Novak *et al.*, 2000). The online and offline consumers all have different social and work environment. For instance, there will be a high intention to buy online among consumers who are lacking of leisure time. So that they tend to find the most convenient way to purchase the product (Bellman *et al.*, 2000).

Online consumers are beware and concern with financial risks in buying on the web such as credit card fraud (Bhatnagar *et al.*, 2000). Also perceive a risk of online shopping and perceived ease of use have shown a strong influence on customer's attitude towards online shopping (Heijden *et al.*, 2001). By the same token, online consumers have unique needs which reflect their online environments (Koufaris, 2002).

Case Study of Thai Consumer Behaviour Towards the Use of Social Network (Instagram)

There are results from the survey of reliable sources mentioned in the literature above (Zocialrank, 2015) reported that most of Thai Instagram users use Instagram 1 to 5 times per day which equal to 41.8

percent. The most using time is 20:01-23:00 pm and take place at home just for entertainment reason (Monwaratch and Peerayut, 2015). Moreover, an interesting survey (its24hrs, 2014) results had found that

- For Thai teenagers, 9 out of 10 people indicated that they check smartphones innumerably.
- 91 percent of participants feel nervous if lacking of smartphones
- 100 percent of participants check their smartphone in bed
- 98 percent of participant use smartphones for texting, checking emails and social network before and after having meals
- 98 percent of participant indicated that they contact friends via online channel than fac-to-face interaction
- 9 out of 10 teenagers order products online
- 100 percent of participants indicated that social network application such as Facebook and Instagram play a vital role in their daily life

From the survey outcome above, it is inevitable to conclude that Thai people are addicted to smartphones especially for checking news, facebook and browsing through Instagram.

For Instagram users who use this channel as a way of operating business such as selling clothes, cosmetics or luxury brand products which offers a lower price than traditional stores in the market. Thus, the trend of purchasing brand name product of Thai people keep rising (Zocialrank, 2014) as the product itself is much cheaper than general boutique shops. Especially, some online shop offers the brand name product which is difficult to find in a traditional one such as limited edition items at a reasonable price. The shop owner tends to upload beautiful pictures and labelled them with the price to attract other followers to contact and purchase the product from them. Hence, there are high risk in purchasing expensive product through online channel.

Also, the poll from PwC Consulting Thailand (2015) on Consumer expectations driving the next retail business model found that online market in Thailand had reached 100,000 million Baht which rose from 90,000 million Bah. Likewise, a survey from Matichon (2015) investigated that Thai celebrities also operate their Instagram shop which sell the luxury brand product such as Hermes, Chanel and Prada handbags. They bought and brought products back Thailand for sales.

However, this behaviour lead to a negative effect of an exceed amount towards pre-order products that Thai government has passed a law for Thai people who travelled back from foreign countries. People who owned products worth more than 10,000 THB have to pay the tax (Matichon, 2015).

SUMMARY

After review of the previous literature key considerations can be highlighted such as factors related to online and social media shopping, benefits of using social media as discussed. Instagram application, tendency of using brand name, online consumer behaviour and Thai consumer behaviour towards the use of social media as illustrated in the review.

REFERENCES

Aaker, D. A. (1991). *Managing Brand Equity*. The Free Press.

Aaker, D. A., & Keller, K. L. (1990). Consumer Evaluations of Brand Extensions. *Journal of Marketing*, *54*(1), 27–41. doi:10.1177/002224299005400102

Abratt, R., & Goodey, S. D. (1990). Unplanned buying and in-store stimuli in supermarkets. *Managerial and Decision Economics*, *11*(2), 111–121. doi:10.1002/mde.4090110204

Aggarwal, P. (2004). The effects of brand relationship norms on consumer attitudes and behavior. *The Journal of Consumer Research*, *31*(2), 87–101. doi:10.1086/383426

Alba, J., Lynch, J., Weitz, B., Janiszewski, C., Lutz, R., Sawyer, A., & Wood, S. (1997). Interactive home shopping: Consumer, retailer, and manufacturer incentives to participate in electronic marketplaces. *Journal of Marketing*, *61*(3), 38–53. doi:10.1177/002224299706100303

Alper, M. (2013). War on Instagram: Framing conflict photojournalism with mobile photography apps. *New Media & Society*.

Bakhshi, S., Shamma, D. A., & Gilbert, E. (2014). Faces engage us: Photos with faces attract more likes and comments on Instagram. *Proceedings of the SIGCHI Conference on Human Factors in Computing Systems*, 965-974. 10.1145/2556288.2557403

Bearden, W. O., & Etzel, M. J. (1982). Reference group influence on product and brand purchase decisions. *The Journal of Consumer Research*, *9*(2), 183–194. doi:10.1086/208911

Bellenger, D. N., & Korgaonkar, P. K. (1980). *Profiling the recreational shopper*. J Retail.

Bellenger, D. N., Robertson, D. H., & Hirschmann, E. C. (1978). Impulse buying varies by product. *Journal of Advertising Research*, 15–18.

Bellman, S., Gerald, L. L., & Eric, J. J. (2000). Predictors of online buying behavior. *Comm. ACM*, *42*(12), 32–38.

Bengtsson, A. (2003). Towards a critique of brand relationships. *Advances in Consumer Research. Association for Consumer Research (U. S.)*.

Bhatnagar, A., Sanjog, M., & Raghav, R. (2000). On risk, convenience, and Internet shopping behavior. *Comm. ACM, 43*(11), 98–105.

Boyd, D. M., & Ellison, N. B. (2008). Social Network Sites: Definition History, and Scholarship. *Journal of Computer-Mediated Communication*, 210–230.

Bradley, S. D., Maxian, W., Laubacher, T. C., & Baker, M. (2007). In Search of Lovemarks: The semantic stmcture of brands. In K. B. Sheehan (Ed.), *Proceedings of the American Academy of Advertising*. Eugene, OR: American Academy of Advertising.

Daniells, K. (2012). *Infographic: Instagram statistics*. Digital Buzz Blog.

Darden, W. R., & Ashton, D. (1975). *Psychographic profiles of patronage preference groups*. J Retail.

Drury, G. (2008). Social media: Should marketers engage and how can it be done effectively? *Journal of Direct, Data and Digital Marketing Practice*, *9*(3), 274–277. doi:10.1057/palgrave.dddmp.4350096

Dwyer, F. R., Schurr, P. H., & Oh, S. (1987). Developing buyer-seller relationships. *Journal of Marketing*, *51*(1), 11–27. doi:10.1177/002224298705100202

Eastlick, M. A., & Feinberg, R. A. (1999). Shopping motives for mail catalog shopping. *Journal of Business Research*, *45*(3), 281–290. doi:10.1016/S0148-2963(97)00240-3

Elliot, S., & Fowell, S. (2000). Expectations versus reality: A snapshot of consumer experiences with internet retailing. *International Journal of Information Management*, *20*(5), 323–361. doi:10.1016/S0268-4012(00)00026-8

Garbarino, E., & Johnson, M. S. (2002). The different roles of satisfaction, trust, and commitment in customer relationships. *Journal of Marketing*, *63*(2), 70–87. doi:10.1177/002224299906300205

Gwinner, K. P., Gremmler, D. D., & Bitner, M. J. (1998). Relational benefits in services industries: The customer's perspective. *Journal of the Academy of Marketing Science*, *26*(2), 101–114. doi:10.1177/0092070398262002

Heinonen, K. (2011). Consumer activity in social media: Managerial approaches to consumers' social media behavior. *Journal of Consumer Behaviour*, *10*(6), 356–364. doi:10.1002/cb.376

Herbig, P., & Milewicz, J. (1993). The relationship of reputation and credibility to brand 'Exito'. *Journal of Consumer Marketing*, *10*(3), 18–24. doi:10.1108/EUM0000000002601

Hocutt, M. A. (1998). Relationship dissolution model: Antecedents of relationship commitment and the likelihood of dissolving a relationship. *International Journal of Service Industry Management*, *9*(2), 189–200. doi:10.1108/09564239810210541

Hyman, H. H. (1942). The Psychology of Status. *Archives de Psychologie*, 94–102.

Jarvenpaa, S. L., & Todd, P. A. (1997). Consumer reactions to electronic shopping on the World Wide Web. *International Journal of Electronic Commerce*, 59–88.

Jiang, P., & Rosenbloom, B. (2005). Customer intention to return online: Price perception, attribute-level performance, and satisfaction unfolding over time. *European Journal of Marketing*, *39*(1/2), 150–174. doi:10.1108/03090560510572061

Jones, T. O., & Sasser, E. W. (2005). Why satisfied customers defec. *Harvard Business Review*, 88–99.

Jung, J., & Sung, E. Y. (2008). Consumer-based brand equity: Comparisons among Americans and South Koreans in the USA and South Koreans in Korea. *Journal of Fashion Marketing and Management*, *72*(1), 24–35. doi:10.1108/13612020810857925

Kaplan, A. M., & Haenlein, M. (2010). Users of the world, unite! The challenges and opportunities of Social Media. *Business Horizons*, *53*(1), 59–68. doi:10.1016/j.bushor.2009.09.003

Kaplan, B., & Duchon, D. (1988). Combining qualitative and quantitative methods in information systems research: A case study. *Management Information Systems Quarterly*, *12*(4), 571–586. doi:10.2307/249133

Kolesar, M. B., & Galbraith, R. W. (2000). A services- marketing perspective on e-retailing: Implications for e-retailers and directions for further research. *Internet Research*, *10*(5), 380–424. doi:10.1108/10662240010349444

Kollat, D. T. (1966). *A Decision-Process Approach to Impulse Purchasing, Science, Technology and Marketing*. American Marketing Association.

Kollat, D. T., & Willett, R. P. (1967). Consumer impulse purchasing behaviour. *JMR, Journal of Marketing Research*, *4*(1), 21–31. doi:10.1177/002224376700400102

Kollat, D. T., & Willett, R. P. (1969). Is impulse purchasing really a useful concept for marketing decisions? *Journal of Marketing*, *33*(1), 79–83. doi:10.1177/002224296903300113

Kothari, C. R. (2011). *Research methodology: methods and techniques*. New Age International.

Koufaris, M. (2002). Applying the technology acceptance model and flow theory to online consumer behavior. *Information Systems Research*, *13*(2), 205–223. doi:10.1287/isre.13.2.205.83

Krishnamurthy, S., & Dou, W. (2008). Advertising with User-Generated Content: A Framework and Research Agenda. *Journal of Interactive Advertising*, *8*(2), 1–7. doi:10.1080/15252019.2008.10722137

Liu, C., & Arnett, K. P. (2000). Exploring the factors associated with Web site success in the context of electronic commerce. *Information & Management*, *38*(1), 23–34. doi:10.1016/S0378-7206(00)00049-5

Lohse, G. L., Bellman, S., & Johnson, E. J. (2000). Consumer buying behavior on the Internet: Findings from panel data. *Journal of Interactive Marketing*, *14*(1), 15–29. doi:10.1002/(SICI)1520-6653(200024)14:1<15::AID-DIR2>3.0.CO;2-C

Lohse, G. L., & Spiller, P. (1998). Electronic shopping. *Communications of the ACM*, *41*(7), 81–90. doi:10.1145/278476.278491

Matichon. (2015). Available at: http://www.matichon.co.th/index.php

Monwaratch, J., & Peerayut, O. (2015). *Expectation and Satisfaction towards Instagram of people in Bangkok*. Thammasat University. (in Thai)

Moorman, C., Zaltman, G., & Deshpande, R. (1992). Relationships between providers and users of market research: The dynamics of trust within and between organizations. *JMR, Journal of Marketing Research*, *29*(3), 314–328. doi:10.1177/002224379202900303

Morgan, R. M., & Hunt, S. D. (1994). The commitment- trust theory of relationship marketing. *Journal of Marketing*, *58*(3), 20–38. doi:10.1177/002224299405800302

Newcomb, T. M. (1950). *Social Psychology*. Holt, Rinehart and Winston. doi:10.1037/11275-000

Novak, T. P., Donna, L. H., & Yiu, F. Y. (1998). Modeling the structure of the flow experience among Web users. *Marketing Science*, *19*(1), 22–42. doi:10.1287/mksc.19.1.22.15184

Nowlis, S. M., & Deborah, B. (2000). Online vs. off- line consumer decision making: The effect of the ability to phys- ically touch merchandise. *Second Marketing Sci. Internet Conf.*

Olds, B. M., Moskal, B. M., & Miller, R. L. (2005). Assessment in engineering education: Evolution, approaches and future collaborations. *Journal of Engineering Education*, *94*(1), 13–25. doi:10.1002/j.2168-9830.2005.tb00826.x

Park, C. H., & Kim, Y. G. (2003). Identifying key factors affecting consumer purchase behavior in an online shopping context. *International Journal of Retail & Distribution Management*, *31*(1), 16–29. doi:10.1108/09590550310457818

Park, N., Kee, K. F., & Valenzuela, S. (2009). Being Immersed in Social Networking Environment: Facebook Groups, Uses and Gratifica- tions, and Social Outcomes. *Cyberpsychology & Behavior*, *12*(6), 729–733. doi:10.1089/cpb.2009.0003 PMID:19619037

Patterson, P. G., & Smith, T. (2001). Relationship benefits in service industries: A replication in a southeast asian context. *Journal of Services Marketing*, *15*(6), 425–436. doi:10.1108/EUM0000000006098

Pritchard, M. P., Havitz, M. E., & Howard, D. R. (1999). Analyzing the commitment-loyalty link in service contexts. *Journal of the Academy of Management Science*, *27*(3), 333–348. doi:10.1177/0092070399273004

Protalinski, E. (2012). *Instagram just passed 100 million users*. Available at:https://thenextweb.com/facebook/2012/09/11/markzuckerberg-instagram-just-passed-100-million-users/

Rainie, L., Brenner, J., & Purcell, K. (2012). *Photos and Videos as Social Currency Online*. Pew Research, Tech. Rep.

Ravald, A., & Grönroos, C. (1996). The value concept and relationship marketing. *European Journal of Marketing*, *30*(2), 19–30. doi:10.1108/03090569610106626

Reynolds, J. (2000). eCommerce: A critical review. *International Journal of Retail & Distribution Management*, *28*(10), 417–444. doi:10.1108/09590550010349253

Sale, J. E., Lohfeld, L. H., & Brazil, K. (2002). Revisiting the quantitative-qualitative debate: Implications for mixed-methods research. *Quality & Quantity*, *36*(1), 43–53. doi:10.1023/A:1014301607592 PMID:26523073

Shao, G. (2009). Understanding the Appeal of User-Generated Media: A Uses and Gratification Perspective. *Internet Research*, *19*(1), 7–25. doi:10.1108/10662240910927795

Shemwell, D. J., Yavas, U., & Bilgin, Z. (1998). Customer-service provider relationships: An empirical test of a model of service quality, satisfaction, and relationship-oriented outcomes. *International Journal of Service Industry Management*, *9*(2), 155–168. doi:10.1108/09564239810210505

Sherif, M. (1948). *An Outline of Social Psychology*. Harper & Row.

Sheth, J. N., & Parvatiyar, A. (1995). Relationship marketing in consumer markets: Antecedents and consequences. *Journal of the Academy of Marketing Science*, *23*(4), 255–271. doi:10.1177/009207039502300405

Silva, T. H., de Melo, P. O., Almeida, J. M., Salles, J., & Loureiro, A. (2013). *A picture of Instagram is worth more than a thousand words: Workload characterization and application. Distributed Computing in Sensor Systems*. DCOSS.

Stephenson, P. R., & Willett, R. P. (1969). Analysis of consumers' retail patronage strategies. In *Basics of qualitative research* (2nd ed.). Sage.

Swaminathan, V., Lepkowska, W. E., & Rao, B. P. (1999). Browsers or buyers in cyberspace? An investigation of factors influencing likelihood of electronic exchange. *Journal of Computer-Mediated Communication.*

Szymanski, D. M., & Hise, R. T. (2000). e-satisfaction: An initial examination. *Journal of Retailing, 76*(3), 290–309. doi:10.1016/S0022-4359(00)00035-X

Tarka, P. (2008). Some empirical observations on multidimensional sealing polish and Dutch youth's values. Innovative Management Journal, 28-50.

van der Heijden, H., Tibert, V., & Marcel, C. (2001). Predicting online purchase behavior: Replications and tests of com- peting models. *Proc. 34th Hawaii Internat. Conf. System Sci.* 10.1109/HICSS.2001.927100

Waterman, A. S. (1990). Personal expressiveness: Philosophical and psychological foundations. *Journal of Mind and Behavior, 11*(1), 47–74.

Williams, R. H., Painter, J. J., & Nicholas, H. R. (1978). *A policy-oriented typology of grocery shoppers.* J Retail.

Wolfinbarger, M., & Gilly, M. C. (2001). Shopping online for freedom, control, and fun. *California Management Review, 43*(2), 34–55. doi:10.2307/41166074

Zocialrank. (2015). *Thai consumer behaviour through the use of Social Network.* Available at: http://www.zocialrank.com/

ADDITIONAL READING

Bernard, H. R. (2002). *Research Methods in Anthropology: Qualitative and quantitative methods* (3rd ed.). AltaMira Press.

Biernacki, P., & Waldorf, D. (1981). Snowball sampling: Problems and techniques of chain referral sampling. *Sociological Methods & Research, 10*(2), 141–163. doi:10.1177/004912418101000205

Blackwell, R. D., Miniard, P. W., & Engel, J. F. (2001). *Consumer behavior* (9th ed.). Harcourt College Publishers.

Bland, J. M., & Altman, D. G. (1994). Correlation, regression, and repeated data. *BMJ (Clinical Research Ed.), 308*(6933), 896. doi:10.1136/bmj.308.6933.896 PMID:8173371

Brace, I. (2008). *Questionnaire design: How to plan, structure and write survey material for effective market research.* Kogan Page Publishers.

Brannen, J. (2005). Mixing methods: The entry of qualitative and quantitative approaches into the research process. *International Journal of Social Research Methodology, 8*(3), 173–184. doi:10.1080/13645570500154642

Calder, B. J. (1977). Focus groups and the nature of qualitative marketing research. *JMR, Journal of Marketing Research, 14*(3), 353–364. doi:10.1177/002224377701400311

Carr, L. T. (1994). The strengths and weaknesses of quantitative and qualitative research: What method for nursing? *Journal of Advanced Nursing, 20*(4), 716–721. doi:10.1046/j.1365-2648.1994.20040716.x PMID:7822608

Chang, T. Z., & Wildt, A. R. (2004). Price, product information, and purchase intention: An empirical study. *Journal of the Academy of Marketing Science, 22*(1), 16–27. doi:10.1177/0092070394221002

Cohen, J., Cohen, P., West, S. G., & Aiken, L. S. (2013). *Applied multiple regression/correlation analysis for the behavioral sciences.* Routledge. doi:10.4324/9780203774441

Collis, J., & Hussey, R. (2009). *Business Research: A Practical Guide for Undergraduate & Postgraduate Students* (3rd ed.). Palgrave Macmillan.

Corbin, J., & Strauss, A. (2014). *Basics of qualitative research: Techniques and procedures for developing grounded theory.* Sage publications.

Creswell, J. W. (2013). *Research design: Qualitative, quantitative, and mixed methods approaches.* Sage publications.

Creswell, J. W., & Miller, D. L. (2000). Determining validity in qualitative inquiry. *Theory into Practice, 39*(3), 124–130. doi:10.120715430421tip3903_2

Crosby, L. A., & Stephens, N. (1987). Effects of relationship marketing on satisfaction, retention, and prices in the life insurance industry. *JMR, Journal of Marketing Research, 24*(4), 402–404. doi:10.1177/002224378702400408

DeLone, W. H., & McLean, E. R. (1992). Information system success: The quest for the dependent variable. *Information Systems Research, 3*(1), 60–95. doi:10.1287/isre.3.1.60

Douglas, E. P., Borrego, M., & Amelink, C. T. (2009). Quantitative, qualitative, and mixed research methods in engineering education. *Journal of Engineering Education, 98*(1), 53–66. doi:10.1002/j.2168-9830.2009.tb01005.x

Eberhardt, L. L. (1970). Correlation, regression, and density dependence. *Ecology, 51*(2), 306–310. doi:10.2307/1933669

Elo, S., & Kyngäs, H. (2008). The qualitative content analysis process. *Journal of Advanced Nursing, 62*(1), 107–115. doi:10.1111/j.1365-2648.2007.04569.x PMID:18352969

Eriksson, P., & Kovalainen, A. (2008). Qualitative methods in business research. *Sage (Atlanta, Ga.).*

Faugier, J., & Sargeant, M. (1997). Sampling hard to reach populations. *Journal of Advanced Nursing, 26*(4), 790–797. doi:10.1046/j.1365-2648.1997.00371.x PMID:9354993

Garland, R. (1991). The mid-point on a rating scale: Is it desirable. *Marketing Bulletin, 2*(1), 66–70.

Gehrt, K., & Shim, S. A. (1998). *shopping orientation segmentation of French con- sumers*: Implications for catalog marketing. *Journal of Interactive Marketing, 12*(4), 34–46. doi:10.1002/(SICI)1520-6653(199823)12:4<34::AID-DIR4>3.0.CO;2-O

Goulding, C. (2005). Grounded theory, ethnography and phenomenology. *European Journal of Marketing, 39*(3/4), 294–308. doi:10.1108/03090560510581782

Guarte, J. M., & Barrios, E. B. (2006). Estimation under purposive sampling. *Communications in Statistics. Simulation and Computation, 35*(2), 277–284. doi:10.1080/03610910600591610

Ha, H. Y., & Perks, H. (2005). Effects of consumer perceptions of brand experience on the web: Brand familiarity, satisfaction and brand trust. *Journal of Consumer Behaviour, 4*(6), 438–452. doi:10.1002/cb.29

Hair, J. F. Jr, Anderson, R. E., Tatham, R. L., & Black, W. C. (1998). *Multivariate Data Analysis* (5th ed.). Prentice-Hall Inc.

Hawes, J. M., & Lumpkin, J. R. (1984). Understanding the outshopper. *Journal of the Academy of Marketing Science, 12*(4), 200–217. doi:10.1007/BF02721809

Homburg, C., & Pflesser, C. (2000). A multiple-layer model of market-oriented organizational culture: Measurement issues and performance outcomes. *JMR, Journal of Marketing Research, 37*(4), 449–462. doi:10.1509/jmkr.37.4.449.18786

Hovorka, D. S., & Lee, A. S. (2010). *Reframing Interpretivism and positivism as Understanding and Explanation: Consequences for Information Systems Research*. ICIS.

Hsu, F. M., Lin, Y. T., & Ho, T. K. (2012). Design and implementation of an intelligent recommendation system for tourist attractions: The integration of EBM model, Bayesian network and Google Maps. *Expert Systems with Applications, 39*(3), 3257–3264. doi:10.1016/j.eswa.2011.09.013

Jiuan, T. S. (2006). 'Strategies for reducing consumers' risk aversion in Internet shopping'. *Journal of Consumer Marketing, 16*(2), 163–180. doi:10.1108/07363769910260515

Kim, A. J., & Ko, E. (2010). *Impacts of luxury fashion brand's social media marketing on customer relationship and purchase intention.*

Kim, A. J., & Ko, E. (2010). The impact of design characteristics on brand attitude and purchase intention: Focus on luxury fashion brands. *J Korean Soc Clothing Text, 34*(2).

Kim, A. J., & Ko, E. (2012). Do social media marketing activities enhance customer equity? An empirical study of luxury fashion brand. *Journal of Business Research, 65*(10), 1480–1486. doi:10.1016/j.jbusres.2011.10.014

Kim, H. J., & Lee, H. Z. (2009). The effect of well-being, consumer value orientations, perceived value and brand preference on purchase intention of environment-friendly cosmetics. *J Korean Soc Clothing Ind, 15*(1).

Kim, J., Kim, J. E., & Johnson, K. K. P. (2010). The customer-salesperson relationship and sales effectiveness in luxury fashion stores: The role of self monitoring. *J Glob Fashion Mark, 1*(4), 230–239. doi:10.1080/20932685.2010.10593074

Lee, A. (1994). Electronic Mail as a Medium for Rich Communication: An Empirical Investigation Using Hermeneutic Interpretation. *Management Information Systems Quarterly, 18*(2), 143–157. doi:10.2307/249762

Lee, G. G., & Lin, H. F. (2005). Customer perceptions of e-service quality in online shopping. *International Journal of Retail & Distribution Management, 33*(2), 161–176. doi:10.1108/09590550510581485

Lewis, J. L., & Sheppard, S. R. J. (2006). Culture and communication: Can landscape visualization improve forest management consultation with indigenous communities? *Landscape and Urban Planning, 77*(3), 291–313. doi:10.1016/j.landurbplan.2005.04.004

Maanen, V. (1979). Reclaiming Qualitative Methods for Organizational Research: A Preface. *Administrative Science Quarterly, 24*(4), 520–526. doi:10.2307/2392358

Miles, J. (2013). *Instagram Power: Build your brand and reach more customers with the power of pictures*. McGraw Hill Professional.

Moon, J., Chadee, D., & Tikoo, S. (2008). Culture, product type, and price influences on consumer purchase intention to buy personalized products online. *Journal of Business Research, 61*(1), 31–39. doi:10.1016/j.jbusres.2006.05.012

Moon, J.-W., & Kim, Y.-G. (2001). Extending the TAM for a World-Wide-Web context. *Information & Management, 38*(4), 217–301. doi:10.1016/S0378-7206(00)00061-6

Moutinho, L., & Hutcheson, G. D. (Eds.). (2011). *The SAGE dictionary of quantitative management research*. Sage. doi:10.4135/9781446251119

Newman, I. (1998). *Qualitative-quantitative research methodology: Exploring the interactive continuum.* SIU Press.

Pallant, J. (2013). *SPSS survival manual*. McGraw-Hill Education.

Penrod, J., Preston, D. B., Cain, R. E., & Starks, M. T. (2003). A discussion of chain referral as a method of sampling hard-to-reach populations. *Journal of Transcultural Nursing, 14*(2), 100–107. doi:10.1177/1043659602250614 PMID:12772618

Pope, C., Ziebland, S., & Mays, N. (2000). Qualitative research in health care: Analysing qualitative data. *BMJ (Clinical Research Ed.), 320*(7227), 114–116. doi:10.1136/bmj.320.7227.114 PMID:10625273

Ratnasingham, P. (1998). The importance of trust in electronic commerce. *Internet Research, 8*(4), 291–313. doi:10.1108/10662249810231050

Richter, A., & Koch, M. (2007). *Social software — status quo und Zukunft*. Technischer Bericht, Nr. Fakultät für Informatik. Universität der Bundeswehr München.

Rohm, A. J., & Swaminathan, V. (2004). A typology of online shoppers based on shopping motivations. *Journal of Business Research, 57*(7), 748–757. doi:10.1016/S0148-2963(02)00351-X

Scriven, M. (1991). Pros and cons about goal-free evaluation. *Evaluation Practice, 12*(1), 55–76. doi:10.1016/0886-1633(91)90024-R

Solomon, M., Russell-Bennett, R., & Previte, J. (2012). *Consumer behaviour*. Pearson Higher Education AU.

Straub, D. W. (1989). Validating instruments in MIS research. *Management Information Systems Quarterly*, *13*(2), 147–169. doi:10.2307/248922

Thomas, D. R. (2006). A general inductive approach for analyzing qualitative evaluation data. *The American Journal of Evaluation*, *27*(2), 237–246. doi:10.1177/1098214005283748

Valck, K., Bruggen, G., & Wierenga, B. (2009). Virtual communities: A marketing perspective. *Decision Support Systems*, *47*(3), 185–203. doi:10.1016/j.dss.2009.02.008

Van, T. E., & Hundley, V. (2001). The importance of pilot studies. *Social Research Update*, (35), 1–4.

Wang, R. Y., & Strong, D. M. (1996). Beyond accuracy: What data quality means to data consumers. *Journal of Management Information Systems*, *12*(4), 5–34. doi:10.1080/07421222.1996.11518099

Ward, S. (1974). Consumer socialization. *The Journal of Consumer Research*, *1*(2), 1–14. doi:10.1086/208584

Weijer, C., Dickens, B., & Meslin, E. M. (1997). Bioethics for clinicians: 10. Research ethics. *Canadian Medical Association Journal*, *156*(8), 1153–1157. PMID:9141987

Wind, J., Vithala, R. R., & Paul, E. G. (1991). Behavioral Methods. In T. S. Robertson & H. H. Kassarjan (Eds.), *Handbook of Consumer Research*. Prentice Hall.

Winter, G. (2000). A comparative discussion of the notion of validity in qualitative and quantitative research. *Qualitative Report*, *4*(3), 4.

Zapata, J., & Shippee-Rice, R. (1999). The use of folk healing and healers by six Latinos living in New England: A preliminary study. *Journal of Transcultural Nursing*, *10*(2), 136–142. doi:10.1177/104365969901000207 PMID:10476165

This research was previously published in Trends and Issues in International Planning for Businesses; pages 89-109, copyright year 2020 by Business Science Reference (an imprint of IGI Global).

Index

I

U

V

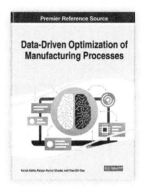
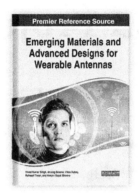

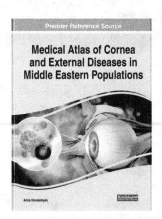

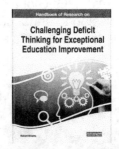

Printed in the United States
by Baker & Taylor Publisher Services